Cases

Strategic Management
Competitiveness & Globalization

9th Edition

Michael A. Hitt
Texas A&M University

R. Duane Ireland
Texas A&M University

Robert E. Hoskisson
Rice University

SOUTH-WESTERN
CENGAGE Learning™

Australia • Brazil • Japan • Korea • Mexico • Singapore • Spain • United Kingdom • United States

SOUTH-WESTERN
CENGAGE Learning

Strategic Management: Competitiveness and Globalization: Cases, Ninth Edition

Michael A. Hitt, R. Duane Ireland, and Robert E. Hoskisson

VP/Editorial Director:
  Jack W. Calhoun

Editor-in-Chief:
  Melissa Acuna

Senior Acquisitions Editor:
  Michele Rhoades

Director of Development:
  John Abner

Senior Editorial Assistant:
  Ruth Belanger

Marketing Manager:
  Nathan Anderson

Senior Marketing Communications Manager:
  Jim Overly

Marketing Coordinator:
  Suellen Ruttkay

Content Project Manager:
  Jacquelyn K Featherly

Media Editor:
  Rob Ellington

Senior Manufacturing Coordinator:
  Sandee Milewski

Production House/Compositor:
  Cadmus Communications

Senior Art Director:
  Tippy McIntosh

Cover and Internal Designer:
  Craig Ramsdell, Ramsdell Design

Cover Image:
  ©Media Bakery

For product information and technology assistance, contact us at
Cengage Learning Customer & Sales Support, 1-800-354-9706

For permission to use material from this text or product, submit all requests online at **www.cengage.com/permissions**
Further permissions questions can be emailed to
permissionrequest@cengage.com

ExamView® and ExamView Pro® are registered trademarks of FSCreations, Inc. Windows is a registered trademark of the Microsoft Corporation used herein under license. Macintosh and Power Macintosh are registered trademarks of Apple Computer, Inc. used herein under license.

Cases ISBN 13: 978-0-538-75311-1
Cases ISBN 10: 0-538-75311-0

South-Western Cengage Learning
5191 Natorp Boulevard
Mason, OH 45040
USA

Cengage Learning products are represented in Canada by Nelson Education, Ltd.

For your course and learning solutions, visit **www.cengage.com**

Purchase any of our products at your local college store or at our preferred online store **www.ichapters.com**

Printed in Canada
2 3 4 5 6 7 13 12 11 10

Our goal in writing each edition of this book is to present a new, up-to-date standard for explaining the strategic management process. To reach this goal with the 9th edition of our market-leading text, we again present you with an intellectually rich yet thoroughly practical analysis of strategic management.

With each new edition, we are challenged and invigorated by the goal of establishing a new standard for presenting strategic management knowledge in a readable style. To prepare for each new edition, we carefully study the most recent academic research to ensure that the strategic management content we present to you is highly current and relevant for use in organizations. In addition, we continuously read articles appearing in many different business publications (e.g., *Wall Street Journal, BusinessWeek, Fortune, Financial Times,* and *Forbes,* to name a few); we do this to identify valuable examples of how companies are actually using the strategic management process. Though many of the hundreds of companies we discuss in the book will be quite familiar to you, some companies will likely be new to you as well. One reason for this is that we use examples of companies from around the world to demonstrate how globalized business has become. To maximize your opportunities to learn as you read and think about how actual companies use strategic management tools, techniques, and concepts (based on the most current research), we emphasize a lively and user-friendly writing style.

Supplements

Instructors

Instructor's Resource DVD (0-538-75315-3) Key ancillaries (Instructor's Resource Manual, Instructor's Case Notes, Test Bank, ExamView™, and PowerPoint®, as well as the Fifty Lessons video collection) are provided on DVD, giving instructors the ultimate tool for customizing lectures and presentations.

New Expanded Instructor Case Notes (0-538-75461-3) To better reflect the varying approaches to teaching and learning via cases, the 9th edition offers a rich selection of case note options:

Basic Case Notes – Each of the 30 cases in the 9th edition is accompanied by a succinct case note designed for ease of use while also providing the necessary background and financial data for classroom discussion.

Presentation Case Notes – For a selection of 13 cases from the 9th edition, a full set of PowerPoint slides has been developed for instructors to effectively use in class, containing key illustrations and other case data.

Rich Assessment Case Notes – Introduced in the 8th edition, these expanded case notes provide details about 13 additional cases from prior editions that are available on the textbook website. These expanded case notes include directed assignments, financial analysis, thorough discussion and exposition of issues in the case, and an assessment rubric tied to AACSB International assurance of learning standards that can be used for grading each case.

Available in Print, on the Instructor's Resource DVD, or Product Support Website.

Instructor's Resource Manual The Instructor's Resource Manual, organized around each chapter's knowledge objectives, includes teaching ideas for each chapter and how to reinforce essential principles with extra examples. This support product includes lecture outlines, detailed answers to end-of-chapter review questions, instructions for using each chapter's experiential exercises and video cases, and additional assignments. Available on the Instructor's Resource DVD or Product Support Website.

Certified Test Bank Thoroughly revised and enhanced, test bank questions are linked to each chapter's knowledge objectives and are ranked by difficulty and question type. We provide an ample number of application questions throughout, and we have also retained scenario-based questions as a means of adding in-depth problem-solving questions. With this edition, we introduce the concept of certification, whereby another qualified academic has proofread and verified the accuracy of the test bank questions and answers. The test bank material is also available in computerized ExamView™ format for creating custom tests in both Windows and Macintosh formats. Available on the Instructor's Resource DVD or Product Support Website.

ExamView™ Computerized testing software contains all of the questions in the certified printed test bank. This program is an easy-to-use test-creation software compatible with Microsoft Windows. Instructors can add or edit questions, instructions, and answers, and select questions by previewing them on the screen, selecting them randomly, or selecting them by number. Instructors can also create and administer quizzes online, whether over the Internet, a local area network (LAN), or a wide area network (WAN). Available on the Instructor's Resource DVD.

Video Case Program. A collection of 13 new videos from Fifty Lessons have been selected for the 9th edition, and directly connected Video Case exercises have been included in the end-of-chapter material of each chapter. These new videos are a comprehensive and compelling resource of management and leadership lessons from some of the world's most successful business leaders. In the form of short and powerful videos, these videos capture leaders' most important learning experiences. They share their real-world business acumen and outline the guiding principles behind their most important business decisions and their career progression. Available on the Instructor's Resource DVD.

PowerPoint® An all-new PowerPoint presentation, created for the 9th edition, provides support for lectures, emphasizing key concepts, key terms, and instructive graphics. Slides can also be used by students as an aid to note-taking. Available on the Instructor's Resource DVD or Product Support Website.

WebTutor™ WebTutor is used by an entire class under the direction of the instructor and is particularly convenient for distance learning courses. It provides Web-based learning resources to students as well as powerful communication and other course management tools, including course calendar, chat, and e-mail for instructors. See http://www.cengage.com/tlc/webtutor for more information.

Product Support Website (www.cengage.com/management/hitt) Our Product Support Website contains all ancillary products for instructors as well as the financial analysis exercises for both students and instructors.

The Business & Company Resource Center (BCRC) Put a complete business library at your students' fingertips! This premier online business research tool allows you and your students to search thousands of periodicals, journals, references, financial data, industry reports, and more. This powerful research tool saves time for students—whether they are preparing for a presentation or writing a reaction paper. You can use the BCRC to quickly and easily assign readings or research projects. Visit http://www.cengage.com/bcrc to learn more about this indispensable tool. For this text in particular, BCRC will be especially useful in further researching the companies featured in the text's 30 cases. We've also included BCRC links for the Strategy Right Now feature on our website as well as in the Cengage NOW product.

Student Premium Companion Site The new optional student premium website features text-specific resources that enhance student learning by bringing concepts to life. Dynamic interactive learning tools include online quizzes, flashcards, PowerPoint slides, learning games, and more, helping to ensure your students come to class prepared! Ask your Cengage Learning sales representative for more details.

Students

Financial analyses of some of the cases are provided on our Product Support Website for both students and instructors. Researching financial data, company data, and industry data is made easy through the use of our proprietary database, the Business & Company Resource Center. Students are sent to this database to be able to quickly gather data needed for financial analysis.

Make It Yours – Custom Case Selection

Cengage Learning is dedicated to making the educational experience unique for all learners by creating custom materials that best suit your course needs. With our Make It Yours program, you can easily select a unique set of cases for your course from providers such as Harvard Business School Publishing, Darden, and Ivey. See http://www.custom.cengage.com/makeityours/hitt9e for more details.

Acknowledgments

We express our appreciation for the excellent support received from our editorial and production team at South-Western. We especially wish to thank Michele Rhoades, our Senior Acquisitions Editor; John Abner, our Development Editor; Nate Anderson, our Marketing Manager; and Jaci Featherly, our Content Project Manager. We are grateful for their dedication, commitment, and outstanding contributions to the development and publication of this book and its package of support materials.

We are highly indebted to the reviewers of the 8th edition in preparation for this current edition:

Erich Brockmann
University of New Orleans

Scott Elston
Iowa State University

Carol Jacobson
Purdue University

Consuelo M. Ramirez
University of Texas at San Antonio

Deepak Sethi
Old Dominion University

Bruce H. Charnov
Hofstra University

Susan Hansen
University of Wisconsin-Platteville

Frank Novakowski
Davenport University

Manjula S. Salimath
University of North Texas

Manisha Singal
Virginia Tech

Len J. Trevino
Washington State University

Marta Szabo White
Georgia State University

Diana J. Wong-MingJi
Eastern Michigan University

Edward Ward
Saint Cloud State University

Michael L Williams
Michigan State University

Wilson Zehr
Concordia University

Finally, we are very appreciative of the following people for the time and care that went into preparing of the supplements to accompany this edition:

Charles Byles
Virginia Commonwealth University

Richard H. Lester
Texas A&M University

Paul Friga
University of North Carolina

Paul Mallette
Colorado State University

Kristi L. Marshall

Michael A. Hitt
R. Duane Ireland
Robert E. Hoskisson

Michael A. Hitt

Michael A. Hitt is a Distinguished Professor and holds the Joe B. Foster Chair in Business Leadership at Texas A&M University. He received his Ph.D. from the University of Colorado. He has more than 260 publications including 26 co-authored or co-edited books and was cited as one of the 10 most-cited scholars in management over a 25-year period in an article published in the 2008 volume of the *Journal of Management.*

Some of his books are *Downscoping: How to Tame the Diversified Firm* (Oxford University Press, 1994); *Mergers and Acquisitions: A Guide to Creating Value for Stakeholders* (Oxford University Press, 2001); *Competing for Advantage,* 2nd edition (South-Western, 2008); and *Understanding Business Strategy,* 2nd edition (South-Western Cengage Learning, 2009). He is co-editor of several books including the following: *Managing Strategically in an Interconnected World* (1998); *New Managerial Mindsets: Organizational Transformation and Strategy Implementation* (1998); *Dynamic Strategic Resources: Development, Diffusion, and Integration* (1999); *Winning Strategies in a Deconstructing World* (John Wiley & Sons, 2000); *Handbook of Strategic Management* (2001); *Strategic Entrepreneurship: Creating a New Integrated Mindset* (2002); *Creating Value: Winners in the New Business Environment* (Blackwell Publishers, 2002); *Managing Knowledge for Sustained Competitive Advantage* (Jossey-Bass, 2003); *Great Minds in Management: The Process of Theory Development* (Oxford University Press, 2005), and *The Global Mindset* (Elsevier, 2007). He has served on the editorial review boards of multiple journals, including the *Academy of Management Journal, Academy of Management Executive, Journal of Applied Psychology, Journal of Management, Journal of World Business,* and *Journal of Applied Behavioral Sciences.* Furthermore, he has served as consulting editor and editor of the *Academy of Management Journal.* He is currently a co-editor of the *Strategic Entrepreneurship Journal.* He is the current past president of the Strategic Management Society and is a past president of the Academy of Management.

He is a Fellow in the Academy of Management and in the Strategic Management Society. He received an honorary doctorate from the Universidad Carlos III de Madrid and is an Honorary Professor and Honorary Dean at Xi'an Jiao Tong University. He has been acknowledged with several awards for his scholarly research and he received the Irwin Outstanding Educator Award and the Distinguished Service Award from the Academy of Management. He has received best paper awards for articles published in the *Academy of Management Journal, Academy of Management Executive,* and *Journal of Management.*

R. Duane Ireland

R. Duane Ireland is a Distinguished Professor and holds the Foreman R. and Ruby S. Bennett Chair in Business from the Mays Business School, Texas A&M University where he previously served as head of the management department. He teaches strategic management courses at all levels (undergraduate, masters, doctoral, and executive). He has over 175 publications including more than a dozen books. His research, which focuses on diversification, innovation, corporate entrepreneurship, and strategic entrepreneurship, has been published in a number of journals, including *Academy of Management Journal, Academy of Management Review, Academy of Management Executive, Administrative Science Quarterly, Strategic Management Journal, Journal of Management, Strategic Entrepreneurship Journal, Human Relations, Entrepreneurship Theory and Practice, Strategic Entrepreneurship Journal, Journal of Business Venturing,* and *Journal of Management Studies,* among others. His recently published books include *Understanding Business Strategy,* 2nd edition (South-Western Cengage Learning, 2009), *Entrepreneurship: Successfully Launching New Ventures,* 3rd edition (Prentice-Hall, 2010), and *Competing for Advantage,* 2nd edition (South-Western, 2008). He is serving or has served as a member of the editorial review boards for a number of journals, including *Academy of Management Journal, Academy of Management Review, Academy of Management Executive, Journal of Management, Strategic Enterprenurship Journal, Journal of Business Venturing, Entrepreneurship Theory and Practice, Journal of Business Strategy,* and *European Management Journal.* He is the current editor of the *Academy of Management Journal.* He has completed terms as an associate editor for *Academy of Management Journal,* as an associate editor for *Academy of Management Executive,* and as a consulting editor for *Entrepreneurship Theory and Practice.* He has co-edited special issues of *Academy of Management Review, Academy of Management Executive, Journal of Business Venturing, Strategic Management Journal, Journal of High Technology and Engineering Management,* and *Organizational Research Methods* (forthcoming). He received awards for the best article published in *Academy of Management Executive* (1999) and *Academy of Management Journal* (2000). In 2001, his co-authored article published in *Academy of Management Executive* won the Best Journal Article in Corporate Entrepreneurship Award from the U.S. Association for Small Business & Entrepreneurship (USASBE).

He is a Fellow of the Academy of Management and is a 21st Century Entrepreneurship Research Scholar. He served a three-year term as a Representative-at-Large member of the Academy of Management's Board of Governors. He received the 1999 Award for Outstanding Intellectual Contributions to Competitiveness Research from the American Society for Competitiveness and the USASBE Scholar in Corporate Entrepreneurship Award (2004).

Robert E. Hoskisson

Robert E. Hoskisson is the George R. Brown Chair of Strategic Management at the Jesse H. Jones Graduate School of Business, Rice University. He received his Ph.D. from the University of California-Irvine. Professor Hoskisson's research topics focus on corporate governance, acquisitions and divestitures, corporate and international diversification, corporate entrepreneurship, privatization, and cooperative strategy. He teaches courses in corporate and international strategic management, cooperative strategy, and strategy consulting, among others. Professor Hoskisson's research has appeared in over 120 publications, including articles in the *Academy of Management Journal, Academy of Management Review, Strategic Management Journal, Organization Science, Journal of Management, Journal of International Business Studies, Journal of Management Studies, Academy of Management Perspectives, Academy of Management Executive, California Management Review,* and 26 co-authored books. He is currently an associate editor of the *Strategic Management Journal* and a consulting editor for the *Journal of International Business Studies,* as well as serving on the Editorial Review board of the *Academy of Management Journal*. Professor Hoskisson has served on several editorial boards for such publications as the *Academy of Management Journal* (including consulting editor and guest editor of a special issue), *Journal of Management* (including associate editor), *Organization Science, Journal of International Business Studies* (consulting editor), *Journal of Management Studies* (guest editor of a special issue) and *Entrepreneurship Theory and Practice*. He has co-authored several books including *Understanding Business Strategy*, 2nd Edition (South-Western Cengage Learning, 2009), *Competing for Advantage,* 2nd edition (South-Western, 2008), and *Downscoping: How to Tame the Diversified Firm* (Oxford University Press, 1994).

He has an appointment as a Special Professor at the University of Nottingham and as an Honorary Professor at Xi'an Jiao Tong University. He is a Fellow of the Academy of Management and a charter member of the Academy of Management Journals Hall of Fame. He is also a Fellow of the Strategic Management Society. In 1998, he received an award for Outstanding Academic Contributions to Competitiveness, American Society for Competitiveness. He also received the William G. Dyer Distinguished Alumni Award given at the Marriott School of Management, Brigham Young University. He completed three years of service as a representative at large on the Board of Governors of the Academy of Management and currently is on the Board of Directors of the Strategic Management Society.

To Ashlyn and Aubrey
Your smiles are like sunshine—they brighten my day.
—**MICHAEL A. HITT**

To my entire family
I love each of you dearly and remain so grateful for your incredibly strong support
and encouragement over the years. Your words and deeds have indeed showed
me how to "keep my good eye to the sun and my blind eye to the dark."
—**R. DUANE IRELAND**

To my wonderful grandchildren (Mara, Seth, Roselyn, Ian, Abby, Madeline,
Joseph, and Nadine), who are absolutely amazing and light up my life.
—**ROBERT E. HOSKISSON**

Case Title	Manu-facturing	Service	Consumer Goods	Food/Retail	High Tech-nology	Internet	Transportation/Communication	International Perspective	Social/Ethical Issues	Industry Perspective
Alibaba		●				●		●		
Baidu		●				●		●		
Barclays		●						●		
Biovail			●		●			●	●	
Blockbuster			●	●		●				●
CEMEX	●						●	●		
Citibank		●			●	●		●		
Computime	●		●			●		●		●
Dell	●		●		●	●				●
eBay, Inc.		●			●	●		●		●
Great Lakes	●								●	
Henkel	●		●					●		
Kroger, Safeway, Costco, and Whole Foods			●	●					●	●
Apple Computer, Inc.	●	●			●	●	●			●
Three Generations of Family-Entrepreneurship	●		●						●	
Cinemaplex		●		●						●
Motorola, Inc.	●		●					●		●
The New York Times Company		●				●	●			●
Nike	●			●				●	●	
Nintendo			●		●	●		●		●
Nucor	●						●	●		
Oasis Hong Kong Airlines		●					●	●		
Pro Clean		●		●						
Room and Board				●					●	
South Beauty Group		●		●				●		
Southwest Airlines		●					●			●
Tesco versus Sainsbury's			●	●				●		
TNK-BP	●									
Under Armour			●					●		●
United Airlines		●					●	●		●

xi

Case Title	Chapter												
	1	2	3	4	5	6	7	8	9	10	11	12	13
Alibaba				●		●		●			●		
Baidu			●		●			●					
Barclays	●	●	●			●						●	
Biovail								●		●	●	●	
Blockbuster			●		●	●	●						
CEMEX		●	●				●	●			●		
Citibank		●	●	●				●	●		●		
Computime	●	●		●							●		●
Dell		●		●	●						●	●	
eBay, Inc.	●				●	●			●				●
Great Lakes	●	●		●								●	
Henkel		●	●				●	●			●		
Kroger, Safeway, Costco, and Whole Foods	●	●								●		●	
Apple Computer, Inc.			●	●	●				●				●
Three Generations of Family-Entrepreneurship	●		●									●	●
Cinemaplex		●	●	●	●				●				
Motorola, Inc.		●		●		●	●					●	●
The New York Times Company	●	●		●					●				
Nike		●		●				●	●		●	●	
Nintendo		●	●	●				●			●		
Nucor		●	●	●	●						●	●	
Oasis Hong Kong Airlines		●	●	●				●					
Pro Clean		●	●	●								●	●
Room and Board			●	●					●			●	●
South Beauty Group	●	●		●								●	●
Southwest Airlines		●	●	●	●							●	●
Tesco versus Sainsbury's					●	●	●	●					
TNK-BP		●				●	●	●		●			
Under Armour	●		●	●				●				●	●
United Airlines		●		●				●	●				

Case Studies

What to Expect From In-Class Case Discussions

As you will learn, classroom discussions of cases differ significantly from lectures. The case method calls for your instructor to guide the discussion and to solicit alternative views as a way of encouraging your active participation when analyzing a case. When alternative views are not forthcoming, your instructor might take a position just to challenge you and your peers to respond thoughtfully as a way of generating still additional alternatives. Often, instructors will evaluate your work in terms of both the quantity and the quality of your contributions to in-class case discussions. The in-class discussions are important in that you can derive significant benefit by having your ideas and recommendations examined against those of your peers and by responding to thoughtful challenges by other class members and/or the instructor.

During case discussions, your instructor will likely listen, question, and probe to extend the analysis of case issues. In the course of these actions, your peers and/or your instructor may challenge an individual's views and the validity of alternative perspectives that have been expressed. These challenges are offered in a constructive manner; their intent is to help all parties involved with analyzing a case develop their analytical and communication skills. Developing these skills is important in that they will serve you well when working for all types of organizations. Commonly, instructors will encourage you and your peers to be innovative and original when developing and presenting ideas. Over the course of an individual discussion, you are likely to form a more complex view of the case as a result of listening to and thinking about the diverse inputs offered by your peers and instructor. Among other benefits, experience with multiple case discussions will increase your knowledge of the advantages and disadvantages of group decision-making processes.

Both your peers and instructor will value comments that contribute to identifying problems as well as solutions to them. To offer relevant contributions, you are encouraged to think independently and, through discussions with your peers outside of class, to refine your thinking. We also encourage you to avoid using "I think," "I believe," and "I feel" to discuss your inputs to a case analysis process. Instead, consider using a less emotion laden phrase, such as "My analysis shows . . . ." This highlights the logical nature of the approach you have taken to analyze a case. When preparing for an in-class case discussion, you should plan to use the case data to explain your assessment of the situation. Assume that your peers and instructor are familiar with the basic facts included in the case. In addition, it is good practice to prepare notes regarding your analysis of case facts before class discussions and use them when explaining your perspectives. Effective notes signal to classmates and the instructor that you are prepared to engage in a thorough discussion of a case. Moreover, comprehensive and detailed notes eliminate the need for you to memorize the facts and figures needed to successfully discuss a case.

The case analysis process described above will help prepare you effectively to discuss a case during class meetings. Using this process results in consideration of the issues required to identify a focal firm's problems and to propose strategic actions through which the firm can increase the probability it will outperform its rivals. In some instances, your instructor may ask you to prepare either an oral or a written analysis of a particular case. Typically, such an assignment demands even more thorough study and analysis of the case contents. At your instructor's discretion, oral and written analyses may be completed by individuals or by groups of three or more people. The information and insights gained by completing the six steps shown in Table 1 often are of value when developing an oral or a written analysis. However, when preparing an oral or written presentation, you must consider the overall framework in which your information and inputs will be presented. Such a framework is the focus of the next section.

Preparing an Oral/Written Case Presentation

Experience shows that two types of thinking (analysis and synthesis) are necessary to develop an effective oral or written presentation (see Exhibit 1). In the analysis stage, you should first analyze the general external environmental issues affecting the firm. Next, your environmental analysis should focus on the particular industry (or industries, in the case of a diversified company) in which a firm operates. Finally, you should examine companies against which the focal firm competes. By studying the three levels of the external environment (general, industry, and competitor), you will be able to identify a firm's opportunities and threats. Following the external environmental analysis is the analysis of the firm's internal organization. This analysis provides the insights needed to identify the firm's strengths and weaknesses.

As noted in Exhibit 1, you must then change the focus from analysis to synthesis. Specifically, you must synthesize information gained from your analysis of the firm's external environment and internal organization. Synthesizing information allows you to generate alternatives that can resolve the significant problems or challenges facing the focal firm. Once you identify a best alternative, from an evaluation based on predetermined criteria and goals, you must explore implementation actions.

In Table 2, we outline the sections that should be included in either an oral or a written presentation: strategic profile and case analysis purpose, situation analysis, statements of strengths/weaknesses and opportunities/threats, strategy formulation, and strategy implementation. These sections are described in the following discussion. Familiarity with the contents of your book's thirteen chapters is helpful because the general outline for an oral or a written presentation shown in Table 2 is based on an understanding of the strategic management process detailed in those chapters. We follow the discussions of the parts of Table 2 with a few comments about the "process" to use to present the results of your case analysis in either a written or oral format.

Table 1 An Effective Case Analysis Process

Step 1: Gaining Familiarity	a. In general—determine who, what, how, where, and when (the critical facts of the case). b. In detail—identify the places, persons, activities, and contexts of the situation. c. Recognize the degree of certainty/uncertainty of acquired information.
Step 2: Recognizing Symptoms	a. List all indicators (including stated "problems") that something is not as expected or as desired. b. Ensure that symptoms are not assumed to be the problem (symptoms should lead to identification of the problem).
Step 3: Identifying Goals	a. Identify critical statements by major parties (for example, people, groups, the work unit, and so on). b. List all goals of the major parties that exist or can be reasonably inferred.
Step 4: Conducting the Analysis	a. Decide which ideas, models, and theories seem useful. b. Apply these conceptual tools to the situation. c. As new information is revealed, cycle back to substeps a and b.
Step 5: Making the Diagnosis	a. Identify predicaments (goal inconsistencies). b. Identify problems (discrepancies between goals and performance). c. Prioritize predicaments/problems regarding timing, importance, and so on.
Step 6: Doing the Action Planning	a. Specify and prioritize the criteria used to choose action alternatives. b. Discover or invent feasible action alternatives. c. Examine the probable consequences of action alternatives. d. Select a course of action. e. Design an implementation plan/schedule. f. Create a plan for assessing the action to be implemented.

Source: C. C. Lundberg and C. Enz, 1993, A framework for student case preparation, Case Research Journal, 13 (Summer): 144. Reprinted by permission of NACRA, North American Case Research Association.

Exhibit 1 Types of Thinking in Case Preparation: Analysis and Synthesis

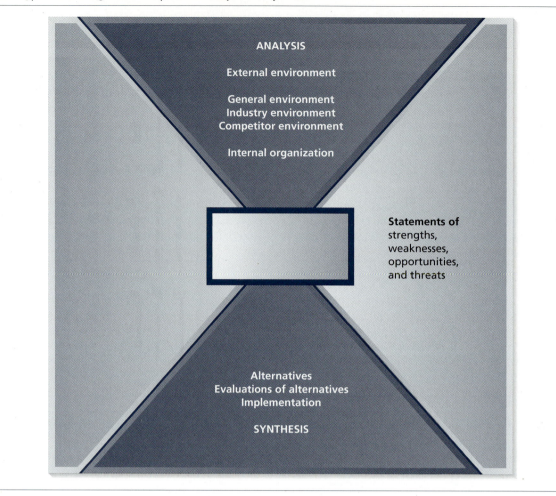

Strategic Profile and Case Analysis Purpose

You will use the strategic profile to briefly present the critical facts from the case that have affected the focal firm's historical strategic direction and performance. The case facts should not be restated in the profile; rather, these comments should show how the critical facts lead to a particular focus for your analysis. This primary focus should be emphasized in this section's conclusion. In addition, this section should state important assumptions about case facts on which your analyses are based.

Situation Analysis

As shown in Table 2, a general starting place for completing a situation analysis is the general environment.

General Environmental Analysis. Your analysis of the general environment should focus on trends in the six segments of the general environment (see Table 3). Many of the segment issues shown in Table 3 for the six segments are explained more fully in Chapter 2 of your book. The objective you should have in evaluating these trends is to be able to *predict* the segments that you expect

Table 2 General Outline for an Oral or Written Presentation

I. Strategic Profile and Case Analysis Purpose

II. Situation Analysis
   A. General environmental analysis
   B. Industry analysis
   C. Competitor analysis
   D. Internal analysis

III. Identification of Environmental Opportunities and Threats and Firm Strengths and Weaknesses (SWOT Analysis)

IV. Strategy Formulation
   A. Strategic alternatives
   B. Alternative evaluation
   C. Alternative choice

V. Strategic Alternative Implementation
   A. Action items
   B. Action plan

to have the most significant influence on your focal firm over the next several years (say three to five years) and to explain your reasoning for your predictions.

Industry Analysis. Porter's five force model is a useful tool for analyzing the industry (or industries) in which

Table 3 Sample General Environmental Categories

Technological Trends
- Information technology continues to become cheaper with more practical applications
- Database technology enables organization of complex data and distribution of information
- Telecommunications technology and networks increasingly provide fast transmission of all sources of data, including voice, written communications, and video information
- Computerized design and manufacturing technologies continue to facilitate quality and flexibility

Demographic Trends
- Regional changes in population due to migration
- Changing ethnic composition of the population
- Aging of the population
- Aging of the "baby boom" generation

Economic Trends
- Interest rates
- Inflation rates
- Savings rates
- Exchange rates
- Trade deficits
- Budget deficits

Political/Legal Trends
- Antitrust enforcement
- Tax policy changes
- Environmental protection laws
- Extent of regulation/deregulation
- Privatizing state monopolies
- State-owned industries

Sociocultural Trends
- Women in the workforce
- Awareness of health and fitness issues
- Concern for the environment
- Concern for customers

Global Trends
- Currency exchange rates
- Free-trade agreements
- Trade deficits

your firm competes. We explain how to use this tool in Chapter 2. In this part of your analysis, you want to determine the attractiveness of an industry (or a segment of an industry) in which your firm is competing. As attractiveness increases, so does the possibility your firm will be able to earn profits by using its chosen strategies. After evaluating the power of the five forces relative to your firm, you should make a judgment as to *how* attractive the industry is in which your firm is competing.

Competitor Analysis. Firms also need to analyze each of their primary competitors. This analysis should identify competitors' current strategies, strategic intent, strategic mission, capabilities, core competencies, and a competitive response profile (see Chapter 2). This information is useful to the focal firm in formulating an appropriate strategy and in predicting competitors' probable responses. Sources that can be used to gather information about an industry and companies with whom the focal firm competes are listed in Appendix I. Included in this list is a wide range of

publications, such as periodicals, newspapers, bibliographies, directories of companies, industry ratios, forecasts, rankings/ratings, and other valuable statistics.

Internal Analysis. Assessing a firm's strengths and weaknesses through a value chain analysis facilitates moving from the external environment to the internal organization. Analysis of the primary and support activities of the value chain provides opportunities to understand how external environmental trends affect the specific activities of a firm. Such analysis helps highlight strengths and weaknesses (see Chapter 3 for an explanation and use of the value chain).

For purposes of preparing an oral or a written presentation, it is important to note that strengths are internal resources and capabilities that have the potential to be core competencies. Weaknesses, on the other hand, are internal resources and capabilities that have the potential to place a firm at a competitive disadvantage relative to its rivals. Thus, some of a firm's resources and capabilities are strengths; others are weaknesses.

When evaluating the internal characteristics of the firm, your analysis of the functional activities emphasized is critical. For instance, if the strategy of the firm is primarily technology driven, it is important to evaluate the firm's R&D activities. If the strategy is market driven, marketing functional activities are of paramount importance. If a firm has financial difficulties, critical financial ratios would require careful evaluation. In fact, because of the importance of financial health, most cases require financial analyses. Appendix II lists and operationally defines several common financial ratios. Included are tables describing profitability, liquidity, leverage, activity, and shareholders' return ratios. Leadership, organizational culture, structure, and control systems are other characteristics of firms you should examine to fully understand the "internal" part of your firm.

Identification of Environmental Opportunities and Threats and Firm Strengths and Weaknesses (SWOT Analysis).

The outcome of the situation analysis is the identification of a firm's strengths and weaknesses and its environmental threats and opportunities. The next step requires that you analyze the strengths and weaknesses and the opportunities and threats for configurations that benefit or do not benefit your firm's efforts to perform well. Case analysts and organizational strategists as well seek to match a firm's strengths with its opportunities. In addition, strengths are chosen to prevent any serious environmental threat from negatively affecting the firm's performance. The key objective of conducting a SWOT analysis is to determine how to position the firm so it can take advantage of opportunities, while simultaneously avoiding or minimizing environmental threats. Results from a SWOT analysis yield valuable insights into the selection of a firm's strategies. The analysis of a case should not be overemphasized relative to the synthesis of results gained from your analytical efforts. There may be a temptation to spend most of your oral or written case analysis on results from the analysis. It is important, however, that you make an equal effort to develop and evaluate alternatives and to design implementation of the chosen strategy.

Strategy Formulation—Strategic Alternatives, Alternative Evaluation, and Alternative Choice.

Developing alternatives is often one of the most difficult steps in preparing an oral or a written presentation. Developing three to four alternative strategies is common (see Chapter 4 for business-level strategy alternatives and Chapter 6 for corporate-level strategy alternatives). Each alternative should be feasible (i.e., it should match the firm's strengths, capabilities, and especially core competencies), and feasibility should be demonstrated. In addition, you should show how each alternative takes advantage of the environmental opportunity or avoids/buffers against environmental threats.

Developing carefully thought out alternatives requires synthesis of your analyses' results and creates greater credibility in oral and written case presentations.

Once you develop strong alternatives, you must evaluate the set to choose the best one. Your choice should be defensible and provide benefits over the other alternatives. Thus, it is important that both alternative development and evaluation of alternatives be thorough. The choice of the best alternative should be explained and defended.

Strategic Alternative Implementation–Action Items and Action Plan.

After selecting the most appropriate strategy (that is, the strategy with the highest probability of helping your firm in its efforts to earn profits), implementation issues require attention. Effective synthesis is important to ensure that you have considered and evaluated all critical implementation issues. Issues you might consider include the structural changes necessary to implement the new strategy. In addition, leadership changes and new controls or incentives may be necessary to implement strategic actions. The implementation actions you recommend should be explicit and thoroughly explained. Occasionally, careful evaluation of implementation actions may show the strategy to be less favorable than you thought originally. A strategy is only as good as the firm's ability to implement it.

Process Issues.

You should ensure that your presentation (either oral or written) has logical consistency throughout. For example, if your presentation identifies one purpose, but your analysis focuses on issues that differ from the stated purpose, the logical inconsistency will be apparent. Likewise, your alternatives should flow from the configuration of strengths, weaknesses, opportunities, and threats you identified by analyzing your firm's external environment and internal organization.

Thoroughness and clarity also are critical to an effective presentation. Thoroughness is represented by the comprehensiveness of the analysis and alternative generation. Furthermore, clarity in the results of the analyses, selection of the best alternative strategy, and design of implementation actions are important. For example, your statement of the strengths and weaknesses should flow clearly and logically from your analysis of your firm's internal organization.

Presentations (oral or written) that show logical consistency, thoroughness, and clarity of purpose, effective analyses, and feasible recommendations (strategy and implementation) are more effective and are likely to be more positively received by your instructor and peers. Furthermore, developing the skills necessary to make such presentations will enhance your future job performance and career success.

Appendix I Sources for Industry and Competitor Analyses

Abstracts and Indexes	
Periodicals	ABI/Inform Business Periodicals Index InfoTrac Custom Journals InfoTrac Custom Newspapers InfoTrac OneFile EBSCO Business Source Premiere Lexis/Nexis Academic Public Affairs Information Service Bulletin (PAIS) Reader's Guide to Periodical Literature
Newspapers	NewsBank—Foreign Broadcast Information NewsBank-Global NewsBank New York Times Index Wall Street Journal Index Wall Street Journal/Barron's Index Washington Post Index
Bibliographies	Encyclopedia of Business Information Sources
Directories	
Companies—General	America's Corporate Families and International Affiliates Hoover's Online: The Business Network www.hoovers.com/free D&B Million Dollar Directory (databases: http://www.dnbmdd.com) Standard & Poor's Corporation Records Standard & Poor's Register of Corporations, Directors, and Executives (http://www.netadvantage.standardandpoors.com for all of Standard & Poor's) Ward's Business Directory of Largest U.S. Companies
Companies—International	America's Corporate Families and International Affiliates Business Asia Business China Business Eastern Europe Business Europe Business International Business International Money Report Business Latin America Directory of American Firms Operating in Foreign Countries Directory of Foreign Firms Operating in the United States Hoover's Handbook of World Business International Directory of Company Histories Mergent's International Manual Mergent Online (http://www.fisonline.com—for "Business and Financial Information Connection to the World") Who Owns Whom
Companies—Manufacturers	Thomas Register of American Manufacturers U.S. Office of Management and Budget, Executive Office of the President, Standard Industrial Classification Manual U.S. Manufacturer's Directory, Manufacturing & Distribution, USA
Companies—Private	D&B Million Dollar Directory Ward's Business Directory of Largest U.S. Companies

Appendix I Sources for Industry and Competitor Analyses (*Continued*)

Companies—Public	Annual Reports and 10-K Reports *Disclosure (corporate reports) Q-File* Security and Exchange Commision Filings & Forms (EDGAR) http://www.sec.gov/edgar.shtml *Mergent's Manuals:* • *Mergent's Bank and Finance Manual* • *Mergent's Industrial Manual* • *Mergent's International Manual* • *Mergent's Municipal and Government Manual* • *Mergent's OTC Industrial Manual* • *Mergent's OTC Unlisted Manual* • *Mergent's Public Utility Manual* • *Mergent's Transportation Manual* Standard & Poor's Corporation, *Standard Corporation Descriptions:* http://www.netadvantage.standardandpoors.com • *Standard & Poor's Analyst Handbook* • *Standard & Poor's Industry Surveys* • *Standard & Poor's Statistical Service*
Companies—Subsidiaries and Affiliates	*America's Corporate Families and International Affiliates* *Ward's Directory* *Who Owns Whom* *Mergent's Industry Review* *Standard & Poor's Analyst's Handbook* *Standard & Poor's Industry Surveys* (2 volumes) U.S. Department of Commerce, *U.S. Industrial Outlook*
Industry Ratios	Dun & Bradstreet, *Industry Norms and Key Business Ratios* *RMA's Annual Statement Studies* *Troy Almanac of Business and Industrial Financial Ratios*
Industry Forecasts	International Trade Administration, *U.S. Industry & Trade Outlook*
Rankings & Ratings	Annual Report on American Industry in *Forbes* *Business Rankings Annual* *Mergent's Industry Review* http://www.worldcatlibraries.org *Standard & Poor's Industry Report Service* http://www.netadvantage.standardandpoors.com *Value Line Investment Survey* *Ward's Business Directory of Largest U.S. Companies*
Statistics	*American Statistics Index (ASI)* Bureau of the Census, U.S. Department of Commerce, *Economic Census Publications* Bureau of the Census, U.S. Department of Commerce, *Statistical Abstract of the United States* Bureau of Economic Analysis, U.S. Department of Commerce, *Survey of Current Business* Internal Revenue Service, U.S. Treasury Department, *Statistics of Income: Corporation Income Tax Returns* *Statistical Reference Index (SRI)*

Appendix II Financial Analysis in Case Studies

Table A-1 Profitability Ratios

Ratio	Formula	What It Shows
1. Return on total assets	$\dfrac{\text{Profits after taxes}}{\text{Total assets}}$ or $\dfrac{\text{Profits after taxes} + \text{Interest}}{\text{Total assets}}$	The net return on total investments of the firm or The return on both creditors' and shareholders' investments
2. Return on stockholder's equity (or return on net worth)	$\dfrac{\text{Profits after taxes}}{\text{Total stockholder's equity}}$	How profitably the company is utilizing shareholders' funds
3. Return on common equity	$\dfrac{\text{Profits after taxes} - \text{Preferred stock dividends}}{\text{Total stockholder's equity} - \text{Par value of preferred stock}}$	The net return to common stockholders
4. Operating profit margin (or return on sales)	$\dfrac{\text{Profits before taxes and before interest}}{\text{Sales}}$	The firm's profitability from regular operations
5. Net profit margin (or net return on sales)	$\dfrac{\text{Profits after taxes}}{\text{Sales}}$	The firm's net profit as a percentage of total sales

Table A-2 Liquidity Ratios

Ratio	Formula	What It Shows
1. Current ratio	$\dfrac{\text{Current assets}}{\text{Current liabilities}}$	The firm's ability to meet its current financial liabilities
2. Quick ratio (or acid-test ratio)	$\dfrac{\text{Current assets} - \text{Inventory}}{\text{Current liabilities}}$	The firm's ability to pay off short-term obligations without relying on sales of inventory
3. Inventory to net working capital	$\dfrac{\text{Inventory}}{\text{Current assets} - \text{Current liabilities}}$	The extent to which the firm's working capital is tied up in inventory

Table A-3 Leverage Ratios

Ratio	Formula	What It Shows
1. Debt-to-assets	$\dfrac{\text{Total debt}}{\text{Total assets}}$	Total borrowed funds as a percentage of total assets
2. Debt-to-equity	$\dfrac{\text{Total debt}}{\text{Total shareholders' equity}}$	Borrowed funds versus the funds provided by shareholders
3. Long-term debt-to-equity	$\dfrac{\text{Long-term debt}}{\text{Total shareholders' equity}}$	Leverage used by the firm
4. Times-interest-earned (or coverage ratio)	$\dfrac{\text{Profits before interest and taxes}}{\text{Total interest charges}}$	The firm's ability to meet all interest payments
5. Fixed charge coverage	$\dfrac{\text{Profits before taxes and interest} + \text{Lease obligations}}{\text{Total interest charges} + \text{Lease obligations}}$	The firm's ability to meet all fixed-charge obligations including lease payments

Table A-4 Activity Ratios

Ratio	Formula	What It Shows
1. Inventory turnover	$\dfrac{\text{Sales}}{\text{Inventory of finished goods}}$	The effectiveness of the firm in employing inventory
2. Fixed-assets turnover	$\dfrac{\text{Sales}}{\text{Fixed assets}}$	The effectiveness of the firm in utilizing plant and equipment
3. Total assets turnover	$\dfrac{\text{Sales}}{\text{Total assets}}$	The effectiveness of the firm in utilizing total assets
4. Accounts receivable turnover	$\dfrac{\text{Annual credit sales}}{\text{Accounts receivable}}$	How many times the total receivables have been collected during the accounting period
5. Average collecting period	$\dfrac{\text{Accounts receivable}}{\text{Average daily sales}}$	The average length of time the firm waits to collect payment after sales

Table A-5 Shareholders' Return Ratios

Ratio	Formula	What It Shows
1. Dividend yield on common stock	$\dfrac{\text{Annual dividend per share}}{\text{Current market price per share}}$	A measure of return to common stockholders in the form of dividends
2. Price-earnings ratio	$\dfrac{\text{Current market price per share}}{\text{After-tax earnings per share}}$	An indication of market perception of the firm; usually, the faster-growing or less risky firms tend to have higher PE ratios than the slower-growing or more risky firms
3. Dividend payout ratio	$\dfrac{\text{Annual dividends per share}}{\text{After-tax earnings per share}}$	An indication of dividends paid out as a percentage of profits
4. Cash flow per share	$\dfrac{\text{After-tax profits + Depression}}{\text{Number of common shares outstanding}}$	A measure of total cash per share available for use by the firm

Ali Farhoomand

University of Hong Kong

China is a place where miracles are made.

JACK MA, FOUNDER AND CHAIRMAN OF ALIBABA GROUP[1]

On November 6, 2007, Alibaba.com debuted on the Hong Kong Stock Exchange, raising US$1.5 billion to become the world's biggest Internet stock offering since Google's initial public offering (IPO) in 2004. On the first trading day, frenzied purchases of the stock pushed prices up by 193 percent, the fourth-largest first-day gain in Hong Kong's stock exchange in three years. The closing price of US$5.09[2] per share gave Alibaba.com a value of about US$25.6 billion, making it the fifth-most-valuable Internet company and the largest in Asia outside Japan. It also made the company's stock among the most expensive on the Hong Kong exchange,[3] trading at 306 times its projected 2007 earnings of US$83.6 million.[4] In contrast, Yahoo!, a globally recognized "dot-com" brand that held a 39 percent stake in pre-IPO Alibaba.com, and Japan's SoftBank, which owned 29.3 percent of Alibaba.com prior to the IPO, traded at only around 60 times their projected earnings. In other words, shareholders had displayed extreme optimism about Alibaba.com's prospective earnings by paying a significant premium to own the company's shares.

Barely a week after the IPO, Alibaba.com was already reported to be in talks with SoftBank to set up a joint venture in early 2008 in Japan. Although the Japanese telecom giant disclosed no details regarding the proposed venture, it was likely that Alibaba.com would expand its service to mobile users in Japan, a market that had been impenetrable to the Chinese e-commerce company.[5] On its home turf, parent company Alibaba Group had already proven its mettle by topping EachNet, an older rival backed by global leader eBay.[6] Founder and Chairman

Jack Ma had made it his aim to make the Alibaba Group one of three largest Internet companies in the world and a Fortune 500 company.[7] Could the IPO be the first step to Alibaba.com's global market dominance, or would it be overtaken just as quickly as it rose to regional pre-eminence?

Internet and E-Commerce in China

The world's most populous nation had 162 million Internet users as of June 2007.[8] Although the Chinese Internet-using population was second only to that of the United States,[9] China's Internet penetration rate of 12.3 percent significantly trailed those of the United States, Japan, and South Korea, whose penetration rates were all more than 65 percent.[10] Nevertheless, with the penetration rate growing at around three percentage points annually (see Exhibit 1), China was expected to experience even more rapid growth in the scale of penetration, having crossed the critical threshold of 10 percent and heading into the steep phase of the S-curve.[11]

Similarly, e-commerce was still in its infancy in China. Official figures estimated that only 25.5 percent of Internet users in China had engaged in online shopping, whereas the figure was 71 percent in the United States. The utilization rate of online sales and marketing was also very low—a mere 4.3 percent compared to 15 percent in the United States. The only exception to the trend was the rate of online stock transactions, which was 14.1 percent, narrowly beating the U.S. rate of 13 percent. The official explanation was the frenzy over the financial markets in China that started around 2006.[12]

Ricky Lai prepared this case under the supervision of Professor Ali Farhoom and for class discussion. This case is not intended to show effective or ineffective handling of decision or business processes.

Exhibit 1 China's Internet Penetration Rate

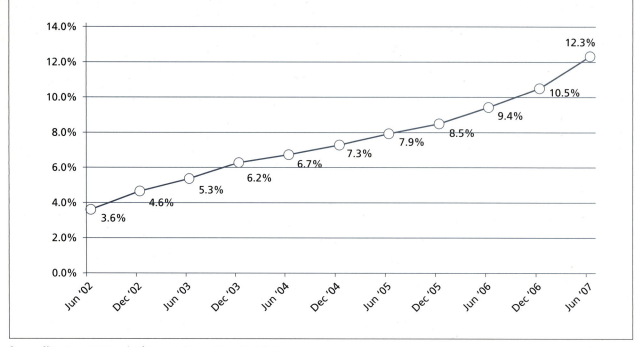

Source: China Internet Network Information Center, 2007, The 20th CNNIC Statistical Survey Report on the Internet Development in China, http://www.cnnic. net.cn/download/2007/20thCNNICreport-en.pdf (accessed November 19, 2007).

Chinese Internet media market researcher, iResearch Consulting Group, valued the Chinese online shopping market at US$1.5 billion in the first quarter of 2007. The online shopping market comprised the customer-to-customer and business-to-customer segments, with the former accounting for US$1.3 billion, or 89.7 percent of the market in China. Overall, the Chinese online shopping market recorded a 14.8 percent rise in the first quarter of 2007 compared to the preceding quarter and a massive 64.1 percent jump over the previous year (see Exhibit 2).[13] By comparison, the online business-to-business (B2B) market was much bigger, valued at US$65.7 billion in the second quarter of 2007, increasing 10.4 percent quarter-on-quarter and a staggering 69.8 percent year-on-year (see Exhibit 3).[14]

SMEs in China

Small and medium-sized enterprises (SMEs) have been a key driving force in the booming Chinese economy. In 2004, SMEs contributed 68.8 percent to the nation's gross industrial output (in current prices).[15] iResearch estimated that the number of SMEs in China would rise from 31.5 million in 2006 to 50 million in 2012 (see Exhibit 4).[16] Out of these 31.5 million Chinese SMEs, a mere 8.8 million, or 28 percent, utilized

third-party B2B e-commerce platforms. With the Chinese government's "11th Five-Year Planning for the Development of E-Commerce" encouraging SMEs to use third-party e-commerce platforms, however, the numbers were expected to rise to 41 million and 82 percent, respectively, in 2012 (see Exhibit 5).[17] The implication was that e-commerce had plenty of room for growth in China, at least among SMEs, where the market was expected to almost quadruple between 2007 and 2012.

The rising popularity of e-commerce among SMEs in China was fueled by several challenges in the traditional trade environment, including:

- Limited geographic presence restricting SMEs' ability to develop customer and supplier relationships beyond their immediate vicinity
- Fragmentation of suppliers and buyers, which made it difficult to find and communicate with suitable trading partners
- Limited communication channels and information sources through which to market and promote products and services or to find new markets and suppliers
- A relatively small scale of operation, limiting SMEs' resources for sales and marketing
- Absence of efficient mechanisms for evaluating the trustworthiness of trading partners[18]

Exhibit 2 Growth of the Chinese Online Shopping Market

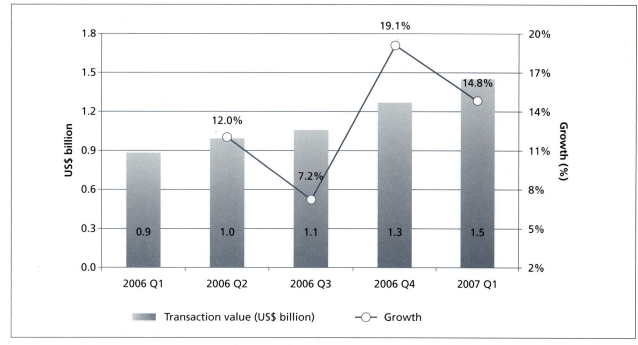

Exhibit 3 Growth of the Chinese B2B E-Commerce Market

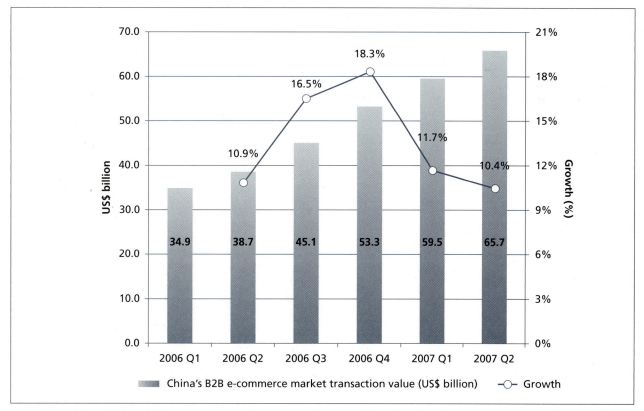

Exhibit 4 Growth of Chinese SMEs

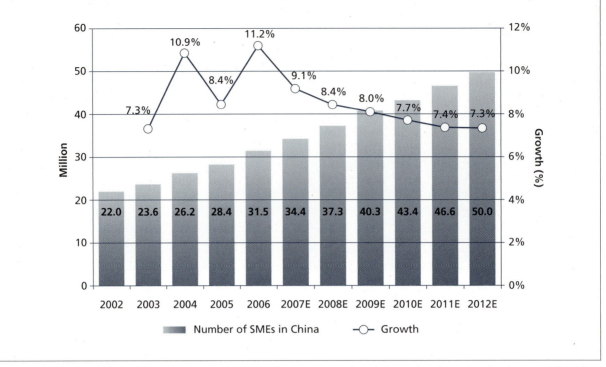

Source: iResearch Inc., 2007, China SME number to reach 50 million in 2012, http://www.iresearchgroup.com.cn/Consulting/others/DetailNews.asp?id=65361, June 6 (accessed November 22, 2007).

Exhibit 5 Usage of Third-Party E-Commerce among Chinese SMEs

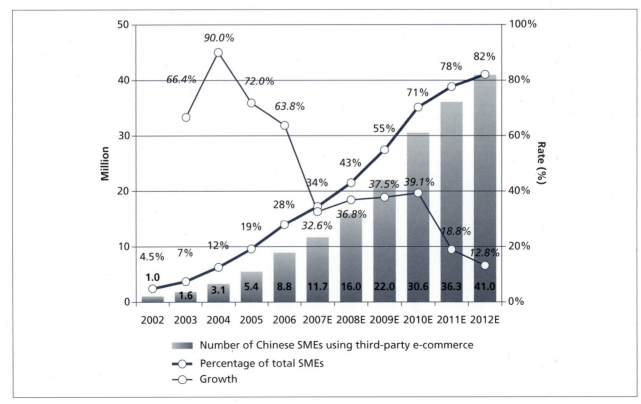

Source: iResearch Inc., 2007, B2B e-commerce should start with interest of SMEs, http://www.iresearchgroup.com.cn/html/Consulting/B2B/DetailNews_id_67225.html, July 12 (accessed November 22, 2007).

Alibaba.com

History

Alibaba's first online marketplace was launched as Alibaba Online in December 1998. Originally, the China-based Web site operated as a bulletin board service for businesses to post, buy, and sell trade leads. In June 1999, Jack Ma and 18 other founders formed the parent company, Alibaba Group, inaugurating its Web site in simplified Chinese to serve the Chinese mainland market. Three months later, a major operating subsidiary in China, Alibaba China, was established to carry out the business of operating B2B marketplaces. Within months, three more sites were launched: an English site for international users, a Korean site for Korean users, and a traditional Chinese site for Chinese users outside of China. In October 2000, Alibaba launched the Gold Supplier membership service for Chinese exporters, followed in August 2001 by the launch of International TrustPass, a membership service catering to exporters outside of China. China TrustPass was launched in March 2002 to serve SMEs engaged in domestic trade.

In September 2006, to facilitate the IPO of its B2B business, Alibaba underwent a restructuring of its B2B arm, Alibaba.com (see Exhibit 6). The principal company emerging from the restructuring, Alibaba.com Limited, became 17 percent–owned by public shareholders, with the remaining shares of the company held by the parent company, employees, and consultants.

Jack Ma

Lead founder and chairman of Alibaba Group, Jack Ma is a native of Hangzhou, located about 100 miles southwest of Shanghai, where the company's headquarters are located.

Exhibit 6 Corporate Structure of Alibaba.com Before and After Restructuring

(Continued)

Exhibit 6 Corporate Structure of Alibaba.com Before and After Restructuring (*Continued*)

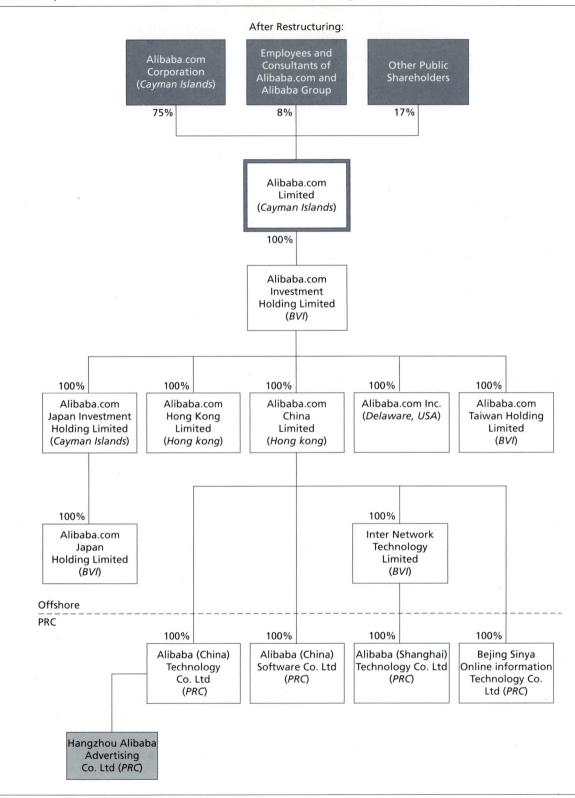

Notes:

_____ Denotes equity ownership

_ _ _ _ _ Denotes contractual relationship

* Formerly known as Alibaba.com E-Commerce Corp.

Source: Alibaba.com, 2007, Global Offering Prospectus, 63–64.

Growing up during China's Cultural Revolution, Ma became interested in learning English. Starting at age 12, and for the next 8 years, he rode his bicycle 40 minutes every morning to a hotel near the West Lake and worked on his English by giving free tours to foreigners. In spite of this effort, he failed his university entrance examinations twice before being accepted to a teachers' university.[19] The low-paying teaching job he was offered after graduation did not interest Ma, and in 1995 he found himself employed by the Chinese government to settle a dispute between a Chinese firm and its U.S. partner. Purportedly, Ma was held captive by the U.S. partner at gunpoint for two days before he regained his freedom by agreeing to become a partner in an Internet startup in China, even though he had no concept of the Internet at all.[20]

Although he never carried out his end of the deal, Ma came into his first contact with a computer and the Internet in Seattle, Washington, and was surprised to find nothing when he searched for "beer" and "China." He then returned to China, borrowed US$2,000, and started a company and Web site called China Pages. The Web site shared a strikingly similar ideology with Alibaba.com: to list Chinese companies on the Internet and help foreigners find their Web sites. Eventually, China Telecom would buy out Ma's stake and he would end up returning to civil service to promote e-commerce. Always looking for a chance to fulfill his dream of setting up his own e-commerce company, Ma stepped out of the civil service again in 1998 and resumed work on his vision to connect Chinese companies to the world through the Internet. This vision was realized in December of that year with the launch of Alibaba Online.

Business Model

By the second quarter of 2007, Alibaba.com was the largest online B2B e-commerce company in China, based on the number of registered users and market share by revenue.[21] The international marketplace was served by their English-language Web site, Alibaba.com, which focused on global importers and exporters. The Chinese marketplace was served by their Chinese-language interface, Alibaba.com.cn, which focused on suppliers and buyers trading domestically in China.

The two B2B marketplaces provided a platform to facilitate e-commerce between business sellers, whom Alibaba.com referred to as "suppliers," and wholesale buyers (see Exhibit 7 for Alibaba. com's value proposition). Suppliers and buyers used the marketplaces to establish their presence online, identify potential trading partners, and conduct business with each other. Suppliers and some buyers used the marketplaces to host their company profiles and catalogues in standardized formats known as "storefronts" and post "listings" such as products, services, and trade leads. Users could view storefronts and listings in over 30 industry categories and nearly 5,000 product categories by either searching for keywords or browsing through the online industry directory (see Exhibit 8 for a typical trading process). For many suppliers, their storefront or listing was their only presence on the Internet. As of June 30, 2007, there were more than 2.4 million storefronts. In the first half of 2007, users posted a monthly average of 2.9 million new listings on the marketplaces.

Through active listings, inquiry exchanges, instant messaging, discussion forums, and other user-friendly community features, suppliers and buyers formed large, interactive online communities on Alibaba.com's marketplaces. In June 2007, Alibaba.com registered more than 540,000 peak simultaneous online users of TradeManager, an instant messaging tool for trade communications. The two marketplaces collectively hosted more than 200 online forums and more than 4.2 million registered users.

To enhance the breadth and depth of the marketplaces, Alibaba.com offered basic features and services to all registered users free of charge. Revenue was generated from suppliers who purchased services, primarily membership packages that provided priority placement

Exhibit 7 Alibaba.com's Value Proposition

Suppliers		Buyers
• Access to active global buyer community		• Access to active global supplier community
• Targeted marketing to reach buyers		• Broad selection of listings
• Customer service and training	**Alibaba.com**	• Access to high-quality, organized information • Easy-to-use interface
• Always online		• Convenient, real-time medium
• Budget certainty through a fixed subscription fee model		• Authentication and trust profiles of suppliers

Source: Alibaba.com, 2007, Global Offering Prospectus, 78.

Exhibit 8 Typical Trading Process in the Alibaba.com Marketplace

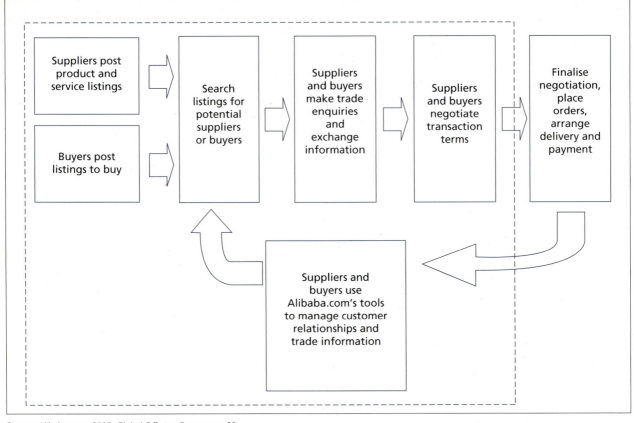

Source: Alibaba.com, 2007, Global Offering Prospectus, 83.

of storefronts and listings in the industry directory and search results. These paying members generated additional revenue by subscribing to value-added services, including purchases of additional keywords to improve their rankings in search results and premium placement on Alibaba.com's Web pages for enhanced exposure and visibility.

Results

Alibaba.com experienced significant growth in the number of registered users (Table 1) and in the number of paying members (Table 2) from 2004 to mid-2007.[22]

For the international marketplace, as of the end of June 2007, about 17.7 percent of users were based in the United States, followed by 8.7 percent from the European Union (excluding the United Kingdom), 8.2 percent from India, 6.2 percent from the United Kingdom, and 2.7 percent from Canada.

For the Chinese marketplace, as of the end of June 2007, Guangdong led in the regional breakdown of registered users with a 21.5 percent share, followed by Zhejiang with 8.5 percent, Jiangsu with 6.6 percent, Shandong with 5.3 percent, and Shanghai with 4.6 percent.

Revenue increased at a staggering cumulative annual growth rate of 94.8 percent from US$48.3 million at the end of 2004 to US$183.2 million at the end of 2006. According to Alibaba.com's detailed financial data (see Exhibit 9), the international marketplace had been

Table 1 Growth in the Number of Alibaba.com's Registered Users

	End of 2004	End of 2005	Year-on-Year	End of 2006	Year-on-Year
Total registered users	6.0 million	11.0 million	+82.6%	19.8 million	+80.2%
International marketplace	1.2 million	1.9 million	+67.2%	3.1 million	+59.8%
Chinese marketplace	4.8 million	9.0 million	+86.3%	16.6 million	+84.6%

Table 2 Growth in the Number of Alibaba.com's Paying Members

	End of 2004	End of 2005	Year-on-Year	End of 2006	Year-on-Year
Total paying members	77,922	141,614	+81.7%	219,098	+54.7%
International marketplace	11,450	19,983	+74.5%	29,525	+47.8%
Chinese marketplace	66,472	121,631	+83.0%	189,573	+55.9%

Exhibit 9 Alibaba.com Financial Data, 2004–2007

	Year ending 31 December						Six months ending 30 June			
	2004		2005		2006		2006		2007	
	Amount	% of revenue	Amount	% of revenue	Amount	% of revenue	Amount	% of revenue	Amount	% of revenue
							(unaudited)			
				(in thousands of Rmb, except percentages)						
Revenue										
International marketplace	254,765	70.9	527,227	71.4	991,869	72.7	431,481	72.7	695,398	72.6
Chinese marketplace	104,670	29.1	211,070	28.6	371,993	27.3	162,156	27.3	260,965	27.3
Others	—	—	—	—	—	—	—	—	1,353	0.1
Total	359,435	100.0	738,297	100.0	1,363,862	100.0	593,637	100.0	957,716	100.0
Cost of revenue[1]	(62,569)	(17.4)	(126,509)	(17.1)	(237,625)	(17.4)	(109,131)	(18.4)	(122,717)	(12.8)
Gross profit	296,866	82.6	611,788	82.9	1,126,237	82.6	484,506	81.6	834,999	87.2
Sales & marketing expenses[1][2]	(194,773)	(54.2)	(393,950)	(53.4)	(610,198)	(44.8)	(299,034)	(50.3)	(307,428)	(32.1)
Product development expenses[1][2]	(19,151)	(5.4)	(35,678)	(4.8)	(105,486)	(7.7)	(47,256)	(8.0)	(58,278)	(6.1)
General and administrative expenses[1][2]	(57,639)	(16.0)	(101,082)	(13.7)	(159,969)	(11.7)	(59,820)	(10.1)	(88,432)	(9.2)
Other operating (loss) income, net	(426)	(0.1)	14,465	1.9	17,645	1.3	800	0.1	1,190	0.1
Profit from operation	24,877	6.9	95,543	12.9	268,229	19.7	79,196	13.3	382,051	39.9
Interest income	3,591	1.0	7,876	1.1	23,159	1.7	10,340	1.7	17,699	1.8
Profit before income taxes	28,468	7.9	103,419	14.0	291,388	21.4	89,596	15.1	399,705	41.7
Income tax credits (charges)	45,393	12.6	(32,965)	(4.5)	(71,450)	(5.3)	(28,253)	(4.8)	(104,543)	(10.9)
Profit for the year/period attributable to equity owners	73,861	20.5	70,454	9.5	219,938	16.1	61,283	10.3	295,207	30.8

Notes:
(1) Includes share-based compensation expenses, which are allocated as follows:

(Continued)

Exhibit 9 Alibaba.com Financial Data, 2004,2007 *(Continued)*

	Year ending 31 December						Six months ending 30 June			
	2004		2005		2006		2006		2007	
	Amount	% of revenue	Amount	% of revenue	Amount	% of revenue	Amount	% of revenue	Amount	% of revenue
							(unaudited)			
				(in thousands of Rmb, except percentages)						
Cost of revenue	1,936	0.5	8,766	1.2	23,335	1.7	13,258	2.2	6,207	0.7
Sales & marketing expenses	5,259	1.5	26,920	3.6	50,068	3.7	21,975	3.7	21,517	2.2
Product development expenses	1,382	0.4	5,126	0.7	16,344	1.2	7,727	1.3	6,582	0.7
General and administrative expenses	2,838	0.8	8,079	1.1	24,157	1.8	10,442	1.8	20,183	2.1
Total share-based compensation expenses	11,415	3.2	48,891	6.6	113,904	8.4	53,402	9.0	54,489	5.7

(2) Includes expenses of Alibaba Group not related to the B2B business as follows:

	Year ending 31 December						Six months ending 30 June			
	2004		2005		2006		2006		2007	
	Amount	% of revenue	Amount	% of revenue	Amount	% of revenue	Amount	% of revenue	Amount	% of revenue
							(unaudited)			
				(in thousands of Rmb, except percentages)						
Sales & marketing expenses	—	—	35,959	4.9	83,186	6.1	58,661	9.9	—	—
Product development expenses	—	—	1,414	0.2	6,748	0.5	3,705	0.6	—	—
General and administrative expenses	9,594	2.7	29,972	4.0	47,573	3.5	18,818	3.2	—	—
Total	9,594	2.7	67,345	9.1	137,507	10.1	81,184	13.7	—	—

Source: Alibaba. Com, 2007, Globl Offering Prospectus, 102–103.

steadily contributing slightly more than 70 percent of revenue, while the Chinese marketplace brought in just short of 30 percent. Specifically, Alibaba.com derived around 71 percent of its revenue from Gold Supplier members of the international marketplace, who paid at least US$5,373.60 per year for a standard package and US$8,060.40 for a premium package. Alibaba.com indicated that it would merge the two tiers of membership beginning November 2007, with the new rate starting at US$6,717.00 per year.[23]

Strengths

Alibaba.com believed that it had certain competitive strengths to merit such moves as the membership merger, which would effectively produce more revenue.

First, Alibaba.com had built a premier brand in the e-commerce domain, boasting the highest traffic among all online B2B marketplaces. According to Internet statistics compiler Alexa.com, Alibaba.com was the most visited site in the e-commerce and international business and trade categories,[24] in addition to being the largest online B2B company in China. Alibaba.com attracted suppliers on the strength of the large number of potential buyers that used the marketplaces, which in turn attracted more buyers to sign up with Alibaba.com. Alibaba.com's breadth and depth in its marketplaces were difficult to replicate, thus creating an effective barrier to new entrants and a virtually insurmountable lead over competitors.

Second, Alibaba.com focused exclusively on the highly lucrative SME sector. Providing tools and solutions tailored to SMEs, Alibaba.com was confident in the value proposition of its service offerings. For example, Alibaba.com provided trust ratings for suppliers and buyers, thus facilitating the process of selecting potential trading partners. The fixed subscription fee model also gave budget certainty to SMEs, which were often budget-sensitive and averse to ad-hoc expenditures. Users and subscribers had responded positively, leading to the formation of interactive communities at the online marketplaces. Alibaba.com had also installed staff dedicated to enhancing the community experience of users to build up loyalty to and trust in the brand.

Third, Alibaba.com was confident about its sales force and customer service support in attracting and retaining users, especially those who paid for subscriptions. As of mid-2007, Alibaba.com maintained more than 1,900 full-time field salespeople in 30 cities across China, more than 800 telephone salespeople, and more than 400 full-time customer-service employees, all of whom were grouped into teams in direct, daily contact with current and prospective customers. The customer service arm provided customer feedback to the sales force which, in turn, made use of the findings and worked with the product development team to deliver services that more closely met customers' needs. For example, a number of services available to Alibaba.com users, such as e-mail and instant messaging, had initially been proposed by customers and later developed by Alibaba.com.

Strategy

Alibaba.com's mission was to make it easy to do business anywhere.[25] To accomplish this mission, Alibaba.com set forth a multi-pronged strategy to make its online marketplaces more effective for SMEs around the world.

First, Alibaba.com tried to increase the size of its marketplaces through the expansion of its user base and active listings. The company believed that the breadth and quality of users and listings were critical to the success of the marketplaces. To that end, Alibaba.com continued to leverage the networking aspect of its online marketplaces, its leading market position, and the "Alibaba" brand name to increase its user base worldwide. It also planned to conduct targeted marketing to potential users in specific industries and geographic locations.

Second, Alibaba.com planned to enhance community experiences to further improve user loyalty and activity through continued development and introduction of new features and tools. Specifically, it planned to invest further in the existing instant messaging service, online forums, and other communication services. Alibaba.com also planned to continue organizing regular meetings, training, and offline events for registered users and paying members to further build the sense of community.

Third, Alibaba.com was keen to monetize its user base after providing years of free service to the majority of its members. The company would strive not only to convert more users into paying members, but also to generate more revenue from existing paying members through sales of value-added services, such as additional keyword listing and premium listing placement.

Fourth, Alibaba.com planned to selectively expand its sales and customer service capabilities into international markets, either directly or through third-party agents, to acquire more paying members and sell premium services outside China. The company had already taken the first step by offering Gold Supplier membership packages to Hong Kong suppliers in 2007. Alibaba.com was already in talks with Japanese telecommunications giant SoftBank about a joint venture to tap the Japanese market, for which significant upgrades to Alibaba.com's Japanese language Web site were already in the pipeline.

Fifth, Alibaba.com believed that its online marketplace platform could be extended beyond pure trade marketing to address users' daily business processes, such as customer relationship management and internal operations. It aimed to enhance the loyalty of its users by providing business applications through the marketplace platform and becoming an integral part of users' business operations. For example, it launched an Internet-based business management application called Alisoft Export Edition, developed by sister company Alisoft, for users based in China.

Finally, Alibaba.com was set to expand its business through acquisitions, investments, licensing arrangements, and partnerships. The underlying objectives would be to expand its user and revenue base, widen geographic coverage, enhance content and service offerings, advance its technology, and strengthen its talent pool. Alibaba.com also considered leveraging its relationship with parent company Alibaba Group to seek cross-selling, cross-marketing, and licensing arrangements and other opportunities.

Competition from Global Sources

Despite Alibaba.com's dominance in the online B2B market in China, the company was not immune to competition from both domestic and international competitors (see Exhibit 10). Chief among Alibaba.com's competitors in the international marketplace was international B2B giant Global Sources, whose online

directory was bolstered by the many other B2B services it offered, such as print business directories and exhibitions.

Founded in Hong Kong in 1971 as a monthly trade magazine for consumer products made in Asia for export to Western markets, Global Sources claimed to have a community of over 647,000 buyers and 160,000 suppliers as of the end of September 2007.[26] Global Sources also boasted the following:

- It enabled suppliers to sell to hard-to-reach buyers in over 230 countries.
- It delivered information on 2 million products annually.
- It operated 14 online marketplaces that delivered more than 23 million sales leads annually.
- It published 13 monthly magazines and over 100 sourcing research reports per year.
- It organized 9 trade-specific exhibitions that ran 22 times a year across seven cities.

In mainland China, Global Sources had over 2,000 staff members in 44 locations and a community of over one million registered online users and magazine readers of its Chinese-language media.

Global Sources clearly posed a threat to Alibaba.com because it was earning more and more of its revenue online, as evidenced by its 2006 annual report demonstrating that its online businesses generated more than 40 percent of its total revenue (Table 3).

Exhibit 10 Market Share of China's Online E-Commerce Market, by Revenue

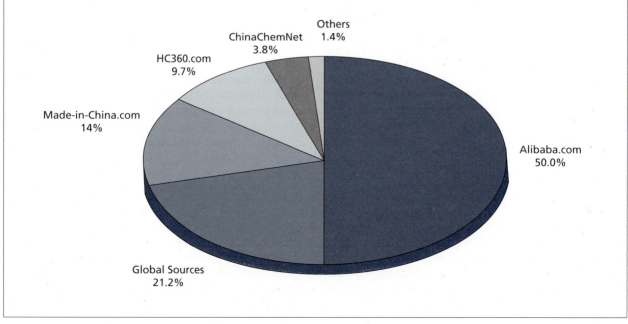

Source: iResearch Inc., 2007, China's B2B e-commerce market reached RMB 489.1 Billion in Q2 of 2007, http://www.iresearchgroup.com.cn/html/consulting/B2B/DetailNews it 72299 html, November 5 (accessed November 20, 2007).

Table 3 Contributors to Global Sources's 2006 Revenue[27]

	Revenue (US$ million)	% of total
Online	64.4	41.2
Print	48.7	31.1
Exhibitions	42.1	26.9
Miscellaneous	1.3	0.8
Total	156.5	

The growth strategy of Global Sources was built around four key foundations:[28]

- Market penetration through increasing revenue from exhibitions by selling more booths and increasing the average revenue per booth; cross-selling to clients not using online, print, or shows, particularly the large number of new clients patronizing only exhibitions; and expanding the online customer base by offering new services and pricing packages for the new Global Sources Online 2.0.
- New product development: Global Sources actively increased its online marketplaces, magazines, and exhibitions. In 2007, it added 11 new online marketplaces, monthly publications, and trade shows and announced eight new exhibitions to be launched in 2008 and 2009.
- Expansion into China's domestic B2B market: domestic trade in China was an attractive growth market and was synergistic with Global Sources's existing media serving China's export and import sectors. Global Sources launched new exhibitions in China in the hopes of attracting volume buyers as attendees. To complement these exhibitions and other vertical, industry-focused markets, the company launched China Global Sources Online to enable international suppliers to sell to China's domestic B2B market.
- Acquisitions and alliances: Global Sources, like Alibaba.com, was on the lookout for complementary businesses, technologies, and products that would help it to achieve and maintain leading positions in the markets it served. In 2007, in support of its plans to expand online business within China, Global Sources acquired the business and Web site assets of a Beijing-based online media company, Blue Bamboo China Ventures.

Given the similarities between the current positioning and growth strategies of Alibaba.com and Global Sources, competition between the two companies for the vast and growing Chinese market is bound to intensify.

Other Competition and Constraints

Competitors in Alibaba.com's Chinese marketplace include domestic B2B e-commerce platforms such as HC360.com, the Web site operated by HC International. As a generalized e-commerce platform, Alibaba.com also had to contend with specialized platforms that focused on vertical coverage of specific industries, such as ChinaChemNet, which catered to the chemical industry in China. Because Alibaba.com founded its success on the breadth of its horizontal coverage of industries, it would be tremendously difficult for it to pursue vertical coverage of a specific industry without upsetting its basic business model. In addition, there was indirect competition from other marketing service providers, such as Internet search engines and traditional trading channels, including exhibitions, trade magazines, classified advertisements, and outdoor advertising.

As Alibaba.com served mostly Chinese SMEs, it was also captive to the same problems that impeded offline commerce, ranging from China's credit and foreign exchange controls to the deficient national distribution network. Many procedures involved in a successful business deal, such as financing and shipping, were simply beyond Alibaba.com's scope. Alibaba.com also faced other issues with online commerce, such as fears about fraud, privacy, and trust that discouraged businesses from adopting the Internet as a medium of commerce.

Internally, Alibaba.com's executives regarded their charismatic and visionary founder and chairman Jack Ma as the company's cornerstone. However, Ma has indicated that his plan is to eventually exit to make room for the next generation of leadership. Despite the fact that many senior executives and potential future leaders of Alibaba.com were handpicked by Ma, questions remained over the issue of succession, especially with Ma's departure looming on the horizon.

At the end of 2007, Alibaba.com experienced a reshuffling of its senior management, with several executives going on study sabbaticals outside of China. Some industry watchers believed the move was a precursor to taking the company global by equipping its Chinese executives with international experience. Such speculation was heightened by reports that Alibaba.com had encountered difficulties in recruiting international business talent.[29]

The Way Forward

Four months into a record-breaking IPO that significantly raised both the capital and profile of the company, Alibaba.com's share price had slipped to around half of the launch value. Could investor optimism about

Alibaba.com be slipping? How could Alibaba.com best utilize the proceeds from the IPO to scale new heights in the B2B e-commerce industry and beyond?[30] Would it be able to emerge from the shadows of its totemic founder and mature into an international conglomerate? Would Alibaba.com thrive under a rising Chinese economy, or would its success only last for "One Thousand and One Nights"?

NOTES

1. R. Kwong & T. Mitchell, 2007, Alibaba shares soar on first day of trading, *Financial Times* (Asia Edition), November 7.
2. US$1 = HK$7.76425 on November 6, 2007.
3. R. Kwong & T. Mitchell, 2007, Alibaba shares soar on first day of trading, *Financial Times* (Asia Edition), November 7.
4. US$1 = RMB 7.4638 on November 6, 2007.
5. R. Kwong, 2007, SoftBank and Alibaba in Talks, *Financial Times* (Asia Edition), November 14.
6. B. Liu, 2007, US Giant eBay Loses Ground to Taobao, *China Daily*, April 17.
7. J. Macartney, 2007, Workaholic's road to fortune "like riding on a blind tiger," *The Times, London*, November 7.
8. China Internet Network Information Center, 2007, The latest statistics, http://www.cnnic.net.cn/en/index/0O/index.htm (accessed November 19, 2007).
9. CIA, 2007, *The World Fact Book*, https://www.cia.gov/library/publications/the-world-factbook/rankorder/2153rank.html (accessed November 19, 2007).
10. China Internet Network Information Center, 2007, The 20th CNNIC statistical survey report on the Internet development in China, http://www.cnnic.net.cn/download/2007/20thCNNICreport-en.pdf (accessed November 19, 2007).
11. China Internet Network Information Center, 2007, The 20th CNNIC statistical survey report on the Internet development in China, http://www.cnnic.net.cn/download/2007/20thCNNICreport-en.pdf (accessed November 19, 2007).
12. China Internet Network Information Center, 2007, The 20th CNNIC statistical survey report on the Internet development in China, http://www.cnnic.net.cn/download/2007/20thCNNICreport-en.pdf (accessed November 19, 2007).
13. iResearch Inc., 18 June 2007, China's Online Shopping Market Worth Rmb 10.8 Billion in Q1 of 2007, http://www.iresearchgroup.com.cn/html/Consulting/Online_Shopping/DetailNews_id_65929.html (accessed 20 November 2007).
14. iResearch Inc., 2007, China's B2B e-commerce market reached RMB 489.1 billion in Q2 of 2007, http://www.iresearchgroup.com.cn/html/consulting/B2B/DetailNews_id_72299.html, November 5 (accessed November 20, 2007).
15. National Statistics Bureau of China, 2006, *China Statistical Yearbook*, Chapter 14–1.
16. iResearch Inc., 2007, China SME number to reach 50 million in 2012, http://www.iresearchgroup.com.cn/Consulting/others/DetailNews.asp?id=65361, June 6 (accessed November 22, 2007).
17. iResearch Inc., 2007, B2B e-commerce should start with interest of SMEs, http://www.iresearchgroup.com.cn/html/Consulting/B2B/DetailNews_id_67225.html, July 12 (accessed November 22, 2007).
18. Alibaba.com, 2007 Global Offering Prospectus, 74–75.
19. R. Fannin, 2008, How I did it—Jack Ma, Alibaba.com, *Inc.*, 30(1): 105.
20. C. Chandler, 2007, China's Web king, *Fortune*, December 10, 172.
21. iResearch Inc., 2007, Alibaba IPO Financial Research Report, http://www.iresearchgroup.com.cn/html/Consulting/B2B/Free_classi__id_1076.html, November 5 (accessed December 11, 2007).
22. Alibaba.com, 2007, Global Offering Prospectus, 102.
23. Alibaba.com, 2007, Global Offering Prospectus, 24.
24. Alexa.com, 2008, Browse: E-Commerce, http://www.alexa.com/browse?&CategoryID=298214; Alexa.com, 2008, Browse: International business and trade, http://www.alexa.com/browse?&CategoryID=42647 (accessed January 2, 2008).
25. Alibaba. com, 2007, Global Offering Prospectus, 80.
26. Global Sources, 2007, Investor Relations Factsheet, http://www.corporate.globalsources.com/IRS/IRFACT.HTM (accessed January 22, 2008).
27. Global Sources, 2006, Annual Report, 24–25.
28. Global Sources, 2007, Investor Relations Factsheet, http://www.corporate.globalsources.Com/IRS/IRFACT.HTM (accessed January 22, 2008).
29. S. So, 2008, Alibaba reshuffle a precursor to global expansion, *South China Morning Post*, January 29.
30. Alibaba.com stated its intention to allocate the net proceeds from the IPO as follows: 60 percent for strategic acquisitions and business development initiatives, 20 percent to increase the existing businesses both in China and internationally, 10 percent to purchase computer equipment and development of new technologies, and 10 percent to fund working capital and for general corporate purposes. Source: Alibaba.com, 2007, Global Offering Prospectus, 130.

Jinxuan Zhang

We've been the No. 1 Web site in China for a number of years, and in fact we are the largest Web site outside of the U.S. When people get to know about the Internet, the first Web site they learn is about Baidu in China.

—ROBIN YANHONG LI, COFOUNDER, CHAIRMAN, & CEO, BAIDU[i]

We were late entering the China market, and we're catching up . . . . Our investment is working and we will eventually be the leader.

—ERIC SCHMIDT, CHAIRMAN & CEO, GOOGLE[ii]

By far China's most popular search engine, Baidu .com Inc. (Baidu) continued to dominate that market with a 60.4 percent market share in 2007,[iii] more than double that of Google Inc. (Google). In 2005, Google, the world's leading search engine, entered the Chinese market. While Google was catching up, Baida continued to grow. BNP Paribas observed: "Baidu and Google are winning at the expense of other search engines [in China] . . . Baidu gained market share at the expense of all players except for Google."[iv]

According to *BusinessWeek's* list of "The Best (and) Worst Leaders of 2006," Li was ranked third and his company was described as the "Best Answer to Google." Bill Gates and Steve Ballmer might want to have a sit-down with Chinese entrepreneur Robin Li. The founder and CEO of Baidu.com has achieved something that Microsoft's top brass have yet to manage—beating Google.[v]

On January 31, 2008, Ballmer made a proposal to Yahoo! to acquire outstanding shares of the company's common stock for per-share consideration of $31 in the hope of rapidly expanding Microsoft's presence in the online search advertising market dominated by Google.[vi]

On May 20, 2008,[vii] Baidu traded at a price to earnings ratio of 153. This is four times more than Google, over seven times more than Microsoft, and almost three times more than Yahoo! Was the price justified? Would it last?

Global vs. Local

Embarking on a Journey for Search

Google is a leading global Internet search and online advertising company. In January 1996, the company was founded by Larry Page and Sergey Brin, who started it as a research project when they were doctoral students at Stanford University. On September 7, 1998, it was formally incorporated as Google Inc. Google was able to win its audience because of the quality of its search results. Google's search algorithm[1] took into account relevance and other qualitative elements that other search engines did not.

Baidu—often referred to as "China's Google"—was incorporated in the Cayman Islands on January 18, 2000, by cofounders Robin Yanhong Li and Eric Yong Xu.[2] Both were Chinese nationals who had studied and worked overseas before returning to China. Baidu began as a provider of Internet search solutions to other Chinese portals. Then, it tapped into the unexplored Chinese online search market and gained a first-mover advantage by coming up with a search engine that provided information in local Chinese languages. Baidu initially became popular because of its multimedia content,

Research Associate Jinxuan (Ann) Zhang prepared this case under the supervision of Professor Didier Cossin as a basis for class discussion rather than to illustrate either effective or ineffective handling of a business situation.

This case was sponsored by the Securities Commission Malaysia (Suruhanjaya Sekuriti). Copyright © 2008 by IMD – International Institute for Management Development, Lausanne, Switzerland. Not be used or reproduced without written permission directly from IMD.

[1] In computer science, a search algorithm is an algorithm that takes a problem as input and returns a solution to the problem, usually after evaluating a number of possible solutions.

[2] Li earned a master's degree in computer science from the State University of New York at Buffalo and worked at search engine Infoseek for more than two years before returning to China. Xu, a biochemist who was well connected in the Silicon Valley, was not involved in the management of the company.

including MP3 music and movies, but was criticized for being "weak on piracy, strong on censorship."[viii]

A "1 followed by 100 zeros" vs. "Hundreds of Times"

The name Google originated from the mathematical term "Googol" for a 1 followed by 100 zeros. It reflected Google's mission "to organize the world's information and make it universally accessible and useful."[ix]

The literal meaning of Baidu is "hundreds of times." It was inspired by an ancient Chinese poem and represented a persistent search for the ideal. The name was chosen so that the world would remember Baidu's Chinese heritage. By focusing on what it knew best, Baidu aimed "to provide the best way for people to find information"[x] by applying an avant-garde technology to the world's most ancient and complex language.

Growing, But Not Yet on the Same Scale

Even though Baidu is growing quickly, it still remains tiny in comparison to Google's global size. Baidu earned about $86 million in net income in 2007 on $239 million in revenue,[xi] compared with Google's $4.2 billion in net income on $16.6 billion in revenue.

Products & Services

Baidu's homepage was strikingly similar to Google's—a search bar at the center of a mostly empty page (see Exhibit 1). Both Baidu and Google provided a wide range of products and services that gave users a better search experience with a view to increasing traffic and user stickiness. Their offerings could be placed into three categories: search, community, and other enhancements. While Google has started to experiment with other markets, such as radio and print publications, Baidu looked towards consumer-to-consumer (C2C) and mobile search.

Business Model

Baidu and Google essentially utilized the same business model—selling ads tied to user searches (see Exhibit 2). Both companies primarily derived their revenues from online marketing activities on their Web sites, principally auction-based pay-for-performance (P4P)[3] search advertisements.

Baidu introduced "pay-for-placement," which allowed companies to bid for search-result placement based on relevant keywords. Google believed that "you can make money without doing evil"[4,xiii] and did not allow ads to

be displayed on its results pages. Advertising produced by certain searches was clearly identified as a "sponsored link" and displayed above or to the right of the results.

In addition, Baidu and Google also expanded their search platforms to include a network of third-party Web sites that incorporated their search box or toolbar in a revenue-sharing model. This enabled both companies to use their advertising platforms to generate user traffic and enlarge their paid-search networks. According to BNP Paribas estimates, Baidu already derived 25 percent of its revenue from its partner Web sites,[xiv] while Google about 10% to 15% from such partner Web sites (see Exhibit 3 for the Google revenue breakdown).[xv]

Growth Strategy

Since 2001, Google has acquired some small startup companies with innovative teams and products—for example, Deja, Pyra Labs, and Sprinks. Since its IPO[5] in 2004, it also has entered into a wide array of products and services outside its sponsored-search domain. Google has attempted to keep pace with changing times and identify future growth opportunities both organically, by launching Gmail and Orkut,[6] and by acquiring YouTube and DoubleClick (see Exhibit 4 for a list of Google's major acquisitions). In April 2004, Google knocked on Baidu's door. Two months later, Google acquired a 2.6 percent stake in Baidu for $5 million (at the time, Baidu was not well known outside its homeland).

For its part, Baidu pursued strategic acquisitions of businesses, assets, and technologies that complemented its existing capabilities and business. In August 2004, it acquired the domain name hao123.com. Headquartered in Shanghai, hao123.com was Baidu's largest traffic contributor and its largest distributor of its P4P services.[7] Both companies also actively formed strategic alliances with market leaders in other business sectors to further broaden their customer bases and product and service offerings.

Geographic Expansion

Google has built up its international presence to the point that international revenues accounted for approximately 48 percent of Google's total revenue in 2007 and surpassed its domestic revenues in Q1 2008 (see Exhibit 3). More than half of its user traffic also came from outside the United States (see Exhibit 5 for a user traffic breakdown). Baidu, for its part, focused on offering searches in Chinese. However, on January 24, 2008, Baidu made

---

[3] P4P customers bid for priority placements of links to their Web sites among relevant search results.

[4] "Don't be evil" was the informal corporate motto or slogan for Google.

[5] Initial Public Offering.

[6] A social networking service run by Google and named after its creator—a Google employee.

[7] Baidu's ability for acquiring local companies was subject to foreign exchange regulations on mergers and acquisitions in China.

Exhibit 1 Homepages of Baidu and Google

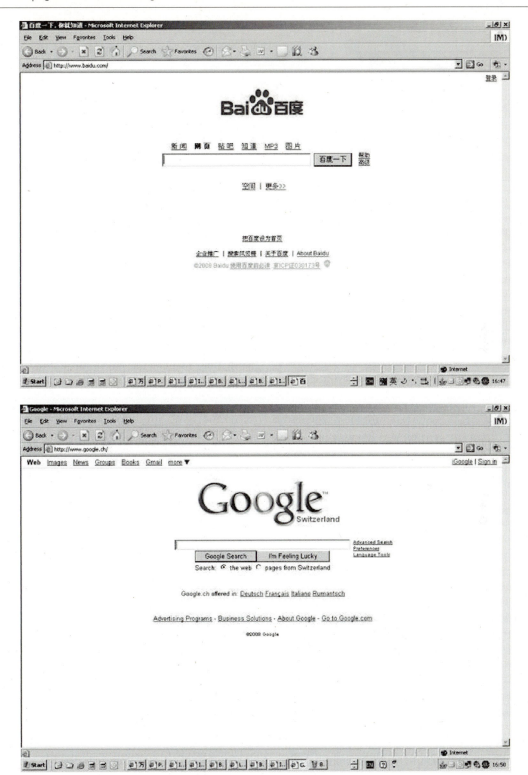

Exhibit 2 Business System of a Search Engine

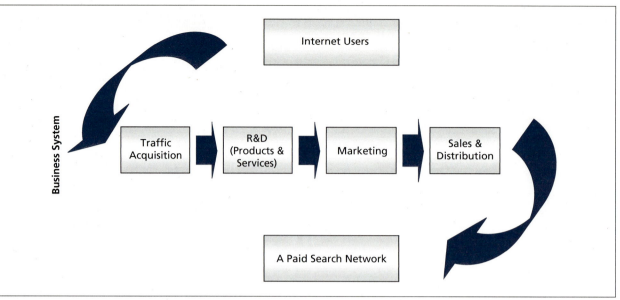

Source: IMD Research.

Exhibit 3 Google's Revenue Breakdown

By Source	2003	2004	2005	2006	2007	2008Q1
Revenues (in $ million)						
Google sites' advertising revenues	$792	$1,589	$3,377	$6,333	$10,625	$3,400
Google network advertising revenues	629	1,554	2,688	4,160	5,788	1,686
Total advertising revenues	1,421	3,143	6,065	10,493	16,413	5,087
Licensing and other revenues	45	46	74	112	181	99
Total revenues	$1,466	$3,189	$6,139	$10,605	$16,594	$5,186
As % of total revenues						
Google sites' advertising revenues	54%	50%	55%	60%	64%	66%
Google network advertising revenues	43%	49%	44%	39%	35%	33%
Total advertising revenues	97%	99%	99%	99%	99%	98%
Licensing and other revenues	3%	1%	1%	1%	1%	2%

Exhibit 3 Google's Revenue Breakdown *(Continued)*

By Source	2003	2004	2005	2006	2007	2008Q1
By Location (in $ million)						
U.S.	$1,038	$2,119	$3,757	$6,030	$8,629	$2,541
International	428	1,070	2,382	4,575	7,965	2,645
Total revenue	$1,466	$3,189	$6,139	$10,605	$16,594	$5,186
As % of total revenues						
U.S.	71%	66%	61%	57%	52%	49%
International	29%	34%	39%	43%	48%	51%

Source: Google's annual reports and quarterly results, dollar value in millions.

Exhibit 4 Google's Major Acquisitions

Acquisition Date	Company	Business	Country	Value	Derived Services
February 12, 2001	Deja	Usenet	USA		Google Groups
September 2001	Outride	Web search engine	USA		Google Personalized Search
February 2003	Pyra Labs	Web software	USA		Blogger
April 2003	Neotonic Software	Customer relationship management	USA		Google Groups, Gmail
April 2003	Applied Semantics	Online advertising	USA	$102 million	AdSense, AdWords
September 30, 2003	Kaltix	Web search engine	USA		iGoogle
October 2003	Sprinks (a division of Primedia)	Online advertising	USA		AdSense, AdWords
October 2003	Genius Labs	Blogging	USA		Blogger
May 10, 2004	Ignite Logic	HTML editor	USA		Google Page Creator
June 23, 2004	Baidu	Chinese language search engine	CHN	$5 million	Sold in 2006
July 13, 2004	Picasa	Image organizer	USA		Picasa, Blogger
September 2004	ZipDash	Traffic analysis	USA		Google Ride Finder
October 2004	Where2	Map analysis	USA		Google Maps

(Continued)

Exhibit 4 Google's Major Acquisitions *(Continued)*

Acquisition Date	Company	Business	Country	Value	Derived Services
October 27, 2004	Keyhole, Inc.	Map analysis	USA		Google Maps, Google Earth
March 28, 2005	Dodgeball	Social networking service	USA		Google Mobile, Google SMS
March 12, 2005	Urchin Software Corporation	Web analytics	USA		Google Analytics
July 2005	Reqwireless	Mobile browser	CAN		Google Mobile
July 7, 2005	Communications Group	Broadband Internet access	USA	$100 million	Internet Backbone
August 17, 2005	Android	Mobile software	USA		Google Mobile, Google SMS
November 2005	Skia	Graphics software	USA		Picasa
November 17, 2005	Akwan Information Technologies	Broadband Internet access	BRA		Internet Backbone
December 20, 2005	AOL	Broadband Internet access	USA	$1,000 million	
December 27, 2005	Phatbits	Widget engine	USA		Google Desktop
December 31, 2005	allPAY GmbH	Mobile software	GER		Google Mobile
December 31, 2005	bruNET GmbH dMarc	Mobile software	GER		Google Mobile
January 17, 2006	Broadcasting	Advertising	USA	$102 million	AdSense
February 14, 2006	Measure Map	Weblog software	USA		Google Analytics
March 9, 2006	Upstartle	Word processor	USA		Google Documents
March 14, 2006	@Last Software	3D modeling software	USA		Google Sketchup
April 9, 2006	Orion	Web search engine	AUS		Google Search
June 1, 2006	2Web Technologies	Online spreadsheets	USA		Google Spreadsheet
August 15, 2006	Neven Vision	Computer vision	USA		Google Maps
October 9, 2006	YouTube	Video sharing	USA	$1,650 million	Google Video
October 31, 2006	JotSpot	Web application	USA		Google Sites
December 18, 2006	Endoxon	Mapping	CHE	$28 million	Google Maps

Exhibit 4 Google's Major Acquisitions *(Continued)*

Acquisition Date	Company	Business	Country	Value	Derived Services
January 4, 2007	Xunlei	File sharing	CHE	$5 million	
February 16, 2007	Adscape	In-game advertising	USA	$23 million	AdSense
March 16, 2007	Trendalyzer	Statistical software	SWE		Google Analytics
April 13, 2007	Double Click	Online advertising	USA	$3,100 million	AdSense
April 17, 2007	Tonic Systems	Presentation program	USA		Google Documents
April 19, 2007	Marratech	Videoconferencing	SWE		Google Talk
May 11, 2007	GreenBorder	Computer security	USA		Internal Use
June 1, 2007	Panoramio	Photo sharing	ESP		Blogger
June 3, 2007	FeedBurner	Web feed	USA	$100 million	Google Reader
June 5, 2007	PeakStream	Parallel processing	USA		Server (computing)
June 19, 2007	Zenter	Presentation program	USA		Google Documents
July 2, 2007	GrandCentral	Voice over Internet Protocol	USA	$45 million	Google Mobile
July 9, 2007	Postini	Communications security	USA	$625 million	Gmail
July 20, 2007	Image America	Aerial photography	USA		Google Maps
September 27, 2007	Zingku	Social network service	USA		Google Mobile
October 9, 2007	Jaiku	Micro-blogging	FIN		Google Mobile

its first international move by launching its Japanese version—Baidu.jp[8]—with the primary objective of serving Chinese small and medium-sized enterprises (SMEs) doing business in Japan. Its focus remained on product development to meet the needs of Japanese users and operating costs and expenses of RMB30 million ($4.3 million) were incurred for Q1 2008 (no revenue was expected for fiscal year 2008).[xvii]

Google in China vs. "China's Google"

Google's Answer to Its Chinese Question

Google launched its Chinese language version in 2000 and its popularity quickly grew through word

of mouth among Chinese Internet surfers. The company did well until September 2002, when Google was blocked by the "Great Firewall of China"[9]—a political rift over censorship with the Chinese government—and was denied rights to China. While Google's company Web site proclaimed, "Google—the closest thing the Web has to an ultimate answer machine," it did not have an answer to its one big China question: how can we go into China and yet not do evil?[xviii]

"They [Google] can't afford to not be in China . . . They are facing a hard choice. They really don't want to be seen as doing something that is evil, but no one goes into China on their own terms."[xix]

According to Eric Schmidt, Google actually did "an evil scale" and finally reached the decision that "not to serve [users in China] at all was a worse evil."[xx] It

[8] With four products only: a Web page, images, videos, and blogs.

[9] Also referred to as the "Golden Shield Project," a censorship and surveillance project operated by the Ministry of Public Security of China.

Exhibit 5 User Geographic Breakdown & Traffic Rank

User Geographic Breakdown				Traffic Rank			
Baidu.com		Google.com		Baidu.com		Google.com	
Market	%	Market	%	Market	Rank	Market	Rank
China	89.1%	U.S.	43.0%	China	1	U.S.	1
South Korea	2.8%	India	8.2%	South Korea	9	Algeria	1
U.S.	1.6%	Brazil	3.7%	Macao	9	Iran	2
Japan	1.0%	U.K.	3.2%	Hong Kong	14	India	3
U.K.	0.7%	Germany	3.0%	Singapore	14	South Africa	3
Taiwan	0.7%	Iran	2.8%	New Zealand	19	U.K.	4
Canada	0.6%	China	2.3%	Taiwan	22	Germany	4
Hong Kong	0.5%	Japan	2.3%	Malaysia	22	Spain	4
Australia	0.4%	Canada	1.8%	Australia	40	Australia	4
Malaysia	0.3%	Italy	1.7%	Canada	47	Indonesia	4
Germany	0.3%	Spain	1.4%	Nigeria	47	Pakistan	4
Singapore	0.3%	France	1.3%	U.K.	71	Saudi Arabia	4
Italy	0.1%	Australia	1.1%	Japan	125	Brazil	5
New Zealand	0.1%	Mexico	1.1%	U.S.	225	Italy	5
Indonesia	0.1%	Turkey	1.1%	Thailand	255	Turkey	5
Thailand	0.1%	Indonesia	1.0%	Indonesia	260	Netherlands	5
Macronesia	0.1%	Russia	0.9%	Germany	283	Canada	6
Spain	0.1%	Pakistan	0.8%	Netherlands	401	South Korea	6
Nigeria	0.1%	Algeria	0.7%	Italy	445	Mexico	9
India	0.1%	Saudi Arabia	0.7%	Spain	920	France	10
France	0.1%	South Africa	0.7%	France	1,024	Poland	10
Netherlands	0.1%	Netherlands	0.7%	Russia	1,226	Japan	11
Russia	0.1%	South Korea	0.7%	India	1,603	Russia	11

Exhibit 5 User Geographic Breakdown & Traffic Rank *(Continued)*

User Geographic Breakdown				Traffic Rank			
Baidu.com		Google.com		Baidu.com		Google.com	
Market	%	Market	%	Market	Rank	Market	Rank
Other markets	0.6%	Poland	0.5%			China	12
	100.0%	Argentina	0.4%			Argentina	12
		Other markets	14.9%				
			100.0%				

was finally granted the rights to open offices in China in January 2005, headed by Taiwan-born Kaifu Lee, a former Microsoft executive, who in 1998 was a founder of Microsoft Research Asia.[10] Several months later, Google introduced a new version of its search engine for the Chinese market by purging its search results of any Web sites of which the Chinese government did not approve.

"Gu Ge" in China

Consumer surveys showed that Chinese Internet users had a wide range of imaginative pronunciations of Google in English, including "gougou" (dog dog), "gugou" (ancient dog), "guoguo" (fruit fruit), and "gougou" (check check).[xxi] In fact, Google had been working on a Chinese name since 2002. After extensive internal debates, external consultations, and consumer surveys, in spring 2006 Google finally announced its Chinese name: Gu Ge. "Gu Ge" meant "song of the grain," expressing the abundance of harvest, or "song of the valley," a reference to the company's Silicon Valley roots.[xxii] This was the first time Google used a non-English name.

Because Google had now been able to enter China using its own name (or something like it), it decided to create on its own Web site there. In June 2006, Google sold its stake in Baidu for more than $60 million. Google spokeswoman Debbie Frost commented: "We have disposed of our modest investment in Baidu … It has always been our goal to grow our own successful business in China and we are very focused on that."[xxiii]

Being Local, Understanding Local

Unlike Google, which offered multi-language search, Baidu focused on searches in Chinese. Interestingly, Chinese is one of the Asian languages based on syllables requiring two bytes to store each character while English only requires one byte. There were fundamental differences in algorithms and behavior between single-byte and double-byte searches. In addition, regular changes necessitated by these algorithms required manpower trained in the local language, which took time for outside companies to develop. CEO Robin Yanhong Li believed that Baidu's understanding of the Chinese language and culture gave it an advantage in that market over Google.[xxiv] On the other hand, Kaifu Lee, Vice President over Google's China operations, felt that his challenge was to help the leadership of Google understand the Internet in China—specifically, Chinese users.[xxv]

Channels

In China, most SME customers[11] were not accustomed to conducting business online. In addition, the payment and logistic infrastructure of e-commerce was far from perfect and required a lot of user education and support, at least initially, especially on how to navigate the Internet. Baidu had built up a direct sales force of more than 3,000 people located in seven major cities[12],[xxvi] to better serve its customers and assist in these areas. It also had a much higher penetration of distributors than Google (see Exhibit 6 for a comparison of channel strength in China), who only had one Chinese distributor in mid-2005 and also generally adopted its global model of customer self-service for China.

---

[10] Microsoft sued Google and Kaifu Li for the move but the case was resolved in a confidential settlement.

[11] Only 100 out of 161,000 of Baidu's online marketing customers were big advertisers as of Q1 2008, but their spending started to outpace its traditional SME customers, especially the financial services, IT, electronics, and automobile industries.

[12] Beijing, Shanghai, Guangzhou, Shenzhen, Taiyuan, Tianjin, and Pooshan by the end of 2007.

Exhibit 6 Comparison of Channel Strength in China

	Baidu	Google China
Number of distributors	~200[20]	24
Number of provinces covered	24	8
Number of direct sales force employees	~3,000	0
Revenue from distributors in Q3 2007 (%)	32	48
Number of paid advertisers in Q3 2007	143,000	38,00
Revenue from top 10 channel partners (%)	10	93

Source: BNP Paribas estimates according to industry sources.[xxxix]

Corporate Structure, Financial Performance, and Valuation

Corporate Structure

To comply with the foreign ownership restrictions on providing Internet content and advertising services in China, from the outset, Baidu operated its Web sites and provided online advertising services in China through contractual arrangements with its local subsidiary, Baidu Netcom. Baidu Netcom, set up on June 5, 2001, was wholly owned by Li and Xu[13] and had the necessary licenses and approvals to operate in China[14] (see Exhibit 7). Google.com operated under a license owned by Google's local partner, Ganii.com.[xxvii]

Financial Performance

Exhibits 8a through 9c provide detailed financial information for Baidu and Google for fiscal years 2003 to 2007. Exhibit 10 contrasts the financial performance and valuation of Baidu and Google across several indicators for fiscal year 2007.

Revenue Drivers

Exhibit 11 shows that Baidu's revenue growth was mainly driven by an enlarged active online marketing customer base effectively served by its direct sales force and third-party distributors and through increasing revenue per online marketing customer. Baidu started to improve its monetization algorithm in 2006 by implementing dynamic bidding and dynamic starting bid prices, and incorporating quality factors in ordering sponsored links as a way of improving its revenue per search.

Breakdown of Costs

Traffic acquisition costs (TAC) remained a key component of Baidu's and Google's cost of revenues. Baidu's TAC continued to rise, reflecting continued growth of revenue contribution from Baidu Union[15] member partners (faster growth than from its own platform).[16] About 70 percent of Google's cost of revenue was TAC. BNP Paribas estimated that Baidu's TAC would continue its upward trend and close the gap with Google worldwide (see Exhibit 12).[xxviii]

Impact of RMB Revaluation

Baidu's reporting currency was the RMB (China's currency). Its revenues and costs were mostly denominated in RMB while a significant portion of its financial assets were denominated in U.S. dollars. Considerable international pressure on the Chinese government to permit the free floatation of the RMB resulted in a significant appreciation of the RMB against the U.S. dollar (see Exhibit 13).

Taxation

As a foreign-invested enterprise registered in a high-tech zone and a "new or high-technology enterprise," Baidu enjoyed preferential tax benefits[17] and a much lower effective tax rate (in the single-digit range, around 4 percent in fiscal years 2004 to 2007 and 7 percent for Q1 2008[xxix]) than Google.

Financial Policies

Baidu relied entirely on dividends and other fees paid by its subsidiaries and affiliates in China. Like Google, it did not pay dividends to its common shareholders.[18]

---

[13] Baidu funded the initial capitalization of Baidu Netcom in the form of a long-term shareholder loan of RMB 2 million ($0.24 million) to Li and Xu.

[14] Under the current Chinese laws and regulations on advertising, P4P was not classified as a form of advertising. The company may not be operated through Baidu Netcom and/or would be subject to higher effective taxation if the laws and regulations were to be changed.

[15] Baidu Union was the network of third-party Web sites and software applications, with five categories: proprietary Web sites, software, Internet cafes, carriers, and other ad networks.

[16] Baidu had the flexibility to turn on or off of the Union traffic and partnerships based on its assessment of the ROI for customers and advertisers, and the return for its profitability and revenue growth.

[17] An exemption from enterprise income tax: 7.5 percent for the first three years and a further 15 percent as long as it maintained its status as a "new or high-technology enterprise." Eligibility for potential tax refunds for Baidu Online on revenues derived from its technology consulting services.

[18] In China, offshore remittance of dividends was also subject to foreign exchange control by the State Administration of Foreign Exchange (SAFE).

Exhibit 7 Ownership and Corporate Structure of Baidu

* A limited liability company incorporated in China.
___ Equity interest
---- Contractual arrangements including business cooperation agreement, operating agreement, license agreements, proxy agreement, and exclusive technology consulting service agreement.
- - - Contractual arrangements including proxy agreement, equity pledge agreement, option agreement, operating agreement, loan agreement, and irrevocable power of attorney.

Source: Developed from Baidu IPO prospectus and SEC filings.

Valuation

IPO

While Baidu regarded its IPO more as a branding event to raise company profile, the outcome far exceeded expectations. When Baidu completed its IPO on NASDAQ on August 5, 2005, its share price soared to $122.54, up 354 percent from its IPO price of $27 on the first trading day, which made it immensely popular among investors. As one investor remarked:

"It's just been amazing. It could be over-enthusiasm, it could be the way Google charted, but there is obviously a lot of speculative buyers who think this could be an Asian Google."[xxx]

In December 2007 Baidu became the first Chinese company to join the NASDAQ 100 Index. Baidu traded at a much higher premium than Google—three times Google's P/E ratio (see Exhibit 14).

Equity Share Ownership

At the end of fiscal year 2006, Li still retained 21.5 percent ownership of the common stock of Baidu. Other directors and officers together owned 6.7 percent of the common stock shares.[xxxi]

Dual-Stock Structure

Like Google, Baidu had a dual-stock structure—two classes of ordinary shares with identical rights except for voting and conversion rights. As a result, it was reported that Baidu may not be in compliance with the listing rules in Hong Kong.[xxxii]

Secondary Listings

There was no clear timeline for Baidu's initial listing in Hong Kong after it was postponed. The goal of listing in Hong Kong would be to help raise the company profile and fund expansion into new areas, such as online auctions. Its plan for an IPO in Shanghai was unlikely due to regulatory huddles that effectively blocked foreign-owned firms (due to its listing on the NASDAQ) from selling stocks on Chinese exchanges.

Still Too Early to Declare A Winner...

On May 3, 2008, Microsoft withdrew its offer to acquire Yahoo! and chose not to pursue a hostile bid (see Exhibit 15). Microsoft had increased its offer to $33 per share (about $47.5 billion) but the two parties still could not reach an agreement. In addition, a recent successful Google–Yahoo! paid-search test and potential deal made the acquisition even more complicated for Microsoft. Two weeks after withdrawing its offer to purchase Yahoo!, Microsoft reopened the door to the possibility of a potential new investment in Yahoo! (not a total acquisition) while discussions were still ongoing between Yahoo! and Google.

Robin Yanhong Li, cofounder, chairman, and CEO of Baidu,[xxxiii] feels that Baidu will someday pose a similar threat, saying, "If he [Bill Gates] is worried about Google he will probably be more worried about Baidu somewhere down the road. . . . When the Chinese market stops growing faster than other countries in world, we will look outside. The reason we focus here now is that this is the fastest growing market we can access."

In recent years, the Chinese search ad market has grown quickly (see Exhibits 16a and 16b) and is also becoming more concentrated. The combined market share of the top three search engines increased from 78 percent in Q1 2006 to 95 percent in 2007 (with Baidu 60.4 percent, Google 21.2 percent, and Yahoo! China/Alibaba 13.8 percent[19]).[xxxiv] In November 2007 the Chinese search market already exceeded the United States in the number of search requests, and by February 2008 in the number of internet users. As Sukhinder Singh Cassidy, the vice president for Asia Pacific and Latin American Operations for Google has said, "We're in sort of inning one of a nine-inning game. . . . It is very early to call a winner in the China search market."[xxxv]

I had no intention of keeping Baidu inside China from the start. Now that we have won over 60 percent share [Q4 2007] in China, I think it's natural that we turn to overseas markets.
—**Robin Yanhong Li, Co-Founder, Chairman & CEO, Baidu** [xxxvi]

Whatever Baidu does, it does not matter to us. The internet is not the same as other IT businesses. [Between] Google and users will turn to whoever does the better, and they will change again when they find someone even better.
—**Kaifu Lee, VP and President for Greater Google China** [xxxvii]

Is it just a matter of time before there is a Baidu.us portal? In this regard Russia's search engine, Yandex, has operations in the United States near Google's headquarters. What will happen if Microsoft acquires (or fails to acquire) Yahoo!? What will Baidu's considerations be for its next choice of secondary listing? How should investors evaluate the stock? These decisions and events will help determine the global, regional, and country battle shaping up in the search engine markets.

---

[19] Alibaba, a leading Chinese e-commerce company, acquired the entire assets of Yahoo! China in 2005, including its search technology, the Web site, its communications and advertising business, and 3721.com (a real-name search engine) Web site. Alibaba also received a $1 billion investment from Yahoo! as well as the exclusive right of using the Yahoo! brand. In return, Yahoo! took 40 percent of Alibaba's shares but only 35 percent of voting rights.

Exhibit 8a Baidu: Consolidated Income Statement (Fiscal Year Ending December 31, 2007)

BAIDU FINANCIALS	RMB Million (except for share, per share information)					$ Million (except for share, per share information)				
INCOME STATEMENT	2003	2004	2005	2006	2007	2003	2004	2005	2006	2007
Exchange rate						8.2767	8.2765	8.072	7.8051	7.3041
Revenues										
Online marketing services	31.8	106.9	307.4	828.5	1,741.0	3.8	12.9	38.1	106.1	238.4
Other services	8.8	10.6	11.9	9.4	3.4	1.1	1.3	1.5	1.2	0.5
Total Revenues	**40.6**	**117.5**	**319.2**	**837.8**	**1,744.4**	**4.9**	**14.2**	**39.5**	**107.3**	**238.8**
Operating costs and expenses										
Cost of revenues	23.3	41.2	104.4	245.5	645.4	2.8	5.0	12.9	31.5	88.4
Business tax and surcharges	1.9	6.5	20.8	51.8	108.8	0.2	0.8	2.6	6.6	14.9
Traffic acquisition costs	10.6	10.9	21.2	75.2	204.7	1.3	1.3	2.6	9.6	28.0
Bandwidth costs	2.2	8.5	21.3	40.0	117.6	0.3	1.0	2.6	5.1	16.1
Depreciation costs	4.1	7.1	25.3	51.6	147.1	0.5	0.9	3.1	6.6	20.1
Operational costs	3.7	6.5	14.9	25.5	65.5	0.4	0.8	1.8	3.3	9.0
Share-based compensation expenses	0.6	1.7	1.0	1.4	1.7	0.1	0.2	0.1	0.2	0.2
Selling, general and administrative	19.6	50.7	134.8	250.2	411.2	2.4	6.1	16.7	32.1	56.3

Exhibit 8a Baidu: Consolidated Income Statement (Fiscal Year Ending December 31, 2007) *(Continued)*

BAIDU FINANCIALS	RMB Million (except for share, per share information)					$ Million (except for share, per share information)				
INCOME STATEMENT	2003	2004	2005	2006	2007	2003	2004	2005	2006	2007
Research and Development	7.0	14.5	44.2	79.2	140.7	0.8	1.8	5.5	10.2	19.3
Total operating costs and expenses	49.9	106.4	283.4	575.0	1,197.3	6.0	12.9	35.1	73.7	163.9
Operating profit	(9.3)	11.0	35.8	262.9	547.2	(1.1)	1.3	4.4	33.7	74.9
Other income (and expenses)										
Interest income	0.3	1.1	13.6	42.4	49.0	0.0	0.1	1.7	5.4	6.7
Foreign exchange loss, net	–	–	(0.7)	(0.1)	–	–	–	(0.1)	(0.0)	–
Other, net	0.1	0.3	0.8	4.2	20.1	0.0	0.0	0.1	0.5	2.7
Total other income (and expenses)	0.4	1.5	13.7	46.5	69.1	0.0	0.2	1.7	6.0	9.5
Net income before income taxes and cumulative effect of change in accounting principle	(8.9)	12.5	49.5	309.4	616.2	(1.1)	1.5	6.1	39.6	84.4
Income taxes	–	0.5	1.9	12.3	(12.8)	–	0.1	0.2	1.6	(1.7)
Income before cumulative effect of change in accounting principle	(8.9)	12.0	47.6	297.2	629.0	(1.1)	1.5	5.9	38.1	86.1
Cumulative effect of change in accounting principle	–	–	–	4.6	–	–	–	–	0.6	–

Exhibit 8a Baidu: Consolidated Income Statement (Fiscal Year Ending December 31, 2007) (Continued)

BAIDU FINANCIALS	RMB Million (except for share, per share information)					$ Million (except for share, per share information)				
INCOME STATEMENT	2003	2004	2005	2006	2007	2003	2004	2005	2006	2007
Net income	(8.9)	12.0	47.6	301.8	629.0	(1.1)	1.5	5.9	38.7	86.1
Net income per Class A and Class B ordinary shares										
Basic (prior to cumulative effect of change in accounting principle)	(0.87)	1.09	2.40	8.92	18.57	(0.11)	0.13	0.30	1.14	2.54
Basic (cumulative effect of change in accounting principle)	–	–	–	0.14	–	–	–	–	0.02	–
	(0.87)	1.09	2.40	9.06	18.57	(0.11)	0.13	0.30	1.16	2.54
Diluted (prior to cumulative effect of change in accounting principle)	0.43	0.43	1.49	8.62	18.11	0.05	0.05	0.18	1.10	2.48
Diluted (cumulative effect of change in accounting principle)	–	–	–	0.13	–	–	–	–	0.02	–
	0.43	0.43	1.49	8.75	18.11	0.05	0.05	0.18	1.12	2.48
Weighted average number of Class A and Class B ordinary shares outstanding										
Basic	10,188,850	10,983,478	19,808,058	33,290,696	33,872,611	10,188,850	10,983,478	19,808,058	33,290,696	33,872,611
Diluted	10,188,850	28,124,327	32,042,888	34,506,594	34,724,364	10,188,850	28,124,327	32,042,888	34,506,594	34,724,364

(Continued)

*2007 results were unaudited results.
Source: Baidu annual reports and quarterly results.

Exhibit 8b Baidu: Consolidated Balance Sheet (Fiscal Year Ending December 31, 2007)

BAIDU FINANCIALS	RMB Million					$ Million				
BALANCE SHEET	2003	2004	2005	2006	2007	2003	2004	2005	2006	2007
Exchange rate						8.2767	8.2765	8.072	7.8051	7.3041
ASSETS										
Current assets										
Cash and cash equivalents	62.8	200.2	900.6	1,136.3	1,350.6	7.6	24.2	111.6	145.6	184.9
Short-term investments	–	–	–	85.3	242.0	–	–	–	10.9	33.1
Accounts receivable, net of allowance	1.9	9.6	22.4	23.1	64.3	0.2	1.2	2.8	3.0	8.8
Prepaid expenses and other current assets	0.9	2.4	11.0	32.3	66.0	0.1	0.3	1.4	4.1	9.0
Deferred tax assets, net of valuation allowance	–	–	1.4	1.7	2.6	–	–	0.2	0.2	0.4
Total current assets	65.7	212.3	935.4	1,278.7	1,725.5	7.9	25.6	115.9	163.8	236.2
Non-current assets										
Fixed assets, net	11.0	35.9	96.4	191.7	678.9	1.3	4.3	11.9	24.6	92.9
Prepayment for land use rights	–	–	77.2	92.4	96.5	–	–	9.6	11.8	13.2
Intangible assets, net	–	13.0	13.3	44.4	40.5	–	1.6	1.6	5.7	5.5
Goodwill	–	–	9.3	47.3	51.1	–	–	1.2	6.1	7.0
Investments, net	–	–	2.0	–	15.4	–	–	0.3	–	2.1

Exhibit 8b Baidu: Consolidated Balance Sheet (Fiscal Year Ending December 31, 2007) (Continued)

BAIDU FINANCIALS														
	RMB Million						**$ Million**							
BALANCE SHEET	2003	2004	2005	2006	2007		2003	2004	2005	2006	2007			
Deferred tax assets, net	–	–	2.8	5.8	15.7		–	–	0.4	0.7	2.2			
Other non-current assets	–	1.1	–	7.7	32.3		–	0.1	–	1.0	4.4			
Total non-current assets	11.0	49.9	201.1	389.3	930.4		1.3	6.0	24.9	49.9	127.4			
TOTAL ASSETS	76.7	262.2	1,136.4	1,668.1	2,655.9		9.3	31.7	140.8	213.7	363.6			
LIABILITIES AND SHARE-HOLDERS' EQUITY														
Current liabilities														
Customers' deposits	8.4	26.0	70.3	141.2	257.6		1.0	3.1	8.7	18.1	35.3			
Accrued expense and other liabilities	3.8	21.9	53.1	153.1	359.3		0.5	2.6	6.6	19.6	49.2			
Deferred revenue	7.5	6.3	7.7	2.6	11.8		0.9	0.8	0.9	0.3	1.6			
Deferred income	–	–	0.1	4.1	2.5		–	–	0.0	0.5	0.3			
Total current liabilities	19.6	54.2	131.2	301.0	631.2		2.4	6.5	16.3	38.6	86.4			
Non-current liabilities														
Long-term payable for acquisitions	–	–	–	7.0	3.0		–	–	–	0.9	0.4			
Deferred income	–	–	0.1	2.8	0.3		–	–	0.0	0.4	0.0			
Total non-current liabilities	–	–	0.1	9.8	3.3		–	–	0.0	1.3	0.5			

Exhibit 8b Baidu: Consolidated Balance Sheet (Fiscal Year Ending December 31, 2007) *(Continued)*

| BAIDU FINANCIALS | RMB Million | | | | | $ Million | | | | |
BALANCE SHEET	2003	2004	2005	2006	2007	2003	2004	2005	2006	2007
Total liabilities	19.6	54.2	131.4	310.8	634.5	2.4	6.5	16.3	39.8	86.9
Commitments	0					0	0	0	0	0
Redeemable convertible preferred shares	91.622	211.4				11.1	25.5	0	0	0
Shareholders' equity										
Class A ordinary shares outstanding at year-end	0.004	0.004	0.004	0.009	0.01	0.0005	0.0005	0.0005	0.0012	0.0014
Class B ordinary shares outstanding at year-end	0	—	0.01	0.005	0.004	0.0012	—	0.0012	0.0006	0.0005
Additional paid-in capital	24.046	43.3	1,009.5	1,088.2	1,171.6	2.9	5.2	125.1	139.4	160.4
Accumulated other comprehensive income (loss)	0	—	(5.5)	(33.7)	(82.0)	—	—	(0.7)	(4.3)	(11.2)
Retained earnings (accumulated losses)	(58.6)	(46.6)	1.0	302.8	931.7	(7.1)	(5.6)	0.1	38.8	127.6
Total shareholders' equity	(34.6)	(3.3)	1,005.1	1,357.3	2,021.4	(4.2)	(0.4)	124.5	173.9	276.7
TOTAL LIABILITIES AND SHAREHOLDERS' EQUITY	76.7	262.2	1,136.4	1,668.1	2,655.9	9.3	31.7	140.8	213.7	363.6

* 2007 results were unaudited.

Source: Baidu annual reports and quarterly results.

Exhibit 8c Baidu: Consolidated Cashflow Statement (Fiscal Year Ending December 31, 2007)

BAIDU FINANCIALS	RMB Million					$ Million				
STATEMENT OF CASH FLOWS	2003	2004	2005	2006	2007	2003	2004	2005	2006	2007
Exchange rate						8.2767	8.2765	8.072	7.8051	7.3041
Cash flows from operating activities										
Net income	(8.9)	12.0	47.6	301.8	629.0	(1.1)	1.5	5.9	38.7	86.1
Adjustments to reconcile net income to net cash generated from operating activities										
Depreciation of fixed assets	4.9	8.9	30.7	64.1		0.6	1.1	3.8	8.2	
Amortization of intangible assets	–	1.1	3.1	6.3		–	0.1	0.4	0.8	
Disposal of fixed assets	–	0.1	0.0	0.9		–	0.0	0.0	0.1	
Share-based compensation	5.1	16.5	33.6	48.3		0.6	2.0	4.2	6.2	
Provision for doubtful accounts	–	0.6	4.3	(0.3)		–	0.1	0.5	(0.04)	
Foreign exchange loss	–	–	0.6	0.1		–	–	0.1	0.01	
Impairment loss on investment		–	–	2.0		–	–	–	0.3	
Cumulative effect of change in accounting principle	–	–	–	(4.6)		–	–	–	(0.6)	
Change in operating assets and liabilities	n/a				n/a					n/a
Accounts receivable	(1.5)	(8.4)	(17.5)	(0.4)		(0.2)	(1.0)	(2.2)	(0.05)	
Prepaid expenses and other assets	0.3	(1.5)	(8.5)	(23.5)		0.0	(0.2)	(1.1)	(3.0)	
Customers' deposits	6.3	17.6	44.2	70.9		0.8	2.1	5.5	9.1	

(Continued)

Case 2: Baidu: Beating Google at Its Own Game

Exhibit 8c Baidu: Consolidated Cashflow Statement (Fiscal Year Ending December 31, 2007) (Continued)

BAIDU FINANCIALS	RMB Million					$ Million				
STATEMENT OF CASH FLOWS	2003	2004	2005	2006	2007	2003	2004	2005	2006	2007
Accrued expenses and other liabilities	1.6	10.7	27.1	62.3		0.2	1.3	3.4	8.0	
Deferred tax assets, net	–	–	(4.3)	(3.2)		–	–	(0.5)	(0.4)	
Deferred revenue	5.0	(1.2)	1.4	(5.1)		0.6	(0.1)	0.2	(0.7)	
Deferred income	–	–	0.2	6.7		–	–	0.0	0.9	
Net cash generated from operating activities	12.7	56.5	162.4	526.1		1.5	6.8	20.1	67.4	
Cash flows from investing activities						–	–	–	–	–
Acquisition of fixed assets	(6.4)	(25.4)	(88.7)	(127.5)		(0.8)	(3.1)	(11.0)	(16.3)	
Acquisition of business	–	–	(10.5)	(43.3)		–	–	(1.3)	(5.6)	
Acquisition of intangible assets	–	(11.9)	(2.1)	(21.9)		–	(1.4)	(0.3)	(2.8)	
Capitalization of internal use software costs	(1.6)	(2.2)	(0.6)	(1.0)		(0.2)	(0.3)	(0.1)	(0.1)	
Acquisition of long-term investments	–	–	(2.0)	–		–	–	(0.3)	–	
Acquisition of marketable securities	–	–	–	(85.3)		–	–	–	(10.9)	
Prepayment for land use rights	–	–	(77.2)	(15.2)		–	–	(9.6)	(1.9)	
Net cash used in investing activities	(8.0)	(39.5)	(181.1)	(294.3)		(1.0)	(4.8)	(22.4)	(37.7)	
Cash flows from financing activities				n/a						n/a

Exhibit 8c Baidu: Consolidated Cashflow Statement (Fiscal Year Ending December 31, 2007) (Continued)

BAIDU FINANCIALS	RMB Million					$ Million				
STATEMENT OF CASH FLOWS	2003	2004	2005	2006	2007	2003	2004	2005	2006	2007
Issuance of Series C convertible preferred shares	–	119.7	–	–		–	14.5	–	–	–
Proceeds from initial public offering (IPO), net of expenses	–	–	716.3	–		–	–	88.7	–	–
Payments for expenses in connection with IPO	–	–	–	(0.6)		–	–	–	(0.1)	
Proceeds from exercise of share options	0.1	0.6	8.0	32.8		0.0	0.1	1.0	4.2	
Net cash generated from financing activities	0.1	120.3	724.3	32.2		0.0	14.5	89.7	4.1	
Effect of exchange rate changes on cash and cash equivalents	–	–	(5.2)	(28.4)		–	–	(0.6)	(3.6)	
Net increase in cash and cash equivalents	4.8	137.4	700.4	235.7		0.6	16.6	86.8	30.2	
Cash and cash equivalents at the beginning of the year	58.0	62.8	200.2	900.6		7.0	7.6	24.8	115.4	–
Cash and cash equivalents at the end of the year	62.8	200.2	900.6	1,136.3		7.6	24.2	111.6	145.6	–
Supplemental cash flow information										
Cash paid during the year for income tax	–	–	4.7	24.2		–	–	0.6	3.1	–
Insurance of ordinary shares in purchase of intangible assets	–	2.1	–	–		–	0.3	–	–	–

* 2007 results not available.
Source: Baidu annual reports.

Exhibit 9a Google: Consolidated Income Statement

GOOGLE FINANCIALS INCOME STATEMENT	Year Ended 31 December				
$ Million (except for share, per share information)	2003	2004	2005	2006	2007
Revenues					
Advertising revenues	1,420.7	3,143.3	6,065.0	10,492.6	16,412.6
Licensing and other revenues	45.3	45.9	73.6	112.3	181.3
Total Revenues	1,465.9	3,189.2	6,138.6	10,604.9	16,594.0
Operating costs and expenses					
Cost of revenues	634.4	1,469.0	2,577.1	4,225.0	6,649.1
Research and Development	229.6	395.2	599.5	1,228.6	2,120.0
Sales and marketing	164.9	295.7	468.2	849.5	1,461.3
General and administrative	94.5	188.2	386.5	751.8	1,279.3
Contribution to Google Foundation	–	–	90.0	–	–
Non-recurring portion of settlement of disputes with Yahoo	–	201.0	–	–	–
Total costs and expenses	1,123.5	2,549.0	4,121.3	7,054.9	11,509.6
Income from operations	342.5	640.2	2,017.3	3,550.0	5,084.4
Interest income and other, net	4.2	10.0	124.4	461.0	589.6
Income before income taxes	346.7	650.2	2,141.7	4,011.0	5,674.0
Provision for income taxes	241.0	251.1	676.3	933.6	1,470.3
Net income	105.6	399.1	1,465.4	3,077.4	4,203.7
Net Income per share					
Basic	0.77	2.07	5.31	10.21	13.53
Diluted	0.41	1.46	5.02	9.94	13.29
Number of shares used in per share calculations					
Basic	137,697	193,176	275,844	301,403	310,806
Diluted	256,638	272,781	291,874	309,548	316,210

Source: Google annual reports.

Exhibit 9b Google: Consolidated Balance Sheet

GOOGLE FINANCIALS BALANCE SHEET	Year Ended 31 December				
$ Million	2003	2004	2005	2006	2007
ASSETS					
Current assets					
Cash and cash equivalents	149.0	426.9	3,877.2	3,544.7	6,081.6
Marketable securities	185.7	1,705.4	4,157.1	7,699.2	8,137.0
Accounts receivable, net of allowance	154.7	311.8	688.0	1,322.3	2,162.5
Income taxes receivable	–	70.5	–	–	145.3
Deferred income taxes, net	22.1	19.5	49.3	29.7	68.5
Prepaid revenue share, expenses and other assets	48.7	159.4	229.5	443.9	694.2
Total current assets	560.2	2,693.5	9,001.1	13,039.8	17,289.1
Prepaid revenue share, expenses and other assets, non-current	17.4	35.5	31.3	114.5	168.5
Deferred income taxes, net, non-current	–	11.6	–		33.2
Non-marketable equity securities	–	–	–	1,031.9	1,059.7
Property and equipment, net	188.3	378.9	961.7	2,395.2	4,039.3
Goodwill	87.4	122.8	194.9	1,545.1	2,299.4
Intangible assets, net	18.1	71.1	82.8	346.8	446.6
TOTAL ASSETS	871.5	3,313.4	10,271.8	18,473.4	25,335.8
LIABILITIES AND SHAREHOLDERS' EQUITY					
Current liabilities					
Accounts payable	46.2	32.7	115.6	211.2	282.1
Accrued compensation and benefits	33.5	82.6	198.8	351.7	588.4
Accrued expense and other liabilities	26.4	64.1	114.4	266.2	465.0
Accrued revenue share	88.7	122.5	215.8	370.4	522.0

(Continued)

Exhibit 9b Google: Consolidated Balance Sheet *(Continued)*

GOOGLE FINANCIALS BALANCE SHEET	Year Ended 31 December				
$ Million	2003	2004	2005	2006	2007
Deferred revenue	15.3	36.5	73.1	105.1	178.1
Income taxes payable	20.7	–	27.8	–	–
Current portion of equipment leases	4.6	1.9	–	–	–
Total current liabilities	235.5	340.4	745.4	1,304.6	2,035.6
Long-term portion of equipment leases	2.0	–	–	–	–
Deferred revenue, long-term	5.0	7.4	10.5	20.0	30.2
Liability for stock options exercised early, long-term	6.3	6.0	–	–	–
Deferred income taxes, net	18.5	–	35.4	40.4	–
Income taxes payable, long-term	–	–	–	–	478.4
Other long-term liabilities	1.5	30.5	61.6	68.5	101.9
Commitments and contingencies					
Redeemable convertible preferred stock warrant	13.9	–			
Shareholders' equity					
Convertible preferred stock, $0.001 par value, 100,000 shares authorized; no shares issued and outstanding	44.3	–	–	–	–
Class A and Class B common stock at 31 December of each year	0.2	0.3	0.3	0.3	0.3
Additional paid-in capital	725.2	2,582.4	7,477.8	11,882.9	13,241.2
Note receivable from officer/stockholder	(4.3)	–	–	–	–
Deferred stock-based compensation	(369.7)	(249.5)	(119.0)	–	–
Accumulated other comprehensive income	1.7	5.4	4.0	23.3	113.4
Retained earnings	191.4	590.5	2,055.9	5,133.3	9,334.8
Total shareholders' equity	588.8	2,929.1	9,419.0	17,039.8	22,689.7
TOTAL LIABILITIES AND SHAREHOLDERS' EQUITY	871.5	3,313.4	10,271.8	18,473.4	25,335.8

Source: Google annual reports.

Exhibit 9c Google: Consolidated Cashflow Statement

GOOGLE FINANCIALS CASHFLOW STATEMENT	Year Ended 31 December				
$ Million	2003	2004	2005	2006	2007
Operating activities					
Net income	105.6	399.1	1,465.4	3,077.4	4,203.7
Adjustments					
Depreciation and amortization of property and equipment	43.9	128.5	256.8	494.4	807.7
Amortization of intangibles and other	11.2	20.0	37.0	77.5	159.9
Stock-based compensation	11.6	11.3	200.7	458.1	868.6
Excess tax benefits from stock-based award activity	229.4	278.7	433.7	(581.7)	(379.2)
Deferred income taxes	–	191.6	21.2	(98.5)	(164.2)
Other, net	–	201.0	22.0	12.5	(39.7)
Changes in assets and liabilities, net of effects of acquisitions					
Accounts receivable	(90.4)	(156.9)	(372.3)	(624.0)	(837.2)
Income taxes, net	(6.3)	(125.2)	66.2	496.9	744.8
Prepaid revenue share, expenses and other assets	(58.9)	(99.8)	(51.7)	(289.2)	(298.7)
Accounts payable	36.7	(13.5)	80.6	95.4	70.1
Accrued expenses and other liabilities	31.1	86.4	166.8	291.5	418.9
Accrued revenues share	74.6	33.9	93.3	139.3	150.3
Deferred revenue	7.0	22.0	39.6	30.8	70.3
Net cash provided by operating activities	395.4	977.0	2,459.4	3,580.5	5,775.4
Investing activities					
Purchase of property and equipment	(176.8)	(176.8)	(838.2)	(1,902.8)	(2,402.8)
Purchase of marketable securities	(316.6)	(316.6)	(12,675.9)	(26,681.9)	(15,997.1)
Maturities and sales of marketable securities	219.4	219.4	10,257.2	23,107.1	15,659.5

(Continued)

Exhibit 9c Google: Consolidated Cashflow Statement *(Continued)*

GOOGLE FINANCIALS CASHFLOW STATEMENT	Year Ended 31 December				
$ Million	2003	2004	2005	2006	2007
Investments in non-marketable equity securities	–	–	–	(1,019.1)	(34.5)
Acquisitions, net of cash acquired and purchases of intangible and other assets	(40.0)	(40.0)	(101.3)	(402.4)	(906.7)
Net cash used in investing activities	(314.0)	(314.0)	(3,358.2)	(6,899.2)	(3,681.6)
Financing activities					
Net proceeds from stock-based award activity	2.3	15.5	85.0	321.1	23.9
Net proceeds from stock-based award activity	–	–	–	581.7	379.2
Net proceeds from public offerings	–	–	4,287.2	2,063.5	–
Payment of note receivable from office/stockholder	–	–	–	–	–
Payments of principal on capital leases and equipment loans	(7.4)	4.7	(1.4)	–	–
Net cash flow by financing activities	8.1	1,194.6	4,370.8	2,966.4	403.1
Effect of exchange rate changes on cash and cash equivalents	1.7	7.6	(21.6)	19.7	40.0
Net increase (decrease) in cash and cash equivalents	91.2	277.9	3,450.3	(332.5)	2,536.9
Cash and cash equivalents at beginning of year	57.8	149.0	426.9	3,877.2	3,544.7
Cash and cash equivalents at end of year	149.0	426.9	3,877.17	3,544.67	6,081.59
Supplemental disclosures of cash flow information					
Cash paid for interest	1.7	0.7	0.2	0.3	1.3
Cash paid for taxes	247.4	183.8	153.6	537.7	882.7
Acquisition-related activities					
Issuance of equity in connection with acquisitions, net	73.5	25.7	22.4	1,173.2	–

Source: Google annual reports.

Exhibit 10 Selected Financial Indicators (fiscal year ending 31 December 2007)

Key Facts	$ Million (except for per-share data)	
	Baidu	Google
Sales	230.1	16,594.0
Operating income	72.2	5,084.4
Net income	83.0	5,268.4
Total assets	361.5	25,302.6
Total liabilities	84.7	2,612.9
EBITDA	100.7	6,642.8
Enterprise value	13,087.0	175,662.0
Headcount	5,200	16,805
Stock price year end	389.8	691.5
Shares outstanding (million)	34.1	312.9
Year-end market cap	13,305.0	216,375.3
EPS	2.5	13.3
Return on assets		
Operating margin (%)	31.4	30.6
Return on assets (ROA) (%)	28.9	19.2
Asset turnover	0.64	0.66
Operating margin (%)		
Costing of goods sold to sales	28.6	34.2
Depreciation	8.7	5.8
Research and development	8.4	12.8
Selling, general and administrative expenses	24.5	16.5
Operating income	31.3	25.6

(Continued)

Exhibit 10 Selected Financial Indicators (fiscal year ending 31 December 2007) *(Continued)*

Key Facts	$ Million (except for per-share data)	
	Baidu	Google
Asset turnover		
Days accounts receivable (relative to sales)	n/a	39.9
Days inventoried (relative to net cost of sales and services)	n/a	n/a
Asset turnover	0.64	0.66
ROE (rate of return on equity)		
Profit margin	36.1	25.3
Asset turnover	0.64	0.66
Financial leverage	1.3	1.1
Return on equity (ROE) (%)	36.9	21.2
Financial risk indicators		
Days accounts payables	n/a	23.0
Current ratio	2.7	8.5
Debt/equity	–	–
Times interest earned (EBIT/Interest expenses)	n/a	4,717.5
Cash flow/debt	n/a	n/a
Per share data		
Common stock price (close)	389.8	691.5
Common stock price (high)	389.0	747.2
Common stock price (low)	388.0	437.0
Equity shares	34.1	312.9
Earning per share	2.5	13.3
Book value of equity per share (end of year)	8.1	70.8
Stock market acceptance		
MVE/BVE (price/book)	48.1	9.8

Exhibit 10 Selected Financial Indicators (fiscal year ending 31 December 2007) *(Continued)*

Key Facts	$ Million (except for per-share data)	
	Baidu	Google
Price/earnings	148.1	52.0
Price/sales	57.8	13.0
Price/cash flow	129.0	50.2
EV/EBITDA	130.0	30.4
EV/EBIT	161.0	35.6
EV/cash flow	127.8	37.0
Relative equity risk of company ('Beta')	3.31	2.42
Common stock price (end of year)	389.9	691.5
Equity shares (millions)	34.1	312.9
Market value of equity (end of year)	13,305.0	216,375.3
Book value of equity (end of year)	276.7	22,079.1
Stern Stewart Performance Indicators		
Market value added (MVA)	13,028.3	194,296.2
After-tax return on invested capital (ROIC) (%)	n/a	21.17
Weighted average cost of capital (WACC) (%)	25.42	21.16
Economic value added (EVA)	(12.7)	(1,187.4)

Note: Figures here were taken mainly from Thomson Financials for comparison purposes, certain figures may be subject to change once Baidu's annual report becomes available.
Source: Thomson Financials, Company annual reports.

Exhibit 11 Baidu: Revenue Drivers

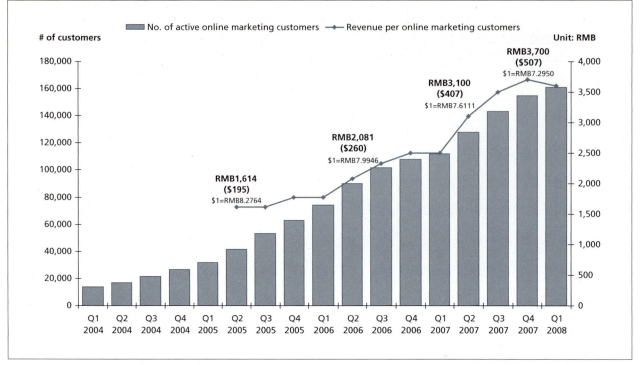

Source: Baidu's annual reports and quarterly results.

Exhibit 12 Comparison of Traffic Acquisition Costs

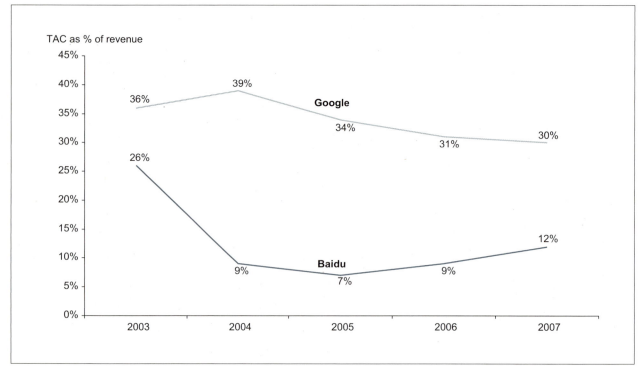

Source: Google's and Baidu's annual reports and quarterly results.

Exhibit 13 Evolution of USS vs. RMB Exchange Rate and Trend[xl] (forward quotation for indication purpose only)

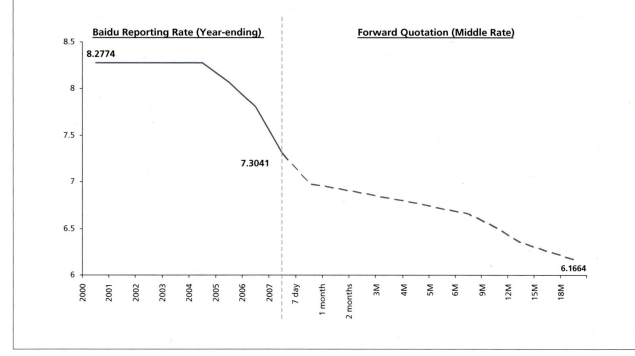

Source: Baidu's annual reports, quarterly results, and http://www.forex.com.

Exhibit 14 Share Performance and Selected Indexes

Source: Datastream.

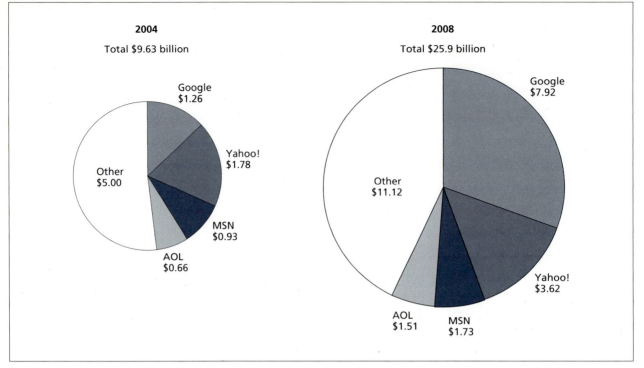

Exhibit 15 U.S. Online Ad Market

2004

Total $9.63 billion

Google
$1.26

Yahoo!
$1.78

Other
$5.00

MSN
$0.93

AOL
$0.66

2008

Total $25.9 billion

Google
$7.92

Other
$11.12

Yahoo!
$3.62

AOL
$1.51

MSN
$1.73

Source: *Wall Street Journal.*[xli]

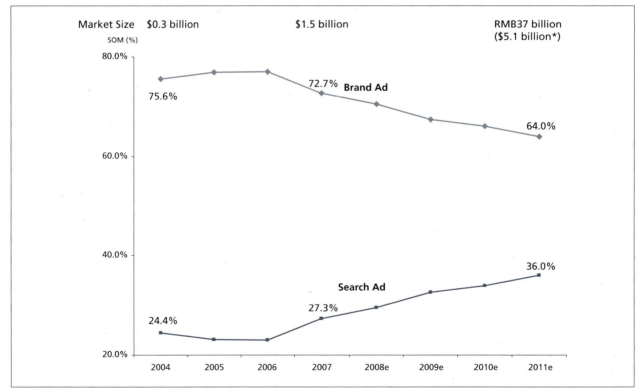

Exhibit 16a China's Online Ad Market Size

Market Size | $0.3 billion | $1.5 billion | RMB37 billion ($5.1 billion*)

SOM (%)

75.6%

72.7% **Brand Ad**

64.0%

24.4%

27.3%

Search Ad

36.0%

2004 | 2005 | 2006 | 2007 | 2008e | 2009e | 2010e | 2011e

Note: Converted at the 2007 year-end rate: $1 = 7.3041, did not take into consideration the effect of RMB revaluation.

Exhibit 16b China's Search Ad Market Size

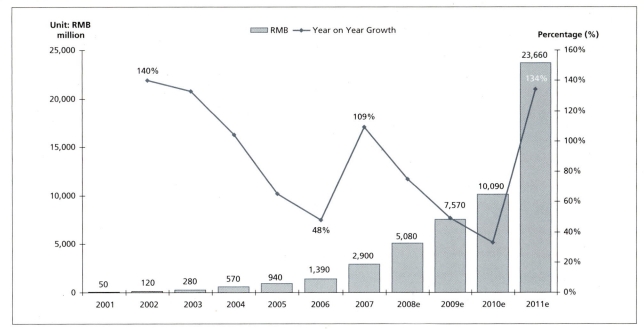

Source: iResearch.[xlii]

NOTES

i. L. Chao & E. Smith, New tune: Google aims to crack China with music push, *Wall Street Journal,* February 6, 2008.

ii. L. Chao & E. Smith, New tune: Google aims to crack China with music push, *Wall Street Journal,* February 6, 2008.

iii. iResearch China Online Search Annual Report 2007.

iv. BNP Paribas report, January 15, 2008.

v. Best Answer to Google, *BusinessWeek,* http://images.businessweek.com/ss/06/12/1207 bestleaders/source/4.htm (accessed May 17, 2008).

vi. Microsoft company press release. January 31, 2008, letter Microsoft sent to Yahoo! board of directors.

vii. Thomson Financials.

viii. Jonathan Watts in Beijing, 2005, Interview: Robin Li, founder of Baidu.com, *The Guardian,* December 8.

ix. Google company Web site.

x. Baidu company Web site.

xi. Baidu company press release.

xii. Google Web site.

xiii. Google Web site.

xiv. BNP Paribas report, January 15, 2008.

xv. Google annual reports.

xvi. BBC, 2006, Google offloads Baidu investment, http://news.bbc.co.uk/2/hi/asia-pacific/4715044.stm, February 15 (accessed May 12, 2008).

xvii. Preliminary Transcript: BIDU—Q1 2008 Baidu Earnings Conference Call, Thomson Street Events, April 24, 2008.

xviii. John Battelle, 2005, 2006, *The Search: How Google and Its Rivals Rewrote the Rules of Business and Transformed Our Culture,* London: Nicholas Brealey Publishing, 2005.

xix. John Battelle, *The Search: How Google and Its Rivals Rewrote the Rules of Business and Transformed Our Culture,* London: Nicholas Brealey Publishing, 2005, 208.

xx. Stacy Cowley, 2006, Google CEO on censoring: 'We did an evil scale,' IDG *News Service,* http://www.infoworld.com/article/06/01/27/74_874 HNgoogleceocensoring_ l html, January 27 (accessed May 16, 2008).

xxi. David Pescovitz, 2006, Chinese Google is song of the grain, http://www.boingboing.net/2006/04/14/chinese-google-is-so.html, April 14 (accessed May 11, 2008).

xxii. David Pescovitz, 2006, Chinese Google is song of the grain, http://www.boingboing.net/2006/04/14/chinese-google-is-so.html, April 14 (accessed May 11, 2008).

xxiii. A. Yeh, 2006, Google disposes of Baidu stake, *Financial Times,* http://www.ft.eom/cms/g/G/6756285a-026d-lldb-al41-0000779e2340.html7nclick_check=l, June 23 (accessed May 12, 2008).

xxiv. J. Watts, 2005, Interview: Robin Li, founder of Baidu.com, *The Guardian,* December 8.

xxv. Baidu 'not a great competitor," says Li Kaifu, *China Wire,* http://www.telecomasia.net/article.php?id article=6759 (accessed May 11, 2008).

xxvi. Baidu.com Q4 2007 Earnings Call Transcript—Seeking Alpha, http://seekingalpha.com/article/64687-baidu-com-q4-2007-earnings-call-transcript?page=-l (accessed May 17, 2007).

xxvii. 2006, Google defends China search site, BBC, http://news.bbc .co.Uk/2/hi/technology/4735662.stm, February 21 (accessed May 12, 2008).

xxviii. BNP Paribas report, January 15, 2008.

xxix.   Preliminary Transcript: BIDU—Q1 2008 Baidu Earnings Conference Call, Thomson StreetEvents, April 24, 2008, and Baidu SEC Filings.

xxx.   China's google Baidu soars in Nasdaq debut, ChinaDaily .com, http://www.chinadailY.com.cn/english/doc/2005-08/08/ content_467140.htm (accessed May 12, 2008).

xxxi.   Baidu annual report.

xxxii. 2008, Baidu was said not in compliance with the Hong Kong listing rules, Sina.com.cn, http://tech.sina.com.en/i/2008-05-20/l 1522205926.shtml, May 20.

xxxiii. J. Watts, 2005, Interview: Robin Li, founder of Baidu.com, *The Guardian*, December 8.

xxxiv. iResearch, China Online Search Annual Report 2007.

xxxv.   Q. Leheng, 2006Baidu vs. Google, r 2006, http://web2 .commongate.com/post/Baidu_vs_Google/, December 6 (accessed May 11, 2008).

xxxvi. C. Hui & H. Kaneko, 2008, Baidu CEO talks about Japanese market, Tech-On!, February 5.

xxxvii. Baidu 'not a great competitor,' says Li Kaifu, *China Wire*, http:// www.telecomasia.net/article.php?id_article=6759 (accessed May 11, 2008).

xxxviii. http://www.alexa.com/data/details/trafficdetails/baidu.com, http:// www.alexa.com/data/details/traffic_details/google.com (accessed May 12, 2008).

xxxix. BNP Paribas report, January 15, 2008.

xl.   Baidu IPO Prospectus, annual reports, and forward quotation from http://forex.hexun.com/2008-04-23/105491657.html (accessed May 13, 2008).

xli.   K. J. Delaney, M. Karnitschnig, & R. A. Guth, 2008, Giving up on Yahoo!, Microsoft rethinks its Internet options, *Wall Street Journal*, May 6, 2008.

xlii.   K. J. Delaney, M. Karnitschnig, & R. A. Guth, 2008, Giving up on Yahoo!, Microsoft rethinks its Internet options, *Wall Street Journal*, May 6, 2008.

Mtina Buechel

IMD–International Institute for Management Development

Late October, 2001, Matt Barrett, CEO of Barclays, was preparing for a seminal event that was to take place the following week. After 24 months in office, he was comtemplating how best to introduce the Group strategy that he had developed with Marakon Associates to the wider organization.

According to Barrett, his key challenge in transforming Barclays was to move it from a large U.K. bank dabbling overseas to a global bank which happened to have a strong U.K. franchise. Barrett's aim was to improve Barclays's performance rapidly and significantly so it could be a predator and not a victim in the industry consolidation that he felt sure was coming.

From the start, he had worked on changing the mind-set and culture of Barclays. His next step was to try to convince the top 100 company executives that the current model for running the business was inadequate for reaching its goals. He passionately believed that a more fact-based, value-growth orientation to running Barclays was essential. This event was key to ensuring that Barclays's new management model would be widely used within the businesses across the Group.

Barclays History

The history of Barclays dates to 1690 when John Freame and Thomas Gould started trading as Goldsmith bankers on Lombard Street in London. In 1896, the company joined with 19 other private banking businesses to form a new joint-stock bank called Barclay and Company Limited. Almost 30 years later, Barclays began its global expansion. In 1981, it became the first foreign bank to file with the Securities and Exchange Commission in Washington, D.C.

After years of expansion, including the acquisitions of the stockbrokers De Zoete & Bevan in 1986 and Wells Fargo Nikko Investment Advisors in 1995,

Barclays faced a leadership challenge. Between 1995 and 1999, Barclays had five different CEOs. In October 1999, Barclays appointed Matt Barrett, a Canadian/Irish citizen who had been the CEO of the Bank of Montreal for the previous decade. Matt was enjoying his retirement when he received the invitation to run Barclays and saw it as a great opportunity. Having been in the financial services industry from the start of his career, Matt had deep vocational knowledge about how a bank, with its multiple businesses and functions, works.

Business Overview

In 2000, Barclays PLC was one of the four dominant retail and commercial banks in the United Kingdom. It was the ninth-largest bank in Europe by assets, with total assets exceeding £320 billion.

The Group consisted of four divisions, of which Retail Financial Services contributed 61 percent of earnings (see Exhibit 1). Its retail franchise included direct relationships with one in five personal customers in the United Kingdom.

In the corporate banking market, Barclays had a direct relationship with more than 25 percent of U.K. businesses, which it served via a network of more than 1,200 relationship managers.

In 1997, Barclays sold the cash, equities, and corporate finance businesses from its investment banking division—Barclays de Zoete Wedd—to Credit Suisse First Boston. As a result, by 2000, the rebranded Barclays Capital had become a collection of sub-scale businesses united by a focus on debt products.

In 2000, Barclays Global Investors (BGI) offered advanced active and indexed asset management services to about 1,800 institutional clients in 36 countries. It introduced the world's first index fund and was managing £529 billion of assets.

Professor Mtina Buechel wrote this case as a basis for class discussion rather than to illustrate either effective or ineffective handling of a business situation.

Exhibit 1 Barclays PLC Corporate Structure (2000)

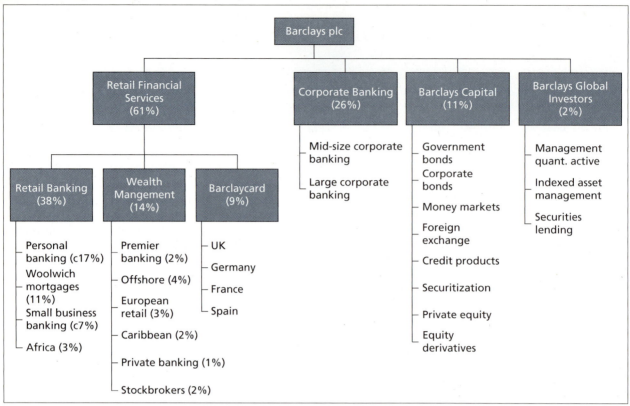

Note: Percentages represent estimated earnings contributions, including pro forma Woolwich.

Source: Company data and Credit Lyonnais Securities Europe estimates.

By 2000, 78 percent of Group revenue and 80 percent of Group profits came from the United Kingdom. Continental Europe generated 10 percent of sales and profits, primarily from high-net-worth retail banking operations in Spain, France, and Portugal. The United States and various African businesses generated the remaining balance.

Situation Assessment

When Barrett joined Barclays, he came across an organization that, according to him, had lost confidence due to years of underperformance and several significant corporate crises. During the 20 years leading up to Matt's arrival, the bank executed 57 divestitures and only two acquisitions. Barclays's global market capitalization rank had fallen from four in 1980 to 22 in 2000 (see Exhibit 2). As a result, predators were circling the company as a potential takeover target and the investor community was increasingly losing patience.

Barclays had lost its way—it had gone from "one of the best" to "one of the rest." Given a prolonged period of underperformance and revolving doors for CEOs, Barclays had become an easy target for the media. Institutional investors were unhappy, employees were demoralized, and the front-line and senior executives had lost confidence. There was at base, however, a great brand and reputation as well as a strong domestic franchise.

Exhibit 2 Barclay's Market Capitalization Rank*

	1980	1985	1990	1995	2000
Rank*	4	13	13	19	22
Mkt Cap (£ bn)	2.0	3.4	7.4	12.4	34.3

*Barclays's rank among the top 100 financial services players globally for any given calendar year.

Source: Marakon Associates.

The Group had no coherent strategic plan, ineffective performance standards and woefully inadequate MIS [management information systems]. We had very little indication where we were losing money and where value was being created. It was like flying a 747 without any controls—exhilarating but life-threatening.

—*Matt Barrett*

One of Barrett's early discoveries was the excessive cost base. For more than 10 years, Barclays had struggled to make significant inroads into reducing its cost base. By 2000, its cost to income ratio was significantly higher than that of competitors (see Exhibit 3). Part of the reason for the excessive cost base was that divisions set up their own HR, IT, and finance divisions to protect themselves from erratic Group governance. Barrett quickly realized that he had a major task ahead of him—to clean up management incompetence and fix the core infrastructure. Indeed, he soon realized that the bank needed a shift in culture and mind-set, a new strategic direction, a structural overhaul, and an improved communications policy.

Building the Foundation

During his first three months in office, Barrett engaged with employees throughout the Group in what he termed "open forums." These were sessions of two to three hours where he would meet up to 1,000 employees from various functions and hierarchical levels. These sessions would typically start with Barrett summarizing his understanding of the current situation. He would then take questions from the audience. In an effort to prepare the organization for the changes he wanted to make, he would also pose provocative questions to his employees, such as "Do you feel that there are people in your area who do not pull their weight?" and "Is it fair that these people are paid the same as you are?" Barrett met approximately 10,000 employees during this initial three-month period to transmit the message that everyone was in this transformation together. There were no second-class citizens.

At the same time, Barrett developed his own vision for the bank—"earn, invest, and grow." He planned to double Barclays's economic profit in four years.[1] In order to finance growth, he planned to reduce costs by £1 billion (from a cost base of £5.5 billion). He emphasized that the money saved from cost reductions created an opportunity for people to shape their destiny, as they could decide which business areas were worth investing in.

In February 2000, six months after Barrett became CEO, the first top 100 executive event was organized in Brighton. Barrett spoke to the group about his vision for the future and explained the company's new financial and strategic goals. These goals were met with skepticism. As one top executive reflected, "I was initially thinking, if I keep my head down, this too will pass." To those who thought the challenge was too great, Barrett's approach was sympathetic but unyielding. Barrett said, "I recognized that it was a significant challenge, and I

Exhibit 3 Barclays Operating Expense as a Percentage of Income in Comparison with Competition

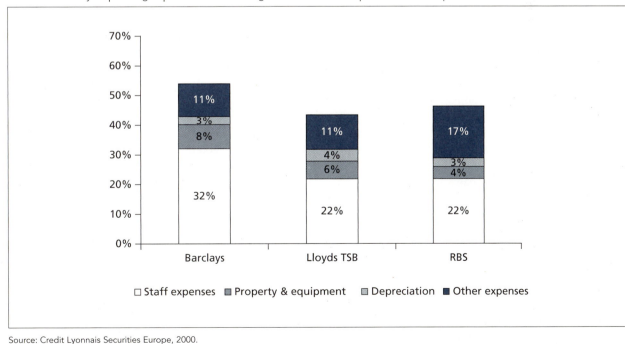

Source: Credit Lyonnais Securities Europe, 2000.

told them that each and every one could count on my support, but that the goal was non-negotiable."

A week later, Barrett publicly committed to these goals to ensure that there would be no scaling back of the commitments. The organization and the top team, while skeptical, were now on the hook to deliver. The goals were to apply equally to him, top management, and everyone in the organization.

Changes at the Top

Barrett started by focusing on his direct reports and spelling out what he believed in—sincerity, encouraging people to take risks, and learning from mistakes. He led as if he had to be reelected the next day. He had to show that he was deeply involved and that he cared.

Barrett quickly turned his sights to realigning the mind-set, and, ultimately, the composition of the top team. He felt that the executive committee (ExCo) was not performing as decision makers but as an administrative body. Each meeting seemed more like a series of bilateral discussions with the CEO than multilateral, high performance dialogues.

At an early ExCo dinner, while the team was having its appetizers, Barrett launched into a direct discussion. He suddenly said he was thinking of disbanding the ExCo meetings if he couldn't make them more productive. There was silence in the room. The team seemed shocked at the prospect of having a FTSE 100 firm that was no longer run by an ExCo (and of each potentially losing his seat at the top table). The team came out vocally against Barrett's proposal and immediately took up his challenge—from then on, their commitment to making the ExCo work became a shared goal. This was reflected in the decision to make co-managing the Barclays Group the primary task of the ExCo and managing their business unit responsibilities the second task. To reflect this change, Barrett realigned ExCo members' rewards, placing more weight on overall company results.

With respect to team composition, Barrett rapidly engineered significant changes on the ExCo. His aim was to undermine opposition to change by bringing in new perspectives and disconnecting existing members from their traditional power bases. Gary Dibb, who had worked for the Bank of Montreal, soon followed Barrett and became the chief administrative officer. John Varley was appointed Group finance director and given ExCo responsibility for delivering cost, productivity, and economic profit goals. This appointment, in particular, was an important step toward building broad organizational confidence in the Group's ability to deliver on its new goals. By spending significant time with the top 100, Barrett was also able to spot and promote young talent to the ExCo, including Gary Hoffman and David Roberts,

who in their late thirties, considerably reduced the average age of the top team.

From an investor's perspective, changes to the senior management team raised concerns about pace and velocity of change. It was, however, positively viewed by equity analysts, such as Credit Lyonnais: "Barclays is undergoing a significant process of change that requires a fresh look and innovative solutions. It can only be assisted by a new senior team."

Gaining Confidence

In October 2000, Barclays acquired Woolwich, a leading mortgage business in the United Kingdom, for £5.4 billion. The acquisition expanded Barclays's product and service portfolio and strengthened an area in which Barclays was weak—residential mortgages. As Barclays had primarily divested in the last 20 years, another purpose of this acquisition was just to show that Barclays could *grow*, not just divest. The Woolwich CEO, John Stewart, moved into Barclays to head Retail.

Value-Based Management Underpins Strategy Development

In the second half of 2000, Barclays Strategic Planning Group, on behalf of the ExCo, reviewed bids from potential advisors to accelerate both the understanding of value and the push for value growth. As Matt Barrett reflected afterwards: "We needed to have tools to make fact-based decisions. There was no cross-organizational discussion of value-adding activities. Barclays was run as four separate pillars and each had its own head office. I used to joke that I was never lonely at the top—there were dozens of 'CEOs.'"

After reviewing the proposals, Barrett and the ExCo decided to work with Marakon Associates, the advisory firm that pioneered "managing for value." Barrett knew Marakon well as he had worked successfully with the company when he was at the Bank of Montreal. Marakon and the ExCo set about looking at all businesses and activities from a value perspective, identifying where value was being created and where it was being destroyed. By assessing all businesses, the supertanker was broken down into a "flotilla of highly maneuverable speedboats," or 20 to 25 smaller value-creating entities, which could be analyzed and managed. The goal was to enable a thorough analysis of each business's potential contribution to the Group.

The value-based approach to developing and delivering strategy was applied within each business. At ExCo meetings, each of the four divisional heads was asked to present two or three alternatives for each business. Each of these strategic options was to be grounded in analysis of industry and company data. Varley characterized the environment as follows: "We are having to up our game, and that is pulling lots of us out of our comfort zones …. All the time we are asking: What makes money and what doesn't? Where are the weaknesses in the business? It had a profound effect— energizing and clarifying …."

As one of the outcomes, it was expected that every investment decision—whether a project, geographic expansion, or new product introduction—presented to the ExCo would have to be assessed using the new value-based management approach. Implicitly, this led to an evaluation of every manager and business unit leader in that sound reasoning had to be used as the foundation for every strategic decision. This method was wildly unpopular at first because it challenged the managers' beliefs. However, as Barnett noted, "We needed to institutionalize the approach. Every meeting we ran had to involve the same questions. Only then would it become part of the DNA."

In the analyst community, the change in management approach did not go unnoticed. As Commerzbank's James Alexander commented: "Value-based management depends on risks and expected profitability, bad debts, and your view of the economy. It's still an art rather than a science. It doesn't entirely help avoid mistakes, but it makes the decision-making process more rigorous."

Developing the Group Strategy

Under Barnett's leadership, and with the help of Marakon's systematic, fact-based approach, the ExCo developed a long-term strategic direction during the first half of 2001. Five full-day ExCo meetings were devoted to debating and agreeing upon a Group strategy. In addition, key opinion formers from across the organization were engaged to provide input and challenge. This resulted in a new strategic direction that called for change along multiple dimensions, including:

- Greater presence outside the United Kingdom, complementing continued strong growth within the U.K. market.

- Greater diversity of sources of economic profit across different product/customer markets, with a greater contribution from asset accumulation and capital markets.
- Growth driven by a more balanced combination of organic and acquisitive moves.
- Selected businesses with full global reach (e.g., Barclays Capital and Barclays Global Investors) leading the way and complementing strong "local" businesses (e.g., UK Retail/Commercial).
- Greater bias of Barclays's personal customer base toward the highly profitable affluent and high-net-worth segments.
- Strongly differentiated customer offers with clearly articulated value for clients, supported by a strong brand and improved distribution, sales, and information.

To drive change, a series of medium-term themes and near-term priorities were developed. As an example, one of the near-term priorities was to develop a "second home market" in continental Europe. This was part of a broader theme to change Barclays's European franchise. Another priority was to expand capital market activities as part of a broader theme to establish world-class global product/customer businesses.

Each of the near-term priorities had a value creation goal attached to it and was led by an ExCo sponsor who had full responsibility for delivering on expectations.

Implementing the Group Strategy

The work with Marakon led to the formal articulation of a Group strategy (see Exhibit 4). In October 2001, this Group strategy was disseminated at the "top 100" meeting in Canary Wharf. Barnett had achieved buy-in from the eight ExCo members, but how would the wider organization receive the Group strategy?

Exhibit 4 Group Strategy Framework

Objective of Our Group Strategy
Our overarching Group Strategy objective is to maximize the economic value of the Group. Accordingly, our Group Strategy has been developed using our value-based strategy development framework and standards.

Components of Our Group Strategy
Our Group Strategic Direction ("Where we are heading")
+Our View of the Future
+Long-Term Direction (5–10 years)
+Medium-Term Strategic Themes (next 2–5 years)
+Near-Term Priorities (next 12 months)

(Continued)

Exhibit 4 Group Strategy Framework (*Continued*)

Our Group Management Model ("How we will run the business")

Group Goals

Our aspiration is to deliver top quartile Total Shareholder Returns vs. our peers over time. However, we do not believe we will be able to continue to deliver against a four-year double-value goal over a 10-year period from our existing business portfolio. As a result, we expect to face a "value gap" in 2010 in the region of £40 billion (£16 billion in today's money) of incremental value creation (as opposed to market capitalization)—broadly equivalent to adding another business of the size of Barclays today over the next 10 years. We expect an economic profit gap of at least £1.5 billion in 2010.

Group Structure

The Group ExCo will have greater involvement in managing cross-Group synergies and "top-down" strategy development; the recent restructuring of the Group into the current model of Clusters, SBUs, and SSUs (Shared Service Units), and the acquisition of Woolwich reflect this evolution.

Group Mission, Beliefs, Practices, and Behaviors

We aspire to be one of the most admired financial services organizations in the world, recognized as an innovative, customer-focused company that delivers superb products and services, ensures excellent careers for our people and contributes positively to the communities in which we live and work. In addition, there are 18 beliefs and practices that outline more specifically the expected operating mode, e.g. Practice 14: We ensure all decisions are fact-based and value-maximizing through our strategy development and agenda management processes. The management team defined an acceptable set of behaviors for the Group. These were—Drive Performance, Build Pride and Passion, Delight Customers, Grow Talent and Capability, Execute at Speed, and Protect and Enhance our Reputation.

Group Decision Rules

Rule 1: Select the strategy/investment alternative which creates the highest economic value (EV).
Rule 2: Select the EV alternative if it meets or exceeds Group/SBU goals for EV, economic profit (EP),[1] and cosW savings.
Rule 3: Select the EV alternative if it is aligned with the Group Strategic Direction.
Rule 4: Select the highest EV if it is aligned with the Group Management Model.
Rule 5: Select the highest EV alternative if it complies with the Group operating policies and standards (e.g., brand, risk, compliance).

Source: Framework developed by Marakon Associates for Barclays.

NOTE

1. Economic profit = net profit after tax less the equity charge, a risk-weighted cost of capital.

Richard Ivey School of Business
The University of Western Ontario

John G. McIntyre leaned back from his computer and considered the just-released Statements of Allegations of the Staff of the Ontario Securities Commission and the U.S. Securities and Exchange Commission against Biovail Corporation and four of its current and former executives. His firm, McIntyre and Associates, was a boutique accounting firm that specialized in providing analysis and recommendations to legal firms representing various classes of shareholders in class action lawsuits. McIntyre had the pending Biovail allegations on his radar since late 2003, when Banc of America issued a "sell rating" on Biovail stock, citing the company's aggressive accounting practices. In light of these new charges, McIntyre was convinced that his firm would be engaged by one of his law firm clients to provide the forensic accounting analysis to them as the legal representatives of shareholders in a suit. McIntyre needed to review the multitude of information accumulated in the Biovail files and determine which of the many issues should be investigated more fully to support any case.

The Pharmaceutical Industry

The pharmaceutical industry was one of the largest and fastest growing manufacturing industries in Canada, contributing approximately $6 billion to Canadian GDP in 2005 and boasting an annual industry growth rate of 7.7 percent.[2] The industry was highly competitive and included brand-name corporations, generic drug manufacturers, smaller biopharmaceutical companies, and well-known research and clinical trial organizations. Exhibit 1 provides summary information from some of the largest, multinational players in the industry.

Most large pharmaceutical companies with locations in Canada were clustered in metropolitan areas such as Montreal and Toronto. The pharmaceutical industry was research and development (R&D) intensive. In 2007, the pharmaceutical industry was responsible for $1.96 billion, or 19 percent of total Canadian R&D spending.[3] The highly skilled Canadian workforce and the Canadian government's commitment to funding pharmaceutical research, either directly or via research and development tax credits, made Canada an attractive investment location for multinational pharmaceutical companies.[4] Furthermore, the North American Free Trade Agreement provided these multinational companies with tariff-free access to the large North American market, enhancing this industry's competitiveness.

Each new drug required a great deal of R&D before it could be approved. The approval process started with preclinical testing. This stage consisted of laboratory tests to show the efficacy and safety of the drug. Following successful preclinical testing, a company filed an Investigational New Drug application (IND) with the Food and Drug Administration (FDA) before it could begin to test the drug on humans. After approval was granted, three phases of clinical trials were conducted. These experimental phases studied the dosage, efficacy and side effects associated with the drug. The clinical trials included up to 3,000 human volunteers. Lastly, a company had to file a New Drug Application (NDA) with the FDA. In the United States, only five in 5,000 compounds that entered preclinical testing made it to human testing. Moreover, only one of those five tested on people was approved.[5] A company's bottom line could suffer drastically if the FDA did not grant approval.

Biovail Company Background

Eugene Melnyk started his first company in 1982 when he was just 23 years old. As the son of a Toronto doctor, he recognized the need of physicians to have a more time-efficient way to read the lengthy medical literature available to them. On this idea, Melnyk founded a publishing company called Trimel, which focused on creating crib notes for physicians who did not have time to read the extensive medical literature available to them.

In October 1990, Melnyk sold Trimel for Cdn$ 6.5 million and shifted focus toward the drug technologies of the pharmaceutical field. With a particular interest in the area of controlled-release drug delivery,[6] Melnyk acquired the proprietary technology. Melnyk then purchased a half-interest in Biovail SA, a financially troubled but well-respected Swiss pharmaceutical company.[7] The new company's operations were consolidated under the name Biovail.

Initially, Biovail licensed its products early in the development cycle to pharmaceutical companies that conducted clinical trials, regulatory processes, and the manufacturing and sale of their products. However, by the mid-1990s, Biovail had become an international, full-service pharmaceutical company based in Mississauga, Ontario.

In December 2001, Melnyk assumed the position of chief executive officer (CEO) of Biovail. The period during Melnyk's tenure as CEO was the focus of numerous civil, criminal, and regulatory investigations that severely increased expenses and legal fees and distracted the Biovail board and management. Melnyk stepped down from his role of CEO in October 2004.

Melnyk was also chairman of the board of directors during his tenure as CEO, and he remained as chairman until his resignation from the board in June 2007. As the reason for his resignation, however, Melnyk told shareholders at the company's annual meeting that he "can point to a dozen successful business deals in the last dozen years, but [he has] a hard time remembering a dozen quality days at home in the last six months."[8]

As of 2008, Biovail invested over 12 percent of its product sales back into research and development of drug technologies. The company's current commercial portfolio included Zovirax® Cream, Zovirax® Ointment, Wellbutrin XL®, Ultram® ER, Cardizem® LA, and a variety of generic[9] medications for therapeutic categories, including cardiology, depression and the central nervous system.[10]

In 2007, Melnyk, who was by this time a 48-year-old multi-millionaire and owner of the Ottawa Senators, was named the 70th wealthiest person in Canada with a net worth of $759 million.[11] In that year, Biovail reported revenues of US$801 million and net income of US$195.5 million.[12] Exhibit 2 includes condensed financial statements for the years 2006 and 2007.

The Truck Accident

On October 1, 2003, a fatal traffic accident occurred involving one of Biovail's delivery trucks. Before long, Biovail would blame this accident for its weak third-quarter revenues. Eight people were killed and 16 people were injured when an 18-wheeler truck crashed into a tour bus. The tour bus, in turn, crashed into Biovail's contract carrier. Though no one was hurt in Biovail's tractor-trailer, the vehicle (which had left the plant on September 30, 2003, F.O.B. destination) was loaded with finished goods that management claimed were severely damaged and, therefore, not salable.

Shortly after the accident, Biovail issued a press release[13] warning that the company's revenues for the third quarter of 2003 would be lower than previously expected. According to management, Biovail's ill-fated shipment contained $15 million to $20 million of one of the company's main revenue drivers, Wellbutrin XL®, an anti-depression medication.

The latest appearance of Biovail in the news, including pictures of the damaged truck, was fueling the fire for skeptical analysts who questioned the timing of the truck accident as well as the quantity of inventory involved. One analyst was quoted as saying "it is a curious thing when a company's financials are so dependent on one truckload of products that it just happens to be shipping on the last day of the quarter."[14]

Regardless of the most recent events, by 2003, Biovail had earned a questionable reputation. With a number of class action lawsuits outstanding and a chief executive officer whose conduct was constantly challenged by analysts, Biovail received widespread scrutiny from the media. Furthermore, Biovail's accounting methods were being questioned, leading investors to wonder whether the company had actually achieved the level of success that was previously reported in their statements.

The Banc of America Research Report

On October 8, 2003, seven days after the accident, Biovail's stock dropped 33 percent on the TSX to $25.20 per share. The plummet in stock value was assumed to be due to the aftermath of the inability for Biovail to meet its earnings forecast and to the October 2003 Banc of America research report that labelled Biovail's stock with a "sell rating." A TSX stock chart and historical prices for Biovail are presented in Exhibit 3.

The Banc of America report sought out the opinions of three forensic accounting experts who studied Biovail's press releases, transcripts, and most recent public filings. In the final report, one expert noted that Biovail's practices may be "aggressive but legal"; another noted that while Biovail's practices did not show that there was any widespread accounting impropriety, there was "perhaps aggressiveness beyond what we have observed at peer companies."[15]

The forensic accountants went on to criticize the company in many areas. The experts questioned the truck accident, noting that after they undertook further investigation, the situation seemed even more surprising. Having studied the photographs and video of the accident scene, they noted that, contrary to Biovail's high damage estimates, one-third to one-half of the truck interior appeared to be empty.

In addition to the peculiar traffic accident, the Banc of America report referenced many other reasons for the sell rating. For example, the experts noted that Biovail's product sales growth had become negative in 2003. Product sales growth, normally the company's primary growth driver, had significantly slowed for Biovail. In the company's statements, overall sales appeared solid but had been helped by royalties and licensing revenue gains. The experts questioned the sustainability of these two types of revenue streams.

Other areas of criticism included Biovail's declining R&D spending, its highly leveraged balance sheet and the company's low tax rate. The experts reported that Biovail's research and development spending had dropped substantially in the past few years. In addition, the report noted that in 2003, each of Biovail's top 10 selling products was purchased rather than developed in-house. The company's balance sheet contained an extremely high level of debt relative to its peer companies. Additionally, Biovail's tax rate was 6.9 percent, as compared to the next lowest tax rate in its peer group at 19.8 percent, and the report questioned whether or not this lower rate was sustainable.[16]

Finally, the area of analysis that was most troubling to the experts concerned Biovail's quality of earnings. The forensic accountants wrote about Biovail's long history of reporting operating earnings results that differed substantially from its GAAP earnings results. The accounting team was particularly concerned with the company's reliance on pro forma earnings.[17] While regulatory filings, including quarterly and annual reports, are prepared using Generally Accepted Accounting Principles (GAAP), press releases and conference calls provide management with other opportunities to communicate with investors about a company's performance using information that was generally not audited prior to its release.

As noted by Biovail management:

Management utilizes a measure of net income and earnings per share on a basis that excludes certain charges to better assess operating performance. Each of the items excluded is considered to be of a non-operational nature in the applicable period. Management has consistently applied this measure when discussing earnings or earnings guidance and will continue to do so going forward. Management believes that most of the Company's shareholders prefer to analyze the Company's results based on this measure, as it is consistent with industry practice. Earnings excluding charges are also disclosed to give investors the ability to further analyze the Company's results.[18]

Banc of America contended that the gap between Biovail's pro forma earnings and its GAAP earnings was among the largest in its peer group. Skepticism surrounded the non-GAAP earnings which portrayed a company that was growing faster than its underlying organic growth.[19] Exhibit 4 provides actual and pro forma financial statements for Biovail for the years 2001 and 2002 and the second quarter of 2003. Exhibit 5 provides select information from the Banc of America research report for Biovail and two of its competitors, Abbott Laboratories and Cephalon, Inc. Exhibits 6 and 7 provide earnings releases for the same two competitors.

Pointing Fingers

"As it has been throughout his career, Melnyk's entrepreneurial drive could be inspiring and effective in his organization. It could also be annoying and frustrating even to his own shareholders because Melnyk would not let even the slightest criticism from regulators and analysts pass."[20]

In March 2006, while he was executive chairman to the Biovail board of directors, Melnyk brought action against 22 defendants, alleging a market manipulation scheme was the reason for the drastic decline in Biovail's stock market price in recent years.[21] Specific allegations were released against Banc of America Securities in response to their October 2003 report. Melnyk accused reporters of influencing independent analysts to broadcast materially false and misleading information about Biovail.[22]

In early April 2006, weeks after Melnyk's market manipulation allegations, Melnyk found himself at the center of media attention as the OSC and SEC acknowledged probable suspicious trading activity.[23] Melnyk was accused of failing to file insider trading reports and acting contrary to public interest by failing to disclose his holdings to the public and understating his ownership stake in the company. The investigation encompassed a large number of trades in Cayman Island trust accounts where Melnyk was believed to be a beneficiary.[24] These trades occurred throughout Melnyk's tenure as chief executive officer from December 2001 through to October 2004.

On May 14, 2007, Eugene Melnyk and other Biovail executives received Wells Notices[25] from the U.S. Securities and Exchange Commission. The Wells Notices encompassed alleged violations of federal securities laws in accounting and disclosure practices.[26] Specific enforcement action against Melnyk was expected regarding his trading and reporting ownership positions of Biovail securities.

On May 18, 2007, Melnyk settled allegations from the Ontario Securities Commission concerning his failure to disclose US$1.3 billion in trades of Biovail shares. To settle this dispute, Melnyk paid the OSC Cdn$1 million and agreed to step down as executive chairman of the board, Biovail Corporation, and from all other director and officer roles relating to Biovail subsidiaries.[27]

On June 30, 2007, Melnyk retired from the board of Biovail Corporation. Since then, the role of executive chairman was assumed by Dr. Douglas Squires.[28] Squires had served Biovail as a director since 2005 and as lead director since 2007. Other new appointments included William Wells as the chief executive officer. Appointments were decided and announced by the Compensation, Nominating, and Corporate Governance Committee of the board of directors.[29] This committee was designed to insure independence and strategic appointments for Biovail leadership.

On February 25, 2008, Melnyk resigned as director and officer of BLS, another Biovail subsidiary. As of February 25, 2008, Melnyk was no longer employed by or a director of Biovail Corporation or any of its subsidiaries.

OSC and SEC Charges Laid

On March 24, 2008, not unexpectedly, both the Ontario Securities Commission and the U.S. Securities and Exchange Commission released a Statement of Allegations targeting Biovail Corporation and four former and current executives[30] and the company's financial reports for 2001, 2002 and Q1 and Q2, 2003. See Exhibit 8 for a summary of the key allegations.

The SEC's statement was particularly scathing, accusing the company and its management team of chronic fraudulent conduct, including financial reporting fraud and other intentional public misrepresentations as a result of their obsession with meeting quarterly and annual earnings targets. The SEC continued by alleging that when it "ultimately became impossible to continue to conceal the company's poor performance, Biovail actively misled investors and analysts as to its cause"[31] referring to the October 1, 2003, truck accident.

The alleged financial reporting fraud involved three accounting schemes that affected reporting periods from 2001 to 2003, including the improper use of a special purpose entity, revenue manipulation, and an intentional misstatement of foreign exchange losses.

Biovail created a special purpose entity, Pharmaceutical Technologies Corp. (Pharmatech), a development-stage company, to undertake an estimated $125 million[32] in research and development activities on behalf of Biovail in return for royalties in mid-2001. Pharmatech's sole shareholder, a past consultant for Biovail, invested US$1 million of which $350,000 was immediately refunded as a fee. The remainder was fully secured by Biovail.[33] As well, the company entered into a share option agreement with the sole shareholder of Pharmatech permitting Biovail to purchase all of the stockholder's Pharmatech shares at any time until December 31, 2006, in exchange for a fixed purchase price. On December 27, 2002, as a result of Pharmatech's banker's refusal to extend financing directly to Pharmatech, Biovail exercised its purchase option and repaid the bank (which also happened to be the company's principal bank) in full. As a result of these transactions, the SEC concluded that Biovail's financial reports were materially false and misleading, causing net income to be overstated by approximately 50 percent in the third quarter of 2001, 32 percent in the 2001 annual financial statements, 15 percent in the first quarter 2002, 18 percent in the second quarter 2002, and 16 percent in the third quarter 2002, and understated by approximately 17 percent in the 2002 annual financial statements.[34]

In October 2001, Biovail entered into an agreement with a distributor whereby Biovail would produce Wellbutrin XL (WXL), which had not yet received FDA approval, and then sell it to the distributor. Biovail was to produce sample products (sold at cost), which the distributor could distribute to physicians as a promotional tour as well as trade products (sold at normal markups) packaged and labeled for commercial sale. By June 2003, the FDA had indicated that WXL was "approvable" subject to some labeling changes. Final approval was not received until August 29, 2003. On June 19, 2003, Biovail contacted its distributor and requested that, prior to June 30, 2003, the distributor place an order for trade WXL. Biovail committed to segregating the specific inventory related to the purchase order in a separate location in its Manitoba warehouse.[35] Biovail further indicated that if the distributor failed to place such an order, the company would not fully commit its manufacturing facilities to producing WXL tablets in advance of the product launch. The distributor sent Biovail a purchase order, and Biovail invoiced the distributor for approximately US$8 million, resulting in an increased second quarter operating income of US$4.4 million.[36] Subsequent to the receipt of the purchase order, management became concerned about the expiry date on the segregated inventory. The segregated inventory was then used to fill orders from the distributor for sample products (at sample- or cost-based prices).

In December 2002, Biovail acquired the rights to certain drugs and assumed a liability denominated in Canadian dollars. Since Biovail reported its results in U.S. dollars, it was required to account for this liability in its financial statements in U.S. dollars by converting the liability at the current rate at each balance sheet date. On March 31, 2003, the Canadian dollar had strengthened against the U.S. dollar compared to its December 31, 2002, rate. Though the company correctly accounted for the liability on its 2002 year-end balance sheet, it continued to use the exchange rate from December 2002 on its March 31, 2003, and June 30, 2003, balance sheets. As a result, the quarterly financial statements for first two quarters of 2003 did not reflect the resultant exchange loss or an accurate statement of the liability. Biovail overstated its net income by approximately US$5 million and US$4 million in the first and second quarters of 2003, respectively. According to the OSC and the SEC, the chief financial officer (CFO) at the time became aware of the error in early July 2003, but took no steps to correct the error or to disclose the error until the company's March 3, 2004, press release.

As McIntyre pondered the two Statements of Allegations in front of him, he found it particularly interesting that Biovail's claim that the truck accident had caused the company to miss its third quarter earnings target appeared to have precipitated the OSC and SEC's investigation. Much of both documents focused on the allegations that the statements made in the company's October 3, 2003, press release were materially misleading or untrue.

Class Action Law Suit

McIntyre and Associates had significant experience in providing forensic accounting analysis to law firms involved in class action lawsuits against corporations accused of breaching securities laws by making false and misleading statements about the state of their business. A class action lawsuit organized the claims of numerous people, in this case shareholders, with a common interest to engage corporate entities in legal action to rectify any immoral actions committed by these entities.[37]

The typical process for a class action lawsuit involved the hiring of legal representation and soliciting the court for "class action" case certification. The certification of "class action" was contingent on the number of shareholders involved in the suit, the extent of commonality in damages experienced by these shareholders and whether the legal representation was aligned with and representative of the shareholder interests.[38] A time period was established for the start and end of the claims period, and only holders of shares during that period were eligible to participate in the class action lawsuit. Once class-action certification was granted, all eligible shareholders were informed and prompted to contribute input into the case. Eligible shareholders then became entitled to a pro-rated portion of any awards received, net of legal expenses.

Class action claims could be settled through negotiation agreements with the corporation, or they could be brought to trial where a judge would render a decision. In order to gain negotiating leverage, the plaintiff had to prove that management intentionally misled shareholders through their actions or through the information that they distributed and that those actions lead to a destruction of shareholder value.[39]

McIntyre's Task

As he sifted through the Biovail files, McIntyre knew there were several issues to consider when preparing the supporting arguments for a law firm to take the lead in a possible class action suit on behalf of Biovail shareholders. Much of what he had read about the actions of Biovail executives might be construed as just poor management judgment; on the other hand, as noted by the OSC and SEC, perhaps this was a case of fraudulent conduct. McIntyre would also have to identify a period of time for which the issues would have impacted shareholders and new purchasers of Biovail shares. The chosen time period would determine the eligible members of the class action suit and the market value destruction that had occurred to their investments in Biovail. McIntyre took a sip of his cappuccino and began to investigate the issues that he believed warranted further examination.

Exhibit 1 Forbes 2000 Largest Companies Drug & Biotechnology Industry (in US$ billions)

Global Rank	Company	Country	Sales	Profits	Assets
57	Pfizer	United States	48.42	8.14	115.27
58	Johnson & Johnson	United States	61.10	10.58	80.95
67	Sanofi-aventis	France	40.95	7.68	104.98
72	Novartis	Switzerland	40.22	12.62	71.89
74	Roche Holding	Switzerland	40.65	8.60	67.72
79	GlaxoSmithKline	United Kingdom	45.07	10.35	57.16
148	AstraZeneca	United Kingdom	29.21	5.53	46.91
162	Merck & Co.	United States	24.20	3.28	48.35
167	Abbott Laboratories	United States	25.91	3.61	39.71
171	Wyeth	United States	22.40	4.62	42.72
228	Amgen	United States	14.77	3.17	34.64
229	Eli Lilly & Co.	United States	18.63	2.95	26.79
257	Bristol-Myers Squibb	United States	19.35	2.17	26.17

Source: http://www.forbes.com/lists, accessed September 27, 2008.

Exhibit 2 Biovail Corporation Consolidated Statements of Income in accordance with United Stated Generally Accepted Accounting Principles (All dollar amounts expressed in thousands of U.S. dollars)

	2007	2006
REVENUE		
Product sales	$801,046	$1,021,278
Research and development	23,828	21,593
Royalty and other	17,944	24,851
	842,818	1,067,722
EXPENSES		
Cost of goods sold	223,680	211,152
Research and development	118,117	95,479
Selling, general and administrative	161,001	238,441
Amortization	48,049	56,457
Legal settlements, net of insurance recoveries	95,114	14,400
Asset impairments, net of gain on disposal	9,910	143,000
Restructuring costs	668	15,126
Contract costs (recovery)	(1,735)	54,800
	654,804	828,855
Operating income	188,014	238,867
Interest income	24,563	29,199
Interest expense	(9,745)	(35,203)

(Continued)

Exhibit 2 Biovail Corporation Consolidated Statements of Income in accordance with United Stated Generally Accepted Accounting Principles (All dollar amounts expressed in thousands of U.S. dollars)

	2007	2006
Foreign exchange gain	5,491	(2,360)
Equity loss	(2,528)	(529)
Other income (expense)	2,944	—
Income from continuing operations before provision for income taxes	208,739	229,974
Provision for income taxes	13,200	14,500
Income from continuing operations	195,539	215,474
Loss from discontinued operation	0	–3,848
Net income	$ 195,539	$ 211,626

Sources: http://www.biovail.com.

Exhibit 2 (*Continued*) Biovail Corporation Consolidated Balance Sheets in accordance with United Stated Generally Accepted Accounting Principles (All dollar amounts expressed in Thousands of U.S. dollars)

	2007	2006
ASSETS		
Current	2007	2006
Cash and cash equivalents	$ 433,641	$ 834,540
Marketable securities	3,895	—
Accounts receivable	111,114	129,247
Insurance recoveries receivable	62,942	—
Inventories	80,745	78,871
Prepaid expenses and other current assets	14,680	15,056
	707,017	1,057,624
Marketable securities	24,417	5,677
Long-term investments	24,834	56,442
Property, plant and equipment, net	238,457	211,979
Intangible assets, net	630,514	697,645
Good will	100,294	100,294
Deferred tax assets, net of valuation allowance	20,700	—
Other long-term assets, net	35,882	62,781
	$ 1,782,115	$ 2,192,442
LIABILITIES		
Current		
Accounts payable	50,415	44,988
Dividends payable	—	80,222

(Continued)

Exhibit 2 (*Continued*) Biovail Corporation Consolidated Balance Sheets in accordance with United Stated Generally Accepted Accounting Principles (All dollar amounts expressed in thousands of U.S. dollars)

	2007	2006
Accrued liabilities	74,363	101,219
Accrued legal settlements	148,000	14,400
Accrued contract costs	45,065	54,800
Income taxes payable	647	41,596
Deferrend revenue	49,088	61,916
Current portion of long-term liabilities	—	11,146
	$ 367,578	$ 410,287
Deferred revenue	55,653	73,621
Income taxes payable	54,100	—
Long-term obligations	—	399,379
Other long-term liabilities	6,965	6,898
	484,296	890,185
SHAREHOLDER'S EQUITY		
Common shares, no par value, unlimited shares authorized,161,023,729, and 160,444,070 issues and outstanding at December 31, 2007 and 2006, respectively	1,489,807	1,476,930
Additional paid in capital	23,925	14,952
Deficit	(278,495)	(232,733)
Accumulated other comprehensive income	62,582	43,108
	$ 1,782,115	$ 2,192,442

Sources: http://www.biovail.com.

Exhibit 2 (*Continued*) Biovail Corporation Consolidated Statements of Cash Flows in accordance with United Stated Generally Accepted Accounting Principles (All dollar amounts expressed in thousands of U.S. dollars)

	2007	2006
CASH FLOWS FROM OPERATING ACTIVITIES		
Net income	$195,539	$211,626
Adjustments to reconcile net income to net cash provided by continuing operating activities		
Depreciation and amortization	94,985	92,150
Amortization and write-down of deferred financing costs	4,821	2,300
Amortization and write-down of discounts on long-term obligations	962	1,291
Accrued legal settlements, net of insurance recoveries	78,652	14,400
Gains on disposal of investments and intangible assets	24,356	4,000
Impairment charges and asset write-offs	21,268	151,140

(Continued)

Exhibit 2 (*Continued***)** Biovail Corporation Consolidated Statements of Cash Flows in accordance with United Stated Generally Accepted Accounting Principles (All dollar amounts expressed in thousands of U.S. dollars)

	2007	2006
Stock-based compensation	10,633	14,794
Accrued contract costs	9,735	54,800
Premium paid on early extinguishment of debt	7,854	—
Equity loss	2,528	529
Loss from discontinued operations	—	3,848
Other	5,578	2,083
Changes in operating assets and liabilities		
Accounts receivable	18,052	4,688
Insurance recoveries receivable	7,994	—
Inventories	3,023	10,906
Prepaid expenses and other current assets	376	311
Accounts payable	3,273	12,999
Accrued liabilities	26,496	13,694
Income taxes payable	7,514	3,897
Deferred revenue	30,796	42,319
Net cash provided by continuing operating activities	340,853	522,517
CASH FLOWS FROM INVESTING ACTIVITIES		
Proceeds on disposals of investments, net of costs	52,669	—
Additions to property, plant, and equipment, net	35,086	44,802
Additions to marketable securities	34,534	3,196
Proceeds from sales and maturities of marketable securities	3,282	4,854
Additions to long-term investments	1,376	1,303
Proceeds on disposals of intangible assets	—	4,000
Acquisitions of intangible assets	—	—
Net cash provided by (used in) continuing investing activities	15,045	40,447
CASH FLOWS FROM FINANCING ACTIVITIES		
Redemption of Senior Subordinated Notes	406,756	1,098
Dividends paid	321,523	80,062
Repayments of other long-term obligations	11,250	25,280
Issuance of common shares	11,217	15,634
Repayment of deferred compensation obligation, net	338	175
Financing costs paid	—	1,275
Payment on termination of interest rate swap	—	—

(Continued)

Exhibit 2 (*Continued***)** Biovail Corporation Consolidated Statements of Cash Flows in accordance with United Stated Generally Accepted Accounting Principles (All dollar amounts expressed in thousands of U.S. dollars)

	2007	2006
Net cash used in continuing financing activities	728,650	92,256
CASH FLOWS FROM DISCONTINUED OPERATION		
Net cash used in operating activities	—	558
Net cash used in investing activities	—	—
Net cash used in discontinued operation	—	558
Effect of exchange rate changes on cash and cash equivalents	1,943	5
Net increase (decrease) in cash and cash equivalents	400,899	389,251
Cash and cash equivalents, beginning of year	834,540	445,289
Cash and cash equivalents, end of year	$ 433,641	$ 834,540

Sources: http://www.biovail.com.

Exhibit 3 Biovail Stock Price History

Source: http://ca.finance.yahoo.com/q/bc?s. Copyright 2008 Yahoo! Inc., http://finance.yahoo.com.

Exhibit 4 Biovail Corporation Earnings Release Income Statement (US$ millions)

	2001	2002	2003 2Q cum
Revenue			
Product sales	$521.2	$646.0	$284.6
Research and development	14.6	28.4	6.3
Co-promotion, royalty and licensing	47.5	113.6	117.8
	583.3	788.0	408.7
Expenses			
Cost of goods sold	126.0	164.7	48.7
Research and development	51.0	52.2	39.8
Seling, general and administrative	110.1	165.7	103.1
Amortization	44.5	71.5	86.4
Write-down of assets	80.5	31.9	—
Acquired research and development	—	167.7	84.2
Settlements	—	—	(34.1)
	412.1	653.7	328.1
Operating income (loss)	171.2	134.3	80.6
Interest income	2.7	3.6	4.7
Interest expense	(36.2)	(32.0)	(19.5)
Other income	—	3.4	6.7
Debt conversion premiums	(34.9)	—	—
Income (loss) before provision for income taxes	102.8	109.3	72.5
Provision for income taxes	15.3	21.5	10.4
Net income (loss)	$87.5	$87.8	$62.1
Diluted earning per share	$0.58	$0.55	$0.39
Net income (loss)	$ 87.5	$87.8	$62.1
Add (deduct) certain items			
Write-down of assets	80.5	31.9	—
Acquired research and development	—	167.7	84.2
Other income	—	(3.4)	—
Debt conversion premiums	34.9	—	—
Net income excluding certain items	$202.9	$284.0	$146.3
Diluted earnings per share excluding certain items	$1.35	$1.77	$0.91

Source: www.sedar.com, Biovail press release.

Exhibit 5 Excerpts from Banc of America Research Report Earnings Quality Analysis

Aggregate ProForma Earnings versus Aggregate GAAP Earnings from 1998 to 2002				
Company	**ProForma EPS**	**GAAP EPS**	**Absolute Difference**	**Relative Earnings Ratio***
Median**	$4.07	$3.05	$0.53	12%
Abbott Labs	$8.90	$7.63	$1.27	14%
Cephalon	$(3.83)	$(5.60)	$1.77	46%
Biovail	$4.75	$(0.59)	$5.34	112%

*Calculated as (ProForma earnings – GAAP earnings)/ProForma Earnings.
**Median represents the median return on invested capital for 16 companies in Biovail's peer group.

Return on Invested Capital*—GAAP Earnings versus ProForma Earnings				
ROIC – GAAP Earnings				
Company	**2000**	**2001**	**2002**	**2003 2Q**
Median**	13.20%	11.40%	14.10%	14.40%
Abbott	29.70%	13.50%	19.90%	15.70%
Cephalon	N/A	−2.80%	13.80%	9.20%
Biovail	−18.90%	10.40%	8.00%	4.20%
ROIC – ProForma Earnings				
Company	**2000**	**2001**	**2002**	**2003 2Q**
Median**	14.90%	13.70%	16.30%	17.90%
Abbott	29.70%	24.10%	22.90%	20.90%
Cephalon	N/A	2.40%	7.40%	4.40%
Biovail	14.80%	20.90%	21.40%	17.70%

*Return on Invested Capital is calculated using the formula: (Net Income – Dividends)/Total Capital.
**Median represents the median return on invested capital for 16 companies in Biovail's peer group.

Source: Banc of America Research Report, October 10, 2003.

Exhibit 6 Abbott Laboratories Earnings Release Income Statement (US$ millions)

	2001	**2002**
Net sales	$16,285.2	$17,684.7
Cost of products sold	7,748.4	8,506.3
Research & development (R&D)	1,577.5	1,561.8
Acquired in-process R&D	1,330.4	107.7
Selling, general & administrative	3,734.9	3,978.8
Total operating cost and expenses	14,391.2	14,154.6
Operating earnings	1,894.0	3,530.1
Net interest expense	234.8	205.2
Net foreign exchange loss	31.4	74.6

(Continued)

Exhibit 6 Abbott Laboratories Income Statement (US$ millions)

	2001	2002
(Income) from TAP Pharm. Products Inc. joint venture	(333.8)	(666.8)
Other (income)/expense, net	78.5	243.7
Earnings before taxes	1,883.1	3,673.4
Taxes on earnings	332.8	879.7
Net earnings	$1,550.3	$2,793.7
Net earnings excluding acquired in-process R&D and other one-time charges	$2,942.8	$3,242.5
(Note 1)		
Diluted earnings per common share (US GAAP)	$0.99	$1.78
Diluted earnings per common share excluding acquired in-process R&D and other one-time charges	$1.88	$2.06
Average no. of common shares outstanding plus dilutive common stock options	$1,566.0	$1,573.3

Note 1: Year 2002 excludes a non-cash charge of $0.05 for acquired in-process research and development related to the acquisition of Biocompatibles' stent business and the Medtronic alliance, $0.06 for one-time charges related to the consent decree with the FDA, $0.09 non-cash charge related to the decline in the value of certain equity investments, and $0.08 related to previously announced restructuring expenses. Year 2001 excludes non-cash charge of $0.56 for acquired in-process research and development, $0.17 for a one-time adjustment to income from TAP joint venture and $0.16 for other one-time charges related to the acquisition of the pharmaceutical business of BASF.

Source: http://www.abbott.com.

Exhibit 7 Cephalon Inc. Earnings Release Income Statement (US$ millions)

	2001	2002
Revenues		
Product sales	$226.1	$465.9
Other revenues	35.9	41.0
	262.0	506.9
Cost and Expenses		
Cost of product sales	44.9	74.2
Research and development	83.0	128.3
Selling, general and administrative	96.2	172.8
Merger and integration costs	0.1	—
Acquired in-process research and development	20.0	—
	244.2	375.3
EBITDA (a)	17.9	131.6
Depreciation and amortization	(14.4)	(35.5)
Debt exchange expense	(52.4)	—
Gain (charge) on early extinguishment of debt	3.0	(7.1)
Other income (expense), net	(9.4)	(26.6)

(Continued)

Exhibit 7 Cephalon Inc. Earnings Release Income Statement (US$ millions)

	2001	2002
Income (loss) before income taxes	(55.4)	62.4
Income tax benefit (expense), net	—	112.6
Income before cumulative effect of changing inventory costing method	(55.4)	175.0
Cumulative effect of changing inventory costing method from FIFO to LIFO	—	(3.5)
Net income (loss)	(55.4)	171.5
Dividends on convertible exchangeable preferred stock	(5.7)	—
Income (loss) applicable to common shares	$(61.1)	$ 171.5
Basic income (loss) per common share		
Income (loss) per common share excluding cumulative effect of changing inventory method	$(1.27)	$3.17
Cumulative effect of changing inventory costing method	$ —	$(0.06)
	$ (1.27)	$ 3.11
Diluted income (loss) per common share		
Income (loss) per common share excluding the effect of changing the inventory method	$ (1.27)	$ 3.07
Cumulative effect of changing inventory costing method	$ —	$ (0.06)
	$ (1.27)	$ 3.01
Weighted average number of common shares outstanding	48.3	55.1
Weighted average number of common shares outstanding - assuming dilution	48.3	57.0
Reconciliation of Income (loss) applicable to common shares to adjusted net income:		
Income (loss) applicable to common shares	$ (61.1)	$ 171.5
Certain charges:		
Deferred tax valuation adjustment	—	(116.7)
CNS joint venture (b)	—	6.5
Short-term bridge financing and other merger related expenses	1.6	—
Acquired in-process research and development	20.0	—
Debt exchange expense	52.4	—
(Gain) charge on early extinguishment of debt	(3.0)	7.1
Cumulative effect of changing inventory costing method	—	3.5
Adjusted net income	$ 9.9	$ 71.9
Basic adjusted net income per common share	$ 0.20	$ 1.31
Diluted adjusted net income per common share	$ 0.19	$ 1.26

(a) Earnings (loss) before net interest, depreciation, amortization, debt exchange expense, foreign currency exchange, dividends on convertible exchangeable preferred stock and cumulative effect of changing inventory costing method.
(b) Includes $3,508,000 from selling, general and administrative expense and $2,973,000 from other expense.

Source: Cephalon, Inc.

Exhibit 8 Summary of Key Allegations in the OSC and SEC Reports

Biovail Corporation engaged in chronic fraudulent conduct including financial reporting fraud and other intentional public misrepresentations. Obsessed with meeting quarterly and annual earnings guidance, Biovail executives repeatedly overstated earnings and hid losses in order to deceive investors and create the appearance of achieving that goal. When it became impossible to conceal the company's poor performance, Biovail actively misled investors to create the appearance of meeting their goals.

The financial reporting fraud involves three accounting schemes that affected reporting periods from 2001 to 2003. They are:

1. A transaction through which Biovail, over a period of several reporting periods in 2001 and 2002, improperly moved off its financial statements to the statements of a special purpose entity known as Parmatech. Revenent transactions included the movement of expenses incurred in the R&D of Biovail products that totaled $47 million through September 30, 2002 and liabilities that exceeded $51 million through that date.
2. A fictitious bill and hold transaction that Biovail created to record approximately $8 million in revenue in the second quarter.
3. An intentional misstatement of foreign exchange losses that caused Biovail's second quarter 2003 loss to be understated by about $3.9 million.

In October 2003, Biovail intentionally and falsely attributed nearly half of its failure to meet its third quarter 2003 earnings guidance to a truck accident involving a shipment of Wellbutrin XL®. Biovail intentionally misstated in press releases and public statements both the effect of the accident on Biovail's third quarter earnings as well as grossly overstating the value of the product involved in the truck accident. The accident, in fact, had no effect on third quarter earnings.

Each of the fraudulent accounting schemes had a material effect on Biovail's financial statements from the relevant quarter and years and was engineered by Biovail's senior management in order to manage Biovail's earnings. In effecting these schemes, Biovail management also intentionally deceived its auditors as to the true nature of the transactions. The truck accident misstatements were intended to and did mislead analysts and the investing public concerning the significance of Biovail's failure to meet its own guidance.

Biovail's then-chairman and chief executive, Eugene Melnyk, also violated share ownership disclosure provisions by failing to identify his beneficial ownership held by several trusts in which he continued to exercise both investment and trading authority.

Source: Statement of Allegations of Staff of the Ontario Securities Commission in the Matter of Biovail Corporation, Eugene N. Melnyk, Brian H. Crombie, John R. Miszuk, and Kenneth G. Howling at March 24, 2008; Securities and Exchange Commission against Biovail Corporation, Eugene N. Melnyk, Brian Crombie, John Miszuk, and Kenneth G. Howling at March 24, 2008.

NOTES

1. This case has been written on the basis of published sources only. Consequently, the interpretation and perspectives presented in this case are not necessarily those of Biovail Corporation or of any of its employees.
2. http://www.ic.gc.ca/epic/site/lsi-isv.nsf/en/li00256e.html, accessed October 20, 2008.
3. http://www.newswire.ca/en/releases/archive/October2008/23/c8768.html, accessed November 17, 2008.
4. Ibid.
5. http://www.allp.com/drug_dev.htm, accessed June 23, 2003.
6. Rather than an individual taking several doses of the same pill in one day, controlled-release technology allows people to take only one dosage of medication, and the technology releases the drug at a controlled pace.
7. Report on business, *The Globe and Mail*, October 2008.
8. http://www.cbc.ca/money/story/2007/05/16/biovailmelynk.html, accessed October 2, 2008.
9. A generic drug is the proven bioequivalent to its branded counterpart. Generic drugs are offered at a lower price.
10. http://www.biovail.com, accessed October 23, 2008.
11. http://www.canadianbusiness.com/after_hours/article.jsp?content=2 0071128_210746_3160&page=2, October 23, 2008.
12. *Triangle Business Journal*, April 21, 2003.
13. Known as the "October 3, 2003" press release.
14. Ibid.
15. Banc of America report, October 10, 2003.
16. Ibid.
17. Pro forma reporting had long been used by companies to paint a "what if" picture, where pro forma numbers were used to show the comparability of financial information in a year when a company acquired or divested of another company to how the financial statements would have looked had the merger taken place at an earlier time or not at all. In recent years companies, including Biovail, have been using unregulated pro forma earnings as a means of showing shareholders a more sustainable view of company profits. Pro forma earnings were often higher than GAAP earnings since companies often excluded a number of expenses they considered to be non-recurring, such as asset write-downs, litigation settlements, merger/acquisition-related expenses, restructuring charges, amortization expenses, research and development charges and stock-related compensation expenses.
18. Biovail press release, March 4, 2003.
19. Ibid.
20. Report on Business, *The Globe and Mail*, October 2008.

21. http://www.sedar.com, Notice of Annual Meeting of Shareholders & Management Proxy Circular, June 25, 2008.
22. http://www.globeandmail.com, March 28, 2006.
23. http://www.globeandmail.com, April 4, 2006.
24. http://www.globeandmail.com, July 31, 2006.
25. A Wells Notice is a letter that the U.S. Securities and Exchange Commission sends to people or firms when it is planning to bring an enforcement action against them.
26. http://www.reportonbusiness.com, May 14, 2007.
27. http://www.globeandmail.com, March 24, 2008.
28. http://www.sedar.com, Management Discussion and Analysis, November 2007.
29. http://www.sedar.com, Biovail Press Release, June 28, 2007.
30. Executives included Eugene Melnyk, Brian Crombie (former CFO), John Miszuk (VP, Controller and Assistant Secretary), and Kenneth Howling (Senior VP and CFO).
31. Securities and Exchange Commission, Statement of Allegations, March 24, 2008.
32. Ontario Securities Commission, Statement of Allegations, March 24, 2008.
33. Ibid.
34. Securities and Exchange Commission, Statement of Allegations, March 24, 2008.
35. Hence the designation of this transaction as a "bill and hold" transaction.
36. Ontario Securities Commission, Statement of Allegations, March 24, 2008.
37. http://www.classaction.ca, accessed November 17, 2008.
38. http://classactiondefense.jmbm.com/2006/05/defending_against_class_action_4.html, accessed November 17, 2008.
39. http://www.web-access.net/~aclark/frames45.htm, accessed November 17, 2008.

Florence Nightingale,
Vara Vasanthi

ICFAI Business School

Blockbuster is committed to keeping pace with the changing needs of customers by offering them an expanding array of convenient ways to access entertainment content." [1]

— *JAMES W. KEYES, CHAIRMAN AND CEO OF BLOCKBUSTER*

Blockbuster Inc. is a leading global provider of in-home movie and game entertainment, with approximately 8,000 stores located throughout America, Europe, Asia, and Australia. The video rental market has undergone many changes and continues to constantly change with new product offerings from companies. The biggest change in the video rental market is the transition from store-based video rental to online video rental. To tackle the changes taking place in the industry, Blockbuster wanted to identify and implement initiatives designed to regenerate the company's activities and enhance its organizational structure to improve profitability. As part of these initiatives, in August 2007 Blockbuster acquired Movielink, a movie download service provider. This acquisition enabled Blockbuster to offer video downloading services to its customers. Blockbuster acknowledged that this acquisition was its next logical step in the planned transformation of the company.[2] It, however, remains to be seen if the acquisition will generate the expected synergies.

The Video Rental Market

In-home filmed entertainment includes video rentals and purchases of various video products such as DVDs with rentals being the most significant portion of this market. A key driver of this market is the affordability and improvement of high-quality DVD technology. Consumer spending on video rentals is nearly three times greater than the theatrical box office.[3] The home video market was the largest segment of consumer movie spending in 2007, generating just over $24 billion in revenue.[4] The breakdown for the revenue in the home video market was approximately $15.9 billion in sales and $8.2 billion in rentals.[5] Customer preferences are changing daily, making an exclusively bricks-and-mortar[6] approach to video sales and rentals unprofitable.[7]

In-home filmed entertainment is offered through various distribution channels such as the retail home video industry, the online video industry, movie downloads, the cable industry, and the satellite industry. Of these distribution channels, the retail home video industry includes the sale and rental of movies on DVD (including in the Blue-Ray format) and VHS by traditional video store retailers such as Blockbuster and other businesses. Online video retailers include Blockbuster Online, Movie Gallery, Netflix, Amazon.com, CinemaNow, and other retailers (Exhibit 1).

As home-viewing technology improves and becomes cheaper, downloading movies over the Internet and watching on wide-screen televisions at home is an emerging trend. By using a computer and a broadband link, movies can be downloaded from online video retailers for as low as $2 to $5 and watched by customers on their computers.[8] Online DVD rental services are convenient and allow customers to find, rent, and watch movies whenever they wish. Online video retailers such as Movielink and CinemaNow provide various methods of

This case was written by Florence Nightingale, ICFAI Business School, Chennai and Vara Vasanthi, ICFAI Business School Case Development Centre, under the direction of Doris Rajakumari John, ICFAI Business School, Chennai. It is intended to be used as the basis for class discussion rather than to illustrate either effective or ineffective handling of a management situation. The case was compiled from published sources.

Exhibit 1 Online Video Rental Companies

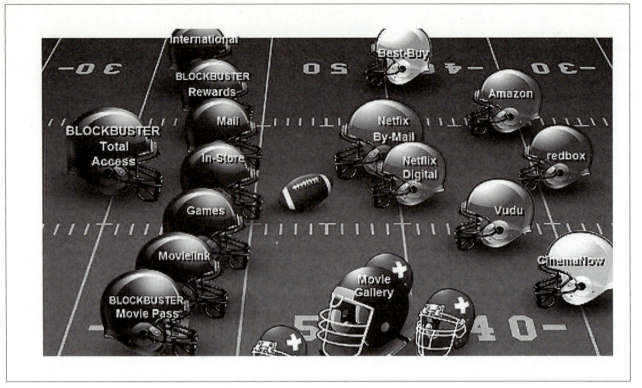

Source: Blockbuster's new paradigm and its impact on competitors, http://finance.paidcontent.org/paidcontent?Page=QUOTE&Ticket=Bbl, November 15, 2007.

access to customers for watching movies. Movielink, for example, offers two options to either buy or rent a movie. It provides a license to watch a movie and also allows for unlimited viewing. The movie can be stored on a hard disc.[9] The price to purchase a movie ranges between $8.99 and $19.99, and a movie rental from $0.99 to $4.99. As technology advances, it is likely to be easier to send a movie from a computer to a television. The major players in movie downloads are Sony, Universal, and Warner Bros., which embarked on a major endeavor to have movies transferred into digital designs. These companies also provide access to movies, similar to online video retailers. CinemaNow.com also provides free movie downloads and allows users to choose from a wide array of movies, ranging from major studio blockbusters to hard-to-find classics.

Despite the emergence of new technologies such as movie downloads and online movie purchases, the online rental business remains popular. The United States (the world's largest market for video rentals) and Europe generated more than $1 billion in consumer spending in this area in 2005.[10] By the end of 2005, there were about 6.3 million online DVD rental subscribers in the United States and Europe.[11] The United Kingdom dominates the European market, followed by Germany and thriving markets in France and Scandinavia. The online sector already accounts for more than 1 in 10 video rentals

in the United Kingdom.[12] According to recent research, 70 percent of Americans prefer watching movies at home, and Americans rented about 10 million movies in September 2007.[13] It is expected that by the end of 2009, more than half of the United Kingdom's rental transactions and rental spending will be online.[14]

The growth in the sector is further aided by customer-friendly strategies adopted by retailers. The retailers no longer insist on return dates or charge late fees for DVD rentals, thereby giving customers more freedom to keep the DVDs as long as they desire. The online rental companies allow customers to pay a monthly fee for access to unlimited rentals, which arrive and are returned by mail. In this fast-growing video rental market, Blockbuster Inc. was one of the early players and was the largest video rental chain in the United States.

The Blockbuster Business Model

Headquartered in Dallas, Texas, Blockbuster Inc. was founded by David Cook in 1982. In October 1985, Cook opened the first Blockbuster Video outlet in Dallas, with 8,000 tapes covering 6,500 titles. At the start of 1987, Blockbuster owned 15 stores and franchised 20 other stores. By the end of 1987, Blockbuster was operating 133 stores and had become the fifth-largest video chain in terms of revenue in the United States.[15] The company's basic revenues were from their stores and from late fees charged for rentals. In August 2004, Blockbuster introduced an online DVD rental service to compete with the established market leader, Netflix. Blockbuster offers services primarily through traditional retail outlets, online retailers, and cable and satellite providers. The company owns various trademarks such as Blockbuster, Blockbuster Video, "torn ticket" Logos, Blockbuster.com, Blockbuster Online, Blockbuster Night, Blockbuster GiftCards, Blockbuster Game Pass, Blockbuster Movie Pass word marks and logos, Blockbuster Rewards, related Blockbuster Family of Marks, Game Rush word mark and logo, and Life After Late Fees.[16]

Blockbuster's business model features a state-of-the-art distribution network and 41 distribution centers in the United States, which can reach most customers with one-day delivery, and an online recommendation system that lets customers select from 65,000 video titles. Blockbuster introduced a package that could travel as first-class mail, making it easy for customers to return DVDs at no charge to them. Blockbuster later launched a new online movie rental program to provide customers both Internet convenience and in-store benefits (see Exhibit 2). Blockbuster projects itself as a home entertainment enterprise with a diversified set of products and services, which includes an expanded games selection, DVD sales, online rentals, game trading, and various other businesses.

Later, the company introduced Blockbuster Total Access, a movie rental program that gives online customers the option of exchanging their DVDs through the mail or returning them to a nearby Blockbuster store in exchange for free in-store movie rentals, which was different from the existing model (Appendix I). In addition, most of Blockbuster's online subscribers had the option of exchanging their online movies for discounted in-store game rentals as well as free in-store movie rentals at more than 5,000 Blockbuster stores. Blockbuster reported, "We want to give consumers the most convenient access to media entertainment, whether that's through our stores or by mail, and are dedicated to doing that with flexible plans and pricing."[17] With more than 65,000 titles to choose from online, Blockbuster delivers DVDs to the subscribers' mailboxes in prepaid postage return envelopes. To increase its business, Blockbuster launched advertising campaigns and also undertook joint promotions with fast food outlets such as Domino's Pizza and McDonald's.

Blockbuster designed marketing and advertising campaigns to maximize opportunities in the marketplace, working closely with customers to connect and drive business. Blockbuster customized its stores' merchandise selection, quantity, and formats to meet the needs and preferences of local customers. As the new business was gaining ground, Blockbuster underwent several changes in its business-level strategy, focusing mainly on cost-cutting programs and selling products such as DVDs. This strategy made an impact, and the sales of DVDs increased as compared to DVD rentals. The popularity of online video rentals, however, was increasing with

Exhibit 2 Blockbuster Online Movie Rental Plan

Source: Blockbuster Online, http://dvd-rental-review.toptenreviews.com/blockbuster-online-review.html.

video-on-demand (VoD) services gaining prominence. VoD services, in which video is streamed over the Internet, deviated from the firm's existing business model, which depended heavily on store ownership and increasing sales per store. Both VoD and online video-rental services diverted focus from the sale of DVDs.[18] Blockbuster developed a good understanding of how the online rental channel worked and what online customers were doing in their stores.

In 2005, as part of a comprehensive business transformation initiative, Blockbuster engaged Accenture, a global management consulting and technology services company, to develop the systems and processes and to launch the online business.[19] Both companies jointly built a network of distribution centers fully dedicated to service online customers. Blockbuster wanted to offer a "one-day" delivery to as many customers as possible. Working with Accenture, Blockbuster also identified sites for distribution centers that enhanced its customer service. The company's online rental program was unique and encouraged former customers to return to Blockbuster's stores.

Blockbuster reported worldwide revenues of more than $5.5 billion and a profit of $54.7 million in 2006.[20] In the same year, Blockbuster Online had about 1.4 million online subscribers.[21] To concentrate more on its online subscriber business, Blockbuster closed nearly 300 stores in the United States in 2006. Blockbuster continued to invest in its Total Access program and added more than 700,000 online subscribers[22] and more than 4 million total subscribers[23] in 2006. This action facilitated Blockbuster's efforts to compete with Netflix. Blockbuster reported, "We have invested heavily in Total Access during the first half of 2007 to capture market share in the overall video rental market and to set the stage for the expected future profitability of our online rental business."[24] Blockbuster's Total Access had a positive impact on its online movie rental revenue. In the first quarter of 2007, revenues reached about $108.9 million.[25] Total Access also helped Blockbuster generate more cross-channel sales and traffic. The average store had about 4,800 shoppers and 45,000 rentals per month. Blockbuster reported, "Growing the revenue of Total Access had helped to offset the in-store revenue decline."[26]

Michael Pachter, an analyst at Wedbush Morgan Securities,[27] said, "Under Keyes, Blockbuster will likely be looking for ways to maximize its customer base and leverage its chain of stores—the main differentiator with Netflix—all while also preparing for the fact that physical DVD rentals may not be its core business in just a few years."[28] Blockbuster focused on protecting its core rental business, developing new retail opportunities, and becoming the preferred provider of digital entertainment.[29] In 2007, Blockbuster had 27 percent of the U.S. video rental market and served more than 87 million customers in the United States, its territories, and 25 other nations.[30]

While Blockbuster tried to make its mark in the online movie rental business, the firm encountered stiff competitions from Apple, Amazon.com, and Wal-Mart, as well as market leader Netflix. In 2007, Netflix was already an established player with 75 percent[31] of the market. Netflix's success was attributed to the firm's business model. Netflix's innovative subscription service, for example, allowed customers to keep videos as long as they wished. There are no due dates or late fees nor does the customer incur any shipping charges. Netflix's success inspired a number of other DVD rental companies both in the United States and abroad (see Exhibit 3).

Both Blockbuster and Netflix offer three movie rentals for a monthly fee of $17.99 (the price of this service changes in response to competitive challenges) and allow customers to return their rentals by mail. However, as part of the Total Access program, Blockbuster accepts returns at its stores and rewards subscribers with a free rental for each store return. Consumers were willing to pay a premium for convenience, and Blockbuster capitalized on that. As a result, Blockbuster gained subscribers from Netflix, which had no bricks-and-mortar presence and could not match with Blockbuster's Total Access plan.

Netflix, for its part, still posted a 36 percent increase in revenue to $305.3 million for the year 2007. Netflix was also investing more than $40 million in new digital download technology.[32] Blockbuster responded to these competitive actions by aggressively trying to take customers away from Netflix.[33] Reducing its prices and enhancing the layouts of its retail stores are examples of the competitive actions Blockbuster decided to initiate while competing against Netflix. Blockbuster also provides printable e-coupons for two free in-store movie or game rentals, and other special offers. Both companies were organized to focus on the key considerations such as selection, price, and customer satisfaction (see Exhibit 4).

Pachter said, "Netflix has tried to grab the lead in the digital distribution channel, but Blockbuster is signaling it's not going to give that up easily."[34] Blockbuster and Netflix offer similar plans and have repeatedly lowered prices or modified services in an effort to win customers. Blockbuster, in addition to the entertainment content provided through its stores and by mail, had taken an important step towards making movie downloading available to computers, portable devices, and directly to televisions in homes.

In 2007, Blockbuster introduced a wider range of subscription plans, including Blockbuster Total Access

Exhibit 3 Netflix—How it Works

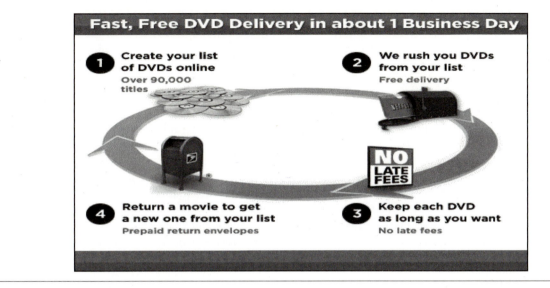

Source: Netflix—How it works, http://www.netflix.com/HowItWorks.

Exhibit 4 Comparison of Blockbuster Online DVD Rentals and NetFlix.com

	BLOCKBUSTER Online **Blockbuster Online DVD Rental**	**NETFLIX.** Netflix
No Late Fees	Keep the DVDs as long as you want **No Late Fees**	Keep the DVDs as long as you want **No Late Fees**
Selections	Over 40,000 titles	Over 40,000 titles
Turn-around Time	1 Day	1 Day
Unlimited DVD Rentals	YES	YES
Delivered to Your Mailbox	YES	YES
Free Shipping & Postage	**Free** first-class postage both ways	**Free** first-class postage both ways
No Return Dates	YES	YES
Distribution Centers	23 across the United States Will start using their **4,500** stores in coming year	35 across the United States.
Free In-Store Coupons	**YES** – Two e-coupons for **FREE** in-store movie or game rentals. Print coupons yourself.	**NO**
Gift Subscriptions	YES	YES
Special Offers	**$9.99 for First Month**	2-week free trial
$$ Cost $$	**$17.99 – 3 titles out** $29.99 – 5 titles out $37.49 – 8 titles out	$11.99, 4 DVDs a month, 2 titles out **$17.99 – 3 titles out** $29.99 – 5 titles out $47.99 – 8 titles out *Eight subscription plans offered*

Source: DVD Rental Services Comparison, http://www.acmetech.com/shopping/movies/dvd_rental.php.

Premium™, Blockbuster Total Access™, and Blockbuster® by Mail. The new subscription plans were available to all current and new subscribers to Blockbuster's online rental service with pricing as low as $4.99 a month[35] (see Appendix 2). Blockbuster's online movie rentals increased by 121.3 percent from $174.2 million in 2006 to $385.5 million in 2007.[36] Despite the increase in the online movie rentals, Blockbuster reported losses in 2007 (see Appendix 3).

According to the projected figures for 2008 in the Online DVD rental report published by *Online DVD Rental Reviews 2008*, Netflix ranked first, with Blockbuster second (see Appendix 4). To survive in the market, Blockbuster needed to increase its market share and establish its reputation in the online download business. According to PricewaterhouseCoopers, by 2010, annual revenue for the online video download business is expected to increase by $3.7 billion and DVD rentals and sales are expected to increase to about $29.5 billion.[37] For these reasons, Blockbuster decided to acquire Movielink.

Movielink Acquisition: The Strategic Rationale

When Blockbuster released its financial results for the year 2007, the firm's shareholders questioned the long-term sustainability of the company's current business model. In response to these concerns, company officials said, "Our goal is to continue to increase our membership base by providing even more ways for customers to get the entertainment they want through our stores, through the mail, and through new technologies."[38] As part of this goal, in August 2007, Blockbuster acquired Movielink, a leading movie downloading service.

Movielink offers movies for download through its video-on-demand Internet distribution service. Movielink was founded as a joint venture among five studios—Paramount Pictures, Sony Pictures Entertainment, MGM, Universal Studios, and Warner Bros.—who were responding to consumers' adoption of high-speed Internet access.[39] Movielink offers about 400 movies, which take 30 to 90 minutes to download, but the customers have the option of watching the movie after 10 minutes of downloading.[40] The Movielink Web site has two stores, a purchase store and a rental store, with a common home page. At the rental store, customers can browse the site and view trailers of movies without any charge. The customer can register with Movielink and pay for the rental by credit card.

Bruce Anderson, Movielink's vice president of engineering and operations, said, "As Movielink's business continues to grow, it is vital that our content delivery infrastructure continues to provide the quality of service our customers have come to expect."[41] Movielink has distribution agreements with the five studios that founded it, as well as Lionsgate and 20th Century FOX. Blockbuster's chief executive, James W. Keyes, said, "The acquisition immediately puts us in the digital download business. Clearly, our customers have responded favorably to having other convenient ways to access movies and entertainment."[42] The acquisition provided Blockbuster with a way to send movies straight to televisions and computers, complementing its store and movie-by-mail operations. Pachter stated, "The acquisition is a defensive move by Blockbuster to keep up with Netflix."[43]

Movielink CEO Jim Ramo said, "The studios' goal with the Movielink service has always been to make digital entertainment content more conveniently, more widely, and more securely available to consumers. This acquisition should further that goal."[44] He added, "With Blockbuster's ability to leverage its store network, online assets, and marketing expertise, Blockbuster should be able to grow the market for digitally-delivered entertainment content, and we believe that's good news for consumers and content providers alike."[45]

Blockbuster believed that the 1,400 movie titles in the Movielink catalog gave it a strong presence among firms offering movies for digital download via online capabilities. Customers are allowed to rent movies for $0.99, and they can store the movie for 30 days on their computers. Movielink announced that it was working on a plan that would allow customers to copy films to DVD.

Movielink's services, however, failed to catch on because the only way to watch films from Movielink on a television was to buy a set-top box. The company offered a network between a PC and television. Analysts felt the issue was that Movielink downloads could not be burned to discs.[46] Movielink did not provide a download-and-burn[47] service because of a misunderstanding between Movielink and the five studios.[48] In contrast, Blockbuster's competitor Netflix's movie download service was favorably received by customers. Movielink ended up failing to reach a wide audience and posted a net loss of $10.16 million in 2007.

Blockbuster's acquisition of Movielink failed to immediately expand the firm's business beyond the store-based movie-rental market. Competition from cable providers offering video-on-demand and DVD-rental services such as Netflix also posed problems for Blockbuster. Whether Blockbuster can use the Movielink acquisition to increase its market share and profitability in the video rental market and whether this acquisition offers Blockbuster an increased online presence remains to be seen.

NOTES

1. C. Metz, 2007, Blockbuster reels in MovieLink, http://www
.theregister.co.uk/2007/08/09/blockbuster_buys_netflix, August 9.
2. K. Regan, 2007, Blockbuster chases online box office with movielink
buy, http://www.ecommercetimes.com/story/58751.html, August 9.
3. EMA's 2007 Annual Report is now available, http://www.entmerch
.org/annual_reports.html.
4. Ibid.
5. The Entertainment Merchant Association, http://www.entmerch.org/
annual_reports.html.
6. Companies that have a physical presence can offer face-to-face
consumer experiences.
7. G. Millman, 2005, Blockbuster's bricks and clicks, http://
www.accenture.com/Global/Research_and_Insights/Outlook/
BlockbustersClicks.htm, June.
8. Blockbuster's bricks and clicks, op.cit.
9. D. Gynn, 2006, Download movies with Movielink/Optaros and
reduce risk, http://opensource.syscon. com/read/256611.htm,
August 8.
10. A. Wood & H. J. Davis, 2005, The outlook for online DVD rental:
A strategic analysis of the U.S. and European markets, http://www
.screendigest.com/reports/05onlinedvdrental/readmore/view.html,
November.
11. Ibid.
12. The outlook for online DVD rental: A strategic analysis of the U.S.
and European markets, op.cit.
13. 2007, Frost & Sullivan Commends DVDPlays Innovative Services in
the Automated DVD Rental Machine Market, http://www.frost.com/
prod/servlet/press-release.pag?docid=110114449, October 23.
14. Ibid.
15. Blockbuster Inc., http://www.fundinguniverse.com/company-
histories/Blockbuster-Inc-Company-History.html.
16. Blockbuster Inc., 2007, http://custom.marketwatch.com/custom/
nyt-com/htmlcompanyprofile. asp?MW=http://marketwatch.
nytimes.com/custom/nyt-com/htmlcompanyprofile. asp&symb=BBI
&sid=153477#compinfo, August 11.
17. 2007, Blockbuster announces expanded online subscription
offerings, http://goliath.ecnext.com/coms2/summary_0199-
6786323_ITM, July 26.
18. Diversity, http://www.blockbuster.com/corporate/diversity
19. Blockbuster's bricks and clicks, op.cit.
20. 2006, Blockbuster profit, 1.4 million online subscribers, http://www
.hackingnetflix.com/2006/07/blockbuster_pro.html, July 27.
21. Ibid.
22. C. Spielvogel, 2007, Blockbuster Q4 income down, revenue up,
http://www.videobusiness.com/article/CA6419949.html, February
27.
23. 2007, Blockbuster emphasizes its online program over stores,
http://www.internetretailer.com/dailyNews.asp?id=22946, June 29.
24. Blockbuster profit, 1.4 million online subscribers, op.cit.
25. Ibid.
26. 2007, Blockbuster Q1 2007 Earnings Call Transcript, http://www
.seekingalpha.com/article/34304-blockbuster-q1-2007-earnings-
call-transcript, May 2.
27. It is recognized among securities professionals as a leading
investment banking and brokerage firm.
28. Blockbuster chases online box office with movielink buy, op.cit.
29. 2007, Blockbuster reports third quarter 2007 results, new
strategic initiatives and decisive actions taken to improve
near-term profitability, http://www.b2i.us/profiles/investor/
ResLibraryView.asp?BzID=553&ResLibraryID=22067&Category=1
027, November 1.
30. Blockbuster Inc., op.cit.
31. J. M. Spool, 2006, Innovation is the new black, http://www.uie.com/
articles/innovation_from_experience_design/, June 1.
32. Blockbuster emphasizes its online program over stores, op.cit.
33. J. Love, 2006. E-retailing's brightest stars at IRCE 2007, http:
//www.internetretailer.com/internet/marketing-conference/89902-
e-retailings-brightest-stars-at-irce-2007.html, December.
34. Blockbuster chases online box office with movielink buy, op.cit.
35. Blockbuster announces expanded online subscription offerings,
op.cit.
36. 2007, Blockbuster turns in a weaker third quarter performance,
http://www.internetretailer.com/dailyNews.asp?id=24278,
November 1.
37. Video download service, http://videodownloadservice.net.
38. A. Chowdhry, 2007, Blockbuster revenue drops 5.7 percent;
focusing on membership gain, http://pulse2.com/category/
blockbuster, November 3.
39. Movielink, LLC Company Profile, http://biz.yahoo.com/
ic/106/106424.html.
40. Movielink, http://dvd-rental-review.toptenreviews.com/movielink-details
.html
41. 2005, Equinix to provide connectivity infrastructure for Movielink
video-on-demand service, http://findarticles.com/p/articles/mi_
m0EIN/is_2005_Jan_17/ai_n8694997, January 17.
42. 2007, Blockbuster acquires Movielink, http://www.nytimes.
com/2007/08/09/business/09movie.html?_r=1&n= Toppercent2f
Newspercent2f Businesspercent 2fCompanies percent 2fBlockbu ste
rpercent20Incpercent2e&oref=slogin, August 9.
43. Ibid.
44. Blockbuster reels in Movielink, op.cit.
45. Ibid.
46. G. Sandoval, 2007, Blockbuster acquires Movielink, http://www
.news.com/2100-1026_3-6201609.html, August 8.
47. The service allows the consumers to purchase, download, and burn
a complete DVD for instant gratification.
48. E. Bangeman, 2007, Is action better than inaction? Blockbuster
buys Movielink for a song, http://arstechnica.com/news.ars/
post/20070809-is-action-better-than-inaction-blockbuster-
buys-movielink-for-asong.html?rel, August 9.

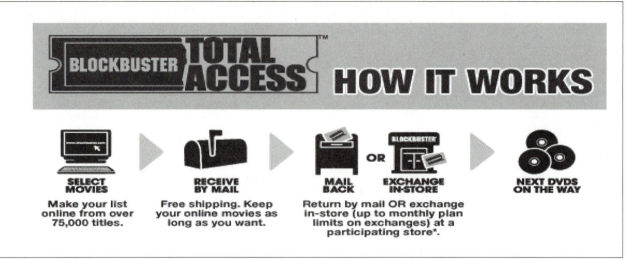

Rent Online – Return by Mail Or In-Store with Blockbuster Total Access™

Only Blockbuster Total Access™ gives the convenience of renting movies online and the choice of how to return them: by mail or bringing them to participating Blockbuster store, where customers can exchange them for new movies or discounted game rentals on the spot (up to monthly plan limits on exchanges).*

In-Store Exchanges

For only $17.99 a month (plus taxes) customers can receive up to 3 DVDs at a time with up to 5 in-store exchanges for free movie rentals or discounted game rentals. When customers finish watching a DVD, they can send it back in the provided postage-paid envelope or return it to a participating Blockbuster store.

Special In-Store Monthly Offers

As a Blockbuster Online member, customers are eligible for exclusive deals and discounts each month at participating Blockbuster stores.

More than 75,000 Titles, Including New Releases

Online DVD library has more than 75,000 titles, and it is growing every week. Customers can find classic cinema, modern favorites, television shows, children's programming, health and fitness workouts, and of course, the hottest new releases from Blockbuster.

Delivered Right to the Mailbox

Renting DVDs is as easy as picking up the mail. DVDs usually arrive within 1–2 business days**. Return the DVD by placing the DVD in the provided postage paid envelope and send it back through the mail or return it to a participating store. Then, the next DVD will be on its way.

Free Shipping and Postage

Shipping is always free. Both ways. There are no postage charges.

No Return Dates on Online Rentals

Blockbuster online rental members can keep online rentals out as long as they want. There are never any due dates*. Watch the DVD when it is convenient for you, and send it back only when you are ready for a new selection.

No Extended Viewing Fees or Late Fees on Online Rentals

As a Blockbuster Online rental member, customers pay a flat monthly rate. There are no extended viewing fees or late fees on DVDs rented online.

* Separate, complimentary in-store membership required for in-store rentals. In-store movie rentals are subject to store rental terms and conditions, including due dates and charges which may apply to rentals not returned by the due date. See store for complete in-store rental terms and conditions. Free in-store rentals must be returned to the store where they were originally rented.

** One business day delivery for Blockbuster based on more than 90 percent of our subscribers being within one-day postal delivery zone. Certain subscribers may experience longer delivery times.

Source: Blockbuster Movies, https://www.blockbuster.com/signup/rp/howItWorks.

Appendix 2 Blockbuster Membership Plans

Blockbuster Online offers the following membership plans:

- $4.99 per month—offers 2 DVD rentals per month and allows 1 movie rental at a time.
- $8.99 per month—offers unlimited DVD rentals per month and allows 1 movie rental at a time.
- $13.99 per month—offers unlimited DVD rentals per month and allows for 2 movie rentals at a time.
- $16.99 per month—offers unlimited DVD rentals per month and allows for 3 movie rentals at a time.

Blockbuster Total Access offers the following membership plans:

- $7.99 per month—2 DVD rentals per month, allowing 1 movie rental at a time or 2 in-store exchanges 1 movie at a time.
- $9.99 per month—offers unlimited DVD rentals per month, allows 1 movie rental at a time and up to 2 in-store exchanges per month.
- $14.99 per month—offers unlimited DVD rentals per month, allows 2 movie rentals at a time and up to 3 in-store exchanges per month.
- $17.99 per month—offers unlimited DVD rentals per month, allows 3 movie rentals at a time and up to 5 in-store exchanges per month.

Blockbuster Total Access Premium plans include:

- $16.99 per month—offers unlimited DVD rentals per month, unlimited in-store exchanges, 1 movie at a time.
- $21.99 per month—offers unlimited DVD rentals per month, unlimited in-store exchanges, 2 movies at a time.
- $24.99 per month—offers unlimited DVD rentals per month, unlimited in-store exchanges, 3 movies at a time.

Source: Blockbuster Online, http://dvd-rental-review.toptenreviews.com/blockbuster-online-review.html.

Appendix 3 Blockbuster Income Statement – 2007

All amounts in millions except per-share amounts	Q3–2007 09/2007	Q2–2007 06/2007	Q1–2007 03/2007	Q4–2006 12/2006
Operating Revenue	1,238.20	1,263.20	1,473.00	1,463.10
Total Revenue	1,238.20	1,263.20	1,473.00	1,463.10
Adjustment to Revenue	0.00	0.00	0.00	0.00
Cost of Sales	396.30	441.00	531.60	536.90
Cost of Sales with Depreciation	570.40	627.70	711.00	699.90
Gross Margin	667.80	635.50	762.00	763.20
Gross Operating Profit	841.90	822.20	941.40	926.20
R&D	0.00	0.00	0.00	0.00
SG&A	603.20	624.30	654.50	610.70
Advertising	27.50	54.80	76.60	47.50
Operating Profit	−5.60	−13.70	−18.40	50.10
Operating Profit before Depreciation (EBITDA)	211.20	143.10	210.30	268.00
Depreciation	217.00	234.50	228.70	212.80
Depreciation Unreconciled	42.90	47.80	49.30	49.80
Amortization	0.00	0.00	0.00	0.00
Amortization of Intangibles	0.00	0.00	0.00	0.00
Operating Income After Depreciation	−5.80	−91.40	−18.40	55.20

(Continued)

Case 5: Blockbuster Acquires Movielink: A Growth Strategy?

Appendix 3 Blockbuster Income Statement – 2007 (*Continued*)

All amounts in millions except per-share amounts	Q3–2007 09/2007	Q2–2007 06/2007	Q1–2007 03/2007	Q4–2006 12/2006
Interest Income	1.30	1.90	1.90	2.60
Earnings from Equity Interest	0.00	0.00	0.00	0.00
Other Income, Net	−1.10	1.70	−0.40	1.60
Income Acquired in Process R&D	0.00	0.00	0.00	0.00
Interest Restructuring and M&A	0.20	77.70	0.00	0.00
Other Special Charges	0.00	0.00	0.00	−5.10
Total Income Available for Interest Expense (EBIT)	−5.40	−10.10	−16.90	54.30
Interest Expense	20.70	21.10	23.60	24.40
Income Before Tax (EBT)	−26.10	−31.20	−40.50	29.90
Income Taxes	8.70	3.00	8.50	10.30
Minority Interest	0.00	0.00	0.00	0.00
Preferred Securities of Subsidiary Trust	0.00	0.00	0.00	0.00
Net Income from Continuing Operations	−34.80	−34.20	−49.00	19.60
Net Income from Discontinued Operations	−0.20	−1.10	2.60	−6.70
Net Income from Total Operations	−35.00	−35.30	−46.40	12.90
Extraordinary Income/Losses	0.00	0.00	0.00	0.00
Income from Cumulative Effect of Accounting Change	0.00	0.00	0.00	0.00
Income from Tax Loss Carryforward	0.00	0.00	0.00	0.00
Other Gains (Losses)	0.00	0.00	0.00	0.00
Total Net Income	−35.00	−35.30	−46.40	12.90
Normalized Income	−35.00	−111.90	−49.00	24.70
Net Income Available for Common	−37.60	−37.00	−51.80	16.70
Preferred Dividends	2.80	2.80	2.80	2.90
Excise Taxes	0.00	0.00	0.00	0.00
Per-Share Data				

Appendix 3 Blockbuster Income Statement – 2007 (*Continued*)

All amounts in millions except per-share amounts	Q3–2007 09/2007	Q2–2007 06/2007	Q1–2007 03/2007	Q4–2006 12/2006
Basic Earnings Per Share (EPS) from Continuing Operations	−0.20	−0.19	−0.27	0.09
Basic EPS from Discontinued Operations	0.00	−0.01	0.01	−0.04
Basic EPS from Total Operations	−0.20	−0.20	−0.26	0.05
Basic EPS from Extraordinary Income	0.00	0.00	0.00	0.00
Basic EPS from Cumulative Effect of Accounting Change	0.00	0.00	0.00	0.00
Basic EPS from Other Gains (Losses)	0.00	0.00	0.00	0.00
Basic EPS Total	−0.20	−0.20	−0.26	0.05
Basic Normalized Net Income/ Share	−0.20	−0.62	−0.27	0.11
Diluted EPS from Continuing Operations	−0.20	−0.19	−0.27	0.09
Diluted EPS from Discontinued Operations	0.00	−0.01	0.01	−0.04
Diluted EPS from Total Operations	−0.20	−0.20	−0.26	0.05
Diluted EPS from Extraordinary Income	0.00	0.00	0.00	0.00
Diluted EPS from Cumulative Effect of Accounting Change	0.00	0.00	0.00	0.00
Diluted EPS from Other Gains (Losses)	0.00	0.00	0.00	0.00
Diluted EPS Total	−0.20	−0.20	−0.26	0.05
Diluted Normalized Net Income/ Share	−0.20	−0.62	−0.27	0.11
Dividends Paid per Share	0.00	0.00	0.00	0.00
Additional Data				
Basic Weighted Shares Outstanding	190.60	190.00	189.40	187.10
Diluted Weighted Shares Outstanding	190.60	190.00	189.40	189.00

Source: Blockbuster Inc. Income Statement, http://finance.google.com/finance?fstype=ii&q=BBI.

Appendix 4 Projected Figures – 2008 Online DVD Rental Report

Legend:
- ■■■■ Excellent
- ■■■□ Very Good
- ■■□□ Good
- ■□□□ Fair
- □□□□ Poor

	Netflix	Blockbuster Online	DVD Avenue	GameznFlix	CafeDVD.com	eHit.com	Intelliflix	Peerflix	Number Slate	iLetYou
Rank	GOLD	SILVER	BRONZE	4	5	6	7	8	9	10
Reviewer Comments	READ REVIEW	READ REVIEW	READ REVIEW	READ REVIEW	READ REVIEW	READ REVIEW	READ REVIEW	READ REVIEW	READ REVIEW	READ REVIEW
Lowest Price	BUY $4.99	BUY $4.99	BUY $9.99	BUY $8.99	BUY $14.95	BUY $13.99	BUY $24.95	BUY Varies	BUY $9.95	BUY Varies
Overall Rating	■■■■□	■■■■□	■■■□	■■■□	■■□□	■■□□	■■□□	■■□□	■■□□	■■□□
Ratings										
Inventory	■■■■	■■■■	■■■□	■■■□	■■■□	■■□□	■■■□	■■□□	■■■□	■■□□
Membership Features	■■■■	■■■■	■■■□	■■■□	■■□□	■■■□	■■■□	■■□□	■■□□	■□□□
Movie Arrival Time	■■■■	■■■■	■■■□	■■■□	■■■□	■■■□	■■□□	■■□□	■■□□	■■□□
Movie Information	■■■■	■■■■	■■■□	■■■□	■■□□	■■■□	■■■□	■■□□	■■■□	■■□□
Search Capabilities	■■■□	■■■□	■■■□	■■■■	■■■□	■■■□	■■■□	■■□□	■□□□	■□□□
Inventory										
DVDs	✓	✓	✓	✓	✓	✓	✓	✓	✓	✓
Games				✓			✓			✓
TV Series	✓	✓			✓		✓	✓		✓
Movie Titles	85,000	75,000	25,000	28,000	13,000	5,000	60,000	unknown	5,000	unknown
Membership Features										
Unlimited DVDs per month	✓	✓	✓	✓	✓	✓	✓		✓	
Monthly Plans	✓	✓	✓	✓			✓	✓	✓	
Pay Per Movie				✓			✓	✓		✓
No Due Date	✓	✓	✓	✓			✓		✓	
No Late Fees	✓	✓	✓	✓			✓		✓	
Free Two-Way Shipping	✓	✓	✓	✓			✓	✓		
Free Trial	✓	✓	✓	✓			✓		✓	
Number of Plans	4	11	4	4	4	4	4	1	1	1
Option to Purchase DVD	✓	✓		✓	✓			✓		
Download Movies	✓									
Average Days to Receive your DVD	1–2	1–2	2–5	2–5	2–4	2–4	1–3	varies	varies	varies
Movie Information										
Title	✓	✓	✓	✓	✓	✓	✓	✓	✓	✓
MPAA Rating	✓	✓	✓	✓	✓	✓	✓		✓	✓
Critic Rating		✓								
Movie Synopsis	✓	✓	✓		✓	✓	✓	✓	✓	✓
Actors	✓	✓	✓	✓	✓	✓	✓	✓	✓	✓
Director	✓	✓	✓	✓	✓	✓	✓	✓	✓	✓
Genre	✓	✓	✓	✓	✓	✓	✓	✓	✓	
Movie Studio	✓	✓		✓						
Awards	✓	✓	✓							
Movie Reviews (Critics)	✓			✓		✓	✓		✓	
Trailers/Previews	✓	✓								

Appendix 4 Projected Figures – 2008 Online DVD Rental Report (*Continued*)

	Netflix	Blockbuster Online	DVD Avenue	GameznFlix	CafeDVD.com	eHit.com	Intelliflix	Peerflix	Number Slate	iLetYou
Search Capabilities										
Title	✓	✓	✓	✓		✓	✓	✓		✓
Actor	✓	✓	✓	✓		✓	✓	✓		✓
Director	✓	✓	✓	✓			✓	✓		✓
Year							✓			
Rating		✓		✓		✓	✓			
Synopsis			✓				✓			
Genre	✓	✓	✓	✓	✓	✓	✓	✓	✓	✓
New Releases	✓	✓		✓	✓	✓		✓	✓	✓
Coming Soon				✓						✓
Production Studio				✓						
Screen Format				✓						
Language			✓	✓		✓	✓			
Subtitles				✓			✓			
Awards		✓					✓			
Support/Documentation										
Phone Support	✓		✓	✓						✓
FAQ	✓	✓	✓	✓	✓	✓	✓	✓	✓	✓
eMail/Online Form		✓	✓		✓	✓	✓	✓	✓	

Source: Top Ten Reviews, http://dvd-rental-review.toptenreviews.com/index.html#anchor, 2007.

Lourdes Casanova, Henning Hoeber

INSEAD

"What has globalisation meant for us? To summarise a long, complex process, we have harnessed the force of globalisation to transform a Mexican-based company with a few international operations into one of the largest global companies in our industry"[1]
   —LORENZO ZAMBRANO, CEO
   AND CHAIRMAN OF CEMEX

At the beginning of 2004, the Mexican corporation CEMEX was the world's third-largest building materials company by revenues, and the only global cement player from an emerging market. By selling its fine grey powder, this emerging multinational had achieved a compound annual growth rate of 18 percent in sales, operating income, and EBITDA,[2] and of 52 percent in free cash flow over a 15-year period. The Monterrey-based corporation ended fiscal 2003 with US$7.1 billion in revenues, EBITDA at US$2.1 billion, and free cash flow at an impressive US$1.1 billion, which is the highest cash flow generation among its industry peers (see Exhibit 1).

At first glance, the incredible success of a company from an emerging market may seem somewhat counterintuitive. How was it possible that a once-small player from a difficult and volatile home market became one of the most profitable businesses in a commodity industry? What was CEMEX's magic formula for success?

CEMEX

CEMEX's growth strategy was driven by worldwide acquisitions following a similar pattern of other "Global Latinas."[3] During its expansion from a local Mexican cement producer to a multinational company, it gained a reputation for excellence in mergers and acquisitions, and for its ability to deliver solid results in difficult times and volatile markets.

Exhibit 1   CEMEX Key Financials

	2003	2002	Change
Net Sales	7,164	6,543	9%
Operating Income	1,455	1,310	11%
EBITDA	2,108	1,917	10%
Consolidated Net Income	659	557	18%
Free Cash Flow	1,143	948	21%
Total Assets	16,016	15,934	1%
Net Debt	5,641	6,122	(8%)
Stockholders' Equity, Majority Interest	6,234	5,744	9%
Earnings per ADR	1.99	1.74	15%

Source: CEMEX Annual Report, 2003. In $US million, except for ADR data.

Origins

CEMEX's origins trace back to 1906, to the founding of Cementos Hidalgo near Monterrey in northern Mexico. In 1920, company founder Lorenzo H. Zambrano Gutiérrez established another cement plant, Cementos Portland Monterrey. Eleven years later, Zambrano merged the two companies to create Cementos Mexicanos, later known as CEMEX.

The Monterrey-based company remained a local player until the 1960s, when it began expanding and

This case was written by Henning Hoeber, Visiting Researcher at INSEAD and Scholar of the Heinrich Hertz-Foundation, under the supervision of Lourdes Casanova, Lecturer in the Strategy Department at INSEAD. It is intended to be used as a basis for class discussion rather than to illustrate either effective or ineffective handling of an administrative situation.

vertically integrating cement and concrete production throughout Mexico. CEMEX's domestic growth was driven by plant construction and strategic acquisition, most importantly, Cementos Maya (1969) and Cementos Guadalajara (1976). The company was listed on Mexico's stock exchange in 1976. In 1980, further growth was facilitated by the Mexican government's import-substitution policies, especially the "Programme for the Promotion of the Cement Industry," which encouraged national players to fulfill the needs of the Mexican market and restricted foreign competition.

With limited growth opportunities abroad, CEMEX started to diversify. In the 1980s, it became a large-scale conglomerate with assets in engineering, hotels, mining, and petrochemicals. In 1982, a severe economic crisis in Mexico forced the government to liberalize the economy to attract foreign investment, after decades of protecting domestic firms. European cement majors were waiting in the wings to claim their share of the lucrative Mexican market.

In the 1990s, CEMEX resolved to become bigger to reduce the likelihood of becoming a takeover target. The man who accomplished this goal was Lorenzo Zambrano, the founder's grandson. An engineering graduate with a Stanford MBA, he was appointed CEO in 1985. Together with a new management team, the strong leadership of Zambrano put CEMEX on course towards becoming a Global Latina.

From Local to Global

The expansion of CEMEX occurred in different phases, each focusing on a particular market or area with distinct characteristics. By internationalizing (see Exhibit 2), CEMEX hoped to lessen its dependence on the Mexican market, leverage more stable cash flows, build scale and scope, and thus establish itself as a global player in the cement sector.

Domestic Market Consolidation: Attack Is the Best Defense. Facing threats from foreign rivals, CEMEX first consolidated its domestic position through the takeover of two leading Mexican cement manufacturers—Cementos Anáhuac (1987) and Cementos Tolteca (1989)—and a 49 percent stake in Control Administrativo Mexicano (1987), which in turn held 93 percent of northern producer Cementos de Chihuahua.[4] All were established players in the national market, but the motivations for their respective acquisitions were different. Anáhuac was targeted because of its large-scale cement plants and its significant exports to the United States, while in Tolteca CEMEX acquired Mexico's most-established cement brand and assets in the southern United States. The two acquisitions cost CEMEX roughly US$1 billion. The stake in Cementos

de Chihuahua allowed CEMEX to expand its reach into a region that had formerly been dominated by this single player. Thanks to these transactions, CEMEX controlled roughly 60 percent of Mexico's cement market and was among the 10 biggest cement companies in the world.

With its newly developed scale, CEMEX was ready to internationalize its operations. Furthermore, in the late 1980s, Zambrano decided to divest all noncement holdings, divert the proceeds to the cement core business, and concentrate on geographic diversification. Several years later, the CEO reflected on the company's moves: "We suddenly found ourselves competing with very large international companies at a time of consolidation in the world cement industry. There were few independent producers left. Either we became large and international, or we would end up being purchased by a bigger player."[5]

Natural Markets in the Americas and Europe. Countries in geographic proximity and those of similar culture and language were natural markets[6] for CEMEX, but the key consideration was market characteristics. CEMEX's international expansion began just north of the Mexican border. In 1986, the company entered into a joint venture with Houston-based producer Southdown Inc. in the southern United States. The two operating companies, Southwestern Sunbelt Cement and Texas Sunbelt Cement, ground imported clinker and marketed the cement output. A similar venture was established with Heidelberg Cement, Danish Aalborg Cement, and American Lehigh, which eventually became the market leader in white cement throughout the United States. The acquisition, of Anáhuac, and its terminal infrastructure in the Gulf of Mexico, facilitated exports to its northern neighbor, and so was further developed. Based on its success in the region, in 1989 CEMEX acquired four cement, concrete, and aggregates companies in the Houston area to complement Cementos Tolteca's existing asset base.

But CEMEX soon suffered a setback to its U.S. ambitions. Following some disagreements over prices and profits, it took over Southdown's share in 1989 and ran the Sunbelt business on its own. Soon after, disappointed Southdown brought an anti-dumping suit against CEMEX and the Mexican company had to pay heavy duties on its products.

This experience convinced Zambrano that he needed to broaden the company's geographic reach. CEMEX's milestone year in this regard was 1992. It first turned its attention to Spain, an ideal target in Europe not only because of its culture and language, but because of its potential for growth in cement demand. With syndicated financing led by Citicorp, Zambrano completed a major transaction: a US$1.8 billion

Exhibit 2 CEMEX's Major Transactions until 2004

Year	Target Home Country	Mode of Entry	Target of Partner	Size mm $
1969	Mexico	Acquisition	Cementos Maya	n.a.
1976	Mexico	Acquisition	Cementos Guadaiajara	n.a.
1986	USA	Joint Venture	Southdown	n.a.
1987	Mexico	Stake 49%	Correcy of Cem, de Chihuahua	n.a.
1987	USA	Joint Venture	Heidelberger, Aalborg, Lehigh	n.a.
1987	**Mexico**	**Acquisition**	**Cementos Anáhuac**	**1.000**[a]
1989	**Mexico**	**Acquisition**	**Cementos Tolteca**	
1989	USA	Acquisition	Gulf Coast Portland Cement	45[a]
1989	USA	Acquisition	Houston Shell and Concrete	
1989	USA	Acquisition	Houston Concrete Products	
1989	USA	Acquisition	Aggregate Transportation	
1989	USA	Acquisition	Sunbelt (JV w/Southdown)	n.a.
1992	USA	Acquisition	Pharns Sand & Gravel	n.a.
1992	**Spain**	**Acquisition**	**Valenciana**	**1,800**
1992	**Spain**	**Acquisition**	**La Auxiliar de la Construcción**	
1993	Bahamas	Acquisition	Concem	23[b]
1994	USA	Acquisition	Balcones Cement Plant	100
1994	**Venezuela**	**Acquisition**	**Vencemos**	**320**[h]
1994	Trinidad	Stake: 20%	Trinidad Cement	10[b]
1994	Panama	Acquisition	Cemento Bayano	60[b]
1995	Dom. Republic	Acquisition	Cementos Nacionales	111[h]
1996	**Colombia**	**Acquisition**	**Cementos Diamante**	**400**
1996	**Colombia**	**Acquisition**	**Samper**	**300**
1997	Philippines	Stake: 30%	Rizal Cement	93[d]
1998	Indonesia	Stake: 14%	Semen Gresik	114[c]

(Continued)

Exhibit 2 CEMEX's Major Transactions until 2004 (*continued*)

Year	Target Home Country	Mode of Entry	Target of Partner	Size mm $
1998	Philippines	Stake: 40%	Rizal Cement	128[d]
1999	Indonesia	Stake: 8%	Semen Gresik	49[c]
1999	Indonesia	Stake: 4%	Semen Gresik	28[c]
1999	Philippines	Acquisition	APO Cement	400[d]
1999	Costa Rica	Acquisition	Cementos del Pacifico	72[k]
1999	Egypt	Stake: 77%	Assiut Cement	319[a]
1999	Chile	Stake: 12%	Cementos Bio-Bio	34[d]
1999	Haiti	Acquisition	Cement Terminals	n.a.
2000	**USA**	**Acquisition**	**Southdown**	**2.800[d]**
2000	Egypt	Stake: 13%	Assiut Cement	56[e]
2001	Nicaragua	Lease	Nicaraguan Government	n.a.
2001	Thailand	Acquisition	Saraburi Cement	73[d]
2001	Bangladesh	Greenfield	Grinding Mill	26[g]
2001	France	Acquisition	Pastroello Travaux Routiers	n.a.
2001	Japan	Acquisition	Wangan	23[f]
2002	Puerto Rico	Acquisition	Puerto Rican Cement Co.	281[a]
2003	USA	Acquisition	Dixon-Marquette Cement	84[j]

[a] CEMEX S.A.B. de C.V.,"CEMEX – The Centennial Book," Mexico, 2006

[b] http://www.luxner.com/

[c] Pankaj Ghemawat, "The Globalization of CEMEX," 29 November 2004

[d] Deutsche Bank, "Global Cement Review," 11 April 2002

[e] http://www.secinfo.com/dRE54.523w.d.htm

[f] http://findarticles.com/p/articles/mi_hb5563/is_200105/ai_n22866174?tag=artBody;col1

[g] http://findarticles.com/p/articles/mi_m0EIN/is_2000_March_29/ai_60909310

[h] www.eclac.org/publicaciones/xml/2/24302/1cg2309i_Chapter_1V.pdf

[j] http://cementamericas.com/mag/cement_positioning_profit_us/

[k] http://www.cemex.com/ar1999/html/en199928.asp

takeover of Spain's two biggest cement companies, Compañía Valenciana de Cementos Portland and La Auxiliar de la Construcción (also known under its brand name Sanson). The transaction put European incumbents on the alert—there was a new kid on the block.

Beyond creating a solid position in Europe, the deal brought financing advantages as CEMEX was able to raise cheaper funds through the Spanish unit. As a consequence, Valenciana became the umbrella holding company for all future international acquisitions. The new subsidiary proved itself when raising funds became especially challenging for Mexican companies during the peso crisis of 1994–1995. Many Mexican companies went into liquidation, but due to its strong export capabilities and international operations, CEMEX survived. In this regard, CEMEX could be said to have benefited from, and even owed its survival, to, globalization.

In the 1990s, U.S. firms began to reduce investment in the cement sector and diversify into other businesses. This created opportunities for foreign cement makers for two reasons. First, shortages opened up the U.S. market to imported cement. Second, U.S. assets in the sector were now on the market—and CEMEX was definitely a buyer.

In 1992, CEMEX subsidiary Sunbelt purchased Pharris Sand & Gravel, while in 1994, CEMEX paid competitor Lafarge US$100 million for the Balcones cement plant. This Texas plant could help CEMEX bypass some anti-dumping regulations. CEMEX also benefited from the passage of the North American Free Trade Agreement (NAFTA). When NAFTA went into effect in 1994, it opened up new revenue opportunities in the United States and enabled CEMEX to continue lowering the country risk associated with being a Mexico-based corporation.[7]

At the same time, CEMEX was expanding throughout Latin America, where it met fierce competition from Lafarge and Holcim. The 1993 acquisition of Concern, a distribution subsidiary of the Norwegian cement producer Scancem, got CEMEX into Caribbean and Central American markets. In 1994, the company acquired Venezuela's largest cement maker, Corporación Venezolana de Cementos (Vencemos), from distressed conglomerate Grupo Mendoza. CEMEX was a "better parent" for the valuable Venezuelan assets, whose location facilitated cement trading to Central America, Brazil, and the Caribbean. CEMEX entered Panama the same year by acquiring Cemento Bayano in a government auction and purchased a minority stake in Trinidad Cement. The following year, it bought Cementos Nacionales, the largest player in the Dominican Republic and Haiti.

In 1996, CEMEX acquired control of two of Colombia's leading cement manufacturers, Cementos Diamante and Cementos Samper, for about US$700 million. With that transaction, CEMEX became the third-largest cement producer in the world. In 1999, CEMEX took a 12 percent interest in Chile's largest cement producer, Cementos Bío Bío, and bought further assets in Haiti. The company also listed American Depository Receipts on the New York Stock Exchange in the same year, to enhance its visibility to the investor community, and consolidated its presence in Central America and the Caribbean by acquiring a 95 percent stake in Costa Rica's largest cement producer, Cementos del Pacífico. CEMEX entered Nicaragua in 2001 by leasing a cement plant from the government, and the following year bought the Puerto Rican Cement Company. With its acquisitions of companies all over Latin America, Cemex became a so-called "Multi-Latina."

Emerging Markets around the Globe. CEMEX's presence in Latin American markets was to be complemented by asset purchases in the Far East. By the mid-1990s, CEMEX had a significant presence in Asia as a cement trader, but had not yet made an acquisition. The company had weathered Mexico's currency crisis of 1994, thanks to its geographic spread, and was therefore eager to further broaden its international reach.

A major opportunity surfaced with the Asian economic crisis of 1997–1998, which had a negative impact on the construction sector. When local firms began selling off noncore assets in building materials and governments started divesting their stakes in cement operations, CEMEX was a buyer again, as valuations began to fall. The first acquisition was in the Philippines, where in 1997 CEMEX paid roughly US$90 million for a 30 percent stake in Rizal Cement Company. A year later, the company bought an additional 40 percent for US$128 million.

From 1998 to 1999, CEMEX turned to Indonesia, subsequently investing nearly US$200 million for an overall 25.5 percent stake in state-owned Semen Gresik Group, the country's largest cement producer, born of a merger between various regional companies. Indonesia was a low-cost production country, was strategically located for cement exports, and had significant growth potential, and was therefore quite important to CEMEX's development and growth in Asia. However, in 2004, the company was still struggling to gain majority control over Gresik and even filed an arbitration claim against the Indonesian government when the original terms of the agreement to raise its stake to 51 percent were not honored.

At the end of the 1990s, CEMEX completed due diligence of two leading Thai producers, Siam Cement and TPI Polene, but abandoned the acquisitions in view of political concerns and financial discipline. In spite of these setbacks, CEMEX had come to Asia to stay. Trading operations in China, one of the world's greatest consumers and producers of cement, began in 1998. In 1999, CEMEX bought APO Cement Corporation, the lowest-cost producer in the Philippines, for $400 million, making it the biggest cement producer in that country. Venturing into Thailand again in 2001, the firm used its investment vehicle CEMEX Asia Holdings, a partnered fund with third-party capital contributions, to purchase the cement manufacturer Saraburi Cement for an enterprise value of approximately US$73 million.

Thailand was the largest exporter in Southeast Asia and a major cement supplier of the U.S. market.

In North Africa, between 1999 and 2000, the company acquired a 90 percent stake in Egypt's top cement producer, state-affiliated Assiut Cement Company. The acquisition marked a shift in strategy from exporting cement to Egypt, to buying production capacity in one of the fastest-growing cement markets in the region. The Egyptian market was highly fragmented, with Assiut controlling a mere 17 percent. Moreover, cement prices (see Exhibit 3) were regulated to a significant degree by the Egyptian government, which controlled almost 50 percent of the industry's capacity and maintained low price levels. Nonetheless, by 2001, CEMEX had established a competitive position in Northern Egypt with a network of over 500 retailers.

Developed Countries. Unlike its rivals, especially European cement makers Holcim, HeidelbergCement, and Lafarge, CEMEX had a limited presence in developed countries. Most of these markets were relatively mature,

especially in the United States and Western Europe. They also tended to remain quite stable, with a large share of demand stemming from infrastructure projects and government-related spending.

CEMEX strengthened its position in the U.S. market in 2000. It paid US$2.6 billion in a surprising takeover of Southdown Inc.—the same company that had earlier led an anti-dumping campaign against CEMEX. Southdown had merged in March 1998 with Medusa Corporation[8] to become the second-largest U.S. cement producer. The deal instantly made CEMEX the biggest cement producer in North America and gave the company a large portion of its income in U.S. dollars.

Southdown was merged into the existing U.S. business in 2001, creating CEMEX Inc., which that year accounted for nearly 30 percent of the parent company's total revenues. Southdown was integrated in a record time of only four months, largely because of CEMEX's accumulated post-merger expertise. In the same year, the firm obtained its investment grade ranking from

Exhibit 3 Pricing Data on Cement, Ex-works, 2004

Country	Price ($)	Country	Price ($)	Country	Price ($)
Australia	84	Hong Kong	55	Nigeria	80
Belgium	101	Hungary	46–54	Norway	82
Canada	67	Ireland	63–69	Philippines	91
Chile	78	Indonesia	35–37	Poland	54
China	34	Israel	63	Portugal	82
Colombia	90	Italy	71	Singapore	37
Czech Republic	69–86	Japan	61	South Korea	59
Denmark	68	Kenya	81	Spain	66
Egypt	34	Malaysia	52	Switzerland	98
Finland	71	Mexico	121	Thailand	38–41
France	92	Morocco	60	United Arab Emirates	52
Germany	35–40	The Netherlands	72	United Kingdom	86
Greece	63	New Zealand	120	United States	75

Source: CSFB, 2004, Building sector—where will the cycle take us?, September 9.

Standard & Poor's and worked hard to maintain this status. The Southdown deal was CEMEX's first step towards becoming a "Global Latina."

Corporate Strategy

With the exception of its diversification efforts of the 1980s, CEMEX traditionally focused on high-margin product cement and had further exposure to ready-mix concrete, especially in the Mexican market, were it had acquired several concrete companies during its domestic expansion. Aggregates, while also an attractive product in the building materials domain, were not a major contributor to CEMEX's revenues. The company focused increasingly on the overall value chain and considered strengthening the downstream business in order to become a "building materials solution provider" rather than a supplier of isolated products.

CEMEX's strategy called for the company's participation in markets with long-term growth potential. The result of this strategic focus on geographic reach was its expansion into emerging markets. Emerging markets had a number of advantages. Compared with developed economies, emerging markets enjoyed relatively strong growth rates and low degrees of urbanization. High growth went hand-in-hand with infrastructure investments and residential construction, which in turn resulted in greater cement consumption. Furthermore, underperforming cement companies with potential for restructuring were more likely to be found in emerging markets.

The Emerging Markets Advantage

Over the years, CEMEX gained significant experience in emerging markets as a result of its presence in Mexico, Latin America, and Southeast Asia. The company had gained a number of strategically relevant insights about market dynamics and customer profiles in developing nations. Through its exposure to these volatile markets (see Exhibit 4), CEMEX learned to "navigate in troubled waters" and to adapt quickly to diverse environments. Because of its experience, CEMEX was able to understand the strategic meaning of challenging situations and turnaround companies.

The retail nature of cement sales in emerging markets offered CEMEX further advantages. CEMEX's bagged cement brands had strong brand recognition. The ability to market cement as a consumer good in developing countries could be considered one of CEMEX's competitive advantages. The knowledge and capabilities that CEMEX developed over the years in emerging market

Exhibit 4 Emerging Markets: Presence of Cement Majors

	Latin America	Eastern Europe	Asia Pacific
Average cement price (US$)	87	46	45
Total cement capacity (Mt)	175	205	315
Total cement consumption (Mt)	113	96	188
Capacity utilization (%)	65%	47%	60%
Global Four: market share (%)	53%	27%	35%
By company:			
Lafarge (%)	10.9%	8.1%	12.5%
Holcim (%)	17.7%	10.2%	11.4%
CEMEX (%)	24.2%	0.0%	5.8%
HeidelbergCement (%)	0.0%	9.0%	55.0%

environments were, in most cases, transferable to markets with similar characteristics.

In Mexico, CEMEX's deep understanding of the local market was exemplified in 1999 by an important initiative, "Patrimonio Hoy," a microfinance-based housing scheme for low-income customers, who accounted for a large portion of the company's bagged cement sales. Another of its initiatives, "Construrama" (2001), was a building materials retail chain that mainly sold CEMEX products. Store owners were granted significant discounts and brand image advantages when their outlet joined the network.

Such initiatives not only erected high entry barriers to the Mexican market, but strengthened the CEMEX brand in Mexico, secured distribution channels, and retained customers. In 2004, the Construrama chain was rolled out in other countries in Latin America.

"The CEMEX Way"[9]

Throughout its transition from a regional to an international company, CEMEX had to deal with varied business and cultural environments, as well as the integration of several geographically spread and technologically distinct firms. As it expanded, CEMEX borrowed the best practices it encountered when making acquisitions, established technological standards for its cement operations, and created a uniform and innovative business model that helped to build a worldwide platform for its global network. CEMEX also incorporated best practices from other industries when these could be usefully applied to the cement industry.

This approach gained fame as "the CEMEX way." It had three essential features. First, the global standardization of processes in production, administration, and commercial areas; second, the alignment of organization through clear role definitions, the implementation of a common knowledge platform, and the use of a common language (English); and third, the harmonization of accounting and controlling systems without giving up the flexibility to adapt to local legal and fiscal constraints.

The implementation of the CEMEX way allowed the company to expand from local to global, and resulted in reduced costs, more efficient asset utilization, superior customer service, faster integration of acquisitions and new technologies, enhanced quality control, and a better overall ability to take decisions. Business model innovation was part of CEMEX's DNA.

Cement Trading Activities

Cement trading, which aims at balancing worldwide supply and demand among often dispersed plants, is an alternative to capital investments in a particular country. For cement companies, trading was a proven tool to survive local crises through global exports. CEMEX, a leader in the field, had established a network of grinding mills and storage silos, and used a fleet of bulk freighters to redirect excess capacity to where it was needed most. Indeed, in some cases, CEMEX utilized these cement exports, facilitated through its trading division, to establish client relationships and investigate potential target markets before making any decisions about strategic acquisitions or expansionary capital expenditures.

Mergers and Acquisitions at CEMEX

Acquisitions were undeniably an important instrument of the company's internationalization strategy. Over the years, CEMEX developed a state-of-the-art takeover approach and showed the necessary discipline in making—as well as not making—acquisitions.

Since 1992 [...] we have made 15 significant acquisitions. We have learned a lot from each of those transactions, as well as from the transactions we did not do. We have learned how to identify potential value and network synergies in an acquisition opportunity. We have learned

how to stick to our disciplines during the bidding and negotiation process. We have learned how to integrate new acquisitions with increasing speed and efficiency. We have learned how to use our balance sheet to finance an acquisition, as well as how to recover our financial flexibility quickly after the transaction is completed.[10]
—**LORENZO ZAMBRANO**

Acquisition Strategy, Target Identification, and Due Diligence

CEMEX generally targeted undervalued and/or underperforming assets with potential for operational efficiency improvements that fit with the product portfolio, as defined by its corporate strategy. Preferred target companies were well-known competitors with a significant share of the market(s) in which a firm competed. When identifying acquisition opportunities, CEMEX also took a broader view and examined the potential for restructuring the respective market as a whole.[11] The company sometimes took advantage of economic crises to shop for cement assets with lower valuations. As stipulated in its annual report of 2003, targeted assets must:

- provide risk-adjusted returns in excess of the weighted-average cost of capital;
- contribute to greater earnings and free cash flow growth stability;
- maintain financial strength and investment-grade credit quality; and
- benefit from the company's management and turn-around expertise.[12]

A senior CEMEX executive described one of the basic purposes of engaging in acquisitions: "It is all about neutralizing business cycles through diversifying, about choosing our investments carefully, about achieving economies of scale, increasing our efficiency."[13]

To evaluate a potential acquisition in depth, a CEMEX team with diverse skills or competencies was sent to the target firm to evaluate its operations as part of CEMEX's due diligence process. Depending on the size of the target company, the process could take from one week to three months, or even longer.[14] The screening included a strong emphasis on country analysis factors such as population size, growth, business cycles, and GDP development, as these were the constituents of cement and building materials demand. Market intelligence could also be obtained from the trading division if exports to the target country had already taken place.

The process was very thorough and enabled CEMEX to make decisions quickly. This was especially advantageous when there were multiple bidders, for example, in the context of government auctions and privatizations.

The findings from the due diligence process also helped to prepare the initiation of post-merger integration (PMI) activities.

Post-Acquisition Management

Newly acquired entities had to be integrated as fast and as smoothly as possible to the "CEMEX way." To achieve this, standardized applications in post-merger management were developed throughout the company's acquisition history. After completing a transaction, CEMEX involved special interdisciplinary integration teams that were tasked to work closely with the target firm and perform a so-called business process gap analysis—comparing the companies' respective processes and deciding where to implement the CEMEX approach and where to adapt to local needs. Superior processes from the acquired firm were retained and disseminated on a company-wide basis. As of 2004, more than half of CEMEX's standardized business processes came from acquired companies.[15] Besides the

benefit of more rapid integration and cost savings, this approach also actively involved the workforce from the acquired firm. Most acquired companies were renamed CEMEX, except for especially well-established brands, to which a small CEMEX logo was added.

The process proved very successful and CEMEX was often cited as an excellent model for effective post-merger integration. Its track record in successful PMI was impressive: the integration time went from 18 months for Valenciana and Sanson (1992), to six months for Vencemos (1994), to four months for Southdown (2000), down to only two months for the Puerto Rican Cement Company (2002).[16]

CEMEX at the Crossroads

In 2004, CEMEX found itself at a crossroads. It had successfully competed with European incumbents, such as the French company Lafarge, or the Swiss company Holcim, in the major emerging markets around the world

Exhibit 5 Operational Statistics

	CEMEX Asset Base, Geographic Spread, and Market Shares						
	Production Capacity (million metric tons/year)	Cement Plants Controlled	Cement Plants Minority Stake	Ready Mix Plants	Land Distr. Centers	Marine Terminals	Market Share 2004 Cement
Mexico		15	3	211	68	8	56.4%
United States	14.2	13	4	86	49	5	10.7%
Spain	10.8	8	—	77	12	19	23.0%
Venezuela	4.6	3	—	30	12	4	47.2%
Colombia	4.8	5	—	21	2		27.0%
Central America & Caribbean	4.1	5	6	28	11	10	n/a
Egypt	4.9	1	—	3	4	1	15.0%
Philippines	5.8	3	—	1	6	3	21.0%
Indonesia	44		4	9	27	10	30.1%
Thailand	0.7	1	—				0.8%
TOTAL	81.5	54	17	466	191	60	

Source: CEMEX Annual Report 2003; CSFB, 2004, Building sector—where will the cycle take us?, September 9; Deutsche Bank, 2004, Holcim—year of the harvest, January 21.

Exhibit 6 Global Cement M&A Activity, 1993–2004 (completed transactions only)

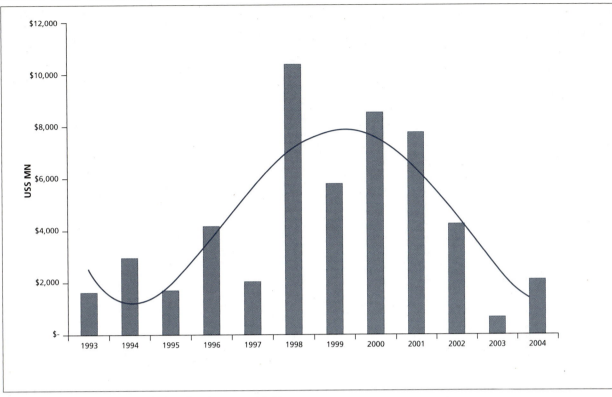

Source: Citigroup, 2004, Cemex S.A. de C.V.—frugal gourmets, July 14.

and had "acquired" its way to the top of the industry. Having established a solid competitive position with its global portfolio of assets (see Exhibit 5), it dominated the majority of the markets in which it operated. But now a critical question arose: Where to go from here?

CEMEX had been using its cash to lower the debt level accumulated with its international purchases. In the two years since the Puerto Rican deal, CEMEX had not made any major acquisitions. Should the company continue to de-leverage to satisfy the financial community? M&A activity soared again in the first quarter of 2004 (see Exhibit 6). CEMEX could choose not to participate in the next round of consolidation, or could choose to actively participate in a new cycle. Should it focus on organic growth, or should it engage in another acquisition spree?

If CEMEX decided to pursue an acquisition, what type of firm and in what geographic location should an acquisition be considered? Should the firm take the next step towards becoming a "global Latina" with a major acquisition in a developed country, or should it build on its emerging markets expertise and search for a turnaround opportunity in a developing economy (see Exhibit 7)?

Exhibit 7 Global Cement Outlook (in million tons, if not otherwise stated)

Country	2000	2001	2002	2003	2004 E	2005 E	2002 Δ	2003 Δ	2004 Δ	2005 Δ	Kg per capita
Western Europe											
Austria	4.5	4.4	4.6	4.5	4.5	4.6	3.6%	–2.2%	1.0%	2.0%	549
Belgium	6.1	5.7	5.4	5.4	5.5	5.6	–5.7%	0.0%	1.0%	2.0%	595
Denmark	1.6	1.5	1.4	1.4	1.4	1.4	–6.7%	0.0%	0.5%	1.0%	289
Finland	1.7	1.6	1.5	1.6	1.6	1.7	–5.3%	4.6%	2.5%	2.5%	326

(Continued)

Exhibit 7 Global Cement Outlook (in million tons, if not otherwise stated) (*Continued*)

Country	2000	2001	2002	2003	2004 E	2005 E	2002 Δ	2003 Δ	2004 Δ	2005 Δ	Kg per capita
France	21.6	21.6	20.7	20.2	21.0	21.3	–4.4%	–2.4%	4.0%	1.5%	365
Germany	35.6	31.5	29.2	27.2	26.0	25.0	–7.3%	–6.8%	–4.4%	–3.8%	354
Greece	9.4	9.9	10.3	11.3	11.2	10.4	4.0%	9.6%	–1.0%	–7.0%	973
Ireland	4.6	4.6	4.4	4.3	4.5	4.6	–5.4%	–1.1%	3.5%	2.5%	1,115
Italy	38.3	39.5	41.3	43.6	44.4	45.1	4.6%	5.6%	1.8%	1.5%	711
Luxembourg	0.5	0.5	0.5	0.5	0.5	0.6	1.9%	0.0%	2.5%	2.5%	1,256
Netherlands	6.3	5.9	5.4	5.3	5.2	5.3	–8.5%	–0.9%	–1.3%	2.2%	330
Norway	1.3	1.2	1.3	1.2	1.2	1.2	2.4%	–3.1%	–1.0%	0.0%	282
Portugal	11.1	10.5	10.5	9.0	9.0	9.2	0.3%	–14.3%	0.3%	1.5%	1,014
Spain	38.4	41.9	44.1	46.1	47.5	48.9	5.2%	4.5%	3.0%	3.0%	1,076
Sweden	1.5	1.6	1.6	1.7	1.8	1.8	–1.8%	6.3%	3.5%	3.0%	179
UK	13.1	13.0	13.0	13.2	13.0	12.9	0.0%	1.8%	–1.5%	–1.0%	215
Switzerland	3.8	3.9	3.7	3.8	3.9	3.9	–5.1%	2.7%	1.5%	1.1%	507
Total Western Europe % change, YoY	**199.5 4.5%**	**198.9 –0.3%**	**198.8 0.0%**	**200.4 0.8%**	**202.2 0.9%**	**203.4 0.6%**					507
Eastern Europe											
Bosnia	1.6	1.6	1.7	1.7	1.8	1.9	3.1%	3.0%	5.5%	5.5%	429
Bulgaria	1.5	1.4	1.6	1.8	1.9	2.0	9.9%	16.1%	4.1%	4.3%	185
Croatia	1.8	1.9	2.3	2.5	2.6	2.8	19.6%	8.7%	3.5%	7.0%	511
Cyprus	0.9	1.1	1.2	1.2	1.3	1.3	13.3%	0.8%	4.5%	4.5%	1,554
Czech Republic	3.6	3.6	3.7	3.8	3.9	4.0	1.0%	4.1%	3.2%	3.0%	354
Hungary	3.6	3.7	3.8	3.9	4.1	4.3	4.1%	2.6%	5.5%	5.0%	373
Iceland	0.2	0.2	0.1	0.1	0.1	0.1	–15.0%	0.0%	3.0%	3.0%	481
Kazakhstan	1.3	2.0	2.3	2.6	2.7	2.8	18.3%	12.3%	4.5%	4.5%	137

(Continued)

Exhibit 7 Global Cement Outlook (in million tons, if not otherwise stated) (*Continued*)

Country	2000	2001	2002	2003	2004 E	2005 E	2002 Δ	2003 Δ	2004 Δ	2005 Δ	Kg per capita
Lithuania	0.4	0.4	0.4	0.5	0.5	0.5	0.0%	7.1%	4.5%	4.5%	120
Poland	14.3	11.4	10.9	11.4	11.8	12.4	−4.4%	4.6%	3.5%	5.0%	282
Romania	4.4	4.4	4.7	4.9	5.2	5.5	6.1%	4.3%	6.0%	6.5%	209
Russia	30.6	33.3	34.0	38.5	40.2	42.2	2.1%	13.2%	4.5%	5.0%	231
Serbia	2.2	2.5	2.2	1.9	1.7	1.9	−10.3%	−13.6%	−8.0%	6.0%	208
Slovakia	1.6	1.6	1.7	1.7	1.8	1.9	2.2%	3.0%	5.0%	6.0%	306
Slovenia	1.2	1.2	1.3	1.4	1.4	1.5	10.2%	3.8%	5.0%	5.5%	644
Ukraine	5.5	5.8	6.3	6.5	7.0	7.5	8.7%	4.0%	7.0%	8.0%	122
Total Eastern Europe % change, YoY	83.7 4.4%	85.3 2.0%	87.9 3.0%	94.7 7.7%	98.8 4.4%	104.0 5.2%					223
Middle East & S. Asia											
Afghanistan	0.7	0.8	0.9	1.1	1.5	1.7	0.6%	31.8%	15.0%	15.0%	36
Iran	21.0	23.4	25.1	26.4	28.2	29.6	7.4%	5.0%	7.0%	5.0%	387
Iraq	4.3	1.8	1.8	1.8	1.8	2.1	0.6%	0.6%	0.0%	15.0%	195
Israel	4.5	4.4	4.5	4.4	4.5	4.7	2.1%	−1.6%	3.0%	3.1%	766
Lebanon	2.6	2.7	2.5	2.5	2.6	2.7	−8.1%	0.0%	4.0%	5.0%	813
Saudi Arabia	15.4	18.0	18.6	18.0	18.6	19.1	3.3%	−3.2%	3.5%	2.5%	738
UAE	6.9	7.5	8.0	8.5	9.5	10.3	6.7%	6.3%	12.0%	8.0%	2,143
Turkey	31.0	25.4	26.2	28.0	32.2	34.8	3.1%	6.9%	15.0%	8.0%	486
Bangladesh	4.8	5.2	6.0	6.5	7.0	7.5	15.6%	8.3%	7.5%	7.0%	39
Brunei	0.4	0.2	0.2	0.3	0.3	0.3	4.3%	4.2%	7.0%	7.0%	1,134
India	92.5	90.3	99.0	110.0	122.1	135.5	9.7%	11.1%	11.0%	11.0%	95
Pakistan	9.9	9.9	10.3	11.2	12.5	13.8	4.0%	8.6%	12.0%	10.0%	61

(*Continued*)

Case 6: CEMEX: Building a Global Latina

Exhibit 7 Global Cement Outlook (in million tons, if not otherwise stated) (*Continued*)

Country	2000	2001	2002	2003	2004 E	2005 E	2002 Δ	2003 Δ	2004 Δ	2005 Δ	Kg per capita
Sri Lanka	2.5	2.7	2.6	2.8	2.9	2.9	−3.0%	8.0%	1.1%	1.1%	135
Total Middle East & S. Asia % change, YoY	**216.7** −2.5%	**214.7** −1.0%	**229.0** 6.7%	**245.7** 7.3%	**281.2** 14.4%	**303.5** 7.9%					
Total China and Hong Kong % change, YoY	**589.5** 5.0%	**624.4** 5.9%	**683.8** 9.5%	**743.9** 8.8%	**795.7** 7.0%	**852.8** 7.2%					450
Total Japan % change, YoY	**72.3** 2.1%	**68.6** −5.1%	**65.0** −5.2%	**62.0** −4.6%	**61.4** −1.0%	**61.4** 0.0%					
Asia Pacific											
South Korea	40.0	50.1	54.3	56.5	58.8	61.1	8.5%	4.1%	4.0%	4.0%	938
Philippines	11.9	11.3	12.9	12.6	13.0	13.7	13.9%	−2.3%	3.5%	5.0%	154
Taiwan	18.5	16.7	16.0	15.5	15.5	15.5	−4.2%	−3.1%	0.0%	0.0%	880
Indonesia	22.5	25.6	27.1	27.2	29.2	31.3	5.7%	0.4%	7.5%	7.0%	85
Malaysia	11.8	11.8	13.0	13.7	14.6	15.6	10.2%	5.0%	7.0%	7.0%	386
Singapore	4.7	4.2	3.8	3.6	3.6	3.7	−9.3%	−5.3%	0.0%	3.0%	1,486
Thailand	17.9	18.5	22.2	23.5	25.1	26.9	19.8%	5.9%	7.0%	7.0%	299
Vietnam	13.7	16.9	19.7	23.0	26.5	28.7	16.6%	16.8%	15.0%	8.5%	139
Total Asia Pacific % change, YoY	**154.9** 7.7%	**162.0** 4.6%	**176.2** 8.8%	**183.1** 3.9%	**194.0** 6.0%	**204.3** 5.3%					
Oceania											
Australia	8.0	7.4	7.5	8.0	8.3	8.6	1.4%	6.7%	4.0%	3.5%	400
New Zealand	1.0	1.0	1.0	1.1	1.1	1.1	1.9%	8.3%	1.0%	1.5%	235
Total Oceania % change, YoY	**9.0** 8.4%	**8.4** −6.7%	**8.6** 1.6%	**9.2** 6.9%	**9.5** 3.6%	**9.8** 3.2%					

(Continued)

Exhibit 7 Global Cement Outlook (in million tons, if not otherwise stated) (*Continued*)

Country	2000	2001	2002	2003	2004 E	2005 E	2002 Δ	2003 Δ	2004 Δ	2005 Δ	Kg per capita
North America											
USA	110.470	112.810	110.020	112.000	120.400	123.410	–2.5%	1.8%	7.5%	2.5%	403
Canada	8.3	8.4	8.6	8.9	9.3	9.5	2.5%	3.2%	4.3%	2.0%	274
Total North America % change, YoY	118.7 1.2%	121.2 2.1%	118.6 –2.1%	120.9 1.9%	129.7 7.3%	132.9 2.5%					390
Latin America											
Argentina	6.2	5.5	4.3	4.8	5.2	5.5	–21.1%	11.6%	8.0%	7.0%	172
Brazil	39.4	38.5	38.8	33.8	33.1	33.9	0.8%	–12.9%	–2.0%	2.2%	238
Costa Rica	1.0	1.2	1.2	1.0	1.1	1.1	0.0%	–14.9%	5.0%	5.0%	280
Chile	3.5	3.6	3.7	3.8	4.0	4.2	1.7%	4.1%	6.5%	5.0%	234
Colombia	5.3	5.4	5.1	5.3	5.5	5.8	–5.6%	3.9%	4.2%	4.2%	141
Ecuador	2.9	3.0	3.1	3.2	3.3	3.5	1.0%	4.9%	4.6%	4.8%	238
El Salvador	1.1	1.2	1.3	1.3	1.4	1.4	2.0%	3.0%	5.0%	5.0%	176
Mexico	29.8	28.3	29.4	30.1	31.3	32.6	3.9%	2.4%	4.0%	4.0%	311
Nicaragua	0.6	0.6	0.6	0.7	0.7	0.7	3.2%	1.6%	5.0%	5.0%	131
Panama	1.0	0.9	0.7	0.9	0.9	1.0	–17.6%	28.6%	4.0%	4.0%	357
Paraguay	0.6	0.6	0.6	0.5	0.5	0.6	–8.1%	–7.0%	3.0%	3.0%	115
Peru	3.6	3.4	3.7	4.0	4.1	4.3	8.8%	9.0%	2.7%	2.9%	147
Puerto Rico	1.6	1.6	1.7	1.8	1.8	1.8	6.3%	2.9%	0.0%	0.0%	421
Venezuela	4.0	4.4	3.7	3.8	4.9	5.5	–15.9%	2.7%	30.0%	12.0%	172
Total Latin America % change, YoY	111.5 0.6%	109.0 –2.3%	108.0 –0.9%	105.6 –2.2%	108.8 3.0%	112.9 3.8%					224

Source: Deutsche Bank, 2004, Global cement update—Mexican wave, November 26.

NOTES

1. Conference on Winning Globally: Organizing for Global Impact. Transcript of a speech of Lorenzo Zambrano, Stanford University, Palo Alto, CA, January 23, 2002.

2. Earnings before Interest, Taxes, Depreciation, and Amortization.

3. The term "Global Latinas" refers to Latin American multinational companies that own operations in the United States, Europe, and Asia and was first introduced in the forthcoming Inter-American Development Bank report with the same title, supervised by Lourdes Casanova.

4. CEMEX S.A.B. de C.V., 2006, CEMEX – The Centennial Book, Mexico.

5. L. Crawford, 1997, Long reach opens new source of finance, *Financial Times*, November 7.

6. As defined by Lourdes Casanova, natural markets for a MNC share a common history or language or have a high level of physical proximity with the country of origin of the MNC.

7. J. Millman, 2000, NAFTA turns Mexico into a global economic force, *Wall Street Journal*, May 9.

8. The merger was valued at US$1 billion.

9. Source: CEMEX S.A.B. de C.V., 2006, CEMEX – The Centennial Book, Mexico.

10. Remarks of Lorenzo Zambrano, Annual Analyst and Investor Meeting, July 1, 2004, Norwalk, CT. Available at http://www.cemex .com, as of May 2008.

11. P. Ghemawat, 2004, The globalization of CEMEX, Harvard Business School, November 29.

12. CEMEX Annual Report, 2003.

13. C. Piggott, 2001, Cemex's stratospheric rise, *LatinFinance*, March.

14. http://www.cemexphilippines.com, as of May 2008.

15. M. Austin, 2004, Global integration the CEMEX way, http://www .thedeal.com/corporatedealmaker/2004/02/global_integration_the_ cemex_w.phpMarch 1.

16. CEMEX S.A.B. de C.V., 2006, CEMEX – The Centennial Book, Mexico.

Citibank's E-Business Strategy for Global Corporate Banking

Dr. Minyi Huang, Ali Farhoomand

The University of Hong Kong

In 2000, in response to intense competition and the dot-com boom, Citibank made a serious push to deliver integrated solutions that enabled its corporate customers to conduct business online. Citibank's e-business strategy ("connect, transform, and extend") was to Web-enable its core services, develop integrated solutions, and reach new markets. Citibank aimed to build a single Web-enabled platform for all customers with similar needs. Following the success of CitiDirect, a corporate banking platform which was developed in 2000 and strengthened in 2003, Citibank started to develop Treasury Vision as a replacement to suit the changing marketplace.

When developing its e-business, Citibank faced constant challenges in serving corporate customers with diverse needs. Sophisticated clients, such as multinational companies (MNCs), required custom-built host-to-host product interfaces. Other customers, such as small and medium-sized enterprises (SMEs), were more conservative and not ready for Web-based solutions. Meanwhile, Citibank was under increasing pressure to cut costs and improve efficiency. Following the outcry over subprime mortgages in October 2007, Citibank faced a very tough business environment.

How could Citibank build a flexible and agile e-business product that could capture its clients' total cash-management and trade-service needs, yet still lower costs and improve efficiency? Given Citibank's enormous global reach, how could it integrate Internet initiatives into its overall strategy and create sustainable competitive advantages?

Global Corporate Banking at Citibank

Citibank was incorporated in 1812 as City Bank of New York. The bank experienced several mergers after its inception. The name Citibank N.A. was adopted in 1976. Following its merger with Travelers Group in 1998, the holding company changed its name to Citigroup Inc. ("Citigroup"). In 2006, Citigroup employed 325,000 staff serving 200 million customers in over 100 countries and had an information technology expenditure of US$3,762 million.

Starting in the 1990s, Citibank's corporate banking activities became more centralized, with more attention focused on 1,400 large global corporations and institutional investors.[1] Citibank transformed from a geography-based organization into a multidimensional one. Customer needs became its first priority, while product types were given second priority.[2]

By most measures, Citibank was the most global U.S. bank. In 1997, Citibank was also one of the most profitable banks in the United States, with an annual profit of US$3.59 billion, of which global corporate banking accounted for US$2.56 billion. Citibank's global corporate banking business continued its healthy growth. The bank's Cash and Trade service was a core product offered to corporate customers. By 2000, Citibank's Cash and Trade division had already exceeded US$1 trillion in financial transactions for customers and counterparts around the world daily. These included foreign exchange transactions, equities, deposits, settlements of trade transactions, and payment of insurance policies. In 2006, the income from its global corporate and investment banking activities reached US$7.127 billion, a three percent increase over 2005.[3]

Citibank's target corporate client base included MNCs, financial institutions, government sectors, local corporations, and SMEs. Citibank differentiated itself from other banks through customer service by offering telephone hotlines, relationship managers who understood clients' needs, and product consultants who provided service expertise. Most importantly, Citibank made continuous investment in technology to support both the front-end and back-end electronic banking system.

For corporate customers, Citibank provided a full range of financial services, except for investment banking services in the United States. The core products were broadly grouped into three categories:[4]

- Transaction services, such as cash management, trade, and custody services
- Corporate finance services, such as working-capital finance, trade finance, and asset-based financing
- Treasury market services, such as hedging and foreign exchange

Citibank aimed to make the organization accessible to its corporate customers by using its unified platform and group-wide expertise. It used a team coverage approach, which allowed Citigroup to work closely with each function in a client's organization.

Cash Management[5]

The main focus of cash management was to find ways to move money around in the most efficient manner possible in order to meet customers' requirements. Two crucial aspects of a corporate treasurer's needs were accounts payable and accounts receivable. In 2000, Citibank focused on developing solutions to address three process areas: accounts receivable process management, accounts payable process management, and liquid-

ity management (Exhibit 1). By 2007, after continuous developments, Citibank's cash management products included Web-enabled payment and receivables solutions, vendor financing, commercial card solutions, and liquidity products designed to help customers to reduce financing costs and achieve greater returns on assets.

To help customers make payments, WorldLink Payment Services had been Citibank's cross-border banking solution for more than 20 years. Using WorldLink Payment Services, payments can be made in more than 135 currencies through a range of payment options including cash, cross-border Automated Clearing House (ACH)[6], checks, or electronic funds transfers. There was no need for multiple foreign currency accounts, and transactions were protected by sophisticated encryption technologies, access restrictions, and authentication procedures. Citibank's QuikRemit Service, a newer service, offered a robust software platform and global distribution network to process fund transfers effortlessly across borders. QuikRemit allowed corporate customers to offer both in-branch and Web-based money transfers to their own customers.

In terms of receiving payments, Citibank's Customer Initiated Payments offered an integrated solution enabling corporate customers to offer Web and telephone payment capabilities to their clients. Corporate customers were able to develop a tailor-made Internet payment application hosted on the Citibank Customer Initiated Payments system that provided one-time or auto-

Exhibit 1 Citibank's Treasury and Cash Management Objectives mated recurring payment initiation. This solution also included a touch-tone telephone payment application for one-time payment initiation as well as a customer service console to enable payment initiation by an operator.

Citibank's commercial cards offered a wide array of Web-based program management tools designed to streamline payment, reporting, spend analysis, global data consolidation, and other critical day-to-day processes. In Asia, commercial cards enabled corporate customers to receive consolidated spend data for all countries within Asia which could be easily leveraged during supplier negotiations. Corporate customers could also work with a single Citibank sales manager responsible for program implementation across all participating Asian countries. Therefore, clients could benefit from consistency in products, delivery, and services. By the end of 2007, Citibank remained the only bankcard issuer that was able to deliver local-currency and local-language programs to clients worldwide by using its own proprietary systems and customer service operations.

Citibank also offered an array of integrated investment options through multiple channels, including automatic orders, branch services, and online services. Through its network of Liquidity Desks, Citibank provided a central point of contact to facilitate investment transactions in every major region. Citibank's Online Investments was a global, secure, Web-based system allowing customers to access a variety of short-term investments using its award-winning electronic banking platform. CitiDirect Online Banking (which was later replaced by Treasury Vision) allowed customers to actively manage their short-term investment portfolios conveniently and efficiently.

Citibank also offered Target Balancing and Notional Pooling as integrated parts of its Global Liquidity and Investments product suite. Target Balancing was an automated process that concentrated end-of-day balances from a source account to a target account, while these services were maintained in-country, regionally, and globally, and encompassed structures operating within a single branch or multiple branches throughout the Citibank network. Notional Pooling was ideal for corporations with decentralized operational structures that wanted to preserve the autonomy of their subsidiaries and accounts. Pool participant accounts in a single currency were aggregated for interest compensation purposes. Funds were not physically moved, but were instead notionally combined. Notional Pooling enabled corporate customers to minimize interest expenses by offsetting debit and credit positions while preserving autonomy, control, and record-keeping. Customers were also able to benefit from offsetting without movement of funds, automating interest reallocation, reducing operating expenses, and concentrating balances. Notional Pooling was used

in conjunction with Target Balancing and Automated Investments to enable corporate customers to fully realize the benefits of a global liquidity structure.

Securities and Fund Services[7]

By 2008, Citibank had developed the financial industry's largest proprietary network, covering 49 markets with more than US$12.5 trillion in assets under custody. Citibank offered international securities trading and investment services to intermediaries. Citibank's Agency and Trust could provide support to help issuers raise short-, medium-, and long-term debts in all major markets. Additionally, Citibank's Depositary Receipts (DR) could provide a wide range of pre- and post-DR program services.

Trade Services and Finance[8]

Back in 2000, Citibank already offered Trade Finance, Trade Services, and Trade Support Services. These product offerings covered the banking service and financing needs of customers who conducted import or export trade transactions (Exhibit 2).

In 2007, Citibank was able to offer efficient services to both importers and exporters due to its global reach and ability to offer secure transactions. For importers, Citibank also provided an array of products to help conduct, monitor, and control international commercial transactions as well as mitigate the associated risks.

Citibank's global electronic banking service was a comprehensive system for initiating transactions and managing financial data activities. Customers could access information and manage all their banking transactions, trade services, cash management, and foreign exchange data from the multiple locations around the world where they conducted their business. They could control the entire trade process, including advising and confirming letters of credit, establishing direct export collections, initiating and tracking payments, retrieving timely status reports, communicating via an online customer service facility, retrieving real-time data worldwide, and customizing reports using data from different systems.

Pricing and Customer Service

Citibank set a standard price for each service, but price discrimination was discretionary based on client volume and value. While some banks competed on price, Citibank emphasized customer service (e.g., response time, technology and support), which gave customers more confidence. Citibank had moved beyond traditional boundaries of banking services by taking over some of the back-office functions of its customers. Customers could move away from the paper-based, labor-intensive payment and collection process, and instead focus resources on their core business of

Exhibit 2 Citibank's Trade Service Products

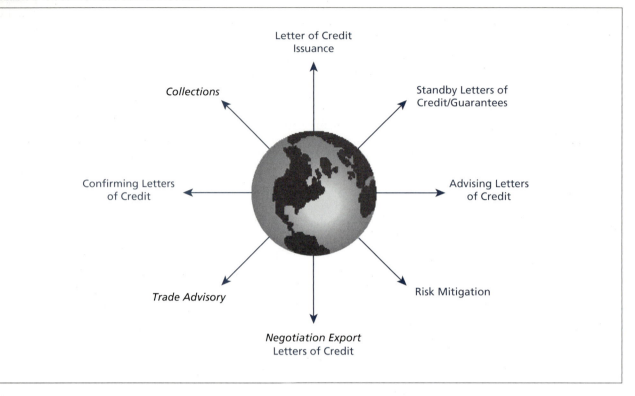

generating sales and revenue. The value to Citibank in offering outsourcing services was to lock in its corporate customers; when a customer outsourced all of its back-end processes to Citibank, Citibank not only secured all the businesses from the customer, but also gained a deeper relationship with the customer. Managing processes for a large number of customers also provided Citibank with economies of scale.

We have the economy of scale and it is viable for us to do all the back-end processes—because the more processes we do for more customers, the lower the unit cost. So our strategy is to get as many outsourcing customers as we can, and by providing the outsourcing, we get the total wallet of the client.

—*CAROLINE WONG, HEAD OF E-BUSINESS GROUP (CASH & TRADE), CITIBANK HONG KONG*[9]

Citibank also used technology to provide customers with better services at lower costs.[10] In 2006, for example, it invested in an electronic communications network that provided state-of-the-art technology for immediate access to liquidity.

A Changing Global Environment

Banks are always under the pressure of revenue and earnings growth to intensify cost-reduction efforts. In an

era of tough competition, banks could not simply use head-count reduction and belt-tightening efforts and needed to find ways to increase operating efficiency while maintaining or even improving services to customers.[11]

Like most other businesses, banks need to increase their profit margins. Net interest margins were falling and fee income growth did not increase as expected. For example, for the 70 largest European banks, net interest margins fell from 2 percent in 2004 to about 1.8 percent in 2006.[12] Meanwhile, competition kept charges for credit cards relatively low; bank customers did not embrace brokerage or life insurance services. Moreover, regulators had made an effort to cap fees or require greater transparency of bank charges.

Between 2005 and 2006, Citigroup's revenue grew 8 percent; however, its operational expenses grew by nearly 15 percent. Therefore, in April 2007, Citibank announced an overhaul of its IT operations and cut 17,000 positions in order to save the company more than US$10 billion over the next three years. Charles Prince, then the company's chairman and chief executive, said that the goal was to identify and eliminate "organizational, technology, and administrative costs that do not contribute to our ability to efficiently deliver products and services to our clients."[13]

Moreover, as a result of the subprime mortgage crisis in the United States, a credit crunch[14] emerged in October 2007. The subprime market was focused on providing loans to those with limited or poor credit histories. During the U.S. housing boom between 2000 and 2006, this market expanded significantly, but a series of interest rate increases in 2006 and 2007 meant that many subprime borrowers could no longer afford their monthly payments, causing them to default on loans.

In November 2007, Prince had to resign after the full extent of Citigroup's subprime mortgage losses began to emerge. Vikram Pandit took up the top job at Citigroup in December 2007. Then, on January 15, 2008, Citigroup announced a US$9.83 billion net loss for the last quarter of 2007. Pandit explained that this loss was due to a US$18.1 billion exposure to bad mortgage debt and was "clearly unacceptable." The group announced that revenues during the fourth quarter had fallen 70 percent from a year earlier to US$7.2 billion.

Smarter and Tougher Customers

Citibank developed expertise and had specific coverage models to serve different market segments. However, as more of Citibank's clients expanded their businesses globally and became e-enabled, it became necessary for Citibank to shift to e-space. In particular, corporations that historically dealt largely through wholesale channels had found that the Internet allowed them to sell directly to customers. Sophisticated corporate customers began to look for an additional range of services. They wanted to collect payments online and have access to more efficient Web-enabled financial processes.[15]

Middle markets were also driving the growing need for Internet banking capabilities. A study by Greenwich Associates in May–June 2001 showed that over half of the middle-market companies in the United States and Canada were using their financial institutions' online banking facilities more often. Nearly 50 percent of respondents said online offerings represented an important component of their banking relationships, and cash management had the steepest gain in usage among mid-size companies.[16] Banks were therefore compelled to identify what companies were looking for and to keep up with the customers with whom they were supposed to develop consultative relationships.

The Business-to-Business (B2B) Market

Sophisticated clients were looking for ways to streamline and improve their traditional payment processes. They demanded electronic invoicing, automatic application of payments to accounts receivable, online payment guarantees, and non-repudiation of transactions that could be enabled by digital receipts stored in archives. On the payment side of transactions, businesses required multi-currency payment management and payment aggregation by invoice and currency. Most companies were interested in technological solutions that allowed them to avoid paper disputes, which meant that the information flowing with a payment was deemed to be as important as the payment itself.[17]

TowerGroup, a research and consulting firm, predicted that payment activities would migrate to the Internet and that there would be US$4 trillion in B2B e-payment activities by 2010. TowerGroup also reported that in 2000, more than 90 percent of all B2B payments were made by check, with 7 percent occurring over the automated clearinghouse (ACH) network, a non-Internet system designed to handle large payments, and the rest using financial Electronic Data Interchange (EDI) services such as Fedwire.[18] The majority of small businesses used traditional payments such as checks; large companies that used ACH did not have the complete data that were necessary for a B2B payment. In addition to checks, various payment methods were available, with clearance time varying according to the method:

- Notes and coins: Notes and coins paid into an account did not require clearing; they had no particular attraction for banks, especially in large volumes, because they were a non-interest-bearing item.
- Banker's draft: This was a check drawn on a bank. Payment by banker's draft was guaranteed.
- Credit cards: Made by voucher or electronically, voucher payments were processed in a way similar to checks.
- Special presentation of checks: This payment method was taken only in cases of extreme doubt about a customer. For example, a payee company could ask its bank to make a special presentation of the check by posting the check to the paying customer's bank.
- Transfers: Funds were transferred from one bank account to another on receipt of instructions (through telephone, subsequently confirmed by writing, on paper, or sent by cable, telex, or an electronic processing center) by the paying bank to make the payment.

Bank-to-corporate connectivity was the biggest hurdle in enabling straight-through processing in treasury- and cash-management across borders.[19] In 1999, corporate customers could access SWIFTNet[20] to exchange confirmations with their banks through Treasury Counterparties. In 2002, access was enhanced by the Member Administrated Closed User Group, where a company could join SWIFTNet if a member bank sponsored it. Though there were no limits on the messages that the corporate customer could exchange with the sponsoring bank, the communication was limited to the sponsoring bank and it was expensive and troublesome for corporate customers to reach an agreement with the banks.

Since the beginning of 2007, most large corporate customers had begun using a new legal model for accessing SWIFTNet: Standardized CORporate Environment (SCORE). Using the SCORE model, a corporate customer could access all participating banks with only one agreement in place. SCORE also laid down rules for the messages that could be sent within the SCORE framework. The only exception was for FileAct message, where the body of a FileAct message could contain any type of messages, such as an EDIFACT[21] or ISO 20022[22] format message. The introduction of SCORE was intended to make it easier, cheaper, and less risky for corporate customers to switch between banks because no technical or format changes were needed for corporate customers in switching banks.[23]

Many banks openly admitted that formats and connectivity were no longer a competitive space but instead a place for cooperation, using standards to reduce costs for their customers as well as themselves. The competition would be in the value-added services that banks sold to customers.[24]

Competition

Some MNCs could not wait for banks to develop Web-enabled financial products, so they started building their own systems and looking for ways to disintermediate banks. Other corporations approached the banks and announced their interest in participating in future developments. New technology, however, required major investments in people, risk, and technological services that some banks were not ready to make. The banking industry's trend toward consolidation meant that fewer banks were competing in the global transaction services marketplace. Deutsche Bank and Citibank were two leading banks that invested hundreds of millions of dollars in the infrastructure required to move and monitor cash balances online. ABN AMRO was also making a serious push to develop its product range.

In early 2001, Deutsche Bank sought to outdo its competitors by building a global payment system capable of accommodating many currencies, languages, and local business practices through its e-bills service. More large banks sought partnerships to provide global business solutions. In international cash management (ICM), companies either partnered with a lead bank that put together a solution for them, or dealt directly with local banks. The majority of companies used a lead bank to provide a solution in four ways: using correspondent banks, acting as an overlay bank, becoming a member of a banking club, or bringing together a network of standardized service providers (Exhibit 3).

Exhibit 3 The Main Trends in ICM in 2000 and 2008

Trends in 2000
• The centralization of cash management and the introduction of shared service centers continued in large companies and were spreading to medium-sized and small companies.
• There was a growing acceptance of the need to outsource ICM operations.
• Companies were realizing that the company-bank relationship was more important than whether or not a bank could offer Internet-based or e-commerce services.
• Companies increasingly wanted to understand and be comfortable with a bank's e-commerce strategy before they were prepared to award them business.
• The use of cross-border zero-balance accounts grew much faster than notional pooling because many companies had sophisticated in-house cash- and treasury-management systems to run them.
• There was a growing realization among some of the major banks that a network of standardized service-provider banks was not always enough; it was also important to have a local branch or branches in countries around the world.
• Banks were walking away from the ICM business where it had ceased to be profitable, producing a growing understanding and acceptance among large companies that banks needed to make reasonable returns; otherwise the standard and quality of services would inevitably suffer.
• As banks' ICM products and memberships of local clearings became similar, the key differentiator in the business became delivery.

Source: D. Danko, J. H. Godwin & S. R. Goldberg, 2002, How to profit from new trends in treasury management, *Journal of Corporate Accounting and Finance*, 14(1): 3–10.

Trends in 2008
• Banks and corporate treasurers were driving the move toward electronic payments in order to better integrate money and information flows.
• Corporate treasury was pushing to integrate the physical and financial supply chains, and there was a parallel convergence in international trade toward open-account, electronic financial supply chains.
• Corporate treasury was focusing on standardizing processes and strengthening internal controls in order to create transparency across a range of business activities to manage risk and ensure financial reporting integrity in compliance with Sarbanes-Oxley.[25]

Source: S. Wilder, 2008, The latest trends in North American cash management, JPMorgan Chase & Co.

Most Fortune 500 companies preferred Citibank when making international e-payments.[26] Although Citibank established itself as a strong contender, technology companies competed heavily by using their technological expertise and interests in providing new services.

Regulatory Scrutiny

Risk management and legal compliance were priorities for banks in 2008.[27] Regulators took an increasingly cross-platform view of risk and therefore expected banks to increasingly connect exposures across channels and payments, which put more pressure on bank architectures where risk management was usually buried at the platform level. For example, the implementation of Basel II[28] increased the pressure on information systems functions and encouraged banks to develop integrated information systems strategies and consequently amend their existing IT infrastructures.[29]

Regulators were also more cautious about privacy issues. They expected banks to be able to identify specific data breaches quickly in order to limit any damage as a result of fraud. In addition, with the growing number of nonbank processors in the marketplace who were generating numerous transactions within the banking systems, regulators scrutinized third-party arrangements much more closely to ensure that banks understood the underlying commercial purpose and ensure that a bank's operations were not hijacked for fraudulent purposes.

Citibank's E-Business Strategy

We are here to serve our clients: whatever our clients want us to do we'll do it for them. We're into e-business not because we're into the dot-com business; we're here because our clients want us to continue performing the basic banking functions for them on the web.

— *CAROLINE WONG, HEAD OF E-BUSINESS GROUP (CASH & TRADE), CITIBANK HONG KONG*[30]

Citibank's vision was to become the world's leading e-business enabler. It wanted to empower local, regional, and global customers and the business-to-business-to-consumer marketplace and provide solutions to help them take advantage of the efficiencies and opportunities created by e-commerce. Citibank's e-business strategy to "connect, transform and extend" was a means to deliver on its vision.

Meanwhile, with technology investments in the global financial service industry growing at a rate of 4.2 percent per year, Citibank tried to manage the overall costs of IT investments. The plan announced in April 2007 to overhaul IT operations included the consolidation of data centers; better use of existing technologies; optimization of global voice and data networks; standardization of its application-development processes; and vendor consolidation. As Citibank stated, "simplification and standardization of Citibank's information technology platform will be critical to increase efficiency and drive lower costs as well as decrease time to market."[32]

Citibank's E-Business Structure

In March 2000, Citigroup chief executive Sanford Weill announced the formation of the Internet Operation Group, a high-level committee charged with spreading

Citibank's E-Business Strategy[31]

CONNECT	TRANSFORM	EXTEND
Web-enable its core services to connect with its customers	Draw on the full range of Citibank's capabilities to deliver integrated solutions	Reach new markets, new customers, and new products

The Six Key Elements of Citibank's E-Business Strategy

- Embed Citibank as the trusted brand within communities
- Build a network of strategic partners
- Help customers to serve themselves
- Web-enable core services
- Create knowledge-based e-services
- 'e-Us'

Exhibit 4 Citibank's Global Transaction Services Awards in Asia, 2007

- Best Custodian in Asia; Best Fund Administrator in Asia (*Asia Asset Management*)
- Best Overall Cash Management Bank across all categories as voted by corporations; Best Electronic Banking Platform; Best at Understanding Business Strategies, Objectives, and Requirements as voted by financial institutions (*Asiamoney*)
- Best Transaction Bank in Asia; Best Cash Management Bank in Asia; Best Corporate Specialist in Asia (*The Asset*)
- Best Cash Management Bank; Best Cash Management Solutions (*FinanceAsia*)
- Asia's Best Investment Management Services; Best Corporate/Institutional Internet Bank in Asia (*Global Finance*)

responsibility for Internet activities more evenly between e-Citi, an incubator for Internet initiatives, and the bank's business units. In April 2000, the group announced the second phase of Citigroup's Internet activity, which involved the creation of two units aimed at infusing the Internet into all consumer and corporate banking activities: e-Consumer and e-Business. Both units were intended to complement e-Citi.[33] In May 2000, two new business units, e-Capital Markets and e-Asset Management, were added.

Jorge Bermudez, executive vice-president and head of Global Cash Management and Trade Services, was appointed to lead the e-Business unit.[34] Bermudez's e-Business unit was responsible for developing Internet software for corporate clients setting up B2B electronic commerce exchanges.

The new business units brought people from the business lines together with people from the Internet side of operations, which combined resources and eliminated duplication and competition. The new strategy of forming high-level committees reversed the centralized approach that Citigroup had pursued under John Reed, the driving force behind the formation of e-Citi.[35] Citigroup's new structure involved traditional business units in formulating Internet strategies and forming

committees to coordinate and synthesize an approach that mirrored that of other banks.[36]

In 2002, Global Transaction Services was created as a division of Citibank's Markets and Banking to integrate Cash, Trade, and Treasury Services and Global Securities Services. It offered integrated cash management, fund services, securities services, trade services, and finance to MNCs, financial institutions, and the public sector around the world (Exhibit 5). The objective was to help corporate customers gain greater control over financial positions both locally and globally, increase efficiency, and reduce costs.

Within just one year, Global Transaction Services was already tapped by 95 percent of Fortune 500 companies and profits grew 38 percent. With a global reach and local presence, Global Transaction Services had assets and businesses in several countries and regions. Its Internet-based cash management, electronic bill payment and online statements, reporting and analytics, securities processing, and other capabilities enabled corporate customers to re-engineer processes, manage working capital more effectively, and improve straight-through processing.

In 2006, Global Transaction Services already supported 65,000 clients, cleared an average of 752,000

Exhibit 5 Citigroup Organizational Structure

securities trades every week, and processed more than US$3 trillion in payments every day. On average, it held US$189 billion in liability balances under administration and US$10.4 trillion in assets under custody and trust, and had the world's largest commercial letter-of-credit portfolio, worth over US$7 billion.

Citibank's Alliance Strategy

Before 2000, Citibank had tried to excel at all facets of e-business—a strategy that failed. The company invested millions of dollars and tried to specialize in each area, including software development, systems development, and front-end services; however, clients and software technology were constantly changing and Citibank was struggling to keep pace with client needs. By 2000, Citibank's strategy focused on alliances and the use of its partners' strengths. Specifically, Citibank partnered with companies that had complementary technology, infrastructure, or access to markets. As Tom Edgerton, head of alliance for Citibank e-business, said, "In the future, it won't be what your company can do, but what the network of companies you work with can provide."[37]

Citibank's key technology players included Oracle, Commerce One Inc., SAP AG, Wisdom Technologies, and Bolero.net. In August 2000, four companies teamed up with Citibank to form FinancialSettlementMatrix .com, a company that connected buyers and sellers in e-marketplaces with payment processing, credit, and other services through multiple participating banks and financial service companies.[38] Citibank's challenge was managing the vendors and suppliers and ensuring that they understood Citibank's strategy and would not exploit the bank's existing strengths in the banking industry. Edgerton said of companies that had approached Citibank to partner with it: "Citibank brings considerable value to potential alliance partners. They're interested in our brand, our financial services expertise, our global presence, our strong customer relationships and position as a trusted provider, as well as our knowledge of specific industries and international markets."[39]

In 2004, Citibank acquired Lava Trading, a leader in electronic execution and sell-side order management systems. This acquisition enabled Citibank to offer institutional clients the benefits of the most sophisticated and robust electronic trading system in the market, with technology that complemented and enhanced their existing platforms and product ranges.

"Connect" in Citibank's E-Business Strategy

Customer convenience was the thrust of the continuous evolution of Citibank's products and services. Key to this goal was providing clients with more channels to access Citibank, and the Internet provided Citibank the flexibility to meet this demand. Jorge Bermudez, Citibank executive vice-president and head of e-Business, stated: "A core part of our e-business strategy is Web-enabling our current services. With CitiDirect, we are building the infrastructure that will serve as the foundation for many of the value-added services we are developing on the Internet."[40]

CitiDirect was designed for corporate customers to do full transactions online anywhere around the world.[41] It was a browser-based delivery channel designed to deliver all of Citibank's cash management and trade products and services online, enabling customers to make inquiries about their account balances, request statements, provide transaction initiation details, and request statement transaction reports online and in real time. CitiDirect allowed customers to perform these functions at any location with Internet access. This was particularly useful for global companies with operations spread out in many countries but wishing to maintain control at regional or global treasury centers.

CitiDirect was piloted in October 2000. In Asia, it was piloted in Singapore, Hong Kong, Australia, Japan, and Malaysia.[42] In 2000, CitiDirect was operating in 36 countries and available in five languages and was expected to be operating in 80 countries and 20 languages and doing a trillion U.S. dollars of business per day by 2002.[43] In May 2001, CitiDirect was already serving 1,000 corporate customers worldwide.

In 2003, Citibank upgraded CitiDirect Online Banking to offer complete payment, receivables, and trade capabilities in emerging markets. The service was made available in 90 countries and in 20 languages, and was awarded Best of the Web for 2003 by Forbes.com in the financial services category. In 2004 alone, this corporate banking platform processed more than 39 million transactions around the world. CitiDirect linked the back-office systems of 90 countries and allowed Citibank to replace its outdated and less-powerful systems and move training and customer services online.

In 2006, Citibank developed TreasuryVision, which was similar to CitiDirect. As Paul Galant, head of Global Cash Management for Citibank, noted, "We are putting a lot of energy behind it and TreasuryVision essentially meets the trends in the marketplace. It connects our clients not only to their internal systems, but it also connects to their enterprise resource planning systems."

TreasuryVision was staffed by world-class employees with expert knowledge of financial data. Once the data were proved by these experts, they would be put into a knowledge warehouse and provided to clients (i.e., corporate treasuries). Therefore, TreasuryVision would not only be an effective way of managing liquidity, but also be a useful channel for knowledge management.

"Transform" in Citibank's e-Business Strategy

Transaction processing, such as cash management, trade finance, and derivatives, was a back-office activity that was not at the forefront of customers' minds. Traditionally, transaction processing for a corporate customer (e.g., the transactional work involved in loan processing) was a function of the bank-customer relationship. Citibank's global presence translated to a huge transactional business and required supporting more than 200 data centers, which did basic, repeatable processes. In 1998, Citibank realized that, similar to any other factory product, this could be commoditized. At that point, Citibank began the transformation.

Regionalization

The transformation process involved consolidating all the data centers within each country and moving them to Singapore. Data were centralized and systems were developed to manage the automatic processing of transactions. By May 1999, the data centers were consolidated down to 60. On the operations side, Citibank began with the regionalization of cash and trade, which afforded Citibank a complete focus on the process. Approaches that Citibank used to decide the location for the regionalized centers were not mutually exclusive. It had considered the following in various combinations:

- Take the biggest infrastructure already existing (i.e., Singapore) and build it up to replace all the smaller centers.
- Ask where to get the best balance of all factors of production and start there from scratch (e.g., Penang)—Greenfield Approach.
- Rely on locally available people and skills (e.g., Sydney).
- Consider the pure cost of labor for lower-skilled areas such as voucher processing.

Singapore, which had back-office operations in several of the bank's business units, was the first processing center that was regionalized, followed by Penang[44] and Sydney's foreign-exchange and derivatives centers. The centers were time-zone-centric, so that decisions were based on the three continental time zones of Europe, Asia, and the Americas.

As a way to lower costs and improve efficiency, in 2006, Citibank reduced the number of data centers by 20 percent. In April 2007, in order to save the company more than US$10 billion, Citibank introduced a plan to overhaul its IT operations. It planned to further consolidate its existing data centers, better use its existing technologies, optimize its global voice and data networks, standardize its application development processes, and consolidate its vendor networks.

The regionalized and specialized processing centers provided Citibank scale and continual improvement opportunities. They reduced the cycle time for transactions, reduced error rates to nearly zero, and yielded new efficiencies for Citibank and its customers. As one manager noted:

We're now able to fragment the process and focus on the little pieces that make the difference, this also means that there's a lot of exchange of information and standardization of processes.

—VENRY KRISHNAKUMAR, CITIBANK VICE-PRESIDENT AND REGIONAL DIRECTOR, OPERATION AND TECHNOLOGY, ASIA-PACIFIC AND JAPAN[45]

Internalizing the Web

Within Citibank, there was a program to promote the e-workplace. The processing centers in particular had taken off through integrating the Web into their business processes. The transformations in the processing cycle focused on workflow automation; employees now had access to information without the need to make phone calls, check paper files, or send faxes. Processing centers had previously required millions of checks and huge reconcilement departments, which were paper-based and labor-intensive. The centralized and specialized processing locations made it easier for Citibank to integrate secure databases into the processing of a transaction. For example, signature-verification and digital-imaging systems were linked with the funds-transfer system.[46]

Straight-Through Automation

Citibank was continuously pushing the limits of straight-through automation by constantly deploying various initiatives. For example, Citibank conducted some artificial intelligence projects, such as prepopulating forms with historical data, which dramatically reduced error rates. It could select rejected transactions and take a look at a customer's history with similar transactions and try to predict what the customer would try to do.[47] The effective implementation of such projects was attributable to the qualified and experienced staff at Citibank.

The benefits of efficiency and cost savings also trickled down to Citibank's customers. In traditional transactions, customers deposited checks into ATMs or opened Letters of Credit by submitting the paperwork to banks, but they did not know when the banks would actually perform the task. With Citibank's straight-through processing, customers' expectations and need to know were matched because the processes took place online and in real time.

Achievements

Proof that Citibank was at the top of its league was the awards it received (Exhibit 4). Citibank was the first company in the financial services industry to receive a quality award for its cash-processing center or regional cash-process management unit (RCPMU).[48] Customer surveys showed that Citibank's RCPMU was rated higher than those of its competitors in the areas of accuracy, timeliness, accessibility, and responsiveness several years in a row. Processing was fast becoming one of Citibank's unique selling propositions. Citibank's commitment to excellence in its processing business translated to greater transparency of the process for customers, allowing them full access to information about the status of their transactions.

"Extend" in Citibank's E-Business Strategy

CitiDirect's roll-out was evidence of Citibank's vision of delivering transaction services online anywhere in the world at any time. Building a new global infrastructure gave Citibank the opportunity to deliver e-products at scale more quickly and efficiently, and any capability improvements in one region would be seamlessly deployed worldwide. Citibank expected CitiDirect to evolve constantly, which would give Citibank the flexibility to continuously enhance the system according to the changing needs of its customers. Other European banks focused mainly on providing pan-European solutions; very few banks wanted to deliver global services.

Citibank's priority was to move all its corporate customers onto CitiDirect because its main goal was to retire the legacy systems of electronic banking. Citibank had to contend, however, with difficulties in migrating customers from using traditional means to using the new products and services. Citibank's corporate clients included top-tier MNCs as well as SMEs. Previously, Citibank had not focused on SMEs; it was in 1997 that it started to consider the SME segment and introduced CitiBusiness.[49] While MNCs dealing in e-business knew what they wanted, SMEs that wanted an e-business presence were unsure how to move forward. Some were not even e-enabled and were still tied up with the legacy systems of the 1970s, 1980s, and 1990s. The greatest concern among most customers was security. Some resisted making the transition because they were skeptical about security, and such behavior was entrenched. CitiDirect had already developed sophisticated security procedures using the latest encryption techniques. Its multilayered security architecture included public and private access keys, single-use passwords, and multiple authorization controls. Despite Citibank's readiness, customer concerns about security did somewhat hinder Citibank's roll-out of Web-based applications.

In 2001, Citibank still provided services using legacy systems for conservative SME customers, while at the same time serving global customers such as MNCs that demanded to transact through the Internet. Citibank was aware that building customers' trust in the Web took years of education. To encourage conservative customers to embrace CitiDirect, Citibank's plan was to build a strategy that included a pricing incentive scheme.

The Citibank Advantage

Global Reach

As part of a global financial institution that employed over 268,000 employees in 100 countries, Citibank was uniquely positioned to serve its customers' global needs. In emerging markets, where 86 percent of the world's population lived and which accounted for 43 percent of the world's purchasing power, Citibank implemented an "embedded bank" strategy. Through this strategy, Citibank established roots in a country as deep as those of any local indigenous bank by building a broad customer base, offering diverse products, actively participating in the community, and recruiting staff and senior management from the local population. This local commitment and history, together with Citibank's global reach and expertise, was a powerful combination that set Citibank apart from its competition. In 2002, Citibank celebrated its 100th year of operations in China, Hong Kong, India, Japan, the Philippines, and Singapore.

Continuous Investment in Technology

Citibank was committed to upholding its position as a premier supplier of cash-management and transactional banking services and invested heavily in technology to improve its services. The main goal was to provide corporate customers the most cost-effective, cutting-edge, reliable, and secure solutions. As a Citibank senior executive explained, "We continuously invest in technology and it's one of our competitive advantages. We've been around a long time, we have been able to invest year after year, and we have seen compounded value from that. A new entrant would have a difficult time investing all at once, but by spending money on infrastructure—not on salespeople or front ends—I think that's how you stay in the position we're in."[50]

Technology was used as a means to achieve a strategic objective for Citibank. With the need to lower costs and improve efficiency, its investment in IT provided better client services at a lower cost. Chuck Prince, former chief executive of Citigroup, said, "One of our goals is to have more common systems and standards across Citigroup so clients can transact with us more easily, no matter what business is serving them or where they're conducting business."[51]

Conclusion

The Internet affected many areas of banking and changed how institutions make strategic decisions. At the same time, technology changed customers' expectations and needs. It was a challenge for Citibank to translate its traditional strengths to the Internet in a way that would add value for its customers. Citibank responded to this challenge by:

- Deploying Web-enabling access points to allow customers to connect seamlessly to Citibank.

- Building a new global infrastructure to deliver products and services online.
- Integrating products in new ways.

In a business environment where change was inevitable and competition was tough, Citibank needed a distinctive strategic direction that would create competitive advantages that would not be easily replicated by its competitors. Citibank also needed to make transformations on a global scale to deliver its e-business strategy and create a business culture that would embrace the e-banking concept, a key element of a highly integrated e-business, within a reasonable budget.

A key question for Citibank is how can it continue to be successful and stay ahead of the competition as Web-enabled technology diffuses through the banking industry? Also, what future trends will emerge that Citibank will need to address in order to continue to be in the lead?

NOTES

1. D. Baron & D. Besanko, 2001, Strategy, organization and incentives: Global corporate banking at Citibank, *Industrial and Corporate Change*, 10(1): 12–14.
2. Ibid.
3. Citigroup 2006 Annual Report.
4. D. Baron & D. Besanko, 2001, Strategy, organization and incentives: Global corporate banking at Citibank, *Industrial and Corporate Change*, 10(1): 12–14.
5. This section adapted from Citigroup, 2008, Global Transaction Services: Cash Management, http://www.transactionservices .citigroup.com/transactionservices/homepage/cash/cash_mgmt.htm (accessed February 18, 2008).
6. Introduced in the 1970s as an alternative to traditional check payments, ACH is a secure network connecting banks to each other. Direct deposits, electronic payments, money transfers, debit-card payments, business-to-business payments, and even tax transactions may be processed through the ACH network.
7. This section adapted from Citigroup, 2008, Global Transaction Services: Securities and Fund Services, "http://www.transactionservices .citigroup.com/transactionservices/homepage/securitiesfunds.htm (accessed February 18, 2008).
8. This section adapted from Citigroup, 2008, Global Transaction Services: Trade Services and Finance, http://www .transactionservices.citigroup.com/transactionservices/homepage/ trade/index.htm (accessed February 18, 2008).
9. Company interview in July 2001.
10. Citigroup 2006 Annual Report.
11. Deloitte, 2007, Global banking industry outlook: Issues on the horizon 2007, http://www.deloitte.com/cda/content/banking.pdf (accessed February 20, 2008).
12. Ibid.
13. J. Vijayan, 2007, Citigroup to lay off 17,000, overhaul IT operations, *ComputerWorld*, April 11.
14. A credit crunch is "a state in which there is a short supply of cash to lend to businesses and consumers and interest rates are high." Princeton University, 2008, Credit crunch, http://wordnet.princeton .edu/perl/webwn (accessed February 20, 2008).
15. C. Cockerill, 2001, Cash management takes to the Internet, *Euromoney*, 381(January): 105.
16. Greenwich Associates was an international research and consulting firm specializing in financial services. Greenwich Associates interviewed 500 corporate treasurers and other executives at middle-market companies in the United States and Canada in May–June 2001. See also: D. Rountree, 2001, Importance of on-line banking, *Bank Technology News*, 14(11): 86.
17. For example, if a company shipped a buyer 100 products at US$10 per piece, but five of the products were defective, the company might simply remit US$50 electronically without any information about the defective products. In such a case, there would be greater possibility of costly payment processes because of back-and-forth inquiries. The solution would be to send a paper explanation; however, this could translate to additional billing inquiries and disputes.
18. To use the ACH network, a company was required to have between US$10 million and US$50 million in annual revenues.
19. J. Jensen, 2007, Bank-to-corporate connectivity: The next stage, http://www.gtnews.com/article/6878.cfm, August 16 (accessed February 13, 2008).
20. SWIFTNet is a general-purpose, industry-standard solution for the financial industry. It provides an application-independent, single window interface to all the financial institutions around the globe.
21. EDIFACT is the international EDI standard developed by the United Nations.
22. ISO is a worldwide federation of National Standards Bodies. ISO20022 (UNIversal Financial Industry [UNIFI] message scheme) provides the financial industry with a common platform for the development of messages in a standardized XML syntax.
23. Ibid.
24. Ibid.
25. The Sarbanes-Oxley Act of 2002 is a U.S. federal law enacted in response to a number of major corporate and accounting scandals, which establishes new or enhanced standards for all U.S. public company boards, management, and public accounting firms.
26. P. Clark, 2001, No longer banking on exchanges, *B to B*, 86(13): 13.
27. S. DeZoysa, 2007, A strategy for future growth: Banking challenges and trends, http://www.gtnews.com/feature/201.cfm, August 16 (accessed February 12, 2008).

28. The Basel Accords are issued by the Basel Committee on Banking Supervision to make recommendations on banking laws and regulations. Basel II is the second of the Basel Accords, discussing how much capital banks need to put aside to prepare for the types of financial and operational risks they face.

29. A. Papanikolaou, 2007, Impact of Basel II on bank's IT strategies, http://www.gtnews.com/article/6875.cfm, August 16 (accessed February 13, 2008).

30. Company interview in July 2001.

31. 2001, CitiDirect online banking—a new era in business banking, *Asiamoney*, May, 84.

32. J. Vijayan, 2007, "Citigroup to lay off 17,000, overhaul IT operations, *Computerworld*, April 11.

33. Robert Willumstad was head of e-Consumer while Edward Horowitz was head of e-Citi.

34. Bermudez reported to Victor Menezes, chairman and chief executive of Citibank, and to the IOG.

35. Reed resigned from his co-CEO post on April 18, 2000.

36. For example, Wells Fargo & Co. and Chase Manhattan Corp. integrated their efforts on using the Internet more closely with their business units.

37. Citibank, 2000, Citibank seeks alliances to accelerate into the e-space, *The Citibank Globe*, http://www.citibank.com/e-business/, November–December (accessed December 3, 2001).

38. Citibank partner companies were Enron Broadband Services (a delivery platform), i2 Technologies (an integrated open-architecture solution), S1 Corporation (a provider of Internet-based payment processing), and Wells Fargo & Company (a provider of complementary services to the entire e-business market).

39. Citibank, 2000, Citibank seeks alliances to accelerate into the e-space, *The Citibank Globe*, http://www.citibank.com/e-business/, November–December (accessed December 3, 2001).

40. Ibid.

41. During the development of CitiDirect, Citibank asked its customers what they wanted from e-commerce and the Internet. Customers put a premium on security, stability, speed, accuracy, and user-friendliness.

42. 2001, CitiDirect online banking—a new era in business banking, *Asiamoney*, May, 83.

43. C. Power, 2000, Citibank deploys its Web troops into business lines, *American Banker*, 165(230), 1.

44. In Singapore, front-end securities processing was also regionalized; however, due to local settlement issues, the back-end processing of securities transactions still needed to be done in individual countries.

45. 2001, Processing comes to the fore, *Finance Asia*, May, 83.

46. A system similar to SWIFT and Forex systems.

47. 2001, Processing comes to the fore, *Finance Asia*, May, 83.

48. The center processed up to US$20 billion worth of transactions daily.

49. CitiBusiness was a one-stop financing solution offered to SME entrepreneurs. Products and services included: CitiBusiness Direct (Internet banking); Cash Management; Trade Services and Trade Finance (trade products); CitiCorp Commercial Finance (asset-based finance); treasury products such as Spot and Forward Foreign Exchange, Interest Rate Hedging, and Yield Enhancement Investment Products; and a customer center. The customer center provided CitiService (an integrated customer inquiry line for after-sales services), Document Collection (an express collection service), CitiFax (a convenient way to update account information) and CitiBusiness Direct (providing online access to account information and transaction initiation).

50. *Finance Asia*, 2001, Processing comes to the fore, May, 83.

51. Citigroup 2005 Annual Report.

From Low Cost to Global Leadership: Computime (Hong Kong) Leads through Innovation

Robert C. Wolcott, Michael J. Lippitz

Northwestern University, Kellogg School of Management

In 2007, Computime management could look back on more than 30 years of steady growth. Founded in 1974 in Hong Kong by mechanical engineer Auyang Ho (hereafter referred to as "Mr. Auyang"), the company had grown from a small manufacturer of digital clocks to a global electronic controls enterprise with operations in Asia, Europe, the Middle East, and North America. Mr. Auyang's son, "Bernie" Auyang Pak Hong (hereafter referred to as "Auyang"), was now CEO. Under their combined leadership, Computime successfully implemented two five-year plans that had brought revenues to more than US$300 million and gained the company a listing on the Hong Kong Exchange.

However, competition in Computime's core markets had markedly increased over the last few years, intensified by the Chinese government's policies encouraging the establishment of new technology companies. Concurrently, overall demand for labor and raw materials in Southeast China had raised costs. Computime's manufacturing centers in Guangzhou, located in mainland China near Hong Kong, no longer benefited from cheap labor compared to that provided farther inland in China or in parts of Southeast Asia.

Auyang realized that Computime needed to find new ways to add value beyond low-cost mass production and small-scale product customization. Computime would need to contribute its own solutions (i.e., conceiving, designing, and manufacturing more of its clients' products) and develop its own brands. In 2004 Computime built a new research and development (R&D) team, followed in 2006 by a dedicated R&D facility in mainland China. The company also introduced its own line of branded products under the Salus name in the United Kingdom.

By 2007 R&D had established its value and Salus had achieved significant success in the United Kingdom with plans for rollout throughout Europe, but challenges remained. How should R&D coordinate with business units? To what extent should R&D engage with customers in Computime's diverse markets? How far beyond the company's core businesses should R&D explore? What would be the implications of transitioning from designing and producing products for customers to producing proprietary branded products?

Surveying the sprawling Hong Kong skyline from afar, Auyang stood prepared to make significant decisions regarding Computime's future. What should they be?

The Contract Manufacturing Industry

Since the late 1970s, companies in many industries had expanded their use of electronic manufacturing services (EMS) (i.e., contract manufacturers) for their electronic components. Typically, an electronics products company such as Philips, Siemens, or Motorola would develop and design new products to precise specifications and then transfer the plans to contract manufacturers for production. The first large player in this space, Solectron, was founded in the United States in the late 1970s.

The trend toward EMS particularly benefited an emerging breed of Asian companies such as Flextronics (Singapore), as well as U.S.-based companies that introduced Asian production, such as Solectron, Jabil, and Sanmina-SCI. Electronics manufacturing was a growth industry, and offered better business opportunities than more traditional ventures such as textile manufacturing for the millions of people who migrated from agricultural to urban industrial settings. Asian governments encouraged the development of technology companies of this sort for the high-quality jobs and technical skills they helped generate.

Until the 1990s, most contract manufacturers did not design new products. Rather, they produced what others had designed. Motivated to increase margins and responding to requests from customers, some contract manufacturers developed in-house design capabilities as a service for their clients. They became known as original design manufacturers (ODMs). As the industry evolved, some branded electronics products companies began relying on ODMs for more and more of their product development, from concept definition through design and manufacturing. By 2005 the contract manufacturing industry had reached global revenues of approximately US$190 billion, representing the combination of EMS ($116.5 billion) and ODM ($73.6 billion)

(see Exhibit 1 for the top 10 EMS and ODM companies worldwide in 2007).[1]

From Digital Clocks to Global Automated Controls Supplier

Computime's First Hit Leads to Growth and New Markets

The digital clock was invented in 1956. Early models used cathode ray tubes to display digits and were employed in expensive instrumentation, often by the military. By the early 1970s, advances in semiconductor technology, light-emitting diodes, liquid crystals, and conductive glass allowed digital clock technology to be realized in consumer electronics, most popularly in digital watches (see Exhibit 2 for a historical summary of Computime sales and major events).

Raymond Auyang, Mr. Auyang's brother, saw an opportunity to produce digital clocks more cheaply in Hong Kong than in the United States, Europe, or Japan.

Exhibit 1 Electronic Manufacturing Services (EMS) and Original Design Manufacturers (ODM) Industry Leaders, 2007 (US$ in millions)

TOP TEN EMSs					
2007 Rank	2006 Rank	Company Name	2007 Annual Revenue	2006 Annual Revenue	Change (%)
1	1	Foxconn	54,706	39,253	39
2	2	Flextronics	33,346	28,876	15
3	4	Jabil	12,432	11,087	12
4	5	Sanmina-SCI	10,138	10,872	−7
5	6	Celestica	8,069	8,811	−8
6	7	Elcoteq	5,740	5,139	11
7	8	Benchmark	2,915	2,907	0
8	9	Venture	2,617	1,971	33
9	10	USI	2,046	1,676	22
10	NA	Plexus	1,624	1,513	7
		Total Top 10	133,633	112,105	19

(Continued)

Case 8: From Low Cost to Global Leadership

Exhibit 1 Electronic Manufacturing Services (EMS) and Original Design Manufacturers (ODM) Industry Leaders, 2007 (US$ in millions) (*Continued*)

			TOP TEN ODMs		
2007 Rank	2006 Rank	Company Name	2007 Annual Revenue	2006 Annual Revenue	Change (%)
1	2	Quanta	23,259	14,170	64
2	1	Asustek	23,033	17,348	33
3	3	Compal	13,634	9,410	45
4	6	Wistron	8,658	6,603	31
5	4	TPV	8,419	7,238	16
6	5	Inventec	7,191	7,167	0
7	7	Lite-On	5,760	5,048	14
8	N/A	Innolux	4,806	3,207	50
9	10	Mitac Intl	2,558	2,540	1
10	8	Inventec App	2,378	3,389	−30
		Total Top 10	99,696	76,120	31

CEO Presentation; Data by iSuppli Corp. 2007 figures are preliminary.

He presented the idea to Mr. Auyang, who had experience in building and managing manufacturing facilities. Mr. Auyang agreed, and in 1974 they gathered a group of 15 engineers to start development and production. Computime became the first company in the region to produce mass-market digital clocks.

Digital clocks soon became standard equipment in automobiles and numerous other products. By 1979 Computime had delivered more than one million devices to customers in North America and Europe. In 1980 it built a manufacturing facility in neighboring Guangzhou, China, making the company an early mover into the newly created special economic zones (SEZs) set up by the Chinese government in the Deng Xiaoping era. Deng's government (Deng never held the official "head of state" position but was recognized during most of this period as China's undisputed leader) instituted widespread economic reforms to transform China from a traditional communist state to a socialist market economy, creating what Deng referred to as "socialism with Chinese characteristics." The SEZs allowed foreign direct investment and other economic liberalizations for specific geographic areas. The National People's Congress

passed "Regulations for the Special Economic Zone of Guangdong Province" in August 1980. Computime completed its Guangzhou facility soon after.

However, Mr. Auyang recognized that the company's products would become commoditized due to intensified competition from other companies making similar products. He decided to create "something that does more than show time." Computime's engineering team expanded the functionality of its product lines to include programmability (i.e., the ability to switch devices on and off at prescribed times). In the early 1980s, Mr. Auyang challenged his company to learn how to make temperature control devices to replace the largely mechanical thermostats of the time. (The Honeywell electronic programmable thermostat had already been invented, but it served a small niche market.) Computime became the first Chinese company to introduce appliance timers and electronic thermostats.

By focusing on manufacturing quality and efficiency, as well as tracking the latest product trends from the United States and Europe, Computime expanded overseas. The company opened its first office in the United States in 1982. It moved its manufacturing

Exhibit 2 Total Computime Sales and Major Events in Company History

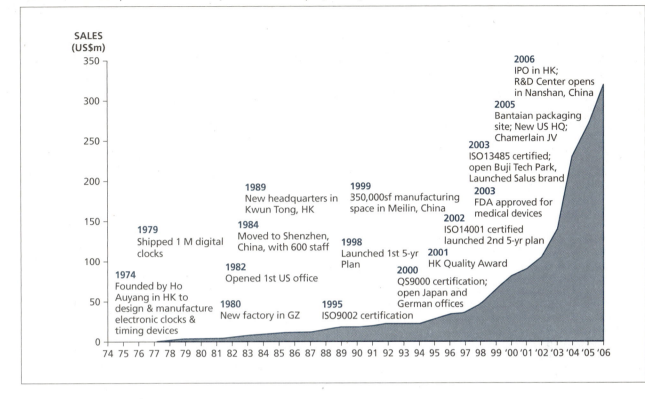

operations and 600 employees to Shenzhen, China, in 1984, further betting on the then-nascent transformation of the Chinese economy. Beginning in 1987, Mr. Auyang vertically integrated development, manufacturing, and sales to enhance quality control, efficiency, and responsiveness. As staff size grew to include more than 1,000 people in 1989, the company opened corporate headquarters in Kwun Tong, Hong Kong, to better access global markets and world-class management expertise.

Computime became an early convert to the International Standards Organization (ISO) certification standards for manufacturing practices. It became ISO 9002 certified in 1995, ahead of many manufacturers of comparable size in the United States and Europe.[2] The company also worked hard to instill the values of teamwork and responsibility for the community promulgated by its founder.

The First Five-Year Plan, 1997–2002

The goal of the first five-year strategic plan was to grow the company to US$100 million in revenues. As part of the plan, Computime expanded its manufacturing capacity and opened its first dedicated offices in Europe and Japan. Its relentless focus on quality and efficiency was

recognized with the Hong Kong Industry Grand Prize for Quality in 2001, ISO 14001 certification in 2002, and U.S. Food and Drug Administration approval for the manufacture of medical devices for the U.S. market in 2003.

The five-year plan also paved the way for new management systems. The company grew over many years by pursuing leading trends in time-based programmable electronics products and building high-quality, efficient manufacturing capabilities. While this strategy worked, it relied largely on the insight and direction of the company founder. Like entrepreneurs worldwide, Mr. Auyang knew that he would eventually need to transfer leadership to the next generation. He also recognized that his growing company required an expanded professional management team.

Mr. Auyang's son Bernie Auyang represented the future. Having started on the production line and in the warehouse, Auyang worked in the finance, sales, and marketing departments before becoming president in 1998 and CEO in 2002. Although Mr. Auyang remained chairman, he provided his son with increasing autonomy, particularly in hiring and setting the overall strategic direction of the company. Computime also added an exceptionally effective chief operations officer (COO), Choi Po Yee (Alice), and invested her with substantial authority over day-to-day operations.

One of Auyang's first hires, in 1998, was Wei Long (W. L.) Ha as chief of engineering. Ha brought experience in new product development for telecommunications products companies, as well as advanced degrees in electronic systems design and industrial management. He developed and implemented a formal new product introduction (NPI) process based on state-of-the-art stage-gate processes and built up Computime's Chinese engineering force. (Computime could hire three mainland Chinese engineers for the same cost as a single Hong Kong engineer.)

In 2000 Computime split into business units in order to better focus on distinct customer groups. The business unit structure evolved as market opportunities changed. In 2002, business units included building and home controls, appliance controls, and commercial and industrial controls. Appliance controls was originally part of building and home controls but split off when the market became large enough to justify an independent division. Ha became president of building and home controls, the largest business unit. Exhibit 3 depicts the 2007 Computime organizational chart and Exhibit 4 lists major product lines by business unit and major OEM customers.

Despite respectable growth from these initiatives, Auyang realized that many new Chinese companies would soon be competing with them in contract manufacturing. More and more companies were becoming proficient at turning a specification into a product with good quality control. If Computime wanted to continue to grow and prosper, it would need to continue to find new opportunities.

The Second Five-Year Plan, 2002–2007

Computime began the development of its new strategic direction by examining how it could maintain its margins and grow to a US$300 million company over

Exhibit 3 Computime's Organization Structure

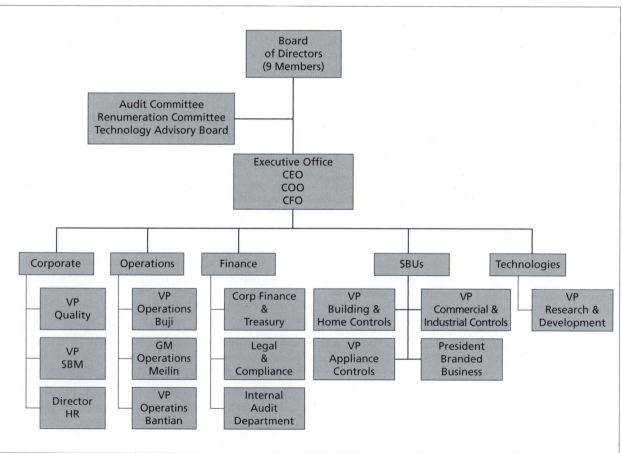

Exhibit 4 Computime's Products and Major Clients

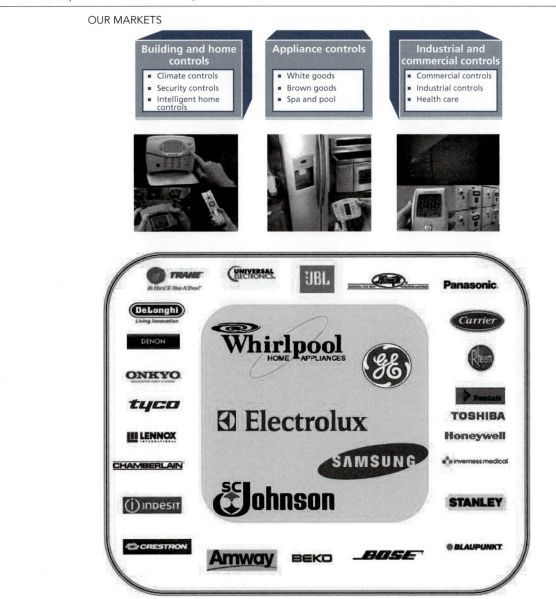

Source: CEO Presentation.

the next five years. Computime management concluded that it would need to create its own opportunities by innovating across its core technology platforms. This would allow it to create new customer solutions, and in certain areas introduce its own branded products. In the past, Computime had assigned patents to its customers. Now it would seek to develop its own intellectual property through R&D. Rather than being strictly an EMS or ODM company, Computime would become an Asian control technology leader (see Exhibit 5 for global locations).

Branded Products

One of the first growth initiatives in the second five-year plan was to move into branded products, in addition to serving as a contract manufacturer. In 2002 Computime formed a partnership with Sensotec of the United Kingdom, a leader in safety electronics, to create Salus Controls plc, with a focus on thermostats, timers, and valves. In 2004, Computime acquired a controlling interest in Salus and in 2006 acquired the remaining stock. Since 2004, Salus doubled its product sales in the United Kingdom. Dean Jepson, managing director of Salus, saw

Exhibit 5 Computime's Global Presence

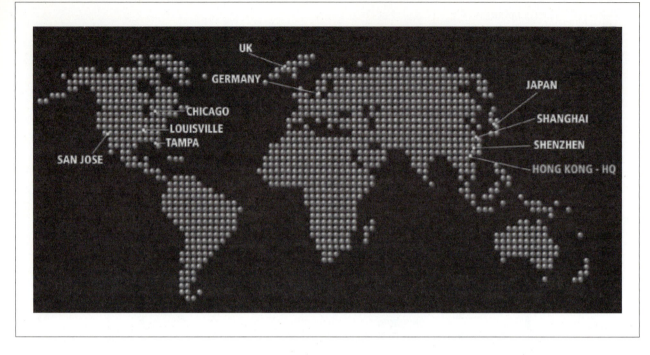

the Computime/Sensotec partnership as helping Salus become "a leading international brand." Commenting on the 2006 equity investment, Jepson said:

It's taken us just two years, in a crowded… market, for Salus to become widely renowned for its unparalleled product offering, technical support, and after-sales service. With additional substantial investment from Computime in product development and ambitious marketing strategies, we look forward to penetrating existing and new markets.[33]

In addition to expanding geographically across Europe, Salus worked on developing solar energy products to take advantage of that fast-growing segment.

Going Public

In order to raise money to finance the company's growth—i.e., its R&D strategy, strategic acquisitions, and geographic expansion—Computime became a publicly traded company on the Hong Kong exchange in October 2006. In its prospectus, it identified high-margin opportunities in "high-technology controls" used in equipment such as power turbines and medical testing devices. Computime indicated that it wanted to acquire "other controls manufacturing technologies" and "proprietary and innovative engineering processes." As for geographic expansion, in 2007 Salus products launched in Germany and France, with plans to eventually be sold throughout Europe. Computime also began seeking partnerships with its OEMs to expand its presence in China and elsewhere.

The IPO was about more than raising capital. Contrary to many family companies' perspectives, Auyang, his father, and the rest of the board believed that building a public company traded on a sophisticated exchange would instill discipline and rigor in management and raise awareness within global capital markets. Computime welcomed the enhanced scrutiny, even as it faced increased pressure to report and perform. Consistent with its move into more technologically sophisticated solutions, the move to the public markets also allowed the company to institute a stock option plan to attract and retain experienced professionals.

Toward an Innovation Capability

Finding the Right R&D Strategy and Organizational Solution

Consistent with the company's heritage, Computime R&D projects were driven by the requirements of customers, as opposed to exploratory research. To jumpstart the process, it acquired a 40 percent stake in an external company, Perception Digital, in 2006. However, it quickly found that the cultures of the two organizations were incompatible and sold its stake in Perception Digital within the year. This experience persuaded Auyang that an internal R&D group made more sense for Computime. It would reflect the existing culture of integrity, teamwork, and a "can-do" attitude. The new R&D focus was expected to enhance this basic culture, not represent a radical change. In Auyang's mind,

Computime had been an innovative leader in contract manufacturing and customization. That early spirit of innovation remained, but the company had become too focused on near-term, tactical objectives.

At first, the engineering departments of the business units argued that they could take on the R&D task as an expansion of their day-to-day responsibilities. Auyang felt that R&D personnel needed to report directly to him, but he agreed to disperse them among the business units. They became a "soft function" within the units. After several months, it became clear that, because R&D engineers were next to the engineering departments in the factories, they were routinely being pulled in to help solve near-term problems or just build minor new features into existing products. Auyang decided that Computime required an external R&D center.

To determine how best to proceed, Auyang worked with senior leadership to select focal areas for technology development. What were the key market drivers in automated controls? Which emerging technologies would be of significance across Computime's business units? Which of these areas represented the best opportunities for the company, given its competencies and customers?

After extensive discussions and benchmarking against industry leaders, Computime's management settled on three pillars—which came to be known as its "3Es strategy"—for its new growth strategy in automated controls:

- Environmentally friendly
- Energy efficient
- Easy to use

Computime also identified five initial technology arenas:

- Wireless (Zigbee[4])
- Variable motor control
- Human-machine interface
- Sensors
- Software control

In 2004 Auyang asked W. L. Ha to become the first head of R&D. Ha was reluctant, as he had already achieved 20 percent growth in the building and home controls unit. He would be giving up business unit leadership in exchange for leadership of a handful of people and a portfolio of R&D projects. He suggested Auyang hire someone from the outside with experience as an R&D lead. However, Auyang wanted to retain continuity and ensure a close working relationship between R&D and engineering. He reasoned that the engineering department would need to adopt R&D projects when they matured and apply them in their markets, so the linkage had to be strong. More importantly, management at Computime relied strongly on trust. It would be important to have an experienced and respected insider lead the new effort.

Ha eventually agreed to make the move to R&D, though he retained his leadership of the building and home controls unit until October 2005. Ha began building an R&D capability by bringing in a small number of top internal people who possessed both technical skill and open-minded personalities. He found that most of these people, by virtue of their forward-thinking tendencies, did not necessarily fit well into the engineering culture of the business units or were not being well managed by their supervisors. He eventually located 10 people inside the company who wanted to be part of the R&D enterprise. (Coincidentally, during this period, the heads of the two other Computime business units were changed, reducing resistance to internal reassignments.)

After Ha selected these 10 internal people, he began hiring from the outside until he had built the organization to 35 people. He hired certain people primarily for their technical skills related to the five initial project areas identified during the strategic planning for the R&D function, while others were hired for their innovative vision.

In June 2006, Computime opened a stand-alone R&D center in Nanshan, China, in the Shenzhen High Technology Park. This enabled most of Computime's R&D personnel to work next door to researchers from other corporate R&D centers, rather than near factory engineers. In addition, a handful of engineers remained in Hong Kong and a few in the United States.

Converting Vision to Action

The creation of a separate R&D center raised the challenge of how to best keep R&D connected to the corporation's strategy. To maintain focus, Auyang repeatedly communicated his clear and simple vision for the company (the 3Es), but now the entire company needed to act. As Bob Cheng, director of engineering, noted, "An idea you act on is innovation. One you don't act on is a dream."

Everyone knew Computime's priorities were technology, manufacturing, and brand (see Exhibit 6). Internal communication regarding the value of R&D initiatives for Computime's success with technology and branding helped build respect within the company for the new center. To critique and adjust the strategic direction, Computime instituted a technical advisory board. Auyang and Ha served on the board with outside experts from local universities and major businesses in Computime's universe of partners.

R&D also needed to synchronize with its business units, a common problem for corporate innovation programs. The mission for R&D was to develop

Exhibit 6 Computime's Business Model: TMB

BUSINESS MODEL

TMB

Technology Research and Development

Technology Product Design and Engineering

Optimized ODM Manufacturing

Brand Management

Low-cost business model with global distribution offers complete "end-to-end" solution at key stages of the production process

technology platforms for incorporation into products three to five years in the future. The business units were more focused on the near-term market potential. Kairy Lei, an up-and-coming young R&D manager, articulated the problem well: "How do you know when it's time to involve the business unit? When should marketing become involved, and how?"

Early on, the R&D center sometimes extended its work into commercialization, though this occasionally caused friction with business unit engineers accustomed to owning projects. There also were concerns over who would take the credit or blame for a project's results. To manage these issues, Ha began personally working with the business units to help transition R&D projects. Computime also developed more defined methods for keeping both R&D and engineering staff appropriately involved and engaged during commercialization, for example, with informal recognition rewards.

Lei said that R&D engineers would be motivated by seeing the results of their work in the marketplace. Stories of which projects succeeded and why were to be actively shared, though by 2007 there were still no *formal* communication channels between R&D and business unit engineers. There were, however, informal exchanges in which business unit engineers made extended visits to the R&D center. An internal meeting on thermostat technology built understanding between R&D and business unit engineers and helped them to synchronize their efforts.

It was also a challenge to train R&D engineers hired in mainland China. While mainland Chinese

engineers tended to have a stronger theoretical basis in their training than their Hong Kong counterparts, they were less accustomed to working in an environment of regular change, where mistakes were tolerated and new approaches and ideas were not only acceptable but necessary. Even Internet access restrictions in China could present real problems interacting with external venues such as interoperability standards organizations. Chinese engineers also tended to be less accustomed to sharing problems, offering ideas, and working in teams. They had typically not been well trained in careful documentation of goals and processes.

Cheng, whose background included design engineering and product development, trained engineers in the R&D center to devise and propose design improvements. He also focused on finding those with an aptitude for English, allowing them to become more directly involved in customer engagements. Hong Kong managers were also integrated into client-facing projects to ensure R&D engineers did not inadvertently reveal intellectual property.

Andrew Li, the head of building and home controls, believed that by 2007 the process was working well. The R&D center's Zigbee wireless platform proved effective at connecting controls throughout the home. Li's engineers piloted technologies from the R&D center and found ways to improve the performance and reliability of their applications. They were able to showcase the new capabilities to potential customers, customizing the message to focus on price for retail markets and reliability for industrial markets.

Business units also began providing feedback to the R&D center. One of Li's customers, seeking ways to improve energy efficiency in fan motors, approached Computime for help. R&D devised an innovative way of controlling air flow and speed. Computime later considered applying the technology to other variable motor control applications.

Where to From Here?

By 2007, Computime had come a long way. The R&D function had gained some credibility. Business unit leadership witnessed R&D's output and support for leading-edge customer needs, but they also experienced a mandated change in priorities. Auyang and his executive team held regular corporate performance reviews attended by business unit heads and second-level directors, which began to include innovation objectives.

Validation also came from customers. As Computime's reputation for innovation grew, customers increasingly approached the company with development challenges. In the future, Auyang and Ha wanted to make this kind of deeper customer interaction more organized rather than dealt with on a case-by-case basis.

They also wondered how Computime could proactively reach out to customers to understand their needs and invest R&D resources in a "customer-leading" fashion, rather than waiting for requests. The company served customers in increasingly varied industries and geographies as the business expanded in Europe, North America, and the Middle East. How could Computime manage such diverse requirements across multiple industries and remain experts?

Other challenges loomed. Ha pointed out that while R&D made great progress since 2004, the development process could be more rigorous. Moreover, while the 3Es and Five Technologies provided an excellent foundation, Auyang and Ha needed to determine how and when to evolve Computime's technology strategy. What role should R&D play in this process? What about the business units—how should projects transition and how should the various groups interact? Moreover, everyone was proud of the solid values they had been able to maintain throughout Computime's growth, and they were mindful of the need to continue maintaining the essence of this successful family-run company (see Exhibit 7).

Perhaps most challenging, how could Computime continue its successful transition from contract

Exhibit 7 Computime's Social Value Statement

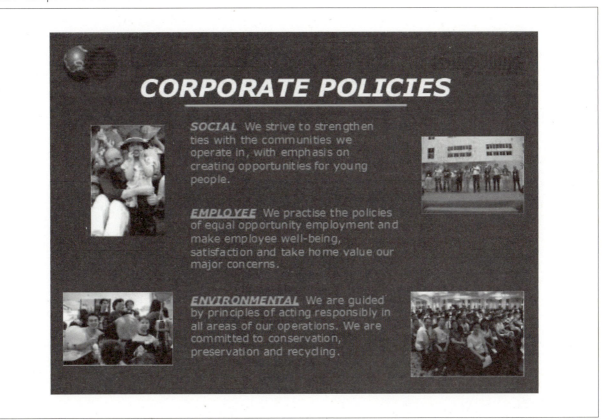

manufacturer to a true global leader offering its own branded products without endangering customer trust? Shen Owyang, business development director, summarized the challenge of Computime's evolution: "Getting over the OEM mentality has been a challenge for Computime, but the relentless management effort from the top is beginning to filter down. Today we learn from our mistakes. There is no shame."

As Auyang prepared for the first annual shareholders meeting since the IPO, he pondered what to do next. In the end, he recognized that innovation meant not only new products, but also new ways of operating, attracting and retaining talent, pleasing customers, and achieving long-term growth. Auyang reasoned, "Innovating is hard work … but it's the only way we'll be a global player in the long run."

NOTES

1. Consultancy iSuppli Corporation, http://www.isuppli.com.
2. ISO 9002 is "maintained by ISO, the International Organization for Standardization, and is administered by accreditation and certification bodies." Some of the requirements include procedures for key business processes, monitoring and record-keeping processes, checking output for defects, and facilitating continual improvement. See Wikipedia, ISO 9000, http://en.wikipedia.org/wiki/ISO_9000.
3. 2007, Salus announces major developments, http://www.buildingtalk.com/news/saz/saz102.html, June 20 (accessed April 5, 2008).
4. Zigbee was a wireless networking protocol for which Computime made compatible products.

*George Griffith, Tiffany Johnson, Rebecca Sebald,
Tracey Cowan, Nick Trotter, and Alfred Wong*

Arizona State University

*It's customers that made Dell great in the first place, and
if we're smart enough and quick enough to listen to customer
needs, we'll succeed.*

—**MICHAEL DELL**

Dell Inc., founded in 1984 by present CEO and chairman
of the board Michael Dell, is a leading technology
provider that designs, develops, manufactures, and
supports PCs, software and peripherals, storage and
servers, and associated services. The public company is
headquartered in Round Rock, Texas, with operations
in three geographic regions: the Americas; Europe, the
Middle East, and Africa (EMEA); and Asia Pacific–
Japan (APJ). Additionally Dell has business centers and
manufacturing sites in more than 20 locations around
the world. Dell operates primarily on a direct customer
sales business model that provides it with in-depth
customer knowledge so that solutions can be effectively
tailored to meet customer needs. Since its founding, Dell
has expanded its core business model by broadening its
product portfolio and adding distribution partners (retail,
value-added resellers, and distributors) that allowed Dell
to reach more than 24,000 retail locations worldwide in
FY09.[1]

Over the past two decades, Dell has been very
successful with the direct customer sales business model,
with an average annual revenue growth of 10 percent
annually. Dell shipped 43 million units in FY09 and held
a 15.1 percent share of the worldwide computer systems
market, enjoying 11.1 percent growth, which exceeded
industry worldwide computer systems growth of
9.7 percent (in terms of sales). In April 2008, Dell was the top
PC provider in the United States and second worldwide in
terms of sales; however, the top position in the United States
was overtaken by Hewlett-Packard (HP) in the first quarter
of 2009.[2] Revenue growth has stalled, with fiscal year 2009
(FY09 ending January 30) revenues of $61.101 billion

compared to FY08 revenues of $61.133 billion. PCs,
their largest product revenue stream, experienced a
12 percent decline. Dell's average selling price (total
revenue per unit sold) also decreased 7 percent year-
over-year, which is attributed to changes in revenue mix
from commercial to consumers, lower selling prices in
retail, and an increasingly competitive environment.
Amidst the economic downturn, corporate IT spending
continues to weaken, with worldwide PC shipments
declining 6.5 percent in the first quarter of 2009. With 80
percent of Dell's sales coming from corporate buyers, the
scaled-back spending has directly impacted Dell's market
share, with Dell shipping 16.7 percent fewer computers
worldwide in Q1 2009 versus Q1 2008.[3]

On December 31, 2008, Dell announced it would reorganize its business units from regional segments to four
globally operated areas—large enterprise, public sector,
small and medium businesses, and global consumer—to
better align with customer needs for "faster innovation
and globally standardized products and services."[4]

History of Dell Inc.

In 1984, while still a student at the University of Texas and
with only $1,000 to his name, Michael Dell founded PCs
Limited, the original name of Dell Inc., and introduced its
first computer, the Turbo, the following year. The company
changed its name to Dell Computer Corporation in 1988
and ultimately to Dell Inc. in 2004 to recognize its expansion beyond a PC-only business. Dell's Web site began
selling computers in 1996, and the company overtook
Compaq as the largest seller of PCs in the United States in
1999. In 2006, Dell acquired computer hardware manufacturer Alienware and both ASAP Software Express Inc. and
EqualLogic in 2008. Since its founding in 1984, Dell Inc.
has grown to employ approximately 78,900 employees.

Note: This case was written to be used as a basis for class discussion rather than to illustrate either effective or ineffective handling of an administrative situation.
We would like to thank Robert E. Hoskisson and Robert E. White for useful feedback in writing this case. Data was collected from publically available sources.

The early business model (1984–1990) was to assemble computers comparable to those of the more widely known IBM and target the price-conscious but tech-savvy consumer segment with lower prices. Dell was able to purchase parts and build their products in house, selling them at a fraction of the price that IBM could offer. It then took orders directly from customers (keeping advertising costs low), built the products to order (keeping inventory costs low), and provided a high level of customer service when delivering the end product.[5] Dell quickly moved into the top position in the direct-mail computer market, specializing in inexpensive PCs.[6] In 1984, Dell grossed $6 million in sales, increasing to $40 million the following year.

In order to sustain growth, the company brought the Tandy Group as consultants in 1987 to create a sales force focused on diversifying their customer base. While profits rose initially, Dell was unwilling to modify its direct customer sales business model to a more traditional sales approach with higher advertising spending and larger sales force, so most of the Tandy Group employees were released within the year. Around the same time, Dell opened new offices in London and Canada, allowing them to garner the attention of corporations, government, and educational consumers. This provided the foundation for the company to go public in June 1988, when they sold 3.5 million shares at $8.50 a share.[7]

Shortly after going public, Dell faced severe competition from several Japanese manufacturers offering similar products at lower prices. In response, Dell increased R&D spending and hired a computer scientist from IBM to manage the R&D staff and increase the technological sophistication of their product offerings. Dell also faced massive holding costs due to underestimating the change in demand the Japanese competition brought. Dell, in fact, had increased capacity substantially to accommodate the previously increasing demand, which resulted in unsold inventory.

To improve its management processes, Dell increased its emphasis on the corporate customer which resulted in a large increase in sales from the corporate segment, from 15 percent of sales in 1987 to 40 percent in 1990.[8] From 1990 to 2000, Dell opened new offices in Italy, France, and Ireland, allowing them to serve Europe, the Middle East, and Africa's larger corporations, offering powerful server solutions. At this time, they also worked to diversify their sales channels by introducing their products in large computer retail stores. As a result, Dell became the sixth-largest PC producer in the United States, and the focus on customer service earned them a #1 rating in J.D. Power and Associates's first survey of PC customer satisfaction.[9] By 1991, Dell had their first laptop PC available for purchase to cater to the fastest-growing segment of the PC market.

In response to the recession and ongoing price wars with PC makers Compaq, IBM, and Apple, Dell made steep price cuts, lowering their profit margins dramatically. Compaq, in particular, had released a lower-end PC that was priced competitively while offering increased customer service, which appealed to Dell's target consumers. Within the next few years, Dell also expanded their product portfolio to include fax machines and compact discs.

In the mid 1990s, "Dell introduced a line of network servers and was soon the fastest-growing company in the server sector."[10] Shortly thereafter, the company implemented an online channel for consumers to place their orders directly. They also strengthened their market position by opening a manufacturing plant in Malaysia. In the late 1990s, they began producing workstations and storage products as well as offering a leasing program that allowed customers to avoid maintaining a system as it became older and more obsolete. In 1998, they built a production and sales facility in China, further extending their global presence. Their final undertakings in the 1990s were to offer Internet access, Dellnet, to their customers as well as adding manufacturing plants in the United States and Brazil.[11] For the fiscal year ending in January 2000, Dell reported net income of $1.86 billion on total revenues of $25 billion.

In the first decade of the twenty-first century, Dell's strategy continued to develop. In late 2001, Dell introduced a new line of products, PowerConnect, which allowed consumers to network within a small business environment. In 2003, they launched their Axim line of handheld computers to compete with competitors' PDAs. In efforts to retain and attract new consumers, Dell set up kiosks in retail shopping malls, opened their first Dell location within a Sears store, created an online music service, and introduced their first line of printers.[12] Dell's diversification, coupled with large increases in shipments of high-profit-margin products such as servers, notebook computers, and storage equipment, propelled the company to new heights in 2004.[13] This diversification allowed annual net income to increase to $2.65 billion. Dell also had an interest in the growing Chinese market and began increasing their presence in rural Chinese areas, capitalizing on subsidies farmers received and has allowed Dell to weather the current tough economic times and boost sales.[14]

Despite the success of the direct sales model, Michael Dell realized the company must keep pace with shifting consumer sentiment and market conditions. Dell told *Forbes* in 2007 that "the old model ran its course, now it's time for a new course."[15] With eyes on the consumer market offering new channels of distribution, Dell brought on a new executive group to accomplish this goal.

Competitive Situation

Key Competitors

Dell faces stiff competition within the computer hardware industry. According to IDC, for Q1 2009, the top five PC shipment vendors worldwide are (in rank order): HP, Dell, Acer, Lenovo, and Toshiba (for U.S. PC shipments, Apple replaces Lenovo as fourth place).[16] For the enterprise market, Dell's standardized desktops and laptops remain the most popular among North American and European enterprises and are a clear leader over HP and Lenovo.[17] Market share data can be found in Exhibits 1 through 3 and competitor revenues from geographic regions can be found in Exhibit 4. The following key competitors will be discussed in order: Acer, HP, Apple, and Lenovo.

Acer Group. Founded in 1977, Acer Group is a Taiwanese company competing with Dell in the desktop PC, notebook computer, server, displays, and information technology (IT) solutions segments. Acer's portfolio of brands includes Gateway and eMachines, which were acquired in October 2007, as well as Packard Bell.

In the first quarter of 2009, Acer had sales of US $3.4 billion, which was down from $3.9 billion in the same quarter in 2008.[18] Their strongest sales came from the EMEA (Europe, Middle East, Africa), where they earned 49 percent of their revenue in the first quarter of 2009. They are the leading manufacturer of notebook computers in the EMEA, with a 26.6 percent market share. In the United States, Acer is the third-ranked maker of both PCs and notebooks with 13.6 percent and 16.8 percent market shares, respectively. Worldwide, for PCs and notebooks, they rank third and second,

Exhibit 1 Worldwide PC Shipments in 2008—Market Share

WW PC Shipments 2008

PC OEM	Market Share	YoY Growth
HP	19.2%	12.7%
Dell	15%	11%
Acer	10.9%	53.3%
Lenovo	7.4%	8.3%
Toshiba	4.6%	25.1%
Others	43%	1.3%

Source: IDC

Exhibit 2 U.S. PC Shipments in 2008—Market Share

U.S. PC Shipments 2008

PC OEM	Market Share	YoY Growth
Dell	29.5%	3.3%
HP	24.9%	1.8%
Acer	9.1%	62.1%
Apple	7.7%	25.7%
Toshiba	5.5%	7.6%
Others	23.4%	−16%

Source: IDC

respectively, with 12.8 percent and 19.6 percent market shares. Notebook sales accounted for 68 percent of their revenue in FY 09 Q1, while PCs accounted for 17 percent, displays 12 percent, and other segments 3 percent.[19]

Acer Group CEO J. T. Wang defines Acer's corporate sustainability as, "A successful global IT company which achieves in triple bottom lines, meaning, outstanding and balanced performance in the economy, environment and society."[20] Most recently, Acer has launched a set of new core values as described by CEO Wang: "The pillars on which we must base our actions include: value-creating, customer-centric, ethical and caring. The way we must act should be: innovative, fast and effective."[21]

Acer has been focusing on the execution of the October 2007 acquisition of Gateway and eMachines by positioning and uniquely segmenting each brand. Acer, which is not known for its direct customer selling, has been evaluating this strategy. However, Gateway has long had a similar direct-selling strategy to Dell but has failed to execute it as effectively. Acer's strategy is to segment their customers based on their needs and tailor one of their brands to meet those needs. Gianfranco Lanci, Acer's president and CEO, stated, "Our channel strategy will be very different from our competitors. The market is changing where users have different needs for our products. We do not want to confuse our customers and think that multiple branding is the future."[22]

Hewlett-Packard. Hewlett-Packard (HP), founded in 1936 and based in the United States, competes directly with Dell in almost every category.[23] HP holds the top position globally in the PC segment with 19 percent market share and recently overtook the top spot in the United States. HP's highest margin business

Exhibit 3 Enterprise Laptop and Desktop Market

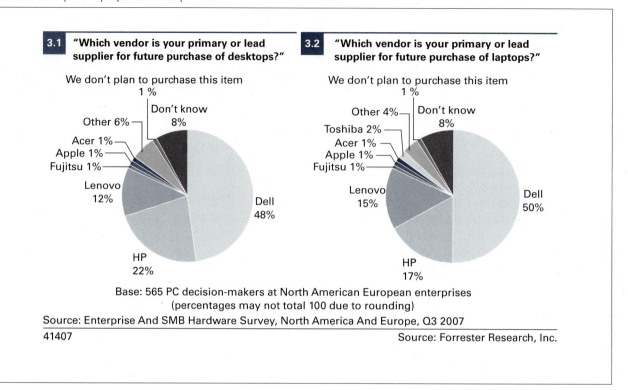

3.1 "Which vendor is your primary or lead supplier for future purchase of desktops?"

We don't plan to purchase this item 1%
Don't know 8%
Other 6%
Acer 1%
Apple 1%
Fujitsu 1%
Lenovo 12%
Dell 48%
HP 22%

3.2 "Which vendor is your primary or lead supplier for future purchase of laptops?"

We don't plan to purchase this item 1%
Don't know 8%
Other 4%
Toshiba 2%
Acer 1%
Apple 1%
Fujitsu 1%
Lenovo 15%
Dell 50%
HP 17%

Base: 565 PC decision-makers at North American European enterprises
(percentages may not total 100 due to rounding)
Source: Enterprise And SMB Hardware Survey, North America And Europe, Q3 2007

41407

Source: Forrester Research, Inc.

has been the imaging and printing business, which contributed 36 percent of earnings but only represented 25 percent of revenues.[24] Their 2008 revenues were $118.4 billion, up from $104 billion in 2007, and break down as follows among their core businesses: Personal

Exhibit 4 Percentage of Revenue by Global Regions and Competitor

Provider	% Sales by Region (2008)		
	Americas	**EMEA**	**APJ**
Dell[7]	47%	22%	12%
Lenovo	28%	22%	50%
HP	42%	42%	16%
Apple*	45%	23%	12%
Acer**	30%	49%	21%

[7]Dell's other operating segment, Global Consumer, accounts for 19% of sales and operates globally.

*Apple's other operating segment, Retail, accounts for 20% of sales and consists of locations in America and International.

**Acer figures based on Q1 2009 results and not annual due to limited availability of information.

Systems Group (PC and handheld devices segment) 35 percent, Imaging and Printing 25 percent, HP Services 19 percent, Enterprise Storage and Solutions 16 percent, HP Software 2 percent, HP Financial Services 2 percent, and Corporate Investments 1 percent.[25] By geographic regions, HP receives 42 percent of its revenue from the Americas (United States, Canada, Latin America), 42 percent from the EMEA, and 16 percent from Asia Pacific. EMEA shows the highest growth, with revenues up 22 percent in 2008 compared to 2007.[26]

In August 2008, HP acquired Electronic Data Services (EDS) for $13 billion, adding strength to their services business. EDS also expanded the breadth of products and services HP offers and gave potential customers, both businesses and at-home consumers, the ability to meet all of their needs. HP is currently going through a four-year restructuring project to improve its efficiency and seek financial savings through shared costs among its business units, and has released plans to cut 24,700 employees from its global workforce.[27]

HP's strategy moving forward is to serve as their corporate customers' only resource for everything IT related. As Mark V. Hurd, the chairman, CEO, and president of HP, stated in the 2008 annual report, "Enterprises are straining to meet ever-growing demand with aging, complex, proprietary and inefficient IT infrastructures. These dynamics are creating a massive disruption in the

IT marketplace and a massive opportunity for HP. With a comprehensive portfolio of hardware, software, and services, HP is well positioned to help customers manage and transform their IT environments."[28]

In their largest revenue business, the PC segment, they are trying to revamp stale sales by introducing new sleek touchscreen computers.[29] "HP is offering the assistance of hardware and software consultants from its services division to help customers come up with new uses for touch technology."[30] As part of this strategy, HP has partnered with Chicago's O'Hare airport and placed 50 touchscreens for patrons to use to access maps and local information. HP is hoping to increase sales from the 400,000 units sold in 2008.

Apple. Apple entered the computer industry in 1976 and has evolved its business strategies of brand loyalty, innovation, marketing advantage, and end-to-end user experience over the past 30 years. In 1998, Apple CEO Steve Jobs took note that their products integrated with very few of the industry standard peripherals, operating systems, and applications, threatening isolation. Jobs decided to adjust their business strategy to focus on product differentiation with offerings that were user friendly, attractively designed, well supported, and comprehensive using Apple products that address specific user needs. The iMac, introduced in 1998, had these qualities and was the catalyst for a turnaround in the company's performance.

While prices of Macs (Apple's computers) are generally more expensive than those of competitors, Apple's competitive strategy is basic: "make the best product possible, and rewards will follow."[31] Without the need to maintain a cost leadership position in the market, Apple is able to focus on differentiating its product, focusing on innovation to cater to the user experience.[32] On average historically, Apple spends 4 to 5 percent of its revenue on R&D, compared to 1 percent by competitors, including Dell.[33] Their current product portfolio now includes iPhones, Macs, notebooks, and iPods, as well as accessories for these core items. Diversification and user-centric design have allowed Apple to hedge the risk of substitutes and to enter markets without excessive marketing expenses traditionally required to target specific market segments or user groups. While Macs currently account for fewer than 5 percent of corporate desktops, many companies responding to an Information Technology Industry Council (ITIC) survey indicate that they are likely to let employees select Macs as business workstations within the next year.[34]

Apple continues to focus on controlling costs through efficient operations. In 2008, Apple outsourced much of its transportation and logistics management outside of the United States. This was done to control costs at the potential risk of losing direct control over production and distribution, potentially compromising quality and quantity of products, and limiting response flexibility to changing market conditions.[35] In 2008, Apple earned first place in the Supply Chain Top 25 ranking by AMR Research. AMR Research stated, "Behind-the-scenes moves like tying up essential components well in advance and upgrading basic information systems have enabled Apple to handle the demands of its rabid fan base without having to fall back on their forgiveness for mistakes."[36]

Apple's total net sales of domestic and international products increased 68 percent from FY06 to FY08 to $32.5 billion while cost of sales increased 50 percent to $4.8 billion.[37] The ratio between domestic and international sales has remained relatively consistent FY06 through FY08, with 43 percent of sales revenue being generated outside of the United States in 2008.[38] Despite strained economic times, Apple's earnings per common share continues to increase year over year. With 31,010 regular employees worldwide in 2008, Apple resource numbers continue to grow as well as research and development expenses (3 percent of net sales in 2008 which is below its historical average).[39]

Lenovo. Founded in 1984, Hong Kong–based Lenovo Legend Group is the largest computer producer in Asia and retains approximately 24,000 employees worldwide. Lenovo acquired IBM's personal computer business in 2005, creating the third-largest personal computer company in the world at the time. Lenovo has been listed on the Stock Exchange of Hong Kong since 1994 and currently controls 25 percent of the Asian computer market due to cost leadership and entry barriers to the Chinese market historically caused by high import tariffs.

Lenovo boasts a "worldsourcing" business model that distributes management, operations, and production into global "hubs of excellence." Strategies for growth in 2009 are outlined to include streamlining and improving the global supply chain and logistics network to control costs, growing customer intimacy to better understand consumer demands, PC focus on workstations and servers, increasing scale to appreciate benefits of economic efficiencies, and building brand recognition and loyalty.[40] Lenovo's product offerings are similar to Dell's (PCs, notebooks, servers, peripherals, and support services), however, it does not offer adjacent product lines (i.e., entertainment, telecommunications, TV), which competitors have begun to offer to hedge the risk of substitute products.

In 2008, Lenovo launched a backwards integration strategy into its supply chain in order to eliminate third parties from the manufacturing process.[41] This move into vertically shoring up its supply chain is aimed at reducing supplier power, thereby increasing control over quality and ability to implement design changes more quickly.

Lenovo sales decreased from FY07 to FY08 (FY ends March 31) by more than 20 percent while operating expenses decreased less than 9 percent.[42] Research and development expenses increased 17.1 percent, indicating a growing focus on innovation and product enhancements. The majority of sales, driven by China, account for nearly 40 percent of total sales while less than 30 percent of sales occur in the United States. Asia Pacific, Europe, Middle East, and Africa account for the remaining 30 percent of sales.

Customer Segments

As alluded to above, Dell serves four main customer segments—Home Users, Large Enterprise, Small and Medium Businesses (SMB), and Public Sector.[43] The segmentation is based on the different needs of each customer sector. As Michael Dell describes it, "Customer requirements are increasingly being defined by how they use technology rather than where they use it. That's why we won't let ourselves be limited by geographic boundaries in solving their needs."[44]

Home Users

The Home Users segment addresses all personal usage of computers and has traditionally been a smaller market than the commercial space. Of all computers shipped worldwide, approximately 75 percent are used professionally while 25 percent are for personal or home use.[45] Despite being a smaller market, the consumer segment "has the potential to expand faster than [Dell's] business with corporations and government agencies."[46]

Large Enterprise

Dell has identified Facebook, Microsoft, Amazon, Akamai, and Baidu as key customers in the corporate servers and data center business segment.[47] The needs of Large Enterprise customers vary from business to business across solutions for data storage, networking, security, or hardware procurement. Being the largest buyers in the IT industry, enterprise customers can demand customized solutions catered to their specific needs. However, with a large amount of resources invested with a specific IT vendor, it is not easy to switch to another vendor without incurring significant change and costs. Curiously, some of Dell's corporate customers also happen to be key vendors, which makes managing "these relationships [a] little challenging," according to Dell's CIO Jerry Gregoire.[48] Enterprise IT spending is expected to remain flat for 2009.[49]

Small and Medium Business

Unlike large enterprises, SMBs do not have a large amount of resources dedicated for IT needs. In fact, the person responsible for IT is often "one of the founding members who is juggling many roles—CFO, sales manager, marketing guy, and so on."[50] Dell has traditionally been a strong player in the SMB market by comprehensively managing SMB's IT needs so the dedicated IT resource can focus on other roles. Dell understands that "SMBs are far more sensitive to cost issues because if their computers are down, that might be all of their systems," as opposed to large enterprises, which would have redundant backup systems with a dedicated IT staff resolving any issues.[51] By having multi-tier service offerings, Dell is able to potentially have more than 72 million SMB customers worldwide.[52] Analysts suggest that SMBs will spend double what big business spends in 2009. HP forecasts show that SMB is "one of the fastest growing IT market opportunities, with 4 to 7 percent growth expected in 2009 for a total available market opportunity of $68 billion."[53] Despite the economic slowdown, competitors such as HP, Lenovo, and Toshiba have all announced plans to target the SMB market in 2009.

Public Sector

In the Public Sector customer segment, Dell has identified government, education, and health care as areas of strategic focus.[54] For these customers, Dell is committed to providing simplified and standardized solutions to satisfy any of their IT requirements. Besides competing in the above segments, Dell is experiencing other competitive issues associated with these segments.

Additional Competitive Issues

Dell offers a broad range of product categories, including mobility products, desktop PCs, software and peripherals, servers and networking, services, and storage.[55] Due to the rapid technological innovations in computer electronics and the high level of dependency of many businesses and home users, there are no clear, direct substitute products for Dell's product portfolio.

While there are no imminent threats from substitute products, there is increasing competition from new entrants in the Home Users market segment. Witnessing the success of new entrants from Taiwan and Japan such as Acer, Asus, Toshiba, and Fujitsu in the late 1990s and early 2000s, many electronics manufacturers continue to attempt to enter the computer manufacturing market. For example, Micro Electronics Inc., the parent company of the computer retailer Micro Center, started selling an in-house line of laptops known as Winbook in 2004.[56,57] Other electronics manufacturers such as

Archos, maker of portable DVD players, made its entry into the portable computing market in 2009 with its Archos 10 netbook.[58] Bigger brands such as Samsung, which is famous for its cell phones, LCD monitors, and TVs, also entered the Home User market with its line of laptops. It is expected that more electronics makers will try to leverage their brand name and enter the home computing market. Furthermore, as the younger population becomes more tech savvy, possible "new entrants" are home or small PC makers that purchase stock parts directly and assemble a customized machine themselves or for a small fee. Ironically, this is how Dell was first founded 25 years ago.[59]

On the other hand, the commercial and public sector markets are experiencing a wave of consolidation. This is evident through major strategic decisions in the industry such as HP's merger with Compaq, Acer's acquisition of Gateway, and IBM's decision to exit the hardware market and focus on IT services. However, there are new competitors in the server market, including producers of supplier products. For example, Cisco systems has signaled that it will enter the server market to more fully serve corporate data centers, which often require integrated solutions based on multiple products.[60]

Economic Downturn and Other Challenges

Dell faces significant challenges in the midst of the current economic recession. Gartner Research predicts the worst-case scenario for IT spending in 2009 will be no growth in the United States, and IT expenditures are expected to shrink in Europe.[61] Forrester Research analyst Andrew Bartels further predicts "the brunt of the slowdown in IT spending will hit servers and PCs,"[62] which is Dell's primary market. In the Home User market, households are reducing their discretionary spending and will opt for low cost PCs with the bare minimum number of features, which may impact Dell's product lineup.

In this difficult economic environment, supplier and customer insolvency is plausible and may result in product delays and reduced demand. Dell also faces risks on the global front due to its international exposure. In FY09, "sales outside the U.S. accounted for approximately 48 percent of [Dell's] consolidated net revenue." Changes in the U.S. monetary policy as well as economic policies around the world may lead to volatile exchange rates, exposing Dell to currency risks despite its foreign currency hedging program.

Also, government and environmental groups have called for corporations to become more "green" and energy efficient. Dell is an industry leader in this area,

as it announced in August 2008 that it has "reached its goal of becoming 'carbon neutral' five months ahead of schedule."[63] While Dell's claim of "carbon neutrality" has been questioned by journalists, Dell is at least taking proactive steps to "set an example by reducing its environmental impact as responsibly and aggressively as it can."[64] Dell's reliance on renewable energy as well as being more energy efficient are estimated to save the company $3 million a year. Dell has also demonstrated itself to be a responsible corporate citizen by participating in programs such as (PRODUCT)RED™, where Dell contributes a part of the proceeds for each product sold associated with the program to a global fund to combat AIDS in Africa.[65]

Other regulatory and legal challenges remain. While Dell is not currently involved in any antitrust lawsuits, its suppliers, such as Microsoft and more recently Intel, have been fined for anti-competitive practices.[66] This can present challenges to Dell as these rulings may affect its pricing arrangements with suppliers as well as how Dell conducts its operations, particularly in Europe.

Finally, on the technological front, computer companies are watching the trend towards mobile computing. Analysts at IDC report that "laptops will overtake desktop PCs as the dominant form of computer in 2011."[67] Despite the economic downturn, IDC expects strong growth in the market of low-cost, small form-factor laptops known as netbooks. The proliferation of wireless infrastructure will also make "Portable PCs as part of a digital lifestyle, rather than just computing device, [which will] sustain growth in both Consumer and Commercial segments."[68] While Dell introduced the Dell Inspirion Mini series in the netbook market in September 2008, it is a follower in this market behind other companies such as Asus's EeePC and Acer's Aspire One.[69]

Dell's Segment Growth Strategies

Upon returning to Dell as CEO in January 2007, Michael Dell resumed control of a company showing signs of struggle in multiple areas including customer service, product quality, and the overall effectiveness of its direct sales model.[70] These issues caused Dell to lose market share to its major rivals. As a first step, Michael Dell identified five large growth areas with at least $5 billion of potential new revenue and reorganized the company around them.[71] The five focus areas for Dell's operations are "consumer business, mobile computers, emerging countries, enterprise, and small/medium business."[72] Dell has also identified and implemented additional company-wide strategic and cost cutting initiatives.

Dell's current strategic initiatives within the consumer market include providing technologically advanced differentiated products that can support price premiums in order to increase profit margins, rapidly detecting shifts in consumer preferences in order to reduce product development time, and increasing distribution via retail channels.

Within the consumer market, Dell is actively seeking to move upmarket to attract technologically savvy customers who are willing to pay a premium to have the newest and best technologies.[73] To support this migration, Dell's products must provide technological superiority compared to its competitors. Dell has increased research and development spending 39.1 percent in 2008 ($693M) versus 2007 ($495M) to facilitate the development of differentiated products.

Dell's historical direct sales model has provided the company with the potential to gather consumer sentiment information directly from consumers rather than through a third-party reseller. Dell is seeking to leverage its direct sales model to detect shifts in consumer preferences earlier than competitors in order to reduce new product development time. Both benefits increase Dell's pricing power and competitive advantage. CEO Michael Dell sees Dell's ability to sense rapidly changing consumer preferences as one of the company's largest potential strategic advantages.[74]

Dell is also seeking to diversify its distribution channels beyond direct sales in an effort to remain competitive as consumers increasingly show preference for shopping for computers at retailers where they can directly compare multiple models.[75] In addition, Dell is able to reach more customers worldwide than would otherwise be possible with a direct-only model. In 2007, Dell began offering its computers at retail outlets ranging from domestic retailers (i.e., Wal-Mart and Staples) to chains in Japan, China, Russia, and the United Kingdom. By 2009, Dell had expanded its retail operations to include 24,000 outlets worldwide. Dell's efforts have led to an 11 percent revenue growth within this segment from 2007 to 2008, a reversal from the 6 percent decrease Dell experienced in 2007. This turnaround in revenue suggests that Dell's efforts directed at the consumer market are having early success.

In regard to mobile computing, the entire computer market is undergoing a gradual transition to more mobility-based computing products. In Q3 of 2008, laptops outsold traditional desktop computers for the first time.[76] Dell's strategic efforts within the mobile computing market include creating new platforms to better meet new consumer and business-user needs in terms of performance, size, weight, and price. To do this, it has separated the product design function for consumer and commercial markets. This strategic change has enabled Dell to produce multiple new product platforms specialized for both consumer and commercial markets, including the Inspirion Mini 3G that targets the rapidly expanding netbook consumer market, and the Latitude XT-2 tablet PC and new thinner and lightweight E-series Latitude laptop for the commercial markets.

In emerging markets, Dell's strategy is to focus on providing region-specific products to meet the needs of emerging markets, particularly in Brazil, Russia, India, and China (BRIC countries). Typically, customers in these markets need a low-cost PC that provides the basic PC functionality, including web-surfing, e-mail, and word processing.[77] Dell has introduced the Vostro-A line of desktop and laptop computers that are specifically focused on the needs of price-sensitive customers within the BRIC market. Dell's marketing and product development efforts targeting BRIC customers have led to 20 percent sales growth within the BRIC market.[78]

Dell provides value to its largest customers by helping them to "simplify their IT environments."[79] To reduce the cost and complexity of large enterprise IT systems, Dell seeks to partner with customers to provide customized solutions including servers, storage, software, and support services. In this way, Dell is potentially building long-term relationships with its most important customers. These complementary products, solutions, and services provide a consistent revenue stream in addition to Dell's traditional hardware lines.

Dell is also seeking to be an innovator in hardware and software products that enable Net 2.0 companies, such as Microsoft, Amazon.com, and Google, as well as "cloud computing" initiatives where companies deliver hosted services over the Internet, usually on a subscription or license basis.[80] These companies are building massive computer networks that require a significant number of servers and IT infrastructure to support their businesses.[81] Michael Dell believes that Dell has "created a whole new business just to build custom products for those customers."[82] He also goes on to state that "now it's a several-hundred-million-dollar business and it will be a billion-dollar business in a couple of years."[83] Supporting these companies with technologically advanced solutions is strategically important to Dell maintaining its leadership in this market.

Similar to the strategy for large enterprise, Dell's small/medium business strategy is to provide the "simplest and most complete IT solution customized for their [specific] needs."[84] To do this, Dell offers a complete line of fully customizable desktop and laptop computers and servers as well as consulting and support services for this market which provide additional revenue streams beyond traditional hardware lines.

In 2008, Dell acquired EqualLogic, Inc. an industry leader in iSCSI SAN storage devices, a key technology for small and medium business customers.[85] Dell executives expect this acquisition to allow them to offer a broader array of storage products specifically tailored for this market. Dell also launched the "Dell Download Store" to enable small and medium-sized businesses to directly obtain third-party software solutions from Dell's Web site.[86]

Dell offers a full set of consulting and support services to support small and medium businesses throughout the product life cycle, including "Dell Pro-Manage" services, which provide "a team that proactively monitors your entire Dell or non-Dell IT infrastructure to prevent downtime before it starts."[87] Dell also makes "a la carte" services available, including services to prevent or address technical problems or hardware failures, protection services for both hardware and data theft, and pre-sale consulting services and IT infrastructure installation.

Cost Initiatives

In addition to strategic efforts aimed at growth, Dell has undertaken a massive cost-cutting campaign to drive down costs while maintaining its supply chain and production cost advantages over its competitors. Dell's current cost-cutting initiative seeks to cut $4 billion in costs by end of FY 2011. They are focused on costs of goods sold (COGS) and Operating Expenses (OpEx), specifically "design-to-value" or designing products that optimize their manufacturing and logistics supply chain as well as reducing total headcount in its sales organization as more and more of its sales are originating from third-party retailers.[88] In design-to-value, "33 percent of the business client and 57 percent of the consumer platforms have been redesigned and cost optimized which now equates to more than 50 percent of [Dell's] total [product] volume."[89] These redesigns led to a 10 percent reduction in average cost per unit in the past 12 months. As Dell's competitors provide pressure to drive down prices, cost initiatives are critical to its competitiveness in the global market for computers and IT equipment.[90]

Changes in Supply Chain Management and Manufacturing

As a computer manufacturer, Dell's manufacturing plants perform computer assembly operations on parts supplied by other companies. These parts could range from instruction manuals to optical drives, which Dell procures and assembles into a final product for its customers. To provide a quality product to its customers, Dell interacts with a large number of suppliers for its many different needs.

To maintain supplier flexibility and manage supplier bargaining power, Dell maintains strategic partnership with a large number of suppliers, procuring parts from multiple sources. While some parts can be easily shipped, Dell requires suppliers of some parts, such as computer motherboards, to be located nearby.[91] Because Dell is often one of their largest customers, Dell's suppliers often open facilities within a 20-mile radius of Dell manufacturing plants. These include Eagle Global Logistics and Cerqa Copyright, which handle computer parts and components and manuals and software, respectively. Due to the oligopolistic/monopolistic nature of the high-tech industry, Dell is forced to contract exclusively with a few suppliers who have control over key capabilities in the value chain. For example, Dell deals almost exclusively with Intel and Microsoft as its suppliers of microprocessors and operating systems. However, Dell is also investigating opportunities with other suppliers. Dell has begun shipping servers equipped with the Linux operating system rather than Microsoft Windows, and while currently Dell only offers "one AMD (Advanced Micro Devices) desktop but no AMD notebooks … a year from now, it's probably going to be different," states Darrel Ward, Dell's director of product management for its business client product group.[92]

As part of its business strategy, Dell has a Supplier Diversity program where "Dell relies on the diversity of its personnel, suppliers … to maximize innovation, growth, competitiveness, and customer satisfaction."[93] This program has earned Dell the number two ranking on DiversityBusiness.com's list of Top 50 Organizations for Multicultural Business Opportunities, which cites, "supplier diversity is a global concern as the leading global systems and services company relies on a worldwide network of quality suppliers to help it build all the products it ships around the globe."[94] Dell also exemplifies industrial leadership in managing supplier relationship by recognizing and rewarding its top suppliers at its annual Worldwide Procurement Supplier Awards. Each year, six suppliers receive awards across the categories of Best Quality, Global Citizenship, Service, Diversity, General Procurement, and Best Overall Supplier.[95]

As noted, Dell has historically utilized a build-to-order approach to supply chain management with a just-in-time manufacturing model where unit pieces were manufactured and stored in inventory but were not pieced together until a consumer request was issued. While this methodology rarely affords the opportunity to maximize economies of scale, it does maintain a low inventory holding cost. In May 2007, Dell began its transition into the retail market when it began selling PCs through Wal-Mart and Sam's Club. Early in 2009, Mike Gray, supply chain director for Dell, made the decision to transition the build-to-order model over to an industry standard build-to-stock methodology to offset increasing manufacturing costs and logistical complexities.[96] This meant that PC units would be put together prior to a custom order in an attempt to decrease costs and compete with other companies selling stock items.

Dell is in the process of moving manufacturing operations from Ireland to Poland in order to better serve customers in Europe, the Middle East, and Africa. With the transition they will be able to automate work and reduce the necessary labor force by 1,900 employees.[97] Pieces of the historically integrated and tightly controlled manufacturing and supply chain process are being outsourced to continue to maintain profits as the profit margin decreases.

Product Lines and Services

Dell offers solutions for PCs, mobility, software, peripherals, storage, and networking servers as well as services. Dell's service offerings include infrastructure consulting, deployment service, asset recovery and recycling, product training, support, and IT management outsourced services. Dell also offers financial services for training and advising on consumer and enterprise financing opportunities. Exhibits 5 through 7 provide a detailed description of Dell's product and service offerings.

The desktop Personal Computer (PC), the flagship product line for Dell since 1984, has traditionally been their largest product revenue stream. Throughout the 1990s, Dell continued to reinvent its PC line with bigger hard drives, faster processors, and better user experiences that cater to several different target market groups. Today, the PC product line includes:

Exhibit 5 Home Office/Consumer Product Comparison

Product Offering	Description	Target Market	Notebooks	Retail Price	Desktops	Retail Price (excludes monitors)	Sales Rep Notes
Inspiron Mini	Consumer Notebook	Cost Leadership, Travel and Portability	Mini9, Mini10, Mini12	$250–$400	None	—	Good for travel and highly portable. Very small screen with small memory but lightweight with good processing speed.
Inspiron	Consumer Desktop and Notebook	Mainstream Consumers	Inspiron13, Inspiron 14, Inspiron15	$350–$700	Inspiron530s, Inspiron 530, Inspiron 531, Inspiron 537s, Inspiron 537	$260–$350	Significantly slower than XPS and more for home use than office.
Studio	High Performance Desktop and Notebook	Enthusiast-Hi Tech Consumer	Studio15, Studio17	$600–$700	Studio Hybrid, Studio Slim, Studio Desktop, Studio One 19	$400–$500	Pre-loaded with antivirus and anti-spyware software.
XPS & Alienware	High end design with unique multimedia capability, high performance gaming systems rivaling HPs gaming division.	Gamers and Innovation Seekers	XPS M1730, XPS 1530, XPS M1330, Studio XPS 13, Studio XPS 16, M17, M15x	$750–$2,000	Studio XPS, XPS ONE, Studio XPS 435, XPS 625, XPS 630, XPS 730x, Alienware ALX X-58	$700–$3,700	Popular with gamers who especially respect the Alienware line. Very competitive against any Gateway and HP products. Great video cards with RunFast software. The newer XPS systems run the latest I7 processor technology.

Source: Dell Web site, http://www.dell.com/; Best Buy Interview performed May 26, 2009, with two customer specialists.

Exhibit 6 Business/Corporate Product Comparison

Product Offering	Description	Target Market	Notebooks	Retail Price	Desktops	Retail Price (excludes monitors)
OptiPlex	Office Desktop	Business, Government, Institutional Users	None	—	360, 740, 760, 960, 160	$300–$850
Vostro	Small Business Desktop and Notebook	Small Business	A90, A860, 1520, 1720, 1320, E5400	$300–$730	220 Mini Tower, 220s Slim Tower, 420 Tower	$300–$530
Latitude	Commercial Enterprise Notebooks	Business, Government, Institutional Users	E5400, E5500, D630, E6400, E6500, E4200, E4300, XT2, E6400 ATG, E6400 XFR	$750–$1,800	None	—
Precision	High performance Notebooks and Desktops	Working Professionals	M2400, M4400, M6400, M6400 Covet	$1,400–$3,400	T3500, T3400, T5500, T5400, T7500, T7400	$750–$1,800

Source: Dell Web site, http://www.dell.com/.

Exhibit 7 Network Server and Storage Solution Comparison

Product Offering	Description	Target Market	Model	Retail Price
PowerEdge Tower Server	Business Server	Cost Leadership	T105, T100, 840, T300, T605, 2900 III, T1610	$400–$1,000
PowerEdge Rack Server	Business Server	Cost Leadership	R200, R300, SC1435, 1950 III, R805, 2950 III, 2970, R905, R900, R710, R610	$650–$3,800
PowerEdge Blade Server	Business Server	Cost Leadership	M605, M600, M805, M905, M1000e, M710, M610	$1,000–$1,800
PowerEdge Rack Infrastructure	Business Server	Cost Leadership	2410, 2420, 4220	$600–$1,000
PowerVault	Direct Attach Storage and Some Network-Attached Storage	Limited Storage, Cost Advantage	MD 1000, MD 1120 DAS, MD 3000 DAS	$2,600–$5,500
PowerConnect	Network Switches	High Quality, Product Differentiation	>51 models	$300–$3,000
Dell/EMC	Storage Area Networks	Mid-level Enterprise Storage	>51 models	$2,000–$4,000

Source: Dell Web site, http://www.dell.com/.

- The **XPS™** and **Alienware** lines targeted at customers seeking innovative designs that cater to user experience.
- The **OptiPlex™** line, which was developed for business, government, and institutional users that are concerned with controlling costs while maintaining security.
- The **Inspiron™** line, which is designed for "mainstream PC users requiring the latest features for their productivity and entertainment needs."
- The **Vostro™** line, launched in July 2007, which caters to the needs of small businesses.
- **Precision™** workstations created for working professionals who demand exceptional performance from hardware platforms and software and application offerings. These professional users are less concerned with cost and are more interested in "three-dimensional computer-aided design, digital content creation, geographic information systems, computer animation, software development, computer-aided engineering, game development, and financial analysis."[98]

In mobile computing, two years after the first Dell laptop debuted in 1989, Dell jumped into the top five computer companies in the world in terms of unit shipments, sending shares skyrocketing. Apple PowerBook designer John Medica led the efforts to create the enhanced Dell Latitude notebook offering. As the industry frontrunner of lithium-ion battery production and the first to introduce a rapid notebook charger, Dell enjoyed financial benefits of a first-mover advantage. Today, the mobility product line includes:

- **XPS™** and **Alienware** laptop lines, which provide customers with the best design and user experience with a high level of gaming capacity. In 2008, the XPS M1330 was introduced with a 13-inch high-definition display with ultra-portable features that earned numerous awards for its unique design.
- **Inspiron™** laptops, which meet customer needs for innovation, style, and high performance at an affordable cost.
- **Latitude™,** developed for business, government, and institutional customers that are interested in security, product lifecycle management, and cost control.
- **Vostro™,** which serves small businesses, was introduced in July 2007.
- **Precision™** serves professionals with exceptional performance in running sophisticated applications that are offered within the line of mobile workstations.

Dell offers "a wide range of third-party software products, including operating systems, business and office applications, antivirus and related security software, entertainment software, and products in various other categories."[99] The primary third-party software provider, ASAP Software Express Inc., historically licensed their software innovations to Dell. In 2008, Dell acquired ASAP and has since released products from more than 2,000 software publishers. Dell packages antivirus and antispyware software from McAfee, Webroot Software, Norton, PC Mover, and other third-party software solutions preloaded with their personal computer units using these software solutions to differentiate the notebooks and desktops.

In 2002, Dell chose to expand its product portfolio to include peripherals that could be value-added components for personal computers. Today, Dell's primary peripherals include printers, projectors, and displays. They first entered the projector segment, shortly followed by entrance into the printer market in 2004, and started using Blu-ray disc technology in 2006. Currently, Dell offers a variety of printers ranging from ink-jet to large multifunction devices for enterprise solutions. Their printers are differentiated by the Dell Ink and Toner Management System™ that streamlines the purchase process by displaying the ink levels of color and non-color cartridges during each print job. Dell offers both branded and non-branded display solutions. To maintain the same level of innovation as Acer and HP, in 2008 Dell introduced cameras and microphones into the external monitors. Since then, Dell has won several awards for "quality, performance, and value" for their monitors.

Dell also offers both network attached storage and peripheral storage. By offering "a comprehensive portfolio of advanced storage solutions, including storage area networks, network-attached storage, direct-attached storage, disk and tape backup systems, and removable disk backup," data can be stored and transitioned over to a new PC or network unit at the end of the prior unit's life cycle. The diversity in the storage options between Dell PowerVault™, Dell EqualLogic, and Dell/EMC storage systems caters to a wide variety of target segments. The options vary based on use, modularity, scalability, encryption options, and backup storage solutions.[100]

In 1994, both Dell and rival HP entered the network and server markets. Throughout the 1990s, Dell expanded their data center offerings to an enterprise solution utilizing the "high-end, fiber channel-based PowerVault™ 650F storage subsystem."[101] In 2004, Dell led a pioneering effort to develop the first Disk Data Format (DDF), a first attempt at a corporate data center server storage solution. By staying at the forefront of the industry and focusing on ease of use, Dell maintains a leadership position in the market. The products are known to be affordable, reliable, scalable, and customizable to meet client needs, demands, and level of understanding and requirement for use. The Dell networking solutions offer both managed and unmanaged connectivity. Current products include:

- The **PowerEdge™** line of servers competes in cost leadership and emphasizes scalability and reliability.
- **PowerConnect™** offers many high-quality features for very large data center customers, with switches that connect computers and servers in small to medium-sized networks.
- **PowerVault™** provides direct attached storage, common interfaces for internal and external storage, high capacity, and possible expansion.

From the time the first PC was introduced in 1985, Dell has relied on customer service as a corporate cornerstone and attributes its consistent success to this focus. In fact, in 2008, every *Fortune* 100 company did business with Dell.[102] Dell caters specifically to user needs in the areas of customer service, financing support, sales support, product support, and international support. In the 2008 annual report, Dell outlined the importance of customer service—to listen to their customers, innovate, and then make the necessary changes In this way, Dell can drive innovation to meet market demands.[103] Businesses and users can call, chat, or e-mail service requests.

Financials

While operating in a very competitive industry, Dell has remained a fiscally stable company. In the last decade, Dell has increased revenues by 142 percent, with recent revenues of $61.1 billion in 2008 with a 10 percent compound annual growth rate (CAGR), and currently has roughly $9 billion in cash.[104] From 1999 to 2008, Dell's net income reached a high of $3.6 billion in 2005 and a low of $1.2 billion in 2001. However, as noted in the introduction, revenue growth has slowed with FY09 revenues of $61.101 billion compared to FY08 of $61.133 billion, with desktop PCs, their largest product revenue stream, experiencing a 12 percent decline. A breakdown of Dell's sales by product segment can be found in Exhibits 9 and 10.

Exhibit 8 Dell Financial Performance (FY00–FY09)

Select Financial Details from Dell's Balance Sheet and Income Statement										
Income Statement ($M)	**FY09**	**FY08**	**FY07**	**FY06**	**FY05**	**FY04**	**FY03**	**FY02**	**FY01**	**FY00**
Revenue	$61,101	$61,133	$57,420	$55,908	$49,205	$41,444	$35,404	$31,168	$31,888	$25,265
Operating Income	$4,193	$4,344	$3,541	$4,740	$4,588	$3,807	$3,055	$2,510	$3,008	$2,613
Net Income	$2,478	$2,947	$2,583	$3,572	$3,043	$2,645	$2,122	$1,246	$2,236	$1,666
Effective Tax Rate	25.5%	22.8%	22.8%	21.9%	31.5%	29%	29.9%	28%	30%	32%
Balance Sheet ($M)	**FY09**	**FY08**	**FY07**	**FY06**	**FY05**	**FY04**	**FY03**	**FY02**	**FY01**	**FY00**
Cash	$9,092	$7,972	$9,546	$7,042	$4,747	$4,317	$4,232	$3,641	$4,910	$3,809
Total Assets	$26,500	$27,561	$17,791	$23,190	$23,215	$19,311	$15,470	$13,535	$13,435	$11,471
Current Liabilities	$14,859	$18,526	$17,791	$15,927	$14,136	$10,896	$8,933	$7,519	$6,543	$5,192
Long-Term Debt	$1,898	$362	$569	$504	$505	$505	$506	$520	$509	$508
% Long-Term Debt of Capitalization	30.8	8.6	11.4	10.9	7.2	7.4	9.4	10.0	8.3	8.7

Source: Dell Annual FY10 1Q Financial Tables, disclosed May 28, 2009.

Exhibit 9 Dell Revenue by Product Line (FY07–FY09)

Annual Revenue by Product Line (in millions, except %)									
	FY09 Fiscal Year Ending: 30 Jan 2009			FY08 Fiscal Year Ending: 1 Feb 2008			FY07 Fiscal Year Ending: 2 Feb 2007		
Product Line	Dollars	% of Revenue	% Change	Dollars	% of Revenue	% Change	Dollars	% of Revenue	
Mobility	18,638	31%	7%	17,423	28%	13%	15,480	27%	
Desktop PCs	17,244	29%	–12%	19,573	32%	–1%	19,815	34%	
Software and Peripherals	10,603	17%	7%	9,908	16%	10%	9,001	16%	
Servers and Networking	6,275	10%	–3%	6,474	11%	12%	5,805	10%	
Services	5,715	9%	7%	5,320	9%	5%	5,063	9%	
Storage	2,626	4%	8%	2,435	4%	8%	2,256	4%	
Net Revenue	61,101	100%	0%	61,133	100%	6%	57,420	100%	

Source: Dell Annual 10-K Report for FY2009, filed March 26, 2009.

In first quarter 2009 (reported as FY10 Q1), Dell released performance in the reorganized globally operating business segments. Large Enterprise, their largest commercial revenue stream, saw quarterly revenues down 31 percent to $3.4 billion (year to year) and operating margins of 5.7 percent. The public sector segment, which includes government, education, and health care, saw revenues down 11 percent to $3.2 billion from the previous year and operating margins of 9.2 percent. Growth in federal and national accounts was offset by the weak performance of remaining accounts. For SMB, revenue fell 30 percent from the previous year to $3 billion, with the strongest demand continuing to be from Asia. Operating margins remained relatively flat at 7.7 percent. The consumer segment saw growth in unit volume (a 12 percent increase) with notebook volume up 32 percent offset by desktop units, which were down 20 percent year to year. Revenues for the consumer segment were down 16 percent to $2.8 billion with operating margins at 0 percent.[105] Detailed financial results for Q1 FY10 can be found in Exhibits 10, 12, and 13.

Publicly traded on the NASDAQ, Dell has been a volatile stock over the past year with a high of $26.04 and a low of $7.84 per share. Dell's 12-month stock performance is –48.29%, which is due in large part to the global recession.[106] At the end of FY09, Dell had 29,542 stockholders, of which 69 percent were institutional owners. Dell has never paid a dividend in its history. In FY09, Dell's percentage of long-term debt to capitalization rose from a decade average of 11.3 percent up to 30.8 percent, earning Dell an A– S&P credit rating.

Dell continues to increase its investment in research and development to improve and expand their product lines in their five key areas (PCs, software and peripherals, servers and networking, services, and storage), spending $693 million in 2008. With the company expanding rapidly in international markets, their customer base is broad and no single customer accounted for more then 10 percent of their sales the last three fiscal years. Dell's sales breakdown by geographic region is available in Exhibit 11.

Key Strategic Leaders

Michael Dell is the youngest CEO ever to earn a ranking on the *Fortune* 500.[107] Dell has held the title of chairman since he founded Dell Inc. in 1984, and served as its CEO for the first 20 years of company history. Dell left his CEO role to Kevin Rollins in July 2004 to work with

Exhibit 10 Dell Revenue by Product Line (Quarterly Results–FY10 & FY09)

	Quarterly Results by Product Line (After Dec. 31st Organizational Announcement)												
	FY10					**FY09**							
Product Line	**May 1, 2009**			**January 30, 2009**		**October 31, 2008**		**August 1, 2008**		**May 2, 2008**			
	Dollars	% of Revenue	% Change Y over Y	Dollars	% of Revenue	Dollars	% of Revenue	Dollars	% of Revenue	Dollars	% of Revenue		
Mobility	$3,875	31.4%	–20%	$3,999	30%	$4,861	32%	$4,895	30%	$4,849	30%		
Desktop PCs	$3,163	25.63%	–34%	$3,538	26%	$4,091	27%	$4,954	30%	$4,781	30%		
Software & Peripherals	$2,246	18.2%	–18%	$2,487	19%	$2,585	17%	$2,790	17%	$2,741	17%		
Servers & Networking	$1,286	10.42%	–25%	$1,431	11%	$1,630	11%	$1,733	11%	$1,718	11%		
Enhanced Services	$1,238	10.03%	–8%	$1,270	9%	$1,365	9%	$1,372	8%	$1,344	8%		
Storage	$534	4.33%	–17%	$703	5%	$630	4%	$690	4%	$644	4%		
Net Revenue	$12,342	100%	–23%	$13,428	100%	$15,162	100%	$16,434	100%	$16,077	100%		

Source: Dell Annual FY10 1Q Financial Tables, disclosed May 28, 2009.

Exhibit 11 Revenue by Global Segments (FY07–FY09)

	Annual Revenue by Business Unit (Prior to Dec. 31st Organizational Announcement)								
	FY09 Fiscal Year Ending: 30 Jan 2009			**FY08** Fiscal Year Ending: 1 Feb 2008			**FY07** Fiscal Year Ending: 2 Feb 2007		
Business Unit	Dollars	% of Revenue	% Change	Dollars	% of Revenue	% Change	Dollars	% of Revenue
Americas Commercial	$28,614	47%	–4.56%	$29,981	49%	5.98%	$28,289	49%
EMEA Commercial	$13,617	22%	0.07%	$13,607	22%	14.9%	$11,842	21%
APJ Commercial	$7,341	12%	2.43%	$7,167	12%	15.17%	$6,223	11%
Global Consumer	$11,529	19%	11.09%	$10,378	17%	–6.22%	$11,066	19%
Net revenue	$61,101	100%	–0.05%	$61,133	100%	6.47%	$57,420	100%

Source: Dell Annual 10-K Report for FY2009, filed March 26, 2009.

Exhibit 12 Revenue by Global Segments (Quarterly Results–FY10 & FY09)

	Quarterly Results by Global Segment (After Dec. 31st Organizational Announcement)													
	FY10					**FY09**								
Global Segment	May 1, 2009			January 30, 2009		October 31, 2008		August 1, 2008		May 2, 2008				
	Dollars	**% of Revenue**	**% Change Y over Y**	**Dollars**	**% of Revenue**	**Dollars**	**% of Revenue**	**Dollars**	**% of Revenue**	**Dollars**	**% of Revenue**			
Large Enterprise	$3,400	27.55%	–31%	$3,889	29%	$4,395	29%	$4,806	29%	$4,921	31%			
Public	$3,171	25.69%	–11%	$3,287	24%	$3,960	26%	$4,510	27%	$3,581	22%			
SMB	$2,967	24.04%	–30%	$3,043	23%	$3,647	24%	$3,958	24%	$4,244	26%			
Consumer	$2,804	22.72%	–16%	$3,209	24%	$3,160	21%	$3,160	19%	$3,331	21%			
Net Revenue	$12,342	100%	–23%	$13,428	100%	$15,162	100%	$16,434	100%	$16,077	100%			

Source: Dell Annual FY10 1Q Financial Tables, disclosed May 28, 2009.

the Michael and Susan Dell Foundation, which manages the family's philanthropic efforts. Amidst poor performance and scandals with accounting practices, Michael Dell returned as CEO in January 2007.

Dell attended the University of Texas but, much like other titans of the computer industry, dropped out of college and went on to found a company based on the idea of selling custom-made computers directly to customers, revolutionizing the way computers were sold.[108] Dell was the first company in the PC business services to offer toll-free technical support and on-site service, which is now considered standard practice throughout the industry. Dell also was able to reduce its inventory costs by ordering the computer parts from nearby suppliers only once an order has been received.

Steven Schuckenbrock joined Dell in January 2007 as Senior Vice President of Global Services, expanded his role to include CIO in September 2007 and currently serves as the president of the division. Schuckenbrock is responsible for all aspects of Dell's support services, which is a potentially quick-growing unit that is responsible for worldwide enterprise service offerings and technology infrastructure.[109] Schuckenbrock is responsible for pioneering Dell's recent "cradle-to-grave policy," offered to enterprise customers, where their systems are updated and maintained for them from the time the machines are purchased until they are retired.

Prior to Dell, Schuckenbrock was a client and competitor as co-COO and Executive VP of Global Sales and Services for Electronic Data Systems Corporation (EDS), one of the largest IT consulting firms. He also brings previous experience as the COO of The Feld Group, an IT consulting organization, from 2000 to 2003 and the CIO for PepsiCo prior to that.

Prior to joining Dell, Ronald G. Garriques worked in Motorola through a number of executive positions, including Executive VP and President of the Mobile Devices Division. As the president of Dell's Global Consumer Group, Garriques is responsible for Dell's portfolio of consumer desktops, laptops, software, and accessories. Garriques is credited with the design of the Motorola RAZR that revived Motorola's line of cell phones in the North American market, and analysts expect Garriques to continue to design revolutionary products for the consumer market for Dell. Garriques holds an MBA degree from The Wharton School of Business at the University of Pennsylvania as well as a master's degree in Mechanical Engineering from Stanford University.

Alan Lafley is the Chairman and CEO of Procter & Gamble (P&G) and has served on the board of Dell since July 2006. When Michael Dell returned as CEO, he recognized the company had issues marketing its products to a consumer market, and utilized this board member connection to learn about consumer marketing from P&G. After spending a day with P&G's marketing group at its Cincinnati headquarters, Michael Dell recalled thinking, "We were doing everything wrong."[110]

Exhibit 13 Operating Performance by Global Segments (Quarterly Results – FY10 & FY09)

	Quarterly Results by Global Segment (After Dec. 31st Organizational Announcement)									
	FY10				FY09					
Global Segment	May 1, 2009		January 30, 2009		October 31, 2008		August 1, 2008		May 2, 2008	
	Operating Income ($M)	Operating Margin	Operating Income ($M)	Operating Margin	Operating Income ($M)	Operating Margin	Operating Income ($M)	Operating Margin	Operating Income ($M)	Operating Margin
Large Enterprise	$192	5.7%	$259	6.7%	$254	5.8%	$259	5.4%	$386	7.8%
Public	$293	9.2%	$289	8.8%	$361	9.1%	$331	7.3%	$277	7.7%
SMB	$230	7.7%	$239	7.9%	$374	10.3%	$330	8.3%	$330	7.8%
Consumer	–($1)	0.0%	$47	1.5%	$142	4.5%	$29	0.9%	$88	2.7%

Source: Dell Annual FY10 1Q Financial Tables, disclosed May 28, 2009.

Strategic Challenges

Michael Dell, with his newly reorganized business and five key areas of growth, is seeking to overcome the issues preventing its continued financial success. Shareholders and the technology world will be carefully watching how Dell and his leadership team deal with these issues. Internally, Dell will need to address operating costs while balancing the expansion into retail distribution channels other than through its traditional direct sales model. The corporate market, which Dell is accustomed to as its core source of revenue, is experiencing little to no growth worldwide, while the consumer market is growing slowly. Externally, the industry is reacting to the current economic downturn and price competition is intensifying. Competitors are aggressively taking market share by providing solutions that match or exceed Dell's technological offerings while meeting evolving customer needs. The globalization of the market is introducing opportunities to move manufacturing and operations to offset costs and open new potential customer markets, but it also exposes Dell to additional competition and risk associated with such emerging markets. With the success of competitors rising and growth in the corporate market declining, how should Dell change its corporate- and business-level strategies to enable growth and meet these challenges?

NOTES

1. 2009, Dell Inc Form 10-K for Fiscal Year 2009, http://i.dell.com/sites/content/corporate/secure/en/Documents/FY09_SECForm10K.pdf, filed March 26, 2009.
2. 2009, B. Charny, H-P dethrones Dell for top sales spot in U.S. Market, *Wall Street Journal* Online, April 16.
3. 2009, Gartner says Worldwide PC shipments declined 6.5 percent in first quarter of 2009, Gartner press release, http://www.gartner.com/it/page.jsp?id=939015, April 15.
4. 2008, Dell globalizes business groups around major customer segments, Dell press releases, http://content.dell.com/us/en/corp/d/press-releases/2008-12-31-00-global-business.aspx, December 31.
5. 2004, *International Directory of Company Histories*, Vol. 63, St. James Press, http://www.fundinguniverse.com/company-histories/Dell-Inc-Company-History.html.
6. 2003, BBC News Channel, Dell's diversification pays off, http://news.bbc.co.uk/1/hi/business/3269299.stm, November 13.
7. *International Directory of Company Histories*, Vol. 63, 2004, St. James Press, http://www.fundinguniverse.com/company-histories/Dell-Inc-Company-History.html.
8. Dell Inc., FY94, Form 10-K for year ending January 30, 1994, http://www.sec.gov.
9. Dell Company History, http://www.referenceforbusiness.com/history2/21/Dell-Computer-Corporation.html.
10. *International Directory of Company Histories*.
11. http://www.fundinguniverse.com/company-histories/Dell-Inc-Company-History.html.
12. 2007, B. Stokes, The history of Dell, http://www.articlealley.com/article_175455_10.html, June 16.
13. *International Directory of Company Histories*.
14. 2009, Bloomberg, Dell to push PCs to China rural areas to boost sales, http://www.bloomberg.com/apps/news?pid=20601080&sid=aJ3XJU_EvYzk&refer=asia, March 26.

15. C. Helman, 2007, The second coming, *Forbes*, December 10, 79–86.
16. http://www.idc.com/getdoc.jsp?containerId=prUS21797609.
17. B. Gray, 2007, How enterprise buyers rate their PC suppliers and what it means for future purchases, Forrester Research, http://www.dell.com/downloads/global/corporate/iar/2007112_Forrester_HowEnterpriseBuyersRate.pdf,_November 12.
18. 2009, Acer Inc. 2009 Q1 Investor Conference Presentation, http://www.acer-group.com/public/Investor_Relations/pdf/2009-4-29AcerQ1-2009-E.pdf, Presented April 29.
19. Acer Inc. 2009 Q1 Investor Conference Presentation.
20. Declaration from Management, http://www.acer-group.com/public/Sustainability/sustainability02.htm.
21. Acer Inc. 2009 Q1 Investor Conference Presentation.
22. Softpedia, 2007, Acer talks about its global strategy, http://news.softpedia.com/news/Acer-Talks-About-Its-Global-Strategy-66563.shtml, September.
23. Hewlett-Packard Web site, http://www.hp.com/hpinfo/abouthp/.
24. 2008, Standard and Poor's, Hewlett-Packard Stock Report, May 9.
25. 2008, Hewlett-Packard, 10-K Annual Report
26. Hewlett-Packard Web site, http://www.hp.com/hpinfo/abouthp/.
27. Ibid.
28. Ibid.
29. J. Scheck, 2009, H-P tries to revive PC sales with touch screens, *Wall Street Journal*, http://online.wsj.com/article/SB124234971369322195.html, May 15.
30. Ibid.
31. 2007, Welcome to planet Apple, *BusinessWeek* Online. http://www.businessweek.com/magazine/content/07_28/b4042058.htm, July 9.
32. L. Grossman, 2007, Invention of the year: The iPhone, http://www.time.com/time/specials/2007/article/0,28804,1677329_1678542,00.html.
33. D. B. Yoffie, 2004, Where does Apple go from here? Harvard Business School Working Knowledge, http://hbswk.hbs.edu/item/3877.html, February 2
34. J. Brodkin, 2009, Apple lacks broad corporate strategy but still sees gains, http://www.networkworld.com/news/2009/010609-apple-corporate-strategy.html, January 6.
35. 2008, Apple Inc, Form 10-Q, http://phx.corporate-ir.net/External.File?item=UGFyZW50SUQ9MzA4OHxDaGlsZEIEPS0xfFR5cGU9Mw==&t=1.
36. S. Murphy, 2008, Apple's supply chain is tops, *Modenr Materials Handling*, http://www.mmh.com/article/CA6574253.html, July 1.
37. 2008, Apple 2008 Annual Report (10-K) filed November 5, http://www.apple.com/investor/.
38. Apple Inc., 2-Year Financial History, FY08/FY06, http://library.corporate-ir.net/library/10/107/107357/items/314467/AAPL_3YR_Q4FY08.pdf.
39. Apple 2008 Annual Report (10-K).
40. Lenovo 2007/2008 Annual Report, http://www.pc.ibm.com/ww/lenovo/pdf/07_08/Lenovo_2007-08_Annual_Report_Final_E.pdf.
41. A. All, 2008, Lenovo's strategy includes no global HQ, more vertical supply chain, *ITBusinessEdge*, http://www.itbusinessedge.com/cm/blogs/all/lenovos-strategy-includes-no-global-hq-more-vertical-supply-chain/?cs=10312, March 3.
42. 2009, Lenovo Interim Report 2008/2009. http://www.pc.ibm.com/ww/lenovo/annual-interim_report.html.
43. Dell Inc., 2009, Dell laptops, desktop computers, monitors, printers and PC accessories, http://www.dell.com/, May 13.
44. Dell globalizes business groups around major customer segments.
45. M. Kanellos, 2002, PCs: More than 1 billion served, CNET News, http://news.cnet.com/2100-1040-940713.html, June 30.
46. Ibid.
47. I. Fried, 2008, Dell racks up Microsoft as data center customer, CNET News, http://news.cnet.com/8301-13860_3-10111860-56.html, December 3.
48. R. Finney, 1999, Dell business strategy secrets (Part 1), The itmWEB Site, http://www.itmweb.com/f031099.htm, February 14.
49. S. Swoyer, 2009, IT spending to hold the line in 2009, Enterprise Systems, http://esj.com/articles/2009/01/20/it-spending-to-hold-the-line-in-2009.aspx, January 20.
50. 2009, Dell: Services targeting SMBs, seeking alpha, http://seekingalpha.com/article/130899-dell-services-targeting-smbs, April 14.
51. A. Patrizio, 2009, Dell targets SMBs with managed service, http://www.internetnews.com/infra/article.php/3815376/Dell+Targets+SMBs+With+Managed+Services.htm, April 15.
52. Dell Inc., 2008, Dell globalizes business groups around major customer segments, http://content.dell.com/us/en/corp/d/press-releases/2008-12-31-00-global-business.aspx, December 31.
53. J. Davis, 2009, More PC makers target SMBs as SMBs pull back IT spending, Channel Insider, http://www.channelinsider.com/c/a/News/More-PC-Makers-Target-SMBs-as-SMBs-Pull-Back-IT-Spending/, March 12.
54. 2008, Simplifying information technology, http://www.egovonline.net/interview/interview-details.asp?interviewid=321, January 3.
55. Ibid.
56. 2004, WinBook W360 Laptop Reviews, CNET Reviews, http://reviews.cnet.com/laptops/winbook-w360/4505-3121_7-30880951.html, May 10.
57. Wikipedia, 2008, Micro Electronics Inc., http://en.wikipedia.org/wiki/Micro_Electronics,_Inc., October 3.
58. J. Stern, 2009, Hands-on with the Archos 10 netbook, http://blog.laptopmag.com/hands-on-with-the-archos-10-netbook, January 14.
59. Wikipedia, 2009, Dell, http://en.wikipedia.org/wiki/Dell, May 12.
60. B. Worthen & J. Scheck, 2009, As growth slows, ex-allies square off in a turf war, *Wall Street Journal*, March 16, A1.
61. C. D. Marsan, 2008, 8 reasons tech will survive the economic recession, CIO.com, http://www.cio.com/article/462919/_Reasons_Tech_Will_Survive_the_Economic_Recession, November 13.
62. PC market continues to resist economic pressures with a boost from low cost portable PCs.
63. K. Johnson, 2008, Dell's green payday: Going carbon-neutral helps bottom line, *Wall Street Journal*, http://blogs.wsj.com/environmentalcapital/2008/08/06/dells-green-payday-going-carbon-neutral-helps-bottom-line/, August 6.
64. J. Ball, 2008, Green goal of "carbon neutrality" hits limit, *Wall Street Journal*, http://online.wsj.com/article/SB123059880241541259.html, December 30.
65. 2008, Introducing (RED) inspired Dell studio laptops, Product (RED), http://www.joinred.com/News/Articles/ArticleDetail/08-11-13/Introducing_RED_inspired_Dell_Studio_laptops.aspx, November 13.
66. Europa Press Release RAPID, 2009, Antitrust: Commission imposes fine of EU1.06Bn on Intel for abuse of dominant position; orders Intel to cease illegal practices, http://europa.eu/rapid/pressReleasesAction.do?reference=IP/09/745&type=HTML&aged=0&language=EN&guiLanguage=en, May 13.
67. BBC News, 2007, Laptops set to outsell desktops, http://news.bbc.co.uk/2/hi/technology/6474581.stm, Mar 21.
68. IDC, 2008, PC market continues to resist economic pressures with a boost from low cost portable PCs, http://www.idc.com/getdoc.jsp?containerId=prUS21420408, September 10.
69. Wikipedia, 2009, Dell Inspiron Mini Series, http://en.wikipedia.org/wiki/Dell_Inspiron_Mini_Series, May 12.
70. L. Lee & P. Burrows, 2007, Is Dell too big for Michael Dell?, *BusinessWeek*, http://www.businessweek.com/magazine/content/07_07/b4021052.htm, February 12.
71. O. Malik, 2008, GigaOM Interview: Michael Dell. Reprinted at Businessweek.com, http://www.businessweek.com/technology/content/jul2008/tc20080727_306498.htm, July 28.
72. PC market continues to resist economic pressures with a boost from low cost portable PCs.
73. A. Ricadela, 2009, Will this bold shakeup save Dell?, *BusinessWeek*, wwwbusinessweek.com, January 1.
74. PC market continues to resist economic pressures with a boost from low cost portable PCs.
75. 2009, Why the big dip at Dell in the first quarter, *Wall Street Journal*, http://blogs.wsj.com/digits/2009/04/15/why-the-big-dip-at-dell-in-the-first-quarter/?mod=crnews, April 15.
76. Suppli.com, 2008, Notebook PC shipments exceed desktops for first time in Q3, http://www.isuppli.com/NewsDetail.aspx?ID=19823, December 23.
77. C. Thompson, 2009, The netbook effect, *Wired*, http://www.wired.com/gadgets/wireless/magazine/17-03/mf_netbooks?currentPage=4, February 23.
78. Dell Inc Form 10-K for Fiscal Year 2009.
79. Ibid.

80. 2008, Michael Dell: A big second half, *BusinessWeek*, wwwbusinessweek.com, July 28.

81. J. Brandon, 2008, What does cloud computing mean for you? *PC Magazine*, http://www.pcmag.com/article2/0,2817,2320619,00.asp, June 23.

82. Why the big dip at Dell in the first quarter?

83. Ibid.

84. Dell Inc Form 10-K for Fiscal Year 2009.

85. Ibid.

86. Ibid.

87. 2009, Dell Web site, http://www.dell.com/content/topics/global.aspx/services/managed/managed_services_overview?c=us&cs=04&l=en&s=bsd.

88. A. Gonsalves, 2009, Dell cost cutting 1 billion as profits fall 48%, http://www.informationweek.com/news/hardware/desktop/showArticle.jhtml?articleID=214700011, February 26.

89. 2009, FY10 Q1 earnings call transcript, http://www.dell.com, May 28.

90. B. Einhorn, 2009, Acer boss Lanci takes aim at Dell and HP, *BusinessWeek*, www.businessweek.com, April 13.

91. M. Harrington, 2004, "Dell Suppliers could be key to deal," *The Business Journal*, http://www.bizjournals.com/triad/stories/2004/10/04/story1.html, October 1.

92. B. Crothers, 2009, Dell offers lesson in Intel-AMD rivalry, CNET News, http://news.cnet.com/8301-13924_3-10240294-64.html, May 13.

93. Dell Inc., 2009, Dell supplier diversity, http://www.dell.com/content/topics/global.aspx/corp/sup_diversity/en/index?c=us&l=en&s=corp, May 13.

94. J. Bowles, 2008, Supplier diversity in action: Best practices of the top organizations for multicultural business opportunities, *BusinessWeek*, advertisement.

95. 2005, Dell recognizes six suppliers in annual awards program, Servigistics press release, http://www.servigistics.com/news/press/2005/04-141.html, April 14.

96. M. Gray, 2008, Dell supply chain director, speaker introduction, http://www.supplychain.eu.com/speakers.asp, June 8.

97. 2009, Limerick, Dell to migrate manufacturing operations from Ireland to Poland and partners by early 2010, http://www.dell.com/content/topics/global.aspx/corp/pressoffice/en/2009/2009_01_08_rr_000?c=us&l=en&s=corp, January 8.

98. Dell Inc. Form 10-K for Fiscal Year 2009.

99. 2009, Dell, Inc. (DELL) description of business, http://www.hotstocked.com/companies/d/dell-inc-DELL-description-52599.html, May 26.

100. 2009, Dell Web site, Data storage and backup, http://www.dell.com/business/storage.

101. 2009, Dell Web site, History, Dell takes on servers and storage, http://www.dell.com/content/topics/global.aspx/about_dell/company/history/history?c=us&l=en&s=corp.

102. Dell Inc. Form 10-K for Fiscal Year 2009.

103. 2008, Dell fiscal year 2008 in review, http://content.dell.com/us/en/corp/d/corp-comm/ir-FY08-in-Review.aspx?c=us&l=en&s=corp&redirect=1, June 1.

104. Standard & Poor's, 2009, Dell stock report, May 9.

105. 2009, FY10 Q1 earnings call transcript.

106. Yahoo Finance, http://www.yahoo.com/finance.

107. Dell, 2009, Michael Dell, Dell executive team, http://content.dell.com/us/en/corp/d/bios/michael-dell-bio.aspx.

108. 2009, Michael Dell biography, A&E Television Networks, http://www.biography.com/articles/Michael-Dell-9542199.

109. Reuters, 2009, Officers and directors for Dell Inc., http://www.reuters.com/finance/stocks/companyOfficers?symbol=DELL.O&viewId=bio.

110. Helman, The second coming.

Kazi Ahmed, Phillip Feller, Tara Ferrin, Jeffrey Fletcher, Fidel Rodriguez, Juliet Taylor, Robin Chapman

Arizona State University

"Our purpose is to pioneer new communities around the world built on commerce, sustained by trust and inspired by opportunity."[1]

Introduction

John Donahoe took over as president and CEO of eBay Inc. in March 2008, during an unfavorable time for the company.[2] Since its inception in 1995, eBay has experienced revenue and earnings growth year after year, but the growth rate has slowed since 2006. For the first time, eBay's revenues fell from the previous year, down by 7 percent in the fourth quarter of 2008.[3] Although eBay is still the industry leader for online retailing with 17 percent market share, it has lost market share to innovative key competitors such as Amazon, Yahoo!, and Google. The expensive acquisition of Skype (a communications software company) did not have the outcome former CEO, Meg Whitman, expected. The company's venture into China failed, and changes in seller fees have not provided the results that eBay executives had anticipated. In addition, there have been lawsuits related to counterfeit products. In March 2008, Meg Whitman stepped down as CEO and was succeeded by John Donahoe, who has to confront the current situation. In a fast-cycle market such as online retailing, how can Donahoe discover new competitive advantages and regain eBay's market share and growth rate while confronting a more complex international and legal environment? In particular, Donahoe now faces a global economic downturn, a struggling e-commerce industry, and company shares trading between $10 and $11 below their prior year price of $40.

Company Leaders and Overview

In 1995, shortly after conducting a successful online auction for a broken laser pointer costing $14.83, Pierre Omidyar realized that the Internet enabled market efficiency by allowing millions of buyers and sellers to view products and conduct transactions. This inspired him to launch AuctionWeb, an online marketplace for buyers and sellers.[4] AuctionWeb officially became eBay in 1997 and hosted more auctions per month in that year than it did in all of 1996. Within four years and with the help of Meg Whitman, eBay grew from a programmer's experiment into a major publicly traded company, trading on NASDAQ with the symbol EBAY[5] (see Exhibit 1 for more details on eBay's history).

Meg Whitman was recruited as eBay's second president and CEO in 1998 and helped bring eBay public in September of that year. At the time eBay's registered users had grown six-fold, to over 2 million, from the prior year. Under Whitman's leadership the company grew to over 200 million users globally and over $7 billion in revenue. During her tenure, Whitman helped eBay enter China, integrated globally recognized brands like PayPal and Skype into the eBay portfolio, and most notably, successfully steered the company through the dot-com bust by staying focused on its core users and core competency—online auctions. She continues to serve on eBay's board of directors.

After a 20-year career at Bain & Company, Donahoe joined eBay in February 2005 as president of eBay marketplaces, where he served for three years. Donahoe's prior executive experience made him an ideal candidate to help expand marketplaces, eBay's core business. Under his leadership eBay acquired Shopping.com, StubHub, Gumtree, and LoQUo, giving it a strategic

The authors would like to thank Professor Robert E. Hoskisson for his support and guidance during the development of this case. This case is not intended to illustrate either effective or ineffective handling of managerial situations. The case is solely intended for class discussion.

Exhibit 1 eBay History

1995: Pierre Omidyar successfully conducted an online auction for a broken laser pointer which cost $14.83. Omidyar realized the Internet enabled market efficiency by allowing millions of buyers and sellers to view products and interact. It was this experiment that led Omidyar to found AuctionWeb, an online marketplace for buyers and sellers.
1996: AuctionWeb expanded greatly, with revenue topping which cost $10,000. In June Omidyar hired Jeff Skoll as president.
1997: AuctionWeb officially became eBay and hosted more auctions per month than it did in all of 1996.
1998: Meg Whitman joined as president and CEO and in September; eBay went public listing on NASDAQ under the symbol EBAY.
1999: eBay started its international expansion with marketplaces in the United Kingdom, Germany, and Australia.
2000: eBay became the number one e-commerce Web site, acquired Half.com to enter into the fixed price market, and continued international expansion with marketplaces in Austria, Canada, France, and Taiwan.
2001: eBay dramatically accelerated its international expansion through marketplaces in Ireland, Italy, Korea, New Zealand, Singapore, and Switzerland.
2002: eBay boosted revenues by acquiring Paypal.com, the primary payment method used on eBay.
2003: eBay expanded into Hong Kong; integrated PayPal Buyer Protection Services, protecting buyers and sellers in the eBay marketplace.
2004: eBay expanded into Malaysia and the Philippines, started strategic alliance in China, and acquired Rent.com. eBay purchased 28 percent ownership in online marketplace rival Craigslist.com for a reported $15 million.
2005: eBay diversified by acquiring Shopping.com, Skype, and foreign classified Web sites LoQUo and Gumtree while launching U.S. classified Web site Kijiji.com.
2006: Launched eBay express adding brand new fixed-price items to its marketplace, thereby further enhancing eBay as a primary shopping location.
2007: eBay acquired online ticket Web site Stubhub.com and Stumbleupon.com, which enhanced its Web presence while strategically partnering to enter India. eBay also partnered with Wal-Mart and Myspace.com to market Skype, and Northwest and Southwest Airlines to make PayPal a payment option. Major League Baseball named StubHub as its official provider of secondary tickets. In June, eBay cancelled its advertising on Google as a result of Google's push for Google Checkout as an eBay payment option.
2008: eBay announced that large-volume sellers with the highest feedback ratings will have preferential search locations and lower fees. eBay removed the option for buyers to receive negative feedback. On March 31, Meg Whitman stepped down as CEO and John Donahoe took over as president and CEO. On October 6, eBay announced a massive stream-lining process which entailed laying off 10 percent of its workforce and restructuring charges of $70 to 80 million. It acquired Bill Me Later and two Danish classified ad Web sites. In mid-2008 eBay signed a deal with Buy.com allowing some sellers to directly negotiate their seller fees, dramatically increasing its items listed, but angering many of its smaller "powersellers." On July 15, a U.S. District Court judge ruled that eBay did not bear legal responsibility for sales of counterfeit goods in its marketplace. On September 16, eBay lowered fees on fixed-cost auctions by more than 70 percent in an effort to better compete with Amazon.com while also eliminating the use of checks and money orders as payments, and shifted to PayPal as the sole payment option for most auctions.

Sources: 2008, eBay history, http://www.ebay.com, November 3; J. Swartz, 2008, eBay to lay off 1,600 employees, cites economy, *USA Today*, October 7, 2B; 2008, eBay 2007 Form 10-K, http://www.ebay.com, November 25, 51; 2008, eBay major direct shareholders, http://finance.yahoo.com, November 26; B. Stone, 2008, Buy.com deal with eBay angers sellers, *New York Times*, July 14, 1; C. Wolf, 2008, eBay cuts fixed-price sales fees by 70%, *Washington Post*, August 21, D03; J. Schofield, 2008, Technology, *The Guardian*, February 21, 3; J. Swartz, 2008, Listings down 13% in boycott of eBay, *USA Today*, February 28, 3B; D. Rushe, 2008, Silicon Valley culture clash as eBay sues Craigslist, *The Times (London)*, April 27, B9; 2008, Judge rules for eBay over fake Tiffany jewelry sales, *International Herald Tribune*, July 15, F12; 2008, Google cancels 'Freedom' party to appease eBay, http://www.techweb.com, June 14; 2008, eBay Fact Sheet, http://www.ebay.com, November 28; 2008, eCommerce marketsize and trends, www.goecart.com/ecommerce_solutions_facts.asp, November 30; 2008, World's most valuable general retailers, http://galenet.galegroup.com. November 30.

presence in the growing online comparison shopping industry, ticket sales, and classifieds. At the time of his transition to CEO, eBay's market share was declining and it had failed to gain in its number of unique visitors. In an attempt to reinvigorate growth, Donahoe shifted eBay's emphasis closer to other competitors by moving from auctions to fixed price listing, which has been the profit engine for Wal-Mart.com, Amazon.com, and Yahoo.com. He also streamlined the organization with a 10 percent workforce reduction and the acquisition of Bill Me Later, a transaction-based credit business with a total payment volume of over $1 billion, as a complementary payment method to PayPal.

Consisting of over 88 million active users in 39 global markets (see Exhibit 2 for eBay marketplace locations), eBay offers anyone the opportunity to be an entrepreneur.[6] The company's marketplace segment operates online auctions, classified ad sites, and other sites where people can conduct commercial transactions. Unlike other e-commerce companies, eBay does not operate the online equivalent of a store; it is more like an online mall or flea market. Its payment segment provides ways for individuals to transfer money to complete an e-commerce transaction. Its third segment, communications, offers technology that enables voice and video communications between computers, and from a computer to an ordinary telephone.[7]

The e-commerce industry is attractive because it is relatively simple to enter. Most of the major players in the industry, including Yahoo!, Google, and eBay, began as small entrepreneurial ventures with little more than an Internet connection and lines of code. Despite relatively low entry barriers, growth is difficult due to strong industry rivalry.

Competitors

Amazon.com Inc.

Amazon.com Inc. (Amazon) was founded in 1994 as an online bookstore. Over the years it expanded to include items ranging from books and CDs to clothing and electronics. This expansion occurred through partnerships with companies including Toys "R" Us, AOL, and Hoover's.[8] Amazon sells other companies' products on its Web site and uses its distribution network to ensure prompt and accurate delivery. After a relatively unsuccessful attempt to add an auction component, Amazon created the Amazon marketplace, which allows sellers to place used items on the site, featuring them alongside identical new items sold by Amazon.[9]

Amazon aims to be the low-cost leader in the e-commerce industry. In order to continue attracting new customers, Amazon continues to add innovative

Exhibit 2 Locations of eBay Marketplaces

Argentina	Malaysia
Australia	Mexico
Austria	Netherlands
Belgium	New Zealand
Brazil	Panama
Canada	Peru
Chile	Philippines
China	Poland
Colombia	Switzerland
Costa Rica	Singapore
Dominican Republic	Sweden
Ecuador	Taiwan
France	Thailand
Germany	Turkey
Hong Kong	United Kingdom
India	United States
Ireland	Uruguay
Italy	Venezuela
Korea	Vietnam

Source: 2008, eBay Web site, http://www.ebay.com.

value-added services such as "frustration-free packaging"—which eliminates difficult-to-open product containers—and the ability for customers to pay with installment payment plans.[10] Amazon is also attempting to vertically integrate as a supplier of kitchenware through its new division, Pinzon.

In 2008, even though third-quarter profit was up 48 percent, Amazon reduced fourth-quarter projections, citing expectations, along with the rest of the retail sector, for a bleak holiday season.[11]

Yahoo! Inc.

Originally known primarily as a search engine, Yahoo! Inc. ventured into the e-commerce industry in 1998 with the purchase of Viaweb. In addition to e-commerce services, Yahoo! products include advertising, e-mail, news and information, photo sharing, and Internet browser toolbars and add-ons.[12] Yahoo! has a presence in more than 20 countries. It appeals to advertisers by creating a Web site that users go to for all of their needs, thereby creating the most exposure for its ads.[13]

While the company currently operates a Yahoo! Shopping site, it discontinued its auction site in the United States and Canada in June 2007. However, Yahoo! still runs auction Web sites in Hong Kong, Singapore, and Taiwan.[14]

In recent years, Yahoo! was involved in a takeover bid by Microsoft. The software giant saw Yahoo! as a way to compete with Google for advertising dollars. After a friendly acquisition was rejected, Microsoft attempted and failed at an unsolicited takeover. Investors have criticized Yahoo!'s board for not dealing more effectively with Microsoft and for not acting in their interest.[15] Although Microsoft is reportedly no longer interested in a full takeover, it may still try to purchase the Yahoo! search engine segment.[16]

Google, Inc.

Google Inc. (Google) is a search engine site that was founded in 1998. It uses proprietary software to "understand exactly what you mean and give back exactly what you want" when searching on the Internet.[17] While Google continually adds applications, such as e-mail and file sharing, 70 percent of its resources are directed toward improving its search engine capabilities. This builds on Google's dominance in this industry, which is derived from its popularity as a search engine. Google also has a strong international presence, with its site available in 116 languages.[18]

From an e-commerce perspective, Google Product Search is an application that will search for items available for purchase on the Internet and display a side-by-side comparison. Google does not have an auction site available, although sellers do have the option of setting a negotiable price for their products. In order to compete with eBay's financial service segment, PayPal, Google launched Google Checkout in 2006 and began charging for its use in February of 2008.[19]

Craigslist

A successful new entrant in the e-commerce industry is Craigslist. A private company, Craigslist began in San Francisco as a way for local residents to list events and classified ads. Craigslist differentiates itself by not charging to list or sell products on its Web site.

All revenue comes from fees for job postings and brokered apartment listings in selected cities such as New York. Craigslist keeps its overhead low in many ways, such as by continuing to operate out of a house instead of an office building and by having a staff of only 25 employees.[20] While confirmed financials are not available, some experts estimate the value of Craigslist to be near $5 billion.[21] As part of eBay's growth and acquisition strategy it has *acquired* a portion, roughly 28 percent, of Craigslist (see Exhibit 3 and Exhibit 4 for competitors' financial data).

Acquisitions

eBay's revenue growth has come largely through acquisitions. The acquisitions have also allowed it to increase its geographic reach, move into related businesses such as online payments, and obtain technology that will strengthen its product differentiation.[22] eBay has completed many acquisitions, and some of the more noteworthy ones are discussed here.

Half.com was one of eBay's first acquisitions and allowed eBay to enter the fixed price marketplace. It was acquired in 2000 for $312.8 million. Half.com allows eBay users to sell used books, games, CDs, and DVDs at fixed prices. Sellers are paid directly by Half.com and eBay operates the Half.com Web site separately from eBay.com but allows eBay.com user profiles to be shared between the Web sites.

In 2002 eBay purchased PayPal for $1.5 billion, thereby enabling sellers of any size to receive online payments from a buyer's credit card or checking account. This greatly reduced the payment and shipment times and provided another source of revenue for eBay. PayPal's transaction fee for transactions less than $3,000 is 2.9 percent of the amount transferred.[23] Revenues for PayPal in 2008 were $2.4 billion, making up 28 percent of eBay's total revenue.[24] In September 2008, eBay announced that PayPal was the sole payment option for a majority of its marketplace listings.[25]

In 2004 eBay acquired Shopping.com, Rent.com, and 28 percent ownership of Craigslist. It purchased Shopping.com for $620 million. Shopping.com allows people to search for products and compare prices (similar to Google's product search formerly known as Froogle). This acquisition gave eBay a new channel for buyers and sellers to interact and a new medium for ad revenue.[26]

eBay acquired Rent.com for $415 million. Rent.com joins landlords with tenants online, charging property owners for each lease produced.[27] The acquisition of Rent.com gave eBay entry into the online classifieds market, while increasing revenue streams and online exposure.

Exhibit 3 Key Competitor Financials

	eBay	Google	Amazon	Yahoo!	Overstock	Craigslist
Annual Sales (in Billions)	8.69	20.92	18.14	7.32	0.873	N/A
Employees	15,500	16,805	17,000	14,300	844	25
Market Value (in Billions)	6.57	86.99	17.84	13.87	0.166	N/A
Total Cash (in Billions)	3.64	14.41	2.32	3.21	0.07	N/A
Beta	1.54	1.57	1.84	1.2	2.54	N/A
Gross Profit Margin (in Billions)	5.91	9.94	3.35	4.13	0.124	N/A
EBITDA (in Billions)	2.93	7.62	1.06	1.29	0.001	N/A
Net Income (in Billions)	1.94	5.05	0.627	0.933	−0.02	N/A
Return on Equity	18.0%	20.8%	38.1%	8.94%	−148%	N/A
Return on Assets	9.7%	14.4%	8.8%	2.51%	−9.03%	N/A
Total Debt/Equity	N/A	N/A	0.172	0.005	N/A	N/A
Market Capitalization (in Billions)	16.34	80.99	18.23	14.16	0.16	N/A

Sources: 2008, Yahoo! Finance, http://finance.yahoo.com, November 24; 2008, Craigslist Fact Sheet, http://www.craigslist.org/about/factsheet, November 24

eBay acquired its partial ownership of Craigslist for an undisclosed amount. eBay's relationship with Craigslist has always been somewhat icy. eBay purchased its shares from an owner that went against the other stockholders' wishes to not sell to a public company. Craigslist alleges that eBay placed a variety of excessive demands on it, such as giving eBay blocking rights on all forms of corporate transactions. In 2008 eBay accused Craigslist of diluting eBay's ownership interest by more than 10 percent; Craigslist countersued a month later accusing eBay of unlawful competition and copyright infringement because it launched the international classified-ad site Kijiji.[28] These lawsuits are yet to be resolved.

eBay acquired Skype in 2005 for $2.6 billion. Skype is an Internet phone provider, allowing users to make calls to almost every country with their computers using Voice Over Internet Protocol (VOIP).[29] eBay's plan for Skype was to integrate it to allow buyers and sellers to communicate prior to transactions.[30] Skype is a free service if both parties are using Skype, but it charges non-Skype users for in-and-out calls.[31] The number of Skype users has increased from 57 million in 2005 to 400 million in 2008.[32] In 2007, eBay declared a $1.4 billion asset impairment for Skype, meaning that either eBay overpaid for

Skype or that the strategic integration of Skype was not going as planned. Thus, to maximize Skype's potential, eBay has announced that it plans to make Skype a stand-alone business and will conduct an initial public offering in the first half of 2010.[33]

eBay acquired Stubhub.com in 2007 for $310 million. Stubhub.com is a secondary ticket marketplace that integrates guaranteed fulfillment and shipment using FedEx.[34] Stubhub partners with American Express for concert tickets and over 60 teams for sporting events.[35] In 2007 Stubhub was named the official secondary market for tickets by Major League Baseball.[36] Stubhub features a season-ticketholder option, encouraging customer loyalty, and an easy method for season ticketholders to resell tickets.[37] eBay operates Stubhub.com independently from eBay.com.

eBay's purchase of Fraud Sciences Ltd. for $169 million in 2008 adds to its technology portfolio. eBay has long operated on the notion that trust is the key to its success, and it has announced plans to improve the level of trust that it provides. Fraud Sciences has developed ways to detect fraudulent purchases and provides eBay with the technology that it needs but lacks the capability to develop.

Exhibit 4 Historical Financial Overview of eBay and its Competitors

eBay.com	2003	2004	2005	2006	2007	2008 Q1	2008 Q2	2008 Q3
Net Revenues	$2,165,096	$3,271,309	$4,552,401	$5,969,741	$7,672,329	$2,192,223	$2,195,661	$2,117,531
Cost of Net Revenues	416,058	614,415	818,104	1,256,792	1,762,972	525,412	562,103	560,963
Net Income (Loss)	441,771	778,223	1,082,043	1,125,639	348,251	459,718	460,345	492,219
Google.com	**2003**	**2004**	**2005**	**2006**	**2007**	**2008 Q1**	**2008 Q2**	**2008 Q3**
Net Revenues	$1,465,934	$3,189,223	$6,138,560	$10,604,917	$16,593,986	$5,186,043	$5,367,212	$5,541,391
Cost of Net Revenues	1,123,470	2,549,031	4,121,282	7,054,921	11,509,586	3,639,808	3,789,247	2,173,390
Net Income (Loss)	105,648	399,119	1,465,397	3,077,446	4,203,720	1,307,086	1,247,391	1,289,939
Amazon.com	**2003**	**2004**	**2005**	**2006**	**2007**	**2008 Q1**	**2008 Q2**	**2008 Q3**
Net Revenues	$5,264,000	$6,921,000	$8,490,000	$10,711,000	$14,835,000	$4,135,000	$4,063,000	$4,265,000
Cost of Net Revenues	4,007,000	5,319,000	6,451,000	8,255,000	11,482,000	3,179,000	3,096,000	3,266,000
Net Income (Loss)	35,000	588,000	359,000	190,000	476,000	143,000	158,000	119,000
Yahoo.com	**2003**	**2004**	**2005**	**2006**	**2007**	**2008 Q1**	**2008 Q2**	**2008 Q3**
Net Revenues	$1,625,097	$5,257,668	$6,425,679	$6,969,274	$6,969,274	$1,817,602	$1,798,085	$1,786,426
Cost of Net Revenues	358,103	2,096,201	2,675,723	2,675,723	2,838,758	755,083	765,911	772,227
Net Income (Loss)	237,879	1,896,230	751,391	660,000	660,000	542,163	131,215	54,348
Overstock.com	**2003**	**2004**	**2005**	**2006**	**2007**	**2008 Q1**	**2008 Q2**	**2008 Q3**
Net Revenues	$234,603	$490,621	$794,975	$780,137	$765,902	$202,814	$188,836	$186,855
Cost of Net Revenues	209,320	424,183	678,502	690,333	641,352	168,843	155,627	154,736
Net Income (Loss)	(11,981)	(4,414)	(25,212)	(106,762)	(48,036)	(4,724)	(7,359)	(1,589)

Sources: 2008, http://www.ebay.com; http://www.google.com; http://www.yahoo.com; http://www.overstock.com; http://finance.yahoo.com; http://www.amazon.com

Also, eBay has expanded into Europe and Asia through acquisitions. It increased its auction reach with Alando in Germany, iBazar in France, Tradera in Sweden, Internet Auction in South Korea, and Baazee in India. eBay incorporated international classified ad Web sites into its portfolio with purchases of Loquo in Spain, Gumtree in the United Kingdom, Marktplaats in the Netherlands, and Den Bla Avis in Denmark. Each international acquisition allows eBay to expand and diversify its revenue base by purchasing established Web sites that the local culture understands.[38] This is an extremely important element when developing any sort of presence in a foreign country as eBay learned through its experience in China (discussed in the Customer Demographics and International Experience subsection).

Alliances

In addition to acquisitions, eBay uses alliances with small entrepreneurs and large companies to increase revenues and enhance the number of items available in the marketplace.

In 2004, eBay established a certified provider program consisting of exams, references, and an annual fee.[39] Partners provide services and products that sellers might need and eBay itself does not wish to offer, such as inventory management software, outbound logistics, or a full consignment business.[40] This helps eBay to attract sellers that might not otherwise use its services, or who wish to conduct a high number of transactions but lack expertise in certain areas. Having these services and products available helps sellers move more product than they would otherwise.[41] Activia is one of the best-known certified companies, providing marketplace listing tools to sellers of multiple items.[42] This alliance allows entrepreneurs to use the eBay name to grow their business while providing eBay fee revenue.

In 2006, eBay aligned with Yahoo! in a marketing alliance to promote revenue growth for both companies. Under the alliance Yahoo! became the exclusive advertising provider on eBay, the companies have a co-branded toolbar, and PayPal became Yahoo!'s preferred payment provider.[43] eBay also aligned with Google in 2006, making Google the primary advertiser on eBay's Web sites outside of the United States.[44] Google has sought to integrate Skype into the alliance as a method to further sales from Web advertising.

In 2007, eBay aligned with Northwest and Southwest Airlines to enable PayPal as a payment option, and with Wal-Mart and Myspace.com to promote the growth of Skype.[45] The alliance with Wal-Mart will allow eBay to sell Skype phone equipment in 1,800 retail locations.[46] These alliances help expand the brand name of both PayPal and Skype while also increasing revenue for eBay.

Although initially many smaller sellers were angered by eBay's 2008 alliance with Buy.com because Buy.com does not pay listing fees and its volume, free shipping, and ability to take returns hurt smaller sellers, this alliance is one of the largest potential revenue generators for eBay. Buy.com is a middle-of-the-market tool that links retailers with buyers, and it immediately added five million fixed-price listings to the eBay marketplace.[47] eBay executives have responded to the objections about its alliance with Buy.com by stating, "eBay is aggressively using price as a lever to improve the value and selection on eBay.com. Consistent with our goals, we have entered into a partnership with Buy.com to bring their new-in-season merchandise onto eBay.com. We expect to learn a great deal from this partnership and we will build upon the results."[48]

It appears that eBay will continue to use partnerships as a large part of its growth strategy. Alliances with online competitors such as Yahoo! have allowed online exposure growth, and certified provider programs have given eBay the opportunity to fill the gaps that they are unable or unwilling to fill.

eBay also seeks growth through internal innovation. Product development accounts for almost 18 percent of the company's operating expenses.

Internal Innovation

eBay's early innovations include My eBay, the feedback forum, and final value fees.[49] My eBay is a personal account on eBay that allows users to track their buying and selling activity, send and receive e-mail, update personal information, and view feedback reports. The feedback forum is intended to form trust between buyers and sellers. Each eBay member has a feedback profile that consists of three main elements: the feedback score, the feedback percentage, and the feedback reports. The feedback score is a rating of a member's trade history—the number of good reports about a member minus the number of bad reports. The feedback percentage is the percentage of users that have reported a positive feedback experience with a seller in a given year. The feedback report displays both positive and negative reports from buyers and sellers who have traded with a member and includes information about each transaction. The final value fees are the portion that eBay takes when an item sells (or ends with a winning bid). For items less than $25, the final value fee is 8.75 percent; for items between $25 and $1,000, the final value fee is 8.75 percent of the initial $25 plus 3.5 percent of the remaining value; for items over $1,000, the final value fee is 8.75 percent of the initial $25 plus 3.5 percent of the initial $25 to $1,000 plus 1.5 percent of the remaining value.

In 2005, eBay unveiled Kijiji.com, an online classified Web site resembling Craigslist. By 2008, Kijiji attracted five million unique monthly visitors and was available in over 1,000 cities across the globe.[50] In 2006, eBay launched eBay Express in the United States, the United Kingdom, and Germany, providing buyers with the ability to buy multiple items, much like Amazon.com. However, due to feedback from both buyers and sellers, eBay closed eBay Express in all three markets in 2008 to focus more on its main eBay site.[51] David Hsu, a management professor at Wharton describes eBay's internal innovation as, "a poor job of identifying synergistic opportunities . . . eBay's research group has not been able to drive much growth by internal innovation. … [eBay] has to get that spark the company had in the early days."[52]

Economic Downturn

When it makes its acquisition, alliance, and innovation decisions, eBay first considers the environmental factors that may influence its success. The increasing unemployment rate and the mortgage crisis have also contributed to a decline in disposable income. This may increase the number of sellers on eBay as those who are unemployed seek ways to make extra money, but fewer people are buying, and those who are demand low prices.[53] Thus, in September 2008 eBay lowered fees on fixed-cost sales by more than 70 percent in an effort to better compete with Amazon.com;[54] and starting in June 2009 infrequent sellers will be able to offer up to five items every 30 days without paying a listing fee.[55]

Customer Demographics and International Experience

An aging population poses potential challenges. Currently, 50 percent of eBay buyers are over the age of 45, 53 percent are male, and 72 percent earn more than $50,000 per year; but as baby boomers age, the number of consumers in this age group will decline.[56]

Additionally, significant shifts in ethnic composition are occurring in the United States. For example, the Hispanic population is growing and is expected to triple over the next 40 years. This will likely alter the type of products desired for purchase on eBay.[57] Furthermore, as eBay continues to pursue international expansion, the products in demand will change and it will need to

broaden its understanding of business practices and levels of service that are required to attract consumers in specific countries.

eBay did not succeed in its first attempt to establish a presence in China, most likely because it lacked insight into the Chinese culture. eBay entered China in 2002 by purchasing a third of China's principal online auction site, Eachnet.com. In 2003, eBay purchased and became the sole owner of Eachnet.com, but by 2005 it had lost significant market share to Taobao, the consumer auction segment of China's largest ecommerce company.[58] eBay failed to understand that its popularity in the United States would not automatically make it successful in China. Some of the complaints were that eBay did not provide phone service or allow bartering, and it did not react quickly enough when Taobao entered the market without charging user fees.[59] Despite its failure with Eachnet.com, eBay is in China for the long haul, as Whitman said, "market leadership in China will be a defining characteristic of leadership globally," and failure to establish itself there would be an "astronomical" setback for the company as a whole.[60] Therefore in 2007 it established a partnership with a Beijing-based Internet company, Tom Online Inc., taking a 49 percent stake in the company and possessing administration rights. This allows eBay to have strong local management that understands the culture and consumer desires. Tom eBay has done much to win the trust of Chinese consumers such as using an escrow service to hold payments until the buyer confirms satisfaction with the product. Whitman stated, "Whatever we do elsewhere to assure trust and safety, in China we have to do more."[61] eBay has had some success in China with Skype; Skype has grown faster in China than anywhere else.[62]

Technology and Competitive Challenges

Various technological trends may pose challenges for eBay. Staying aware of the trends and responding quickly is essential—as eBay learned from its misfortune in Japan. eBay lost significant market share to Yahoo! and pulled out of Japan in 2002 mostly due to failing to be up to date with the technology that Japanese users expected to be available on an auction site.[63] Another possible issue is that Skype's technology may threaten eBay's profitability by giving buyers and sellers an opportunity to conduct the transaction without using eBay and thereby circumventing eBay's fees.

Another aspect of technology that poses a challenge is that retailers have put great effort into improving their Web sites to make online shopping easier for consumers. Stores such as Best Buy, Nordstrom, Target, and Wal-Mart carry items in four out of five of eBay's top volume categories (electronics, computers, clothing/accessories, and home/garden). Consumers may prefer these retailers over eBay because they have greater confidence in their ability to return items and to have some sort of recourse if a purchased item is never received or is broken upon receipt. However, eBay was founded on its judicious use of technology and it has recently developed some technology to help it limit the number of legal proceedings related to counterfeit products.

Legal Issues

Fashion fakes constitute a $600 billion industry worldwide[64] and despite eBay's efforts to crack down on counterfeit merchandise, some eBay users continue to sell it. This has led to lawsuits against eBay from companies such as Rolex, Tiffany & Co., Hermès, Louis Vuitton, and L'Oreal. Lawsuit results have been mixed. Rolex first instigated a trial against eBay in 2001. The original ruling was overturned by a German court in 2007 because the judge believed that eBay could not be held liable for damages, but it should monitor its site to prevent fakes from being sold. Again in early 2009 Rolex brought a case against eBay, but the judge ruled in favor of eBay.[65] In the case against Tiffany & Co. in July 2008, a U.S. District Court judge ruled that eBay did not bear legal responsibility for sales of counterfeit goods in its marketplace and that "it is the trademark owner's burden to police its mark."[66] However eBay was not as fortunate in the French courts in the cases against Hermès and Louis Vuitton. It was ordered to pay Hermès $30,000 in damages because "by failing to act within [its] powers to prevent reprehensible use of the site, both the seller and eBay committed acts of counterfeiting;"[67] eBay was also instructed to compensate Louis Vuitton $63 million for "culpable negligence," and an additional $20 million in damages for unauthorized sales of its perfume.[68] Most recently, though, courts in Paris have ruled in favor of eBay in a case against L'Oreal, stating that "preventing the sale of counterfeit goods on the eBay platform encounters major difficulties when it comes to perfumes and cosmetics."[69]

eBay is dedicated to thwarting the sale of counterfeit products on its site. It has developed a filter program that detects offerings that blatantly violate trademark rights, established a team that works closely with law enforcement agencies, and even launched an anti-counterfeit campaign that aimed to educate buyers on how to avoid counterfeit products.

Tax law also may present challenges for eBay. Currently, if a consumer orders merchandise from a company that does not operate in his or her state of residence, no sales tax is paid on the item.[70] However, there is a possibility that legislation will pass requiring Internet purchases to be taxed. The IRS has also proposed that certain types of Internet companies, including eBay, should be required to collect and report individuals' earnings, allowing the IRS to ensure income taxes are being paid.[71] If this legislation passes, eBay users may move their business to sites that are not required to adhere to this policy.

To this point, eBay has been able to successfully navigate the company through environmental obstacles; it will need to continue to do so in order to remain profitable.

Financial Results

eBay derives most of its income from transaction costs associated with online sales. The product category that brings in the most revenue for eBay is vehicles (see Exhibit 5). Revenues from its businesses outside of the main eBay auction marketplaces have grown to 44 percent of total revenue. In 2008, of its $8.5 billion total net revenues, PayPal made up $2.3 billion (27 percent), Skype made up $551 million (6 percent), and marketplace transactions made up $5.6 billion (66 percent); 46 percent came from the United States, and 54 percent came from international sources.[72] In recent years, more and more of eBay's revenue is generated from international operations (see Exhibit 6).

In 2008 eBay was ranked second among the world's most valuable retail Web sites, only trailing Amazon in unique visitors and year-over-year growth.[73] In annual sales, eBay trails Google ($20.92 billion) and Amazon ($18.14 billion), beating Yahoo! ($7.32 billion) and Overstock ($.873 billion) (see Exhibits 3 and 4). Craigslist is not a public company and thus its sales data is not public information.

Marketplace revenue depends on gross merchandise volume (GMV). eBay breaks down GMV into the number of listings multiplied by the conversion rate (the percentage of items that sold) multiplied by the average sale price.[74] New-listing and GMV growth in 2008 came primarily from the international marketplace (see Exhibit 6). In 2008 eBay marketplaces had 86.3 million active users and 140 million listings at any given time.[75] Vehicles, parts, and accessories made up 31.5 percent of the top 16 GMV categories for the years 2006–2008, while consumer electronics and computers composed 16.4 percent, clothing and accessories was 8.5 percent, and home and garden was 6.8 percent (see Exhibit 5). eBay's expansion into fixed-price sales is positive, as this area increased to 45 percent of total GMV in 2008.[76] Regardless of the positive financial results that eBay

Exhibit 5 eBay Categories and Trends

	30-Sep-06	31-Dec-06	31-Mar-07	30-Jun-07	30-Sep-07	31-Dec-07	31-Mar-08	30-Jun-08	30-Sep-08
				$1 billion categories trend data (in millions)					
Vehicles	12,376	11,552	11,832	13,536	13,328	12,424	12,672	13,532	11,688
Parts and Accessories	3,764	4,172	4,680	5,016	4,596	4,768	5,348	5,392	4,620
Consumer Electronics	3,876	5,872	4,880	4,608	4,620	6,788	5,796	5,200	4,992
Computers	3,600	3,996	4,052	3,688	3,688	4,132	4,248	3,656	3,500
Clothing and Accessories	3,704	4,744	4,540	4,496	4,340	5,564	5,348	5,288	4,652
Home and Garden	3,036	3,496	3,584	3,640	3,700	4,120	4,244	4,184	3,840
Collectibles	2,208	2,804	2,684	2,388	2,380	2,948	2,772	2,468	2,232
Books/Movies/Music	2,780	3,032	3,124	2,720	3,000	3,288	3,456	2,952	2,864
Sports	2,496	2,668	2,584	2,892	2,836	2,884	2,940	3,232	2,992
Business & Industrial	1,752	2,012	2,232	2,220	2,140	2,300	2,584	2,452	2,212
Toys	1,700	2,564	2,136	1,940	1,940	2,748	2,396	2,144	1,952
Jewelry & Watches	1,644	2,184	1,972	1,960	1,924	2,508	2,332	2,216	1,988
Cameras & Photo	1,404	1,636	1,524	1,548	1,504	1,752	1,672	1,672	1,508
Antiques & Art	1,012	1,304	1,352	1,248	1,164	1,484	1,508	1,364	1,096
Coins & Stamps	900	1,044	1,320	1,068	1,028	1,192	1,428	1,188	1,032
Tickets & Travel	972	916	1,088	1,336	1,772	1,980	1,496	2,012	2,260
Total	47,224	53,996	53,584	54,304	53,960	60,880	60,240	58,952	53,428
Percentage Growth		14%	–1%	1%	–1%	13%	–1%	–2%	–9%

Source: 2008, eBay Annual Report, http://www.ebay.com

Exhibit 6 eBay Growth: U.S. vs. International

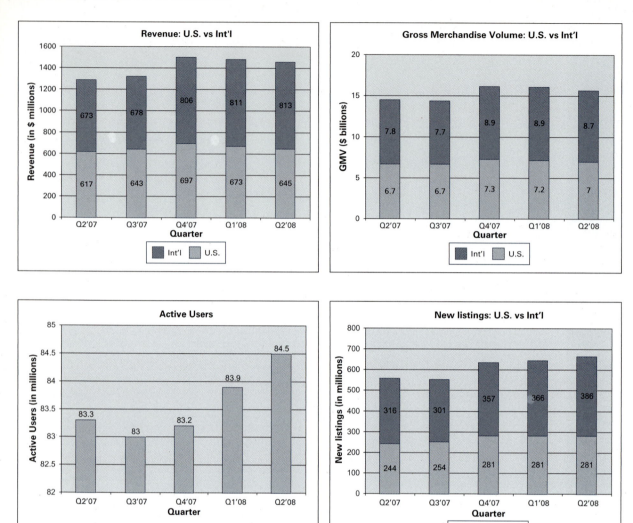

Source: 2008, Investor Relations, eBay company website, http:// www.ebay.com.

posted in 2008, there are some significant challenges for which the new CEO and other leaders must determine solutions.

Overview of Challenges

eBay is currently in a fast-cycle market, causing it to experience extreme external competitive pressure. This competitive pressure is from both dominant Internet companies such as Amazon, Yahoo!, and Google as well as small private companies such as Craigslist. eBay faces the challenge of differentiating itself from these competitors, while at the same time striving to attract

buyers and increasing revenues on each transaction. In an effort to attract more listings and higher revenues, eBay's alliance with Buy.com has sparked boycotts and a loss of some its core customers. eBay needs to find a balance between satisfying buyers and creating economically beneficial cost structures for large strategic alliance partners.

Given the current budget deficits of many states, they may push to overturn the 1992 Supreme Court ruling that liberated mail-order merchants from having to collect sales tax from a consumer in a state in which they do not have a physical presence. This would result in eBay having to ensure that sales tax is collected on each transaction, leading to increased costs and more book-keeping for eBay.[77]

Counterfeit merchandise affects eBay's image as a trustworthy auction site and poses the threat of more time and money spent in lawsuits. Current competition is fierce in the fast-cycle VOIP marketplace and potential government regulations of the VOIP industry could further affect the Skype brand. Additionally, Skype's technology is licensed from third parties and although there are contracts in place, future license renewals could increase costs or make it illogical for eBay to use this third-party software.[78]

eBay is currently at a unique period in company growth as its acquisition strategy has created a large conglomerate of companies that intertwine within the online marketplace arena, while looking for new avenues to gain market share and revenue. The e-commerce industry as a whole is in a growth-stage and competitors are gaining market share as they innovate at a faster pace than eBay. With Meg Whitman's retirement and the company's recent shift toward focusing on the fixed-price marketplace, eBay has entered a defining phase of its business.

NOTES

1. 2008, eBay: The world's online marketplace, http://pages.ebay.com/aboutebay/thecompany/companyoverview.html, December 4.
2. A. Schmidt, 2008, eBay CEO Meg Whitman to retire, MSNBC, http://www.msnbc.com, January 23.
3. R. Waters, 2008, eBay revenue to decline for first time, Financial Times, October 16; F. Ross, 2009, eBay's 4th quarter earnings—The recession? All Business, http://www.allbusiness.com, February 14.
4. 2008, eBay History, http://www.ebay.com, November 3.
5. Ibid.
6. 2008, eBay Form 10-K, http://www.ebay.com.
7. 2008, eBay Form 10-K, http://www.ebay.com.
8. 2008, Hoover's Company Records: Amazon.com Inc., November 1.
9. T. Wolverton, 2000, Amazon, Sotheby's closing jointly operated auction site, Cnet News, http://news.cnet.com, October 10.
10. 2008, Amazon announces beginning of multi-year frustration-free packaging initiative, Forbes, http://www.forbes.com, November 3.
11. B. Stone, 2008, Profit is up at Amazon, but outlook is reduced, New York Times, October 23, B3.
12. 2008, Hoover's Company Records: Yahoo! Inc., November 25.
13. 2008, 2007 Yahoo! Inc. Form 10K, http://www.yahoo.com, February 27.
14. 2007, Yahoo! to close North American auction site, MSNBC, http://www.msnbc.msn.com, May 9.
15. A. Sorkin & S. Lohr, 2008, Pursuing Yahoo! again, Microsoft shows need for a Web franchise, New York Times, May 19, A1.
16. B. Stone, 2008, Now comes the hard part as Yahoo! wrestles with a question of direction, New York Times, November 18, B1.
17. 2008, Corporate information: Our philosophy, http://www.google.com, November 28.
18. Ibid.
19. 2007, Google Inc., Form 10-K, http://www.google.com.
20. 2008, craigslist fact sheet, http://www.craigslist.org, November 16.
21. J. Fine, 2008, Can Craigslist stay oddball? BusinessWeek, May 19, 75.
22. 2008, The Portfolio Story, http://ebayinkblog.com/wp-content/uploads/ThePortfolioStory_24Oct08.pdf, October.
23. 2008, Transaction fees domestic transactions, PayPal company Web site, http://www.paypal.com, December 3.
24. 2008, eBay 2007 Form 10-K, 51.
25. C. Wolf, 2008, eBay cuts fixed-price sales fees by 70%.
26. 2008, eBay to buy Shopping.com for $620 million, http://news.cnet.com, December 3.
27. 2008, eBay to buy Rent.com for $415 million, http://news.cnet.com, December 3.
28. 2008, eBay files corporate governance suit to protect its investment in Craigslist, eBay News, http://www.news.ebay.com, April 22; 2008, Craigslist-eBay suit details icy relationship, PC Magazine, www.pcmag.com, May 13; 2008, eBay goes public with Craigslist complaint, USA Today, http://www.usatoday.com, May 1.
29. 2008, About Skype, Skype company Web site, http://www.skype.com, December 3.
30. 2008, eBay to buy Skype in $2.6bn deal, http://news.bbc.co.uk, December 3.
31. 2008, About Skype.
32. 2009, Skype available on Apple App store, About Skype, http://www.skype.com, March 31; 2008, What to do with Skype, http://news.cnet.com, December 3.
33. 2009, eBay Inc. announces plan for 2010 initial public offering of Skype, About Skype, http://www.skype.com, April 14.
34. 2008, Is Stubhub the ticket for eBay, BusinessWeek, http://www.businessweek.com, December 3.
35. 2008, About Stubhub, Stubhub company Web site, http://www.stubhub.com/, December 3.
36. 2008, eBay 2007 Form 10-K.
37. 2008, About Stubhub.
38. 2008, The portfolio story.
39. Ibid.
40. 2008, eBay certified provider program, http://www.ebay.com, November 16.
41. 2008, Inside eBay's innovation machine—case studies, CIO Insight, http://www.cioinsight.com, November 16.
42. 2008, Certified providers program.
43. 2008, Yahoo!, eBay in Web advertising pact, MSNBC, http://www.msnbc.msn.com, December 3.
44. 2008, Google and eBay form an alliance to tailor adds to every customer, http://www.guardian.co.uk, December 3.
45. 2008, eBay 2007 Form 10-K, http://www.ebay.com, November 25, 51.
46. 2008, Wal-Mart to sell Skype phone gear, MSNBC, http://www.msnbc.msn.com, December 3.
47. B. Stone, 2008, Buy.com deal with eBay angers sellers, New York Times, July 14, 1.
48. R. Smythe, 2008, eBay partners with Buy.com, http://www.ebayinkblog.com, May 3.
49. A. Hsiao, 2009, Understanding the eBay feedback system, About.com, www.ebay.about.com, May 20; 2009, Final value fees, http://www.ebay.com, May 20; 2009, Using My eBay, http://www.ebay.com, May 20.
50. 2008, About Kijiji, http://bayarea.kijiji.com, December 3.
51. 2008, About eBay express, http://www.ebay.com, December 3.
52. 2008, eBay, After Meg, Forbes, http://www.forbes.com, December 3.
53. R. Waters, 2008, Add eBay to the cart, Financial Times, http://www.ft.com, October.
54. C. Wolf, 2008, eBay cuts fixed-price sales fees by 70%, Washington Post, August 21, D03.
55. R. Metz, 2009, eBay cuts auction listing fees for casual sellers, The Boston Globe, http://www.boston.com, May 12.

56. 2008, eBay Seller Central, http://www.ebay.com, November; 2008, The changing nature of retail: Planting the seeds for sustainable growth, *Deloitte Consulting*, http://www.deloitte.com, November 18.

57. 2005, Changing demographics result in shifting consumer habits, http://www.retailforward.com, November 4.

58. K. Hafner & B. Stone, 2006, eBay is expected to close its auction site in China, *New York Times*, http://www.nytimes.com, December 19.

59. Ibid., R. Hof, 2006, eBay's China challenge, *BusinessWeek,* http://www.businessweek.com, December 19.

60. K. Hafner & B. Stone, eBay is expected to close its auction site in China; B. Powell & J. Ressner, 2005, Why eBay must win in China, *Time*, http://www.time.com, August 22.

61. V. Shannon, 2007, eBay is planning to re-enter the China auction business, *New York Times*, http://www.nytimes.com, June 22.

62. Ibid.

63. B. Powell & J. Ressner, Why eBay must win in China; 2001, How Yahoo! Japan beat eBay at its own game, *BusinessWeek*, http://www.businessweek.com, June 4.

64. A. Szustek, 2009, eBay victorious over Rolex in latest counterfeiting lawsuit, *Finding Dulcinea*, http://www.findingdulcinea.com, February 27.

65. D. Woollard, 2009, Rolex loses eBay lawsuit, http://www.luxist.com, February 26.

66. 2008, Judge rules for eBay over fake Tiffany jewelry sales, *International Herald Tribune*, July 15, F12.

67. C. Matlack, 2008, Hermes beats eBay in counterfeit case, *BusinessWeek*, http://www.businessweek.com, June 6.

68. R. Waters, 2008, eBay wins court battle with Tiffany, *Financial Times*, http://www.ft.com, July 14; R.Waters, 2008, Moment of truth for eBay on luxury goods, *Financial Times*, http://www.ft.com, June 30.

69. I. Steiner, 2009, eBay fends off L'Oreal's counterfeiting lawsuit, *Auction Bytes*, http://www.auctionbytes.com, May 13.

70. A. Broache, 2008, Tax-free Internet shopping days could be numbered, *CNET News*, http://www.cnetnews.com, April 15.

71. 2008, Internet broker tax reporting, eBay Government Relations, http://www.ebay.com, November 20.

72. 2008, eBay 2007 Form 10-K, http://investor.ebay.com/annuals.cfm, 51, November 25.

73. 2009, eBay narrows the gap, but Amazon tops in traffic again, Nielsen says, *Internet Retailer*, http://www.internetretailer.com, February 27.

74. 2008, Q3 20008 Earnings Slides, eBay company Web site, http://www.ebay.com, November 16.

75. 2008, eBay 2007 Form 10-K, http://www.ebay.com, 51.

76. 2008, eBay Fact Sheet, http://www.ebay.com, November 28.

77. 2008, Sales tax on the Internet, http://www.nolo.com, December 4.

78. 2008, eBay 2007 Form 10-K, 29.

Jenny Mead, Andrew C. Wicks, Patricia H. Werhane,
R. Edward Freeman

University of Virginia, Darden School Foundation

Hence gout and stone afflict the human race;
Hence lazy jaundice with her saffron face;
Palsy, with shaking head and tott'ring knees
And bloated dropsy, the staunch sot's disease.
　　—A ROMAN POET'S DESCRIPTION OF LEAD
　　　POISONING[1]

Ellie Shannon, the division manager overseeing bromine production for the Indiana-based Great Lakes Chemical Corporation (Great Lakes), faced a thorny dilemma. In a matter of hours, she had to make a recommendation to the company's board of directors on which of three policy options she felt the company should pursue. There was fierce public opposition to the leaded additive that Great Lakes produced via its subsidiary, Octel Associates. In 1997, Octel was one of the few remaining producers of lead additives, which had long ago been banned in the United States and most developed countries, but were still used in many developing countries. There was worldwide pressure, particularly from environmentalists, on Great Lakes to stop producing the lead additive. However, ending production would have a huge negative impact on Great Lakes's profits and some negative effects on countries that had not made the transition from leaded to unleaded gasoline for their cars and machinery.

Great Lakes Chemical Corporation

In the 1930s, Great Lakes was originally founded as an oil and gas exploration company, McClanahan Oil Company. It's name was later changed to Great Lakes Chemical Corporation. In 1948, CEO Charles Hale acquired the Michigan-based Great Lakes Chemical Corporation in an effort to turn the company into a natural resources conglomerate.[2] During the 1950s, Great Lakes focused on petroleum production, but moved out of that field and into the bromine and chemical business. In 1958, Emerson Kampen, who would later become CEO, discovered that southern Arkansas had great quantities of bromine-rich brine deposits. With this resource, Great Lakes became the top presence in the bromine business, eclipsing even Dow Chemical, which sold its bromine business to Ethyl Corporation in 1986. Bromine was used in a variety of retail and industrial products and was particularly important as a fire-retardant additive in textiles and plastics.

By the last decade of the twentieth century, Great Lakes developed and produced a variety of specialty chemical products for such applications as water treatment, specialty household cleaners, flame retardants, polymer stabilizers, fire suppressants, and performance chemicals. Products included methyl bromide, used for agriculture; clear brine fluids for oil drilling; bromine-, phosphorus-, and antimony-based flame retardants and synergists; and fluorine specialties for automotive component systems. Despite a plethora of products, Great Lakes had its greatest success with Octel Associates, a tetraethyl lead (TEL) producer. After acquiring Octel Associates in 1989, it accounted for well over half of the company's total operating profit each year, even as its share of sales declined.

Great Lakes never set out to be a lead additive producer. The company acquired Octel Associates for its capacity to produce bromine. While Octel used that

This case was prepared by Jenny Mead, Senior Ethics Research Associate; Andrew C. Wicks, Associate Professor of Business Administration; Patricia H. Werhane, Ruffin Professor of Business Ethics; and R. Edward Freeman, Elis & Signe Olsson Professor of Business Administration. It was written as a basis for class discussion rather than to illustrate effective or ineffective handling of an administrative situation.

chemical to make the additives, Great Lakes used them in other products such as color stabilizers and fire retardants. Great Lakes was willing, in order to get the bromine-producing capability, to "take on the last years of the production of lead additives—as well as an ethical, and public relations, challenge."[3]

Great Lakes had flourished under the leadership of Emerson Kampen, who became CEO in 1977. At that time, the company was tiny, with barely $50 million in revenues. By 1993, when Kampen's declining health forced him to step down, Great Lakes had become a multinational presence with $1.8 billion in sales. Kampen and other Great Lakes executives had wanted to focus on Octel's unique saltwater bromine-extraction process, but put those plans on hold when it discovered the TEL "gold mine" that Octel provided.

Lead Then and Now

By the end of the twentieth century, leaded gasoline was banned in most of the developed world (see Exhibit 1). Scientific studies in the 1960s proved its harmful effects: brain damage in children, respiratory problems in the elderly, and damage to air quality, among others. Many developing countries still had not eliminated lead as an additive, in part because of a lack of government regulation and further due to cars that used leaded gasoline. Although many Central and South American countries had taken various steps to eliminate lead, these efforts were overshadowed by the lead problems that still existed in China, the Middle East, and many African countries.

Numerous reports outlined the dangers of leaded gasoline, widely considered the fastest and most efficient

Exhibit 1 History of Lead

6500 BC: Lead discovered in Turkey.

3000 BC: First significant production of lead.

500 BC–300 AD: Roman lead smelting produces dangerous emissions. Greek physicians give clinical description of lead poisoning.

1800s: A German chemist discovers tetraethyl lead (TEL) and U.S. medical authorities diagnose childhood lead poisoning, which, in 1904, is linked to lead-based paint.

1900–1929: After automotive scientists find that an alcohol-gasoline blend is a viable motor fuel and, later, that benzene in this mixture prevents engine knocking, it becomes standard fuel for automobiles, even though the National Lead Company admits in 1921 that lead is poisonous. In 1924, 15 workers at New Jersey and Ohio refineries die from exposure to TEL. Throughout the 1920s, experts warn against the dangers of lead in gasoline production and fumes, with the U.S. Surgeon General temporarily suspending the production and sale of leaded gasoline in 1925, but the use of TEL continues for the next five decades.

1930s: By the mid-1930s, 90 percent of gasoline sold in the United States contains TEL.

1940s: Report concludes that eating lead paint chips causes physical and neurological disorders including behavioral, learning, and intelligence problems in children.

1950s: Smog in Los Angeles is identified as the interaction of hydrocarbons and oxides of nitrogen, with car emissions being the biggest source. In the mid-1950s, an automaker pact stifles development of emissions-control devices.

1960s: The study "Contaminated and Natural Lead Environments of Man" offers the first hard proof that high lead levels in industrial nations are man-made and endemic. The Senate Public Works Committee holds first hearings on air pollution. Automakers settle suit by U.S. Justice Department for conspiracy to delay the development of pollution-control devices.

1970s: The Clean Air Act is passed in 1970 and the Lead-Based Paint Poisoning Prevention Act passes in 1971. To avert threatened legislation to restrict use of the internal-combustion engine, GM agrees to add catalytic converters to meet Clean Air Act standards. Active element of converters—platinum—is contaminated by leaded gas, presaging its demise. EPA gives notice of proposed phase-out of lead in gasoline. The new standards are finalized in 1976. The Energy Tax Act (1978) creates ethanol tax incentive, expanding use of ethanol in United States.

1980s: U.S. National Academy of Sciences calls leaded gasoline the greatest source of atmospheric lead pollution. The EPA reports in 1983 that between 1976 and 1980, the amount of lead consumed in gasoline dropped 50 percent and blood-lead levels dropped 37 percent. Benefits of phase-out exceed costs by $700 million. The Reagan administration, which had opposed lead phase-out, reverses its position, and by 1986, the primary phase-out of leaded gas in the United States is complete.

1990s: The United Nations Conference on Environment and Development, commonly known as the Rio de Janeiro environmental summit, calls for worldwide lead phase-out. Study shows that U.S. blood-lead levels declined 78 percent from 1978 to 1991. American Academy of Pediatrics study shows direct relationship between lead exposure and IQ deficits in children. World Bank calls for world phase-out of leaded gasoline.

2000: European Union bans leaded gasoline.

Sources: http://www.ehso.com/ehshome/Lead_effects.htm (accessed July 24, 2008) and J. Lewis, 1985, Lead poisoning: A historical perspective, *EPA Journal*, May, www.epa.gov/history/topics/perspect/lead.htm (accessed July 10, 2008).

means of sending lead particles into the atmosphere to be inhaled and then into the soil, where they could remain indefinitely. Phasing out lead internationally, many experts believed, was necessary to reduce human exposure to lead and prevent lead poisoning.

Indeed, the statistics on leaded gasoline were alarming.[4]

- Lead adversely affects the neurological system, the kidneys, and the cardiovascular system.
- In adults, lead exposure causes increased blood pressure, hypertension, and a higher risk of cardiovascular disease.
- Children are most adversely affected by lead exposure. Children between one and two years of age absorb 40 to 50 percent of ingested lead, whereas adults absorb only 10 to 15 percent of ingested lead.
- In developing countries where leaded gasoline, leaded paint, and other major exposure routes were still common, all children under age two and more than 80 percent between the ages of three and five have blood lead levels that exceeded the World Health Organization (WHO) standard. An estimated 15 million to 18 million children in economically developing countries suffer permanent damage from lead poisoning, resulting in lowered intelligence (as measured by IQ tests), learning disabilities, hearing loss, reduced attention span, and behavioral abnormalities.

In the mid-1990s in Egypt, where leaded gasoline still existed, lead in the air caused 6,500 to 11,600 heart attacks, 800 to 1,400 strokes, 6,300 to 11,100 premature adult deaths, and approximately 820 infant deaths annually.

Great Lakes: TEL Profits and Dilemmas

In 1994, Octel represented 59 percent, or $259 million, of Great Lakes total operating profit of $439 million. Some Wall Street analysts "projected that Octel's share of profits from current operations would not fall below 50% for many years, despite an 8% annual decline in pounds of TEL sold."[5] By 1995, Great Lakes had $5 billion in annual revenue, with consistent and healthy 15 percent operating profit margins. That same year, Standard & Poor's raised Great Lakes's credit rating to AA− from A+.

A key question for Great Lakes, as well as for producers of products such as asbestos, tobacco, and agrichemicals, was "under what conditions should legal products that are being phased out of the developed world to protect people's health or the earth's environment be sold to poorer nations?"[6] Great Lakes never anticipated that it

would be dealing with that question for so many years. Demand for leaded gasoline was still high in developing countries. Great Lakes had no competitors, because other major producers had discontinued making tetraethyl lead (TEL), the additive for gasoline. Without much competition, Great Lakes flourished financially and controlled 90 percent of the market, which was otherwise unappealing because of the environmental issues, the large capital costs involved in building plants, and the unsavory publicity.

Pressure Mounts

For a number of years, Great Lakes capitalized on Octel without much public criticism from environmentalists, most likely because Great Lakes had a low profile as an industrial middleman. By the mid-1990s, environmental groups were putting pressure on the company to stop selling lead. Great Lakes readily admitted that its lead additive was not only its greatest money-maker, but also extremely harmful. They agreed that eventual elimination was necessary but that the environmentalists' call for a worldwide TEL ban by 2010 was unrealistic. This was in large part because, outside of the industrialized world, there were not enough refineries capable of producing unleaded gas. Also, many cars had no catalytic converters; also, if they ran on lower-octane unleaded gasoline, these cars would emit greater amounts of pollutants, such as benzene.[7]

Despite its production of lead additives, Great Lakes declared that it was committed to environmental responsibility (see Exhibit 2 for its vision, mission, and values statements and Exhibit 3 for its environment, health, and safety policy). After all, the company argued, many of the other chemicals it produced were replacements for many existing chemicals far more harmful and noxious than lead. Its largest nonbromine business, for example, recycled agricultural waste into a metal-processing chemical.

Critics of the company, however, said that Great Lakes had too many financial incentives for deluding itself about TEL's harmful effects. Making sure that customers using hazardous products were fully informed about the consequences, critics argued, was the "bare minimum"[8] of ethical corporate behavior. But some critics also acknowledged that, beset with economic and environmental problems, developing countries "are unlikely to be able to make sophisticated judgments about something as arcane as leaded gas, especially when the refineries are often in the hands of governments or ruling elites whose financial incentives are to stay with the status quo."[9]

Environmentalists argued that Great Lakes should contribute some of Octel's profits toward subsidizing a more rapid transition away from TEL. Many organizations,

Exhibit 2 Great Lakes Chemical Company: Goals, Vision, Mission, Values

Goals

At Great Lakes, our goal is to be recognized as the premier company in the markets we serve. Achieving this goal requires a compelling vision, clear priorities, and a commitment to shared values necessary to succeed as a company. We believe these are the same values that help us succeed in the other areas of our lives as well.

Vision

Great Lakes's stated vision was to make the world safer, more productive, and healthier, and to create innovative products, value-added services, and responsible practices.

Mission

The company's stated mission was "to be recognized as the premier company in the markets we serve." The company stated that it planned on reaching its goal by providing "world-class responsiveness" as well as "innovative products" and services; superior financial performance; maintaining a vital corporate culture; and being a "responsible global citizen."

Values

Great Lakes set of stated values included:

- Inspiring trust
- Creating value
- Focusing on results
- Working as a team
- Leading by engaging others
- Actively learning and teaching
- Communicating openly and honestly

Source: Adapted from http://www.greatlakeschemical.com (accessed November 17, 2004). (Great Lakes has since been acquired by Chemtura, so the Web site is no longer available.)

such as the World Bank and WHO, asserted that the cost of transitioning to unleaded gas was not as high as originally thought, and the net impact on economic growth would not be substantial. Indeed, projections were that in the short term, there might be increases in costs and a decline in productivity, but in the longer term, the changeover would be a net positive for developing countries. But as of 1996, leaded gasoline was still sold in large quantities in other countries: It comprised 93 percent of all gasoline in Africa; 94 percent in the Middle East; 30 percent in Asia; and 35 percent in Latin America.[10]

Policy Options

Shannon considered Great Lakes's three policy options. First, the company could continue to supply the lead additives to developing countries for the foreseeable future. Demand probably would remain high and competition minimal, but the vocal opposition from environmentalists and others would likely only grow stronger. Shannon remembered that as the United States itself developed economically, it had used leaded gasoline until switching to unleaded was environmentally necessary and economically feasible. Eventually, she thought, developing countries would reach the same point where the transition would be easier economically. As a result, she wondered why others thought it was Great Lakes's responsibility to bring about this change, especially when supplying the gas additive was helping developing countries' economic development.

Second, Great Lakes could get out of selling leaded gasoline in the near future, without worrying about the preparations or consequences to the developing countries. In short, Great Lakes could simply "wash its hands of the leaded gasoline business and its repercussion."

Exhibit 3 Great Lakes Chemical Company's Energy, Health, and Safety Policy

Great Lakes was committed to "protecting the health and safety" of its employees, communities, and the environment. This commitment, according to Great Lakes, began with "our management, flows through our organization, and is shared by each and every employee."

The company was committed to complying with all legal requirements applicable to their operations and products; protecting the health and safety of employees as well as the public and the environment via robust identification of risks involved in its products and operations; continually improving its environmental, health, and safety performance and reviewing these goals annually; operating according to the "Responsible Care® Guiding Principles and Requirements"; working actively with stakeholders in developing products that provided "benefits to society in accordance with the principles and values expressed in this Policy"; and sharing the policy as well as other information about operations and products with all interested stakeholders.

Source: Adapted from http://www.greatlakeschemical.com (accessed November 17, 2004). (Great Lakes has since been acquired by Chemtura, so the Web site is no longer available.)

This option held the most promise for rescuing its reputation, but the company would take a big financial hit. Environmental groups were pushing the company aggressively toward this option and thought it would provide the shock that governments needed to change their policies and phase out leaded gasoline. Nonetheless, Shannon realized, there was no guarantee that governments in developing countries would be receptive. Even so, she realized, it could be smart for Great Lakes to anticipate a time when government regulation would force her company's hand; it was better, no doubt, to act before the government did.

Third, Great Lakes could aggressively phase out its participation in this marketplace, with a five-year deadline. In the meantime, the company would need to actively work to push developing countries' governments to change their policies and switch to unleaded gasoline. But there was always a good chance that Great Lakes would get pushback from governments and could be unsuccessful in getting them to change. Although it seemed in many respects a prudent "middle path," this option could leave the company with the worst of both worlds—it might not be aggressive enough to create change in governments and prove to its detractors its commitment to environmental responsibility, while also still ending its revenue stream from leaded gas.

Shannon struggled with which option seemed best to recommend to the top brass at Great Lakes. There was nothing illegal in Great Lakes making and selling lead additives, but the company, which had always been low profile, was now developing a black eye from the bad press. Shannon realized that while for now environmental pressure came from the United States and other developed countries, eventually it would also come from the developing countries. Great Lakes placed a great deal of importance in the well-being of its shareholders and remaining a viable company, but it also wanted to be—and to be seen as—a respectable corporate citizen.

NOTES

1. J. Lewis, 1985, Lead poisoning: A historical perspective, EPA Journal, http://www.epa.gov/history/topics/perspect/lead.htm, May (accessed July 10, 2008).
2. Great Lakes Chemical Corporation, *FundingUniverse*, http://www.fundinguniverse.com/company-histories/Great Lakes-Chemical-Corporation-Company-History.html (accessed July 9, 2008).
3. B. J. Feder, 1995, Alchemist's Dream Come True, *New York Times*, August 17, D-1.
4. Information taken from "Get the Lead Out!," 2003, *Ecoforum* 26(1).
5. Feder.
6. Feder.
7. Pollution-reducing catalytic converters, which ran on unleaded fuel, were introduced in 1975 as U.S. automakers began complying with the EPA's lead phase-out timetable. The converters enabled a chemical reaction in an internal combustion engine that converted the toxic by-products to less toxic substances.
8. Feder.
9. Feder.
10. D. Seyferth, 2003, The rise and fall of tetraethyl lead. 2, Organometallics, *American Chemical Society*, 22: 5177.

Marit Loewer

Otto Beisheim School of Management

It was a Friday morning in May 2008 when Andreas Welsch, General Manager of the German department of Henkel Adhesives Technologies for Consumers and Craftsmen, arrived early at the Henkel site in Düsseldorf-Holthausen, Germany (see Exhibit 1).

The chimneys at the enormous production site were already bellowing smoke, even at this early hour. As Welsch walked to the impressive glass building where his office was located, he thought about his upcoming meeting with company marketing executives. A

Exhibit 1 Henkel site in Düsseldorf-Holthausen

Marit Loewer prepared this case under the supervision of Professors Lutz Kaufmann and Matthias Koch to provide material for class discussion. The authors do not intend to illustrate either effective or ineffective handling of a managerial situation. The authors may have disguised certain names and other identifying information to protect confidentiality.

gloomy forecast awaited him in the latest consumer report: Gasoline prices kept rising and further looming price increases caused German consumers to worry about their purchasing power. Concerns about price stability and uncertainty resulting from the financial crisis and the flagging U.S. economy fueled economic fears among German consumers. This news would certainly influence Henkel's business and increase the importance of today's meeting.

Upon his arrival at the conference room, he spoke to his marketing managers:

We are facing a challenging situation. As we already know, the growth of our markets has slowed down in recent years and the raw material price increase puts pressure on our margins. But even worse now, one of our competitors in the adhesives business is just about to enter one of our core categories with very low prices. This will certainly affect our sales numbers. The time has come where we have to develop a long-term strategy in order to escape the constant war for market share with our competitors. Competing for an ever smaller market is not a solution. This new strategy is of utmost importance for the adhesives business, if we want to stay put as market leaders in the long run. It has to be developed quickly as senior management expects it in two days!

Company Profile: Henkel AG & Co. KGaA

Based in Düsseldorf, Germany, Henkel AG & Co. KGaA was an international group with worldwide presence and listed on the London Stock Exchange. Its sales were €13,074 million (see Exhibit 2) and employed approximately 53,000 people in the fiscal year 2007. Henkel was among the most internationally aligned German-based companies in the global marketplace. Consumers in approximately 125 countries around the world trusted in brands and technologies that originated on the Henkel production line. The company was organized into three operational business sectors: Laundry & Home Care, Cosmetics/Toiletries, and Adhesives Technologies (see Exhibit 3). It was the umbrella company for well-known brands such as Persil, Schwarzkopf, Pritt, and Pattex.

History of Henkel

Founded in 1876 as Henkel & Cie in Aachen by 28-year-old merchant Fritz Henkel (see Exhibit 4), the company's first successful product was a washing powder based on water-glass. In contrast to all similar products, which were at that time sold loose, this heavy-duty detergent

Exhibit 2 Key Financial Data of Henkel AG & Co. KGaA for 2006–2007

Key Financials

Henkel
A Brand like a Friend

Figures in mill. euros		2006	2007	Change
Sales		12,740	13,074	+2.6%
Operating profit (EBIT)		1,298	1,344	+3.5%
Return on sales (EBIT)	in %	10.2	10.3	+0.1 pp
Net earnings		871	941	+8.0%
Earnings after minority interests		855	921	+7.7%
Earnings per preferred share [1]	in euros	1.99	2.14	+7.5%
Return on capital employed (ROCE)	in %	14.5	15.4	+0.9 pp
Capital expenditures on property, plant, and equipment		431	470	+9.0%
Research and development expenses		340	350	+2.9%
Employees (annual average)	number	51,716	52,303	+1.1%

[1] basis: share split (1:3) of June 18, 2007   pp = percentage points

© Henkel 2008   1

Exhibit 3 Henkel Business Sectors

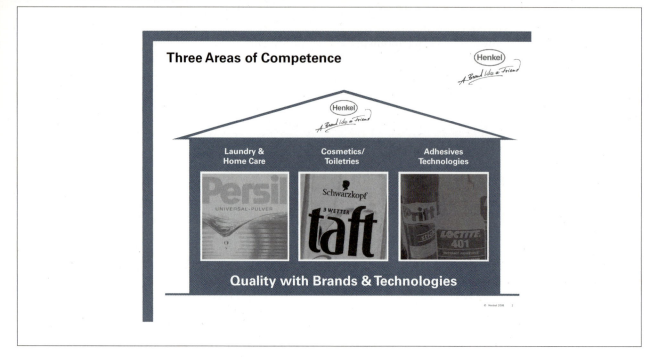

was marketed in handy packets. It was a huge success, and, two years later, Henkel relocated his company to Düsseldorf by the Rhine to take advantage of logistics and better sales opportunities. In the years to come, many innovations were developed at Henkel. In 1907,

Persil, the first self-acting laundry detergent, became the pillar for the company's growth and helped radically simplify the laborious and time-consuming household chore of doing laundry. However, Fritz Henkel did more than revolutionize laundry care. He was also a pioneer

Exhibit 4 The Founder of the company

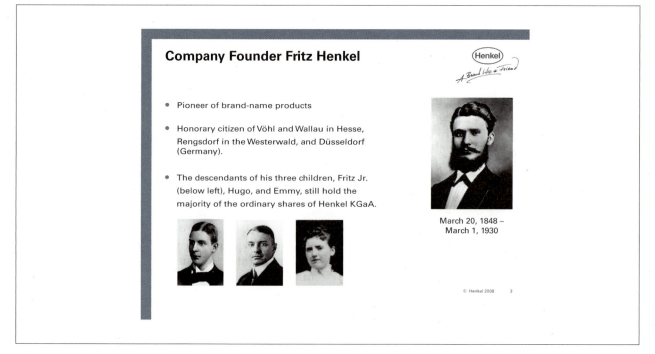

of modern brand management. He systematically raised awareness about Persil in the general public by means of innovative and sensational advertising campaigns. Ever since then, the combination of outstanding product quality and intelligent brand management has been the cornerstone of Henkel's success. In 1922, the product range was extended to adhesives, and, in 1950, Henkel entered the cosmetics markets with the acquisition of TheraChemie (hair colorants). The Henkel brand grew very quickly as a result of international expansion.

Henkel's diverse product range and strengths that ranged from modern consumer products for everyday use to complex chemical and technical system solutions for industrial consumers influenced the company to concentrate on its corporate identity. Branded products and technologies were identified as strategic pillars for the future, and four business sectors were defined: Laundry and Home Care, Cosmetics/Toiletries, Consumer and Craftsmen Adhesives, and Henkel Technolgies (industrial and engineering adhesives, sealants, and surface treatments). The slogan "A Brand Like a Friend" was introduced to convince consumers to embrace the broad variety of Henkel products and facilitate the perception of Henkel as a brand, not a corporation. Henkel's intention was to suggest proximity to the customer and foster their trust in Henkel quality.

The latest major acquisition was completed in March 2008: Henkel took over the Adhesives and Electronic Materials business from Akzo Nobel, previously owned by National Starch. Following the integration, Henkel's Adhesive Technologies business sector was expected to increase to around €7.5 billion in annualized sales in 2008. By completing this acquisition, Henkel further strengthened its leading position in the global adhesives markets, particularly in the industrial segment.

Adhesive Technologies Business Sector

Effective April 1, 2007, the previously separately managed business sectors of "Consumer and Craftsmen Adhesives" and "Henkel Technologies" were merged to form the Adhesive Technologies sector. This enabled the adoption of a unified market approach with better utilization of core competencies of both businesses. The Adhesive Technologies business sector offered adhesives, sealants, and surface treatment products for use in household and office applications for the do-it-yourself populace, professional craftsmen, and for industrial and engineering applications. The new sector was the world leader in its segment, with about €5,711 million in sales in 2007, accounting for 43 percent of Henkel revenues overall (see Exhibit 5). In view of the heavily fragmented competitor landscape with over 1,500 vendors and a relatively small number of global players offering a comparable product portfolio, the business sector saw itself as market leader in each

Exhibit 5 Sales and EBIT by Business Sector

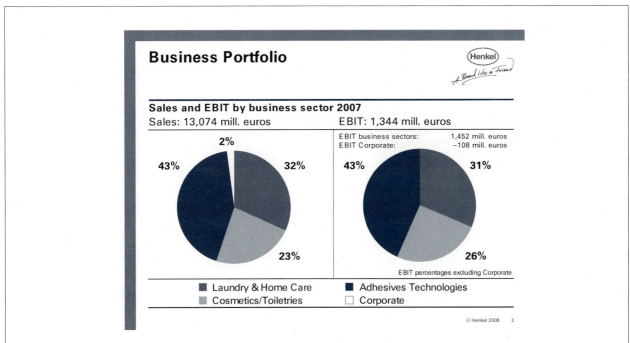

of its product categories. The variety of markets for adhesives was unmatched: the packaging industry, auto manufacturers, aircraft building, power plants, steel-mills, tin-can producers, and powerhouses were all customers of Henkel adhesives. Different competitors existed in each of these markets, and often each competitor only served a special niche and sector. Only very few companies were active in as many segments as Henkel, and this was the reason that Henkel was almost triple the size of its next best competitor.

Adhesive Technologies for Consumers and Professionals in Germany

The market catering to consumers and professionals for adhesive technology in Germany was also complex, with many different segments and sub-segments. Henkel was exceptional in that it offered so many different products under one corporate umbrella (see Exhibit 6).

Products were available for different customer segments. Consumers were divided into the two subgroups of households/offices, which were offered products for repair jobs and handcrafts, and "do-it-yourself" customers with products for renovation and repairing. On the other hand, there were professionals to whom Henkel offered products for construction and intensive usage, such as External Thermal Insulation Composite Systems. Sales channels for the customer segments were very different: products for consumers were sold in do-it-yourself (DIY) stores, specialist

shops, drugstores, and food retailing shops. Driven by the ever-growing discount channel, price had become a key parameter in all trade negotiations and even in the communication of the trade itself.

The products for professionals were sold in specialist stores, and producers had to follow a completely different approach in this channel. Sales representatives would contact the relevant craftsmen—painters, tilers, floorers, and so on—individually, as each one of them chose the products they would use and had to be convinced about the advantages of new products. The craftsmen were a rather conservative group who mostly trusted in products they already knew and worked with for a long time. Thus, they were difficult to convince about the advantages of new products, and it took the sales representatives about five to six visits per person to gain a new customer. Therefore, the quantity and quality of sales representatives were, understandably, key factors in how well a product sold. Professionals tended to stick with products with which they were familiar in order to avoid customer complaints. Craftsmen faced several challenges in earning new customers, including their high hourly wages and the challenge of showing, in advance, that their work was superior to that of others in the field and, as such, worthy of a higher salary. The most common way for customers to make their choice was through looking at ads for craftsmen in the Yellow Pages. No ranking system of any kind existed for craftsmen, and customers were often very hesitant

Exhibit 6 Sub-brands under the Henkel Brand

to order such professional services because they were unsure of the quality they would receive in return.

Henkel offered its customers (the do-it-yourself category and professionals) high-quality products (see Exhibit 7), as this was traditionally the way to differentiate the firm's products from the competition. Many customers were not familiar with Henkel brands, but instead knew the sub-brands, as Henkel did not invest in the overall Henkel name. The Henkel organization was built on these sub-brands because product managers for each sub-unit developed their own marketing strategy for the products of their sub-brand. Therefore, customer confidence had to be established for each sub-brand, and only some were already well known. Brands like Pritt, Pattex, and Ponal were the most popular brands in the DIY segment.

Adding new features to improve their products was another method Henkel used to outperform its competitors. Their product range was constantly expanding and different products had been developed for every possible area of application. However, in the DIY segment, this complexity did not make the task of choosing the "right" product easy for consumers. Information about renovation products in the DIY stores was not always sufficient, and qualified store personnel were sometimes difficult to find. Also, other supplementary information sources were rare. Customers could not access sufficient information about the proper application of a product, the required quantity for a certain renovation job, or

new product information. Most women avoided DIY stores completely because the brand image and product descriptions were very technical. Traditionally, it was a man's task to maintain the house, and although many women were doing craftwork to decorate their homes, they felt less comfortable with renovation work. In addition, women preferred models and concrete samples of how a house would look after renovation so as to get some inspiration, but these samples were hard to come by. Even in the professional segment, the broad product range was not appreciated by all customers: some preferred to have a "universal" product for a certain task, since, from their point of view, many new products did not offer additional value.

Overall, it was difficult for Henkel to increase the number of products sold as its products had already achieved solid market positions. On the other hand, it was difficult to meaningfully influence the size of different markets in that each market was affected by trends associated with primary materials, such as tiles and wallpaper, as well as individuals' overall inclination to build and renovate.

The entire market had undergone a drastic downturn over the past 10 years. The reunion of East and West Germany in 1989 led to several years of strong growth. First, the population of East Germany entered the market and added another 13 million consumers. Second, East Germany was under-served by distribution channels for renovation products and many new DIY

Exhibit 7 Products of Henkel Adhesives Technologies

stores had to be set up. Third, the foundations of most houses in East Germany were very old and in need of renovation. Moreover, many new buildings were erected after the reunion, sponsored by the government through tax incentives. All these factors caused a boom in the industry that lasted until the late 1990s. There were few new competitors because of the entry barriers created by the need for significant capital investments to enter the industry. During the boom, many existing competitors built new capacities to be able to respond quickly and adequately to the high demand.

After 10 years of prosperity in the industry, the German DIY market became saturated with the 3,300 DIY stores that were built over the years and saw a decrease in public building licenses, which in turn reduced the demand for renovation material. Also, the percentage of homeowners in Germany was one of the lowest in Europe. Eventually the market began to shrink and competition intensified to secure and gain larger shares of a declining market.

The competition in the adhesives market for consumers and craftsmen was diversified among different product segments and target groups. In the adhesives segment for households and offices, UHU was the largest competitor in Germany. The company was part of the Bolton Group, a privately owned Italian business. UHU's product range was comparable to Henkel's in this segment. But UHU had one specific advantage—their adhesive "Alleskleber" was well known to every German since childhood and nearly synonymous with household adhesives. It was widely available and sold in supermarkets as well as stationery shops and malls, and, therefore, had the largest market share.

For the professional craftsmen target group, it was important to offer direct contact between the producer and client for support and product enhancements, technical advice, addressing complaints, and warranty support. Product innovations were another factor that companies used to attract customers. Henkel saw itself as an innovator in the industry and built its strategy around innovation. This positioned Henkel in the premium segment, but the strategy often deployed by competitors was to battle over price—the tighter the market, the fiercer the price war. This hurt every competitor. Henkel was very proud of its broad product range, which accentuated its unique image in the competitive landscape. Often, other companies tried to emulate Henkel's advantage by expanding their product portfolio to capture a share of the shrinking market, so as to reduce the factor of differentiation in competition.

Besides shrinking markets, increasing energy prices also cut into profitability. Henkel was highly dependent on energy prices in terms of product manufacturing and transportation. Since oil was the base for many of

Henkel's products, oil prices directly influenced Henkel's profit margins. Employee salaries were also continuously rising. Henkel was a member of the IG Chemie, the industrial union for chemical companies that was very successful in negotiating higher wages.

In the long run, consumer markets were projected to stagnate. Low birth rates in Germany would lead to a lower population and a higher average age in the future. The typical age limit for doing DIY work was just 50 years, and this demographic development would lead to a shrinking target customer group.

The Business Situation for the Adhesives Technologies Department

The overall adhesives market influenced the business situation of Henkel's Adhesives Technologies department. Even if it was able to hold profits at the same level as the previous year, its profitability would be below expectations. In addition to the impact of high raw material costs and increasing salaries negotiated by the IG Chemie, it also had to compete successfully against its competitors in each business segment.

For example, in the tiler segment, the company PCI—a subsidiary of BASF—held a 28 percent market share and was the market leader, while Henkel's market share was at single digits. Even though PCI was the major player, it was not the most aggressive on price. These international companies entered the local market from outside Germany because Germany was still attractive: Requirements for quality standards for renovation work were comparably high. Local professional craftsmen appreciated high-quality products and product innovations offered by these international companies, as compared to other countries, in order to avoid customer complaints.

Italian producer Mapei entered the German market in 2006. It was number one internationally in the tiler segment with €1.3 billion turnover. It acquired several companies, including Soppro, which were already active in the German market and had local knowledge. These companies then received orders at such low prices that none of the local producers could compete with them. For these projects, they then assigned sub-contracts to tilers who had to use Mapei's products for their work. Henkel's strategy was different. It tried to gain market share by developing superior products. Henkel tried to convince tilers of the quality of its products with incremental product innovations. Henkel's developers had produced a "low dust" tile adhesive, which was healthier for tilers to work with. Another innovation was a "lightweight" tile adhesive. The product usage results of 25 kg

(55 lb) were comparative to jobs done with 80 kg (176 lb) of a conventional tile adhesive.

Nevertheless, Henkel's product innovations were not systematically based on current customer needs, but rather on technical feasibility. Market research completed by other departments recognized new trends in consumer behavior, such as the preference for wellness and health products and the awareness for eco-friendly goods. However, these trends were not incorporated during development of new adhesives products. Research and development was laboratory-driven rather than customer-driven. Therefore, products became increasingly specialized and equipped with new features that would allow them to be used with all possible materials and situations. The product range that served the same purpose widened.

In all, products became increasingly comparable throughout the industry. In the long run, incremental improvements would not assure business success because of the saturated market for adhesives. A further specialization in adhesives would not increase demand, but would only take away some market share from an existing product. It was a spiraling race with competitors trying to gain some temporary market share.

As a response to this development, Henkel's strategy was two-fold. First, Henkel strived to be better than its competition. It aimed to gain market share through innovation, POS excellence, distribution expansion, and better marketing concepts. Second, profitability was to be secured by cost-saving projects, simplification of processes, and improvements in the organization.

Andreas Welsch's introductory speech to his marketing executives included a presentation on the current business situation and the latest consumer report. It caused a lively discussion in the room about how to develop a long-term strategy for the department of Adhesives Technologies for Consumers and Craftsmen. Different possibilities were debated, which led to the conclusion that in the long run, the competition could not be beaten by incremental improvements of the existing products. A promising alternative would be to expand the existing market by creating new and uncontested market space where competition would be irrelevant. New target groups would expand the customer pool and alleviate the pressure of fighting with the competitors over the same customers.

Welsch was pleased with the direction the discussion was taking and announced that this meeting should be the kickoff for a Blue Ocean Strategy implementation. A creative but structured process to develop ideas for new markets and customer groups had to be started—and there was no time to lose.

David F. Larcker, Brian Tayan

Stanford Graduate School of Business, Rock Center for Corporate Governance

Retail Grocery Industry

Retail grocery sales represent a significant portion of the U.S. economy. According to Standard & Poor's, there were over 190,000 grocery stores in the United States in 2006, generating $900 billion in sales.[1] The industry was highly competitive, with companies operating on low gross and net margins. Food products—whether fresh produce and meats or packaged foods—were often subject to fierce price competition. As a result, grocery stores were generally under significant pressure to reduce their operating costs in order to maintain profitability.

For the last several decades, the grocery industry grew roughly in line with gross domestic product and was considered a mature industry. In order for companies to succeed, they needed to find effective strategies to steal customers from competitors. Many sought to differentiate themselves through store format, store location, product mix, ancillary services, or quality of customer service. Strategies, however, could easily be imitated by competitors, putting grocery store chains under constant pressure to innovate and remain efficient.

In general, growth also required the expansion into new store locations. Because most markets were already saturated with incumbent players, growth often came through acquisition. Some successful companies with a differentiated strategy, however, were able to grow organically. No matter the route of growth, the retail grocery industry was capital intensive, requiring significant investment in new stores and store remodels.

Companies that failed to grow often went bankrupt or were acquired.

In 2006, the largest sellers of groceries by revenue were Wal-Mart ($127 billion), Kroger ($60 billion), SuperValu ($34 billion), and Safeway ($34 billion).[2] The emergence of Wal-Mart in the grocery business was a relatively recent phenomenon. Already the largest discount merchandiser in the world, the company entered the grocery business in the 1990s through a new store format called the Supercenter, which sold both groceries and general merchandise in one location. In a few short years, Wal-Mart leveraged its Supercenters to catapult itself into the leading position in the grocery industry. In the early 1990s, the company had essentially zero dollars in grocery sales. By 1999, it was the fifth-largest grocery seller, with $15 billion in sales. In 2002, it surpassed Kroger as the industry leader, with $48 billion in sales. By 2006, it had further solidified its lead, generating almost twice the revenue from grocery sales as former industry leader Kroger. As a low-cost provider and the dominant retailer in the United States, Wal-Mart's presence in the grocery industry added to the pressure on all other providers to differentiate their offerings and develop new strategies to survive (see Exhibit 1 for summary statistics of the grocery store industry).

Kroger

In 2006, Kroger was the second-largest seller of food and groceries in the United States after Wal-Mart, with

Exhibit 1 Retail Grocery Industry: Summary Statistics

Grocery Store Sales (2006)	Number of Stores	Sales (in billions)
Supermarkets	**34,019**	**$499.5**
Conventional	27,006	345.5
Limited assortment (under 1,500 items)	2,283	10.4
Natural/gourmet foods	1,358	13.0
Warehouse (low price/service)	442	2.4
Military commissary	172	4.1
Superstore combo (30,000 sq. ft. min.)	2,758	124.0
Other food formats	**159,544**	**$407.2**
Wholesale club stores	1,119	96.0
Grocery (under $2 million)	13,306	17.7
Convenience (excluding gas)	144,703	291.3
Military	416	2.2
Total grocery stores	**193,563**	**$906.7**

Source: Standard & Poor's, 2008, Industry Survey: Supermarkets and Drugstores, January 24.

Top 10 Supermarket Chains*					
1999 Sales (in billions)		2002 Sales (in billions)		2006 Sales (in billions)	
1. Kroger	$42.2	1. Wal-Mart	$48.7	1. Wal-Mart	$126.7
2. Albertson's	31.0	2. Kroger	44.8	2. Kroger	59.8
3. Safeway	28.1	3. Safeway	29.4	3. SuperValu	34.0
4. Ahold USA	19.4	4. Albertson's	28.5	4. Safeway	33.7
5. Wal-Mart	15.7	5. Ahold USA	25.0	5. Ahold USA	24.2
6. Winn-Dixie	14.6	6. Delhaize America	14.7	6. Publix	20.2
7. Publix	12.6	7. Publix	14.5	7. Delhaize America	17.3
8. Food Lion	11.9	8. Winn-Dixie	12.6	8. H. E. Butt Grocery	11.2
9. SuperValu	8.2	9. SuperValu	8.2	9. Winn-Dixie	8.5
10. A&P	7.7	10. A&P	7.8	10. Meijer	7.3

* Estimated data for supermarket items only.

Source: Standard & Poor's, Industry Survey: Supermarkets and Drugstores, December 7, 2000; June 26, 2003; and January 24, 2008.

$66.1 billion in sales. The company operated 2,468 supermarkets in 44 markets. Kroger held the number one or number two market-share position in 38 of these 44 markets. Its store chains were regionally managed under two-dozen brand names, including Kroger, Ralphs, Fred Meyer, Food 4 Less, Fry's, and Dillons. Many of these stores were combination food and drug stores, and 600 of the stores included gas stations. The company also operated 779 convenience stores, 412 jewelry stores, and 42 food processing plants.[3]

The history of the Kroger Company began in 1883 when Bernard H. Kroger opened the Great Western Tea Company in Cincinnati, which became one of the first chain stores in the country.[4] Kroger expanded his company by buying out competitors at depressed prices during times of economic panic. In 1902, he changed the name of the company to the Kroger Grocery and Baking Company. After World War I, he continued his aggressive expansion, and, by 1929, Kroger had over 5,000 stores across the nation.

Throughout the twentieth century, Kroger Company introduced a slew of innovations to improve the economics of its operations and try to gain local competitive advantages. In the early 1900s, it was one of the first grocery stores to also offer bread freshly baked in the store and a fresh meat department. During the Great Depression, to further improve the quality of its produce, it began sending procurement officials to visit its suppliers' fields to inspect crop quality. During the next decade, Kroger consolidated its assortment of company manufactured products under one private label as it sought to build on a reputation for quality. In the 1950s, it began a sweeping effort to replace many of its local neighborhood locations with larger supermarkets. Such efforts, which continued for several decades, led to consistent growth in sales.

Over the years, Kroger made further changes as it sought to stay ahead of the competition. In the 1960s, it entered the pharmacy business, purchasing stand-alone pharmacy chains and adding drug-dispensing departments within its grocery store locations. The company also built on its reputation for quality by adding nutritional information on the packaging of its private label brands and "sell by" dates on perishable items. It also installed electronic scanners to reduce checkout times and improve customer service.

In the 1980s, Kroger became the target of private equity investors who were attracted to the free cash flow generated by its retail stores. Kroger received bids from the Dart Group and Kohlberg Kravis Roberts & Co. (KKR), offering to take it over for as much as $5 billion. To fend off these investors, the company undertook a radical recapitalization in which it took out substantial debt, paid out a significant one-time dividend of $40 per share to shareholders, and increased employee ownership of the company's stock. Following the recapitalization, Kroger had $5.3 billion in debt, a net deficit of over $2.5 billion, and more than 30 percent of its shares were held by employees.

As a result, during the next several years the company was forced to further tighten its operations and focus on debt reduction. It installed new management information systems to better track inventory. It also increased the number of combination food and drug stores, giving it greater scale and return on investment. In 1998, Kroger completed the largest acquisition in its history, purchasing the Fred Meyer chain (with stores primarily in 12 Western states) for $8 billion in stock and the assumption of $4.8 billion in debt. The move helped Kroger expand in the West, where Wal-Mart's presence was minimal.

David Dillon assumed the position of chief executive officer in 2003 and chairman of the board the following year. Previously, he had served as president and chief operating officer at Kroger, having originally come to the company through Kroger's 1982 purchase of Dillon Companies. At the time, Dillon managed Dillon Companies, a family-owned grocery chain based in Kansas.

Under Dillon's leadership, Kroger continued to expand its middle-market position. Faced with competition from natural food providers and boutique grocery stores at the high end and discount grocery providers at the low end, Kroger further expanded its fresh foods and produce departments and added an assortment of prepared meals. Such efforts were intended to cater to the mainstream markets and still protect operating margins. To this end, the company also increased its private-label offerings in product areas where it believed it could offer an attractive product to customers at an economical price.

To increase the frequency of customer visits, the company added fuel stations next to many of its stores. Also, Kroger contracted with Dunnhumby (wholly owned by U.K. grocery giant Tesco) to manage its customer loyalty program and provide advanced analytics. The company reviewed the purchasing patterns of Kroger customers and grouped them into psychographic profiles.

Kroger relied on findings from the data to refine store format, adjust its product mix on a store-by-store basis, and mail promotional coupons to Kroger loyalty cardholders. The company believed that its relationship with Dunnhumby offered it a key advantage.[5]

Under Dillon's tenure as chief executive officer, total company revenue increased from $53.8 billion (fiscal year 2003) to $66.1 billion (fiscal year 2006). Operating income increased from $1.4 billion to $2.2 billion, net income from $315 million to $1.1 billion, and earnings per share from $0.41 to $1.56.[6]

During these years, Kroger decreased its store count from 2,532 to 2,468. Same-store sales growth (excluding sales of gasoline) decreased 0.4 percent in 2003, and then increased 0.8 percent in 2004, 3.5 percent in 2005, and 5.6 percent in 2006. Of note, Kroger weathered a four-and-a-half-month strike by the United Food and Commercial Workers union in southern California in 2004 as it sought to renegotiate its contract agreements. The strike—which affected Kroger, Safeway, and Albertson's—involved 71,000 workers walking off the job and significantly impacted operating results. The three grocery store chains and the labor union eventually signed a new contract agreement, which allowed for a reduction in hourly wages and health care benefits. Kroger common stock, which traded at $17 per share in June 2003 when Dillon became chief executive officer, was at $26 at the end of fiscal year 2006 (see Exhibit 2 for financial and operating results at Kroger).

Executive and Director Compensation at Kroger

The executive compensation program at Kroger included six elements: salary, performance-based annual cash bonus, performance-based long-term cash bonus, equity, retirement and benefits, and perquisites. Dillon received a base salary of $1.15 million in 2006.[7]

The performance-based annual cash bonus allowed for the payment of a cash bonus resulting from the successful achievement of one-year financial and operational targets. For 2006, 30 percent of the plan was earned based on identical sales growth targets; 30 percent was based on EBITDA targets (earnings before interest, taxes, depreciation, and amortization); 30 percent was based on implementation targets for the corporate strategic plan; and 10 percent was based on performance of new capital projects compared to budget. The annual payment was calculated by taking into account performance relative to targets set at the beginning of the year. Independent directors

Exhibit 2 Kroger: Selected Financial Information

(in millions, except per share)	2002	2003	2004	2005	2006
Revenues	$51,760	$53,791	$56,434	$60,553	$66,111
Operating Income	2,573	1,374	843	2,035	2,236
Net Income	1,205	315	(104)	958	1,115
Debt	$8,574	$8,364	$7,971	$7,232	$7,060
Shareholders Equity	3,850	4,011	3,619	4,390	4,923
Earnings Per Share	$1.52	$0.42	$(0.14)	$1.31	$1.54
Dividends Per Share	—	—	—	—	$0.195
Ending Share Price	$15	$19	$17	$18	$26
Average Diluted Shares	791	754	736	731	723
Market Value Equity	$11,865	$14,326	$12,512	$13,158	$18,798
Enterprise Value	20,439	22,740	20,483	20,390	25,858
Store Count	2,488	2,532	2,532	2,507	2,469
Same Store Sales	0%	(0.4%)	0.8%	3.5%	5.6%
Gross Margin Percentage	27.0%	26.3%	25.3%	24.8%	24.2%

Notes: Fiscal year ends January 31 of the following year. Same-store sales exclude gasoline sales, except for 2002 where figure was not disclosed.

Source: The Kroger Co., forms 10-K, filed with the Securities and Exchange Commission. Share price information from Center for Research in Securities Prices (University of Chicago).

retained the right to adjust performance objectives during the year. For 2006, Dillon earned $2.1 million under this plan, or 141 percent of the targeted bonus amount.

The performance-based long-term cash bonus was based on the successful achievement of four-year targets. Measurement of results was made following both the second year (the *phase-in component*) and the fourth year. Targets were established for four undisclosed "key categories, based on results of customer surveys" and the reduction of total operating costs as a percentage of sales (excluding gasoline). The long-term cash bonus plan was implemented in fiscal year 2005 and no payments had been made as of fiscal year 2006.

The equity component of the executive compensation program included stock option and restricted stock grants, which were intended to align the interests of management with the interests of shareholders. The size of the grants awarded was based on a benchmarking report prepared by compensation consultancy Mercer Human Resources Consulting, which in turn was based on comparable grants made by peer companies. The company noted in its 2006 proxy that it had been decreasing the number of stock options and increasing the number of restricted stock awards over the previous few years, because of their greater perceived value and changes in accounting standards.

Retirement and other benefits included a defined contribution program, defined benefit program, deferred compensation plan (which allowed participants to defer up to 100 percent of their cash compensation each year, at an interest rate equal to Kroger's 10-year borrowing rate), and severance and extended health care benefits in the event of a change in control.[8]

Perquisites included personal use of company airplanes (with executives responsible for paying the variable costs of operation), life insurance, reimbursement for the tax costs of participation in the non-qualified retirement plan, and reimbursement of up to $4,500 for financial planning services. This last benefit was discontinued as of 2007. Kroger noted in the proxy that the board "does not believe that it is necessary for the attraction or retention of management talent to provide the named executive officers a substantial amount of compensation in the form of perquisites."

Non-executive directors on the board at Kroger received an annual retainer of $75,000. The chair of each committee received an additional $12,000 annual payment, and each member of the audit committee, as well as the lead director, received an additional $10,000 annual payment. Each non-executive director also received a restricted stock and stock option grant each year in December. Directors who had served since before 1997 received medical and retirement benefits (see Exhibit 3 for compensation figures for Dillon, other named executives at Kroger, and Kroger board members).

Exhibit 3 Kroger: Compensation and Related Information

Compensation for Chief Executive Officer and Other Named Executives							
	Base Salary	Bonus	Stock Awards	Option Awards	Change in Pension/ Deferred Comp	Other	Total
David Dillon Chairman & CEO							
2006	$1,155,991	$2,116,770	$519,160	$3,311,870	$1,008,309	$142,437	$8,254,537
2005	1,100,000	1,940,131	—	2,473,620	NA	105,762	5,619,513
2004	1,083,974	736,361	—	2,786,880	NA	86,156	3,717,791
2003	880,062	244,962	2,517,000	—	NA	50,197	3,692,221
Named Officers (2006)							
CFO	499,099	635,031	97,835	339,653	256,221	31,819	1,859,658
Vice Chairman	809,969	1,340,621	195,956	794,327	360,184	44,530	3,545,587
President & COO	809,969	1,340,621	195,956	811,355	698,272	83,891	3,940,064
Exec. Vice President	575,413	767,496	533,782	576,090	711,031	87,552	3,251,364

Options valued using Black-Scholes pricing model. In 2006, the assumptions were: expected volatility 27.6 percent, risk-free rate 5.07 percent, dividend yield 1.50 percent, and average term 7.5 years.

Exhibit 3 Kroger: Compensation and Related Information (*Continued*)

Chief Executive Officer: Stock Option Exercises						
Year	Shares Acquired	Value Realized	Exercisable Options	Unexercisable Options	Value Exercisable	Value Unexercisable
2006	30,000	$247,950	729,000	716,000	$5,586,010	$5,545,540
2005	172,000	1,669,930	576,000	849,000	1,188,580	1,333,247
2004	—	—	590,000	707,000	2,074,073	336,924
2003	120,000	1,270,500	482,000	515,000	2,443,137	808,941

Non-Executive Director Compensation						
	Fees	Stock Awards	Option Awards	Change in Pension/ Deferred Comp	Other	Total
12-Director Average (2006)	77,316	46,242	52,023	2,758	108	$178,447

Executive and Director Stock Ownership (2006)			
CEO	938,446	729,000	1,667,446
CFO	75,994	167,000	242,994
Vice Chairman	428,320	465,000	893,320
President & COO	224,497	473,500	697,997
Exec. Vice President	116,875	250,833	367,708
Directors	2,500–43,000	0–25,000	2,500–68,000

Other Information (2006)	
Ownership Guidelines	Stock and options in dollar amount equal to five times base salary (CEO), four times base salary (other named executives), and three times base salary or annual retainer (directors).
Severance Provisions	All management who are at least 40 and have more than six years of service are entitled to payment ranging from 9 to 20 months' salary and bonus. All stock options and restricted stock immediately vest.
CEO SERP (Present Value)	None
Largest Shareholders	AXA Financial, 66,457,092 shares, 9.4 percent; Lord, Abbett & Co, 46,202,740 shares, 6.5 percent; Kroger Savings Plan, 40,480,889 shares, 5.7 percent
Number of Directors	16
Number of Independent Directors	13
Staggered Board	No (voted to declassify in 2006)

(*Continued*)

Exhibit 3 Kroger: Compensation and Related Information (*Continued*)

Other Information (2006)	
Lead Director	Yes
Number of Board Meetings	6
Number of Audit Committee Meetings	9
Number of Compensation Committee Meetings	4
Number of Corporate Governance Committee Meetings	4
Compensation Consultant Used	Mercer Human Resources Consulting
Peer Group (Compensation)	Albertson's, Costco, CVS, Great Atlantic & Pacific Tea, Rite Aid, Safeway, SuperValu, Target, Walgreens, Wal-Mart
Peer Group (Stock Performance)	Albertson's, Costco, CVS, Great Atlantic & Pacific Tea, Koninklijke Ahold, Marsh Supermarket Safeway, SuperValu, Target, Wal-Mart, Walgreens, Whole Foods, Winn-Dixie
Five-year Total Return Performance: Kroger	28.31 percent
Five-year Total Return Performance: S&P 500 Index	44.66 percent
Five-year Total Return Performance: Peer Group	2.54 percent

Source: Kroger Co., forms DEF-14A, filed with the Securities and Exchange Commission, Equilar, Inc.

Safeway

Safeway was the fourth-largest seller of food and groceries in the United States, with $40.2 billion in fiscal 2006 sales. The company operated 1,761 food and drug stores primarily in California, Oregon, Washington, Alaska, Colorado, Arizona, Texas, Chicago, the Mid-Atlantic states, Canada, and Mexico (through a 49 percent interest in a joint venture). Safeway store chains operated under regional brand names, including Safeway, Pak'n Save Foods, Vons, Pavilions, Dominick's, Randall's, and Tom Thumb. The company also owned Blackhawk, a niche company that distributed third-party gift cards to Safeway and other retailers. The prepaid cards were branded for use at major retailers such as Barnes & Noble, Best Buy, Gap Inc., Starbucks, and The Home Depot, or for general use under the American Express, MasterCard, and Visa names.[9]

The history of Safeway began in the early 1900s when S. M. Skaggs and, later, his son Marion B. Skaggs opened a chain of retail grocery stores in California.[10] The stores offered an attractive assortment of food products, particularly fresh meats and produce. In 1926, Charles Merrill, cofounder of investment firm Merrill Lynch, approached Skaggs about combining his company with the grocery chain Safeway Stores, which Merrill had recently acquired. Together, the combined operation would have over 650 stores, with Skaggs as its president. Under Skaggs's leadership, Safeway expanded rapidly, aided by acquisitions, and reached over 3,200 stores by 1931.

Over the next several decades, Safeway implemented a series of innovations to increase its competitiveness in the industry. In the 1950s, the company launched a major renovation campaign, replacing older stores with larger supermarkets. Larger-format stores included expanded produce, dairy, meat, and frozen food sections. In the 1960s, it took its expansion overseas, opening stores in England, Australia, Hawaii, and Alaska. In the 1980s,

Safeway invested heavily in updating its management information systems and expanded its consumer marketing programs.

Like Kroger, Safeway found itself the target of private equity buyers in the 1980s. Unlike Kroger, however, Safeway acceded to its suitors, agreeing to be acquired by Kohlberg Kravis Roberts & Co. for $69 per share, valuing the company at $5.3 billion, including the assumption of $1.1 billion in debt.[11] Following the buyout, Safeway's balance sheet was highly leveraged, as nearly all of the company's equity was replaced with debt. In order to reduce leverage, the company made a series of divestitures, including its British operations (which were run separately as Safeway PLC) and several underperforming stores in the United States. The company also aggressively cut costs to improve operating efficiency. The restructuring efforts were so effective that the company found itself more profitable on a smaller revenue base in 1988 than it had been in 1985. In 1990, Safeway went public again.

Steven Burd became chief executive officer of Safeway in 1993 and was still in that position as of 2006. Burd had worked as a consultant to the company while it was under private equity ownership. During the 1990s, he concentrated on increasing sales, holding down operating costs, and further reducing the company's debt load. With a strengthened balance sheet, he embarked on an acquisition binge, purchasing Vons in southern California (1997), Dominick's Supermarkets in Chicago (1998), Carr-Gottstein Foods in Alaska (1999), Randall's Food Markets in Texas (1999), and Genuardi's Family Markets in Pennsylvania, Delaware, and New Jersey (2001).

Burd's tenure was not without its challenges. In the early 2000s, the company struggled with operational issues that affected the results of some of its recently acquired chains. Furthermore, the company faced a series of challenges with its union workforce as it sought to hold down wages and benefits. In 2004, Safeway faced the same four-and-a-half-month strike that affected Kroger and Albertson's. As the principal negotiator with the union, Burd faced considerable public criticism from union sympathizers.

Beginning in 2003, the company announced its most recent strategic initiative: the redesign of every one of its more than 1,700 stores over the following six years. Safeway committed up to $1.6 billion per year over a total of six years to support the remodeling of all of its stores.[12] The new format stores included an upscale design with wood floors to replace the more dated white linoleum. They also offered a wider selection of fresh produce, high-quality meats and fish, prepared meals, and expanded offerings of natural and organic foods. To this end, the company added a private-label O Organics line of products—certified by the USDA—to complement its standard Safeway SELECT brand. Many of the locations also included a Starbucks store-within-a-store.

Under Burd's tenure as chief executive officer, total company revenue increased from $15.2 billion (fiscal year 1993) to $40.2 billion (fiscal year 2006). Operating income increased from $441 million to $1.6 billion, net income from $123 million to $871 million, and earnings per share from $0.25 (adjusted for splits) to $1.94. During these years, Safeway increased its total store count from 1,078 to 1,761. Over 40 percent of its stores had been renovated into the Lifestyle format by 2006. Same-store sales growth (excluding sales of gasoline) decreased 1.3 percent in 2004 and then increased 4.3 percent in 2005 and 3.3 percent in 2006. Safeway common stock, which traded at $4 per share (adjusted for splits) in 1993, was at $35 at the end of fiscal year 2006 (see Exhibit 4 for financial and operating results at Safeway).

Executive and Director Compensation at Safeway. The executive compensation program at Safeway included five elements: salary, annual bonus, equity, retirement, and other benefits. Safeway noted in the proxy that "in comparison to similar companies, we believe our compensation programs place greater emphasis on the achievement of company-wide goals, rather than on the achievement of individual goals." The board of directors also noted that "in compensating our executives, we place greater emphasis than other companies on the objective of increasing the market value of our stock." As a result, the company sought to provide cash compensation that was below the median of its peer group, and to set performance-based equity incentives above the median of its peer group, to the extent that the company achieved outperformance.[13] Burd received a base salary of $1.33 million in 2006.

The annual bonus payment was based on two plans: an operating performance bonus plan and a capital bonus plan. Under the operating bonus plan, the board set annual performance goals for identical-store sales, operating profit, and working capital. For fiscal 2006, Burd was eligible to earn an operating performance bonus up to 170 percent of his annual salary. The actual payment amount was based on the extent to which performance targets were achieved. For example, if Burd achieved targets, he stood to earn 50 percent of the maximum bonus and a bonus payment equal to 85 percent of his salary would be paid. For 2006, performance targets were specified as same-store sales growth of 3.0 percent (excluding sales of gasoline) and operating profit of $1.548 billion. Actual results were 3.3 percent same-store sales group and operating profit of $1.6 billion, and Burd received the maximum bonus allowed.

Under the capital bonus plan, the board set performance goals related to the performance of recent

Exhibit 4 Safeway: Selected Financial Information

(in millions, except per share)	1993	2002	2003	2004	2005	2006
Revenues	$15,215	$34,917	$35,727	$35,823	$38,416	$40,185
Operating Income	441	948	574	1,173	1,215	1,600
Net Income	123	(828)	(170)	560	561	871
Debt	$2,689	$8,436	$7,822	$6,763	$6,359	$5,868
Shareholders Equity	383	3,628	3,644	4,307	4,920	5,667
Earnings Per Share	$0.25	$(1.77)	$(0.38)	$1.25	$1.25	$1.94
Dividends Per Share	—	—	—	—	0.15	0.2225
Ending Share Price	$4	$23	$22	$20	$24	$35
Average Diluted Shares	492	467	442	449	450	448
Market Value Equity	$1,968	$10,741	$9,724	$8,980	$10,800	$15,680
Enterprise Value	4,657	19,177	17,546	15,743	17,159	21,548
Store Count	1,078	1,808	1,817	1,802	1,775	1,761
Same Store Sales	2.1%	(2.4%)	(4.5%)	(1.3%)	4.3%	3.3%
Gross Margin Percentage	27.2%	31.5%	30.0%	29.6%	28.7%	28.8%

Notes: Fiscal year ends December 31. Per share data and share count information adjusted for splits (4-for-1).

Source: Safeway Inc., forms 10-K, filed with the Securities and Exchange Commission. Share price information from Center for Research in Securities Prices (University of Chicago).

capital investments, including store remodels and new store openings. Performance was measured by the return on invested capital achieved by the end of the first and third years. For fiscal 2006, Burd was eligible to earn a capital bonus up to 30 percent of his annual salary. Median targets were set at a weighted average return on assets of 27.2 percent for first-year projects and 30.5 percent for third-year projects. Actual results were 29.5 percent and 30.5 percent, respectively, and Burd received a bonus equal to 95.4 percent of the maximum allowed.

The equity component of the executive compensation program included stock-option and restricted-stock grants. It also included restricted-stock awards tied to performance at the Blackhawk subsidiary. The company noted in its 2006 proxy that the Blackhawk subsidiary, which was 97 percent owned by Safeway, was a "high-growth business that, because of our ownership interest, could produce significant value to the company and its stockholders." The company also explained that restricted stock awards tied to the performance of Blackhawk would give executives incentive to grow the business.

Retirement benefits consisted of a defined benefit pension plan and a supplemental executive retirement program (SERP). Other benefits included deferred compensation plans, limited personal use of company airplanes, a company-provided automobile for commuting and business purposes, a home security system, the cost of physical examinations (up to $2,500), and life insurance. Safeway did not have any severance or change-in-control agreements with its executives.

Non-executive directors on Safeway's board received an annual retainer of $125,000. The lead independent director and chairs of the audit and strategic initiative committees received an additional $25,000 annual payment. Other members of the audit and strategic initiative committees received an additional $15,000. The chairs of the executive compensation committee and nominating and corporate governance committees also received an additional $15,000, and other members of these committees received an additional $10,000. Each member of the executive committee received (excluding Burd) an additional $15,000. Fifty percent of the fees that a director received were automatically deferred into stock units that were equivalent in value to Safeway common stock. At their discretion, directors were also allowed to defer the remaining 50 percent. Finally, new directors received a stock option grant of 20,000 shares (see Exhibit 5 for compensation figures for Burd, other named executives at Safeway, and Safeway board members).

Costco

With approximately $31.9 billion in sales of food and other sundries, Costco was effectively the fourth-largest grocery merchant in the United States in 2006 with total sales of $59 billion. The company operated 458 warehouses in 37 states, Canada, the United Kingdom, Korea, Taiwan, and Japan. The company also operated

Exhibit 5 Safeway: Compensation and Related Information

Compensation for Chief Executive Officer and Other Named Executives							
	Base Salary	Bonus	Stock Awards	Option Awards	Change in Pension/ Deferred Comp.	Other	Total
Steven Burd Chairman & CEO							
2006	$1,332,250	$2,639,825	$208,725	$1,978,553	$632,342	$212,298	$7,003,993
2005	1,300,000	1,951,000	—	7,697,655	NA	283,000	11,231,655
2004	1,144,000	1,146,000	—	—	NA	—	2,290,000
2003	1,000,000	—	—	—	NA	—	1,000,000
2002	1,000,000	258,000	—	—	NA	—	1,258,000
Named Officers (2006)							
CFO	590,928	730,505	570,214	1,066,445	78,795	—	3,036,887
CMO (Marketing)	691,425	854,739	1,208,714	2,192,336	93,751	11,412	5,052,377
Chief Strategist	622,877	770,000	555,304	1,049,619	—	10,000	3,007,800
Retail Operations	593,154	733,256	555,304	916,649	247,833	—	3,046,196

Options valued using Black-Scholes pricing model. In 2006, the assumptions were expected volatility 27.1 percent, risk-free rate 4.43 percent, dividend yield 0.8 percent, and average term 4.5 years.

Chief Executive Officer: Stock Option Exercises						
Year	Shares Acquired	Value Realized	Exercisable Options	Unexercisable Options	Value Exercisable	Value Unexercisable
2006	14,430	$187,215	5,585,833	1,852,334	$72,600,952	$25,428,794
2005	22,862	285,353	5,394,430	1,029,167	45,652,874	5,711,877
2004	1,150,000	17,179,775	4,897,292	520,000	37,366,125	—
2003	850,000	13,041,080	5,467,292	1,100,000	58,581,375	—
2002	264,970	10,968,122	5,737,292	1,680,000	76,752,557	—

(Continued)

Exhibit 5 Safeway: Compensation and Related Information (*Continued*)

Non-Executive Director Compensation				
	Fees Paid in Cash	Stock Awards	Option Awards	Total
Eight-Director Average (2006)	19,746	183,177	21,768	$224,691

Executive and Director Stock Ownership (2006)			
	Shares	Stock Options	Total
CEO	468,400	5,997,466	6,465,866
CFO	90,332	400,184	490,516
CMO (Marketing)	110,723	795,392	906,115
Chief Strategist	113,584	517,789	631,373
Retail Operations	105,808	509,589	615,397
Directors	2,000–1,350,504	13,331–14,272	15,331–1,350,504

Other Information (2006)	
Ownership Guidelines	Stock and options in dollar amount equal to 10 times base salary (CEO), 4 times base salary (other named executives). Directors required to own shares equal to one year's cash compensation.
Severance Provisions	None. Unvested stock options and restricted stock vest in the event of change in control.
CEO SERP (Present Value)	Yes ($8.5 million)
Largest Shareholders	FMR, 51,894,951 shares, 11.7 percent; AXA Financial, 51,016,582 shares, 11.5 percent; Brandes Investments, 35,628,031 shares, 8.0 percent
Number of Directors	9
Number of Independent Directors	8
Staggered Board	No
Lead Director	Yes
Number of Board Meetings	5
Number of Audit Committee Meetings	8
Number of Compensation Committee Meetings	4
Number of Corporate Gov. Committee Meetings	2
Number of Executive Committee Meetings	3

Exhibit 5 Safeway: Compensation and Related Information (*Continued*)

Other Information (2006)	
Number of Strategic Initiatives Meetings	3
Compensation Consultant Used	Towers Perrin
Peer Group (Compensation)	Best Buy, Colgate Palmolive, CVS, Federated Dept. Stores, Fortune Brands, Gap, General Mills, Home Depot, IAC/Interactive, J.C. Penney, Johnson & Johnson, Kohl's, Kroger, Limited Brands, McDonald's, Office Depot, PepsiCo, Sears Holdings, Sherwin-Williams, Staples, SuperValu, Target, Walgreens.
Peer Group (Stock Performance)	Great Atlantic & Pacific Tea, Kroger
Five-year Total Return Performance: Safeway	−16.01 percent
Five-year Total Return Performance: S&P 500 Index	22.16 percent
Five-year Total Return Performance: Peer Group	11.75 percent

Source: Safeway Inc., form DEF-14A, filed with the Securities and Exchange Commission, Equilar, Inc.

29 warehouses in Mexico through a 50 percent interest in a joint venture. In addition to food and sundries, Costco warehouses sold a variety of hard-line goods such as appliances, electronics, and office supplies, as well as soft-line goods such as apparel and jewelry. Most warehouses also offered ancillary services, including food stands, one-hour photo centers, pharmacies, optical centers, and gas stations.[14]

In 1983, James Sinegal and Jeffrey Brotman opened the first Costco warehouse in Seattle, Washington. The concept of the *warehouse club* had been pioneered by Sol Price, who founded Price Club in 1976. Operating on a membership basis, the club sold goods in bulk to small business owners, who also used their membership to buy items for personal use. Sinegal had worked for Sol Price since 1954, first on a part-time basis at Price's Fedmart while he was still a student at San Diego State University, and then at Price Club as an executive. Under Price's mentorship, Sinegal learned the practices of discount retailing. In the early 1980s, he was introduced to Brotman, and the two founded Costco.

Costco's strategy was to sell items on a low-margin, high-volume basis. While a typical retailer operated on a 25 to 40 percent gross margin, Costco marked up products by no more than 14 percent above cost. In order to make such sales profitable, the company had to sell large volumes of product. It did so by using a couple of techniques. First, it increased packaging size. Whereas the standard retailer might sell Tide detergent in 100–fluid ounce containers, Costco would sell Tide detergent in 300–fluid ounce containers. To deliver

value to customers, Costco would only sell in bulk sizes if the per-unit price of the item was lower than the per-unit price offered by competitors, typically 10 to 20 percent cheaper. Second, it offered only a limited number of SKUs (stock-keeping units). While a standard grocer offered 40,000 SKUs or more, Costco limited its selection to only 4,000 basic items. This led to greater inventory turnover. High turnover meant that customers often purchased and paid for items before Costco was required to pay its suppliers, reducing its investment in working capital.

Customers of Costco were required to purchase a one-year membership in order to access the items in its warehouses. A basic one-year membership cost $50 and an executive membership cost $100, which included additional benefits, such as a 2 percent cash rebate on most items. Costco sought to increase the value of its membership over time by adding ancillary services to its warehouses, such as one-hour photo centers, tire departments, and pharmacies. Such services broadened Costco's offerings, and, more importantly, they increased the frequency of visits that members made to its stores.

The Costco model had other operating efficiencies compared to a traditional retailer. The limited selection of bulk items meant that the company could transport items directly from the delivery truck to the shop floor on pallets. As a result, Costco employees did not have to devote significant time to stocking shelves. Even fresh produce was displayed in stacked cardboard boxes that were not unpacked and sorted. Costco also limited marketing activities, relying instead on reputation to generate new memberships. Both of these allowed the company to keep its operating costs low and therefore further reduce prices.

While the club warehouse model was a compelling shopping destination for many customers, Costco was not the only retailer that operated under this model. It faced competition from Sam's Club (owned by Wal-Mart) and BJ's Wholesale Club. In total, there were over 1,200 warehouse clubs in the United States and Canada. Costco also faced competition from local grocery store chains that offered greater selection and convenience.

Costco went public in November 1985 with Sinegal as chief executive officer and Brotman as chairman of the board. Under their tenure, total company revenue increased from $762 million (fiscal year 1986) to $59.0 billion (fiscal year 2006). Operating income increased from $5.6 million to $1.6 billion, net income from $3.6

million to $1.1 billion, and earnings per share from $0.025 (adjusted for splits) to $2.30. During these years, Costco increased its total store count from 22 to 458. Results were aided by Costco's 1993 merger with Price Club. Same-store sales growth (including sales of gasoline) increased 10 percent in 2004, 7 percent in 2005, and 8 percent in 2006. Costco common stock, which went public at $1.70 per share (adjusted for splits) in 1985, was at $47 at the end of fiscal year 2006 (see Exhibit 6 for financial and operating results at Costco).

Executive and Director Compensation at Costco.

The executive compensation program at Costco included four elements: salary, annual cash bonus, equity, and other benefits and perquisites. Sinegal received a base salary of $350,000 in 2006, and Brotman, as executive chairman, received a base salary of $356,731.[15] Executives

Exhibit 6 Costco: Selected Financial Information

(in millions, except per share)	1986	2002	2003	2004	2005	2006
Revenues, Net	$747	$37,995	$41,695	$47,149	$51,879	$58,963
Membership Fees	15	769	853	961	1,073	1,188
Operating Income	5.6	1,132	1,157	1,386	1,474	1,626
Net Income	3.6	700	721	882	1,063	1,103
Debt	$136	$1,314	$1,337	$1,015	$765	$257
Shareholders Equity	89	5,694	6,555	7,625	8,881	9,143
Earnings Per Share	$0.025	$1.48	$1.53	$1.85	$2.18	$2.30
Dividends Per Share	—	—	—	0.20	0.43	0.49
Ending Share Price	$1.6	$33	$32	$41	$43	$47
Average Diluted Shares	144	479	479	482	492	480
Market Value Equity	$230	$15,807	$15,328	$19,762	$21,156	$22,560
Enterprise Value	366	17,120	16,665	20,777	21,921	22,817
Store Count	22	374	397	417	433	458
Same Store Sales	NA	6%	5%	10%	7%	8%
Gross Margin Percentage	11.17%	10.55%	10.69%	10.73%	10.66%	10.55%

Notes: Fiscal year ends August 31. Per-share data and share count information adjusted for splits (6-for-1). Fiscal year 1986 share price end of trading following initial public offering in November 1985. Store count excludes Mexico warehouses owned through 50 percent interest in joint venture, which are accounted for on equity basis. Same-store sales growth includes sales of gasoline. Net revenue is net of membership fees.

Source: Costco Wholesale Corp., form 10-Ks, filed with the Securities and Exchange Commission. 1986 financial results adjusted to exclude one-time benefit from tax loss carryforward. Share price information from Center for Research in Securities Prices (University of Chicago).

were eligible for an annual cash bonus of up to $200,000. The company noted in its proxy that no specific formula was used in determining actual bonus amounts. In general, Sinegal requested his bonus, based on what he considered to be an appropriate amount. In 2006, he requested that no bonus be paid. Brotman received a cash bonus of $200,000.

The equity component of the executive compensation program included restricted stock grants, which were awarded based on the achievement of certain performance metrics. The metrics included minimum thresholds for total sales growth and growth in pretax income.

Benefits and perquisites included a deferred compensation program (which allowed an executive to defer up to 100 percent of salary and bonus and to receive a match of up to 50 percent of the deferred amount, with such match capped at $5,000), a defined contribution pension plan, life insurance, health care, and a vehicle allowance.

Costco's board of directors did not employ compensation consultants in setting executive compensation levels. The board reviewed compensation packages at a set of peer companies, but did not rely on mid-point ranges or other quantitative comparisons in setting pay levels, instead reviewing such data for "general reference." The compensation committee noted in the 2006 proxy that it "believes that Mr. Sinegal and Mr. Brotman are underpaid. Accordingly, their compensation levels for fiscal 2006 are fair to the Company." The following year, the company noted in its proxy: "The Committee … wishes to respect Mr. Sinegal's wishes to receive modest compensation, in part because it believes that higher amounts would not change Mr. Sinegal's motivation and performance."

Non-executive directors on the board at Costco received an annual retainer of $30,000 and $1,000 for each meeting attended. Each non-executive director also received an annual grant of restricted stock (see Exhibit 7 for compensation figures for Sinegal, Brotman, other named executives at Costco, and Costco board members).

Whole Foods

In 2006, Whole Foods was the largest seller of natural foods and groceries in the United States, with total company revenues of $5.6 billion. The company operated 186 stores in 31 states, Canada, and the United Kingdom. All stores operated under the Whole Foods brand name.[16]

John Mackey opened the first Whole Foods Market in Austin, Texas, in 1980.[17] While natural foods stores had been in existence since the late 1960s, the typical natural foods market was poorly maintained and primarily offered a limited selection of organic produce and grains. By contrast, Mackey's Whole Foods Market was 12,500 square feet—comparable in size to a local supermarket—and carried a broad selection of fresh fish and meats, locally baked bread, cheeses, beer, and coffee. The store attracted a more affluent clientele that was willing to pay premium prices for natural foods that were minimally processed or free from artificial ingredients and preservatives.

Over the next few years, Whole Foods expanded at a modest pace opening stores in Texas at a rate of approximately one per year. It was not until 1988 that the company ventured beyond Texas, purchasing a store in New Orleans and later opening one in Palo Alto, California. In 1992, Mackey began to charter a more aggressive expansion strategy and took the company public to raise capital for growth. At the time, Whole Foods still operated off a small base of 10 stores, generating sales of $92.5 million and net income of $1.6 million. Following the public offering, however, Whole Foods expanded into new regions, including New England, Illinois, and Florida, while also increasing its presence in California. Expansion primarily came through acquisition, with Whole Foods purchasing regional chains and converting them to the Whole Foods name and format.

By 1998, Whole Foods and its competitor Wild Oats (based in Boulder, Colorado) had acquired most regional natural food store chains. Whole Foods was the larger of the two, with 70 percent more stores and almost five times the sales revenue. The incremental sales per store were due in part to Whole Foods's ability to charge premium pricing and its wide selection of products, including an extensive array of prepared meals which appealed to affluent and health-conscious shoppers.

Mackey remained chief executive officer and chairman of the board throughout Whole Foods's history as a public company. His business philosophy combined a belief in cooperative effort with an intense capitalistic drive. Operating decisions were decentralized, with store managers given discretion to adjust their product mix to local tastes. Managers were also given generous financial incentives, including stock options, to maximize the profitability of their stores. Mackey wanted his company to dominate the natural food retail category. He also staunchly opposed the idea of unions at Whole Foods, saying that "fundamentally they're parasites."[18]

Under Mackey's tenure as chief executive officer of the public Whole Foods, total company revenue increased from $120 million (fiscal year 1992) to $5.6 billion (fiscal year 2006). Operating income increased from $4.6 million to $319 million, net income from $3.1 million to $204 million, and earnings per share from $0.11 (adjusted for splits) to $1.41. During these years, Whole

Exhibit 7 Costco: Compensation and Related Information

Compensation for Chief Executive Officer and Other Named Executives							
	Base Salary	Bonus	Stock Awards	Option Awards	Change in Pension / Deferred Comp	Other	Total
James Sinegal CEO							
2006	350,000	—	—	—	NA	104,629	$454,629
2005	350,000	100,000	—	2,937,255	NA	47,971	3,435,226
2004	350,000	200,000	—	3,035,580	NA	28,016	3,613,596
2003	350,000	—	—	2,834,790	NA	25,460	3,210,250
2002	350,000	—	—	4,005,330	NA	23,756	4,379,086
Named Officers (2006)							
Chairman (Brotman)	356,731	200,000	1,307,750	—	NA	146,258	$2,010,739
COO-Global Ops	535,096	102,396	—	—	NA	103,948	741,440
CFO	519,808	—	—	—	NA	131,642	651,450
COO-Merchandising	535,096	81,917	—	—	NA	86,559	703,572
COO-East & Canada	504,519	78,511	—	—	NA	88,051	671,081

Options valued using Black-Scholes pricing model. In 2005, the assumptions were: expected volatility 38 percent, risk-free rate 4.28 percent, dividend yield 1.11 percent, and average term 6.6 years.

Chief Executive Officer: Stock Option Exercises						
Year	Shares Acquired	Value Realized	Exercisable Options	Unexercisable Options	Value Exercisable	Value Unexercisable
2006	300,000	$12,787,230	1,200,000	300,000	$15,426,715	$2,147,400
2005	100,000	3,749,070	1,350,000	450,000	20,772,050	2,252,475
2004	—	—	1,300,000	450,000	22,676,445	2,669,550
2003	90,000	1,503,900	1,140,000	460,000	13,815,620	276,000
2002	—	—	1,060,000	480,000	16,509,120	251,400

Non-Executive Director Compensation			
	Fees Paid in Cash	Stock Awards	Total
Nine-Director Average (2007)	40,556	137,659	$178,215

2006 director compensation not available.

Exhibit 7 Costco: Compensation and Related Information (*Continued*)

Executive and Director Stock Ownership (2006)			
	Shares	**Stock Options**	**Total**
CEO	2,421,058	1,200,000	3,621,058
Chairman	1,945,748	1,200,000	3,145,748
COO-Global Ops	108,535	564,000	672,535
CFO	20,962	420,000	440,962
COO-Merchandising	60,914	545,000	605,914
COO-East & Canada	12,500	—	12,500
Directs	14,500–175,833	18,000–120,000	32,500–295,833

Other Information (2006)	
Ownership Guidelines	None
Severance Provisions	Unvested stock options and restricted stock vest
CEO SERP (Present Value)	No
Largest Shareholders	Davis Advisers, 58,261,745 shares, 12.8 percent; Barclays, 40,026,498 shares, 8.8 percent
Number of Directors	13
Number of Independent Directors	7
Staggered Board	Yes
Lead Director	No
Number of Board Meetings	5
Number of Audit Committee Meetings	7
Number of Compensation Committee Meetings	2
Number of Corporate Governance Committee Meetings	4
Compensation Consultant Used	None
Peer Group (Compensation)	Wal-Mart, Home Depot, Target, BJ's Wholesale, and Lowe's
Peer Group (Stock Performance)	BJ's, Home Depot, Lowe's, Best Buy, Office Depot, Staples, Target, Kroger, Wal-Mart
Five-year Total Return Performance: Costco	40 percent (estimated)
Five-year Total Return Performance: S&P 500 Index	42 percent (estimated)
Five-year Total Return Performance: Peer Group	5 percent (estimated)

Source: Costco Wholesale Corp., forms DEF-14A, filed with the Securities and Exchange Commission, Equilar, Inc., performance measures provided in graph form only, not numerically.

Foods increased its total store count from 20 to 186. Same store sales growth increased 14.5 percent in 2004, 11.5 percent in 2005, and 10.3 percent in 2006. Whole Foods common stock, which traded at $3 (adjusted for splits) following its 1992 initial public offering, was at $59 at the end of fiscal year 2006 (see Exhibit 8 for financial and operating results at Whole Foods).

Executive and Director Compensation at Whole Foods.

The executive compensation program at Whole Foods consisted of three elements: base salary, cash bonus, and equity. Whole Foods noted in its 2006 proxy that in addition to attracting and retaining qualified employees, the company "endeavors to ensure that our compensation program is perceived as fundamentally fair to all stakeholders." As a result, the cash compensation that executives could receive was subject to limitations. In 2006, the cash compensation for all executives was capped at 19 times the average hourly wage of all full-time

employees. Between 2000 and 2005, this cap had been 14 times the average hourly wage, and, prior to 2000, the cap had been 10 times.[19] In 2006, Mackey received a base salary of $287,600.

The amount of bonus earned by executives was based on a calculation of *economic value added* (EVA). Although Whole Foods did not disclose its methodology for calculating EVA, it indicated that "in its simplest form, EVA is equivalent to net operating profits after taxes minus a charge for the cost of capital necessary to generate those profits." The amount of bonus earned under the EVA plan was contributed to a pool for each individual, with a portion paid out annually. The annual payout, in combination with the base salary, was subject to the cap of 19 times the average wage for all employees. In 2006, the average hourly wage was $15.38, which translated to an annual salary of $31,990. As a result, executive cash compensation was capped at $607,800. If the bonus to be paid out to each executive caused

Exhibit 8 Whole Foods: Selected Financial Information

(in millions, except per share)	1992	2002	2003	2004	2005	2006
Revenues	$120	$2,690	$3,149	$3,865	$4,701	$5,607
Operating Income	4.6	141	167	217	230	319
Net Income	3.1	80	99	130	136	204
Debt	$0.5	$168	$169	$171	$19	$9
Shareholders Equity	36	563	745	950	1,366	1,404
Earnings Per Share	$0.109	$0.66	$0.79	$0.99	$0.99	$1.41
Dividends Per Share	—	—	—	0.30	0.47	2.45
Ending Share Price	$3	$21	$28	$43	$67	$59
Average Diluted Shares	28	127	131	135	140	145
Market Value Equity	$84	$2,667	$3,668	$5,805	$9,380	$8,555
Enterprise Value	85	2,835	3,837	5,976	9,399	8,564
Store Count	20	135	145	163	175	186
Same Store Sales	10%	8.7%	8.1%	14.5%	11.5%	10.3%
Gross Margin Percentage	30.9%	34.7%	34.3%	34.7%	35.1%	34.9%

Notes: Fiscal year ends September 30. Per-share data and share count information adjusted for splits (8-for-1). The 1992 share price is at end of trading following initial public offering. Company paid special $2 per share dividend in 2006 in addition to regular quarterly dividend of $0.15 per share.

Source: Whole Foods Market Inc., forms 10-K, filed with the Securities and Exchange Commission. Share price information from Center for Research in Securities Prices (University of Chicago).

total cash compensation to exceed the cap, the amount in excess of the cap was forfeited. The full amount of the EVA bonus, whether paid or forfeited, was still subtracted from the pool balance. Furthermore, the accumulated balance in the pool for each individual was also limited to the amount of the cap. Executives had the right to take time off without pay in order to reduce their cash salary, thereby increasing the amount of bonus that they could be paid within the cap.

The equity component of the executive compensation plan consisted of stock options. For the most part, all executives received the same number of options, with small additional grants made to reward continued employment with the company. The size of the options grants was at the discretion of the board and not determined by a formula. Whole Foods did not use compensation consultants to benchmark pay packages or for plan design. In its proxy, the board of directors noted that "stock price performance has not been a factor in determining annual compensation because the price of the company's common stock is subject to a variety of factors outside our control."

Beginning in 2007, Mackey announced that his salary would be reduced to $1 per year and that he would no longer receive cash bonuses or stock option awards. Non-executive directors on the board at Whole Foods received a quarterly retainer of $2,756 and $4,978 for each meeting attended in person. The lead director also received an additional $7,738 quarterly retainer. Directors received additional payments depending on their roles and their attendance. Directors also received stock option grants (see Exhibit 9 for compensation figures for Mackey, other named executives at Whole Foods, and Whole Foods board members).

Exhibit 9 Whole Foods: Compensation and Related Information

Compensation for Chief Executive Officer and Other Named Executives							
	Base Salary	Bonus	Stock Awards	Option Awards	EVA Pool Earned Not Received	Other	Total
John Mackey Chairman & CEO							
2006	$287,600	$320,200	—	$427,000	$312,176	—	$1,346,976
2005	356,000	126,000	—	733,713	NA	460,000	1,675,713
2004	342,000	118,000	—	441,651	NA	—	901,651
2003	326,000	41,000	—	211,887	NA	—	578,887
2002	302,000	150,000	—	104,462	NA	4,891	561,353
Named Officers (2006)							
CFO	268,500	339,300	—	405,000	449,532	—	1,462,332
co-COO	310,900	296,900	—	420,000	369,861	—	1,397,661
co-COO	371,600	236,200	—	426,000	347,598	—	1,381,398
Business Dev.	333,600	274,200	—	405,000	437,761	—	1,450,561
Global Support	303,100	304,700	—	489,000	493,845	—	1,590,645

Options valued using Black-Scholes pricing model. In 2006, the assumptions were: expected volatility 29.4 percent, risk-free rate 5.04 percent, dividend yield 1.26 percent, and average term 3.22 years.

(Continued)

Exhibit 9 Whole Foods: Compensation and Related Information (*Continued*)

Chief Executive Officer: Stock Option Exercises						
Year	Shares Acquired	Value Realized	Exercisable Options	Unexercisable Options	Value Exercisable	Value Unexercisable
2006	36,000	2,437,547	71,876	50,353	2,536,640	635,685
2005	52,000	1,804,571	86,500	67,000	4,416,650	1,316,040
2004	37,080	1,013,893	124,000	38,000	3,878,600	492,135
2003	92,000	1,909,849	162,000	34,000	2,939,725	215,885
2002	—	—	235,000	37,000	3,408,069	330,346

Non-Executive Director Compensation				
	Fees Paid in Cash	Options Awards	Other	Total
Seven-Director Average (2006)	40,233	3,512	1,608	$ 45,353

Executive and Director Stock Ownership (2006)			
	Shares	Stock Options	Total
CEO	1,147,230	79,252	1,226,482
CFO	116,816	77,000	193,816
co-COO	8,012	61,128	69,140
co-COO	37,482	88,840	126,322
Business Dev.	137,256	69,000	206,256
Global Support	12,228	93,866	106,094
Directs	1,756–14,892	30,800–67,344	32,556–82,236

Other Information (2006)	
Ownership Guidelines	N/A
Cap on Executive Compensation	2006–$607,800 (19 times average wage) 2005–$436,800 (14 times) 2004–$426,900 (14 times) 2003–$409,700 (14 times) 2002–$398,700 (14 times)
Severance Provisions	Lump sum payment equal to salary plus prior year bonus and immediate vesting of stock options.
CEO SERP (Present Value)	None
Largest Shareholder	Janus, 10,169,761 shares, 7 percent
Number of Directors	8

Other Information (2006)	
Number of Independent Directors	6
Staggered Board	No
Lead Director	Yes
Number of Board Meetings	4
Number of Audit Committee Meetings	8
Number of Compensation Committee Meetings	4
Number of Corporate Governance Committee Meetings	3
Compensation Consultant Used	None
Peer Group (Compensation)	Not disclosed
Peer Group (Stock Performance)	S&P Food Retail Index. Data not disclosed for 2006.

Source: Whole Foods Market Inc., forms DEF-14A, filed with the Securities and Exchange Commission, Equilar, Inc.

NOTES

1. Standard & Poor's, 2008, Industry survey: Supermarkets and drugstores, January 24.
2. Ibid. Grocery sales shown here are estimated to exclude revenues from nongrocery items and differ from total revenue figures shown later in the case.
3. The Kroger Co., 2006 form 10-K, filed with the Securities and Exchange Commission, April 4, 2007.
4. History from:The Kroger Co., 2005, *International Directory of Company Histories*, vol. 65, Chicago: St. James Press.
5. C. Rohwedder, 2007, What makes Tesco, Kroger more than just rivals?, *Wall Street Journal*, December 24.
6. Fiscal 2003 results included $560 million in goodwill and asset impairment charges.
7. Information on executive and director compensation in this section from Kroger Co., 2006 form DEF-14A, filed with the Securities and Exchange Commission, May 15, 2007.
8. Severance provisions were defined under The Kroger Co. Employee Protection Plan (KEPP) and applied to all management and administrative employees with at least one year of service who were not covered by a collective bargaining agreement. Severance amounts were based on pay level and other benefits. Eligible participants who were at least 40 years old and had more than six years of service were entitled to severance payments ranging from 9 to 20 months' salary and bonus.
9. Safeway Inc., 2006 form 10-K, filed with the Securities and Exchange Commission, February 26, 2007.
10. History from: Safeway Inc., 2007, *International Directory of Company Histories*, vol. 85, Chicago: St. James Press.
11. Safeway stock soars $4.625 after accord set with kohlberg, 1986, *Wall Street Journal*, July 29.
12. J. Hibbard, 2006, Put your money where your mouth is; Safeway wanted a fresher, healthier image. The first step was to become fresher and healthier, *BusinessWeek*, September 18.
13. Information on executive and director compensation in this section from: Safeway Inc., 2006 form DEF-14A, filed with the Securities and Exchange Commission, April 4, 2007.
14. Costco Wholesale Corp., 2006 form 10-K, filed with the Securities and Exchange Commission, November 17, 2006. Sales of food and other sundries included sales of fresh food (meat, baked goods, deli products, and produce), food (dry and institutionally packaged foods), and sundries (candy, snack food, tobacco, alcoholic and nonalcoholic beverages, and cleaning and institutional supplies).
15. Information on executive and director compensation in this section from: Costco Wholesale Corp., 2006 form DEF-14A, filed with the Securities and Exchange Commission, December 20, 2006, and 2007 form DEF-14A, filed with the Securities and Exchange Commission, December 18, 2007.
16. Whole Foods Market Inc., 2006 form 10-K, filed with the Securities and Exchange Commission, December 8, 2006.
17. History from: Whole Foods Market, Inc., 2003, *International Directory of Company Histories*, vol. 50, Chicago: St. James Press.
18. S. Lubove, 1998, New age capitalist John Mackey says he wants to make the world a healthier and happier place. The unions want to put him out of business, *Forbes*, April 6.
19. Information on executive and director compensation in this section from: Whole Foods Markets Inc., 2006 form DEF-14A, filed with the Securities and Exchange Commission, January 22, 2007.

Robin Chapman, Robert E. Hoskisson

Arizona State University

"This will go down in history as a turning point for the music industry," said Apple Computer CEO Steve Jobs. "This is landmark stuff. I can't overestimate it!"[1] Jobs was referring to the April 2003 debut of Apple's iTunes Online Music Store, the first legal online music service to have agreements with all five major record labels. Although initially available only for Macintosh users, iTunes sold more than 1 million songs by the end of its first week in operation. Not only did iTunes change the nature of the music industry, it also added greatly to Apple's revenues by way of promoting the purchase of the iPod—a portable digital music device that can store downloaded iTunes songs. In 2007, Apple controlled more than 70 percent of the digital music market,[2] and its net income was $3.5 billion (see Exhibits 1 and 2). Jobs hopes further that the success of iTunes will flourish with the launch of Apple TV and iPhone in 2007. In May 2007, Apple was named by *BusinessWeek* as the most innovative company for the third year in a row. Apple's focus on innovation has helped it maintain a competitive advantage and marketing prowess over other industry players that have historically been much stronger than Apple.[3] However, Apple must beat the competition on a number of levels. iTunes faces stiff competition from new and existing online music and video download services both legal and illegal. The iPod, Apple TV, and iPhone all face the threat of lower-priced rivals and possible substitutes. Apple's innovative ability and the quality of its marketing strategy will likely determine the outcome of the company's foray into the music, mobile phone, and video-on-demand businesses.

Early Company History

On April 1, 1976, Steve Jobs and Stephen Wozniak began the partnership that would eventually become Apple Computer. Both electronics gurus, Jobs and Wozniak had known each other since high school and had worked together previously on other projects.[4] In early 1976, Wozniak had been working on combining video monitors with computers. His idea was to invent a user-friendly computer that ordinary consumers could buy. Wozniak, who worked for Hewlett-Packard (HP) at the time, decided to approach his employer with his idea. HP, however, did not see a future for personal computers (PCs) and soundly rebuffed him. At that point, Steve Jobs told his friend Wozniak that they should go into business together and sell computers themselves.[5]

Their first computer, the *Apple I*, was built in the garage of Jobs's parents (see Exhibit 3). Known as a "kit computer," the original Apple consisted merely of a circuit board and did not even have an exterior casing. It was intended to be sold to hobbyists only. Jobs called the computer an "Apple" in honor of his days working at an orchard while seeking enlightenment—and because neither he nor Wozniak could come up with a better name.[6] The *Apple I* received mixed responses from hobbyists, and the duo decided it was time to expand the market for personal computers by building a more attractive and useful machine, the *Apple II*.[7]

Growth

After taking on new partners to fund expansion plans, the company officially became Apple Computer, Inc., in early

* This case is intended to be used as the basis for class discussion rather than to illustrate effective or ineffective handling of an administrative or strategic situation. We appreciate the previous input on an earlier case focused only on the music industry by Jeff Berrong, Marilyn Klopp, Max Mishkin, Jimmy Pittman, and Adrian Ray under the direction of Professor Robert E. Hoskisson.

Apple Computer, Inc., by Robin Chapman and Robert E. Hoskisson. Reprinted by permission of the authors.

1977.[8] Within months, the recapitalized company introduced the *Apple II*, the first computer to come with a sleek plastic casing and color graphics.[9] Annual sales increased dramatically to $10 million, and the company began to grow quickly in size, adding thousands of employees.[10] On December 12, 1980, Apple became a public company. On the first day of trading, its share price increased from an initial $22 offering to $29.[11] By the end of the year, Apple reached $100 million in annual sales.[12] The fledgling company, however, soon faced some experienced competition.

In 1981, IBM released its first personal computer. IBM's sheer size ensured its domination of the young PC market. Steve Jobs realized that Apple would have to move fast in order to remain a viable company. Over the next few years, the company released several new computer models, most notably the *Apple III* and the *Lisa*. Neither of these models sold particularly well.

In 1983, Jobs recruited Pepsi-Cola CEO John Sculley as Apple's president and CEO. Jobs hoped that this change would bring more structure and

Exhibit 1 Consolidated Statements of Cash Flows

(In millions)	Three Fiscal Years Ended September 29		
	2007	2006	2005
Cash and cash equivalents, beginning of the year	$ 6,392	$ 3,491	$ 2,969
Operating Activities: Net income	3,496	1,989	1,328
Adjustments to reconcile net income to cash generated by operating activities:			
Depreciation, amortization, and accretion	317	225	179
Stock-based compensation expense	242	163	49
Provision for deferred income taxes	78	53	50
Excess tax benefits from stock options	—	—	428
Gain on sale of Power School net assets	—	(4)	—
Loss on disposition of property, plant, and equipment	12	15	9
Changes in operating assets and liabilities:			
Accounts receivable, net	(385)	(357)	(121)
Inventories	(76)	(105)	(64)
Other current assets	(1,540)	(1,626)	(150)
Other assets	81	(1,040)	(35)
Accounts payable	1,494	1,611	328
Other liabilities	1,751	1,296	534
Cash generated by operating activities	5,470	2,220	2,535

Source: Apple's 2007 Fiscal Year 10K, www.apple.com/investor.

organization to the young company.[13] Apple's biggest computer achievement, the Macintosh (Mac), was released. After initially opposing it, Jobs had personally taken on the task of developing the Mac, which became the first PC featuring a graphical interface and a mouse for navigation. Apple first presented the now-famous Macintosh computer with a riveting January 1984 Super Bowl commercial. The memorable commercial featured an Orwellian *1984* world filled with stoic human zombies, all watching a large-screen image of "Big Brother." A young woman rushes into the room and dramatically destroys the screen. Apple used this *1984* imagery to depict IBM's computer dominance being destroyed by the new Macintosh.[14] With features that made the Mac easy to use for publishing and a marketing strategy that concentrated on universities, the new computer sold very well, pushing Apple's fiscal 1984 sales to an unprecedented $1.5 billion.[15]

Shake-Up

By 1985, however, Jobs and Sculley began to disagree over the direction they wanted the company to take. After Jobs's attempt to remove Sculley failed, Jobs left Apple in May to start his own new business, NeXT Computers. Meanwhile, Microsoft benefited from Apple's poor negotiation of a contract that cleared the way for successive versions of the Windows operating system to use graphical user interface (GUI) technology similar to that of the Mac. With this agreement, "Apple had effectively lost exclusive rights to its interface design."[16]

In 1990, Microsoft released Windows 3.0, the first universal software that could run on nearly every PC regardless of the manufacturer. Although Apple's worldwide sales had reached $7 billion by 1992, Apple soon found itself fighting an uphill battle against the movement toward standardized software. More and more businesses and consumers wanted compatible operating

Exhibit 2 Apple Computer, Fourth-Quarter Fiscal 2007 10Q Report

Net Sales (net sales in millions and unit sales in thousands)	Three Months Ended		
	12/29/07	12/30/06	Change
Net Sales by Operating Segment:			
Americas net sales	$ 4,298	$ 3,521	22%
Europe net sales	2,471	1,712	44%
Japan net sales	400	285	40%
Retail net sales	1,701	1,115	53%
Other segments net sales (a)	738	482	53%
Total net sales	$ 9,608	$ 7,115	35%
Unit Sales by Operating Segment:			
Americas Macintosh unit sales	841	625	35%
Europe Macintosh unit sales	705	491	44%
Japan Macintosh unit sales	91	70	30%
Retail Macintosh unit sales	504	308	64%
Other segments Macintosh unit sales (b)	178	112	59%
Total Macintosh unit sales	2,319	1,606	44%

Exhibit 2 Apple Computer, Fourth-Quarter Fiscal 2007 10Q Report (*Continued*)

Net Sales (net sales in millions and unit sales in thousands)	Three Months Ended		
	12/29/07	12/30/06	Change
Net Sales by Product:			
Desktops (c)	$ 1,515	$ 955	59%
Portables (d)	2,037	1,455	40%
Total Macintosh net sales	3,552	2,410	47%
iPod	3,997	3,427	17%
Other music-related products and services (e)	808	634	27%
iPhone and related products and services (f)	241	—	NM
Peripherals and other hardware (g)	382	297	29%
Software, service, and other sales (h)	628	347	81%
Total net sales	$ 9,608	$ 7,115	35%
Unit Sales by Product:			
Desktops (c)	977	637	53%
Portables (d)	1,342	969	38%
Total Macintosh unit sales	2,319	1,606	44%
Net sales per Macintosh unit sold (i)	$ 1,532	$ 1,501	2%
iPod unit sales	22,121	21,066	5%
Net sales per iPod unit sold (j)	$ 181	$ 163	11%
iPhone unit sales	2,315	—	NM

(a) During the third quarter of 2007, the Company revised the way it measures the Retail Segment's operating results to a manner that is generally consistent with the Company's other operating segments. Prior period results have been reclassified to reflect this change to the Retail Segment's operating results along with the corresponding offsets to the other operating segments. Further information regarding the Company's operating segments may be found in Notes to Condensed Consolidated Financial Statements at Note 7, "Segment Information and Geographic Data."

(b) Other Segments include Asia Pacific and FileMaker.

(c) Includes iMac, eMac, Mac mini, Mac Pro, Power Mac, and Xserve product lines.

(d) Includes MacBook, iBook, MacBook Pro, and PowerBook product lines.

(e) Consists of iTunes Store sales, iPod services, and Apple-branded and third-party iPod accessories.

(f) Derived from handset sales, carrier agreements, and Apple-branded and third-party iPhone accessories.

(g) Includes sales of Apple-branded and third-party displays, wireless connectivity and networking solutions, and other hardware accessories.

(h) Includes sales of Apple-branded operating system, application software, third-party software, AppleCare, and Internet services.

(i) Derived by dividing total Mac net sales by total Mac unit sales.

(j) Derived by dividing total iPod net sales by total iPod unit sales.

Source: Apple Company, 2007 4Q Form 10Q, hwww.apple.com/investor, 22.

Exhibit 3 Select Apple Product Releases

1976	Apple I
1977	Apple II
1980	Apple III
1983	Lisa
1984	Macintosh Graphical user interface (GUI)
1986	Macintosh Plus
1987	Macintosh II
1991	Macintosh Quadra PowerBook 100
1994	PowerMac 6100
1997	PowerBook G3
1998	iMac
1999	iBook
2001	iTunes iDVD iPod
2003	iLife suite iTunes 4 (online music store w/200,000 downloadable songs)
2004	iPod Mini eMac iPod (Click Wheel) iPod (U2 Special Edition) iPod Photo
2005	iPod Shuffle iPod nano iPod color iPod with video
2006	MacBook Mac mini
2007	Apple TV iPhone

Source: www.apple-history.com.

systems, but the Macintosh still ran exclusively on Mac OS, a system not available to other computers. By 1993, Apple's board of directors replaced Sculley as CEO. Apple moved through two CEOs over the next five years.

During this time, Apple partnered with IBM and Motorola to produce the PowerPC chip, which would run the company's new line of PowerMacs, allowing it to outperform computers powered by Intel microprocessors.[17] Despite this and Apple's attempts to reorganize, losses mounted in 1996 and 1997. In December 1996, Apple acquired NeXT, with the plan of using its technology as the basis for a new operating system. After being gone for more than a decade, Jobs returned to the company he had originally cofounded with Wozniak.

Jobs's Return

One of the first problems Steve Jobs moved to fix was the ongoing dispute between Apple and Microsoft over the Windows graphical user interface (GUI). Microsoft not only paid an undisclosed amount to Apple, but also made its Office 98 suite compatible with Macintoshes.[18] Jobs then proceeded to change the company's sales strategy in 1997 to encompass direct sales—both online and by phone. In a flurry of product releases, Apple introduced the new generation of PowerMacs, PowerBooks, and the highly anticipated iMac and iBook, which were less expensive computers aimed at the low-end computer market. After an entire year without showing a profit, the first quarter of 1998 began three years of profitable quarters for Apple.[19]

Jobs stated that he wanted to transform the company by making the Mac "the hub of [the consumers'] digital lifestyle." To do this, Apple introduced iLife in 2002, a software suite including applications such as iPhoto, iMovie, iTunes, and eventually the iPod. With the advent of Napster and peer-to-peer music sharing, Apple saw a way to capitalize on the emerging trend of cheap music downloads by creating a legal online music distribution network. iTunes would be the key to exploiting this market. Once downloaded by way of iTunes, music could then be transferred only to an iPod (due to encryption). With iTunes, Apple has quite possibly revolutionized the distribution of music and hopes to do the same with the distribution of movies on demand. Similar changes may be expected with the iPhone in the mobile or smartphone industry segments and with Apple TV in the mobile media and set-top box industry segments.

iTunes: Apple's Online Music Store

Apple ventured into the market of legal downloads with the introduction of its iTunes Music Store.[20] iTunes offers downloads at a specified price without requiring a subscription or monthly fees. Originally offered exclusively on Apple's own Mac, iTunes can now be installed on PCs as well. The idea behind iTunes was to provide a solution to the illegal pirating of music and software from rival sources such as Kazaa.

iTunes offers its users a selection of more than 6 million songs, with new songs continually added.[21] Titles are from just about every genre of music. Users can perform a search by type of music, artist name, or title of track or album. Each song available can be previewed without making a purchase. Purchasers have the option of purchasing an entire album or single songs. Each song is $0.99, and a complete album starts at $9.99. Downloads can be made not only to a Mac or PC, but also directly to an iPod. All new song additions are encoded in AAC format, which many say is superior to MP3, although iTunes does still carry the MP3 format on some of its older selections.

Once songs are downloaded, they are stored as a digital music library. As this collection grows, this list of songs can be arranged in many different ways. Songs can be arranged by personal rating, artist, or genre. This feature allows for a customizable playlist for playback or burning to a CD.

In addition iTunes offers a collection of more than 10,000 audiobooks ranging in price from $2.95 to $15.95, including many different language lessons. Also available are downloadable versions of public radio shows. Gift certificates are also available in different denominations and can be sent electronically through e-mail.

As previously mentioned, in its first week of existence, the number of downloads from iTunes surpassed the 1 million mark. This feat is amazing considering that at the time of iTunes' introduction, the download service was available only for the Mac. In addition, at that time, Mac users comprised less than 5 percent of U.S. computer users.[22] When iTunes became available for use on the PC, sales increased even more rapidly. iTunes PC downloads reached the 1 million mark in three days, less than half the time it took for the Mac version. But the success of iTunes is not measured in number of downloads sold per day or week, since after paying royalties, Apple makes only approximately 10 cents per song. iTunes is simply used as a means to boost the sale of iPods, iPhones, and Apple TVs, which generate a substantial profit per sale. For example, the iPod has been labeled "the profit machine" for Apple, as it tends to produce a 50 percent profit margin, per unit, before marketing and distribution costs.[23]

iTunes, iPod, iPhone, and Apple TV

iPod

For music lovers, the iPod is the greatest invention since the Walkman. With up to 160 GB of storage, it allows users to carry up to 40,000 songs or 200 hours of video wherever they go.[24] There are currently four different iPod styles: the iPod shuffle, iPod classic, iPod nano, and iPod touch. iPod owners can purchase accessories such as the armband, the radio remote, and the universal dock and remote to make using the iPod even more enjoyable. In 2007, with more than 100 million products sold, the closest competitor to Apple's iPod had only 8 percent of the market share, leaving Apple with the vast majority. While others are seeking to simply duplicate the complementary and innovative relationships between iPod and iTunes, Apple continues to innovate with new products such as the iPhone and Apple TV.[25] (See Exhibit 4 for more details about the iPod products.)

iPhone

In first-quarter 2007, Apple launched its "revolutionary" product, the iPhone. The iPhone combines three concepts popular with consumers: a mobile phone, a widescreen iPod, and an Internet communication device. The iPhone brags "an entirely new user interface based on a large multi-touch display and pioneering software," which users can control with just their fingers.[26] The iPhone's default Internet browser will be Apple's own Safari,** but it is open to other software as well.[27] The iPhone allows for 8 hours of talk time, 24 hours of audio playback time, and 10 days of standby time.[28] Apple sold 1 million iPhones less than three months after this product was available to consumers. Apple expects this trend to continue during 2008 and to reach sales of 10 million iPhones, stealing 1 percent of the mobile phone market share.[29]

Apple TV

In addition to the iPhone, Apple also introduced the Apple TV in 2007. With this product, Apple intends to revolutionize the Internet video industry, as it did with the music download industry. Users can download movies and TV shows via the iTunes online service or via YouTube as well as view digital photos and home videos.[30] Some negative hype claims that the Apple TV will be a flop just like the Apple III and the Power Mac

---

** Safari is Apple's Internet browser that was introduced in 2003. It is part of Apple's strategy to gain more market share by having both hardware and software products. Apple suggests that Safari is the fastest browser available. It blocks pop-up advertising and has a built-in text reader that reads the site pages aloud. In addition to being the default browser for the iPhone, it is the default browser for the iPod Touch and the Mac computer. Safari's user share was estimated to be 6 percent in early 2008. (P. Festa, 2003, Welcome to the browser jungle, Safari, CNET News, www.news.com, January 7; 2008, Wikipedia, http://en.wikipedia.org.)

Cube. Some of the features that made the first edition unpopular include the following:

- Users are not able to download a movie from iTunes directly to their TV; they have to download it to their PC first.
- It requires an HDTV, but the movies that can be downloaded are of such low resolution that the picture looks fuzzy and old-fashioned.
- It has no DVD drive.

Steve Jobs announced at the Macworld Conference & Expo in January 2008 that the upgraded version of Apple TV will allow owners to order movies directly from the TV rather than having to download to the PC.[31] Also, critics do compliment the fact that the Apple TV plays a slideshow of digital photos.[32]

The price to rent a movie using Apple TV is $2.99 for library titles, $3.99 for new releases, and $1 extra to view the movie in high definition.[33]

One key component that must be in place to have good media content for the three products mentioned is the relationship that Apple has with each of its media and phone service suppliers.

Service Suppliers: iTunes, Apple TV, and iPhone

iTunes

iTunes has agreements with all five major record labels (BMG, EMI, Sony Music Entertainment, Universal, and Warner Bros.) as well as more than 200 independent labels. These agreements allow iTunes to sell the music owned by these labels and pay the record label each time a song is downloaded. This deal is considered a reseller agreement, meaning that Apple is not licensing content from these labels, but rather buying it wholesale and reselling it to consumers.[34] Apple gets to keep its share, while the portion the label receives must be divided among many parties including artists, producers, and publishers. Labels earn approximately 70 cents per song sold on iTunes. This figure may seem small, but it is still greater than losing money to the millions of illegal downloads that nearly crippled the music industry.

The revenues for record label companies have been dropping in the past year due to tough market conditions, and Apple has introduced a strategy that may help increase revenues by at least a small percentage. It has already contracted with EMI to make its entire catalog available to iTunes' users in two formats, the traditional download option, which includes the Fairplay digital rights management (DRM) software and DRM-free versions. The DRM software limits the

number of times a song can be copied, which decreases the quality of the song. The DRM-free versions would deliver greater quality music but would require a higher price tag. iTunes will start the DRM-free songs at $1.29 per song versus the traditional $0.99 per song. Other record labels may enter into the same agreement with Apple depending on how successful this strategy is with EMI.[35]

NBC recently cancelled its agreement with Apple to provide its TV shows on iTunes due to pricing disputes. Walt Disney Studios previously offered its new releases, and Paramount, Metro-Goldwyn-Mayer (MGM), and Lionsgate allowed older library titles to be purchased on iTunes, but the supplier agreements have changed with the launch of Apple TV.[36]

Apple TV

Apple did not have an easy time finalizing with movie studios contracts that will allow Apple to sell movies on iTunes for use on the iPod and Apple TV. Not only were the studios concerned about losing significant revenues from the sales of DVDs and Blu-ray discs, but some studios urged Apple to require a watermark on digital video for it to play on its devices. Their concern is heightened given the pirating experienced in the music download business. One movie-studio executive said, "Our position is, if you want our content, you have to protect our business." Apple, however, responded that it trusts its consumers not to play pirated movies.[37]

The limited number of movie downloads available on iTunes would significantly diminish the success of Apple TV. Thus, Apple's CEO was persistent in his negotiations with the movie studios. Jobs announced at the Macworld Expo in 2008 that Apple had reached agreement with each of the following major studios: Twentieth Century Fox, The Walt Disney Studios, Warner Bros., Paramount, Sony Pictures Entertainment, MGM, Lionsgate, and New Line Cinema.[38] Despite NBC's issues with Apple concerning TV shows, Universal Pictures (owned by NBC and General Electric) has agreed to allow Apple to rent its movies via iTunes.

The supplier agreement between Apple and the movie studios is that new movies will not be available for rent until 30 days after the DVD is distributed. Within a 24-hour period, customers will be able to watch a film as many times as they like once the movie is started. Movies that are downloaded but not started will not be available for viewing after 30 days.[39]

iPhone

Cingular was selected as the exclusive wireless carrier for the iPhone in the United States because, according to Steve Jobs, Cingular is the best and most popular carrier in the United States.[40] Together these companies

Exhibit 4 iPod Product Descriptions

	iPod shuffle		iPod nano		iPod classic		iPod touch	
Capacity[1]	1GB	Up to 240 songs	4GB	Up to 1,000 songs, up to 3,500 photos, up to 4 hours of video, or some of each	80GB	Up to 20,000 songs, up to 25,000 photos, up to 100 hours of video, or some of each	8GB	Up to 1,750 songs, up to 10,000 photos, up to 10 hours of video, or some of each
	2GB	Up to 500 songs	8GB	Up to 2,000 songs, up to 7,000 photos, up to 8 hours of video, or some of each	160GB	Up to 40,000 songs, up to 25,000 photos, up to 200 hours of video, or some of each	16GB	Up to 3,500 songs, up to 20,000 photos, up to 20 hours of video, or some of each
							32GB	Up to 7,000 songs, up to 25,000 photos, up to 40 hours of video, or some of each
Price	1GB $49	2GB $69	4GB $149	8GB $199	80GB $249	160GB $349	8GB $299	16GB $399 32GB $499
Color display			2-inch		2.5-inch		3.5-inch Multi-Touch	
Wireless data[2]							Wi-Fi (802.11b/g)	
Battery life[3]	Up to 2 hours of audio		Up to 24 hours of audio Up to 5 hours of video		Up to 40 hours of audio Up to 7 hours of video		Up to 22 hours of audio Up to 5 hours of video	

1. 1 GB = 1 billion bytes; actual formatted capacity is less. Music capacity is based on 4 minutes per song and 128-Kpbs AAC encoding; photo capacity is based on iPod-viewable photos transferred from iTunes; video capacity is based on H.264 1.5-Mbps video at 640-by-480 resolution combined with 128-Kbps audio; actual capacity varies by content.

2. Internet access is required; broadband is recommended; fees may apply.

3. Testing was conducted by Apple in August 2007 using preproduction hardware and software. For audio playback, the playlist contained 358 unique audio tracks consisting of content imported from CDs using iTunes (128-Kbps AAC) and content purchased from the iTunes Store (128-Kbps AAC); all settings were default except that Ask to Join Networks was turned off for iPod touch. For video playback, video content was purchased from the iTunes Store; all settings were default except that Ask to Join Networks and Auto-Brightness were turned off for iPod touch. Battery tests are conducted with specific iPod units; actual results may vary. Rechargeable batteries have a limited number of charge cycles and may eventually need to be replaced (see www.apple.com/support/ipod/service/battery). Battery life and number of charge cycles vary by use and settings. See www.apple.com/batteries for more information.

Source: www.apple.com/ipod/whichipod.

developed the Visual Voicemail feature that allows users to listen to the voicemails they prefer rather than having to listen to all messages in succession. Since the agreement was made between Cingular and Apple, Cingular was acquired by AT&T. iPhone owners are required to sign a two-year service agreement with AT&T. AT&T offers four different plans, with monthly fees ranging from $59.99 to $119.99. All plans include the visual voicemail, unlimited access to the Internet, and roll-over minutes.[41]

Hardware

Concerning its hardware suppliers, Apple is usually not forthcoming with this information. However, a disassembled iPhone reveals that the microprocessor chip is supplied by Samsung; Philips, Texas Instruments, and Linear Technology all play a role in providing the batteries, and many other companies provide chips that are central to the camera, display, and motion sensor.[42]

Many companies have expressed frustration in working with Apple because Steve Jobs is very clear on his vision for his products and can tend to be controlling. Maintaining good supplier relationships and keeping enough control to provide the quality of products expected of Apple is a balance that Apple will have to find in order to stay ahead of its competitors.

Competitors

iTunes

Since the October 2003 launch of iTunes.com for Windows, Apple has faced a multitude of competitors. During the late 1990s, the emergence of music sharing came about with Napster, a freeware program offering free downloads using peer-to-peer transfers. Peer-to-peer transfers allow users to connect directly with other users without the need for a central point of management.[43] However, in recent years due to legal proceedings, Napster and all other competitors have become a subscription service similar to iTunes.

Napster. In May 1999, 19-year-old Shawn Fanning created Napster while studying at Northeastern University. The name Napster came from the Internet "handle" he had used as a programmer. He created a type of software that allowed music fans anywhere to "share" MP3s in one forum. During the first year of service, Napster was obtaining more than 250,000 new users a week while maintaining a free service.[44] This software creation led to the ever-growing controversy of the availability of MP3s on the Internet. Music sharing exploded in the late 1990s, and Napster's servers were overloaded with millions of requests a day for media downloads. Music artists considered this new "sharing" forum to be a continuous copyright violation. Fanning soon became the target of their animosity and became one of the most disliked people in the music industry.

During 2000, Napster was in and out of court and was finally slated to shut down on July 26, 2000. The decision was reversed two days later on July 28, 2000.[45] In 2001, Konrad Hilbers, a 38-year-old German, became CEO of the rapidly declining music file-sharing site. In June 2001, Napster had more than 26 million users, but growth was declining fast, going from 6.3 billion to 2.2 billion minutes used a day. On March 7, 2002, Napster closed its servers while opting to implement a fee-based service to comply with the federal judge's decision. On June 3, 2002, Napster filed for Chapter 11 bankruptcy in an effort to secure court-ordered protection from creditors. This move was part of the overall financial restructuring strategy of Bertelsmann AG, which was proceeding with its takeover of the once popular file-sharing system. By July 2003, Roxio, Inc., had acquired Napster and was planning a Napster 2.0 launch for December 2003. Napster 2.0 is a successful, legal fee-based service.[46]

Through restructuring and quality legal representation, Napster finally has a legal base that is expected to stand. Currently, Napster 4.0 is online with content agreements from five major record labels and hundreds of independent labels; therefore, its library is made up of more than 5 million songs. Members have unlimited access to the library for $12.95 per month. Napster 4.0 now accommodates the use of its software for Mac and Linux users.

Kazaa. Sharman Networks Limited was founded in January 2002 as a private limited company. Sharman Networks develops and markets world-class Internet applications. Kazaa Media Desktop and Kazaa Plus are products of Sharman Networks. Sharman Networks earns revenue by soliciting companies to advertise on its software. Users that prefer ad-free use of the software can purchase an upgrade, Kazaa Plus for $29.95. This upgrade will also allow for greater search capabilities and more download sources.[47]

Being Australian-based, the company avoided legal intervention in allowing the file sharing, but in 2005, the Federal Court of Australia ruled that Kazaa had knowingly allowed users to illegally download copyrighted songs. The company was charged to change its software to prohibit copyrighted music or videos from being shared.[48] Kazaa owners agreed to pay the four major record labels (Universal Music, Sony BMG, EMI, and Warner Music) $100 million.[49]

Kazaa Media Desktop is a program rumored to be littered with spyware and ad-based programs that "infect" consumer systems; thus many users have become wary of accessing Kazaa's site.[50]

RealNetworks, Inc. RealNetworks, through its RealPlayer Music Store, sought a price war with Apple by dropping the price to $0.49 per song and $4.99 per album compared to Apple's price of $0.99 and $9.99, respectively. Analysts indicated that RealNetworks was pricing below the cost of purchasing the music from the record companies, and eventually it did increase its price to $0.99 per song; however, it still offers, select songs for $0.49 a track. As part of its battle to reduce Apple's market share, RealNetworks launched technology called Harmony, which allows RealNetworks users to translate songs purchased from RealPlayer Music Store into a format that can be played on an iPod. It also allows RealNetworks music to be played on Microsoft formats.[51] RealPlayer is a RealNetworks medium through which it competes in the video-on-demand market. Video can be downloaded from the Web to an iPod, PC, CD, and DVD. RealPlayer customers can subscribe to its SuperPass membership, which combines the benefits of RealPlayer and the RealPlayer Music Store. The $14.99 monthly fee provides subscribers with $10.00 worth of music downloads and full-length movies per month.

Sony. Sony started a music download service called Connect in the spring of 2004. Despite its efforts to compete in the music downloading market, it did not realize significant success; thus, Connect closed at the end of March 2008.[52] Instead, Sony is focusing its attention on gaining market share in the video download segment.[53]

Virgin Media. Virgin offers more than 15,000 record labels in addition to computer games and videos and Blockbuster movies. Similar to iTunes, customers can listen to a 30-second sample before purchase and download exclusive tracks through Virgin's V2 music label before the tracks are released to the general public.[54]

Wal-Mart. Wal-Mart launched its own online music store. It is currently the number-one music retailer in the nation, followed by iTunes.[55] Initially Wal-Mart offered music in MP3 format for $0.88 per song, $0.11 cheaper than Apple, but currently it offers songs for $0.94 and albums starting at $7.88.[56]

Yahoo! Music Unlimited. Subscribers to Yahoo! Music Jukebox have access to more than 2 million songs. Users can listen to 150 LAUNCHcast radio stations or download songs to any PC. After paying a monthly $6.00 fee, subscribers pay only $0.79 per song. Nonsubscribers can also download songs for $0.99 each.[57] At this time, Yahoo! offers only music on its site; video and TV shows are not available.

Apple TV

Amazon Unbox. The Amazon Unbox was introduced in 2006. Users download films or TV shows to the Amazon Unbox Player or on Windows Media Player. In addition, Amazon established a partnership with TiVo in 2007 that allows consumers to purchase movies or TV shows through Amazon's Unbox and send it to the TiVo machine to view. Amazon's service is similar to its competitors in that once a movie or show is downloaded, it must be viewed within 30 days and once it is started, it must be viewed within 24 hours. Amazon also has agreements with most of the major movie studios such as Paramount Pictures, Universal Studios, Warner Bros., CBS, and Fox.[58] NBC contracted with Amazon to offer its TV shows for download after NBC cancelled its agreement with Apple for the iTunes service.[59]

CinemaNow. This company seemed to have been ahead of the game, entering the video download market in 1999. It was the first to offer pay-per-view movies from the major Hollywood studios, the first to offer Download-to-Own services, and the first distributor of Burn-to-DVD movies. It is headquartered in Marina Del Rey, California, and its library consists of more than 10,000 movie titles, television programs, music concerts, and shorts. It has enabled users to download movies to the Microsoft Xbox 360 video game console as part of its strategy of providing multiple platforms on which to download movies. It has recently been creating joint ventures to differentiate itself in the industry. It originated as a distributor of videos via the Internet and has progressed most recently to wireless Internet "infotainment," a new feature available in select new car models. Its agreement with USTelematics, Inc. will allow it to offer a package of features and functions, including the creation of a mobile Wi-Fi Internet hotspot to enable online computer usage in the car, as well as DVD, movies, TV, Xbox, and other computer games.[60]

Disney. Disney, through an agreement made with Microsoft in 2007, offers movie download service for use on the Xbox 360. This service is one of the few that offers movies in high-definition format. Consumers have access to the Walt Disney Studios library, including titles from Walt Disney Pictures, Touchstone Pictures, Hollywood Pictures, and Miramax Films.[61]

HP. HP announced at the beginning of 2008 that it had reached an agreement with Sony Pictures Home Entertainment (SPHE) to deliver movies on demand. HP's manufactured-on-demand service will produce a DVD of any movie, TV show, or other content offered through SPHE. HP believes this service will aid movie studios in trying to match supply and demand for movies it sells on DVD. The current list of items available for order are classic TV shows never released on DVD, foreign movies, specialty cable programming, independent movies, specialty genres such as religion and education, and recently broadcast TV shows.[62]

Movielink. Recently acquired by Blockbuster, Movielink began in 2002 and was owned by five of the top movie studios: Universal Studios, Paramount Pictures, Sony Pictures, MGM, and Warner Bros. It operates as a subsidiary of Blockbuster and offers 3,300 movie titles.[63] Consumers who purchase a movie from Movielink must view it using a computer, a TV connected to a computer, or an Xbox 360 game console or via a set-top box company.

Netflix. Like many of its competitors, Netflix has teamed up with a technology company, LG, to become a stronger player in the video-on-demand market. In January 2008, Netflix announced that through LG's set-top box, customers can stream movies directly on their TVs. The device is expected to be available in the second half of 2008.[64] In the meantime, Netflix subscribers can stream to their PC an unlimited number of movies per month, unconstrained by hourly limits, for a monthly fee with plans starting at $8.99 per month. The on-demand library offers viewers the option of 6,000 titles of movies and TV shows.[65]

Sony. In the United Kingdom and Ireland, Sony offers video-on-demand service through its PlayStation Portable device. It has partnered with British Sky Broadcasting to provide the movies.[66] It also offers this service in Japan, but it is currently not available in the United States.

Vudu. Vudu, headquartered in Santa Clara, California, entered the video-on-demand market in April 2007.[67] Vudu's black box connects to the TV and Internet, and the built-in hard drive gives users the option of viewing 5,000 movie titles instantly. The box costs $400. The service has no monthly service charge, but a rental costs $2.00 to $4.00 per movie. As such, Vudu claims to be the cure-all for the movie rental business; it saves customers from running back and forth from the video store or waiting for the movie to come in the mail from Netflix or Blockbuster; it offers more movie titles than video-on-demand providers; and it is more functional than Internet download services because it does not require a PC. Similar to Vudu's competitors, once a movie is downloaded, it must be viewed within 24 hours.

Vudu offers movies from all major Hollywood studios. But since it is subject to the distribution windows, the time frame in which select movies are available may not match consumer demand. Only some movies have previews, and some are available only for purchase and not for rent.[68]

Wal-Mart. In December 2006, Wal-Mart entered the movie download segment of the entertainment industry, but only a year later it exited the business because it had not caught on with consumers. Raul Vasquez, Wal-Mart's CEO for walmart.com, stated that the download service was an experiment. "We want to understand what the customers want. And I think what we learned is that the initial experience of buying and downloading content needs to be better. We thought it was going to be easier for the customer to understand."

iPhone

Motorola. Motorola has been a long-time leader in mobile phone sales in the United States. However, since Apple's iPhone and Research In Motion's (RIM) Blackberry have been gaining ground, the leader is falling hard and fast. Motorola's RAZR phone has lost its popularity, and its smartphone made in partnership with Microsoft, the Motorola Q, has not performed as expected. Motorola announced in January 2008 that it is seeking alternatives for its handset business, most likely a divestiture.[69]

Palm. Despite the fact that Palm sold 689,000 Treos in the first quarter of 2007, a 21 percent increase from the previous year, Palm is struggling to remain a major player in the smartphone market amid the success of the Blackberry and the iPhone. The competition with the iPhone is especially fierce since AT&T is the phone service provider for both products. Palm introduced its Centro in October 2007 as a low-cost strategy to increase market share. Although the Centro sells for $99, it does not have all of the features of the iPhone. But cost-conscious consumers may choose it over the iPhone given the iPhone's $399 price tag.[70]

Research In Motion. The Blackberry created by Research In Motion (RIM) has been a popular product among corporate consumers who mainly needed e-mail service and a calendar. To stay in the competitive game, however, RIM has been adding features to make its product more appealing to users who want the fun features in addition to the features that aid in their work. Blackberrys now have cameras and can play music. There is a rumor that RIM is going to introduce a Blackberry 9000, which will have a touch-sensitive screen, making it similar to the iPhone.[71] Conversely, Apple has recently released tools that make its iPhone more corporate-user friendly, and it will now be compatible with Microsoft's Exchange platform.[72]

Exhibit 5 illustrates a comparison of the product features for the iPhone relative to its key competitors.

Exhibit 5 iPhone properties and its competitors

	Apple iPhone - $499 to $599	Moto Q - $499	BlackBerry Pearl - $299	Palm Treo 750 - $649
	N/A	FM Radio with Software Sold Separately	No	FM Radio with Software Sold Separately
	Bluetooth Wireless Technology v2.0 + EDR	Bluetooth Wireless Technology v1.2	**Bluetooth Wireless Technology v2.0**	Bluetooth Wireless Technology v1.2
	N/A but most likely	Video Capture/Camcorder QCIF-quality	N/A	Video Capture/Camcorder QCIF
	Full QWERTY Soft Keyboard	QWERTY Keyboard Backlit with thumbwheel	QWERTY Keyboard	QWERTY Keyboard Backlit
	N/A	**Infrared Port**	No	**Infrared Port**
	N/A	**Use Phone as Modem via USB Cable, Bluetooth, or IR**	**Use This Phone as a Modem**	**Use Phone as Modem via USB Cable, Bluetooth, or IR**
	iSynch via Bluetooth or Wi-Fi Mac or PC	PC Synch via Cable: Infrared or Bluetooth: Active Sync	PC Synchronization	PC Synch via Cable: Infrared or Bluetooth: Active Sync
	Full Color Display 3.5" 320 x 480 Pixels at 160 ppi	Color Display 320 x 240 Pixels, 65K Colors, QVGATFT	Color Display 240 x 260 Pixels, 65K Colors	Color Display 320 x 320 Pixels, 65K Colors, TFT
	Multi Touch Screen	No	No	**Touch Screen**
	Speakerphone	**Speakerphone**	**Speakerphone**	**Speakerphone**
	Widgets	To-Do List, Alarm, Calculator, Calendar, etc.	To-Do List, Alarm, Ca culator, Calendar, etc.	To-Do List, Alarm, Calculator, Calendar, etc.
	N/A	**Voice Memo**	N/A	**Voice Memo**
	N/A	Vibrate	Vibrate	Vibrate
	N/A	**Voice recognition**	**Voice-activated Dialing**	No
	Predictive Text Entry with corrector	N/A	**Predictive Text Entry**	No
	Advanced Sensors for Rotation Detection	No	No	No
Messaging & Internet Features				
	Safari Full Rich HTML Browser	Pocket Internet Explorer HTML	**Full HTML Web Browser**	Blazer Browser Supports
	N/A	MMS	MMS	MMS
	SMS	**SMS**	**SMS**	**SMS**
	POP3/IMAP Push Email services	Pocket Outlook Supports POP, IMAP, APOP, ESMTP	**Push Email POP3, IMAP, SMTP**	Pocket Outlook Supports POP, IMAR, APOP, ESMTP
	Google Maps Built in	No	No	No
	Widgets	No	No	No
	Visual Voice Mail	No	No	No
	N/A	IM	IM	IM
Technical Specifications				
	OSX	Windows Mobile 5.0 + BREW	BlackBerry OS with Intel XScale Processor + Java	Palm OS 5.4 with Intel 312 Mhz XScale Processor
	Data Download Speed - EDGE + WiFi (802.11 b/g)	Data Download Speed - EV-DO and 1xRTT	Data Download Speed - EDGE	Data Download Speed - EV-DO and 1xRTT
	GSM Quad Band 850, 900, 1800, 1900	**GSM Quad Band 850, 900, 1800, 1900**	**GSM Quad Band 850, 900, 1800, 1900**	**GSM Quad Band 850, 900, 1800, 1900**
	Built-in Memory - 4GB or 8GB Available	Built-in Memory - 64 MB Available	Built-in Memory - 64 MB Plus Online Photo	Built-in Memory - 123 MB Available
	None	**SecureDigital (SD) Card Format Compatible Slot**	**MicroSD Card Format Compatible Slot**	**SecureDigital (SD) Card Format Compatible Slot**
	Dimension - 115 x 61 x 11.6mm	Dimension - 116 x 63 x 11.5mm	**Dimension - 107 x 50 x 14.5mm**	Dimension - 111.8 x 58.4 x 20.3mm
	Weight - 4.8 oz	Weight - 6.40 oz	**Weight - 3.2 oz**	Weight - 6.40 oz
Battery Life				
	Up to 300 Minutes Talk/Video/Browsing	Talk Time - Up to 240 Minutes	Talk Time - Up to 210 Minutes	Talk Time - Up to 282 Minutes
	N/A	Standby Time - Up to 192 Hours	Standby Time - Up to 360 Hours	Standby Time - Up to 300 Hours
	Up to 16H Audio Playback	N/A	N/A	N/A
	No	**Removable**	**Removable**	**Removable**

iPod

Some of the iPod's major competitors include Rio Karma, Dell Digital Jukebox DJ, Samsung Napster YP-910GS, and the Gateway Jukebox Player DMP-X20 (see Exhibit 6).[73] Some of the differences from the iPod include a longer battery life, such as a 16-hour battery life for the Dell MP3 player. The weight also varies from one competitor to the next, ranging from 7.7 ounces to 5.5 ounces. (For a detailed list of the major competitors' specifications, see Exhibit 7.)

The Microsoft Zune premiered in the fall of 2006. Due to its lack of tremendous success, in the fall of 2007, Microsoft exerted great energy in combating the success of the iPod with its improved Zune. The Zune offers options of 4, 8, or 80 gigabytes of storage with prices ranging from $150 to $300. The newest edition of the Zune is smaller, has a better viewing screen, and allows users to wirelessly synchronize the gadget with the music on their computers. It also includes a touch-sensitive pad that allows users to navigate through songs with more precise control than the iPod, according to Microsoft executives.[74] But critics suggest that the Zune does not pose a significant threat to the iPod because it does not offer any significant technological breakthroughs.[75] Only 1.2 million Zunes sold during 2007 while Apple sold more than 41 million iPods. Apple's success can likely be attributed to its marketing competency.

Marketing

Up until this point, Apple's marketing endeavors have earned it awards, product sales, and a devoted base of customers, both new and old. In 2003, Apple was awarded *Advertising Age's* Marketer of the Year for its upbeat, original, and (most importantly) memorable advertisements for both its iPod and iTunes.[76] Apple has been hailed as one of the best marketers by many different sources and has had a reputation over the years of being a brand that can gain customers through its well-thought-out and carefully executed marketing strategies.

Marketing has been one of Apple's strengths; however, staying on top of the game will become more difficult as Apple develops a broader range of products and markets them to the mainstream customer rather than just the "tech-savvy fanatics" in fields such as education and design.[77] "The customer base is now more diverse, including students and mainstream consumers, and it's harder to satisfy as a whole," says Lopo L. Rego, a marketing professor at the University of Iowa.[78] Business leaders today have a daunting job in balancing shareholder demands and running a successful company. Businesses want to market new products aggressively to try and ensure their products' success. Apple heavily promoted the iPhone when it was introduced in July 2007. Customer and investor expectations, due to Apple's reputation, boosted the stock price. But when customers don't believe that the marketing promises have been delivered, stock price, brand equity, and investor confidence are significantly affected.[79] Apple's success lies in a carefully thought-out plan.

Marketing Plan

A marketing plan begins with design of the product.[80] In an industry of low profit margins and cost cutting, Apple takes a different approach to the design of its products. While competitors are doing everything they can to keep costs down, Apple does what it can to make its product different. In 2007, for the third year in a row, Apple was named as the Most Innovative Company by *Business-Week*.[81] Its CEO, Steve Jobs is "a legend for his design sense."[82] Even employees of one of Apple's biggest competitors, Microsoft, have recognized Apple's dominance in the design of eye-catching products. The employees created a mock promotion for the iPod had it been created by Microsoft and circulated it on YouTube.[83]

Steve Jobs is essential to the public relations and promotional aspect of Apple, especially with the iPod.[84] He maintains relationships with the media and has been called the "public face and champion of the brand."[85] He is an expert when it comes to talking with the press, maintaining relationships with magazine editors, and continually creating new relationships.[86] Because of his dynamic, high-energy personality, he usually holds a new idea that he is energetic about and is always ready and willing to share the idea to gain exposure.

Jobs also takes action in response to customer feedback to show that he is listening and concerned. For example, three months after the iPhone was available in stores, Apple cut the price of this product by one-third. This was a strategic move to increase demand and meet sales goals; it was not the result of a faulty product. Consumers who had purchased the iPhone in the first three months for the higher price expressed great dissatisfaction. Jobs responded by promising these consumers a $100 Apple store credit.[87]

A more recent advantage in Apple's marketing strategy is its retail stores. Apple has opened more than 200 retail stores located worldwide. At the time that Apple opened its first retail store in 2001, analysts predicted that Apple would report huge losses and shut the store within two years. At the time, no computer manufacturer had proved profitable in running its own branded store.[88] However, Apple's retail stores contributed an estimated $200 million, 15 to 16 percent of its profits during the past two years (see Exhibit 8).[89] Apple's philosophy behind the stores is brand exposure. Apple believes that the more people can touch an Apple product

Exhibit 6 Products of Competitors to iPod

Creative Nomad
Jukebox Zen NX (20 GB)

Samsung Napster
YP-910GS (20 GB)

Rio Karma (20 GB)

iRiver iHP-120

Dell Digital Jukebox
DJ (20 GB)

Gateway Jukebox Player
DMP-X20 (20 GB)

Source: http://reviews.cnet.com/4520-6497-5093864.html.

and see what it can do with their own eyes, the greater the potential market share.[90] In addition, the stores provide free group workshops, personal training, and personal assistance for Apple customers.[91]

Apple offers a One-to-One program for an annual fee of $99; subscribers can attend a tutorial session with an Apple expert for an hour once a week for one year. Apple customers can also consult with the staff at the "Genius Bar" by appointment. The Genius Bar is where Apple product users meet face-to-face with Apple's "geniuses" for answers to technical questions and for problem troubleshooting. In addition, customers wanting to purchase a new computer or other equipment can schedule an appointment with a shopping assistant, who helps ensure that the customer selects the right equipment for his or her needs. Apple has apparently struck a chord with customers because its staff conducts more than 50,000 training sessions per week.[92] "Apple has become the new gathering place," said Steven Addis, chief executive of Addis Creson, a brand strategy and design firm in Berkeley. "You can't help but get caught up with it when you first walk in."[93]

As so eloquently stated in a *USA Today* article, "Apple's arsenal of attention-getting tools holds lessons for any company: design cool, innovative products. Have

Exhibit 7 Details of Products of Competitors to iPod

Basic Specs	Creative Nomad Jukebox Zen NX (20 GB)	Samsung Napster YP-910GS (20 GB)	Rio Karma (20 GB)	iRiver iHP-120	Dell Digital Jukebox DJ (20 GB)	Gateway Jukebox Player Product DMP-X20 (20 GB)
Product type	Digital player	Digital player / recorder / radio	Digital player	Digital player / voice recorder / radio	Digital player / voice recorder	Digital player / voice recorder / radio
PC interface(s) supported	Hi-Speed USB	Hi-Speed USB	Hi-Speed USB	Hi-Speed USB	Hi-Speed USB	Hi-Speed USB
Flash memory installed	8 MB	Info unavailable	Info unavailable	Info unavailable	Info unavailable	Info unavailable
Storage capacity	20 GB	20 GB	20 GB	20 GB	20 GB	20 GB
Digital formats supported	MP3	MP3	MP3	MP3	MP3	MP3
Weight	7.2 oz	6 oz	5.5 oz	5.6 oz	7.6 oz	7.7 oz
Resolution	132 × 64	Info unavailable	160 × 128	Info unavailable	160 × 104	160 × 128
Battery technology	Lithium ion	Lithium polymer	Lithium ion	Lithium polymer	Lithium ion	Lithium ion
Mfr estimated battery life	14 hour(s)	10 hour(s)	15 hour(s)	16 hour(s)	16 hour(s)	10 hour(s)
Software included	Creative MediaSource	Drivers & Utilities	Drivers & Utilities	Drivers & Utilities	Drivers & Utilities	Drivers & Utilities

Source: http://reviews.cnet.com/4520-6497-5093864.html.

a streamlined product line. Invest in memorable ads. Work your customer base to make customers feel special and create word-of-mouth agents. Most important: keep the world and media surprised, to generate gobs of attention."[94]

Finally, Apple has garnered major success for iPod and iTunes by way of strategic partnerships with other well-known brands. Apple has created marketing agreements with Volkswagen of America, Burton Snowboards, Nike, and Starbucks. By affiliating itself with different brands, Apple gains consumer confidence as well as exposure through marketing partner advertisements.

Strategic Agreements

All of the strategic agreements that are currently known by the public are agreements related to the iPod. It remains to be seen what alliances or joint ventures Apple enters in order to create awareness for the iPhone and Apple TV.

Volkswagen. In early 2003, Volkswagen of America (VW) offered a free iPod to customers who purchased a 2003 hardtop Beetle 10. The ad campaign was aptly named "Pods Unite."[95] The deal brought iPod enthusiasts (and people who just wanted to learn more about the iPod) into the Volkswagen stores, and both products benefited from the advertisement. For three months, iPods were shown in Volkswagen showrooms.[96] Also, the Volkswagen sold iPod connectivity wiring and a cradle for the iPod to be used in the new VW Beetle.[97] Because both brands are known for unique design, it is likely that the promotion brought in consumers who highly value the design aspect of a product, whether it is a car or a digital music player.

Exhibit 8 Retail Sales as a Contribution to Overall Apple Revenue

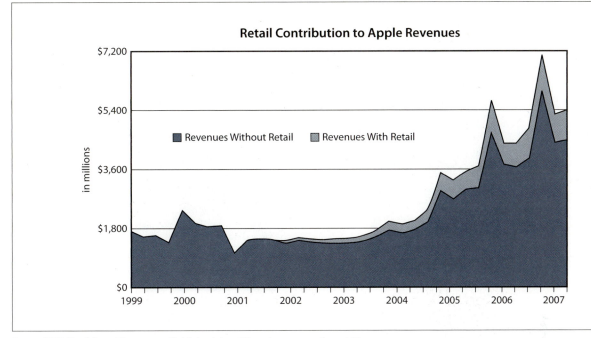

Source: 2007, Retail Stores' Importance Highlighted, http://ifoapplestore.com, August 17.

In the fall of 2007, rumors came out that Apple and VW were in discussions about furthering their relationship to create an iCar. This car would feature products that Steve Jobs fashioned. No details have been specified by either company's leaders.[98]

Burton Snowboards. In January 2004, Burton released a snowboarding/snow-skiing jacket made especially for use with the iPod (Exhibit 9). The jacket has a built-in iPod control electronic system on the sleeve of the jacket so that the wearer can operate the iPod without removing gloves, digging in pockets, or fumbling with zippers.[99] The iPod rests in a protected chest pocket in the inner lining of the jacket. With this jacket, Apple places a product into the hands of those who use iPods and creates exposure for the iPod by way of young snowboarders and skiers showing off and wearing the special jacket.

Nike. Nike and Apple have teamed up to create a smart running shoe. When runners combine a pair of Nike athletic shoes, an iPod nano, and the iPod Sport Kit, they are able to track their run in real time, with time, distance, pace, and calories burned displayed on the iPod. The iPod Sport Kit became available in 2006. Users' playlists can be selected based on the desired workout. If runners need a sudden burst of energy, they can press the Power Song button. An additional feature is the voice feedback that tells runners when they reach a personal best, whether it is in regard to pace, distance, time, or calories burned.[100] The personal data can be uploaded to Nike's Web site, and runners can compete virtually against one another.[101] The most recent partnership between Nike and Apple will shift to the gym. Teaming up with gym equipment makers and 24-Hour Fitness and Virgin Athletic Clubs, Apple and Nike will allow club members to plug their iPod nanos into the cardio equipment to track workouts, upload the information to Nike's Web site, and set goals based on personal history or to compete with others tracked on the Web site.[102]

Starbucks. In September 2007, Starbucks and Apple announced a joint venture that allows Starbucks customers to access (at no cost) the iTunes Wi-Fi Music store at more than 600 participating Starbucks locations. Customers can browse, search, and preview all songs available on the iTunes store, including the "Now Playing" service, which displays the name of the song playing at that moment in Starbucks. "Getting free access to the iTunes Wi-Fi Music Store and the 'Now Playing' service at Starbucks is a great way for customers to discover new music," said Steve Jobs.[103] If customers have to leave the Starbucks store before the download of a song is complete, their personal computer will complete the download automatically at a later time. Every song purchased in a Starbucks participating location syncs back to the users' computer the next time they connect.

In addition to these agreements with domestic companies, Apple is seeking opportunities to create demand for its products in the global market.

Exhibit 9 Complementary Product Advertised with iPods

Source: www.burton.com/Burton/gear/products.asp?productID=728.

Going Global

To stay on top of its game, Apple is pursuing opportunities to sell the iPhone globally. Apple has a goal of capturing 1 percent of the global cell phone business by the end of 2008. It already has partnership agreements with cell phone carriers in France, Germany, and Great Britain. It has also entered the Middle East and Africa regions, ranking fifth next to Nokia, Research In Motion, HTC, and Motorola.[104] Considering that Japan is one of the world's largest and most demanding mobile phone markets with almost 100 million mobile phone users, Steve Jobs has been meeting with officials in Japan in hopes of making a partnership agreement with some of the major telecommunications companies in Japan. This market will be difficult to penetrate, as many other foreign companies have tried unsuccessfully to compete with the 10 domestic handset makers in Japan. Some analysts wonder whether Apple will be able to develop a relationship with the Japanese carriers due to Apple's tight control over the design of the phone, but others believe Apple will succeed. Apple already has a positive brand image in Japan related to the Macintosh computer and the iPod and has seven Apple retail stores already in place.[105]

Stephen Kobrin, a Wharton Multinational management professor explained in a recent interview that companies that are high-tech and driven by technology that demands that they expand into many countries simultaneously are "born global." He clarifies by further stating, "Companies that are born global 'tend to have high-tech products that immediately find acceptance in many different cultures and societies.'"[106] Thus, it is likely that the iPhone will experience success in many different markets, as will the Apple TV and other new products that Apple may launch when they become part of its global strategy.

Future Opportunities and Challenges

As Apple tries to expand its product line to include media and software in addition to hardware and as it tries to reach many different consumers rather than its traditional niche of "cult followers," the tech-savvy consumers who work in fields such as education and design, the company will find it more difficult to keep a positive brand image among all consumers. The technology and entertainment industries are constantly and rapidly changing. Will Apple be able to keep its reputation related to innovative design and continually launch products that will be the "latest hit"? Competition has become extremely fierce in the technology sector, and Apple needs to be concerned not only about major competitors, but also about start-up companies. For example, in relation to the iPhone, GotVoice is a Web-based company that allows subscribers to record voicemail messages in MP3 format and send those messages to their e-mail account to view the subject line and the message length. This capability rivals Apple's Visual Voicemail on the iPhone, and the service is free unless users prefer to pay $10 to avoid ad pop-ups.[107]

Interestingly, GotVoice has an advantage over Apple's Visual Voicemail in that it works not only with cell phones, but also with home and work phones.[108] It will be a challenge for Apple to maintain its competitive advantage in new product hardware and to create strong relationships with powerful suppliers of media and other services as well as fend off startups such as GotVoice in software and other areas.

NOTES

1. D. Leonard, 2003, Songs in the key of Steve, *Fortune*, April 28.
2. D. Chmielewski & M. Quinn, 2007, Technology; Movie studios fear the sequel to iPod; They see risk that new Apple TV signals effort to control distribution, *Los Angeles Times*, June 11, C1.
3. R. E. Hoskisson, 2007, Strategic Focus: Apple: Using innovation to create technology trends and maintain competitive advantage, Hitt, Ireland, & Hoskisson, *Strategic Management: Competitiveness and Globalization*, 8th Edition.
4. Ibid.
5. Apple history, www.apple-history.com/frames.
6. Ibid.
7. L. Kimmel, 1998, Apple Computer, Inc.: A History, www.geocities.com/Athens/3682/applehistory.html.
8. Ibid.
9. http://apple-history.com.
10. Apple Computer History Weblog, http://apple.computerhistory.org.
11. L. Kimmel, 1998, Apple Computer, Inc.: A history.
12. Apple Computer History Weblog.
13. http://apple-history.com.
14. Ibid.
15. Apple Computer History Weblog.
16. http://apple-history.com.
17. Ibid.
18. Ibid.
19. Ibid.
20. http://www.apple.com/itunes.
21. 2008, iTunes store, www.apple.com/itunes/store/, January 8.
22. P. Hardy, 2003, Apple launches Windows-based iTunes, *Music & Copyright Magazine*, October 29.
23. A. Hesseldahl, 2005, Unpeeling Apple's Nano, *BusinessWeek*, www.businessweek.com, September 22.
24. 2007, www.apple.com.
25. R. E. Hoskisson, Strategic Focus: Apple.
26. 2007, Apple reinvents the phone with iPhone, Apple Inc. press release, www.apple.com/pr/library/2007/01/09iphone.html, January 9.
27. K. Allison, 2007, Apple encroaches on Window's turf, *The Financial Times*, www.ft.com, June 11.
28. 2007, iPhone delivers up to eight hours of talk time, Apple Inc. press release, www.apple.com/pr/library/2007/06/18iphone.html, June 18.
29. 2007, In three months, iPhone sales top a million, *New York Times*, www.nytimes.com, September 11.
30. Ibid.
31. M. Quinn & D. C. Chmielewski, 2008, Studios join Apple's movie-rental service, *Los Angeles Times*, www.latimes.com, January 16.
32. B. Schlender, 2007, The trouble with Apple TV, *Fortune*, June 11,155(11): 56.
33. 2008, www.apple.com/appletv/rentals.
34. W. Cohen, www.rollingstone/news/newsarticle.asp?nid =18075.
35. K. Regan, 2007, EMI revenue falls but DRM-free iTunes sales promising, *Ecommerce Times*, www.ecommercetimes.com, August 6.
36. M. Garrahan & K. Allison, 2007, Apple signs film deal with Fox studio, *Financial Times*, www.ft.com, December 27.
37. D. C. Chmielewski & M. Quinn, 2007, Technology; Movie studios fear the sequel to iPod; They see risk that new Apple TV signals effort to control distribution, *Los Angeles Times*, June 11, C1.
38. 2008, Apple premieres iTunes movie rentals with all major film studios, Apple press release, www.apple.com/pr/library, January 15.
39. M. Quinn & D. C. Chmielewski, Studios join Apple's movie-rental service.
40. 2007, Apple chooses Cingular as exclusive U.S. carrier for its revolutionary iPhone, Apple Inc. press release, www.apple.com/pr/library/2007/01/09cingular.html, January 9.
41. 2008, www.apple.com/iphone.
42. A. Hesseldahl, 2007, Take the iPhone apart, *BusinessWeek*, www.businessweek.com, July 2.
43. 2001, Napster's History, http://w3.uwyo.edu/~pz/nap2.htm.
44. 2001, The history of the Napster struggle, www.theneworleanschannel.com/news/457209/detail.html.
45. 2003, Napster 2.0 to launch by Christmas, www.roxio.com/en/company/news/archive/prelease030728.jhtml.
46. Ibid.
47. J. Ketola, 2003, Kazaa Plus service launched, www.afterdawn.com, August.
48. 2008, Wikipedia, http://en.wikipedia.org/wiki/kazaa.
49. 2006, Kazaa settlement, *BBC News*, http://news.bbc.co.uk., July 27.
50. 2003, Kazaa Usage Map, http://tools.waglo.com/kazaa.
51. N. Wingfield, 2004, Price war in online music, *Wall Street Journal*, www.wsj.com, August 17.
52. 2008, http://musicstore.connect.com.
53. Y. I. Kane, 2007, Sony to challenge Apple in TV, movie downloads, *Wall Street Journal*, www.online.wsj.com, September 4.
54. 2008, www.virgin.com/VirginProducts/Shopping/Musicdownloads.aspx.
55. 2008, iTunes now the number two music retailer in the United States, Apple press release, www.apple.com/pr/library.
56. 2008, http://musicdownloads.walmart.com.
57. 2008, http://music.yahoo.com.
58. B. Stone, 2007, Amazon and TiVo in venture to put downloaded movies on TV, *New York Times*, www.nytimes.com, February 7.
59. G. Sandoval, 2007, NBC says goodbye to Apple, hello to Amazon, www.news.com, September 4.
60. 2008, CinemaNow Inc., *BusinessWeek*, http://investing.businessweek.com, March 14; 2008, www.cinemanow.com; 2008, Wikipedia, http://en.wikipedia.org; A. Gonsalves, 2007, *Information Week*, www.informationweek.com, July 18.
61. 2007, The Walt Disney Studios to offer movie rentals on demand through Xbox Live starting now, *MicrosoftNews*, www.microsoft.com/presspass, July 10.
62. 2008, HP and Sony Pictures Home Entertainment announce manufactured-on-demand content licensing agreement, *HP News Release*, www.hp.com/hpinfo/newsroom, January 24.
63. 2007, Blockbuster acquires Movielink, *New York Times*, www.nytimes.com, August 9.
64. 2008, Netflix and LG unveil video-on-demand service, *Appliance Magazine*, www.appliancemagazine.com, January 7.
65. 2008, Netflix now offers subscribers unlimited streaming of movies and TV shows on their PCs for the same monthly fee, Netflix press release, www.netflix.mediaroom.com, January 14.
66. Leipzig, 2007, PSP (PlayStation Portable) video download service, Sony Computer Entertainment Europe press release, www.scei.co.jp/corporate/release, August.
67. 2008, Wikipedia, http://en.wikipedia.org.

68. D. Pogue, 2007, High-speed video store in the living room, *New York Times*, www.nytimes.com, September 6.
69. J. Goldman, 2008, Motorola hangs up on handsets, www.cnbc.com, January 31; A. Hasseldahl, 2008, Blackberry vs. iPhone: Who wins? *BusinessWeek*, www.articles.moneycentral.msn.com, January 3.
70. E. M. Rusli, 2007, Palm wilts, *Forbes*, www.forbes.com, October 2.
71. A. Hesseldahl, 2008, Blackberry vs. iPhone: Who wins?
72. J. Goldman, 2008, iPhone vs. Blackberry: Apple launches new software, www.cnbc.com, March 6.
73. www.reviews.cnet.com/html.
74. N. Wingfield, 2007, Microsoft tunes its Zunes to catch up with iPod, *Wall Street Journal Online*, www.wsj.com, October 3, D8.
75. Ibid.
76. A. Cuneo, 2003, Apple transcends as lifestyle brand, *Advertising Age*, December 15.
77. 2007, A bruise or two on Apple's reputation, *BusinessWeek*, www.businessweek.com, October 22.
78. Ibid.
79. J. Quelch, 2007, How marketing hype hurt Boeing and Apple, *Harvard Business*, http://discussionleader.hbsp.com, November 2.
80. Ibid.
81. J. Smykil, 2007, *BusinessWeek* names Apple most innovative, http://arstechnica.com, May 6.
82. L. Gomes, 2006, Above all else, rivals of Apple mostly need some design mojo, *Wall Street Journal*, May 24, B1.
83. Ibid.
84. Cuneo, Apple transcends as lifestyle brand.
85. Ibid.
86. Ibid.
87. 2007, In 3 months, iPhone sales top a million.
88. R. Stross, 2007, Apple's lesson for Sony's stores: Just connect, *New York Times*, www.nytimes.com, May 27.
89. Ibid.; 2007, Retail stores' importance highlighted, http://ifoapplestore.com, August 17.
90. Cuneo, Apple transcends as lifestyle brand.
91. www.apple.com/findouthow/retail/.
92. J. Boudreau, 2008, Apple tutorial classes help create bond with customers, *The Mercury News*, www.mercurynews.com, March 3.
93. Ibid.
94. J. Graham, 2007, Apple buffs marketing savvy to a high shine, *USA Today*, www.usatoday.com, March 3.
95. Wong.
96. Ibid.
97. Ibid.
98. C. Campellone, 2007, Apple and Volkswagen team up for possible iCar, http://media.www.theloquitur.com, September 20.
99. Ibid.
100. www.apple.com/ipod/nike/run.html.
101. E.C. Baig, 2006, Apple, Nike exercise iPods to track workouts, *USA Today*, www.usatoday.com, May 23.
102. 2008, Nike, Apple plug iPods into gym equipment, *USA Today*, www.usatoday.com, March 4.
103. 2007, Apple and Starbucks announce music partnership, Apple press release, www.apple.com/pr/library, September 5; http://www.apple.com/itunes/starbucks.
104. N. Gohring, 2008, Apple beats Microsoft and Motorola in 4Q phone sales, IDG News Service, February 6.
105. Y. I. Kane & N. Wingfield, 2007, For Apple iPhone, Japan could be the next big test, *Wall Street Journal Online*, www.wsj.com, December 19, B1.
106. 2007, What makes a global leader? *India Knowledge at Wharton*, http://knowledge.wharton.upenn.edu/india, October 4.
107. M. S. Lasky, 2007, iPhone versus your phone: Tips to avoid iPhone envy, *PC World*, www.pcworld.com, June 27.
108. 2008, www.gotvoice.com.

From Swords to Ploughshares: Three Generations of Family Entrepreneurship, Conflict, Transition, and Connection

Randel S. Carlock, Elizabeth Florent-Treacy

INSEAD

An Entrepreneurial Family: The Early Years

Harry McNeely Jr. grew up in the 1920s and 1930s in a genteel Irish Catholic community in St. Paul, Minnesota. His parents were contemporaries of F. Scott Fitzgerald, who lived, wrote, and drank in their neighborhood (Fitzgerald described his own house as "below the average on a street above the average"). Harry's father, like many well-off Irish Catholics of the period, had earned, not inherited, his wealth. The McNeelys were the epitome of the American dream—an immigrant family whose success at running a small but growing business gave them, within one generation, an entry into old-money gentry in St. Paul.

In 1916, Harry McNeely Sr. borrowed $5,000—a great sum of money in that era—from his father-in-law to start a warehousing and drayage business in downtown St. Paul. He named it the St. Paul Terminal Warehouse Company. Harry Sr.'s brother-in-law and fellow company executive, Paul Frenzel, was also a founding shareholder, although his ownership interest constituted a minority share.

The company leased a warehouse to store and distribute freight via the nearby Soo Line Railroad, and business grew quickly. By the mid-1920s it was also doing contract pickup and delivery work for trucking companies. The company was not asset-rich at that time—it owned trucks, tractors, and trailers but almost no real estate.

Just prior to World War II, with real estate prices low and war production starting up, Harry Sr. made several key real estate purchases in St. Paul, including a warehouse company and an International Harvester

This case was written by Professor Randel S. Carlock, Berghmans Lhoist Chaired Professor in Entrepreneurial Leadership, and Elizabeth Florent-Treacy, Research Project Manager, both at INSEAD. It is intended to be a basis for class discussion rather than to illustrate either effective or ineffective handling of a business situation.

The active cooperation and contributions of the McNeely family are greatly appreciated. The support of the Berghmans Lhoist family, the Wendel International Centre for Family Enterprise, and the INSEAD Research and Development Committee are gratefully acknowledged.

plant (a manufacturer of trucks and tractors). The subsequent production boom, during and just after the war, was very profitable for companies like the McNeelys in the warehouse, storage, and transportation business.

In the 1950s and 1960s, the company, now called Space Center (and later renamed Meritex) continued to expand both in size and in the scope of its core businesses. For example, when the Whirlpool plant in St. Paul, which produced refrigerators and the like, required a large warehouse in which to store and mix loads for shipment to distributors, Space Center purchased land from the Burlington-Northern Railroad and built, then managed, Whirlpool's 244,000-square-foot warehouse.

In addition, old buildings were continually acquired and rehabilitated. One executive explained: "We have a special talent for going in and taking a property or building that has seen better days, and fixing it up to create value. It's called adaptive reuse." For example, several of the company's original warehouses were rehabilitated into office buildings and leased to the State of Minnesota.

In Quincy, Illinois, Space Center acquired an interest in a subsurface industrial space, where it set up a distribution center. Clients quickly came to appreciate the advantages of subsurface space (which were originally limestone caves), including safety and environmental stability. Steve Dorff, an asset manager, said: "Old limestone caves provide a secure storage opportunity for a variety of products. There's a massive amount of space. The caves just go on forever and ever; they're amazing. We just get 'rock doctors'—engineers who understand mining and rock development—to develop the space. They can work with those dimensions. Clients really like the space."

The company continued to acquire buildings all across the United States, following an opportunistic strategy that often combined the purchase of under-utilized real estate with the operation of a public warehouse, or provision of third-party logistics services. The original public warehouse business had many closely related offshoots, including multiple financial and transportation companies.

The Next Generation of Entrepreneurs

Harry McNeely Sr. was the head of the company into the early 1960s. His eldest child, Don, had joined the company in 1937 as a top executive. Harry Jr., the youngest of his four children, graduated from Yale, then served in the U.S. Navy and was on the staff of the U.S. Ambassador to Australia before joining the family firm in 1949 (see Exhibit 1). Harry Jr. described the organization at that time as a family-run operation:

My mother was secretary and my father was chairman and president. My uncle, Paul Frenzel, was a member of the board, along with two outsiders: the financial vice president of the company and the company's legal counsel. The board pretty much just fulfilled the required functions. I joined the board very late in the 1970s. It continued to be very much an inside board. It functioned to fulfill the legal requirements of having an annual meeting for shareholders and those sorts of things.

—*HARRY MCNEELY JR.*

Don McNeely worked very closely with his father and later succeeded him as president. When his much younger brother Harry Jr. finally joined the company, it was as a junior executive. Toward the end of Harry Sr.'s life, Don became the de facto head of the company, to the point that when Harry Sr. needed to travel for business or pleasure, Don would barely wait until his father was out the door before getting on the phone and making deals on his own—which drove his father crazy.

Whereas the sons were taken into the company as shareholders, Harry Sr. made provision for his two daughters in the form of a generous case settlement, making them completely independent with no financial or legal ties to the family firm. However, after his death, his daughters, Jean and Audrey, hired a law firm to contest the will and sue their mother and brothers for unduly influencing their father—despite the fact that they had known they would not be included in his will.

Threatened with a lawsuit, their mother agreed to give each daughter a gift of stock in the company to avoid the notoriety such a lawsuit would bring. Jean and Audrey became minority shareholders; each with a 10.5 percent stake in the company. Their brothers Don and Harry Jr. each had 31.3 percent (with the McNeely family trust and the Frenzel family holding the remaining shares).

The real trouble began shortly thereafter.

Exhibit 1 McNeely Family Genogram, 2009

// = divorce

Three generations of McNeelys in 2006

Family Conflict

Fifteen years after Harry Sr.'s death, the company faced a serious threat to its survival: a classic family business battle of minority against majority shareholders, with a painful subplot of sibling rivalry. A long-time family acquaintance, who later became a board member, commented:

It's the old story of the [family] in the business and the [family] out of the business. The people in the business say to the outside family members, 'Why are you giving us all this trouble? You're just sitting there collecting dividends!' The outsides say, 'Well, we're family members too ....'

The following account, from a St. Paul newspaper, is typical of the press coverage at that time:

Court orders liquidation for city warehouse firm

A Ramsey County District Court judge ruled Thursday that Space Center Inc. should be placed in receivership and sold to resolve a long, bitter dispute among members of a family who control the St. Paul warehouse company.

Space Center was founded in 1916 as St. Paul Terminal Warehouse Co. by Harry McNeely Sr. (who died in 1968). The children are now fighting for control of the company. Donald G. McNeely, son of the company's founder, is chairman of Space Center, president of a holding company, and head of more than 40 subsidiaries. His brother, Harry McNeely Jr., is vice president of the holding company, and a director of Space Center. Together, they own a majority of the company's stock.

The two men are being sued by the minority shareholders, led by their own sisters. They argued in court that their brothers had frozen them out of the company's management and any significant share of the profits, and that the brothers were running the company for their own benefit. Specifically, the sisters claimed that the brothers had avoided paying significant dividends, failed to disclose required information, and misused corporate assets for their own gain. None of the minority shareholders has served on the company's board. The lawyer representing the McNeely brothers said, "If this decision of Judge Lynch is permitted to stand, it will be the demise of a company that provides jobs for 750 families. What we have is minority shareholders who have lived most of their lives in Europe and just want to get money out of their holdings."[1]

—*St. Paul Pioneer Press Dispatch*

Harry McNeely Jr., the youngest of the four siblings, tried very hard for years to reconcile his elder sisters and brother. According to Harry's children, the real conflict between Don and his sisters was about family issues not fully understood by anyone: the business was simply the stage on which the family struggle was played out. Even during the court proceedings, Harry continued to have dinner with his sisters and try to find a way to resolve the problem. His daughter said: "It was tough for Dad because he was trying to get everybody back at the table rather than [taking the dispute to] a courtroom. It was hard because he is a real family man and his family was having a terrible fight. This had been going on for years in fact. The aunts would fly in from Europe and make waves, then leave. He tried to be the peacemaker."

To no avail.

For the sisters, the issue was that the minority shareholders had no representation on the board. As a result, they argued, the company never paid them dividends, they had no access to liquidity, and they were never a part of planning and decision making. When they ventured to ask what the company was doing or where it was headed, they were ignored.

This, in turn, exposed a fundamental difference between the brothers: Harry wanted to address the issues but Don would not entertain any of the sisters' grievances. He wouldn't even talk about them. He refused to deal with his sisters; they were a pain. His attitude seemed to be that they had no right to take action against him.

Harry McNeely Jr. said: "The family members simply had different needs. You have to listen and respect those needs in a business family, but that wasn't happening with the siblings in my father's family. And that is what led inevitably to the lawsuit. Emotions were heightened– and then, you know how Americans are: 'Hit that speed dial to the lawyer!'"

As a result, what had been a family ownership conflict became a very public courtroom drama. It was a terrible period for Harry Jr. and his children, who watched as the family legacy turned to ashes. Harry recalled the trial:

I was in my office. The case was being heard at the district court nearby. One of my colleagues walked in my office and said, "You're never going to believe what I just heard." I sat down and I said, "Okay, tell me." And he said, "Your brother Don, on the witness stand, swore under oath that he didn't have any sisters, and they were sitting in the courtroom in front of him." That was in the first ten minutes of the trial, and it never got any better.

Immediately following the court decision, the McNeely brothers, who served as CEO and vice president of the family firm, developed a strategy to save the business by liquidating assets and transferring property to their sisters to settle the judgment. The company survived the bitter lawsuit, but it had poisoned the elder brother's thinking about family businesses. Don McNeely later called a meeting with his own and his brother's children to declare that Space Center was no longer a family business and that none of the third generation would be involved, a decision allegedly made without consulting his younger brother. As one of Harry's daughters noted, "When you think about the generational differences and goals (between the brothers), you could look back and say, 'You know, we should have just ended our relationship with him right then and there,' but our family tie was too strong."

From the Courtroom to the Boardroom

Both Don and Harry wanted to put the lawsuit behind them and return to business as usual. Soon after the lawsuit concluded, Don started working on a unique solution for creating a partnership between the brothers' holdings. His goal was to divide Space Center Inc. into two businesses, taking specific properties for himself and leaving others to Harry. An acquaintance recommended a "355 restructure" (with reference to Section 355 of the U.S. Internal Revenue Code), which would allow the separation to take place on a tax-free basis. Don and Harry agreed that it should work and preliminary documents were drawn up. A great deal of time and careful planning went into preparing for the split and the subsequent relationship of the two new entities (Space Center for Don, and Space Center Enterprises for Harry). In tense negotiations between the brothers, key executives acted as middlemen to overcome numerous hurdles and conflicts of interest. Finally, in December 1989, Space Center Inc. held its last board meeting as an integrated company and approved the separation into two distinct entities.

A curious thing was that both businesses had grown dependent on the talents of professional non–family managers for their success. The retention of these individuals was a key element of the restructuring and a challenge in its own right. None of the managers had received any form of the equity interest promised several years earlier. And yet, once again, they were enduring another trying and protracted negotiation between two siblings with very different interests and leadership styles.

In the end, each brother had his own holding company and the senior management team created a third separate entity, known as Space Center Company, which contracted with each brother's company for a fee based on revenues. Walt Richey, one of its top executives and a trusted advisor to both Don and Harry, was made the principal of the third entity, which was created in part

to meet the need to retain key managers and provide a means of attracting new talent to grow the businesses. (That the contract had a 15-year duration and imposed a prohibitive breakup fee on the management company was testimony to the toll taken by years of family strife on the company as a whole.)

Al Trostel, later a member of the Space Center Enterprises board of directors, described it as an "elegant solution":

With Harry and Don's agreement, the third entity managed the assets of the two brothers' Space Center companies. The fee for managing was based on the revenues that each company was able to generate. In addition, the management company could take a piece of new investments.

How much of a piece, and at what price, was negotiated on a case-by-case basis. But the question of price was a tough issue. The managers did not have the cash to buy in to the same degree as the McNeelys, so the issue was always, what was the worth of the managers' "sweat equity"? In the end, the managers had two incentives, an incentive to increase cash flow and an incentive to make money on the investments.

A Framework for Governance Outsiders Join the Board

Harry believed that he needed an independent board of directors for Space Center Enterprises; his company should not have the typical family business board composed of top family executives, an accountant, a family lawyer, and a good friend. Instead, he turned to four very experienced executives he knew and said, in effect, "I'm trying to handle a major transition in my company. I don't know how to do it, and I need help." Al Trostel, who joined the board at that time, pointed out, "All kinds of top, experienced people will sign up to be on your board if you approach them that way."

Eventually, in 1992, a board was formed that included a majority of independent directors for the first time. Harry signed up an executive from both Honeywell and Pillsbury who had prior business relationships with the company. Another director was a venture capitalist. Al Trostel, the fourth member, was a professor at the University of St. Thomas School of Business. The selection of outside directors and their subsequent influence on the firm's governance process was a critical turning point, and Harry's principal contribution. According to Trostel, Harry really listened to the board: "Harry was willing to expose himself to a great degree. It was very uncomfortable for him at times. The board would take him to task, and he would listen. Sometimes he'd drag his feet on an issue for months on end, but he stuck with us."

As could be expected, the new outside directors looked long and hard at the 1990 management agreement as a part of the task of familiarizing themselves with all the business, governance, management, ownership, and finance aspects of the company. Over time, they developed concerns about the three-entity structure—the management company and the two brothers' property companies—as they considered management's reports and proposals.

Another even more important issue loomed: Harry and Don were both of retirement age and Don had already said that he didn't want any of the third-generation siblings—neither his own children nor Harry's—to continue in his business. Harry, on the other hand, felt that his children should have the opportunity to continue the family legacy, provided they had relevant experience and that, as a group, they agreed to develop an effective governance structure for addressing business decisions and family issues such as career conflicts, dividends and liquidity issues, and ownership responsibilities.

However, although Harry was nearing his 70th birthday, he had not said when exactly he intended to retire, nor had he identified potential successors. At the time, none of Harry's children had worked in the company, although several were on the board. Additionally, if the management company remained a separate entity there would be few opportunities or openings for family members who wanted to take an active role in running the company.

Moreover, the continued existence of the three-part structure was increasingly questioned. For some time, Don had expressed dissatisfaction with the management company. By 1994 it became clear that he wanted to end his company's relationship with the management company, and in effect also terminating any association with his brother's company. Once again, there was considerable tension between family members and, in addition, with the nonfamily professional managers.

In early 1995, Don's company left the three-entity relationship. Looking back, Harry said that he wished he had understood earlier how different he and his brother's expectations were for the family business. If the assets had been divided 25 years earlier, he and his brother might have been more productive and entrepreneurial. Whatever the case, the past was now history.

One of Harry's daughters said:

I think that the two brothers' decision to divide the business in two in 1995 was a good decision. It satisfied their desire to finally separate. They really had very different goals both in terms of business strategy and also how involved they wanted their families to be. They were finally able to go down their own paths and yet not abandon a lifetime of work building the company.

The board of Harry's company Space Center Enterprises now had to face the reality that the separate management company structure was possibly too elegant; one board member called it "an unsustainable arrangement." Once Don's company had pulled out of the three-entity structure, Harry's company was forced to shoulder all the costs for the management company. In addition, the board could not overlook the conflict of interest that the situation engendered. The executives had established their own corporation, their own board of directors, and their own objectives. They were also free to make deals with other companies. Professor Trostel said:

The people in the management company were all quite talented and because their management company was employee-owned it became their vehicle for building personal wealth. When Don pulled his assets out, Harry's company had to pick up the extra cost of the management—costs that had originally been scaled for both holding companies. Some managers went with Don but it was not feasible to cut back further in proportion to the reduction in assets under management.

In addition, we came to realize that there was a very unhealthy conflict of interest for the managers. Sure, they had a stake in the new investments, but there was always the double negotiation: the negotiation with the seller of the property, and the negotiation with Harry's company as to how much of the deal they would get.

Harry was well aware of these problems. He noted at one board meeting that because the business was managed by the people in the management company, no management expertise or candidates for succession were being developed within his family's Space Center Enterprises holding company. He also wondered what would happen if the management company terminated its agreement with Space Center Enterprises and went off on its own. At another board meeting, his eldest son Paddy expressed similar concerns on behalf of shareholders about the separation of intellectual capital and financial capital between the two entities, and the shareholders' lack of leverage to revise or terminate the management agreement. They were also concerned about succession within the management company as they had little or no influence over CEO selection in that organization.

The Return of the Third-Generation Successor

Harry Jr.'s son, Harry McNeely III, known as Paddy, spent 10 years in the banking industry before joining the family firm. His expertise was in loans to commercial enterprises, both public and private. He never decided at any point that he definitely would (or would not) work for the family company one day. As he commented, "I think that fate could have taken a different path, and I could have not ended up here [in the family business] as well." Harry seemed to be willing to let Paddy find his own path: "My father didn't show any particular outward signs, either to me or anyone else, that he hoped I would join him."

When Paddy joined Space Center Enterprises in 1991—after a restructuring at the bank left him with a nice severance package but no immediate prospects in the banking industry—he joined the family firm as a kind of "free agent" with no real assignment. He recalled: "It was somewhat of an awkward situation, and I think that's almost to be expected. I just kind of dropped in from outer space and there was no real spot on the organizational chart for me. So initially I attended a great number of meetings and was given a broad exposure to the business."

Reflecting on that time, a board member said:

When Paddy came over from the bank where he had worked before coming to Space Center Enterprises, he joined the management team—but not really. He was never considered one of them, and he did not, in my opinion, have a real executive position. Paddy was not part of the club and was treated with disdain. I can remember a statement from one of the managers—we were discussing how difficult it was for family members other than Harry to be involved with the company—"That was not an unintended consequence" the manager said. That's an exact quote!

Despite the career issues and uncertainties that he faced, Paddy felt there was a long-term opportunity for him in the company if he could contribute to the restructuring and transitions that were occurring. He knew he had to earn his father's trust as well as demonstrate his capabilities to the board and nonfamily managers at Space Center Enterprises if he wanted to earn a senior management position.

Harry McNeely's overriding goal was to ensure that his company stayed in the family and that it would be professionally managed. The independent directors on the board had been charged with driving the succession process, assessing the pros and cons of the management company–holding company partnership, and advising the family on the eventual ownership transition to Paddy and his siblings. The stakes were high because the outcome of any one of these tasks could threaten the future of the family-controlled company, and to make things more difficult they had to be resolved virtually simultaneously.

In July 1996, after a long planning process, the Space Center Enterprises board decided to merge the management company into the holding company to create one organization. The McNeely family lawyer recalled:

The trigger that prompted the decision came when Walt Richey, the [management company] CEO, announced to the board that he planned to retire [and named the man he had chosen to be his successor]. After Walt left the meeting, a director asked Harry if he was comfortable not having a voice in the selection of the CEO of the company that managed the largest part of his net worth. The board quickly began addressing the ownership and management of the company specifically and with greater urgency. After that, Harry and the board began to plan for the buyout of the management company and focused on the leadership question.

In a significant way, the restructuring of the company created the first opportunity for Paddy to demonstrate his commitment and business acumen. Over the following year, he negotiated the buyout of the management company and successfully reintegrated the executives into Space Center Enterprises, a task he described as "gruesome":

I became the point man for resolving the organizational issues and providing exit vehicles, and negotiating long-term incentive plans for the managers who agreed to stay. You just kind of buckle down and work through it, but I was not a real happy person at that time. It was not a lot of fun but it was absolutely essential. All but one of the managers were my age; most of them had left other jobs and relocated here to St. Paul to join our company. And here I am, having to carry out this role of unwinding their dreams of stock ownership. It was very awkward.

The buyout of the management company was concluded on March 2, 1998. Subsequently, the name of Space Center Enterprises was changed to Meritex (which had been the name of the management entity) to avoid confusion with Don's similarly named Space Center Inc.

Some in the family and on the board began to wonder whether Paddy could be the logical successor to Harry, as one board member commented:

The management company may have seemed like a very elegant solution but the buyout created a very tough situation for Paddy. He did an exemplary job of carrying out that negotiation. He never lost his cool, even though he had plenty of provocation. It was then that we began to realize that even though he had not had much operating management experience, he had some very special talents that would serve the company well.

Paddy's trial by fire tested his leadership skills. It was at this time that he began to see himself as a potential successor to his father. Representing his family had allowed him to experience a new challenge. Now he was sure he wanted to run the family company. But what Harry and the next generation of owners wanted was less clear, at least to the board members. They had several meetings where they discussed Paddy's role in management succession scenarios but never the larger issues of what the shareholder group wanted. They had concerns about Paddy's credentials and experience. The family didn't make clear what they wanted.

While Harry wasn't clear about what his or Paddy's future role should be, he did make it very plain, even to outsiders, that the board would be responsible for choosing the next CEO. In a newspaper interview, he declared, "It is not predetermined that Paddy will be CEO of the company. That's why you have a board; its most important job is to pick the CEO."

But other people in the company had noticed the change in Paddy. He seemed to have decided that he wanted to run the company now—not at some undetermined time in the future.

There was, however, one important person standing in his way: his father. It was obvious to the board and the McNeely family that Harry was reluctant to hand over the reins. At a board meeting just after the brothers' companies were separated and restructured, Harry had said that he hoped to retire in 1998. Now it was 1998 but he seemed to have changed his mind. He looked set to stay on indefinitely. Paddy's frustration finally boiled over:

In July 1998, I threw my hands up and called in an outside family business consultant for expert advice. I told him that my father had given no indication at all about his plans for succession, other than saying, "I'm staying here as CEO forever." I said to my father, "If that's your plan, then I'm out of here." We had no documented succession plan. We did not have a strongly defined strategy. It was frustrating to me personally; there was no end date in sight.

It was a tense meeting. Harry and I agreed that we needed to take some action and so we decided that Wayne Brusewitz, a long-time senior executive with the company, would become interim president and I would serve as number two. We acted without first consulting the board. They didn't rebel [when they heard the decision], but some politely said, "Well, OK, you've done that. We'll do our best to make the business as good as we can, but understand we didn't pick this person. Now we need to start talking about accountability."

After the meeting, Paddy continued his official role as chief administrative officer and at the same time Wayne Brusewitz became his mentor. There was still no question that the family and board needed to start working on a leadership transition and developing a stronger business strategy. The family company had been merged with the management company; the CEO was working beyond his stated retirement date; some decisions were being made without consulting the board; and there was no agreement on a successor. The good news, as one director remarked, was that something had happened. The bad news was that it was not a strategic decision and the board's role had been seriously compromised. The board of directors was left to wonder where the company was headed. They felt they had to make a change and could not wait for Brusewitz, who was also about ready to retire, to leave on his own.

In addition, the independent board members felt a parallel and sometimes conflicting responsibility to the present and future owners of the company; they had to support the senior family CEO who was implementing the business strategy and help train the younger siblings to be effective board members in their own right (there were seats for two siblings on the board). After all, they could be dismissed from the board by the family whenever they chose. They decided it would be best if everyone worked as a team.

Building on the idea of teamwork, the board began to review the succession process. They determined that Harry's support was the key success factor. They became more proactive in challenging Harry to consider the future implications of his actions. As one board member recalled: "The first step in the transition process was to get a new CEO in place soon. It wasn't really about the choice between Paddy or an outsider; it was about getting a permanent CEO."

The Making of a Family CEO

At a meeting in August 2000, the board voted to formally begin the process of identifying a new CEO to put the business on track to meet the shareholders' stated growth objectives. The board, as Paddy knew, was not convinced that he should be CEO.

Meritex now owned and managed 7 million square feet of buildings and several underground spaces throughout central United States. The company had diversified into three main businesses all related to warehouse applications but requiring very specialized management skills. It operated standard warehousing and manufacturing facilities, offices, and high-tech "clean room" laboratories for everything from cans to computer chips. It provided third-party logistics to consumer product manufacturers requiring flawless execution in timing and deliveries of products and materials. Furthermore, the company continued to acquire and adapt old properties for new uses. It was a complex organization requiring a capable general manager, a successful deal maker, and a decisive leader. The board challenged Paddy to demonstrate his aptitude for the CEO position by presenting his plans for the company at its November 2000 meeting. In fact, several meetings took place over the next six months. Paddy met with the board, outlined his strategy, and discussed his potential role as CEO and chairman. Eventually, all the shareholders were informed of these discussions and the matter was formally reviewed at two board meetings. Simultaneously, the board was in effect discussing Harry's exit from the formal leadership of the company. The board worked through these issues methodically and in a very transparent way. Throughout the process, crucial discussions and decisions on succession occurred smoothly and without disruption.

After much deliberation, the board agreed to support Paddy for the CEO's position but stipulated that he must hire an experienced outsider to be president and chief operating officer, describing this person as "...a new person who should bring in a lot of what we need—knowledge, connections and credibility, and the ability to attract capital and put together a strategy. He'll be the head of new business, the acquisitions." The plan was let Paddy develop and see if he could rise to the occasion, but to have a backup plan in place.

In a May 18, 2001, memo to all employees, Harry wrote:

I am pleased to announce that the Board of Directors elected Harry McNeely III (Paddy) Chief Executive Officer and Chairman of the Board, and Wayne Brusewitz, Senior Vice President. As a part of its responsibilities, the board has approved a leadership succession plan that considers the need to grow and strengthen the organisation in the long term. The shareholders and the board share my confidence that Paddy and the management team are well prepared to accomplish this task.

After the process was completed, Paddy offered his perspective on the selection process and the role of the board:

The biggest reason that things will never be the same again is that the board can fire me. They couldn't fire Harry. They couldn't hold him accountable. To them, I'm an employee. They are accountable to me as a shareholder, but I am an employee in their minds. Of course, I'm not

a typical employee because there are all kinds of family entanglements. But if it finally boils down to it, they could shoot me right out the door.

I think the feeling now is "let's go forward." Not just for me as an individual but collectively, the whole board and the rest of the team. We can see that now we are finally ready to begin executing strategy . . . and it's an exciting time. I think we have a winning strategy for the company and there's a strong group of people running the company. There seems to be peace within the family, within the sibling group.

Epilogue: The McNeely Foundation

There is an epilogue that brings the McNeely story full circle. The McNeely Foundation (created in the early 1960s by Harry's parents, Harry G. McNeely Sr. and Adelaide Frenzel McNeely), was established at a time when privately held businesses could use company stock to establish charitable organizations. The main advantage was the tax relief on the gift of stock. The McNeely Foundation was set up to manage McNeely family assets and estate issues, with little planning at that time for the operational side of the foundation.

In the 1970s, the Internal Revenue Service ruled that foundations could not hold private or closely held stock. The change was intended partly to prevent disputes over the value of assets and partly to close a loophole that had previously allowed family foundations to be used as wealth transfer instruments. The McNeely family decided to buy back the stock they had given to their foundation, which meant that, from then on, the foundation had cash to become more operational and participative in the community.

The McNeely Foundation gives grants in the areas of education, human services, the environment, the arts, and community betterment. The foundation matches employees' gifts to charitable organizations, awards educational scholarships to their children, and sponsors fundraising events. Since the transition period in the 1970s, McNeely family members, with Harry's guidance, have played an important operational and governance role in the family foundation, as Harry's daughter, Shannon, explained:

My grandmother, Adelaide, served as chair of the foundation for many years and remained active on the board until late in her life. My father, Harry, served as chair after her resignation. His role was similar to his role in Meritex; he was instrumental in charting the course for both organizations.

On the business side, our father listened to experts regarding the use of an outside board, worked with us on educating the next generation family members, began succession planning and created the structure for continuing family involvement and generational transfers. Within Meritex, this effort has been confined to our nuclear family, due to his split with his brother. I am sure that his ability to direct his own business and foster the involvement of his children in it has been gratifying for him, but I wonder if the work he has done with the blending of family branches within the McNeely Foundation is not an equally or even more satisfying legacy for him.

During his tenure as chair of the McNeely Foundation, he continued the involvement of his brother Don's family branch on the foundation board, represented by Don's son. My father added two of his own children to the board, Paddy and me [Shannon], as well as the only child of his sister, who was also the heir of his other sister who was childless. So, in effect, he had all the descendants of his generation represented within the foundation, all working together as his generation was never able to do.

I think that he satisfied not only his desire to see the extended family sharing the legacy of the foundation, but also made amends for the transgressions of his generation and their inability to mend their differences peacefully during my grandmother's lifetime. I know that the family lawsuit, and even more the personal bitterness among some of her children, was a source of great sadness to my grandmother until the day she died. Our regenerated unity of families and purposes—fueled by a son's desire on a deeply personal level to set things right for his mother—is a symbolic statement to all McNeelys and the outside world that we have moved beyond our history.

When my father resigned as chair and from the foundation board, he handed the chair position to me, thereby transferring leadership to the third generation. I think that the work being done by, and within, the McNeely Foundation demonstrates that family division, litigation and separation in one generation does not have to sound the death knell for the business or the family's relationships with each other. The business and nonprofit ventures in our family have survived all the turmoil, and have begun to excel due to the dedicated work of our patriarch and the willingness of the next-generation cousins to put aside the strife of the previous generation and move on to become stewards of the family legacy in its greatest sense.

And as Harry remarked: "I didn't have any great dream that I was going to do this. But having been through the thorny patches, it just seemed to make an awful lot of sense to try and not replicate what had happened before."

In 1994, the Harry G. McNeely family won the Minnesota Family Business of the Year Award given by the University of St. Thomas in St. Paul. This award is based on successful participation of multiple generations of family members in the business; a demonstrated support for family business education; a commitment to social responsibility and community development, and the practice of professional family business management techniques. In 2008, the Harry McNeely family was named "Family Business of the Year" by *Minnesota Business*.

In one generation, the McNeely family went from enduring the largest court-ordered business liquidation in Minnesota's history to being the recipient of one of the state's most prestigious business awards. With considerable understatement, Harry observed:

Now all the families are represented on the board of the family's foundation by third-generation cousins, it's kind of neat. It's fun seeing all the cousins getting along. And I sit back and I say to myself, if we were all still in one big pot [all involved in the same company], I wonder how well the cousins would get along? This way they seem to get along quite well, so there are some saving graces.

NOTES

1. Excerpt from M. Langberg, 1985, Court orders liquidation for city warehouse firm, *St. Paul Pioneer Press Dispatch*, November 1, 1.

Steve Gove

Virginia Tech

Brett P. Matherne

Loyola University of New Orleans

If the motion picture industry's performance in 2007 were a feature presentation, the marquee would read "Massive Box Office: Smashing Records—the Sequel!" At $9.63 billion, box office revenue set another record in 2007, a full 5 percent above the record set in 2006.[1] An astonishing 1.4 billion tickets were sold in 2007. But beyond the headlines, the industry is a study in contradictions:

- The number of theaters is declining, but the number of screens is at an all-time high.
- Revenues are up, but attendance is largely flat—1.4 billion tickets sold is little improved from 1997, when 1.35 billion tickets were sold, and is a fraction of the 4 billion sold in 1946. In 1946, the average person attended 28 films a year. Today, it is 6.[2] (see Exhibits 1 and 2).
- The U.S. population is increasing, but the size of the market in the core demographic group is growing more slowly (see Exhibit 3).

- Americans spend more time than ever on entertainment—3,500 hours annually—but only 12 of those hours are spent at the movies.[3] The average person watches that much television every three days.

Movies remain as popular as ever, but opportunities for viewing outside the theater have greatly increased. While motion picture studios increased revenues through product licensing, DVD sales, and international expansion, the exhibitors—movie theaters—have seen their business decline. Movies are more available than ever, but fewer are venturing to the theater to see them. Many theaters have ceased operation, driven from the market by consolidation and a lack of patrons.

Will the marquee at the local theater soon change to: "A Horror Show at the Cinemaplex?" How has this come to be? What can exhibitors do to respond?

Exhibit 1 Domestic Tickets Sold and Box Office Gross

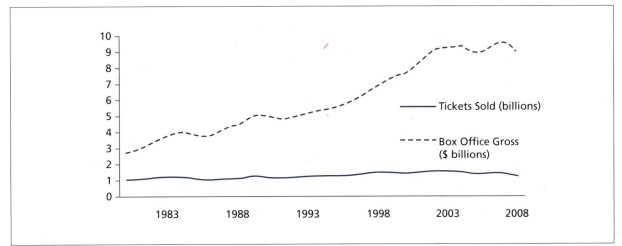

Source: http://boxofficemojo.com & U.S. Census.

Exhibit 2 Average Movie Ticket Price

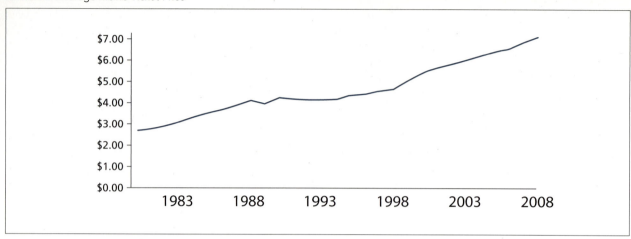

Source: http://boxofficemojo.com.

The Motion Picture Industry Value Chain

The motion picture industry value chain consists of three stages: studio production, distribution, and exhibition. All stages of the value chain are undergoing consolidation.

Studio Production

The studios produce the lifeblood of the industry; they create content. Films from the top 10 studios produce over 90 percent of domestic box office receipts (see Exhibit 4). Studios are increasingly part of larger corporations,

managed as any other profit center. Management is a challenge as investments are large and there is no one formula for success. Because of this, profitability swings wildly. The cost of bringing a typical feature to market is more than $100 million, up 25 percent in the past five years.[4] Typically, marketing expenses are a third of these costs.

Studios know their core audience is 12 to 24 years old. This age group purchases nearly 40 percent of theater tickets. Half are "frequent moviegoers" attending at least one movie per month. Profits are driven by the studios' ability to satisfy this fickle audience. In 2008, films based on two successful comic book characters met

Exhibit 3 Population Trend among 14 to 17 and 18 to 24 Age Groups (Millions)

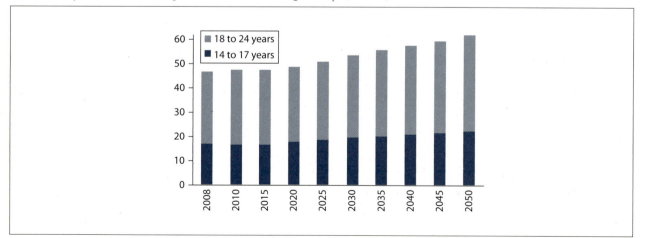

Source: U.S. Census.

Exhibit 4 Market Share of Film Production (2007)

Studio Parent & Label	2007 Combined Share (%)
Time Warner (Warner Brothers & New Line)	19.8
Sony (Sony & MGM)	16.7
Viacom (Viacom & Paramount)	15.5
Disney (Disney, Buena Vista Pictures, & Miramax)	15.4
Universal Studios	11.4
News Corp. (20th Century FOX)	10.5
Lions Gate	3.6
DreamWorks SKG*	0.0
	92.9

Note: *DreamWorks share in 2005 was 5.7%.

Source: Adapted from Mintel Report: Movie Theaters, United States, February 2008.

with wildly different fates.[5] Paramount's successful *Iron Man* was produced for $140 and grossed $318 million at the domestic box office. Warner Brothers's *Speed Racer*, produced for $20 million less and released the following weekend, was a flop, grossing just $44 million.

Demographic trends are unfavorable. The U.S. population will increase 17 percent by 2025, an increase of 54 million people. However, the number of 12- to 24-year-olds is expected to increase only 9 percent—just 4 million more potential viewers. Based on the current number of theaters and screens, this is an increase of less than 700 additional viewers per theater, or roughly 100 per screen.

Distribution

Distributors are the intermediaries between the studios and exhibitors. Distribution entails all steps following a film's artistic completion, including marketing, logistics, and administration. Exhibitors negotiate a percentage of gross from the studio or purchase rights to films and profit from the box office receipts. Distributors select and market film to exhibitors, seeking to maximize potential attendees. Distributors coordinate the manufacture and distribution of the film to exhibitors. They also handle collections, audits of attendees, and

other administrative tasks. There are over 300 active distributors, but much of this work is done by a few major firms, including divisions of studios. Pixar, for example, co-produced *Finding Nemo* with Disney and distribution was handled by Disney's Buena Vista.

Exhibition

Studios have historically sought full vertical integration through theater ownership, allowing greater control over audiences and capturing exhibition profits. A common practice was for the studio to use their ownership to reduce competition by not showing pictures produced by rivals. This practice ended in 1948 with the Supreme Court's ruling against the studios in *United States v. Paramount Pictures*. Theaters were soon divested, leaving them to negotiate with studios for film access and rental.

Theaters are classified according to the number of screens at one location (Exhibit 5). Single-screen theaters were the standard from the introduction of film through the 1980s. They have since rapidly declined in number, replaced by theater complexes. These include miniplexes (2 to 7 screens), multiplexes (8 to 15 screens), and megaplexes (16 or more screens). The number of theaters decreased more than 15 percent between 2000 and 2007, but the number of screens increased because of growth in megaplexes. Nearly 10 percent of theaters are now megaplexes, and the number of screens is at a historical high of 40,077.[6] Many analysts argue the industry has overbuilt and too many theaters and screens exist to make the business profitable.

Movie attendance usually increases as the economy declines. In 2008, there were rapid increases in gas prices, a large stock market decline, and significant layoffs. One summer movie patron commented, "There's not a whole lot you can do for $10 anymore."[7] Movies do remain a

Exhibit 5 Number of Theaters by Complex Size

	2000	2007	% Change
Single Screens	2,368	1,748	−26.18%
Miniplexes (2–7 Screens)	3,170	2,296	−27.57%
Multiplexes (8–15 Screens)	1,478	1,617	9.40%
Megaplexes (16+ Screens)	405	616	52.10%
Total	7,421	6,277	−15.42%

Sources: Developed by author from: Entertainment Industry, 2007 Report, Motion Picture Association of America, and Mintel Report "Movie Theaters, United States, February 2008."

Exhibit 6 Exhibition Market Leaders

Company	Theater Brands	# U.S Theater Locations	# U.S. Screens	Avg. Screens per Theater
Regal	Regal, United Artists, Edwards	526	6,355	12
AMC	AMC, Loews	315	4,585	14
Cinemark	Cinemark, Century	284	3,606	12
Carmike	Carmike	280	2,412	8
	Total for four leading companies	1,405	16,958	
	Industry total	7,421	40,077	

Source: Mintel Report "Movie Theaters, United States, February 2008," SEC filings and author estimates.

bargain in the entertainment business. Four tickets to a movie can cost under $27 (depending on the time of day and location) compared to $141 for an amusement park or $261 for a pro football game.[8] For many, the air-conditioned comfort of a dark theater and the latest Hollywood release offer a break not just from the summer heat, but from reality. "It's escapism, absolutely. It's probably a subconscious thing, and people don't realize it. But there's just so much going on, with people trying to pay their mortgages and get by. It's an escape for a couple of hours."[9]

Declining ticket sales and the increased costs associated with developing megaplexes led to a wave of consolidation among exhibitors. There are now four dominant exhibitors: Regal, AMC, Cinemark, and Carmike. While operating 1,405 theaters in the country (just 19 percent), these companies control 42 percent of screens. This market share provides these exhibitors with negotiating power for access to films, prices for films and concessions, and greater access to revenues from national advertisers.

There is little differentiation in the offerings of the major theater exhibitors—prices within markets differ little, the same movies are shown at the same times, and the food and services are nearly identical. Competition between theaters often comes down to distance from home, convenience of parking, and proximity to restaurants. Innovations by one theater chain are quickly adopted by others. The chains do serve different geographic markets and do so in different ways.[10] Regal focuses on mid-size markets using multiplexes and megaplexes. Regal's average ticket price of $7.43 is the highest among the leaders. AMC concentrates on urban areas with megaplexes and on large population centers, such as those in California, Florida, and Texas. Cinemark

serves smaller markets, operating as the sole theater chain in over 80 percent of its markets. Cinemark's average ticket price last year of $5.11 was the lowest of the majors. Carmike concentrates on small to mid-sized markets, targeting populations of less than 100,000 that have few other entertainment options. Carmike's average ticket price in 2007 was $5.89, but at $3.05, their average concession revenue per patron is the highest among the majors.

The different approaches of the companies are reflected in the cost of fixed assets per screens. These costs result from decisions made on how to serve customers, such as the level of technology and finish of the theater—digital projection and marble floors cost more than traditional projectors and a carpeted lobby.[11] Despite multi- and megaplex facilities, Regal's cost per screen is the highest at $430,000. Carmike, the rural operator, is the lowest at just $206,000. Cinemark is in the middle at $367,000. Data is not available for AMC, but costs are thought to be near or above those of Regal.

The Business of Exhibition

There are three primary sources of revenue for exhibitors: box office receipts, concessions, and advertising. Managers have low discretion; their ability to influence revenues and expenses is limited. Operating margins among exhibitors average a slim 10 percent. This is before significant expenses such as facility and labor costs. The result is marginal or negative net income. Overall, the business of exhibitors is best described as loss leadership on movies: the firms make money selling concessions and showing ads to patrons who are drawn by the movie.

Box Office Revenues

Ticket sales constitute two thirds of exhibition business revenues. The return on these receipts, however, is quite small. A power imbalance results in contracts that return the vast majority of box office receipts to the studios. The record-setting revenues at the box office have been the result of increases in ticket prices and have flowed back to the studios.

Concessions

Moviegoers frequently lament the high prices for concessions. Concessions average 25 to 30 percent of revenues. Direct costs are less than 15 percent of the selling price, making concessions the largest source of exhibitor profit. These are influenced by the three factors: attendance, pricing, and material costs. The most important is attendance: more attendees equal more concession sales. Sales per patron are influenced by prices. The $3.75 price point for a large soda is not by accident, but the result of market research and profit-maximization calculation. Costs are influenced by purchase volume, with larger chains able to negotiate better prices on everything from popcorn and soft drinks to cups and napkins.

Advertising

Exhibitors also generate revenue through pre-show advertising. Though this constitutes just 5 percent of revenues, it is highly profitable. Mintel reports that advertising revenues among exhibitors are expected to increase at a rate of approximately 10 percent over the coming decade.[12] Audiences signal consistent dislike for advertising at the theater. Balancing the revenues from ads with audience tolerance is an ongoing struggle for exhibitors.

Overall, the exhibitor has limited control over both revenues and profits. Box office receipts are the bulk of revenues, but yield few profits. Strong attendance numbers allow for profitable sales of concessions and advertisements, but there are significant caps on the volume of concession sales per person and selling prices seem to have reached their maximum. Advertising remains an attractive avenue for revenues and profits, but audiences loathe it.

The Process of Exhibition

The fundamentals of film exhibition have changed little since the early 1940s. To show a picture, each theater receives a shipment of physical canisters containing a "release print" from the distributor. Making these prints requires $20,000 to $30,000 in up-front costs and $1,000 to $1,500 for each print. Thus, a modern major motion picture opening on 2,500 screens simultaneously requires $2.50 to $3.75 million in print costs. This is borne by the studios, but paid for by movie attendees.

Each release print is actually several reels of 35-mm film, which are manually loaded onto projector reels, sequenced, and queued for display by a projector operator. The film passes through the projector, which shines intense light through the film, projecting the image through a lens that focuses the image on the screen. A typical projection systems costs $50,000, with one needed for each screen.

Digital cinema is becoming economically viable. Digital cinema involves a high resolution (4096 × 2160) digitized image projected onto the screen. Basic digital systems cost $150,000 to $250,000 per screen. Conversion of an existing eight-screen theater to digital thus involves an investment of $1.2 to $2 million. The costs for digital "release prints" are far lower than traditional film, but these costs savings most directly benefit the studio whereas the exhibitors must pay any costs to convert theaters. The number of digital theaters is expanding rapidly. In 2004, there were less than 100, and there are now approximately 4,600, or 12 percent of screens. Because of the cost involved, most theaters use a mixture of technologies, with a minority of screens in any one facility featuring digital projection.

The Theater Experience

For a significant number of moviegoers, the draw of the theater is far more than what film is showing. Moviegoers describe attending the theater as an experience, with the appeal based on:[13]

- the giant theater screen
- the opportunity to be out of the house
- not having to wait to see a particular movie on home video
- the experience of watching the movies with a theatrical sound system
- the theater as a location option for a date

The ability of theaters to provide more than what audiences can experience at home appears to be diminishing. Of the reasons why people go to the movies, only the place aspects—the theater as a place to be out of house and as a place for dating—may be immune from substitution. Few teenagers want to watch a movie and eat popcorn with their date at home with their parents next to them on the sofa.

The overall "experience" currently offered by theaters falls short for many. Marketing research firm Mintel reports the reasons for not attending the theater more frequently are largely the result of the declining experience. Specific factors include the overall cost, at-home viewing options, interruptions such as cell phones in the theater, rude patrons, the overall hassle, and ads prior to the show.[14] A recent *Wall Street Journal* article reported on interruptions ranging from the intrusion of soundtracks in adjacent theaters to cell phones. "The interruptions capped a night of moviegoing already marred by out-of-order ticketing kiosks and a parade of preshow ads so long that, upon seeing the Coca-Cola polar bears on screen, one customer grumbled: 'This is obscene.'"[15] Recounting bad experiences is a lively topic for bloggers. A typical comment: "I say it has gotten worse. I hate paying $9.00 for a ticket and the movie is 90–100 minutes long, people talking on the cell phone, the people who work at the theaters look like they are bored, and when you ask them a question, the answer is very rude. I worked as an usher in the late '60s and we had to wear uniforms and white gloves on Friday and Saturday nights, those days are long gone."[16]

A trip to the local cinemaplex can be eye opening even for industry insiders. In 2005, Toby Emmerich, New Line Cinema's head of production, faced a not-so-common choice: attending "War of the Worlds" in a theater or in a screening room at actor Jim Carrey's house. Said Emmerich in an *LA Times* article, "I love seeing a movie with a big crowd, but I had no idea how many obnoxious ads I'd have to endure—it really drove me crazy. After sitting through about 15 minutes of ads, I turned to my wife and said, 'Maybe we should've gone to Jim Carrey's house after all.'"[17]

The unique value proposition offered by movie theaters—large screens, the long wait for DVD release, and advantages of theatrical sound systems—also appears to be fading. Increasingly larger television sets, DVD content, and the adoption of high-definition technology are all part of this change. One blogger posts, "Whereas the electronics industry has been innovating to create immersive experiences from the comfort of our own home, the US theater industry has been dragging their feet."[18]

Home Viewing Technology

Home television sets are increasingly large, high-definition sets coupled with inexpensive, yet impressive audio systems. In 1997, the screen size of the average television was just 23 inches. Currently, almost half of LCD televisions sold have screens 36 inches or larger.[19] Because set size is measured as the diagonal screen size, increases in viewable area are greater than the measurement suggests. In recent years, the viewing area of sets doubled from 250 inches to 550 inches.

The FCC requirement that all broadcasters convert to digital broadcasts by June 12, 2009, is widely credited with starting a consumer movement to upgrade televisions. Since the 1950s, television transmissions were formatted as 480 interlaced vertical lines (480i) of resolution. The new digital format is high definition (HD), providing up to 1080 vertical lines of resolution (1080p).[20] Three quarters of all televisions sold since 2006 are HD capable.

As LCD technology became the standard for both computer and television screens, manufacturing costs declined. Wholesale prices for televisions fell 65 percent from the late 1990s to 2007.[21] In 2006, the average television retailed for $29 per diagonal inch of set size. This is expected to decrease to $22 within five years.[22] Consumers, however, are actually spending more on every television, consistently electing to purchase larger sets to achieve a better viewing experience. Sharp, a leading manufacturer of televisions predicts that by 2015 the average screen will reach 60 inches.[23]

Large screen televisions, DVD players, and audio and speaker components are commonly packaged as low-cost home theaters. The average DVD player now costs just $72[24] and high-definition DVD players are beginning to penetrate the market. Retail price wars during the 2008 Christmas season led to HD Blu-Ray players dropping below $200. These home theater systems offer a movie experience that rivals many theaters, all for $1,000 to $2,000. Says Mike Gabriel, Sharp's head of marketing and communications: "People can now expect a home cinema experience from their TV. Technology that was once associated with the rich and famous is now accessible to homes across the country."[25]

Content Availability and Timing

Even the best hardware offers little value without content for display. Rental firm Netflix advertises a selection of more than 100,000 titles extending well beyond new and classic films to include television shows, sports, and music performances. HD content is increasingly available to maximize the experience offered by those HD televisions. Satellite and cable television providers have engaged in a game of one-upmanship to provide the greatest percentage of HD content available to subscribers. By the end of 2009, 2,000 movies were available on Blu-Ray DVD.[26]

Movie fans no longer have to wait long for the summer's blockbuster to appear on DVD. The time period between theatrical and DVD release has declined 40 percent since 2000. The top five films in 2000 were released on DVD an average of 37 weeks after their box office opening. In 2007, the lag was just 23 weeks. And, studios are experimenting with simultaneous releases to theaters, pay per view, and DVD.

Overall, the visual and audio experience available in the home is rapidly converging with that available at the movie theater. As a blogger on the movie fan site Big Picture posted:

I used to go to the movies all the time—even my blog is called the Big Picture. Then I started going less—and then less still and now—hardly at all. My screen at home is better, the sound system is better, the picture is in focus, the floors aren't sticky and the movies start on time. My seat is clean. And there's no idiot chattering away 2 rows behind me, and (this is my favorite) THERE'S NO CELL PHONES RINGING. EVER.[27]

Is this a horror show at the cinemaplex?

NOTES

1. Motion Picture Association of America (MPAA), 2007, Entertainment industry market statistics.
2. A. Serwer, 2006, Extreme makeover: With big screens and high-def in more and more living rooms, movie theaters are taking radical new measures to woo filmgoers, *Fortune*, 153: 108–116.
3. Mintel Report, 2008, Movie theaters—U.S., February.
4. MPAA, 2007, Entertainment industry market statistics.
5. All data on these two films from http://www.boxofficemojo.com.
6. Developed by author from: Entertainment Industry, 2007 Report, Motion Picture Association of America.
7. J. Woestendiek & C. Kaltenbach, 2008, $10 is small price for a big escape: Movie box office figures are flourishing despite, or because of, economic worries, *Baltimore Sun*, July 8.
8. MPAA, 2007, Entertainment industry market statistics.
9. J. Woestendiek & C. Kaltenbach, 2008, $10 is small price for a big escape: Movie box office figures are flourishing despite, or because of, economic worries, *Baltimore Sun*, July 8.
10. Data on the firms, screen sizes, location, from Web sites and SEC filings.
11. All data is from SEC filings, based on net property, plant, and equipment reported in 2007 balance sheet and on the number of screens.
12. Mintel Report, 2008, Segment performance: cinema advertising, Movie theaters—U.S., February.
13. Mintel Report, 2008, Reasons to go to the movies over watching a DVD, Movie theaters—U.S., February.
14. Mintel Report, 2008, Reasons why attendance is not higher, Movie theaters—U.S., February.
15. K. Kelly, B. Orwall, & P. Sanders, 2005, The multiplex under siege, *Wall Street Journal*, December 24, P1.
16. Blog comment, Over the past years…, http://cinematreasures.org/polls/22/ (accessed December 11, 2008).
17. Incident reported in Patrick Goldstein, 2005, Now playing: A glut of ads, *Los Angeles Times*, July 12, E-1.
18. Designs of the week: The Movie Theater Experience, 2008, November 23, http://www.sramanamitra.com/2008/11/23/designs-of-the-week-the-movie-theater-experience/.
19. DuBravac, 2007.
20. DuBravac, 2007.
21. DuBravac, 2007.
22. B. Keefe, 2008, Prices on flat-screen TVs expected to keep falling, *Atlanta Journal-Constitution*, March 15.
23. Average TV size up to 60-inch by 2015, says Sharp, TechDigest, http://www.techdigest.tv/2008/01/average_tv_size.html (accessed December 11, 2008).
24. MPAA, 2007, Entertainment industry market statistics.
25. Average TV size up to 60-inch by 2015, says Sharp, TechDigest, http://www.techdigest.tv/2008/01/average_tv_size.html (accessed December 11, 2008).
26. http://www.movieweb.com.
27. The Big Picture, Why is movie theatre attendance declining?, http://bigpicture.typepad.com/comments/2005/07/declining_movie.htm (accessed December 11, 2008).

Aaron Christensen, Victor Delagarza,
Aric Griggs, Lubka Robertson,
Tamara Stuart, Michael Valverde

Arizona State University

In November 2008, Motorola announced the post-ponement of its highly publicized spinoff of the Mobile Device segment, a struggling business segment that is pulling down the results of the entire firm. In light of the challenging economy, Motorola faces the decision of if and when to spin off this division and which new market opportunities to explore in order to return to the profitable company it was for so many years.

Company History

In 1928, Paul and Joseph Galvin incorporated Galvin Manufacturing[1] after acquiring "battery elimina-tor operations"[2] from the bankrupt Stewart Storage Battery Company.[3] A battery eliminator is a device that allows "battery-powered radios [to] run on a stan-dard household electric current"[4] instead of batter-ies. Galvin Manufacturing used the technology as the groundwork for its first car radio named Motorola.[5] The name Motorola is a combination of "'motor' (for motor car) and 'ola' (which implied sound)."[6] Galvin Manufacturing introduced its first Motorola car radio in 1930, the Motorola Police Cruiser radio in 1936,[7] and home radios in 1937.[8] By the end of 1937, B. F. Goodrich had partnered with Galvin Manufacturing to become the first national Motorola dealer.[9]

Starting in 1940, Galvin Manufacturing expanded its product line to include two-way communication devices.[10] The first product was the Handie-Talkie SCR536 AM Radio, which was used extensively by the military during World War II.[11] The success of the Handie-Talkie and a strong belief in the sustainable demand for its communication products led Galvin Manufacturing to create a separate product division and establish a sales subsidiary, Motorola Communications

and Electronics, Inc.[12] Leveraging its experience with military radios, Galvin Manufacturing introduced its first commercial line of Motorola FM vehicular two-way radio systems and equipment in 1941.[13] By the end of 1943, Galvin Manufacturing successfully completed its first initial public offering with its stock selling for $8.50 per share.[14] Building upon earlier success, Galvin Manufacturing produced the world's first portable back-pack FM radio (SCR300), more commonly known as a "walkie-talkie."[15] In 1946, Galvin Manufacturing part-nered with Bell Telephone Company to enable car radio-telephone service via Motorola communication equip-ment for the Chicago area.[16]

Galvin Manufacturing officially changed its name to Motorola, Inc. in 1947.[17] As part of a diversifica-tion strategy, Motorola acquired the car radio manu-facturer Detrola, a supplier to Ford Motor Company, and entered the television market with the Golden View VT71.[18] Motorola sold more than 100,000 Golden View television units within the first year and became the fourth-largest U.S. television manufacturer.[19] Motorola illustrated its commitment to product development and innovation through the establishment of its R&D opera-tions in Phoenix, Arizona, in 1949.[20] This R&D effort led to advances in semiconductor and transistor tech-nology, including the germanium transistor technology Motorola used in its 1955 car radios.[21] The germanium transistor "was the world's first commercial high-power transistor . . . [and] Motorola's first mass-produced semiconductor."[22]

By 1954, Motorola had outgrown its existing orga-nizational structure, causing Paul Galvin to decide to reorganize the company[23] into product-line divisions.[24] The following year, Galvin's son, Robert, became Motorola's president.[25] Robert Galvin continued to

Note: This case was written to be used as a basis for class discussion rather than to illustrate either effective or ineffective handling of an administrative situation. We would like to thank Robert E. Hoskisson and Robert E. White for useful feedback in writing this case. Data was collected from publically available sources.

lead the company by following its communication and television expertise but "shifted the company's strategy toward selling directly to government and business."[26] In 1958, Motorola introduced the Motrac vehicular radio that "enabled the radio to transmit without running the vehicle's engine."[27] Motorola also introduced a three-amp power transistor,[28] a small radio receiver used extensively in hospitals (more commonly known as a pager[29]) and color television sets[30] during the 1950s and 1960s. In 1969, Motorola's radio transponder on *Apollo 11* "relayed the first words from the Earth to the Moon . . . [and] transmitted telemetry, tracking, voice communications, and television signals from the Earth to the Moon."[31]

By 1968, frustrations over limitations concerning car-based communication technology led the Federal Communications Commission (FCC) to propose allocating bandwidth to new technologies that would address this problem.[32] Thus, Motorola pioneered the cellular phone industry by creating the first commercial cellular phone, the Motorola DynaTAC phone.[33]

Motorola continued its pioneering efforts in the world of manufacturing. In 1968, Motorola developed the Six Sigma quality improvement process.[34] Six Sigma is an analytical, statistical approach that is used to improve the quality of manufacturing processes and to eliminate defects.[35] Since its introduction, Six Sigma has become a global standard.[36]

During the 1990s Motorola extended its traditional product offerings into the digital arena. Motorola acquired General Instrument Corporation, the company that developed the all-digital high-definition television (HDTV) technical standard.[37] In 1991, Motorola developed the first digital cellular phone prototype[38] and by 1994 Motorola produced its Integrated Digital Enhanced Network (iDEN) digital radio, which combined paging data, cellular communications, and voice dispatch in a single radio network and handset.[39] Motorola continued to enhance product features and produce phones with more integrated features through the end of the 1990s.[40]

In 2000, Motorola partnered with Cisco Systems, Inc. to expand operations into the United Kingdom with BT Cellnet by supplying the "world's first commercial General Packet Radio Service (GPRS) cellular network."[41] Motorola then introduced the wireless cable modem which allowed computer networking, a 700-MHz high-speed data system for public safety, a cellular PDA handset that combined Linux and Java technology, and demonstration of the first WiMAX mobile hand-offs.[42]

In 2004, Motorola's introduction of the RAZR (see Exhibit 1) was a huge success as indicated by the facts that the firm sold more than 750,000 units in the first 90 days and held a 16 percent share of the cell phone

Exhibit 1 Motorola RAZR Phone

Source: 2009, http://www.motorola.com.

market until 2007.[43] Motorola tried to extend the RAZR's success by introducing the Q in 2005, but it ultimately failed to invoke the same response as its predecessor.[44] In 2006, Motorola expanded its international product offerings again by introducing the MING touch screen smartphone with advanced handwriting software and the Chinese alphabet targeted for the Asian market.[45] Despite continued efforts in the mobile device market segment, Motorola's market share decreased from 22.2 percent in 2006 to 12 percent in 2007.[46]

Edward Zander, the first non-Galvin CEO, was hired by the board of directors in January 2004 to replace Chris Galvin when he retired.[47] Zander steered the company toward products that focused on combining Internet technologies with wireless phone technologies.[48] In 2007, Motorola merged with Symbol Technologies in order to expand its product offerings in mobile computing, advanced data capture, and radio frequency identification (RFID).[49] Motorola also acquired Good Technology in 2007 to expand access to enterprise applications, intranets, and corporate applications for mobile employees.[50] Disappointing returns in 2007 led Motorola's second largest shareholder, Carl Icahn, to demand changes in the organization and the board of directors.[51] Greg Brown replaced Zander in January 2008.[52] Prior to being appointed as CEO, Brown held the president and COO positions. Brown possessed almost 25 years of high-tech experience and had been with Motorola since 2003.[53] However, his appointment did not help ease shareholder frustrations over Motorola's struggling mobile device business, and during his tenure there has been significant turnover in upper management positions, ultimately affecting the company.[54] Therefore, Motorola leaders have thoughtfully considered the direction the company should take, specifically which products it should offer, in order to resume successful operations.

Product Offerings

In 2007 when Motorola restructured the organization, it aligned its business into three operating segments: Home and Networks Mobility, Enterprise Mobility Solutions, and Mobile Devices.[55] The firm's product portfolio consists of wireless handsets, accessories, and access systems as well as digital entertainment devices, voice and data communications systems, and enterprise mobility products.[56]

The Home and Networks Mobility segment competes in the cable set-top box, broadband cable modem, cellular infrastructure, and wireless broadband systems industries.[57] In the third quarter of 2008, this division contributed 32 percent of Motorola's net sales.[58]

The Enterprise Mobility Solutions segment competes in areas such as two-way radio, wireless broadband systems, and private networks for both enterprise and government use.[59] Furthermore, Motorola provides broadcast interactive networks, third-party switching for broadband networks to include: Code Division Multiple Access (CDMA),[60] Global System for Mobile Communication (GSM), and Universal Mobile Telecommunications System[61] (UMTS), all of which are technologies used for mobile communication networking.[62] This division contributed 27 percent of Motorola's net sales in the third quarter of 2008.[63]

The Mobile Devices segment competes in the wireless handset industry. This segment manufactures and sells analog and digital two-way radios, voice and data communication products for private networks, and intellectual property in the form of licenses and patents.[64] This segment comprised 42 percent of Motorola's net sales in third quarter 2008.[65] In the same quarter Motorola held approximately 8.4 percent market share (25.4 million units) in the global handset market. There are several competitors that have taken market share from Motorola.

Competitors

In the wireless handset industry, Motorola's top competitors are Nokia, Samsung, and Sony Ericsson Mobile Communications. LG Electronics, Apple Inc., Research

in Motion and HELIO are also competitors but do not pose as large a threat.

Nokia[66]

In 1998 Nokia became and has since been the leading cell phone manufacturer. In 2008 it had net sales of $70.5 billion from 468 million units shipped. This was a seven percent increase over 2007. In 2008 Nokia controlled 39 percent of the mobile communication device market. In 2008 alone Nokia introduced 26 different phones that were focused in five different categories. Smartphone sales made up 13 percent of total cell phones shipped, totaling 61 million units. Nokia is especially dominant in the European and Asian Pacific markets.

Nokia started a joint venture with Siemens in 2007 to provide industry leading consumer Internet service. Nokia has been actively acquiring other businesses to expand its dominance in the mobile phone industry. Since 2006, Nokia has acquired nine businesses in the consumer software field that range from file sharing and music services to advertising and security. Nokia has been affected by the global crisis that started toward the end of 2007; however, the firm has been able to reduce the negative effects of the crisis through its effective use of strategic acquisitions, partnerships, and industry-leading research and development.

Samsung Electronics[67]

Samsung produces and sells products ranging from televisions to home appliances to mobile devices. It is also a major supplier for both LCD screens and memory-based semiconductor chips. Samsung's Telecommunication Networks division, which manufactures and sells the firm's wireless handsets, generates approximately 23 percent of Samsung's sales revenue. With strong brand awareness, consumer-driven design, and aggressive expansion into developing markets, Samsung increased its net profit by 42 percent from 2006 to 2007.

Samsung has been able to launch premium products and rapidly penetrate emerging markets with its mid-range products. As such, it is currently the world's second-largest mobile phone maker, with a 14.3 percent market share. Its premium products, such as the Ultra Edition smartphone, have captured the attention of consumers with features such as a touchscreen, high megapixel cameras, and music capabilities. Samsung was voted "best brand" six years in a row in the United States and captured the number one market spot in France and Russia.

Sony Ericsson Mobile Communications[68]

With the joint venture between Sony and Ericsson in 2001, Sony Ericsson Mobile Communications was able to offer a variety of mobile handsets and other mobile devices that supported multimedia applications and other personal communication services. This is in line with the firm's vision to "be the prime driver in an all-communicating world … in which all people can use voice, text, images and video to share ideas and information whenever and wherever they want."

China, the United States, and India are Sony Ericsson's top three markets. However, by increasing the sales of lower-priced handsets in emerging markets such as Latin America, Sony Ericsson sold over 100 million handsets in 2007—an increase of 18 percent from the previous year. Sony Ericsson believes it is in a prime position to build on its recent strong performance and continues to develop its mid- to low-range products while establishing brand awareness with its high-end products.

LG Electronics[69]

The Mobile Communications division of LG Electronics (LG) is a global leader in the worldwide mobile market.[70] By strategically reallocating its resources, LG plans on becoming a member of the "Global Top 3." LG aims to anticipate customer needs and surpass them with products using the latest technology and presenting consumers with stylish product designs. This strategy seems to be effective as illustrated by a 13 percent increase in mobile handset sales worldwide and a 10 percent increase in global revenue in 2007.

Apple Inc.[71]

Most commonly known for designing and producing software, computers, computer peripherals, and portable music players, Apple Inc. entered the mobile communications devices market with the introduction of the iPhone through a partnership with AT&T Mobility LLC. The iPhone combines cellular communications, a portable music player, and Internet access using Wi-Fi into a single product, all through the control of a touchscreen. Many well-established companies have tried to imitate the capabilities of the iPhone in their respective smartphones.

For fiscal 2008, Apple generated annual revenue of $32 billion versus 2007 annual revenue of $24 billion. Profit margins increased from 14.6 percent in 2007 to 14.9 percent in 2008. Also, Apple's handset division revenue jumped up from approximately $250 million to $1.8 billion in 2008.

Research in Motion[72]

Founded in 1984, Research in Motion (RIM) is a leading designer and manufacturer of innovative wireless solutions.[73] RIM is best known for its telecommunication handheld device, the BlackBerry. It supports mobile telephony, text messaging, e-mail, and Web browsing.

By the end of fiscal year 2008, Blackberrys were available in more than 135 countries. Hardware generates 79 percent of RIM's revenue, which amounted to $6 billion in fiscal 2008, nearly double the revenue of 2007. Profit margins for 2008 were 21 percent versus 27 percent for 2007. The company plans on expanding its selection of mobile devices with several new smartphones as well as enhancing software and services to gain new market share.

HELIO, Inc.[74]

In January 2005, HELIO, Inc. was formed via a joint venture between EarthLink, Inc. and SK Telecom Co., Inc. with the purpose of developing wireless telecommunications services, including but not limited to handsets. Services that are included are integrated Imaging, an Ultimate Inbox, and other popular applications such as MySpace and YouTube.[75] A 282 percent increase in equipment sales and other revenue from 2006 to 2007 indicates that HELIO has successfully established itself in the U.S. market.

In addition to the main competitors in the handset market, Motorola is constantly faced with competition from emerging technologies such as Mobile Internet Devices (MIDs).

Mobile Internet Devices (MIDs)[76]

MIDs are devices that allow consumers to "communicate with others, enjoy [their] favorite entertainment, and access information on-the-go" by connecting to wireless hotspots around town. This new technology provides all of the Internet capabilities consumers want as well as the ability to have a conversation using Voice over Internet Protocol (VoIP). Industry-leading companies, such as Intel, are forming a Mobile Internet Device Innovation Alliance.[77] The MID Alliance is comprised of industry-leading original manufacturers as Asus, BenQ, Compal, Elektrobit, HTC, Inventec, and Quanta.[78] The members of the alliance are working together to solve engineering challenges with respect to power management, wireless communications, and software integration.[79]

Each of these firms is vying for business from the customers Motorola seeks to serve as it operates in its three business segments.

Motorola's Customers

Motorola's Mobile Device Segment has several large customers including Sprint Nextel, Verizon, China Mobile, AT&T, and America Movil. Motorola has stated that "the loss of one or more of [these companies] could have a material adverse effect on the Company."[80] Sales to these five companies accounted for 42 percent of total revenue in the Mobile Devices segment.[81]

Customers of the Home and Networks Mobility segment include Comcast, Verizon, KDDI, China Mobile, and Sprint Nextel. Sales to these five customers account for 43 percent of total net sales for this division. Similar to the Mobile Devices segment, the loss of any one customer could be detrimental.[82]

Enterprise Mobility Solutions segment customers include the U.S. government, Scansource, IBM, Ingram Micro, and Wal-Mart.[83] Sales to these customers generate 19 percent of the division's net sales. Other customers include resellers and distributors, who then sell to the commercial enterprise market.

Because of the late 2008 financial crisis and the tightening of credit, Motorola is concerned that customers will defer purchases, be unable to obtain financing, and submit more requests for vendor financing by Motorola.[84]

Motorola's Suppliers

Motorola's suppliers include Freescale, Qualcomm, ATI, Spansion, Texas Instruments, and STMicroelectronics. One drawback is that some of the inputs required to manufacture Motorola's products are only available from a single supplier. In 2003 and 2004, Motorola suffered from product delays due to supply shortages caused by a lack of a sufficient number of suppliers.[85] Also, with the current financial crisis, Motorola is concerned that its suppliers may become capacity constrained because of credit issues and thus cause possible product delays.[86]

However, Motorola actively works with suppliers to assist them in reducing lead times and improving efficiency. David Buck, the director of procurement, states "We look for opportunities for our suppliers to be more successful."[87] Motorola works with suppliers early in the design phase of a product, enabling a fast ramp-up of production. At times, "purchasers involved in design are co-located with designers."[88] These activities contribute directly to Motorola's bottom line since parts can be ramped up and delivered faster, with increased quality and lower cost.

Financial Performance

Motorola reported financial losses and a decline in annual sales in 2007 (see Exhibit 2). Net sales in 2007 totaled almost $36.7 billion, down 15 percent compared to net sales of $42.8 billion in 2006.[89] The Mobile Devices segment's net sales in 2007 were $19 billion, representing 52 percent of the Company's consolidated net sales, but experiencing a 33 percent decrease from the previous year. The Home and Networks Mobility segment's net sales in 2007 were $10 billion, representing 27 percent of the Company's consolidated net sales, a 9 percent increase from the previous year. The Enterprise Mobility Solutions segment's net sales in 2007 were $7.7 billion, representing 21 percent of the Company's consolidated net sales, a 43 percent increase in net sales from the previous year.[90]

Additionally, Motorola reported operating losses of $553 million (see Exhibit 2). In the previous year, the firm reported operating earnings of $4.1 billion.[91] Operating margins were 1.5 percent of net sales in 2007 compared to 9.6 percent in 2006—another substantial decline.[92]

Exhibit 2 Motorola, Inc. and Subsidiaries

Income Statement			
	Years Ended December 31		
(In millions, except per share amounts)	**2007**	**2006**	**2005**
Net sales	$ 36,622	$ 42,847	$ 35,310
Costs of sales	26,670	30,120	23,881
Gross margin	9,952	12,727	11,429
Selling, general and administrative expenses	5,092	4,504	3,628
Research and development expenditures	4,429	4,106	3,600
Other charges (income)	984	25	(404)
Operating earnings (loss)	(553)	4,092	4,605

Exhibit 2 Motorola, Inc. and Subsidiaries (*Continued*)

Income Statement			
		Years Ended December 31	
(In millions, except per share amounts)	2007	2006	2005
Other income (expense)			
Interest income, net	91	326	71
Gains on sales of investments and businesses, net	50	41	1,845
Other	22	151	(109)
Total other income (expense)	163	518	1,807
Earnings (loss) from continuing operations before income taxes	(390)	4,610	6,412
Income tax expense (benefit)	(285)	1,349	1,893
Earnings (loss) from continuing operations	(105)	3,261	4,519
Earnings from discontinued operations, net of tax	56	400	59
Net earnings (loss)	$ (49)	$ 3,661	$ 4,578
Earnings (loss) per common share			
Basic			
Continuing operations	$ (0.05)	$ 1.33	$ 1.83
Discontinued operations	0.03	0.17	0.02
	$ (0.02)	$ 1.50	$ 1.85
Diluted			
Continuing operations	$ (0.05)	$ 1.30	$ 1.79
Discontinued operations	0.03	0.16	0.02
	$ (0.02)	$ 1.46	$ 1.81
Weighted average common shares outstanding			
Basic	2,312.7	2,446.3	2,471.3
Diluted	2,312.7	2,504.2	2,527.0
Dividends paid per share	$ 0.20	$ 0.18	$ 0.16

Source: Motorola 2007 Annual Report, http://www.motorola.com.

The firm incurred a loss from continuing operations of $105 million which resulted in $0.05 per diluted common share.[93] This was down from the stated $1.30 per diluted common share in 2006 with continuing operations of $3.3 billion, as shown in Exhibits 2 and 3.

Another significant decrease from previous years occurred in the stated operating cash flow of $785 million in 2007 (see Exhibit 4). Generated operating cash flows from 2005 through 2007 are $4.3 billion, $3.5 billion, and $785 million, respectively, showing a continuation of a decreasing trend.[94]

The less-than-stellar financial situation has led management to consider different strategies that would best solve this predicament.

Exhibit 3 Motorola, Inc. and Subsidiaries

Balance Sheet		
	December 31	
(In millions, except per share amounts)	2007	2006
Assets		
Cash and cash equivalents	$ 2,752	$ 2,816
Sigma Fund	5,242	12,204
Short-term investments	612	620
Accounts receivable, net	5,324	7,509
Inventories, net	2,836	3,162
Deferred income taxes	1,891	1,731
Other current assets	3,565	2,933
Total current assets	22,222	30,975
Property, plant and equipment, net	2,480	2,267
Investments	837	895
Deferred income taxes	2,454	1,325
Goodwill	4,499	1,706
Other assets	2,320	1,425
Total assets	$34,812	$38,593
Liabilities and stockholders' equity		
Notes payable and current portion of long-term debt	$ 332	$ 1,693

Balance Sheet		
	December 31	
(In millions, except per share amounts)	2007	2006
Accounts payable	4,167	5,056
Accrued liabilities	8,001	8,676
Total current liabilities	12,500	15,425
Long-term debt	3,991	2,704
Other liabilities	2,874	3,322
Stockholders' equity		
Preferred stock, $100 par value	—	—
Common stock, $3 par value	6,792	7,197
Issued shares:	2,264	2,399
Outstanding shares:	2,236	2,397
Additional paid-in capital	782	2,509
Retained earnings	8,579	9,086
Non-owner changes to equity	(706)	(1,650)
Total stockholders' equity	15,447	17,142
Total liabilities and stockholders' equity	$34,812	$38,593

Source: Motorola 2007 Annual Report, http://www.motorola.com.

Exhibit 4 Motorola, Inc. and Subsidiaries

Statement of Cash Flows			
	Years Ended December 31		
(In millions)	**2007**	**2006**	**2005**
Operating			
Net earnings (loss)	$ (49)	$ 3,661	$ 4,578
Less: Earnings from discontinued operations	56	400	59
Earnings (loss) from continuing operations	(105)	3,261	4,519
Adjustments to reconcile earnings (loss) from continuing operations to net cash provided by operating activities:			
Depreciation and amortization	903	558	540
Non-cash other charges	213	49	106
Share-based compensation expense	315	276	14
Gains on sales of investments and businesses, net	(50)	(41)	(1,845)
Deferred income taxes	(747)	838	1,000
Change in assets and liabilities, net of effects of acquisitions and dispositions			
Accounts receivable	2,538	(1,775)	(1,303)
Inventories	556	(718)	(19)
Other current assets	(705)	(388)	(721)
Accounts payable and accrued liabilities	(2,303)	1,654	2,405
Other assets and liabilities	170	(215)	(388)
Net cash provided by operating activities from continuing operations	785	3,499	4,308
Investing			
Acquisitions and investments, net	(4,568)	(1,068)	(312)
Proceeds from sale of investments and businesses	411	2,001	1,538
Capital expenditures	(527)	(649)	(548)

(Continued)

Exhibit 4 Motorola, Inc. and Subsidiaries (*Continued*)

Statement of Cash Flows			
		Years Ended December 31	
(In millions)	2007	2006	2005
Proceeds from sale of property, plant and equipment	166	85	103
Proceeds from sales (purchases) of Sigma Fund investments, net	6,889	(1,337)	(3,157)
Proceeds from sales (purchases) of short-term investments	8	(476)	8
Net cash provided by (used for) investing activities from continuing operations	2,379	(1,444)	(2,368)
Financing			
Net proceeds from (repayment of) commercial paper and short-term borrowings	(242)	66	11
Repayment of debt	(1,386)	(18)	(1,132)
Net proceeds from issuance of debt	1,415	—	—
Issuance of common stock	440	918	1,199
Purchase of common stock	(3,035)	(3,826)	(874)
Excess tax benefits from share-based compensation	50	165	—
Payment of dividends	(468)	(443)	(394)
Distribution from (to) discontinued operations	(75)	(23)	283
Net cash used for financing activities from continuing operations	(3,301)	(3,161)	(907)
Effect of exchange rate changes on cash and cash equivalents from continuing operations	73	148	(105)
Discontinued Operations			
Net cash provided by (used for) operating activities from discontinued operations	(75)	(16)	297
Net cash used for investing activities from discontinued operations	—	(13)	(16)
Net cash provided by (used for) financing activities from discontinued operations	75	23	(283)
Effect of exchange rate changes on cash and cash equivalents from discontinued operations	—	6	2
Net cash provided by (used for) discontinued operations	—	—	—

Exhibit 4 Motorola, Inc. and Subsidiaries (*Continued*)

Statement of Cash Flows			
	Years Ended December 31		
(In millions)	2007	2006	2005
Net increase (decrease) in cash and cash equivalents	(64)	(958)	928
Cash and cash equivalents, beginning of year	2,816	3,774	2,846
Cash and cash equivalents, end of year	$ 2,752	$ 2,816	$ 3,774
Cash Flow Information			
Cash paid during the year for:			
Interest, net	$ 312	$ 322	$ 318
Income taxes, net of refunds	440	463	703

Source: Motorola 2007 Annual Report, http://www.motorola.com.

Motorola's Strategies

Motorola's current strategies are framed around efforts to return the firm to profitability. In the past couple of years there has been much discussion about spinning off the Mobile Devices segment as an independent company, similar to what Motorola had previously done with Free Scale. In a press release, Greg Brown stated the following: "Creating two industry-leading companies will provide improved flexibility, more tailored capital structures, and increased management focus—as well as more targeted investment opportunities for our shareholders."[95] However, as a result of the 2008 economic downturn, Motorola postponed the spin-off until the third quarter of 2009.[96]

Motorola is going to direct its efforts to better understand consumer demand.[97] In addition, it plans to pursue a product upgrade cycle and initiate operational changes to cut costs and make the company leaner.[98] This entails cutting approximately 3,000 jobs—2,000 of which will be from the handset division.[99] In addition, Motorola is considering reducing its emphasis on the European market.[100]

Motorola also invested heavily in the newly developed WiMax technology.[101] There are high expectations for WiMax as the next-generation wireless technology because it supports high-speed data transmission.[102] WiMax is capable of transmitting data at speeds from 1 to 5 megabits per second.[103] Furthermore, it works on

a radius of over 20 miles.[104] Motorola believes competing in this technological and product domain is crucial for its mobility strategy.[105] In November 2008, Motorola announced the deployment of its first trial network in Vietnam.[106] Dr. Ray Owen, head of Technology for Asia and general director of Motorola Vietnam, said: "Launching the trial network for Vietnam Datacommunications Company is another milestone in Motorola's long history of leading WiMAX development in the industry."[107]

Historically, Motorola has not limited the number of operating systems it supports in the Mobile Devices segment. However, recently the firm reduced the number of operating systems it supports to only P2K (Motorola's legacy platform for low-end devices),[108] Windows Mobile, and Android.[109] Motorola has been a featured partner with Google since the inception of the Android platform alliance.[110] Android will feature social networking applications such as Facebook and MySpace.[111] Moreover, analysts believe that social networking phones are expected to be a hit with the 16- to 34-year-old age segment, expected to comprise 23 percent of cell phone users by the end of 2012.[112]

Motorola's cost-reduction actions may expose the firm to additional risks.[113] Similar to most firms in this very competitive market, Motorola is confronted with an uncertain future.

Exhibit 5 Competitor Financials*

Competitor Financials

Key Numbers	Sony Ericsson Mobile	Nokia	Nokia (Mobile Phones)	Samsung	Samsung (Telecom)	RIM (2008)	RIM (Devices) (2008)	Apple (2008)	Apple (Headsets) (2008)	LG (Headsets)		
Annual Sales ($ mil.)	47.50	75,203.30	32,309.00	105,018	16,114	6,009.40	4,914	32,479	1,800	3,136		
Net Income ($ mil.)			5,434.00	8,446	2,407	1,294.00	370	4,834				
Employees		100,534	3,614			8,387		35,100				
Market Cap ($ mil.)				48,700								
Profitability											Industry	Market
Gross Profit Margin		33.90%									33.40%	52.70%
Pre-Tax Profit Margin		16.20%									0.50%	4.70%
Net Profit Margin	7.40%	14.10%	7.45%	8.04%	11.60%	21.53%	7.53%	14.88%		6%	-0.30%	2.70%

* Aside from Motorola, Nokia is the only publicly traded company on the U.S. exchanges; therefore, those companies traded on non-U.S. exchanges are not required by the Securities and Exchange Commission to report all necessary financials.

Source: 2008, http://hoovers.com; 2008, http://www.samsung.com; 2008, http://www.apple.com; 2008, http://www.lge.com; 2008, http://www.rim.net.

The Future for Motorola

Motorola has struggled to maintain pace with the change in technology that consumers desire. Indeed, the firm has struggled to have a top-performing product within the Mobile Devices segment since its introduction of the RAZR. Will a spinoff of this division help the rest of Motorola's business improve its financial performance? Can the new CEO and top-management team establish a positive reputation and limit the turnover that has taken place in upper management since he took over? These and other questions are at the forefront of the minds of the board of directors and stockholders alike.

NOTES

1. 2008, Motorola Inc Timeline, *Motorola Inc,* http://www.motorola.com.
2. 2008, Motorola – Early History, *Free Encyclopedia of Ecommerce,* http://ecommerce.hostip.info/pages/751/Motorola-Inc-EARLY-HISTORY.html.
3. Ibid.
4. 2008, Motorola Inc. Timeline.
5. 2008, Motorola Inc.—Early History.
6. 2008, Motorola Inc. Timeline.
7. Ibid.
8. 2008, Motorola Inc.—Early History.
9. Ibid.
10. 2008, Motorola Inc. Timeline.
11. Ibid.
12. 2008, Motorola Inc.—Early History.
13. 2008, Motorola Inc. Timeline.
14. Ibid.
15. Ibid.
16. Ibid.
17. Ibid.
18. 2008, Motorola Inc.—Early History.
19. Ibid.
20. Ibid.
21. 2008, Motorola Inc. Timeline.
22. Ibid.
23. 1990, Paul Galvin: Motorola, *American National Business Hall of Fame,* http://www.anbhf.org/laureates/pgalvin.html.
24. 2006, Illinois Hall of Fame; Paul Galvin, *Illinois Review,* http://illinoisreview.typepad.com/illinoisreview/2006/11/illinois_hall_o_2.html.
25. 2008, Motorola Inc. Timeline.
26. 2008, Motorola Inc., *Encyclopedia Britannica,* http://www.britannica.com, November 30.
27. 2008, Motorola Inc. Timeline.
28. 2008, Motorola Inc.—Early History.
29. Ibid.
30. 2008, Motorola Inc. Timeline.
31. Ibid.
32. 2008, Motorola DynaTAC—35th Anniversary, Motorola Inc., http://www.motorola.com.
33. 2008, Motorola Inc. Timeline, Motorola Inc., http://www.motorola.com/content.jsp?globalObjectId=7632.
34. 2008, Motorola Inc. Timeline, Motorola Inc., http://www.motorola.com/content.jsp?globalObjectId=7632.
35. 2008, Six Sigma: Motorola does it right, Motorola Inc., http://www.motorola.com.
36. 2008, Motorola Inc. Timeline.
37. Ibid.
38. Ibid.
39. Ibid.
40. Ibid.
41. Ibid.
42. Ibid.
43. 2008, 20 Moments in Motorola History, *ChannelWeb,* http://www.crn.com/networking/206906014;jsessionid=F0MYJEPAOMV5UQSNDLPCKH0CJUNN2JVN?pgno=3.
44. Ibid.
45. 2008, Motorola Inc. Timeline.
46. 2008, CCID Consulting reviews Motorola performance in the mobile phone market, *Reuters,* http://www.reuters.com, June 11.
47. 2008, 20 moments in Motorola history.
48. Ibid.
49. 2008, Motorola Inc. Timeline.
50. 2008, 20 moments in Motorola History.
51. Ibid.
52. Ibid.
53. 2007, Motorola names Greg Brown CEO, *BusinessWeek,* http://www.businessweek.com, November 30.
54. A. Dannin, 2008, Motorola Inc., http://library.morningstar.com.ezproxy1.lib.asu.edu/stocknet/MorningstarAnalysis.aspx?Country=USA&Symbol=MOT.
55. 2008, Motorola Inc. company description, *BusinessWeek,* http://investing.businessweek.com.
56. 2008, Motorola 2007 Annual Report, http://www.motorola.com.
57. 2008, Form 10-Q: Motorola, Inc., United States Securities and Exchange Commission, http://sec.gov/Archives/edgar/data/68505/000095015208008426/c47113e10vq.htm.
58. Ibid.
59. Ibid.
60. 2008, CDMA – Code Division Multiple Access, Birds-Eye.net, http://www.birds-eye.net/definition/c/cdma-code_division_multiple_access.shtml.
61. 2008, UMTS – Universal Mobile Telecommunications System, Birds-Eye.net, http://www.birds-eye.net/definition/u/umts-universal_mobile_telecommunications_system.shtml.
62. 2008, Motorola Inc. company description, *BusinessWeek.*
63. 2008, Form 10-Q: Motorola, Inc.
64. 2008, Motorola Inc. company description.
65. 2008, Form 10-Q: Motorola, Inc.
66. 2008, Nokia Annual Report, http://www.nokia.com; 2007, Nokia in 2007, *Nokia,* http://media.corporate-ir.net/media_files/irol/10/107224/reports/ann_acc_2007.pdf_.
67. Samsung Electronics 2007 Annual Report, http://www.samsung.com.
68. Ericsson Annual Report 2007, http://www.ericsson.com.
69. LG Annual Report 2007, http://www.lg.net.
70. 2008, About LG: Mobile communications, http://www.lge.com.
71. 2007, Apple Form 10-K, Securities and Exchange Commission, http://www.sec.gov, December 31.
72. Research in Motion 2008 Annual Report, http://www.rim.net.
73. 2008, RIM: Company, Research in Motion, http://www.rim.com.
74. 2008, Helio, Inc, and Helio LLC Exhbit 99.1, Helio, http://documents.scribd.com/docs/qk9y5wyxvrrcweuad2d.pdf
75. 2008, Don't call us a phone company, Helio, http://www.helio.com.
76. 2008, Mobile internet devices, Intel Corporation, http://www.intel.com.
77. Ibid.
78. Ibid.
79. Ibid.
80. 2008, SEC Form 10-Q: Motorola, Inc, *AOL Money and Finance,* http://finance.aol.com.
81. Ibid.

82. Ibid.
83. Ibid.
84. 2008, Motorola Form 10-Q.
85. T. Krazit, 2004, After delays, Motorola brings V400 to North America, *InfoWorld*, http://www.infoworld.com, January 16.
86. 2007, Motorola Form 10-Q.
87. P. Teague, 2007, The ABCs of spend analysis: Change the way you source, *Purchasing*, http://www.purchasing.com, May 3.
88. J. Carbone, 2007, Time-to-Market is key, *Purchasing*, http://www.purchasing.com, March 15.
89. 2008, Motorola 2007 Annual Report.
90. Ibid.
91. Ibid.
92. Ibid.
93. Ibid.
94. Ibid.
95. Ibid.
96. A. Dannin, Motorola Inc.
97. J. Zounis, 2008, Motorola Inc., http://library.morningstar.com.ezproxy1.lib.asu.edu/stocknet/AnalysisArchive.aspx?docId=234200&Year=2008&Country=USA&Symbol=MOT.
98. Ibid.
99. O. Kharif, 2008, Motorola's turnaround plans meet with skepticism, *BusinessWeek*, http://www.businessweek.com, October 31.
100. Ibid.
101. A. Dannin, Motorola Inc.
102. M. Reardon, 2005, Motorola, Intel team on mobile WiMax, CNET News, http://news.cnet.com, October 27.
103. Ibid.
104. Ibid.
105. Ibid.
106. Motorola Media Center, 2008, Motorola deploys its First WiMAX 802.16e trial network in Vietnam, http://www.motorola.com, November 27.
107. Ibid.
108. http://www.funambol.com/blog/capo/2008/10/motorola-focusing-on-android-why-it-is.html.
109. A. Dannin, Motorola Inc.
110. D. Gardner, 2008, Motorola reportedly trimming operating systems in favor of android, *Information Week*, http://www.informationweek.com, October 29.
111. O.Kharif, 2008, Motorola readies its own android social smartphone, *BusinessWeek*, http://www.businessweek.com, October 17.
112. Ibid.
113. Ibid.

The New York Times Company

Mike Apostol, Jami Clement, Cory Edwards, Mairah Meller, Sam Park, Phil Rogers, Doug Trucha, Robin Chapman

Arizona State University

The New York Times Company

Arthur O. Sulzberger Jr., chairman and publisher for The New York Times Company, left work on November 5, 2008, reeling from amazement over the events of the day. Although since the 1980s[1] print circulation had rapidly declined in the newspaper industry, this day had been very different. Thanks to the post-election front page headline declaring, "OBAMA – Racial Barrier Falls in Decisive Victory," *The New York Times* had flown off shelves at a rate not seen since November 11, 1918, when the newspaper, then owned by Sulzberger Jr.'s grandfather, announced the end of World War I.[2] Even more significant is the fact that copies of the Obama-headlined newspaper were selling on eBay for more than $600.[3]

However, Sulzberger Jr. did not dwell on the good fortune of this particular day. The excitement in the newsroom over the paper's interest did not erase or even ease the current crisis at The New York Times Company. In September 2008 total company revenues from continuing operations decreased 8 percent compared with the same month in 2007, and advertising revenues decreased 13 percent.[4] Unlike the challenges that his forebears had faced, today's challenges could not be solved simply by investing money in the company with the hope that high-quality journalism would prove more profitable.[5] The company was fast approaching the point where it would have to manage its business primarily to conserve cash (with only $46 million in cash on the books) and avoid defaulting on its debt (approximately $1.1 billion). Furthermore, Sulzberger Jr. realized that the situation would only worsen as advertising revenue was widely projected to keep falling.[6]

According to The New York Times Company's policy on ethics in journalism, the core purpose of the company is to "enhance society by creating, collecting and distributing high-quality news, information and entertainment."[7] For 100 years the company had been able to fulfill this purpose and has set the standard for print publications in the United States as well as around the world by spending big money not only on the addition of new sections and color illustrations but also on a highly gifted editorial staff (salaries are thought to exceed $300 million a year[8]).

Sulzberger Jr. pondered on how great it would be if the company could return to the "good old days," when the newspaper was a profitable business simply due to subscriptions and advertising income.

History

Former banker George Jones and journalist/politician Henry Jarvis Raymond founded *The New York Times* on September 18, 1851.[9] From 1851 to 1860 the newspaper was published Monday through Saturday. However, demand for daily news became so great during the Civil War that *The New York Times*, along with other major dailies, began publishing Sunday issues.[10] In the 1880s the newspaper moved from supporting Republican candidates to a more politically independent position (although the newspaper supported Grover Cleveland, a Democratic presidential candidate, in 1884, a decision that temporarily damaged readership).[11]

In 1896 *The New York Times* was purchased by Adolph Ochs, publisher of *The Chattanooga Times*, thus beginning the Ochs-Sulzberger family ownership of the newspaper. In 1897 Ochs coined the newspaper's slogan "All the news that's fit to print."[12] This motto, which can still be found on the front page of each daily issue of *The New York Times*, was a shot by Ochs at competing newspapers, which were known for downplaying legitimate news in favor of eye-catching headlines that sold more newspapers.[13]

The authors would like to thank Professor Robert E. Hoskisson for his support and guidance during the development of this case. This case is not intended to illustrate either effective or ineffective handling of managerial situations. The case is solely intended for class discussion.

Entering the twentieth century there were many "firsts" which allowed *The New York Times* (now called the "*Gray Lady*" by some due to its staid appearance and style), under Ochs's guidance, to achieve international scope, circulation, and reputation. In 1904 the newspaper received its first wireless transmission from a battle at sea during the Russo-Japanese war. *The New York Times* began its first regular air delivery to Philadelphia in 1910. In 1920 the newspaper made its first trans-Atlantic delivery.[14]

In 1935, in the midst of the Great Depression, Ochs passed away, leaving his son-in-law, Arthur Hays Sulzberger, as the newspaper's publisher.[15] Sulzberger got to work right away, pushing the newspaper's editors to begin an editorial barrage on President Roosevelt's plan to pack the Supreme Court with hand-selected individuals. This editorial crusade is still remembered as one of the most intense periods in *The New York Times'* history, and cemented the newspaper's commitment to "hard-hitting, ground-breaking journalism."[16]

During the 1940s, *The New York Times* extended its reach by introducing daily crossword puzzles and a fashion section. An international edition was published for the first time in 1946, and continued until the following year when *The New York Times* collaborated with the *New York Herald Tribune* and *The Washington Post* to publish the *International Herald Tribune* in France. In 1946, the newspaper also purchased a radio station (WQXR).[17]

The 1960s are remembered for the paper's involvement in the 1964 libel case, *The New York Times v. Sullivan.* This case resulted in one of the key U.S. Supreme Court decisions supporting freedom of the press.[18] In 1967 *The New York Times* went public and founded The New York Times Company.[19]

The company experienced a period of substantial change after going public. In the 1970s it acquired magazine publications such as *Golf Digest* and *Tennis Magazine*, book publishing companies like Cambridge, various daily newspapers, and even television stations.[20] Throughout the 1980s the company continued to aggressively acquire media outlets, and in the late 1980s investors were rewarded by two stock splits and many repurchases.[21]

Early in the 1990s, The New York Times Company began to advance its digital strategy, and in 1995 the company launched its domain, nytimes.com, on the World Wide Web. The New York Times Company has tried to exploit the Internet by spending more than $500 million on acquisitions and investments in new media from 2005 to 2008. 2005 saw The New York Times Company acquisition of About.com (an online consumer information provider), and in 2007 it acquired consumeresearch.com (an online aggregator and publisher of product reviews).

The New York Times Company also owns 53 percent of BehNeem (a Web-based software package that supports the day-to-day learning activities of students and faculty, including networking, object/file sharing, and storage and blogging), 14 percent of Indeed (a vertical meta-search for help-wanted listings), and less than 10 percent in several other new media companies.

The company's revenue stream changed during the first decade of the twenty-first century as advertising revenues declined in traditional print operations. In 2007 they created a new alliance with Monster.com to promote jobs on nytimes.com as a supplement to its declining classified revenues.[22]

In 2008, The New York Times Company announced a joint venture called quadrantONE with the Tribune Company, the Gannett Company, and the Hearst Corporation as an attempt to make it simpler for advertisers to do business with any of the four media groups. The challenge being that Internet giants such as Google, Yahoo!, and Microsoft are increasingly stealing advertising dollars through simple online advertising programs such as Google AdWords.[23]

As of 2008, The New York Times Company is a leading media company. It holds sole ownership of *The New York Times* (the third largest daily newspaper in United States, with a circulation of 1.1 million on weekdays and 1.6 million on Sundays[24]), *The International Herald Tribune*, *The Boston Globe*, 16 other daily newspapers, and a radio station.[25] *The New York Times* syndicate sells columns, magazine and book excerpts, and feature packages to more than 2,000 newspapers and other media to clients in more than 50 countries. It is the largest syndicate in the world specializing in text, photos, graphics, and other noncartoon features.[26] The New York Times Company also co-owns Discovery Civilization Channel[27] and has a 17.5 percent stake in New England Sports Ventures, which owns the Boston Red Sox and 80 percent of New England Sports Network, a cable network that televises Red Sox games.[28]

The company has also strived to put the right people in top leadership positions in order to meet the challenges facing the industry, but certain aspects of leadership have created some additional challenges.

Key Strategic Leaders

Arthur Ochs Sulzberger, Jr., Chairman & Publisher

Sulzberger Jr. became a correspondent for *The New York Times* in 1978. After serving in various reporting and business positions he was promoted to assistant editor in 1987, became publisher in 1992, and succeeded his father, Arthur Ochs Sulzberger, as chairman of the board of The New York Times Company in 1997.[29]

Due to the dual stock structure using Class A and Class B stocks to limit voting power, the Ochs-Sulzberger family has been able to maintain control of The New York Times Company since it went public in 1967. Prominent stakeholders such as Harbinger and Firebrand have been trying to change the dual stock structure, but six trustees must vote in favor of the change, which will not occur as long as the Ochs-Sulzberger family controls eight of the seats.[30]

Janet L. Robinson, President & CEO
Janet Robinson joined The New York Times Company in 1983. She became president and general manager in 1996, and was elected to the company's board of directors in December 2004. At that time she was also appointed to be the company's president and CEO.[31]

Since Robinson's appointment as CEO, traditional print media and the U.S. economy have endured significant losses. In 2004 the stock price was $47, down from a high of $53.80 in 2002. The price tumbled even further to around $6.65/share in November 2008. Robinson has attempted to offset the losses of traditional print media by placing emphasis on and expanding the company's new media operations. According to Robinson, expanding the company's Internet businesses is an "absolute priority."[32] Under Robinson, the company has grown its Internet businesses, but it has not liquidated assets as quickly as desired by some investors.

James Follo, Senior Vice President and CFO
Prior to taking his post as senior vice president and CFO in January 2007, James Follo was chief of finance at both Martha Stewart Living Omnimedia and General Media International.[33] Given the financial difficulties The New York Times Company is currently facing, Follo has publicly stated that with the exception of The New York Times, The New York Times Company is willing to sell any of its assets.[34] However, Follo recognizes that in the current economy, selling assets would do little to alleviate long-term financial troubles and has been negotiating with bankers to secure loans for the company.[35]

Vivian Schiller, Senior Vice President and General Manager
Vivian Schiller has been with The New York Times Company since May 2002. She was appointed as senior vice president and general manager of nytimes.com in May 2006. In this role she has led the day-to-day operations of the The New York Times most significant Web site overseeing product technology, marketing, classifieds, strategic planning, and business development. Schiller previously served as senior vice president of television and video for The New York Times and also executive vice president and general manager for the

Discovery Times. In November 2008, Shiller announced that she would be leaving the company for the post of CEO at National Public Radio. This is a critical loss at a time when strategic Internet leadership is needed more than ever.

Dissident Investors and Harbinger Capital Partners
After enduring a loss of $29 per share, Morgan Stanley sold its 7 percent stake in The New York Times Company. However, many dissident investors are still on board and plan to make changes to return The New York Times to its once proud and profitable state. One of these investors, Harbinger Capital Partners, has a 19 percent stake in the company.[36] Philip Falcone, lead at Harbinger Capital Partners, "has a long record of buying into troubled firms and then relentlessly pushing for change despite the odds."[37] The primary complaints of investors are the dual stock system that limits their access to controlling votes, slower than expected online expansion, and unprofitable holdings such as The Boston Globe. They also do not like the Company's stake in the Boston Red Sox because, though profitable, it is an unrelated business.

The Harbinger Group aims to transform the company in five years from one that does about 10 percent of its business in digital to one that does most of its business in digital. However, friction within the board of directors impedes the company's ability to make quick decisions, and since the Ochs-Sulzberger family owns the majority of shares, it is believed that "the company is going to do what the family wants it to do."[38]

The board is influenced not only by the Ochs-Sulzberger family, but also by the actions that competitors take.

Key Competitors

The New York Times Company's competitors are primarily in the publishing industry. The company also competes in the "information collection and delivery" and "Internet content provider" sectors. Top competitors include Gannett Co., Inc.; News Corporation; and The Washington Post Company.[39]

Gannett Co., Inc.[40]
Founded by Frank Gannett in 1906 and made public in 1967, Gannett is not only the largest newspaper publisher in the United States (as measured by total daily circulation), but a leading international news and information company. Approximately 8,900 shareholders in the United States and several foreign countries hold the company's more than 230 million outstanding shares of common stock. Total revenues in 2007 were $7.4 billion. (See Exhibit 1 for Gannett Financials 2005–2007.)

Exhibit 1 Gannett Financials 2005–2007

Gannett Income Statement	2007	2006	2005
Revenue ($ mil.)	7,439.5	8,033.4	7,598.9
Gross Profit ($ mil.)	3,275.4	3,595.1	3,537.7
Operating Income ($ mil.)	1,650.9	1,998.2	2,048.1
Total Net Income ($ mil.)	1,055.6	1,160.8	1,244.7
Diluted EPS (Net Income)	4.52	4.90	5.05

Gannett Quarterly Statements	Quarter Ending Jun 08	Quarter Ending Mar 08	Quarter Ending Dec 07
Revenue ($ mil.)	1,718.0	1,676.9	1,856.5
Gross Profit ($ mil.)	729.5	690.4	828.8
Operating Income ($ mil.)	(2,133.6)	327.6	372.7
Total Net Income ($ mil.)	(2,290.8)	191.8	245.3
Diluted EPS (Net Income)	(10.01)	0.84	1.06

Gannett Financial Ratios	Company	Industry Median	MarketMedian[1]
Price/Sales Ratio	0.32	0.45	1.04
Price/Earnings Ratio	—	9.00	10.88
Price/Book Ratio	0.34	0.82	0.98
Price/Cash Flow Ratio	1.84	4.14	6.46

[1] Public companies trading on the New York Stock Exchange, the American Stock Exchange, and the NASDAQ National Market.

Source: 2008, Gannett, *Hoover's*, November 13.

In the United States, Gannett publishes 85 daily newspapers with a total circulation of 6.9 million, as well as nearly 900 nondaily publications. Major U.S. newspapers owned by Gannett include *USA Today* (the largest daily newspaper with a circulation of more than 2.2 million), *The Arizona Republic,* and the *Detroit Free Press.* In addition, Gannett owns 23 television stations in the United States that reach more than 20 million households, publishes periodicals and inserts, and operates approximately 150 news and Internet advertising sites customized to the markets they serve. In January 2008, Gannett's total U.S. Internet audience was 25.8 million unique visitors, reaching about 15.9 percent of the Internet audience.

Gannett's newspaper publishing operations in the United Kingdom, through its subsidiary Newsquest, include 17 daily newspapers and approximately 300 weekly newspapers, magazines, and trade publications, as well as classified business Internet sites. In addition to its publishing and broadcasting businesses, in line with its mission "to successfully transform Gannett to the new environment,"[41] Gannett has also advanced in its digital strategy through business acquisitions including PointRoll (a provider of media marketing services to online advertisers) and Ripple6, Inc. (a social media services provider), partnerships with companies such as CareerBuilder (for employment advertising), ShopLocal (an online marketing solutions provider), and ShermansTravel (an online travel service).

Although Gannett has been aggressively cutting costs for some time and growing revenue from Internet sources, its newspaper advertising revenue decreased 14 percent in the first nine months of 2008 because of the movement of readers to the Internet as well as the weakening U.S. economy. In October 2008 Gannett reported that third-quarter profit fell 32 percent from the same quarter in 2007. In addition, the company announced that revenue and operating profit would likely experience double-digit percentage declines in 2009.[42] In response, Gannett planned to lay off 10 percent of its daily newspaper employees (up to 3,000 workers) by December 2008. These layoffs follow the elimination of more than 1,000 jobs since August 2008 in the company's most troubled division: U.S. publishing. However, Gannett is quick to point out that the layoffs amount to only 3 percent of the division's employees, and other publishers have made much more drastic eliminations (for example, since June 2008, the *Miami Herald* has carried out two rounds of 10 percent layoffs).[43] To further emphasize the company's dedication to cut costs, Gannett's chairman, president, and CEO Craig Dubow recently announced that he is taking a voluntary salary cut of $200,000 from now through 2009 as well as freezing the 2009 salaries of all company and divisional officers.[44]

News Corporation[45]

Created in 1980 by Rupert Murdoch, News Corporation is the world's third largest media conglomerate with total revenues of $33 billion in 2008. (See Exhibit 2 for News Corporation Financials 2006–2008.) The company is publicly traded and listed on the New York Stock

Exhibit 2 News Corporation Financials 2006–2008

News Corp. Income Statement	2008	2007	2006
Revenue ($ mil.)	32,996.0	28,655.0	25,327.0
Gross Profit ($ mil.)	12,465.0	10,010.0	8,734.0
Operating Income ($ mil.)	5,381.0	4,452.0	3,868.0
Total Net Income ($ mil.)	5,387.0	3,426.0	2,314.0
Diluted EPS (Net Income)	1.80	1.14	0.76

News Corp. Quarterly Statement	Quarter Ending Jun 08	Quarter Ending Mar 08	Quarter Ending Dec 07
Revenue ($ mil.)	8,589.0	8,750.0	8,590.0
Gross Profit ($ mil.)	3,361.0	3,298.0	(1,261.0)
Operating Income ($ mil.)	1,478.0	1,438.0	1,418.0
Total Net Income ($ mil.)	1,129.0	2,694.0	832.0
Diluted EPS (Net Income)	0.42	0.88	0.27

News Corp. Financial Ratios	Company	Industry Median	Market Median[1]
Price/Sales Ratio	0.46	0.48	1.06
Price/Earnings Ratio	4.60	10.41	11.20
Price/Book Ratio	0.53	1.01	1.03
Price/Cash Flow Ratio	3.84	4.79	6.54

[1] Public companies trading on the New York Stock Exchange, the American Stock Exchange, and the NASDAQ National Market.

Source: 2008, NewsCorp, *Hoover's*, November 13.

Exchange, the Australian Securities Exchange, and the London Stock Exchange. Nearly 40 percent of the company is controlled by Murdoch and his family.

News Corporation's newspaper and information services include News International (which publishes four national newspapers in the United Kingdom), News Limited (which publishes more than 110 national, capital city, and suburban newspapers in Australia), the *New York Post* (the fifth largest daily in the United States), and the *Wall Street Journal* (an English-language daily with a worldwide circulation of more than 2 million). Its publishing businesses include HarperCollins (a global English-language book publisher) and Dow Jones & Co. (a provider of global business news and information services). Additionally, News Corporation has operations in film, television, cable network, and direct broadcast satellite television segments. It owns Fox Filmed Entertainment (a global film and television production and distribution operation), Fox Broadcasting Company (the largest broadcasting network in the United States with more than 200 affiliate stations), the more than 30 television stations in the Fox Television Stations group, 23 percent of Premiere AG (a German pay-television company), 35 percent of British Sky Broadcasting (the U.K.'s largest digital pay-television platform), and nearly 100 percent of SKY Italia (Italy's most popular pay-television company).

New media properties held by News Corporation include Fox Interactive Media (an interactive services company including MySpace, a lifestyle and social-networking site which attracts 230,000 new users per day), NDS Group (a supplier of open end-to-end digital pay-television solutions), and News Outdoor (the largest outdoor advertising company in Eastern Europe). In November 2008, News Corporation announced that despite strong increases in first-quarter cable network operating income (31 percent) as well as newspaper and information services income revenue (37 percent, driven by the company's December 2007 acquisition of Dow Jones & Company), first-quarter profit fell 30 percent from the same quarter the previous year due to declining television and newspaper advertising revenue, a weaker performance by Fox Filmed Entertainment, and investment losses in Premiere AG. Additionally, the company announced that revenue and operating profit would probably see double-digit percentage declines in 2009.[46]

Although Murdoch has not provided much detail on cost-cutting techniques that will be employed, he has said that he is considering merging the back-office operations of the *Wall Street Journal* and the *New York Post* as well as closing 10 of the 17 U.S. printing plants that produce the *Wall Street Journal*.[47] Additionally, Murdoch has said that more emphasis needs to be placed on the

international expansion of Dow Jones & Company, as well as subscription-based businesses that have the benefits of twin revenues from subscribers and advertisers. "We will be looking to start new channels where there are opportunities, and we certainly see that on a big scale internationally."[48]

The Washington Post Company[49]

With a history dating back to 1877, The Washington Post Company is an education and media company publicly traded on the New York Stock Exchange since 1971. Apart from chairman Donald Graham and his family, who have voting control over the company, Warren Buffett and his Berkshire Hathaway corporation is also a substantial shareholder with 18 percent of the publicly traded shares. Total revenue in 2007 was $4 billion. (See Exhibit 3 for Washington Post Financials 2005–2007.)

Although The Washington Post Company is best known as the publisher of *The Washington Post*, the company also owns other media operations including *Newsweek*, six television stations, and the online publishing operations of Newsweek Interactive (WPNI) (a subsidiary whose products include washingtonpost.com, Newsweek.com, Slate, BudgetTravel.com, and Sprig.com). It owns nonmedia operations including Kaplan, Inc. (an international provider of educational and career services for individuals, schools, and businesses) and CableOne (a cable television and Internet service with approximately 700,000 subscribers in 20 U.S. markets).

In October 2008, The Washington Post Company reported an 86 percent decline in third-quarter profit compared with the same quarter in 2007. However, the company notes that if the $59.7 million goodwill impairment charge at some of its newspapers and the $12.5 million accelerated depreciation charge of *The Washington Post's* printing presses were to be excluded, its publishing division would be cash flow–positive with $3.8 million in profit for the quarter.[50]

At *The Washington Post*, advertising revenue fell 14 percent during the third quarter of 2008.[51] However, under Graham's leadership as well as that of his close advisors (namely Warren Buffet, who has publicly stated "The present model—meaning print—isn't going to work,"[52]) the company has been preparing for the industry's present crisis for some time. In addition to investing millions into its digital business (WPNI) since the mid-1990s, The Washington Post Company has labored to rebrand itself as a company associated with innovation in digital media and technology.

In March 2008 it announced that it would sponsor LaunchBox08, a global challenge for digital startups to submit innovative ideas in order to receive funding and

Exhibit 3 *Washington Post* Financials 2005–2007

Washington Post Income Statement	2007	2006	2005
Revenue ($ mil.)	4,180.4	3,904.9	3,553.9
Gross Profit ($ mil.)	2,297.4	1,862.5	1,644.3
Operating Income ($ mil.)	477.0	459.8	514.9
Total Net Income ($ mil.)	288.6	324.5	314.3
Diluted EPS (Net Income)	30.19	33.68	32.59

Washington Post Quarterly Statements	Quarter Ending Jun 08	Quarter Ending Mar 08	Quarter Ending Dec 07
Revenue ($ mil.)	1,106.2	1,063.1	1,125.5
Gross Profit ($ mil.)	598.2	572.0	596.9
Operating Income ($ mil.)	4.8	66.9	149.3
Total Net Income ($ mil.)	(2.7)	39.3	82.9
Diluted EPS (Net Income)	(0.31)	4.08	8.74

Washington Post Financial Ratios	Company	Industry Median	Market Median[1]
Price/Sales Ratio	1.17	1.44	1.56
Price/Earnings Ratio	31.16	19.02	15.82
Price/Book Ratio	1.51	2.99	1.52
Price/Cash Flow Ratio	8.84	13.62	9.88

[1] Public companies trading on the New York Stock Exchange, the American Stock Exchange, and the NASDAQ National Market.

Source: 2008, Washington Post Company, *Hoover's*, November 13.

participate in a business-building program with access to professional mentors and advisors.[53] Additionally, The Washington Post Company has steered away from investing in its print operations, but instead heavily investing in its nonmedia operations. Kaplan Inc. and CableOne now provide 53 percent and 16 percent, respectively, of total revenue.[54]

Nontraditional Media Competitors

While The New York Times Company has long fought its peers in the traditional print industry, the advent of the Internet created news opportunities for other companies beyond The New York Times Company and its traditional competitors. The second generation of the Internet brought with it new online mediums such as blogs, social networks, and online communities that allowed for anyone to self-publish for the world to see. With more than 112 million blogs now online, the avenues for advertisers to get their advertisements to niche audiences has risen dramatically. Bloggers add new blog entries with an astounding frequency of 1.6 million posts each day.[55] Recognizing the importance of the new online medium, *The New York Times* editor Bill Keller stated, "We must do whatever we can to strengthen our competitive position . . . [and ensure] among other things, that we are well equipped to navigate the passage to our digital future."[56]

Internet giants such as Google, Yahoo!, and Microsoft have increasingly encroached on the turf of traditional media by offering their own news sites. Sites such as Google News function without an editorial staff, instead leveraging an automated aggregation system that takes current, high-ranking stories and sorts them automatically into sections of the Google News page. "No human is involved in the altering of the front page or story promotion, beyond tweaking the aggregation algorithm.[57]"

The Google News site, which leverages more content from *The New York Times* than any other source (without paying for it), is said to be valued at more than $100 million, even though it generates no advertising revenue for Google directly.[58] Some have predicted a long drawn-out battle between Internet giants and the traditional print media.[59] The traditional print media has recognized this challenge and has suggested that perhaps partnering with Internet giants such as Google would be in their best interest. Jeff Jarvis, NYU journalist professor, and Edward Roussel, manager of digital content for *The Telegraph* said of print media's efforts to go online:

"It's hard to imagine a newspaper creating better technology than Google. And the service is proving to be brilliant at ad sales—so why not outsource those departments to Google so a paper can concentrate on its real job—journalism …. Ideally every newsroom would be able to think of Google and all its capabilities as their own.[60]"

Current Market Dynamics

Historically, The New York Times Company, like most of its primary competitors, has been deeply entrenched in the traditional print media industry where two consistent revenue streams exist: circulation unit sales and advertising related revenue. However, the Internet has truly become a disruptive technology in the information dissemination market. Internet subscriptions are replacing the daily newspaper expenditure in many households.

Unlike national newspapers such as *USA Today* and the *Wall Street Journal,* which have tended to hold their ground better, and for small-market dailies where competition from other media is not usually as intense, *The New York Times* has posted steep declines in circulation in recent years.[61] In October 2008 it was reported that its weekday circulation fell 3.6 percent from the previous year, and its Sunday circulation dropped 4.1 percent.[62] *The New York Times* has countered decreases in circulation with increases in subscription prices of more than 25 percent in recent years. As a result, it has not seen a decrease in circulation revenue. In fact, October 2008

circulation revenue increased 3.9 percent from the same period in 2007.[63]

As previously indicated, since the early 1990s the company has taken steps to profitably advance its digital strategy. In the past three years alone The New York Times Company has spent more than $500 million on acquisitions and investments in new media and the company's Internet operations. According to Nielsen Online, http://nytimes.com had 20 million unique visitors in September 2008, an increase of about 37 percent over the same period the previous year, and online advertising revenues climbed by approximately $10 million to $79 million. The popularity of the site stems not only from its content and format (which has benefited from the expertise of *The New York Times's* editorial staff), but also the reputation of *The New York Times* as a newspaper committed to "hard-hitting, ground-breaking journalism," something that cannot be easily replicated by competitors.

The New York Times Company also has the benefit of long-standing relationships with advertisers who may be wary of continuing a relationship with the company's traditional print media operations, but are eager to take advantage of the wide audience reached by the company's new media.

Despite the relationships *The New York Times* Company has maintained with advertisers and the reputation it has for employing great journalists, the financials indicate that the company has been more affected by its challenges than its assets.

Financials

Advertising revenues are typically elastic by nature. As the economy surges, companies advertising budgets expand. Unfortunately, economic challenges mean ad revenues generally decrease. Between October 2007 and October 2008, advertising revenues for The New York Times Company declined by 16.2 percent, with classified advertising revenue down 34.7 percent as offers for jobs, real estate, and automobiles each plunged at least 34 percent.[64]

The two major operating groups, News Media Group and the About Group, have seen divergent revenue paths during the past several years, with the About Group growing and becoming increasingly profitable while the News Media Group contracts and records net losses (see Exhibit 4 for New York Times Company Revenue Comparison by Segment).[65]

Advertising revenue for the About Group increased by 13.8 percent (see Exhibit 5) during the past year and has maintained double digit revenue growth since inception. However, this division of the company is

Exhibit 4 New York Times Company Revenue Comparison by Segment

Time Period	News Media Group Ad Revenue ($000s)	% Change	About Group Ad Revenue ($000s)	% Change	Circulation Revenue ($000s)	% Change
Q1–Q3 2008	1,231,411	−12.7	79,502	+16.5	676,486	+1.8
Q1–Q3 2007	1,410,208	−4.4	68,217	+28.2	664,539	+1.5
Q1–Q3 2006	1,474,408	−1.5	53,196	+102.4	654,994	+.01
Q1–Q3 2005	1,496,608		26,278		655,971	

Source: 2008, New York Times Company, http://morningstar.com, November 22.

Exhibit 5 New York Times Company Advertising Revenue Comparison 2007 v. 2008

The New York Times Company 2008 Q3 Advertising Revenues[a] ($ 000s)						
	September			Year to Date		
	2008	2007	% Change	2008	2007	% Change
News Media Group						
New York Times Media Group	$103,048	$116,753	−11.7	$781,607	$867,774	−9.9
New England Media Group	27,167	32,577	−16.6	240,591	289,414	−16.9
Regional Media Group	19,204	24,657	−22.1	209,212	253,020	−17.3
Total News Media Group	149,419	173,986	−14.1	1,231,410	1,410,208	−12.7
About Group[b]	8,739	7,878	+10.9	79,502	68,216	+16.5
Total Ad Revenues From Continuing Operations	$158,158	$181,864	−13.0	$1,310,912	$1,478,425	−11.3
Discontinued Operations: Broadcast Media Group[c]	0	0	N/A	0	45,745	N/A

(a) Numbers may not add due to rounding.
(b) Includes the Web sites of About.com, ConsumerSearch.com, UCompareHealthCare.com, and Calorie-Count.com.
(c) On May 7, 2007, the Company sold the Broadcast Media Group, consisting of nine network-affiliated television stations, their related Web sites and the digital operating center for approximately $575 million.

Source: 2008, New York Times Company, http:// www.nytco.com, November 22.

too small to make up for the decline in the traditional media group. As a result, total revenues for the company declined 8.9 percent in the third quarter of 2008, with circulation revenues up 1 percent because of the newspaper price increase (see Exhibits 6 and 7). Net income has decreased by 82.1 percent when compared to the same quarter in 2007, and net profit has decreased from $505 million in 1998 to $185 million in 2007 (Exhibit 8).

Total assets showed no growth at $3.5 billion in 2007, while total liabilities increased from $1.9 billion in 1998 to $2.4 billion in 2007 (see Exhibit 9). Debt-to-equity ratio increased from 0.39 in 1998 to 0.69 in 2007 (see Exhibit 10). At the end of third quarter in 2008, the company had $46 million in cash, $1.1 billion in debt, and a debt-to-equity ratio of 0.85. Of particular concern is the fact that $400 million of that debt is due in 2009.[66] Standard & Poor's threatened to downgrade the company's rating to junk status, causing insult to injury and raising the amount of interest expense The New York Times Company will be forced to pay on its debt.[67]

The company's quick ratio of 0.43 clearly shows the inability of the company to cover short-term cash needs. Further, the company's liquidity has decreased from the same period 2007, ironic given the fact that presidential election years typically create an advertising and circulation sales gain.

Exhibit 6 New York Times Company Revenue Comparison 2007 v. 2008

The New York Times Company 2008 Q3 Total Company Revenues[a] ($ 000s)			
	Third Quarter		
	2008	**2007**	**% Change**
Advertising Revenues			
News Media			
National	$188,666	$212,910	−11.4
Retail	86,507	97,191	−11.0
Classified	82,778	117,157	−29.3
Other Ad Revenue	13,658	14,423	−5.3
Total News Media Group	371,608	441,681	−15.9
About Group[b]	26,588	23,362	13.8
Total Ad Revenues from Continuing Operations	398,196	465,043	−4.4
Circulation Revenues	225,689	223,420	+1.0
Other Revenues[c]	63,157	65,896	−4.2
Total Company Revenues from Continuing Operations	$687,042	$754,359	−8.9
Discontinued Operations: Broadcast Media Group[d]	0	0	N/A

(a) Numbers may not add due to rounding.

(b) Includes the Web sites of About.com, ConsumerSearch.com, UCompareHealthCare.com, and Calorie-Count.com.

(c) Primarily includes revenues from wholesale delivery operations, news services/syndication, commercial printing, digital archives, direct mail advertising services, and rental income.

(d) On May 7, 2007, the Company sold the Broadcast Media Group, consisting of nine network-affiliated television stations, their related Web sites, and the digital operating center for approximately $575 million.

Source: 2008, New York Times Company, http://www.nytco.com, November 22.

Exhibit 7 New York Times Company Statement of Cash Flow 1998–2007

Cash Flow	1998	1999	2000	2001	2002	2003	2004	2005	2006	2007	TTM
Cash Flows from Operating Activities $Mil											As originally reported
Net Income	278.9	310.2	397.5	444.7	299.8	302.7	292.6	259.8	(543.4)	208.7	(32.5)
Depr & Amort	135.2	197.5	228.0	194.0	153.4	47.8	146.8	143.8	169.9	189.6	155.1
Deferred Taxes	(12.6)	(44.6)	(28.2)	(52.9)	88.1	53.5	3.6	(29.6)	(139.9)	(11.6)	—
Other	49.9	138.1	(7.5)	(114.5)	(267.9)	(37.7)	1.1	(79.6)	935.8	(276.0)	103.2
Cash from Operations	451.5	601.1	589.9	471.2	273.3	466.3	444.0	294.3	422.3	110.7	225.8
Cash Flows from Investing Activities $Mil											
Cap Ex	(81.6)	(73.4)	(85.3)	(90.4)	(160.7)	(120.9)	(153.8)	(221.3)	(332.3)	(380.3)	(213.2)
Purchase of Business	0.0	—	(296.3)	(2.6)	(176.9)	(65.1)	0.0	(437.5)	(35.8)	(34.1)	(5.7)
Other	25.4	(9.5)	186.6	430.4	(23.3)	(60.0)	(38.4)	163.4	79.4	562.6	(2.7)
Cash from Investing	(56.2)	(82.9)	(195.0)	337.4	(360.9)	(245.9)	(192.2)	(495.5)	(288.7)	148.3	(221.6)
Cash Flows from Financing Activities $Mil											
Net Issuance of Stock	(441.9)	(395.8)	(543.1)	(591.4)	(62.7)	(175.3)	(252.1)	(43.0)	(52.3)	(4.0)	(2.7)
Net Issuance of Debt	222.5	103.9	331.3	—	195.1	49.9	107.4	658.6	61.1	0.0	—
Dividends	(69.6)	(72.0)	(75.4)	(77.0)	(80.3)	(85.5)	(90.1)	(94.5)	(100.1)	(125.1)	(133.1)
Other	(177.1)	(126.5)	(102.5)	(157.3)	20.5	(7.7)	(14.4)	(316.7)	(14.9)	(151.5)	122.8

(Continued)

Exhibit 7 New York Times Company Statement of Cash Flow 1998–2007 (*Continued*)

Cash from Financing	(466.1)	(490.4)	(389.7)	(825.7)	72.6	(218.7)	(249.2)	204.4	(106.2)	(280.5)	(13.0)
Currency Adj	—	—	—	—	—	—	—	—	—	—	—
Change in Cash	(70.8)	27.9	5.2	(17.1)	(15.0)	1.7	2.7	3.2	27.5	(21.6)	(8.7)
Free Cash Flow $Mil											
Cash from Operations	451.5	601.1	589.9	471.2	273.3	466.3	444.0	294.3	422.3	110.7	225.8
Cap Ex	(81.6)	(73.4)	(85.3)	(90.4)	(160.7)	(120.9)	(153.8)	(221.3)	(332.3)	(380.3)	(213.2)
Free Cash Flow	369.9	527.7	504.6	380.9	112.6	345.4	290.2	73.0	90.0	(269.6)	12.6

S&P Index Data: S&P 500 Copyright © 2008

Source: 2008, New York Times Company, http://morningstar.com, November 22.

Exhibit 8 New York Times Company Income Statement 1998–2007

Income Statement — As originally reported

	1998	1999	2000	2001	2002	2003	2004	2005	2006	2007	TTM
Revenue	2,936.7	3,130.6	3,489.5	3,016.0	3,079.0	3,227.2	3,303.6	3,372.8	3,289.9	3,195.1	3,042.6
COGS	1,461.6	1,378.8	1,458.1	1,362.9	1,352.6	1,428.8	1,475.6	1,540.4	1,529.5	1,341.1	1,325.4
Gross Profit	1,475.1	1,751.8	2,031.4	1,653.1	1,726.4	1,798.4	1,828.1	1,832.4	1,760.4	1,854.0	1,717.2

Operating Expenses $Mil

	1998	1999	2000	2001	2002	2003	2004	2005	2006	2007	TTM
SG&A	959.8	1,180.5	1,395.5	1,278.7	1,181.5	1,258.9	1,318.1	1,474.3	1,466.6	1,397.4	1,374.8
R&D	—	—	—	—	—	—	—	—	—	—	—
Other	0.0	NaN	0.0	0.0	NaN	0.0	(NaN)	(122.9)	814.4	229.1	194.7
Operating Income	515.2	571.3	635.9	374.4	544.9	539.6	510.0	481.1	(520.6)	227.4	147.7

Other Income and Expense $Mil

	1998	1999	2000	2001	2002	2003	2004	2005	2006	2007	TTM
Net Int Inc & Other	(9.70)	(32.80)	37.20	(34.60)	(53.50)	(31.50)	(33.60)	53.30	50.70	(39.80)	7.30
Earnings Before Taxes	505.50	538.50	673.10	339.90	491.40	499.90	476.70	446.10	(551.90)	185.00	(44.30)

(Continued)

Exhibit 8 New York Times Company Income Statement 1998–2007 (Continued)

Income Taxes	218.90	228.30	275.60	137.60	191.60	197.80	183.50	180.20	16.60	76.10	(3.40)
Earnings After Taxes	286.60	310.20	397.50	202.20	299.80	302.10	293.20	265.90	(568.50)	108.80	(40.80)
Acctg Changes	—	—	—	—	—	—	—	(5.90)	0.00	0.00	—
Disc Operations	—	—	—	242.50	0.00	0.00	—	—	24.70	99.80	8.70
Ext Items	(7.70)	0.00	0.00	—	—	—	—	—	—	—	—
Net Income	278.90	310.20	397.50	444.70	299.80	302.70	292.60	259.80	(543.40)	208.70	(32.50)
Diluted EPS, Cont Ops$	1.49	1.73	2.32	1.26	1.94	1.98	1.96	1.82	(3.93)	0.76	(0.29)
Diluted EPS$	1.45	1.73	2.32	2.78	1.94	1.98	1.96	1.78	(3.76)	1.45	(0.23)
Shares	192.00	179.00	171.00	160.00	154.00	152.00	149.00	145.00	144.00	144.00	143.00

S&P Index Data: S&P 500 Copyright © 2008

Exhibit 9 New York Times Company Balance Sheet 1998–2007

Balance Sheet									As originally reported		
Assets $Mil											
	1998	1999	2000	2001	2002	2003	2004	2005	2006	2007	Latest Qtr
Cash and Equiv	36.0	63.9	69.0	52.0	37.0	39.5	42.4	44.9	72.4	51.5	45.9
Short-Term Investments	—	—	—	—	—	—	—	—	—	—	—
Accts Rec	331.9	366.8	341.9	318.5	358.3	387.7	389.3	435.3	402.6	437.9	364.6
Inventory	32.3	28.7	35.1	31.6	23.3	29.0	32.7	32.1	36.7	26.9	27.5
Other Current Assets	121.8	155.7	164.8	157.8	144.5	147.2	149.6	145.5	673.3	148.1	139.3
Total Current Assets	522.0	614.9	610.8	559.9	563.1	603.3	613.9	657.8	1,185.0	664.5	577.3
Net PP&E	1,326.2	1,218.4	1,207.2	1,166.9	1,197.4	1,187.3	1,367.4	1,468.4	1,375.4	1,468.0	1,354.8
Intangibles	1,327.6	1,305.0	1,480.1	1,410.2	1,393.1	1,474.4	1,464.6	1,851.0	784.4	811.9	737.2
Other Long-Term Assets	289.4	357.5	308.7	301.7	480.3	539.8	504.0	555.9	511.2	528.7	552.4
Total Assets	**3,465.1**	**3,495.8**	**3,606.7**	**3,438.7**	**3,633.8**	**3,804.7**	**3,949.9**	**4,533.0**	**3,855.9**	**3,473.1**	**3,221.7**
Liabilities and Stockholders' Equity $Mil											
Accts Payable	163.8	191.7	178.3	171.0	177.7	176.6	190.1	201.1	242.5	202.9	160.7
Short-Term Debt	124.1	0.0	291.3	158.3	178.1	228.0	335.4	496.5	546.7	111.7	397.9
Taxes Payable	—	—	—	225.2	8.4	10.6	—	—	—	—	—
Accrued Liabilities	257.0	298.8	318.1	242.2	253.7	267.3	264.7	285.5	321.3	335.4	258.7
Other Short-Term Liabilities	82.9	183.0	89.7	64.2	117.9	77.9	329.6	83.5	187.5	325.7	131.8

(Continued)

Exhibit 9 New York Times Company Balance Sheet 1998–2007 (*Continued*)

Total Current Liabilities	627.8	673.5	877.4	860.9	735.7	760.4	1,119.8	1,066.5	1,298.0	975.7	949.1
Long-Term Debt	513.7	512.6	553.4	517.1	648.6	646.9	393.6	822.0	720.8	672.0	672.5
Other Long-Term Liabilities	792.1	861.0	894.7	911.1	980.2	1,005.2	1,036.0	1,128.3	1,017.3	847.1	803.0
Total Liabilities	1,933.6	2,047.1	2,325.5	2,289.0	2,364.5	2,412.5	2,549.3	3,016.8	3,036.1	2,494.9	2,424.6
Total Equity	1,531.5	1,448.7	1,281.2	1,149.7	1,269.3	1,392.2	1,400.5	1,516.3	819.8	978.2	797.1
Total Liabilities & Equity	3,465.1	3,495.8	3,606.7	3,438.7	3,633.9	3,804.7	3,949.9	4,533.0	3,855.9	3,473.1	3,221.7

S&P Index Data: S&P 500 Copyright © 2008

Source: 2008, New York Times Company, http://morningstar.com, November 22.

In comparison to industry competitors, The New York Times Company is underperforming in sales growth and net profit margin while capital spending is higher. Despite an effort to improve its financial situation, capital spending reached $213 million in 2008, up from $82 million in 1998 (see Exhibit 7).

Not unexpected with these financial results, the company's stock price has underperformed. In an effort to curb the steady stock devaluation, The New York Times Company announced in March 2007 that it would increase its dividend by 31 percent hoping that such a drastic increase in an already generous dividend would help stabilize, if not increase, the stock price.[68] It did not work. Since then the stock dropped from $24/share to just over $5/share in November 2008, when the company announced that it would need to cut its dividend by 74 percent.[69] Financial analysts have favorably viewed this dividend reduction, upgrading the stock and commenting that the move alone should recoup $100 million in annual revenue.[70]

The New York Times Company's market cap is just under $1 billion, an astonishingly low figure given that far smaller media companies have sold for far more. Earlier this year for example, CBS acquired the consumer

Exhibit 10 New York Times Company Liquidity Ratios 1998–2007

Liquidity/Financial Health											
	1998	1999	2000	2001	2002	2003	2004	2005	2006	2007	Latest Qtr
Current Ratio	0.83	0.91	0.70	0.65	0.77	0.79	0.55	0.62	0.91	0.68	0.61
Quick Ratio	0.59	0.64	0.47	0.43	0.54	0.56	0.39	0.45	0.37	0.50	0.43
Financial Leverage	2.26	2.41	2.82	2.99	2.86	2.73	2.82	2.99	4.70	3.55	4.04
Debt/Equity	0.39	0.41	0.50	0.52	0.57	0.52	0.34	0.59	0.97	0.69	0.85

Source: 2008, New York Times Company, http://morningstar.com, November 22.

technology reviews company CNET Networks for $1.8 billion,[71] nearly twice The New York Times Company's market cap.

The company's financial condition makes it difficult for it to support growth at competitive rates, let alone to simply continue operations.

Strategic Challenges and the Future

The New York Times Company lacks any clear differentiators when compared to its market competitors. Moreover, its primary competitors are in stronger financial positions as the economy is in a period of turbulence and certain change is coming to the traditional print industry. In addition, the company lacks a defined strategic intent; clearly defined goals with respect to where

and how it intends to compete in the market. The New York Times Company will see significant headwinds as it enters various digital market segments. It will face a multitude of new (nontraditional) competitors, some with unique strategies and better capitalization to enter these markets and create new product offerings, vying for the same advertising dollars.

As Sulzberger Jr. looks beyond the momentary good fortunes of *The New York Times* owing to the Obama-headlined newspaper of November 5, 2008, he must address the serious challenges facing The New York Times Company. How can he influence the board of directors to act in unison? What long-term strategy should they implement? How can the company differentiate itself from competitors? How can it leverage the competencies of the new media outlets it has acquired to help improve its financial situation?

NOTES

1. L. Han, 2008, Newspaper circulation falls Again, *Forbes*, April 28.
2. 2008, Sulzberger Family, *Wikipedia*, November 20.
3. 2008, *Guardian,* November 6.
4. 2008, New York Times Company reports September revenue, *Yahoo Finance*, October 23.
5. 2005, The future of the New York Times, *BusinessWeek*, January 17.
6. H. Blodget, 2008, Cash crunch at the New York Times, *Silicon Alley Insider*, November 8.
7. 2008, New York Times Company: Press www.nytco.com, November 25.
8. A. Bianco, J. Rossant, & L. Gard, 2005, The future of the New York Times, *BusinessWeek*, January 17.
9. 2008, New York Times Company, *Hoovers,* November 18.
10. 2008, New York Times Company, *Wikipedia*, November 14.
11. Ibid.
12. New York Times Company, *Hoovers.*
13. New York Times Company, *Wikipedia.*
14. 2008, New York Times Company: Company Milestones 1981–1910, www.nytco.com, November 14.
15. 2008, New York Times Company: Company Milestones 1911–1940, www.nytco.com, November 14.
16. 2008, New York Times Company: Company Milestones 1941–1970, www.nytco.com, November 14.
17. 2008, New York Times Company: Company Milestones 1971–1980, www.nytco.com, November 14.
18. 2008, *Times v. Sullivan*, Cornell University, November 14.
19. New York Times Company: Company Milestones 1971–1980.
20. Ibid.
21. New York Times Company: Company Milestones 1981–1990.
22. R. Gavin, 2007, New York Times Co. partners with Monster, *The Boston Globe*, February 14.
23. L. Story, 2008, 4 news companies ally to sell ads on the Internet, *New York Times*, February 15.
24. New York Times, *Wikipedia.*
25. 2008, New York Times Company, www.nytco.com, November 20.
26. 2008, New York Times Company, www.answers.com November 25.
27. 2002, New York Times Company and Discovery Communications, Inc. announce joint venture in Discovery Civilization Channel, *Business Wire*, April 5.
28. L. Haul, 2008, New York Times CEO: Red Sox a good investment, *Forbes*, March 11.
29. 2008, Arthur Ochs Sulzberger, Jr., *Wikipedia*, November 15.
30. J. Yarow & J. Fine, 2008, How can the New York Times be worth so little?, *BusinessWeek*, July 25.
31. 2008, Janet L. Robinson, *Wikipedia*, November 15.
32. 2008, NY Times CEO: Focused on online growth, *Forbes*, March 11.
33. 2008, New York Times Company, www.nytco.com, November 20.
34. NY Times CEO: Focused on online growth.
35. C. Douglas, 2008, Globe shows red ink as Times faces cash crunch, *Boston Business Journal*, November 13.
36. R. Perez-Pena, 2008, Two funds raise their stake in Times Company to 19%, *New York Times*, February 26.
37. E. Hessel, 2008, Times Tussle, *Forbes*, February 15.
38. 2008, Dissident investors increase Times Co. stake, www.boston.com, February 21.
39. 2008, New York Times Company, *Hoovers*, November 13.
40. 2008, Gannett, www.gannett.com, November 14.
41. Ibid.
42. R. MacMillian, 2008, Gannett profit falls short on weak advertising, *News Daily*, October 24.
43. 2008, Gannett laying off 10% of newspaper staff; Dicky warns in memo: 'fiscal crisis is deepening,' http://Gannettblogspot.com, October 28.
44. 2008, Gannett Chairman Dubow takes $200,000 pay cut, *Editor and Publisher*, November 3.
45. 2008, NewsCorp, www.newscorp.com, November 13.
46. D. Wilkerson, 2008, News Corp shares plunge after outlook cut, *MarketWatch*, November 6.
47. R. MacMillian, 2008, News Corp slashes outlook, profits dive, *Reuters*, November 5.
48. D. Wilkerson, News Corp shares plunge after outlook cut.
49. 2008, Washington Post Company, www.washpostco.com, November 13.
50. F. Ahrens, 2008, Washington Post Co. earnings plummet in third quarter, *washingtonpost*, October 31.
51. A. Jesdanon, 2008, Ad sales drop squeezes 3Q earnings for Post, Belo, www.boston.com, October 31.
52. M. Gunther, 2007, Can the Washington Post survive?, http://money.cnn.com, July 26.
53. 2008, Washington Post Co. Sponsors LaunchBox08 Startup Competition, *Business Wire*, March 10.

54. Lin E., 2008, S&P: Washington Post Co. outlook negative, *Shaping the Future of the Newspaper*, October 28.

55. 2008, Technorati, www.technorati.com, November 26.

56. J. Koblin, 2008, Layoffs at The New York Times; Keller Says 'We Hope Worst is Behind Us,' *New York Observer*, May 7.

57. 2008, Google News, *Wikipedia*, November 18.

58. J. Fortt, 2008, What's Google News Worth? $100 Million, *Fortune Magazine*, July 22.

59. M. LaMonica, 2004, Googlezon: The Future of Media, *CNET*, December 27.

60. J. Jarvis, 2008, The Host With the Most, *Guardian*, July 21.

61. S. Sitel, 2008, New York Times Circulation Plummets, *The Huffington Post*, April 28.

62. R. Perez-Pena, 2008, Newspaper Circulation Continues to Decline Rapidly, *The New York Times*, October 27.

63. 2008, Internet Revenue At New York Times (NYT) Needs To Be Going Up 100%, But It's Not, *247wallst*, November 20.

64. 2008, New York Times Company: Investor Relations Financials, www.nytco.com, November.22.

65. Ibid.

66. C. Douglas, 2008, Globe Shows Red Ink as Times Faces Cash Crunch, *Boston Business Journal*, November 13.

67. J. Yarrow & J. Fine, How Can The New York Times Be Worth So Little.

68. Ibid.

69. D. Wilkerson, 2008, New York Times Co. Shares Tumble to New Low, *MarketWatch*, November 21.

70. M. Peer, 2008, NY Times' High Dividend Is Old News, *Forbes*, November 24.

71. M. Arrington, 2008, CBS to Acquire CNET for $1.8 Billion, *TechCrunch*, May 15.

Nike's Global Women's Fitness Business: Driving Strategic Integration

Lyn Denend

Stanford Graduate School of Business

My goal, in golf terms, was to get the women's business on Nike's leader board. Over the past 15 years, it has come and gone as an initiative. But we've finally gotten it embedded as one of the biggest growth opportunities for the company.

—DARCY WINSLOW, GENERAL MANAGER OF NIKE'S GLOBAL WOMEN'S FITNESS BUSINESS

In the summer of 2006, Nike announced a major corporate reorganization that would shift the company's focus from a product orientation to a category-driven approach. The six major business categories were running, men's training, basketball, soccer, women's fitness, and sportswear. While these categories did not encompass the entirety of Nike's business (e.g., golf would continue to be run as a separate, stand-alone business as it had since its inception),[1] these six areas were chosen because they were expected to account for 90 percent of the company's growth. Smaller business categories (e.g., tennis, children's products) ultimately would be incorporated into the new organization structure after it became established in these critical growth areas and was operating effectively.

For years, Nike had organized its business around footwear, apparel, and equipment. Integration between these three business units was inconsistent, and typically driven by special events and initiatives (e.g., the Olympics, World Cup). The goal of the reorganization was to take a more consumer-oriented approach to the market, optimizing the company's activities to give customers a holistic collection of everything they want and need in a particular sports category. This would require the organization to break down its product-oriented silos and collaborate on a more formal, ongoing basis.

The reorganization also represented a change in Nike's traditional business priorties. The elevation of women's fitness to a major focus for the famously testosterone-driven company was a substantial victory for the team that been fighting for the increased prominence of this potentially lucrative market segment for the past several years. Darcy Winslow, general manager of Nike's global women's fitness business, and a semi-virtual team of individuals across the company had been working across traditional boundaries within Nike's complex, matrixed organization to achieve the required level of cross-business integration to deliver cohesive collections of footwear apparel and equipment to the women's market. While it was not always easy to get disparate product/business units and multiple geographic regions working on the same schedule toward a common goal, they had made it happen, despite organizational barriers, leadership challenges, and the need for extensive manual interventions and workarounds.

As Winslow looked back on her experiences as the leader of the global women's fitness team and prepared to transition to her new executive position, she contemplated what recommendations she would make to help the new leader sustain and improve the level of strategic integration that had been achieved. Because her new role would focus on implementing Nike's new, category-driven organization, she also needed to reflect on the lessons she had learned over the past several years—how to shape a new organization to support the defined business strategy, stimulate cross-business collaboration, and sustain innovation—so that she could capitalize on the most successful strategies and avoid common pitfalls that might hinder Nike's progress in 2007 and beyond.

Lyn Denend prepared this case under the supervision of Professor Robert Burgelman as the basic for class discussion rather than to illustrate either effective or ineffective handling of an administrative situation.

About Nike

Company History

Nike was founded by Bill Bowerman and Phil Knight. The two men met when Bowerman was coaching track and field at the University of Oregon and Knight was a middle-distance runner on his team. After earning an MBA from Stanford (GSB 1962), Knight returned to Oregon and approached Bowerman with an idea to bring in low-priced, high-tech athletic shoes from Japan to compete in the U.S. athletic shoe market (which was dominated by German imports at the time).[2] With a handshake and a $500 investment by both men, Blue Ribbon Sports (BRS) was born in 1964. BRS began importing shoes from Onitsuka Tiger, with Knight making sales at high school track meets and Bowerman relentlessly looking for ways to improve the product designs. Before long, their competitive spirits got the better of them and they branched out on their own, forming a new company in 1972 that would design, produce, and sell its own shoes.

By 2006, that company, called Nike for the Greek goddess of victory, had grown into the one of the world's most well-known brands and a dominant competitor in the global athletic footwear, apparel, and equipment market. Nike's fiscal year 2006 sales reached $15 billion (up 9 percent from FY 2005), with net income of $1.4 billion (compared to $1.2 billion the previous year).[3] The company, headquartered in Beaverton, Oregon, had approximately 26,000 employees worldwide and operations in 120 countries (see Exhibit 1 for select Nike financials).

Exhibit 1 Fiscal Year 2006 Consolidated Financial Statements (period ending May 31, 2006)

Income Statement	Quarter Ending			Year Ending		
	05/31/2006	05/31/2005	% Chg	05/31/2006	05/31/2005	% Chg
Revenues	$4,005.4	$3,721.4	8%	$14,954.9	$13,739.7	9%
Cost or sales	2,252.0	2,038.7	10%	8,367.9	7,624.3	10%
Gross margin	1,753.4	1,682.7	4%	6,587.0	6,115.4	8%
	43.8%	45.2%		44.0%	44.5%	
Selling and administrative expense	1,232.1	1,139.2	8%	4,477.8	4,221.7	6%
	30.8%	30.6%		29.9%	30.7%	
Interest (income) expense, net	(16.3)	(3.6)	—	(36.8)	4.8	—
Other expense, net	26.4	9.2	—	4.4	29.1	—
Income before income taxes	511.2	537.9	–5%	2,141.6	1,859.8	15%
Income taxes	178.4	188.4	–5%	749.6	648.2	16%
	34.9%	35.0%		35.0%	34.9%	
Net income	332.8	349.5	–5%	1,392.0	1,211.6	15%
Diluted EPS	1.27	1.30	–2%	5.28	4.48	18%
Basic EPS	1.29	1.34	–4%	5.37	4.61	16%
Weighted average common shares outstanding						
Diluted	261.4	268.5		263.8	270.3	
Basic	257.2	261.1		259.0	262.6	
Dividends declared	0.31	0.25		1.18	0.95	

Note: All figures in millions, except per share data.

Source: Nike, Inc. reports fiscal 2006 earnings per share growth of 18 percent, June 27, 2006, http://www.nike.com/nikebiz/investors/earnings/docs/q406.pdf; bsessionid=TLLCDPGTWYSGCCQFTC2SF5AKAWMLQIZB (accessed February 7, 2007).

Nike's corporate mission was "to bring inspiration and innovation to every athlete in the world." In this written statement, there was an asterisk after the word "athlete" with a note that clarified, "If you have a body, you are an athlete." The company's brand was built on inspiring (and even challenging) individuals to get out and realize their physical potential. Nike's products were designed to give them a competitive edge in doing so. Innovation was at the heart of the company's values, and innovative products were at the center of its competitive advantage. As stated on the Nike Web site, "For three decades, we have been committed to giving athletes of every make, model and body style, who compete and recreate in ways never before imagined, the very best performance products. Products of the pure imagination. Products that move the needle of performance. Products that help us be the athletes we know we are."[4]

Organization

Given this intense focus on products and product innovation, it was no surprise that Nike had organized its business around a product orientation, with three primary business units focused on footwear, apparel, and equipment. In fiscal 2006, footwear accounted for roughly 66 percent of the business, apparel 28 percent, and equipment 6 percent.[5] In the global branded footwear market, some estimates placed Nike's market share at approximately 38 percent, with Adidas/Reebok (which joined forces when Adidas acquired Reebok in 2006) following at 34 percent.[6] Other footwear competitors, including Puma, Asics, Mizuno, and Umbro, trailed significantly in their market share. Because the apparel and equipment markets were more fragmented than footwear, with many more competitors of all sizes vying for share, Nike owned a smaller piece of the market

in these product areas. For example, 2005 estimates indicated that together Nike, Adidas, and Reebok held a total of approximately 15 percent of the sports apparel market in the United States.[7]

Nike's business units represented the lead dimension of the company's matrixed organization structure, along with a handful of global functions (sales, brand, customer service, operations, logistics, etc.). Its four geographic regions—the United States, Europe, Middle East, and Africa, Asia-Pacific, and the Americas—represented the second dimension.[8] Nike's nine sports categories—which included running, basketball, tennis, soccer, and golf—made up the third aspect of the matrix.

Within this matrixed structure, decision making and priority setting were dominated by the business units, in keeping with Nike's desire to optimize innovation and execution around its primary products. Members of the footwear, apparel, and equipment teams collaborated across business unit boundaries to some extent, but this was most commonly done in support of particular projects. "As a company, Nike is very initiative-driven," commented Steve Lesnard, global concept director for women's fitness.[9] (See Exhibit 2 for biographies of Nike employees.) Product groups would work together, involving the global functions and executing through the regions, to create a collection for a special event, such as the World Cup, U.S. Open, or the Olympics, but then go back to their silos as soon as the common goal was achieved. "Everybody comes together around something like Beijing [site of the last Olympics] because we know it's coming, and we understand the stakes," said Lesnard. "But it's different when you're talking about supporting an ongoing strategy." Underscoring the disintegrated nature of day-to-day operations, Winslow said, "I use the example that for all the years

Exhibit 2 Biographies of Nike Employees Interviewed for the Case Study

Mindy Grossman, Vice President of Apparel

A 30-year veteran of the retail and apparel industries, Mindy Grossman was appointed chief executive officer of IAC Retailing in April 2006. In this capacity, Grossman oversees operations which, in aggregate, represent more than $3 billion in revenues annually and comprise HSN, Cornerstone Brands, Shoebuy, and IAC's international retailing business. Grossman joined IAC from Nike, Inc., where she served as vice president and head of the company's $4 billion global apparel business. Among her numerous accomplishments during her tenure at Nike was the development and growth of Nike's women's business. Previously, Grossman was president and CEO at Polo Jeans Company. She also worked as vice president of new business at Polo Ralph Lauren Corporation, as president of the Chaps Ralph Lauren division of Warnaco's menswear division, and as vice president of sales and merchandising at Tommy Hilfiger. Grossman attended Manhattanville College and George Washington University.

Seana Hannah, Category Footwear Leader Women's Training

Seana Hannah is responsible for leading the global team of marketers, designers, and developers who create exciting products for women in the gym and girls training for sport. Over her 16-year tenure at Nike, she has held several positions, including retail associate, EKIN (Nike spelled backwards!—the role is a footwear technical rep who knows the shoes frontward and backward), product line manager in kids and running, and product director of women's running. Hannah received her BS in Sociology from Amherst College.

(Continued)

Exhibit 2 Biographies of Nike Employees Interviewed for the Case Study (*Continued*)

Steve Lesnard, Global Concepts Director for Global Women's Fitness

Steve Lesnard worked as marketing director for a women's luxury apparel brand before joining Nike in 1997. He worked first with the company's global footwear division and then with the EMEA regional footwear team. Next, Lesnard joined the EMEA brand team as the apparel and women's regional marketing manager, followed by a position as the U.S. senior brand manager for apparel, women's, tennis, and kids. More recently, he moved into the role of global concept director for women's fitness.

Emma Minto, Director of Strategic Planning for Nike Brand's U.S. Apparel Division

A specialist in business strategy, new business development, and marketing, Emma Minto is the director of strategic planning for Nike Brand's U.S. apparel division. Minto joined Nike, Inc., as director of strategic planning for its global women's fitness division where she helped to build and establish the organization to drive the global women's fitness sports businesses. Before joining Nike, Minto helped to build TeamOn Systems, a messaging technology startup, as VP of marketing and professional services and was a management consultant at Corporate Decisions Inc. and Mercer Management Consulting. Minto began her career as a product marketer at Colgate Palmolive. She holds an MBA from Harvard Business School and a Bachelor of Commerce from Queen's University in Ontario, Canada.

Maithili Shenoy, Global Director of Supply Chain Strategy and Development

With Nike since 2002, Maithili Shenoy is primarily responsible for strategy development, process redesign, performance management, and education for the supply chain area. Prior to coming to Nike, she spent more than 10 years in management consulting at Deloitte Consulting and Accenture, specializing in supply chain strategy consulting and business process reengineering for *Fortune* 500 clients in the consumer products and retail industries. Shenoy received her BS in Operations Research from Columbia University and a Master's in International Business from Sophia University in Tokyo.

Jodi Sittig, Marketplace Development Director, Global Women's Fitness

In her 14 years with Nike, Jodi Sittig has been instrumental in delivering and implementing brand, retail, and event strategies. In her role as marketplace development director for global women's fitness, she aligned retail and sales strategies around the globe for the women's fitness business. Prior to that role, as the women's brand manager for the United States, Sittig led the alignment of the U.S. women's business. She started in Nike's retail group as director of marketing and events, moving within two years to retail director of marketing, where she led teams in the creation and execution of national strategic plans for NIKETOWN and the factory store markets. Sittig also played a role in the creation and implementation of the marketing strategy for the first Nike Goddess (now Nike Women) store. Sittig earned her BS in Fashion Merchandising from Kent State University.

Mary Slayton, Director of Market Intelligence

In her role as director of market intelligence, Mary Slayton oversees market, consumer, and competitive information and analysis for Nike on a global basis. Over her 12-year tenure with Nike, she has held many positions, including general manager of the accessories business, marketing director for the Jordan brand, director of strategic planning for the U.S. region, director of strategic planning for subsidiaries, and director of consumer insights. Slayton received her BS in Economics from Colorado College and her MBA from Northwestern's Kellogg School of Business. Prior to Nike, she worked at Pillsbury, McKinsey & Company, and Wilson Sporting Goods.

Barbara Sumner, Creative Director for Integrated Footwear, Apparel, and Equipment

Barbara Sumner leads design in men's and women's styles across all sport categories and Nike's sport culture business. Prior to this, her roles included creative director for the U.S. women's business, creative director for global apparel, and creative director for integrated footwear, apparel, and equipment. She attended the University of Oregon and the Fashion Institute of Technology in New York.

Jim Sutton, Senior Director of Global Organization and Leadership Development

Jim Sutton leads Nike's talent management processes for leadership development, assessment, executive coaching, succession management, performance management, and learning/training. Prior to this role, he was the HR director for Nike's global apparel and equipment business units. Sutton worked at San Francisco-based Levi Strauss & Company for 25 years, where he held senior HR generalist leadership roles. He was HR director for Levi's USA prior to joining Nike in 1997. Sutton has a Bachelor's in Business Administration from Texas A&M University and holds a coaching certification from the Hudson Institute of Santa Barbara.

Hans van Alebeek, Vice President, Global Operations & Technology

Hans van Alebeek joined Nike as director of operations of Europe in 1999 and was appointed vice president, operations and administration in EMEA in 2001; vice president, global operations in 2003; vice president, global operations and technology in 2004; and corporate vice president in November 2005. Prior to joining Nike, he worked for McKinsey & Company as a management consultant, and at N.V. Indivers in business development.

(Continued)

Exhibit 2 Biographies of Nike Employees Interviewed for the Case Study (*Continued*)

Darcy Winslow, Global General Manager for Women's Footwear, Apparel, and Equipment

As Nike's global general manager for women's footwear, apparel, and equipment, Darcy Winslow oversees all aspects of the value creation chain in women's fitness—innovation, product creation, marketing, supply chain, retail, and sales. She has worked at Nike for 18 years and has held many positions within the business, including biomechanical research assistant, director of footwear and apparel product testing, product development manager, core team member of Nike's business reengineering initiative, director of advanced research and development, global director for footwear research, design and development, general manager of sustainable business strategies, and global women's footwear director. Winslow received her BS in Exercise science and an MS in Exercise Physiology and biomechanics. She is also a 2003 graduate of the Stanford Executive Program.

Pat Zeedick, General Manager of Equipment and Women's for the EMEA Region

Pat Zeedick has held several different positions over the past 19 years of her career with Nike. As of late 2006, she was the general manager of equipment and women's for the Europe, Middle East, and Africa region. Prior to that, she was the general manager of Nike Canada, director of sales for the Americas region, global director of sales training and development, national development sales director for the United States, Western regional apparel sales manager, and territory sales manager in the Nike Rocky Mountains region. She started her career with the company as an apparel rep. Prior to Nike, Zeedick worked in retail as a buyer and general manager at Joslins department store in Colorado. She grew up in Pennsylvania and completed her education at Indiana University of Pennsylvania.

that I was leading women's footwear, I never even met the person running women's apparel. Our businesses ran that separately."

One of the causes for these barriers arose from the different timelines each business had for bringing its products to market. Winslow explained:

In general, footwear runs on an 18-month product-creation cycle, from a seasonal kickoff to when product actually hits retail. In apparel, product development is decentralized, so they have four different product-creation engines: a global product-creation engine, a U.S. product-creation engine, an EMEA product-creation engine, and an Asia-Pacific product-creation engine. And they're all on different calendars. Some are 12 months, some are 14, and some are 16. Then, in the equipment business, they have seven different calendars because they have so many different product types—bags, socks, gloves, hand weights, and things like that. So you can see why it's so difficult to work together.

The challenges of coordinating across these calendars and different dimensions of the matrix were compounded by the fact that Nike developed products for four seasons a year, which meant that each business was managing multiple seasons at any given time.

Within each business unit (e.g., footwear, apparel, equipment), collaboration was not much easier. Ongoing collaboration was required between a business unit and critical functions at both the global and regional level. However, functional representatives were not always involved in important business activities on a timely basis. For example, the apparel team for running might not include individuals from brand marketing in the product creation process until designs were nearly finalized, which challenged Nike's ability to deliver an integrated point of view to the consumer. Furthermore, the global functions within the business units did not always share the same priorities with the regional teams. This meant that global programs were not always executed as planned, if the regions elected to adapt plans based on local issues, opportunities, and needs (see Exhibit 3 for an illustration of this situation).

Over the years, Nike considered adding gender to its matrixed organizational structure as a fourth dimension. However, each time this change was discussed, the company decided against it. "We felt like it would add too

Exhibit 3 Illustrative Representation of Centralized and Decentralized Functions within Nike's Footwear and Apparel Businesses

	Product Design	Product Development	Demand Planning	Manufacturing	Distribution	Sales	Customer Service
Footwear	C	C	D	C	D	D	D
Apparel	D	D	D	C	D	D	D

C = Centralized
D = Decentralized

Source: Compiled by authors based on information provided by Nike.

much additional complexity to an already complicated organization structure," recalled Winslow. As a result, efforts to more effectively address the women's market within Nike's male-dominated culture had been marked by "lots of fits and starts." According to Mindy Grossman, the company's former vice president of global apparel, "Some of the issue in the past was that there was a faction within the company that felt if we were successful in the women's business, it would erode our men's business and we would lose some of our testosterone. Clearly, that's not the case. If we can communicate through product and messaging to the female consumer, but do it in an appropriate Nike voice, we will enhance the brand, not detract from it." She continued:

To give the company credit, Nike has been a force in women's sports and fitness for a very long time. If you look at the efforts [with] Title IX[10] and the iconic "If You Let Me Play" ads, we've had a huge impact on the perception of women in sports. But we were not able to translate that success into a major impact on the business of our women's products. Nor were we able to have a broader impact on the consumer relative to her believing that Nike was a brand for her. There was a lot of verbal commitment within the company, but not a lot of true commitment, all the way, to defining what it really meant to be a brand for women.

For example, one of Nike's moves to better address the women's market came in the early to mid-1990s, when the company created a women's team within its product marketing group and signed endorsement contracts with female athletes such as Sheryl Swoopes, Lisa Leslie, Gabrielle Reece, and Mia Hamm. "They organized as a women's team, but we didn't change anything else in the system. There was no delineation between men's and women's product development, product design, or innovation. It was put a pink bow on it, and then call it a day," joked Mary Slayton, director of market intelligence. Winslow concurred, "It was merely a marketing effort: 'How do we create a dialogue with female consumers?'"

Next, in 1997, the footwear business dedicated three resources to bringing a women's perspective to its running category as more and more women were becoming active in that sport. A product line manager, a designer, and a developer were focused on creating running shoes for women (versus more than 12 resources dedicated to the men's running market). That small team slowly started building momentum.

"We had a designer who really helped influence our small team," recalled Seana Hannah, category footwear leader of women's training, who worked as part of the initial group. "I think because she was new to Nike, she could come in and just say, 'OK. Let's do this.' And she could sketch it out, and then people could start visualizing it and say 'You know what? That does feel different. It looks really different. And I could see women wanting to wear it.'" Before long, the team had developed a series of feminine yet athletic styles that sold just as well as Nike's traditional models at competitive price points. "But I still got the question every single day from within the organization: 'Why are we doing women's shoes again?'" said Hannah. "It was incredibly frustrating at times, and we had several shoes dropped early on in the process. It wasn't until a few key shoes sold extremely well that the larger team started truly paying attention to the women's opportunity."

After a few other experiments within the company, including strides made in the apparel business, Nike created its global women's footwear division in 2001. "That's when things really started to change," said Winslow. "There was a distinct delineation between our men's and women's teams, from innovation, design, marketing, development, product testing, all the way down." Until this time, many of the women's shoes had been built using molds for men that were then "taken down" to fit a women's foot, despite the fact that for any given foot length, women weighed 15 to 40 percent less than men (and therefore required different shoe designs and dynamics). But Winslow explained, "When we started the women's footwear division, every single shoe was made based on a woman's biomechanics. They had Shox™ for her, and the air bags were engineered with the right pounds per square inch, based on female rather than male weight. This was the point in time when all of this became nonnegotiable in our women's products." According to Hannah, who joined Winslow's women's footwear team from the running group, "The best part was not having to justify why we were doing women's shoes anymore[... being] dedicated to innovation for the women's market was also a big improvement, so we could take that technology and translate it into a fantastic product…."

As Winslow began building the global women's footwear business, another idea for addressing the women's market emerged: a retail and marketing project called Nike Goddess, which was intended to help the company rethink the way it sold its products to women.[11] In contrast to the male-oriented Niketown stores, Nike Goddess stores were meant to be women-only destinations (the name of these stores would later be changed to Nike Women). "We wanted them to be like a Starbucks for women, where they would want to go, hang out, and stay. And we wanted to offer one-on-one clienteling instead of the traditional customer service they'd get at another store," said Jodi Sitting, marketplace development director for global women's fitness, who was involved in helping develop the concept behind the marketing and customer service approach for the initial

Goddess stores. With a modern yet distinctly residential or "homey" feeling, the Goddess stores offered footwear, apparel, and equipment to its customers, loosely unified via Nike's corporate color palette.

When *Fast Company* wrote an article in mid-2002 that provided publicity for Nike's Goddess stores beyond the southern California market where they were located, Winslow remembered:

I started getting all these phone calls asking, "Where can I find the Goddess clothes?" And I said, "Goddess is a store where you can find Nike apparel and footwear." But I started thinking, "Why don't we have a Goddess collection?" So I pulled together a small team across footwear, apparel, [and] equipment to create these very small, very specialized, higher-priced collections that we would only sell at Nike women's stores to see if women would respond to them and buy from head to toe. We started planning our first Sport Lux collection in fall 2003 totally under the radar. But when it hit the market on February 14, 2005, it sold out almost immediately. That's when we knew for sure that we were on the right track.

Changing the Game

Concurrent with some of these important grass-roots efforts taking place within Nike to better address the women's market, Nike's senior management team initiated a study to identify the next big growth opportunities for the company. For about six months, a cross-functional team analyzed new sports categories and geographic markets, as well as the possibility of moving more aggressively into women's products. From this analysis, the five ideas with the highest potential were chosen to be part of a larger assessment project called "Change the Game." The senior management team wanted to know which of the five high potential opportunities—outdoor, bags, men's training, value footwear, and women—had what it would take to outpace growth in the rest of the business and drive the company's next leap forward. In March 2004, they designated a cross-functional task force for each of the five areas and gave them the mandate to validate the opportunities and present a case for how to enter this business.[12] Winslow was chosen to lead the women's "Change the Game" initiative with Grossman, Nike's highest-ranking female executive, serving as the executive sponsor.

The women's task force was made up of a core team of five or six men and women from different parts of the business who worked on the project as a "second job." Emma Minto, an external consultant brought on to play the role of the strategic lead, was the team's only dedicated resource.

Phase One

Minto described the first phase of the team's work, which occurred over the course of approximately six weeks:

Phase one started with getting a read internally on where we had been with the women's business: What had been our successes? What had been our challenges? I spent a lot of time talking to 40 or 50 people across the company about what the barriers had been to pushing the women's business forward in a bigger way. The second piece of the analysis was to get an external take on what was going on in the market. How do we define the market? How do we size it? We also spent a lot of time trying to understand our competitive position. The third piece was looking at the consumer. Around the globe, a lot of different work had been done [on] consumers in the women's market, but none of it had been pulled together. So we collected the internal research that we could find, as well as what was available externally.

Internally, the team confirmed that there were great initiatives under way in the business, the regions, and in specific categories to address the women's market, "But they were happening in their own pockets," said Winslow. "They weren't integrated, so we weren't leveraging our collective power."

In terms of the market, Winslow recalled, "It was clear that we were missing a huge business opportunity." Nike defined the women's fitness market as encompassing all of the fitness activities women performed in the gym, as well as running and walking outdoors (see Exhibit 4). While this definition clarified the scope of the Change the Game proposal, it did not easily correspond to available market data. Apparel data was particularly challenging due to the blurry boundaries between fitness and active wear. For example, "When you look at active wear, you start bringing in The Gap and Old Navy," said Winslow. "So we had to draw a line around the exact market that we were looking at and define who we felt were our true competitors. In the end, after a lot of triangulation, we estimated that it was about a $13 billion market, with most of this coming from the U.S., the big-five countries in Europe, and one or two countries in Asia." Roughly 25 percent of the market opportunity would be in footwear, with 70 percent in apparel, and the remainder coming from equipment. As for growth, the team estimated that the market was expanding at a rate of 5 to 8 percent per year, driven by trends in women's participation rates in new and established sports, gym memberships, and other related changes (see Exhibit 5).

From a competitive perspective, Nike faced off against a handful of traditional but well-respected brands in women's footwear, with Nike maintaining a leading position in some categories but not others. For example, Reebok dominated the market in women's aerobics, but

Exhibit 4 Definitions for Nike's Women's Business

women's fitness: Encompasses all the fitness sports women may choose to do for general fitness—in the gym plus outdoor running and walking.

fitness sport: One of several possible fitness activities performed by women to keep fit. Her equivalent of a man's "*sports.*" Activities she cares about.

portfolio: A group of related yet independent businesses, such as fitness sports.

sweat beauty: Nike's women's fitness target consumer. She's 22 … SUPER CONFIDENT, active, full-on, sassy, try anything, someone you'd go drinking with, sexy, adventurous, dynamic, youthful, fun … and she works out 3 to 5 times/week.

fitness dance: A fusion of dance styles and music blended with traditional cardio workout techniques; an outlet for creativity and expression beyond traditional fitness sports.

sexy: (slang) Highly appealing or interesting; attractive: "The clothes make me feel sexy."

full alignment: Arrangement of people, process, and technology to successfully deliver an integrated collection of FW, AP, and EQP to our consumer.

Source: Information provided by Nike.

Nike led in women's running from a market share and revenue perspective. However, "In apparel it's a much more fragmented business so our market share is much, much lower," said Winslow. The primary take-away for the team was that no single company, Nike included, had a dominant "mindshare" in the women's fitness market. For this reason, many of the company's competitors also appeared to be rethinking their positioning in the space. Adidas had started taking a different approach to the women's market by bringing on celebrity designer Stella McCartney to create fashionable athletic wear. While some argued that her designs were not practical from a performance perspective, they were successful in "waking up the fashion performance business," said Winslow. Puma introduced its Olive brand to try to break into the yoga market. Around the same time, New Balance launched cause-related marketing to attract women via connections to Race for the Cure.[13]

"In addition to the traditional competitors in our industry, there were lots of new and smaller competitors

Exhibit 5 Market Data–Women's Fitness

The Women's Fitness Market Is Growing Geometrically

Expanded Consumer Base
- 12 of the top 30 sport/activity participation categories are fitness related.
- Participation grew in every "fitness" sport activity between 2001 and 2002.
- 53 percent of the 36.3 million members at U.S. gyms are women. Membership doubled in 15 years.
- More than 40 percent of all Americans age 16 and over work out 2 or 3 times/week

Expanded Locations
- The number of U.S. gyms grew 20 percent from 2002 to 2003 to 22,000. The majority of the new facilities are targeted at women or are yoga/dance studios.
- A new *Curves* women's gym franchise opens every four hours. *Curves* is the fastest-growing franchise in the world. There is one *Curves* gym for every one-and-a-half McDonald's in the United States, and 25 percent of all gyms in the United States are *Curves* gyms.
- Conservatively, there are 63,000 gyms worldwide.
- The number of gyms in China tripled in two years to 350 in 2003. Imagine the growth by the 2008 Olympics.

Expanded Activity and Demands
- Pilates and Yoga represent two of the top three growth fitness activities. From 1998 to 2002, participation growth was 169 percent for Pilates training and 95 percent for Yoga/Tai Chi. Nearly 13.5 million people participated in Yoga in 2003: 83 percent were women.
- The number of gyms offering funk/hip hop dance classes increased 150 percent from 2001 to 2003, up to 33 percent.
- Dance/aerobic exercise was second only to cardio equipment in area expansion at U.S. gyms in 2002. Cardio, strength, and dance are priorities for area expansion in 2003 to 2004.
- In 2002, the number of personal trainers in the United States increased 20 percent to 80,000. Ninety-one percent of gyms offered personal training in 2003 versus 87 percent in 2002.
- Fitness has a significant halo on the total $13 billion Women's Active Sports Market.
- The global Women's Fitness Sport Market is $6.1 billion.

Source: IHRSA, Idea Fit, SGMA, Yankleovich Group, Time, June 2003, CBS on August 19, 2003; information provided by Nike.

that we also had to consider," commented Winslow. "Companies like Lulu Lemon, Under Armour, and Danskin were either taking a singular focus by category … or had entered the market through one category, but were now expanding into others. The competitive landscape was changing dramatically, and that altered how we needed to develop our competitive attack plan."

As Nike turned its attention to the female consumer, one of the most compelling statistics dealt with the sheer spending power of women—in the United States alone, the team calculated that women spent $7 trillion each year. The global brand team had recently defined Nike's target female customer: a 22-year-old, confident, slightly irreverent woman who wanted to work out hard and look good. The company referred to her as the "Sweat Beauty" consumer (see Exhibit 4). The women's Change the Game team did not have to research and redefine this target—it needed to figure out what she wanted, how she shopped, and how the company could connect with her. "We also had to figure out how she approached sports," added Minto.

According to Winslow, one of the things the team learned was that:

Women don't do fitness. They run, they walk, they do cardio machines, they dance, they go to yoga. So that's what led us to a micro-segmentation approach. Previously, most of our women's products were nonspecific, so women's real needs got marginalized. We discovered that we had to get much more specific regarding what's different about dance versus running versus cardio. Because any woman can tell you, for example, that it doesn't work to wear running shorts during yoga.

Minto concurred and summarized some of the other lessons from the team's consumer research:

We realized that the way that we were approaching the market was not in line with the consumer. She wanted to shop at the mall, in catalogs, and at boutiques on "High Street," but most of our distribution was through retail sporting goods stores. She wanted to have great athletic products made specifically for each of her sports, but we were offering her products for general "fitness." She wanted collections of footwear, apparel, and equipment, and we were cobbling existing products together. She also wanted to hear from us on a consistent basis and for us to really have a relationship with her, and we were still thinking in terms of initiatives (see Exhibit 6).

Finally, Nike had to figure out a new way to talk to female consumers. "If you look at the approach that Nike has taken over the years, which has been very successful, it's very, very competitive and uses the male elite athlete, hero-worship model. But that really doesn't work for women, so we had to think about a different way

Exhibit 6 Nike's Vision for Changing the Game in the Women's Market: Accelerating Women's Fitness to Women's Sports

From	To
"Initiative"	"A sustainable, profitable, brand enhancing portfolio of sport businesses where we are the aspirational brand of choice for her."
• Inconsistent Relationship with Consumer	• The Dominant Brand in Her Mind
• Color-based Collections	• Integrated, Concept-based Collections
• Inconsistent Retail Experience	• Consistent Defining Retail Experience Globally
• Isolated Initiatives	• Aligned Global Strategy
• Inconsistent, Inadequate Commitment and Resources	• Integrated, Fully Resourced Global Team
• Incremental, Isolated Business Opportunities	• Accelerated Global Business Opportunities

Source: Information provided by Nike.

to create a dialogue and an emotional connection with women," said Winslow.

Ultimately, the vision that the Change the Game team presented to the senior management team at the end of the first phase (April 2004) was to shift the focus of women's fitness from a series of broad initiatives to a sustainable, profitable, brand-enhancing portfolio of sports businesses that, in combination, would make Nike the aspirational brand of choice for women.

"We told them, 'If we continue to run the business the way we have been, we will continue to see incremental growth,'" recalled Winslow. "But, if we really want to take a leadership position, we're going to have to do things differently." The team proposed taking a three-tiered approach to the market. Tier one would be focused on dance. While this was nowhere near the largest micro-segment in the market, "We felt it had good revenue potential. It absolutely had energy associated with it. And nobody owned it. So this would become our 'sharp point' in terms of communicating with women," said Winslow. According to Slaytou, this decision also carried with it some important internal benefits:

The women's business was going to continue to languish unless they could find a way to fit it into the Nike mold.

Dance was young and edgy, and there were celebrity athletes to focus on in the space. So the executives could relate and see how dance would put something into Nike's brand bank rather than taking something out. Mindy and Darcy found a sharp point that fit the brand, knowing that underneath they would have to build a foundation of slightly less sexy stuff to pays the bills.

Tier two would include the categories where Nike already had some ownership in the market, yet there were opportunities to expand the business. These core fitness sports included cardio, running, walking. Tier three included other, smaller micro-segments where Nike had a presence (swim, cycling, Pilates) or wanted to focus to elevate the category to tier two (yoga) over time (see Exhibit 7).

"This way of organizing the women's business became a very powerful image for us as we started to think about going to market differently," explained Winslow. "Typically, when we went to market with a footwear product, we were on the footwear wall. Apparel was in another department, and bags were somewhere else. So, as part of our pitch to the senior executives, we talked about merchandizing by sport and have the apparel, the footwear, and the equipment all merchandised in the same area." Grossman referred

to this collection-based approach to retail as creating a "store within a store" for Nike's products. "It seemed so simple, but this represented a major change and was sure to be some of our most difficult work because retailers had been locked into their own way of doing business for decades," continued Winslow. It would also be a challenge internally since Nike operated its supply chain "as an item-driven business," said Maithili Shenoy, global director of supply chain strategy and development, and a part-time member of the Change the Game team who represented Nike's global operations group. "Our systems and processes are different across the businesses and are not set up to be able to deliver an integrated collection of products to the same place at the same time," she added.

According to Minto, Nike's senior executives were energized by the team's initial presentation "They told us, 'Okay, great. We like where you're going with your insight, so start building plans that will enable you to better line up with the consumer.'" The team was given until July to complete the next phase of business case development.

Phase Two
During phase two, the team focused on developing an overarching plan for approaching the women's market.

Exhibit 7 Nike's Proposed Approach to the Women's Fitness Market

Source: Compiled by authors based on information provided by Nike.

"Basically, we had to think through everything we'd do in product, in sales and retail, in marketing, and in the organization to get after the business," Minto summarized. Primary emphasis was placed on the team's sharp point, dance, as well as the three highest potential areas after that—cardio, running, and yoga.

One of the biggest challenges facing the team was how it would deliver its vision of presenting integrated collections to female consumers. "One of our big insights was this vision of delivering integrated head-to-toe collections of apparel and equipment, but we had to figure out how we were going to do that in an environment with three independent product engines all working on different timelines. So, we had a sub-team that went to work on trying to align the calendars and the processes and get everybody on the same page, with the same vision, the same priorities, for a given season against our specific sports," explained Minto.

As team members started to reach out to other parts of the organization to talk about calendar alignment, it became clear that there were few formal mechanisms in place that would help enable an integrated, cross-business approach to developing and bringing a women's collection to market. On the front end, as referenced earlier, the product creation engines in footwear, apparel, and equipment did not work together. When the company tried to bring something to market in a coordinated fashion (e.g., driven by a special initiative), "Footwear and equipment would be on the edge of their seats, saying 'We need to start working together right now because the gun's about to go off for us to create our line plans, our briefs, and our contracts.' But apparel would be sitting back saying, 'Okay, we understand that this is important, but it's not top of mind for us right now. We've got another five months before our line plans are due.' If we were really going to move forward with integrated collections, we had to get out in front of footwear and equipment," said Winslow.

On the back end, Nike's supply planning, sourcing, manufacturing, and delivery mechanisms also were not aligned across the businesses or regions. "Our supply chain was somewhat of a blunt instrument that was able to deal with averages," said Hans van Alebeek, Nike's executive vice president for operations and technology. "It was not a highly precise instrument that could deliver assortments to exactly the same date. It could do it reasonably well, but not precisely enough for the team looking at opportunities in women's fitness to feel as though they were delivering powerful stories to the retail floor through complete collections."

Despite these barriers, there were examples within the company where the concept of delivering integrated collections was working. In Europe, under the leadership of Loredana Ranza, the regional women's team had learned how to "manually handhold the process to make sure it delivered the core of a collection to the stores when they wanted it there," noted van Alebeek. The Change the Game team studied the European process and used it as a basis for developing a similar process that could be leveraged across all regions, which they called the Integrated Calendar Alignment process. "There were lessons learned in Europe that convinced us this was feasible," said Shenoy, who worked for van Alebeek. The proposed approach took a 21-month view of the product creation and delivery processes across footwear, apparel, and equipment as well as brand marketing. Critical activities and decisions were synchronized through the creation of six joint milestones (see Exhibit 8):

1. **Seasonal Kickoff and Creative Direction** (end of month 2) – Integrated meeting to set seasonal creative direction, confirm seasonal themes, and build key stories.

2. **Design Review** (end of month 9) – Integrated creative meeting to review product design in all fitness sports, across all business units.

3. **Prototype Review** (end of month 10) – Planning and prioritization for the brand, retail, sales, and the regions.

4. **Go-to-Market Strategy** (beginning of month 12) – Presentation of the go-to-market plan by brand, retail, sales, and the regions.

5. **Prelines** (middle of month 13) – Product groups and brand presents an integrated collection to key accounts in multiple regions.

6. **Brand Execution and Post-Season Review** (beginning of month 15) – Brand plans presented and evaluation of seasonal planning and booking results.

The process was designed to culminate six months later with the delivery of the integrated collections to retail, as well as Nike's other distribution channels. Activities between these key milestones would be coordinated through weekly virtual team meetings in which individuals from each business, region, and function were expected to report on their progress and raise issues that would help sustain alignment.

After working through this process, Winslow (as the head of global women's footwear) and Jamie Shierk (as the head of global women's apparel) made a decision to initiate the development of an integrated collection of footwear, apparel, and equipment in the women's dance category prior to receiving approval from Nike's executive team to formally organize around the women's business. "Nobody was really in charge. But Jamie and I assumed responsibility, with Mindy's sponsorship, because we felt like we had to push it forward," recalled Winslow.

Exhibit 8 Global Women's Fitness-Integrated Calendar Alignment Process

Grossman explained: "I felt that there was support for where we were going, so there was limited risk to our decision. Even if we didn't get approval to formally pursue the women's business from an integrated perspective, a dance collection would still provide a better consumer proposition. The only potential downside was that it would require a tremendous amount of additional work from certain members of the organization because we didn't have a syncopated process or structure yet."

Under the radar, the team brought together the right individuals from across the businesses, regions, and functions in July 2004 for a spring 2006 seasonal kick-off. Winslow recalled the excitement: "Everyone sitting around that table came to participate, not because their managers told them to, but because they knew this was the right path forward." Then, with a common vision, they quietly got to work on developing the company's first integrated dance collection.

Concurrently, the Change the Game team made its next presentation to Nike's senior executives. The group presented an overall strategy for approaching the women's market, as well as the detailed plans for executing the strategy. Again, the executives were supportive and told the group to prepare the final aspects of its business case for presentation in three months.

Phase Three

In preparing for the third and final presentation to Nike's executive team, Minto described the team's effort.

"Between August and October, we focused on two primary work streams: (1) how we would organize and, (2) how much money we needed. It was one thing for everyone to say in July, 'We love your ideas.' But we were asking for more than just support to organize. We needed the company to make an investment in the women's business," she said.

Minto spent a great deal of time creating models to estimate the amount of additional revenue the women's business could expect to drive through an integrated approach, as well as how much of an incremental investment would be required to support the vision. "Then I went out to the regions again, and talked with representatives from footwear, apparel, and equipment to perform a sanity check on the numbers," she recalled. "It was important to do that because, when we were going to ask for money, I needed to make sure that the four regional VPs and the three BU VPs would all say, 'Yes, I've talked to this group and I'm comfortable with the projections that are being made.'"

The other piece of work was designing the organization. Jim Sutton, global HR director for apparel, was brought on to the team to help think through what structure, positions, and people would be required to enable the new group to execute the strategy. "In the past, we might assign a highly respected, key person to take charge of driving a virtual team," Sutton explained. That model had worked successfully on certain initiatives, but had not been as well received for efforts that were meant to be sustained over a longer period of time. "We relatively quickly determined that the women's business was too large an opportunity with significant complexity to work on a virtual team basis. We needed a core team of dedicated resources to make it work," he said. "But that meant we would exist outside the matrix," recalled Minto, which was a "big deal" because it could significantly limit the team's formal authority to drive decisions and make things happen. "Ultimately, we proposed what I would call a semi-virtual organization," said Grossman. Until the women's team could prove its model (by outpacing growth in the rest of the company), it recognized that creating a dedicated, cross-functional unit that added another dimension to the matrix was out of the question. "There was obviously a part of the organization that would have to work via influence. But there would be a group of people, not just an individual, along with other resources that would help make things easier," she added (see Exhibit 9).

The next challenge was to define the specific positions that would make up the global women's fitness core team (or "virtual leadership team," as it was called) and then develop high-level position descriptions outlining the responsibilities of each role (see Exhibit 10). The first position created was the role of the general manager to lead the global women's fitness business and report to Grossman, who would continue as the acting sponsor for women's fitness. One of the next positions developed was the role of the strategic planner to manage strategic integration, operations, and finance. To address the issues associated with the collection-based approach, Winslow and the team also proposed a new position,

called the global marketplace development director, who would be responsible for developing and executing the new retail and merchandising strategy. They also created an ongoing, part-time role for a member of the operations team to work with global women's fitness, helping the group get product collections to market.

In an effort to have a lean core team, Winslow experimented with the creation of "leveraged positions." She described the model this way:

We started looking at how we could leverage existing people to take on a slightly greater amount of responsibility across the business units. For example, there was a creative director for women's footwear, a creative director for women's apparel, and several creative directors in equipment. What we didn't want to do is create an additional creative director role that only would be responsible for organizing the efforts of these individuals, rather than actually designing footwear, apparel, or equipment. So what we decided was to take the strongest person within the design function and make that job a leveraged director role. We did the same thing in innovation and merchandising.

The people who ultimately filled these leveraged roles would maintain their business unit–specific responsibilities while also coordinating across BUs to ensure that a cohesive design, innovation, and merchandising agenda and story were achieved in each of the women's sports categories. To make the model work, a small percentage of their regular duties would be offloaded to create bandwidth for the new aspects of the role.

When actually preparing the final presentation for the executive team, said Minto, "The other thing we did

Exhibit 9 Global Women's Fitness: Proposed Organization

Source: Information provided by Nike.

Exhibit 10 Global Women's Fitness Proposed Core Team Position Descriptions

Corporate Women's Fitness Sponsor
- Champion of Women's Fitness business at corporate level
- Direct manager of Women's Fitness GM
- Communication to PHK & BOD, Co-President and VPs
- Provides strategic direction
- Facilitates buy-in at CSR
- "Down Field Blocking"
- Owns $ and integration with Supply Chain and Retail

Women's Fitness GM
- Creates and drives execution of the Women's Fitness strategy
- Owns portfolio of fitness-sport businesses
- Owns alignment process across business units and regions
- Drives global vision for retail presentation and rollout for Women's Fitness
- Leads efforts globally to identify and drive new channels of distribution
- Manages Women's Fitness leadership team (direct & indirect reports)
  - Contributes to HRP/Org Development
- Ambassador for Nike's Women's Fitness Sport businesses, internally and externally

Director, Marketplace Development
- Develops and drives vision for retail presentation in market
- Creates and manages global showrooms
- Identifies and helps to develop priority markets for Women's Fitness
- Leads efforts globally to identify and drive new distribution channels for Women's Fitness
- Leads integration of sales into Global Women's Fitness

Director, Strategic Planning
- Partners with Women's Fitness GM to develop overarching and portfolio global business plans
- Owns financial planning and reporting for Women's Fitness
- Drives strategic analysis (competitive/consumer/channel/market size, etc.)
- Drives business development—integration with existing businesses and new business
- Works with global operations strategic planning to drive supply chain and demand planning with regions

  (Note: The directors of marketplace development and strategic planning reported directly to the GM of Women's Fitness.)

Innovation Director
- Functional lead for Women's Fitness GM for Innovation
- Leads the thinking around creative problem solving for Women's Fitness Sports consumer
- Organizes the logistics to work successfully across FW, AP, & EQP
- Demonstrates the ability to see, understand, and drive toward the vision of the new retail reality for the targeted consumer
- Owns integrated innovation map (3 to 5 years) for Women's Fitness Sports

Creative Director
- Functional lead for Women's Fitness GM for Creative Design Direction
- Leads the thinking around creative problem solving for Women's Fitness Sports consumer
- Organizes the logistics to work successfully across FW, AP, & EQP
- Demonstrates the ability to see, understand, and drive toward the vision of the new retail reality for the targeted consumer
- Owns seasonal creative direction across FW, AP, & EQP

Merchandizing Director
- Functional lead for Women's Fitness GM for Merchandising
- Leads the thinking around creative problem solving for Women's Fitness Sports consumer
- Organizes the logistics to work successfully across FW, AP, & EQP
- Demonstrates the ability to see, understand and drive toward the vision of the new retail reality for the targeted consumer
- Primary communicator for FW, AP, & EQP
- Aligns flow, delivery, and color across FW, AP, & EQP
- Aligns consumer profiles across FW, AP, & EQP

Operations Director
- Functional lead for Women's Fitness GM for Operations
- Coordinates communication and shared learning across global product engines, regional product engines, and regional operations
- Leads creation of a formalized process for collection delivery (versus current ad hoc systems)

Note: These positions reported directly to their business unit or global function leaders, with a secondary reporting relationship to the GM of Women's Fitness.

Source: Information provided by Nike.

was look at all the great work we had already begun for the global launch of an integrated dance collection and we used it to say, 'Guess what? The strategy has already been initiated. We've already got the shared vision and a shared approach to the business. We've identified how we're going to align, and check out what we've already done for spring 2006.' And the reaction was, 'Wow, it's already happening. It's moving. It's possible to do.'" Winslow added, "We had learned a lot from our first integrated kickoff meeting and the work we did together over the next three months before the October presentation. So we had some real anecdotes to share with the executives to support our case."

Then Grossman made the pitch. According to Minto, "She said, 'Here's the investment I'm asking for, and here's why and how it's going to give you a payback.' She went in with the attitude, 'You either say yes or no now. But we're not going to continue to develop the business case. You're either in or you're out, because we want to get going.'" In the end, the team's passion and direct approach paid off. "Out of the five Change the Game opportunities, women's fitness was the only group that got the green light to go forth and organize," said Winslow. "We were given enough money to create 20 new positions [out of the 24 the team requested], not only for the core team, but also for roles within the business units and regions to ensure that we had adequate resources to execute on the business strategy that we had developed and presented." Summarizing the outcome, Grossman said, "This was truly a Change the Game commitment that would enable us to work toward a dominant position in the women's business and create an incredible emotional attachment to that consumer."

Making It Happen

Following this important approval milestone, one of the first things Grossman did was to hire Winslow in the GM role for global women's fitness, effective January 1, 2005. She explained the choice:

Darcy had tremendous credibility. She'd been at the company for some time. She was respected for her knowledge of the brand, meaning she wouldn't do anything that wouldn't be right for Nike. She had huge technical knowledge, as well as leadership and people skills. She had already been running the women's business in footwear and had achieved success. And, she really had a passion for it. Plus, she had been working closely with me on leading the Change the Game project and had presented to the executives. I think if it wasn't Darcy, it would have been a surprise because of how strong a leader she had been.

Winslow next began building her team. According to Grossman, "Darcy needed a dream team to staff these core positions. She needed people who, like her, had influence in the organization, solid reputations, good communication skills, and a deep passion for the women's business. It was very important that anyone on that core team be able to get the buy-in across the organization for what they wanted to do." Using these criteria, Winslow hand-picked Minto to fill the strategic planning role and Sittig to fill the marketplace development position. These two women, along with an administrative assistant, would report directly to Winslow, while all other members of the semi-virtual team would have dual reporting relationships, with a secondary responsibility to the women's team.

Early on, Winslow, Minto, and Sittig created a "people map" to help them navigate Nike's complex internal organization. "The people map reflected who the major decision-makers were by product type, region, and function that were associated with the women's business," Winslow explained. "But one of the challenges was that almost every person on the map had multiple responsibilities. So they weren't just dedicated to women's." While this could make it harder to get their mindshare in supporting the women's business, the map was useful in helping the team identify those with whom they should be working and all the players within the organization that needed to be better coordinated.

"Having been here for so long, many of us knew a large percentage of the community," said Winslow. "For example, the fact that I started in the sport research lab doing testing and research on athletes and then moved into product-testing gave me a real in-depth knowledge of how those two areas function. I also had some good old buddies down there—I still do—who could help us drive important changes." She continued, "But there were still important players in the company that none of us had ever met. We found that it was more challenging to engage these people, particularly in a way that was not threatening or controlling, but more engaging and collaborative." One strategy used by the team was to spend more time listening than talking or trying to influence them in some of the early meetings. "You can't just jump in and start influencing people," said Sittig. "You have to prove yourself and earn their trust by really listening and helping them by adding value. For the first six months, we spent a lot of time understanding other peoples' needs and building these types of relationships."

Even among the core team's known allies, however, some individuals wanted to proceed cautiously regarding the women's fitness business. Winslow offered as an example the reaction she got from her boss, the executive in charge of global footwear, when she made the move to global women's fitness:

Footwear had a lot at stake. It's the biggest part of Nike's business. And none of us really knew if the changes in our women's fitness strategy potentially would put other parts of the business at risk or negatively affect day-to-day operations. I mean, if our goal was just to grow the women's fitness business, we could cannibalize the women's running business to make this happen. We could trade off between our own businesses instead of taking market share from our competitors. So that's why my boss told me I had 51 percent of his support. This was a symbolic way of saying "I'm with you, but I've got some reservations."

The challenge to the women's fitness team was to make "believers" out of these kinds of supporters and skeptics alike. To help accomplish this, Winslow recognized the need for an integrated strategy for the global women's fitness team. However, because each of the areas represented in Nike's matrix created their own strategies somewhat in isolation of the others, this would be no easy feat to accomplish. Typically, Nike developed a three-year corporate strategy that was then used by the regions and businesses to develop their own strategies that supported the overall corporate plan. Winslow described it as a "trickle-down process." She went on to explain the approach she took to crafting a complementary strategy for women's fitness: "What I had to do was take the footwear, apparel, and equipment business strategies and the regional ones as they applied to the women's business and then start to cut across to build our own strategy that supported the corporate strategy. We did not go off-track, for example, from what footwear's plan was. But we did make it more specific and enhanced it relative to the women's fitness market."

Simultaneously, the team worked to define metrics and incentives to help motivate, drive, and track desired performance related to global women's fitness. "We developed a scorecard around the women's business," said Grossman, "that captured market share, financial goals, commitment to marketing, and growth." Winslow was held accountable for meeting these numbers, "even though, ultimately, I have very little direct control," she commented. "My job is to drive the organizations to come together in an integrated fashion to have an overall impact on the business. So, in some ways, I'm being measured against the process." Minto and Sittig were similarly measured on the results of the overall women's fitness business, although accessing the required data proved to be difficult. "Our systems weren't set up to be able to capture integrated results. It turned out to be relatively time-intensive and manually intensive to figure out what kind of an impact we were having on the business," noted Winslow.

Most of the other members of the global fitness women's team continued to be measured first and foremost on the results they achieved that supported their primary reporting relationships. "For those people on the team who reported into footwear and apparel, even though they knew the importance of the integrated women's collection, their number one goal was to sell shoes or clothes. Their number one goal was *not* to

integrate," offered Barbara Sumner, creative director for integrated footwear, apparel, and equipment, as an example. That said, Winslow provided input into their performance reviews and had a voice in recognizing outstanding performance, as well as raising issues.

As for incentives, "There were added responsibilities for some roles, but there were not a lot of added incentives," said Sittig. "As a group, Darcy, Emma, and I opted to reward and thank people who went above and beyond the call of duty in their second role as a part of the global women's fitness team, but this was not part of the regular bonus structure. We were able to give cash bonuses to some people, but they didn't know at the beginning of the year that they would be getting them." Shierk concurred, "There was not a lot of attention paid to additional motivation, if you will. Large scale change management is not necessarily one of Nike's strengths—it's something we're still learning." However, as she pointed out, "The women's team was so passionate that there wasn't a pervasive need to motivate. The motivation was already there. And, if anything, the fact that the company was now directly investing in this market made it even more motivating."

Operationally, the integrated product development process was already in motion with the spring 2006 dance collection. However, it required constant attention to keep the effort aligned considering the vast inherent differences in how the groups were used to working. Using an analogy, Slayton explained, "You go to a chiropractor and you get adjusted. But it's not over. You have to go back the next week and get readjusted because your body will naturally go back to the way it's accustomed to aligning. You have to keep going back. Our organization is the same way. Unless we keep getting adjusted, we always go back to being footwear-focused and male-focused because that is our core skeleton."

Sumner provided another specific example: "One time I saw a piece of footwear that was supposed to be part of the collection but I didn't even recognize it. It had completely changed through the footwear process and the information was not shared with the rest of the group." Weekly or bi-weekly meetings (depending on the needs of each sub-team) were meant to help prevent such disconnects, but things still slipped through the cracks as people juggled heavy meeting schedules and competing priorities.

This problem intensified as the global women's fitness team sought to expand beyond the spring 2006 season to additional categories and multiple seasons. "We had started with one season but, after we got approval, we had to start adding multiple seasons. So it very quickly got more complex, and it took a lot more energy to keep everything lined up," said Minto. Shierk added, "People underestimated the impact that it was going to have to people's travel schedules and their meeting schedules, which are already crazy at Nike because we are a matrixed organization and we work in these teams that have to influence each, other in the absence of direct reporting structures. So, it had a broader impact on people's physical time in their job than we initially accounted for."

Another challenge for the women's fitness business was that it was no longer about providing generic "training" products to female consumers. "We were about cardio, running, yoga, and dance. And we needed to start treating these categories like four discrete businesses," said Minto. "To drive this mentality, we set up virtual fitness sport teams and named captains from the various product groups to lead the focus in these areas through integrated teams." Winslow elaborated:

To move from a product-based organization to a consumer-based organization, we needed these team captains to step up and run the categories across the business units, regions, and functions. And so it was another example of asking somebody to take on additional duties, and to work across the organization. For example, when it was time for a seasonal kickoff, the captain for the category would pull together the right people and craft a three-year business plan for that particular sport. This helped us make sure that the right people came together at the right time and went out into the market to gather trend data, inspiration, and ensure that they kicked the season off holding hands. It's a tough proposition for someone to manage, but we looked at it as a developmental opportunity to learn how to affect change in a business through influence and relationship-building.

This additional layer of structure added even more meetings and demands on everyone's time. However, as Winslow and Grossman promoted the global women's fitness concept through a "road show" throughout the company, enthusiasm and commitment remained high. "People wanted it to be successful. And so they came to meetings. They showed up and they brought the people that we needed from their teams, too," said Minto. Sittig added:

But what happened about six to nine months into the project was that everyone stopped talking about it. The road show was over and senior management stopped talking about it purposely, so that we could actually do the work. And I think that spooked people a little bit. It gave the team the feeling that this was not a primary focus for the company anymore and maybe helping us wasn't a priority, which was exactly the opposite of what was intended. We had to say, "We're still a focus—they're just letting us do our work and giving us a break from doing internal presentations!"

This issue was compounded by changes within the semi-virtual team. "As different people came in and out of the business, it was challenging to replicate the same level of passion and involvement that we had with the original team," said Minto. "How do you keep a new player aligned with the strategy when they want to rethink their individual piece of the business? How do you keep the same level of momentum and goodwill when they haven't been involved since the beginning?" she added. This challenge was particularly pronounced at the higher levels of the organization. "When you start getting disengagement from the senior team, that's when you create a lot of unnecessary work and tension by virtue of the lack of organizational accountability or support," noted Lesnard.

Commenting on the overall reaction the global women's fitness team received from the Nike organization, Grossman felt that it was generally positive and supportive. The problem, she said, was just that, "There are so many competing priorities. It's a very complex organization with so many different businesses in a hundred different countries. Every day we have to compete for resources. So any pushback we got was really more about capacity—organizational capacity, resource capacity, and how many things people can be expected to do at any one time."

Delivering the Integrated Dance Collection for Spring 2006

When the Change the Game team decided to develop dance as a category within global women's fitness and initiate the development of the first integrated collection, the team was building on successes that had been realized in the EMEA region. Not only had EMEA started developing and delivering integrated collections, but it had already entered the dance market. "In the three years that we have gone after this plan, we've taken dance from almost nothing to roughly 42 percent of our women's fitness sports business," said Pat Zeedick, general manager of equipment for EMEA and the virtual general manager for the region's women's business. Importantly, EMEA was the only region that had designated a general manager role focused on driving the women's business at the regional level.

According to Zeedick, "When we looked at our consumer in Europe, she wasn't driven by 'I want a perfect body. I want to compete. I'm an athlete.' Her position was, 'Hey, exercise should be social, it should be fun. And, for me that means dance. So talk to me about something that I have a passion for and love to do, but at the same time is a blast and I can do with my friends and then go out afterwards.'" Targeting this consumer with footwear, apparel, and equipment designed especially for dancers' needs and high-energy TV commercials geared to three different segments of consumers (an elite athlete, a group of women seeking exercise as well as a social connection, and an "everywoman"), the European market started to take off.

The global women's fitness team latched on to this positioning as it started to design its first integrated dance collection. "This was a great way for us to make the point that sportswear could be fashionable and trendy, because dancers would rather suffer in order to look good than just get the right product," said Lesnard. Through the "super-human" efforts of the semi-virtual team, the integrated product development effort moved forward, producing a holistic, innovative collection that exceeded even the team's own expectations. However, creating the products was only one part of the challenge. Grossman explained:

The biggest issue in my mind was being able to create at the point of the consumer touchpoint the experience that we wanted the consumer to have. We can develop great products that fit into an integrated collection, but it will be meaningless unless it gets executed effectively at retail so that the customer experiences it as intended. We had our own Nike women's stores where we were able to execute as planned, but that was a limited number. Certainly, on the Web, we could tell an integrated story. But, it was much harder to change the way we communicate to the consumer in a traditional retail store setting.

Not only was there resistance from retailers who were reluctant to change their traditional merchandising practices or allocate more floor space to Nike (at the expense of other suppliers), but also the problems within Nike's supply chain made delivery of the collections difficult. "We tended to work with month-long delivery windows, which meant that our customers could be sitting for three weeks with shoes and shorts but no tops to complement them as intended in the collection," described van Alebeek. "The retailers don't really want to put products out on the floor until they have the complete assortment. What we found was that a lot of micromanagement of our existing processes was needed to make sure that we delivered more complete assortments to customers across product types."

"So, the process had to be manually overridden to ensure that our dance products hit the stores at the same time, in 6,000 doors," said Winslow. "We did it, but the process was not sustainable. There was no way they could manually handle that for each sport for each season, season after season after season. That has sparked a lot of investment in our supply chain operations to figure out how to better integrate our supply chain processes across divisions." Van Alebeek added, "We were able to do it in places where we put experienced people on the project. But it wasn't scaleable. Our next challenge is to scale up our ability to do this for multiple businesses at larger volumes as we move from an items business to a collections business."

Going forward, a greater level of prioritization also would be required. For example, "If you actually do a bit of analysis, you realize that with 20 percent of the styles, you get 95 percent of the business. If you can deliver those on time and as a collection, you've basically taken care of 95 percent of your business. And that means as you start working with factories and prioritizing what needs to be done and what may need to be air-freighted in, you're actually not talking about the whole collection, you're talking about a piece of it, which makes it more manageable," said van Alebeek. Shenoy offered another example, "We've got so many doors to deliver to, that it's not necessarily practical to think that we can do this for everyone. We have to figure out which doors are most important to total sales and give them priority when it comes to delivering a collection. Otherwise, if everything is a priority, then nothing is a priority."

Despite these barriers, the first integrated dance collection was considered a success on multiple levels, including its contribution to Nike's brand in the women's fitness market, the products themselves, and as a catalyst for driving the new, integrated approach to the women's fitness market. Furthermore, as improved integration took root, new opportunities were discovered to increase leverage. For example, in the EMEA region, the team experimented with an integrated sales approach for two of the company's biggest accounts in the United Kingdom. Winslow explained, "Historically, it's always been that footwear, apparel, and equipment did their sales pitch separately to different buyers within a company. But this time, they got together to tell the whole story and pitch the whole line. When the bag buyers saw the dance bag and could see how it went with the apparel and footwear, they bought 200 percent more than normal because they understood the power of the collection." Shortly thereafter, all EMEA countries (except one) had adopted the integrated new sell-in approach, and it was being considered in other regions.

Looking Forward

Reflecting on the experiences of the global women's fitness team, as well as the larger women's effort at Nike over the years, Grossman said, "The biggest issue for me was that the change was slow. Sometimes it felt like we took three steps forward and two steps backwards, because we really had." While also bothered by the pace of change at times, Hannah offered this perspective: "I think that earlier efforts were required to plant the seed. Then we had to do it in running and other parts of the business so that the organization was ready when Darcy and Mindy really stepped up and fought to get the resources. So, as frustrating as it was, I see now how it almost had to be an incremental change to affect the behavior and attitude of the greater organization." "It wasn't just about changing the products," Grossman added. "It was about changing the company's culture, perceptions, and commitment." (See Exhibit 11 for

Exhibit 11 Global Women's Fitness—Sample from 2006 Print Ad Campaign

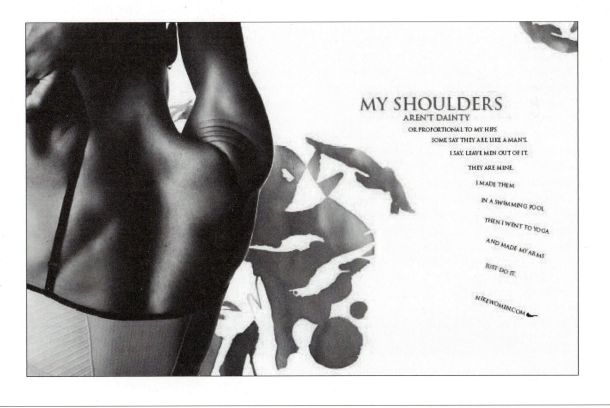

(Continued)

Exhibit 11 Global Women's Fitness—Sample from 2006 Print Ad Campaign (*Continued*)

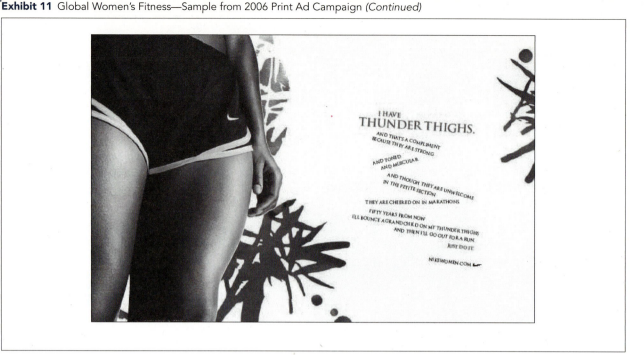

Source: Information provided by Nike.

sample print ads from one of the global women's fitness team's 2006 campaigns.)

As Winslow prepared to transition out of her role as the general manager for global women's fitness as part of Nike's shift to a category-driven organization, she noted, "It's been a challenging two years. But we have learned so much that will be valuable to Nike as we move forward." In fact, the achievements of the global women's fitness team, as well as other groups such as football (soccer) and golf, had served as a model and an important input into the company's decision regarding how to restructure. As Charlie Denson, president of Nike Brand and one of the company's top executives, put it, "We are operating in a very, very complex multidimensional business environment, and one of the things that we feel very strongly about … is that we can do a much better job continuing to grow the business by breaking it down into smaller pieces and getting more focused and deeper involvement and connectivity with key groups of consumers. We've looked at it many different ways, and

we feel that the category approach is the best way to get after this thing."[14]

Having lived through this transition in advance of the rest of the organization, one question facing Winslow was what specific advice and recommendations she could make to help Nike orchestrate the change more quickly and on a larger scale. Another question was what new challenges, barriers, or trade-offs would be uncovered, for global women's fitness as well as the other businesses, as the company abandoned its product-driven mentality in favor of a more consumer-oriented approach. For example, while the women's market would now be formalized as an important part of Nike's corporate strategy, women's running (which had previously been an important and sizable part of Winslow's global women's fitness team) would now be managed by the running category. Nike had to consider how these types of issues would affect the company's efforts in the women's market from both an internal and external perspective.

NOTES

1. When Nike's senior management team established its golf business, the leader appointed to run the group negotiated to have it set up separate from the larger Nike organization, with its own profit-and-loss statement. The golf business has been run this way ever since.

2. Nikebiz.com, 2007, Heritage, http://www.nike.com/nikebiz/nikebiz.jhtml?page=5, February 7.

3. 2006, Nike, Inc. reports fiscal 2006 earnings per share growth of 18 percent, http://www.nike.con/nikebiz/investors/eaniings/docs/q406.pdf, bsessionid =TLL CDPGTWYSGCCOFTC2SF5AKA WMLOIZB, June 27 (accessed February 7, 2007).

4. Nikebiz.com, 2007, Product technology, http://www.nike.com/nikebiz.jhtml?page=6, February 8.

5. Nike, Inc. reports fiscal 2006 earnings per share growth of 18 percent, op cit.

6. 2006, Adidas World Cup shout out, *BusinessWeek Online*, April 3, http://www.businessweek.com/magazine/content/06 14/b3978079 .htm (accessed February 8, 2007).

7. MarketResearch.com, 2005, Performance apparel markets, October 1, http://www.marketresearch.com/product/display .asp?productid=1186623&g=1 (accessed February 8, 2007).

8. Regionally, in fiscal 2006, the United States accounted for approximately 44 percent of Nike's business, EMEA 33 percent, AP 16 percent, and the Americas 7 percent.

9. All quotations from Nike employees are from interviews conducted with the authors in late 2006, unless otherwise cited.

10. Title IX of the Educational Amendments of 1972 bans sex discrimination in school in both academics and athletics.

11. F. Warner, 2006, Finding the goddess within, *Shattered*, September, 53.

12. To "get after" something is a common Nike expression, meaning that the project will be aggressively pursued.

13. The Susan G. Komen "Race for the Cure" (the world's largest series of 5K runs and fitness walks) raises significant funds and awareness for the fight against breast cancer, celebrates breast cancer survivorship, and honors those who have lost their battle with the disease.

14. SeekingAlpha.com, 2006, Nike F1Q07 earnings call transcript, http://retail.seekingalpha.com/article/17351, September 21 (accessed February 7, 2007).

Nintendo's Disruptive Strategy: Implications for the Video Game Industry

Havovi Joshi, Samuel Tsang

The University of Hong Kong, Asia Case Research Centre

For some time we have believed the game industry is ready for disruption. Not just from Nintendo, but from all game developers. It is what we all need to expand our audience. It is what we all need to expand our imaginations.

— **SATORU IWATA**
  PRESIDENT OF NINTENDO CO. LTD[1]

In the 2008 *BusinessWeek*–Boston Consulting Group ranking of the world's most innovative companies, Nintendo Co. Ltd ("Nintendo") was ranked seventh, up from thirty-ninth the previous year.[2] This improvement was in recognition of Nintendo's transformation into an innovative design powerhouse that challenged the video game industry's prevailing business model.

In 2000, when Sony, Microsoft, and Nintendo (the "big three" of the video game console manufacturers) released their latest products, Sony's PlayStation 2 (PS2) emerged as the clear winner, outselling Microsoft's Xbox, and Nintendo's GameCube. In 2006, these players introduced a new generation of video game consoles, precipitating a new competitive battle in the industry. Microsoft and Sony continued with their previous strategy of increasing the computing power of their newest products and adding a more impressive graphical interface. However, Satoru Iwata, president of Nintendo, believed that the video game industry had been focusing far too much on existing gamers and completely neglecting non-gamers. In light of this belief, the company repositioned itself by developing a radically different console, the Wii (pronounced "we"). The Wii was an interesting machine that used a wand-like remote controller to detect players' hand movements, allowing them to emulate the real-life play of such games as tennis, bowling, and boxing.

The new console proved to be a runaway success. By September 2007, Nintendo had become Japan's most valuable listed company after Toyota, and its market value had tripled since the launch of the Wii. In spite of this initial success, however, it was not clear whether Nintendo had really disrupted the industry and significantly changed the dynamics of competition in it.

History of Nintendo, 1889 to 2002

Nintendo's[3] roots could be traced all the way back to 1889 in Kyoto, Japan, when Fusajiro Yamauchi, the founder of the company, started manufacturing playing cards. In 1907, the company began producing Western playing cards, and by 1951, it had become the Nintendo Playing Card Company. In 1959, it began making theme cards under a licensing agreement with Walt Disney Company; by 1963, the company had gone public and taken its current name. During the period 1970 to 1985, Nintendo began focusing on the manufacture of electronic toys and entered the emerging field of video games (see Exhibit 1).

Interestingly, 1991, the year Nintendo launched the highly popular Super NES in the United States, was also the year Nintendo's vision become Sony's opportunity—and the creation of what could be described as Nintendo's "greatest challenge" for over a decade—the Sony PlayStation (PS). Nintendo had wanted to incorporate CD-ROM into its Super NES, and Sony had agreed to create the PS for this purpose. However, over the next two years there were many conflicts of vision between Nintendo and Sony, and the two finally parted ways. Nintendo went ahead with Philips

Exhibit 1 The History of Nintendo, 1889 to 2002

1889	Fusajiro Yamauchi, the founder of the company, began manufacturing and selling Japanese playing cards.
1907	The company began producing Western playing cards.
1951	Begins using the name "Nintendo Playing Card Company Ltd."
1959	Nintendo began making theme cards under a licensing agreement with Disney.
1962–63	The company went public and took its current name.
1970	Nintendo began focusing on the manufacture of electronic toys and entered the emerging field of video games by licensing Magnavox's Pong technology.
1977	Nintendo developed its first home video game machines, Color TV Game 15 and Color TV Game 6.
1980	Nintendo established its U.S. subsidiary, Nintendo of America. Developed and started selling the first portable LCD video games with a microprocessor.
1981	One of Nintendo's most famous coin-operated games, "Donkey Kong," appeared and was an instant hit in both the United States and Japan.
1983	Nintendo expanded its product range from games and arcade machines to home consoles, and the company released Famicom, a technologically advanced home video game system, in Japan. With its high-quality sound and graphics, Famicom was a huge hit, dominating the Japanese market.
1985	Nintendo successfully launched Famicom in the United States as the Nintendo Entertainment System (NES). The company then marketed a follow-up version of "Super Mario Bros." for the NES, and this classic game helped the NES become a resounding success.
1989	Nintendo released a new console, the Game Boy. The Game Boy was the first major product in the handheld game console industry and became immensely popular because of its portability and accessibility.
1990–92	In 1990, Nintendo launched the Super Family Computer game system in Japan, which also did very well. A year later, the same product was launched as the Super NES in the United States. In 1992, Super NES was released in Europe.
1994	Nintendo formed design alliances with companies such as Silicon Graphics. Released the Super Game Boy, a peripheral for the Super NES, which enabled Game Boy software to be played on the TV screen.
1995	Introduced a 32-bit Virtual Immersion System, known as the "Virtual Boy."
1996	Nintendo launched its 64-bit N64 game system. It launched "Pokémon" on the Game Boy: the game involved trading and training virtual monsters and was the first in a hugely popular video-game series. The company also released another blockbuster video game, "The Legend of Zelda: Ocarina of Time." In just six weeks, 2.5 million units of the game were sold.
1997	It introduces the innovative "Rumble Pak" attachment for the N64 controller, which enabled the game player to feel vibrations while playing the game.
1998	Release of Game Boy Color. "Pokémon" is introduced overseas and becomes a smash hit.
2000	Nintendo acquired a 3 percent stake of convenience store operator Lawson in order to leverage Lawson's online operations and network to sell video games.
2001	Launched the new version of the Game Boy, with a 32-bit CPU. Nintendo GameCube is launched in Japan and the United States.
2002	GameCube is launched in the European and Australian markets.

Source: Nintendo Co. Ltd, 2008, Annual Report, http://www.nintendo.co.jp/ir/pdf/2008/annual0803e.pdf (accessed October 3, 2008).

technology,[4] and Sony was left with the PS, which the company decided to continue developing. Given Sony's clout and resources, when the PS and its wide range of games were finally released in Japan in 1994, the console was an instant success. In 1995, Sony released the PS in the United States, totally uprooting Nintendo's established name in the industry.

For many years, Nintendo was a dominant player in the video game industry. It had sold more than two billion games since 1985. Its top-selling series included nonviolent and easy-to-play games such as "Super Mario Bros." and "The Legend of Zelda." Its games were so successful largely because they appealed to all age groups across different cultures. The title of a book published in 1993 summed up Nintendo's supremacy: *Game Over: How Nintendo Zapped an American Industry, Captured Your Dollars, and Enslaved Your Children*. Suddenly, after the debut of the Sony PS, it was no longer the leader of the video game industry.

Nintendo tried various strategies to counter Sony. However, competition continued to intensify, and the PS2 also captured a significant portion of the video game market, maintaining a dominant position in the industry. In May 2001, Microsoft too entered the video game market by introducing the Xbox console, leaving Nintendo with an even smaller piece of the market.

In 2002, Nintendo appointed Satoru Iwata[5] as president of the company. It was hoped that, with his experience and deep insights into how the market evolved, Iwata would help the company develop a brand-new vision and approach.[6]

The Video Game Industry

History

The video game industry was born in the 1970s. In the early days, notable players such as Atari from the United States and Namco from Japan brought video games to teenagers in the form of arcade games found in malls and video game arcades. With the introduction of home consoles, video games began to make their way into households around the globe.

In the 1980s and early 1990s, many new players came to the market. With the increasing popularity of personal computers (PCs), gamers were no longer limited to playing their favorite video game titles on proprietary consoles. Although the market was affected by the introduction of PCs, video game makers achieved steady growth.

Nevertheless, the target customer group of video game consoles was narrowly confined to teenagers. Armed with insightful targeting and positioning, image-conscious branding, and superb graphics technologies, Sony introduced the PS in the mid-1990s. The Japanese electronics giant revolutionized the perception of video game consoles and successfully captured new players, thereby helping the industry grow substantially. Video gaming suddenly became the new popular entertainment. It was especially well received by young adults, mostly males in their late 20s or early 30s, and often with substantial disposable incomes. By the time Sony launched the PS2 in 2000, technology giant Microsoft realized that it could no longer ignore the runaway success of this product or the effect the booming video

game market was having on its traditional PC and software domains. Thus Microsoft's video game console, the Xbox, was launched in 2001.

Since the early 2000s, the convergence of information technology, telecommunications, media, and entertainment has brought dramatic social and technological changes. With the new socio-technological movement and a wider audience base, the big video game console markers such as Sony and Microsoft began to realize that there were new opportunities for their video gaming and console product offerings, which would play a far greater role in people's lives than mere entertainment.

Trends in the Industry

With the broad availability of broadband Internet, increasing sophistication of high-definition (HD) video technologies, and decreasing cost of hard-drive storage, video game console manufacturers realized that their products no longer had to be for gaming only. In fact, many players such as Sony and Microsoft envisioned their game consoles as all-encompassing home entertainment centers. Further, given the increasing speed achieved by broadband connections, Internet users were increasingly able to access large quantities of data files, especially those containing HD audio and video. Consequently, these console producers developed and offered online libraries as a new service enabling users to download and stream a variety of movies, music, and television shows through their consoles.

As top-quality video materials became more readily available through HD broadcasting and Internet downloads, a new recording medium with increased storage capacity was required. Two formats, the Blu-ray format[7] developed by a consortium led by Sony, and the HD-DVD format developed by a consortium led by Toshiba, competed to become the standard in this area.

By offering online games based on new and existing titles, console makers could provide similar social-networking or virtual-world services to get online gamers to play, connect, and form loyal communities. Such communities were expected to help create a perpetual demand for services and products created by the video game makers and their alliance partners. In fact, in-game advertising had already started and offered a new revenue stream to video game developers.

Nintendo: Innovation and the Launch of the Wii

Traditionally, Sony, Microsoft, and Nintendo would enter a new cycle or a new competitive battle every five to six years, and in 2000, Sony's PS2 emerged as the clear winner.[8] Since then, the industry's focus turned even more to the technological advancement of the console hardware, particularly in terms of faster processing speed, higher definition of video quality, and increasing complexity of the games. The relentless pursuit of superior technologies became the driver of the industry's dynamics.

However, the former leader in the video game industry, Nintendo, adopted a vastly different viewpoint about the industry's future development. Some years before the battle that began in 2006, Iwata saw the potential threats facing the industry. He observed that the video game market in Japan was shrinking. Based on various market trends and data, the key factor causing this reduction appeared to be the increasing complexity of video games, which required players to invest a significant amount of their time to learn and play them using increasingly complicated controllers with combinations of buttons and joysticks. Consequently, occasional gamers with busy lives had stopped playing. Further, for novices and non-gamers, the time required to learn and play these games was a major deterrent for potential newcomers to join the camp. Iwata also saw that the video game industry had largely ignored non-gamers and was focused on the existing players. Armed with these insights, Iwata decided to devise a radically new strategy as the foundation for leading Nintendo down an unorthodox path.

The new strategy's objective was to reach out to non-gamers in order to create a bigger market. Iwata's mandate was for simpler games to be developed, targeting all customers, irrespective of age, gender, or gaming experience. These new games were to take no more than a few minutes to set up and play. In addition, they would require an easy-to-use controller. He also wanted the game scenarios to be largely based on real-life situations rather than fantasies.

In order to pilot Iwata's idea, Nintendo first developed a new handheld gaming device called the DS, which stood for "double screen." It was launched in 2004. The DS was positioned as "the machine that enriches the owner's daily life."[9] One of the key features of this device was a touch-screen that gamers could tap or write on with a stylus. This innovative design enabled gamers to play without using complicated sets of buttons or a mini-joystick. The company then launched the Nintendo Wi-Fi Connection, an innovative service that allowed DS system players to play with other users through a wireless network. The DS was a huge success, and by April 2008, more than 70 million units had been sold worldwide.[10]

Among the many DS game titles, the most popular was "Nintendogs," particularly among female gamers. Players of "Nintendogs" could interact with their virtual pets through the DS's built-in microphone and "touch" them via the touch-screen. They could take these dogs for walks, teach them tricks, and enter them into competitions. Another popular game was "Brainage," which featured brain-training games that were basically puzzles.

Following the success of the DS, Nintendo rolled out the DS Lite in 2006. With its mature Game Boy and innovative DS systems, Nintendo remained the leader in the handheld console segment and continued to retain well over 90 percent of the handheld device market that it had captured since 1989.

However, the deciding factor in Nintendo's success was the video game console segment. Since 2000, Nintendo had lost control of the fixed console market to Sony's PS. With its new strategy to capture non-gamers and expand the market, coupled with the lessons learned from the DS handheld device, Nintendo developed its new console, the Wii, which arrived about the same time as the rollout of Microsoft's Xbox 360 and Sony's PS3, and just in time for the 2006 holiday shopping season (see Exhibit 2 for a timeline).

Our goal was to come up with a machine that moms would want—easy to use, quick to start up, not a huge energy drain, and quiet while it was running. Rather than just picking new technology, we thought seriously about what a game console should be. Iwata wanted a console that would play every Nintendo game ever made.

—SHIGERU MIYAMOTO,
MEMBER OF THE WII DEVELOPMENT TEAM[11]

The Wii was an impressive, well-designed, tiny machine that was controlled with a wand-like controller that resembled a TV remote control. Without an elaborate joystick and wire, gamers could navigate the system simply by moving the controller. Motion detectors would then translate the movement of the wand into on-screen action, enabling simulation of real-life games such as tennis, bowling, and boxing. The games were sold on optical discs similar to DVDs. The Wii could also be connected to the Internet for online news and weather updates and to access Nintendo's classic game catalogue, which could be downloaded from the Web. To do this, players could access the Virtual Console service, whereby games originally released for the SNES and N64 could be downloaded from the Wii Shop Channel and accessed from the Wii.

Nintendo positioned the Wii as "a machine that puts smiles on surrounding people's faces," encouraging communication among family members as each of them found something personally relevant and were motivated to turn on the console every day in order to enjoy "the new life with Wii."[12] To promote the Wii, Nintendo adopted the same word-of-mouth strategy that had proven successful in promoting the DS. The company "recruited a handful of carefully chosen

Exhibit 2 Significant Milestones in the Video Game Console Industry

1967	German engineer Baer and co-workers designed the first video game console and developed the first set of games, the Brown Box.
1972	Magnavox approved of the Brown Box and developed Magnavox Odyssey, the first commercial video game console.
1975	Atari, a company founded by Bushnell in 1972, had its first major hit with the arcade game "Pong." "Pong" introduced at-home video games to the masses and Atari became hugely popular.
1977	With Warner Bros. having bought Atari in 1976, the Atari VCS, a cartridge-based system that played multiple games, was developed and released, and became a resounding success.
1980	Mattel entered the market and released Intellivision, a console featuring synthesized voices.
1983–84	Unlicensed games flooded the market and, with many new home systems such as the Atari 5200, the video game industry crashed. Nintendo launched Famicom in Japan.
1985	Nintendo released the NES in the United States.
1989	Nintendo released its second smash hit, the Game Boy.
1991	Nintendo released the Super NES in the United States, a year after its launch in Japan.
1995	Sony launched the PS.
1996	The N64, the last mass-market system to use cartridges, was released by Nintendo.
2000	Sony released the PS2.
2001	Microsoft released the Xbox.
2002	Nintendo released the Game Boy Advance.
2004	Nintendo launched the DS.
2005	In early 2005, Sony released the PSP. In November, Microsoft released the Xbox 360.
2006	Nintendo launched the Wii. Sony launched the PS3.

Source: *Time*, 2005, Video game console timeline—video game history—Xbox 360, http://www.time.com/covers/1101050523/console_timeline/ (accessed August 13, 2008).

suburban housewives to spread the word among their friends that the Wii was a gaming console the whole family could enjoy together."[13] The Wii was also featured in the gamers' self-made video, which was then shared through YouTube and social networking sites. This once-experimental approach was more effective than the traditional advertising or mass-media campaigns used by Sony and Microsoft.

In addition to becoming the home gaming system for the family, Wii also helped expand "exergaming," which was the combination of on-screen action with physical exercise. The origins of exergaming can be traced to 1989, when Nintendo released the Power Pad and Power Glove, two accessories for its gaming console. The Power Pad was a "large plastic platform that plugged into the console and contained pressure sensors on which gamers could step or jump to play sports games."[14] The Power Glove was a "glove-like controller that translated various gestures into on-screen movements."[15] However, these two accessories had not sold well. Now, with the introduction of the Wii into millions of households, boxing, tennis, bowling, golf, and baseball games would require players to act out the physical movements involved in these sports. Consequently, it was predicted that the Wii would spawn a whole new generation of exergaming that would go far beyond the existing games that used dance mats or video cameras to detect players' actions, as the Wii's controller could detect more subtle movements and could be used to record and analyze these movements through intelligent software to determine the players' physical fitness levels.[16]

The Wii proved to be a runaway success and by September 2007, Nintendo became Japan's most valuable listed company after Toyota, at US$72 billion in market value—nearly tripling in value since the launch of the Wii (see Exhibits 3 and 4).[17]

Exhibit 3 Nintendo's Income Statements, 2006 to 2008 (US$ Millions)

	March 31, 2006, Restated	March 31, 2007, Restated	March 31, 2008
Revenues	4,736.0	8,988.8	15,553.5
Cost of Goods Sold	2,735.4	5,289.1	9,043.0
Gross Profit	2,000.6	3,699.7	6,510.6
Selling, General and Administrative Expenses	850.4	1,219.0	1,602.0
R&D Expenses	284.5	350.7	344.1
Depreciation	16.4	24.8	31.7
Other Operating Expenses	1,151.3	1,594.4	1,977.8
OPERATING INCOME	849.3	2,105.2	4,532.8
Interest Expense	0.0	—	—
Interest and Investment Income	209.2	316.1	410.7
Currency Exchange Gains	423.3	239.4	−858.8
Other Non-Operating Income	22.3	28.7	16.5
Earnings before Tax (excluding unusual items)	1,504.1	2,689.3	4,101.1
Gain on Sale of Investments	32.8	5.2	−101.2
Gain on Sale of Assets	−0.2	−1.2	34.1
Other Unusual Items, Total	11.5	—	—
Earnings before Tax (including unusual items)	1,548.2	2,693.3	4,034.1
Income Tax Expense	633.7	1,072.7	1,641.7
Earnings from Continuing Operations	914.9	1,620.9	2,393.3
NET INCOME	914.9	1,620.9	2,393.3

Source: Adapted from *BusinessWeek*, 2008, Financial results for Nintendo Co. Ltd, www.investing.businessweek.com/research/stocks/financials (accessed August 4, 2008).

Key Players in the Video Game Industry

Video Game Hardware

Other than Nintendo, the video game hardware industry (essentially comprising the manufacture of consoles and devices) was dominated by Sony with its PS family, and Microsoft with the Xbox 360.

Sony.[18] For decades, Sony defined the leading edge in gadgetry, producing transistor radios in the 1950s, Trinitron TVs in the 1960s, and the revolutionary Walkman in the 1970s.[19] Similarly, when the company introduced the PS in Japan in March 1994 and in the United States in 1995, it brought the technology of video gaming to a whole new level (see Exhibit 5). With Sony's strategy of attracting older teenagers and young adults (who had significantly more disposable income) by offering more sophisticated and often more violent games, the PS dominated the market.

In 2000, the PS2 was released and completely won over the video game market. The PS2 was not only backward-compatible with the PS, but could also be used to play CDs and DVDs. For most people who bought the PS2, it was their first DVD player. In July 2008, Sony announced that worldwide PS2 console sales exceeded 140 million,[20] making the PS2 the best-selling console in history.

In order to compete against Nintendo, the ruler of the handheld video game market, Sony introduced the PlayStation Portable ("PSP") in 2004. In the meantime, Sony continued to release other electronics, such as Sony Connect, an online music service; Vaio Pocket, a portable music player designed to compete with Apple's iPod; and Network Walkman, which was the first Walkman with a hard drive.

Exhibit 4 Nintendo's Consolidated Sales Information for the Six Months Ending September 30, 2007 (US$ Millions)

		Year Ending March 31, 2007	Six Months Ending September 30, 2006	Six Months Ending September 30, 2007
Hardware	Handheld	3,241	1,349	1,827
	Console	1,356	33	1,741
	Others	470	79	355
	Total	5,068	1,461	3,923
Software	Handheld	2,530	1,019	1,322
	Console	714	93	719
	Others	46	10	44
	Total	3,289	1,121	2,085
Total Electronic Entertainment Products Division		8,357	2,582	6,008
Others (playing cards, etc.)		19	7	13
TOTAL		8,376	2,589	6,021

(US$1 = ¥115.4 on March 31, 2008)

Source: Nintendo Co. Ltd, 2007, Consolidated financial statements for the six months ending September 30, 2007, http://www.nintendo.com/corp/report/FY07FinanciaiP£SiiltsYdf, October 25 (accessed August 1, 2008).

Although the PS product line dominated the market, the sales of Sony's other electronics (e.g., DVD recorders, TVs, and computers) and music products dropped significantly. Consumer demand remained weak as there was a battle over prices, with Apple's iPod undermining the sales of Sony's CD and MiniDisc Walkmans, as well as their TV products. These challenges, in addition to the costs incurred in streamlining operations, significantly decreased Sony's market value, and in 2004 the company reported a loss. Sony, once acknowledged globally for its cutting-edge technological innovations, was coming to be perceived as a bureaucratic conglomerate.

In order to rectify the situation, in 2005 Sony brought in Sir Howard Stringer to replace Nobuyuki Idei as chairman and chief executive. Stringer was the first non-Japanese chief of the company and, prior to this post, had been the head of the company's U.S. and electronics divisions. After taking over, Stringer announced Project Nippon, a corporate restructuring plan designed to revamp Sony's electronics business and foster better collaboration between the company's divisions. His plan called for eliminating 10,000 jobs (the company had 150,000 employees) and closing 11 of Sony's 65 factories. Stringer also revealed plans for improved research-and-development (R&D) with a stronger focus on consumer demand, aiming to reestablish Sony's presence in Japan. Sony's emphasis became HD products for consumers and broadcasters, and

semiconductors designed to improve performance in the company's products.

As one of the major weapons in Sir Stringer's grand plan, Sony planned to introduce and leverage the PS3 to regain its position in the electronics industry. The PS3 was designed to be a multimedia entertainment hub. Thus, people would buy the PS3 to watch movies in addition to playing games. Its computing power would also allow users to chat online, listen to music, and view high-quality animations. The machine would also be backward-compatible with games designed for previous PS consoles. Sony hoped that it would be able to utilize the Cell computer chip, jointly developed with IBM and Toshiba, in other products too, such as selling home servers broadband and high-definition television (HDTV) systems. This powerful chip would power the new PS3, whose games would also be the first mass utilization of the Blu-ray format.[21]

In November 2006, after several delays, Sony's PS3 was released nearly a year after Microsoft's Xbox 360 and within a week of the debut of Nintendo's Wii. However, the results were largely disappointing. Supply problems and the high price tag of the PS3 resulted in Sony losing its dominant position in the console market to Nintendo. To boost sales, the company slashed the price of the PS3 in mid-2007. Around the same time, because of continuous setbacks in terms of delays and inability to ramp up production, Sony fired Ken Kutaragi, who was the chief architect of the PS product line.

Exhibit 5 Evolution of Technology in the Video Game Console Industry's War for Supremacy

First Generation 1972–1977	Simple gameplay and basic visuals, such as Atari's "Pong."
Second Generation 1977–1984	Consoles such as the Atari 2600 were launched. The 8-bit cartridge appeared. This era ended with the video game market crashing.
Third Generation 1983–1987	The 8-bit cartridge continued. The first console war took place between Nintendo's NES and Sega's Master System, with Nintendo emerging as the leader. Games such as "Super Mario Bros." and "Metal Gear" were launched and became huge successes. The handheld market, allowing mobility while playing games, was introduced with Nintendo's Game Boy and Sega's Game Gear.
Fourth Generation 1987–1996	The 16-bit cartridge arrived. Graphics became increasingly well defined. Nintendo again won the war against Sega, with its SNES sales exceeding those of the Sega Mega Drive.
Fifth Generation 1995–2002	32-bit, 64-bit, and 3D graphics were introduced. In this era, Sony launched the PS and the CD format arrived—two events that completely revolutionized the industry. In the format war of CD versus cartridge, the cartridge just did not have the capacity of the CD to store games, which were increasingly complex and featured high-quality graphics. Further, while there was a possibility the CD could be pirated, it had the advantage of being cheaper than the cartridge. Nintendo's N64 was the last cartridge-based console to be produced.
Sixth Generation 1998–2004	The 128-bit era began. Sony launched the PS2, which used the DVD format and got exclusive licenses for games such as "Grand Theft Auto" and "Metal Gear Solid 2," making it the winner of this round of competition. Microsoft launched the Xbox and took second place. Nintendo's Game Cube trailed in third. Sega's Dreamcast lagged at fourth place.
Seventh Generation 2004–2008	The Xbox 360 and the PS3 introduced HD gaming and graphics. The PS3 had now moved ahead from the DVD to the Blu-ray format, and this combination of HD and Blu-ray implied far superior storage capacity and graphics. Nintendo's Wii had motion sensors.

Source: Adapted from D. Lero, 2007, A history of gaming, http://www.gamespot.com/pages/unions/home.php?union_id=Contributions, November 14 (accessed August 13, 2008).

In July 2008, 20 months after the release of the PS3, the console had barely achieved 10 percent of its sales target. At the end of Sony's fiscal year in March 2008, sales were 12.85 million, and the company expected to sell just about 10 million in the fiscal year ending March 2009.[22] Sony's more pressing need was to steer the PS3 to profitability, which was estimated to finally happen by 2009 (see Exhibits 6 and 7). Given the shaky situation, Sony had no plans to cease development of games for the older PS2 system and planned to continue rolling out titles specifically for it.[23]

Microsoft. Entering the video game business in 2001 was one of Microsoft's diversification moves when the company recognized the remarkable success of Sony's PS2 and the potential threat the video game market posed to its stronghold in the PC market. The Xbox was the company's first foray into the industry and was launched to compete directly with Sony's PS2 and Nintendo's GameCube. In November 2002, the company launched Xbox Live, allowing subscribers to play online Xbox games with other subscribers around the world. By mid-2005, the service had attracted about two million subscribers worldwide.

However, by May 2005, the software giant had sold only 21.3 million Xbox units, which put the company in a distant second place behind Sony's PS2 (which had sold 83.5 million units) and slightly ahead of Nintendo's GameCube (with sales of 18.3 million units).[24] By August 2005, Microsoft's Xbox division had cost the company US$4 billion.[25] Soon after, production of the Xbox was ended in favor of the Xbox 360.

Microsoft was determined to capture the top spot in the market with the launch of the Xbox 360 in November 2005, several months ahead of its rivals (Sony's PS3 appeared in the market in late 2006, about a week after Nintendo's Wii). Some believed that the previous success of Sony's PS2 was partly due to its advantage in reaching the market earlier than its rivals; thus, Microsoft imitated this marketing strategy and became the first game console in the new business cycle. Further, having learned a hard lesson from the flop of the original Xbox in Japan, Microsoft worked closely with the producers of Japanese games in an attempt to neutralize the traditional advantages of its two main rivals. The company also abandoned its previous approach of using off-the-shelf parts provided by Intel and NVIDIA to build its consoles because while such an approach was efficient, it lacked the flexibility that Microsoft's rivals enjoyed in reducing costs and increasing profit margins during a console's lifetime.[26] (For instance, Sony had gradually reduced the number of chips required by its

Exhibit 6 Sony's Income Statement, 2006–2008 (US$ Millions)

	March 31, 2006	March 31, 2007	March 31, 2008
Revenue	63,541.2	70,513.4	89,601.3
Cost of Goods Sold	43,786.9	54,652.4	68,885.3
Gross Profit	19,754.3	15,861.0	20,716.0
Gross Profit Margin	31.1%	22.5%	23.1%
Selling, General and Administrative Expenses	12,446.4	8,719.8	9,525.6
Depreciation	5,682.2	6,531.3	7,408.1
Operating Income	1,625.7	609.9	3,782.3
Operating Margin	2.6%	0.9%	4.2%
Non-Operating Income	1,054.6	489.3	1,159.1
Non-Operating Expenses	246.5	231.9	231.6
Income before Taxes	2,433.8	867.3	4,709.8
Income Taxes	1,500.4	458.0	2,055.1
Net Income after Taxes	933.4	409.3	2,654.7
Continuing Operations	1,050.7	1,073.8	3,731.3
Total Net Income	1,050.7	1,073.8	3,731.3
Net Profit Margin	1.7%	1.5%	4.2%

Source: Adapted from C. Colbert, 2008, Sony Corporation, Hoover's Company Information.

PS2 without sacrificing its performance.) Subsequently, Microsoft adopted a new design for its Xbox 360 in the hope that this would achieve a new degree of manufacturing flexibility that could help integrate various components and increase profitability in the future (see Exhibit 8).[27]

Video Game Software

The computer game industry, one of the biggest money-spinners in the global entertainment industry, routinely spent amounts ranging from US$12 million to US$20 million to develop each game. As the consoles became more expensive, the cost of developing games for them also increased. However, Nintendo turned its lower-cost hardware into another competitive advantage. By focusing on characters rather than special effects, developing Wii games cost the company about half what its competition was spending on Xbox and PS games, and thus the expense could be recouped at a much lower sales volume. Nintendo had also thrown in

Exhibit 7 Analysis of Sony's Income Statement for the Year Ending March 31, 2008

Sony's increase in revenues was largely due to the group's electronics segment, comprising televisions and digital cameras, which saw an 8.9 percent increase in sales. The video game segment increased sales by 26.3 percent to US$12.2 billion, largely due to an increase in sales of the PS3. In all, 9.24 million PS3 units were sold during the year, an increase of 5.63 million units over the previous year. With Sony increasing software sales to 57.9 million units (from 44.6 million) and reducing hardware costs, the losses in the PS3 segment declined to US$1.18 billion from US$ 2.21 billion in the previous year.

PSP sales increased by 4.36 million units to 13.89 million, and PSP software sales rose by 0.8 million to 55.5 million units. PS2 sales declined by 0.98 million units to 13.73 million, with PSP software sales decreasing by 39.5 million units to 154 million.

For the year ending March 31, 2009, Sony expected game segment sales to decline and the PS2 business to shrink. However, the company was optimistic that profitability would increase with more titles available for the PS3 and reductions in hardware costs. There would be an estimated 22 percent reduction in profits, taking into account the one-off increase in the March 2008 financials due to property sales and the floating of the group's financial services segment.

Source: Adapted from D. Jenkins, 2008, "Sony's game division sees 26% sales jump, http://www.gamasutra.com/php-bin/news-index.php?story=8638, May 14 (accessed August 11, 2008).

Exhibit 8 Microsoft's Income Statement, 2005–2007 (US$ Millions)

	June 30, 2005	June 30, 2006	June 30, 2007
Revenue	39,788	44,282	51,122
Cost of Goods Sold	6,200	7,650	10,693
Gross Profit	33,588	36,632	40,429
Gross Profit Margin	84.4%	82.7%	79.1%
Selling, General, and Administrative Expenses	18,172	19,257	20,465
Depreciation	855	903	1,440
Operating Income	14,561	16,472	18,524
Operating Margin	36.6%	37.2%	36.2%
Non-Operating Income	2,067	1,572	1,577
Income before Taxes	16,628	18,262	20,101
Income Taxes	4,374	5,663	6,036
Net Income after Taxes	12,254	12,599	14,065
Net Profit Margin	30.8%	28.5%	27.5%

Source: Adapted from S. Shafer, 2008, Microsoft Corporation, Hoover's Company Information.

five simple but highly addictive games, Wii Sports, with each console so that the buyer was getting a "complete" product at a great price. Sony and Microsoft, on the other hand, incurred losses on the consoles they sold, despite their high price. To compensate for these losses, they sold their games with high licensing royalties. As

of July 2008, 6 of the 10 most popular games worldwide were for Nintendo consoles (see Exhibit 9).

Nintendo also focused on developing first-party titles. Nintendo had placed its top software designers at the helm of hardware design. Thus, while Sony and Microsoft relied heavily on third parties to develop titles,

Exhibit 9 Top 10 Games Worldwide, July 2008 (approximate number of units in thousands)

Rank	Console	Game	Publisher	Number of Weeks Since Launch	Sales for the Week Ending July 25, 2008	Sales Since Launch by July 25, 2008
1	Wii	Wii Sports	Nintendo	88	333	26,826
2	Wii	Wii Fit	Nintendo	35	206	6,010
3	DS	Dragon Quest V	Square Enix	2	181	861
4	Wii	Mario Kart Wii	Nintendo	16	167	6,604
5	Wii	Wii Play	Nintendo	87	144	13,840
6	DS	Pokemon Mysterious Dungeon 2	Nintendo	46	117	2,919
7	DS	Guitar Hero: On Tour	Activision	3	116	740
8	Wii	Super Smash Bros. Brawl	Nintendo	26	95	6,430
9	PS2	Powerful Pro Baseball 15	Konami	1	88	88
10	Xbox 360	NCCA Football 09	Electronic Arts	2	84	374

Source: Adapted from VGChartz, 2008, "Worldwide chart for week ending July 25, 2008, http://www.vgchartz.com (accessed August 4, 2008).

Nintendo's consoles were designed to suit the concepts of the games that would run on them, allowing the creation of early first-party titles that really showcased the hardware, including low-profit and offbeat games like Brainage. Such games would have been impossible on another company's hardware.[28]

The sales of hardware consoles such as the Wii, Xbox, and PS were highly correlated to the launch and sale of the video games that could be played on them. For instance, in March 2008, Nintendo launched its exclusive hit game "Super Smash Bros. Brawl" for the Wii and, in that month, along with selling 2.7 million copies of the game, the company sold more video game consoles in the United States than Sony and Microsoft combined.[29]

The Battle Begins

Until the launch of the Wii at the end of 2006, competition in the video game market was straightforward. The leader was the company that introduced a wider array of games with high-quality graphics and increasingly complex gameplay. Then Microsoft introduced the Xbox 360 in November 2005, and Nintendo and Sony followed about a year later with the Wii and PS3. It was apparent that the rules of competition had changed.

Sony continued to claim success in selling the aging PS2 console. Given its long history in the market, the PS2 had outsold both the Xbox 360 and the Wii. Microsoft also remained confident about its Xbox 360. As of May 2008, Microsoft announced its Xbox 360 game machine had beaten the Wii and PS3 to reach 10 million units in U.S. sales.[30] The head start of several months in selling the Xbox 360 gave Microsoft an edge over Sony's PS3 and Nintendo's Wii. The lead time also helped Microsoft and its partners build a vast library of games, which was a major factor for consideration when gamers chose a particular console.

However, within a month of Microsoft's announcement that it was the leader in the U.S. console war, the June 2008 figures were released and it was evident that the Wii had usurped the Xbox 360 as the leader. A total of 10.9 million Wiis were sold in the United States since its launch in November 2006, whereas a total of 10.4 million Xbox 360s were sold since its launch a year earlier.[31] The PS3 came in a distant third with 4.8 million units sold. In the United States, which was Nintendo's largest market,[32] the Wii had taken off the fastest by selling 600,000 units in the first eight days, generating US$190 million in sales.[33] In fact, because of its high demand and market buzz, many consumers found it difficult to get their hands on the machine even months after the launch (see Exhibit 10). The same story about demand existed

Exhibit 10 Sales Figures of Wii, PS3, and Xbox 360 in the United States (approximate number of units in thousands)

	Xbox 360	Nintendo Wii	Sony PS2	Sony PS3
September 2006	259	0	300	0
October 2006	217	0	235	0
November 2006	511	476	664	197
December 2006	1,132	604	1,400	491
January 2007	294	436	299	244
February 2007	228	335	295	127
March 2007	199	259	280	130
April 2007	174	360	194	82
May 2007	155	338	188	82
June 2007	198	382	270	95
July 2007	170	425	222	159
August 2007	277	404	202	131
September 2007	528	501	215	119
October 2007	366	519	184	121

Exhibit 10 Sales Figures of Wii, PS3, and Xbox 360 in the United States (approximate number of units in thousands) (*Continued*)

	Xbox 360	Nintendo Wii	Sony PS2	Sony PS3
November 2007	770	981	496	466
December 2007	1,260	1,350	1,100	798
January 2008	230	274	264	269
February 2008	254	432	352	281
March 2008	262	721	216	257
April 2008	188	714	124	187
May 2008	187	675	133	209
June 2008	220	667	189	406
TOTAL	8,079*	10,853	7,822	4,851

*Cumulative sales of the Xbox 360 from the launch date in November 2005 to September 2006 equaled 2,414 units, bringing the total from launch to June 2008 to 10.5 million units.

Source: Adapted from PVC Forum, 2008, "Games sales chart—monthly console hardware sales in America, www.forum.pcvsconsole.com, July 17 (accessed August 11, 2008).

in other parts of the world, and Nintendo emerged as the clear month-on-month leader with the outstanding success of its new console (see Exhibit 11).

In terms of profitability, Nintendo was in an enviable position of making a profit on each Wii console sold from the first day (see Exhibit 12). Sony, on the other hand, had already slashed the price of the PS3 by US$100 to US$499 to help boost sales of the console. This was still US$20 more than Microsoft's most expensive version of the Xbox 360 and about twice the price of Nintendo's Wii.[34]

Exhibit 11 Worldwide Sales Figures of Wii, PS3, and Xbox Units (approximate number of units in thousands)

	Xbox 360	Nintendo Wii	Sony PS2	Sony PS3
September 2006	446	0	859	0
October 2006	431	0	793	0
November 2006	1,263	1,068	2,016	516
December 2006	2,028	2,418	3,282	843
January 2007	692	1,308	981	546
February 2007	648	1,315	954	389
March 2007	438	900	708	954
April 2007	395	1,060	648	530
May 2007	482	1,522	746	418
June 2007	392	1,245	647	298
July 2007	350	1,371	735	419

	Xbox 360	Nintendo Wii	Sony PS2	Sony PS3
August 2007	636	1,612	882	609
September 2007	837	1,149	754	428
October 2007	1,007	1,234	699	632
November 2007	1,516	2,698	1,334	1,525
December 2007	2,215	4,267	2,456	2,389
January 2008	1,064	2,961	1,271	1,480
February 2008	648	1,606	830	948
March 2008	710	1,730	765	929
April 2008	886	2,545	668	1,189
May 2008	796	2,331	488	939
June 2008	618	1,921	499	995
TOTAL	18,498	35,596	23,015	15,981

Source: Estimated data adapted from VGChartz, July 2008, World hardware sales—weekly comparison, http://www.vgchartz.com/aweekly.php (accessed August 16, 2008).

Exhibit 12 The Economics of the Game: Wii, PS3, and the Xbox 360

Microsoft and Sony were prepared for initial losses in producing their Xbox 360 and PS3 in the hopes that there would be a long-term profit from software sales. However, by integrating hardware and software development, Nintendo made profits on both from the very start. In the United States and Europe, where the Wii's retail price was higher than in Japan and it came bundled with Wii Sports, it was estimated that it made a healthy gross profit margin per console of US$49 in the United States and US$74 in Europe, factoring in currency conversions.[37]

Nintendo also outsourced nearly all production of the Wii and the DS. Its strategy of having more than one supplier for the same part meant that it got the parts cheaper and increasing production was not difficult. Sony, on the other hand, produced an estimated 40 percent of its components in-house.[38] The massive costs of investing in the game console, which was equipped with a Blu-ray player and the powerful Cell chip, meant that Sony continued to incur a loss on each PS3 sold.[39] Electronics supply chain researcher iSuppli's analysis in November 2006 showed that Sony's selling price of US$499 per 20GB PS3 resulted in a unit loss of about US$306.85, not including packaging, controller, and cables.[40]

As for Microsoft, at launch the Xbox 360 was estimated to be losing about US$125 per console.[41] By November 2006, the company streamlined processes and reduced manufacturing costs by almost 40 percent, thereby making an estimated profit of US$75.70 on the retail price of US$399.[42] However, the year ending 2007 remained difficult for the company's Xbox 360 division, which managed both hardware and software sales. The division posted a net loss of US$2 billion. This was primarily due to Microsoft incurring costs exceeding US$1.1 billion by extending the warranty on the product from one year to three years, mainly due to "red ring o' death" issues (a problem that arose due to a defective graphic chip and which caused the console to die while in use). It was only for the year ending June 30, 2008, that a yearly operating profit—amounting to US$426 million—was reported.

Finally, unlike Sony's and Microsoft's reliance on third-party development of games, Nintendo's focus on in-house titles had a pronounced impact on revenues. These were far more profitable than third-party titles, for which the console manufacturer might get only 10 to 15 percent of the price of the game.[43]

It was becoming clear that, in this latest battle between the Xbox 360, PS3, and Wii, the Wii was the clear winner of the game.

Nintendo's Disruptive Strategy

It was not just the video game industry that had felt the impact of the innovative Wii. With the December 2007 release of Wii Fit (an extension of the Wii for exercise activities utilizing the Wii Balances Board peripheral), the potential for capturing yet another class of non-gamers was significantly increased. Wii Fit aimed to integrate health and entertainment and featured approximately 40 different activities, including yoga, pushups, and other exercises. It was described as a way to help get families to exercise together. Within six months of being released, the product had sold two million copies in Japan and had long queues waiting for its delivery in many parts of the world. Its effect on the health industry was already evident, with doctors and therapists recommending it for various purposes, such as body balance, strength training, keeping patients interested in performing repetitive and tedious exercises, and for the elderly to enjoy expanding their range of motion.

Nintendo's business model was also exciting for small, independent software producers. In May 2008, Nintendo made the strategic move of loosening its traditionally tight control over content by launching WiiWare in the United States and Europe. WiiWare, an online channel for distributing downloadable games, enabled users to download new games by independent developers. Reggis Fils-Aime, president of Nintendo of America,[35] said, "Independent developers armed with small budgets and big ideas will be able to get their original games into the marketplace to see if we can find the next smash hit. WiiWare brings new levels of creativity and value to the ever-growing population of Wii owners."

While it was still too early to predict the final results, Nintendo's Wii has revolutionized and changed the nature of competition, and not just in the video-game industry. Would this disruptive transformation of the video game industry leave the competitors in the cold? What course of action was available to them?

Appendix
Disruptive Technology

The term "disruptive technology" was coined by Clayton M. Christensen, a professor at the Harvard Business School. Christensen believed that leading companies, despite having followed all the right practices (i.e., keeping a close watch on competition, listening to their customers, and investing aggressively in new technologies), still lost their top positions when confronted with disruptive changes in technology and market structure. He suggested that, while keeping close to customers was critical for current success, it was paradoxically also the cause for companies' failure to meet the technological demands of customers in the future.

To remain at the top of their industries, managers must first be able to spot disruptive technologies. To pursue these technologies, managers must protect them from the processes and incentives that are geared to serving mainstream customers. And the only way to do that is to create organizations that are completely independent of the mainstream business.[36]

Disruptive technology is an innovation that uses a "disruptive strategy'" rather than a "sustaining" strategy (one which improved the performance of an established product) or a "revolutionary" strategy (one which introduced products with dramatically improved features). Christensen argued that following good business practices could ultimately weaken a great company because truly important breakthrough technologies were often rejected by mainstream customers because they could not immediately use them. Companies with a strong customer focus would thus reject those strategically important innovations. As a result, it was left to the more nimble, entrepreneurial companies to pursue those disruptive opportunities, which might result in worse product performance in the short term, but in the long run were of strategic importance in creating new markets and finding new customers for future products.

NOTES

1. S. Iwata, 2006, GDC keynote address, *Nintendo World Report*, http://www.nintendoworldreport.com/newsArt.cfm, March 23 (accessed July 31, 2008).
2. J. McGregor, 2008, The world's most innovative companies, *BusinessWeek*, http://www.businessweek.com/magazine/content/08, April 17 (accessed July 10, 2008).
3. "Nintendo," loosely translated from Japanese, means "leave luck to heaven."
4. Under this deal, Philips, one of Sony's principal rivals, would produce an add-on device for Nintendo game players allowing them to use optical compact discs with greater storage capacities than game cartridges.

5. Iwata joined HAL Laboratories in 1982 and shortly after became the company's coordinator for software production, where he helped create video games such as "Kirby." In 1993, he became president of HAL, a post he held until 2000, when he joined Nintendo as head of the corporate planning division. When Yamauchi retired in 2002, Iwata became president of Nintendo.

6. C. Colbert, 2007, Nintendo Co. Ltd, Hoover's Company Information; M. Sanchanta, 2007, Nintendo market cap rockets, *Financial Times*, September 26; 2006, Playing a Different Game, *The Economist*, October 26.

7. Blu-ray was a new DVD format derived from the blue laser, which had a short wavelength of 405 nm. Blu-ray discs could store substantially more data than the DVD format, which was derived from red-laser (650 nm) technology.

8. The PS2 had been updated since introduction and was available in a much smaller format than the original.

9. Nintendo, 2007, Consolidated financial statements for the six months ending September 30, 2007, http://www.nintendo.com/corp/report/FY07FinancialResults.pdf, October 25 (accessed August 1, 2008).

10. Data sourced from VGChartz.com (week ending April 5, 2008), Hardware table, http://www.vgchartz.com (accessed August 1, 2008).

11. K. Hall, 2006, The big ideas behind Nintendo's Wii, *BusinessWeek*, http://www.businessweek.com/technolgy/content/nov2006, November 16 (accessed June 25, 2008).

12. Nintendo, 2007, Consolidated financial statements for the six months ending September 30, 2007, http://www.nintendo.com/corp/report/FY07FinancialResults.pdf (accessed August 1, 2008).

13. 2007, "Building buzz: Marketing, 2007, *The Economist*, 383(8525): 64.

14. http://www.wordspy.com/words/exergaming.asp?r=16.9423217396108&svr=9&lang=en_us& (accessed August 1, 2008).

15. Ibid.

16. C. Colbert, 2007, Nintendo Co. Ltd, Hoover's Company Information; 2007, Let's get physical, *The Economist*, March 8.

17. K. Takenaka, 2007, Nintendo becomes Japan's second most valuable company, *Reuters*, http://www.reuters.com/article/technology-media-telco, September 25 (accessed August 1, 2008).

18. This chapter contains excerpts from A. Farhoomand & S. Tsang, 2006, Microsoft's diversification strategy, Asia Case Research Centre, The University of Hong Kong.

19. L. Stahl, 2006, Sir Howard Stringer: Sony's savior? *CBS News 60 Minutes*, http://www.cbsnews.com/stories/2006/01/06/60minutes/main1183023_page3.shtml, January 8 (accessed June 25, 2008).

20. C. Nutall, 2008, Sony sets 150m sales target for PS3, *Financial Times*, http://www.ft.com/cms/s/0/1c46ad2e-5678. July 20 (accessed August 14, 2008).

21. Sony joined Matsushita and Samsung, plus a few other companies, to jointly develop the Blu-ray format. The alliance, formed in 2004, aimed to establish the new DVD format for optical storage media. In late 2004, Disney agreed to use the Blu-ray format.

22. C. Nutall, 2008, Sony sets 150m sales target for PS3, *Financial Times*, http://www.ft.com/cms/s/0/1c46ad2e-5678, July 20 (accessed August 14, 2008).

23. C. Colbert, 2007, Nintendo Co. Ltd, Hoover's Company Information.

24. Data sourced from http://vgchartz.com, 2005, Hardware table, May 28 (accessed July 30, 2008).

25. V. Murphy, 2005, Microsoft's midlife crisis, *Forbes,* http://www.forbes.com/2005/09/12, September 13 (accessed August 1, 2008).

26. Lifetime refers to the complete stages of the product's life cycle: from conception, through design and production, to its service and, finally, disposal.

27. This chapter contains excerpts from A. Farhoomand & S. Tsang, 2006, Microsoft's diversification strategy, Asia Case Research Centre, The University of Hong Kong.

28. R. Ehrenberg, 2007, Game console wars II: Nintendo shaves off profits, leaving competition scruffy, *Seeking Alpha*, http://seekingalpha.com/article/34357-game-console-wars-ii-nintendo-shaves-off-profits-leaving-competition-scruffy, May 3 (accessed August 14, 2008).

29. P. McDougall, 2008, Nintendo Wii sales trounce Xbox 360, Playstation 3, *Information Week*, http://www.informationweek.com/news/hardware/, April 18 (accessed July 15, 2008).

30. D. Wakabayashi, 2008, Xbox 360 sales surpass Wii, PS3, *Reuters*, http://www.reuters.com/article/technologyNews, May 15 (accessed June 25, 2008).

31. T. Ricker, 2008, NPD: Wii usurps Xbox as best selling U.S. game console, pulling away, *Engadget*, http://www.engadget.com/2008/07/18/npd-wii-usurps-xbox-360-as-best-selling-us-game-console, July 18 (accessed August 11, 2008).

32. The United States comprised 36 percent of Nintendo's total sales for the year ending March 2007, followed by Japan with 34 percent.

33. C. Colbert, 2007, Nintendo Co. Ltd, Hoover's Company Information.

34. CNN, 2007, Sony slashes PS3 price tag by about $100, http://www.cnn.com/2007/TECH/fun.games/07/09/sony.prie.reut/index, July 9 (accessed August 11, 2008).

35. J. L. Bower & C. Christensen, 1995, Disruptive technologies: Catching the wave, *Harvard Business Review*, http://www.hbsp.harvard.edu/b01/en/common/item_detail.jhtml, January 1 (accessed August 11, 2008).

36. M. Sanchanta, 2007, Nintendo Wii success helps component makers' score, *Financial Times*, http://ft.com/cms/s/0/4f9a9108-6467-11dc-90ea-00009fd2ac.html, September 16 (accessed August 14. 2008).

37. Ibid.

38. C. Nutall, 2008, Sony sets 150m sales target for PS3, *Financial Times*, http://www.ft.com/cms/s/0/1c46ad2e-5678. July 20 (accessed August 14, 2008).

39. Edge Online, 2006, iSuppli: 60GB PS3 costs US$840 to produce, http://www.edge-online.com/news/isuppli-60gb-ps3-costs-840-produce, November 16 (accessed August 14, 2008).

40. Ibid.

41. J. Mann, 2006, Microsoft makes tiny profit on Xbox 360 hardware, *TechSpot News*, http://www.techspot.com/news/23612-microsoft-makes-a-tiny-profit-on-xbox-360-hardware.html, November 20 (accessed August 14, 2008).

42. R. Ehrenberg, 2007, Game console wars II: Nintendo shaves off profits, leaving competition scruffy, *Seeking Alpha*, http://seekingalpha.com/article/34357-game-console-wars-ii-nintendo-shaves-off-profits-leaving-competition-scruffy, May 3 (accessed August 14, 2008).

43. R. Ehrenberg, 2007, Game console wars II: Nintendo shaves off profits, leaving competition scruffy, Seeking Alpha, http://seekingalpha.com/article/34357-game-console-wars-ii-nintendo-shaves-off-profits-leaving-competition-scruffy, May 3 (accessed August 14, 2008).

Frank C. Barnes

University of North Carolina-Charlotte, Belk College of Business

Beverly B. Tyler

North Carolina State University, College of Management

Nucor was the classic American success story, rising on the world stage while "old steel" gave up. However, in 2009, Nucor and its CEO, Daniel DiMicco, faced challenges as great as any in the company's 54-year history. In December 2008, DiMicco announced earnings for the fourth quarter of 2008 would plunge and told Jim Cramer on CNBC how sales for the steel industry "went off the edge of a cliff." After three record quarters, capacity utilization "immediately" fell to 50 percent. The U.S. mortgage crises led to a global financial meltdown that affected the growth and economic health of both developed and developing economies. Iron ore and scrap metal prices, which had soared only months before due to the voracious demand for infrastructure projects in China and India, plummeted to bargain basement prices along with demand for steel and steel products. With the financial markets in disarray and governments working to bail out financial institutions, consumers who had spent freely on big ticket items suddenly became risk averse. Nucor, which had become the world's tenth largest steelmaker by 2005, dropped to the twelfth largest by 2007, as it and its competitors completed acquisitions around the world. DiMicco, who had led the company during the downs and ups of 2001 and 2005, had a big job ahead—to assess the threats and opportunities facing Nucor and to select the best strategies and structure for the company as it moved into the twenty-first century.

Background

The solid foundation of Nucor was built on the failure of several companies. The first failure involved Nuclear Consultants, a company formed after World War II to ride the wave of growth in "nuclear" technology. When this didn't happen, the renamed Nuclear Corp. of America moved on to the "conglomerate" trend popular at the time. Nuclear acquired various "high-tech" businesses, such as radiation sensors, semi-conductors, rare earths, and air-conditioning equipment. However, the company still lost money, and a fourth reorganization in 1966 put 40-year-old Ken Iverson in charge. The building of Nucor began.

Ken Iverson joined the Navy after high school and transferred from officer training school to Cornell's aeronautical engineering program. After graduation, he selected mechanical engineering/metallurgy for a master's degree to avoid the long drafting apprenticeship in aeronautical engineering. His college work with an electron microscope earned him a job with International Harvester. After five years in that company's lab, his boss and mentor prodded him to expand his vision by going with a smaller company.

Over the next 10 years, Iverson worked for four small metals companies, gaining technical knowledge and increasing his exposure to other business functions. He enjoyed working with the presidents of these small companies and admired their ability to achieve outstanding results. Nuclear Corp., after failing to buy the company Iverson worked for, hired him as a consultant to locate another metals business the firm could purchase. In 1962, Nuclear Corp. acquired a small joist plant in South Carolina that Iverson found. The purchase was completed with the condition that Iverson be allowed to run the operation.

Over the next four years, Iverson built up the Vulcraft division as Nuclear Corporation struggled. The president, David Thomas, was described as a great promoter and salesman but a weak manager. A partner with Bear Stearns actually made a personal loan to the company to keep it going. In 1965, when the company was on the edge of bankruptcy, Iverson, who headed the only successful division, was named president and moved the company's headquarters to Charlotte, North Carolina. He immediately began getting rid of the esoteric, but unprofitable, high-tech divisions and concentrated on the successful steel joist business. The company built more joist plants, and, in 1968, began building its first steel mill in South Carolina to "make steel cheaper than they were buying from importers." By 1984, Nucor had six joist plants and four steel mills, using the new "mini-mill" technology.

The original owner of Vulcraft, Sanborn Chase, was known at Vulcraft as "a scientific genius." He was a man of great compassion who understood the atmosphere necessary for people to be self-motivated. Chase, an engineer by training, invented a number of products in diverse fields. He also established the incentive programs for which Nucor later became known. With only one plant, he was still able to operate in a "decentralized" manner. Before his death in 1960, the company was studying the building of a steel mill using newly developed mini-mill technology. His widow ran the company until it was sold to Nucor in 1962.

Dave Aycock met Ken Iverson when Nuclear purchased Vulcraft and they worked together closely for the next year and a half. Located in Phoenix at the corporate headquarters, he was responsible to Iverson for all the joist operations and was given the task of planning and building a new joist plant in Texas. In late 1963, he was transferred to Norfolk, where he lived for the next 13 years and managed a number of Nucor's joist plants. In 1977, he was named the manager of the Darlington, South Carolina, steel plant. In 1984, Aycock became Nucor's president and chief operating officer, while Iverson became chairman and chief executive officer.

Aycock had this to say about Iverson: "Ken was a very good leader, with an entrepreneurial spirit. He is easy to work with and has the courage to do things, to take lots of risks. Many things didn't work, but some worked very well." For some companies, failure to take a risk is failure—this was the belief of the company's founder and reinforced by Iverson during his time at the helm. Nucor was very innovative in steel and joists. The firm's plant at Norfolk was years ahead of its time in wire rod welding. In the late 1960s, they had one of the first computer inventory management systems and design/engineering programs. They were very sophisticated in purchasing, sales, and managing, and they often beat their competition through the speed of their design efforts.

By 1984, the once-bankrupt conglomerate had become a leading U.S. steel company. It was a fairytale story. Tom Peters used Nucor's management style as an example of "excellence" while the barons of old steel ruled over creeping ghettos. NBC did a feature about Nucor, and *The New Yorker* serialized a book about how a relatively small American steel company built a team that led the whole world into a new era of steelmaking. Iverson was rich, owning $10 million in stock, but with a salary that rarely reached $1 million, a fraction of some other U.S. executives made. The 40-year-old manager of the South Carolina Vulcraft plant had become a millionaire. Stockholders chuckled and non-unionized hourly workers, who hadn't seen a layoff in 20 years, earned more than the unionized workers of old steel and more than 85 percent of the people in the states where they worked.

Nucor owed much of its success to its benchmark organizational style and the empowered division managers. There were two basic lines of business, the first being the six steel joist plants that made the steel frames seen in many buildings. The second line included four steel mills that utilized innovative mini-mill technology to supply the joist plants at first and, later, outside customers. In 1984 Nucor was still only the seventh-largest steel company in America, but it had established the organization design, management philosophy, and incentive system that led to the firm's continued success.

Nucor's Formula for Success, 1964–1999

In the early 1990s, Nucor's 22 divisions, one for every plant, had a general manager, who was also a vice president of the corporation. There were three divisions: joist plants, steel mills, and miscellaneous plants. The corporate staff consisted of less than 25 people. In the beginning, Iverson had chosen Charlotte "as the new home base for what he had envisioned as a small cadre of executives who would guide a decentralized operation with liberal authority delegated to managers in the field," according to *South* magazine. The divisions did their own manufacturing, selling, accounting, engineering, and personnel management, and there were only four levels from top to bottom (see Exhibit 1).

Iverson gave his views on keeping an organization lean:

Each division is a profit center and the division manager has control over the day-to-day decisions that make that particular division profitable or not profitable. We expect the division to provide a contribution, which is earnings before corporate expenses. And we expect a division to earn 25 percent return on total assets employed, before corporate expenses, taxes, interest or profit sharing. And we have a saying in the company—if a manager doesn't provide that for a number of years, we are either going to get rid of the division or get rid of the general manager, and it's generally the division manager.

Nucor strengthened its position by developing strong alliances with outside parties. It did not engage in internal research and development. Instead, it monitored others' work worldwide and attracted investors who brought them new technical applications at the earliest

Exhibit 1 Nucor Organization Chart, 1991

possible dates. Though Nucor was known for economically constructing new facilities, its engineering and construction team consisted of only three individuals. They did not attempt to specify exact equipment parameters, but asked the equipment supplier to provide this information and then held the manufacturer accountable. They had alliances with selected construction companies around the country who knew the kind of work Nucor wanted. Nucor bought 95 percent of its scrap steel from an independent broker who followed the market and made recommendations regarding scrap purchases. Nucor did not have a corporate advertising department, corporate public relations department, or a corporate legal or environmental department; however, it did have long-term relationships with outsiders to provide these services.

The steel industry had established a pattern of absorbing the cost of shipments so that, regardless of the distance from the mill, all users paid the same delivered price. Nucor broke with this tradition and stopped equalizing freight. It offered all customers the same sales terms—price plus actual shipping costs. Nucor gave no volume discounts, feeling that with modern computer systems, there was no justification. Customers located next to the plant guaranteed themselves the lowest possible costs for steel purchases. Two tube manufacturers, two steel service centers, and a cold-rolling facility were located adjacent to the Arkansas plant. These facilities accounted for 60 percent of the shipments from the mill.

The plants were linked electronically to each other's production schedules, thereby allowing them to function in a just-in-time inventory mode. All new mills were built on large enough tracts of land to accommodate collaborating businesses.

Iverson didn't feel greater centralization would be good for Nucor. Hamilton Lott, a Vulcraft plant manager, commented in 1997: "We're truly autonomous; we can duplicate efforts made in other parts of Nucor. We might develop the same computer program six times. But the advantages of local autonomy make it worth it." Joe Rutkowski, manager at Darlington steel, agreed: "We're not constrained; headquarters doesn't restrict what I spend. I just have to make my profit contribution at the end of year."

South magazine observed that Iverson had established a characteristic organizational style described as "stripped down" and "no nonsense." "Jack Benny would like this company," observed Roland Underhill, an analyst with Crowell, Weedon and Co. of Los Angeles, "so would Peter Drucker." Underhill pointed out that Nucor's thriftiness didn't end with its "spartan" office staff or modest offices. "There are no corporate perquisites," he stated, "No company planes, No country club memberships. No company cars."

Fortune noted, "Iverson takes the subway when he is in New York, a Wall Street analyst reports in a voice that suggests both admiration and amazement." The general managers reflected this style in the operation of their individual divisions. Their offices were more like plant offices or the offices of private companies built around manufacturing rather than for public appeal. They were simple, routine, and businesslike.

Division Managers

The corporate personnel manager described management relations as informal, trusting, and not "bureaucratic." There was a minimum of paperwork, a phone call was more common than memos, and no confirming memo was thought to be necessary.

A Vulcraft manager commented: "We have what I would call a very friendly spirit of competition from one plant to the next. And, of course, all of the vice presidents and general managers share the same bonus systems, so we are in this together as a team even though we operate our divisions individually."

The divisions managed their activities with a minimum of contact with the corporate staff. Each day disbursements were reported to corporate office. Payments flowed into regional lockboxes. On a weekly basis, joist divisions reported total quotes, sales cancellations, backlogs, and production. Steel mills reported tons rolled, outside shipments, orders, cancellations, and backlog.

Each month, the divisions completed a brief operations analysis, which was sent to all the managers. Its three main purposes were (1) financial consolidation, (2) sharing information among the divisions, and (3) corporate management examination. The summarized information and the performance statistics for all the divisions were then returned to the managers.

The general managers met three times a year. In late October they presented preliminary budgets and capital requests. In late February they met to finalize budgets and deal with miscellaneous matters. Then, at a meeting in May, they handled personnel matters, such as wage increases and changes of policies or benefits. The general managers, as a group, considered the raises for the department heads, the next lower level of management for all the plants.

Vulcraft: The Joist Divisions. One of Nucor's major businesses was the manufacture and sale of open web steel joists and joist girders at Vulcraft divisions located in Florence, South Carolina; Norfolk, Nebraska; Ft. Payne, Alabama; Grapeland, Texas; St. Joe, Indiana; Brigham City, Utah; and Chemung, New York. Open web joists, in contrast to solid joists, were made of steel angle iron separated by round bars or smaller angle iron (see Exhibit 2). These joists cost less, were of greater

Exhibit 2 Nucor's Vulcraft Group

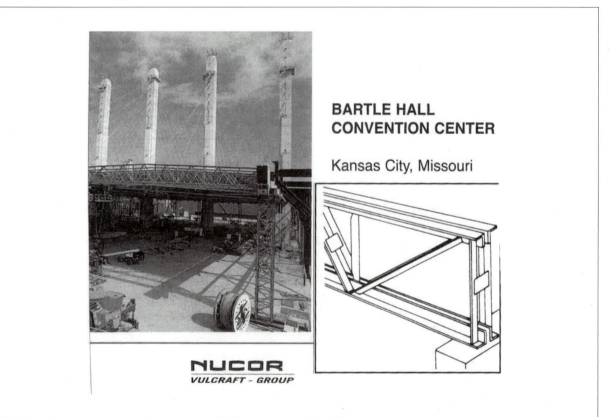

BARTLE HALL CONVENTION CENTER

Kansas City, Missouri

NUCOR
VULCRAFT - GROUP

strength for many applications, and were used primarily as the roof support systems in larger buildings, such as warehouses and shopping malls.

The joist industry was characterized by high competition among many manufacturers for many small customers. With a large percentage of the market, Nucor had been the largest supplier of joists in the United States since 1975. It utilized national advertising campaigns and prepared competitive bids on 80 to 90 percent of the buildings using joists. Competition was based on price and delivery performance. Nucor had developed computer programs to prepare designs for customers and to compute bids based on current prices and labor standards. In addition, each Vulcraft plant maintained its own engineering department to help customers with design problems or specifications. The Florence manager commented, "Here on the East Coast we have six or seven major competitors; of course none of them are as large as we are." He added, "It has been said to us by some of our competitors that in this particular industry we have the finest selling organization in the country."

Nucor aggressively sought to be the lowest-cost producer in the industry. Materials and freight were two important elements of cost. Nucor maintained its own fleet of almost 150 trucks to ensure on-time delivery all over the country, although most business was regional due to transportation costs. Plants were located in rural areas near the markets they served. Nucor's move into steel production was a move to lower the cost of steel used by the joist business.

On the basic assembly line used at the joist divisions, three or four of which might make up any one plant, about six tons of joists per hour would be assembled. In the first stage, eight people cut the angles to the right lengths or bend the round bars to the desired form. These were moved on a roller conveyer to six-man assembly stations, where the component parts would be tacked together for the next stage, which was welding. Drilling and miscellaneous work were done by three people between the lines. The nine-man welding station completed the welds before passing the joists on roller conveyers to two-man inspection teams. The last step before shipment was the painting.

The workers had control over and were responsible for quality. There was an independent quality control inspector who had the authority to reject the run of joists and cause them to be reworked. The quality control people were not under the incentive system and reported to the engineering department.

Daily production might vary widely, since each joist was made for a specific job. The wide range of joists made control of the workload at each station difficult; bottlenecks might arise anywhere along the line. Each workstation was responsible for identifying such bottlenecks so that the foreman could reassign people promptly to maintain productivity. Because workers knew most of the jobs on the line, including the more skilled welding jobs, they could be shifted as needed to avoid bottlenecks.

There were four lines of about 28 people each on two shifts at the Florence division. The jobs on the line were rated on responsibility and assigned a base wage, from $11 to $13 per hour in 1999. In addition, a weekly bonus was paid on the total output of each line. Each worker received the same percentage bonus based on their base wage. The Texas plant had a typical bonus of 225 percent, giving workers an average wage of $27 an hour.

The amount of time required to make a joist had been established over time. As a job was bid, the cost of each joist was determined through the computer program. The time required depended on the length, number of panels, and depth of the joist. At the time of production, the labor value of production, the standard, was determined in a similar manner. The general manager of the South Carolina plant stated, "In the last nine or ten years, we have not changed a standard." The Grapeland plant maintained a time chart based on the time jobs usually take, which was used to estimate the labor required on a job. The plant teams' bonuses were measured against this time.

Steel Divisions. Nucor moved into the steel business in 1968 to provide raw material for the Vulcraft plants. Iverson said, "We got into the steel business because we wanted to build a mill that could make steel as cheaply as we were buying it from foreign importers or from offshore mills." Thus, they entered the industry using the new mini-mill technology after they took a task force of four people around the world to investigate new technological advancements. A case writer from Harvard recounted the development of the steel divisions:

By 1967 about 60 percent of each Vulcraft sales dollar was spent on materials, primarily steel. Thus, the goal of keeping costs low made it imperative to obtain steel economically. In addition, in 1967 Vulcraft bought about 60 percent of its steel from foreign sources. As the Vulcraft Division grew, Nucor became concerned about its ability to obtain an adequate economical supply of steel and, in 1968, began construction of its first steel mill in Darlington, South Carolina. By 1972 the Florence, South Carolina, joist plant was purchasing over 90 percent of its steel from this mill. The Fort Payne, Alabama plant bought about 50 percent of its steel from Florence. Since the mill had excess capacity, Nucor began to market its steel products to outside customers. In 1972, 75 percent of the shipments of Nucor steel were to Vulcraft and 25 percent were to other customers.

Between 1973 and 1981, Nucor built three more bar mills and their accompanying rolling mills to convert the billets into bars, flats, rounds, channels, and other products. Iverson explained in 1984:

In constructing these mills we have experimented with new processes and new manufacturing techniques. We serve as our own general contractor and design and build much of our own equipment. In one or more of our mills, we have built our own continuous casting unit, reheat furnaces, cooling beds, and, in Utah, even our own mill stands. All of these to date have cost under $125 per ton of annual capacity—compared with projected costs for large integrated mills of $1,200-1,500 per ton of annual capacity, ten times our cost. Our mills have high productivity. We currently use less than four man-hours to produce a ton of steel. Our total employment costs are less than $60 per ton compared with the average employment costs of the seven largest U.S. steel companies of close to $130 per ton. Our total labor costs are less than 20 percent of our sales price.

In 1987, Nucor was the first steel company in the world to begin to build a mini-mill to manufacture steel sheet, the raw material for the auto industry and other major manufacturers. This project opened up another 50 percent of the total steel market. The first plant in Crawfordsville, Indiana, was successful, and three additional sheet mills were constructed in 1989 and 1990. During the next several years, these steel plants were significantly modernized and expanded. By 1999, their total capacity was three million tons per year at a capital cost of less than $170 per ton. Nucor's total steel production capacity was 5.9 million tons per year at a cost of $300 per ton of annual capacity. The eight mills sold 80 percent of their output to outside customers and the balance to other Nucor divisions.

The Steelmaking Processing

A steel mill's work is divided into two phases, preparation of steel of the proper "chemistry" and the forming of the steel into the desired products. The typical mini-mill utilizes scrap steel, such as junk auto parts, instead of the iron ore, which would be used in larger, integrated steel mills. The typical bar mini-mill had an annual capacity of 200 to 600 thousand tons, compared with the seven million tons of Bethlehem Steel's integrated plant in Sparrow's Point, Maryland.

In the bar mills, a charging bucket fed loads of scrap steel into electric arc furnaces. The melted load, called a "heat," was poured into a ladle to be carried by overhead crane to the casting machine. In the casting machine, the liquid steel was extruded as a continuous red-hot solid bar of steel and cut into lengths weighing some 900 pounds called "billets." In the typical plant the billet,

about four inches across and about 20 feet long, was held temporarily in a pit where it cooled to normal temperatures. Periodically, billets were carried to the rolling mill and placed in a reheat oven to bring them up to 2,000°F at which temperance they would be malleable. In the rolling mill, presses and dies progressively converted the billet into the desired round bars, angles, channels, flats, and other products. After cutting to standard lengths, they were moved to the warehouse.

Nucor's first steel mill, which employed more than 500 people, was located in Darlington, South Carolina. The mill, with its three electric arc furnaces, operated 24 hours per day, five-and-a-half days per week. Nucor made a number of improvements in the melting and casting operations. Thus, less time and lower capital investment were required at Darlington than at older mini-mills The casting machines were "continuous casters," as opposed to the old batch method.

Not all of Nucor's research projects were successful. The company spent approximately $2,000,000 in an unsuccessful effort to utilize resistance heating. Even more was lost from an effort at induction melting. As Iverson told *Metal Producing*, "That costs us a lot of money. Time wise it was very expensive. But you have got to make mistakes and we've had lots of failures."

The Darlington design became the basis for plants in Nebraska, Texas, and Utah. The Texas plant cost less than $80 per ton of annual capacity. Whereas the typical mini-mill at the time cost approximately $250 per ton, the average cost of Nucor's four mills was under $135. An integrated mill was expected to cost between $1,200 and $1,500 per ton.

The Darlington plant was organized into 12 natural groups for the purpose of incentive pay. Two mills each had two shifts with three groups: melting and casting, rolling mill, and finishing. In melting and casting there were three or four different standards, depending on the material. These standards had been established by the department manager years ago based on historical performance and were never adjusted. The caster, the key to the operation, was used at a 92 percent level—greater than the claims of the manufacturer. For every good ton of billet above the standard hourly rate for the week, workers in the group received a 4 percent bonus. Workers received a 4 to 6 percent bonus for every good ton sheared per hour for the week over the computed standard. A manager stated: "Meltshop employees don't ask me how much it costs Chaparral or LTV to make a billet. They want to know what it costs Darlington, Norfolk, Jewitt to put a billet on the ground—scrap costs, alloy costs, electrical costs, refractory, gas, etc. Everybody from Charlotte to Plymouth watches the nickels and dimes."

Management Philosophy

Aycock, while still the Darlington manager, stated:

The key to making a profit when selling a product with no aesthetic value, or a product that you really can't differentiate from your competitors, is cost. I don't look at us as a fantastic marketing organization, even though I think we are pretty good; but we don't try to overcome unreasonable costs by mass marketing. We maintain low costs by keeping the employee force at the level it should be, not doing things that aren't necessary to achieve our goals, and allowing people to function on their own and by judging them on their results.

To keep a cooperative and productive workforce you need, number one, to be completely honest about everything; number two, to allow each employee as much as possible to make decisions about that employee's work, to find easier and more productive ways to perform duties; and number three, to be as fair as possible to all employees. Most of the changes we make in work procedures and in equipment come from the employees. They really know the problems of their jobs better than anyone else.

To communicate with my employees, I try to spend time in the plant, and, at intervals, have meetings with the employees. Usually, if they have a question, they just visit me. Recently a small group visited me in my office to discuss our vacation policy. They had some suggestions and, after listening to them, I had to agree that the ideas were good.

In discussing his philosophy for dealing with the workforce, the Florence manager stated:

I believe very strongly in the incentive system we have. We are a non-union shop and we all feel that the way to stay so is to take care of our people and show them we care. I think that's easily done because of our fewer layers of management…I spend a good part of my time in the plant, maybe an hour or so a day. If a man wants to know anything, for example an insurance question, I'm there and they walk right up to me and ask me questions, which I'll answer the best I know how.

We don't lay our people off and we make a point of telling our people this. In the slowdown of 1994, we scheduled our line for four days, but the men were allowed to come in the fifth day for maintenance work at base pay. The men in the plant on an average running bonus might make $17 to $19 an hour. If their base pay is half that, on Friday they would only get $8 to $9 an hour. Surprisingly, many of the men did not want to come in on Friday. They felt comfortable with just working four days a week. They are happy to have that extra day off. About 20 percent of the people took the fifth day at base rate, but still no one had been laid off, in an industry with a strong business cycle.

In an earlier business cycle, the executive committee decided in view of economic conditions that a pay freeze was necessary. The employees normally received an increase in their base pay on the first of June. The decision was made at that time to freeze wages. The officers of the company, as a show of good faith, accepted a 5 percent pay cut. Management held meetings with the production workers to explain the economic crisis the company faced and to address any employee questions.

Personnel Policies

Nucor provided an incentive plan and job security. All employees at Nucor received the same fringe benefits and there was only one group insurance plan. Holidays and vacations did not differ by job. Every child of every Nucor employee received up to $1,200 a year for four years if they chose to go on to higher education, including technical schools. The company had no executive dining rooms or restrooms, no fishing lodges, company cars, or reserved parking places.

Jim Coblin, Nucor's vice president of human resources at the time, described Nucor's systems for *HR Magazine* in a 1994 article, "No frills HR at Nucor: a lean, bottom-line approach at this steel company empowers employees." Coblin, as benefits administrator, received part-time help from one of the corporate secretaries in the corporate office. The plants typically used someone from their finance department to handle compensation issues, although two plants had personnel generalists. Nucor plants did not have job descriptions, finding they caused more problems than they solved, given the flexible workforce and non-union status of Nucor employees. Surprisingly, Coblin found performance appraisal a waste of time. If an employee was not performing well, the problem would be dealt with directly. The key, he believed, was not to put a maximum on what employees could earn and pay them directly for productivity. Iverson firmly believed that the bonus should be direct and involve no discretion on part of a manager.

Employees were kept informed about the company. Charts showing the division's results in return-on-assets and bonus payoff were posted in prominent places in the plant. The personnel manager commented that as he traveled around to all the plants, he found everyone in the company could tell him the level of profits in their division. The general managers held dinners at least once a year with their employees. The dinners were held with 50 or 60 employees at a time, resulting in as many as 20 dinners per year for the general managers. After introductory remarks, the floor was opened for discussion of any work-related problems. There was a new employee orientation program and an employee handbook that contained personnel policies and rules. The corporate office sent all news releases to each division where they were posted on bulletin boards. Each employee in the company also received a copy of the annual report. For the last several years, the cover of the annual report contained the names of all Nucor employees.

Absenteeism and tardiness were not a problem at Nucor. Each employee had four days of absences before pay was reduced. In addition to these, missing work was allowed for jury duty, military leave, or the death of close relatives. After this, a day's absence cost the employee bonus pay for that week and lateness of more than a half-hour meant the loss of bonus for that day.

Safety was a concern of Nucor's critics. Nucor plants had 10 fatalities in the 1980s, but after safety administrators were appointed at each plant, safety improved in the 1990s. The company also had a formal grievance procedure, although the Darlington manager couldn't recall the last grievance he had processed.

The average hourly worker's pay was more than twice the average paid by other manufacturing companies in the states where Nucor's plants were located. In many rural communities, Nucor provided better wages than most other manufacturers. The plant in Hertford County illustrated this point. A June 21, 1998, article in *The Charlotte Observer* entitled "Hope on the Horizon: In Hertford County, Poverty Reigns and Jobs are Scarce" reported, "In North Carolina's forgotten northeastern corner, where poverty rates run more than twice the state average, Nucor's $300 million steel mill is a dream realized." The plant on the banks of the Chowan River saw employees earning up to three times the average local manufacturing wage. Nucor's desire to have other companies in the field close by to save on shipping costs led to four companies announcing they would locate close to Nucor's property, adding another 100 to 200 jobs. People couldn't believe such wages, but the average wage for these jobs at the Darlington plant was $70,000 and it was thought that this plant paid similarly. The plant CFO added that Nucor didn't try to set its pay "a buck over Wal-Mart" but instead went for the best workers. The article noted that steelwork is hot and often dangerous, and that turnover at the plant may be high as people adjust to the nature of the work and Nucor's hard-driving team system. He added, "Slackers don't last." The local preacher said, "In 15 years, Baron (a local child) will be making $75,000 a year at Nucor, not in jail. I have a place now I can hold in front of him and say 'Look, right here. This is for you.'"

In early 2009, Nucor's unique policies with its employees were still evident. Despite the economic crisis, performance in 2008 was excellent and $40 million in bonuses were distributed, with an extra bonus on top because of the extraordinary year. The company paid $270 million in profit sharing. Gail Bruce, the new vice president of human resources, explained how Nucor had avoided the layoffs other plants experienced. First, there was a history of open communications and a system designed to deal with the nature of the industry and educate workers about it. If plants were idled, pay automatically went to base pay, which was about half the usual total income with bonuses. No one was laid off and the well-paid workers could adapt, just like the company. He marveled, "The spirit in the operations is extraordinary." The cooperation extended to other solutions. *BusinessWeek* reported, "Work that used to be done by contractors, such as making special parts, mowing the lawns, and even cleaning the bathrooms, is now handled by Nucor staff. The bathrooms, managers say, [were] an employee suggestion." *BusinessWeek* reported that DiMicco and other managers received hundreds of cards and e-mails thanking them for caring about workers and their families.

The Incentive System

There were four incentive programs at Nucor, one each for (1) production workers, (2) department heads, (3) staff people, such as accountants, secretaries, or engineers, and (4) senior management, which included the division managers (VP/general managers of each division). All of these programs were based on group performance.

Within the production program, groups ranged in size from 25 to 30 people and had definable and measurable operations. The company believed that a program should be simple and that bonuses should be paid promptly. "We don't have any discretionary bonuses—zero. It is all based on performance. Now we don't want anyone to sit in judgment, because it never is fair…" said Iverson. Bonuses are based on roughly 90 percent of the historical time it takes to make a particular joist. If, for example, that week the joists are produced 40 percent faster than the standard time, workers get a 40 percent bonus in their pay the following week. The complete paycheck amount, including overtime, was multiplied by the bonus factor. A bonus was not paid when equipment was not operating. The foremen were also part of the group and received the same bonus as the employees they supervised.

The second incentive program was for department heads in the various divisions. The incentive pay here was based on division contribution, defined as the division earnings before corporate expenses and profit sharing are determined. Bonuses were reported to run between 0 and 90 percent (averaging more than 50 percent) of base salary. The base salaries at this level were set at 75 percent of industry norms.

There was a third plan for people who were not production workers, department managers, or senior managers. Their bonuses were based on either the division return-on-assets or the corporate return-on-assets, depending on their unit. Bonuses were typically 30 percent or more of a person's base salary for corporate positions.

The fourth program was for the senior officers. This group had no employment contracts, pension or retirement plans, or other perquisites. Their base salaries were set at about 75 percent of what an individual doing similar work in other companies would receive. Once return-on-equity reached 9 percent (slightly below the average for manufacturing firms) 5 percent of net earnings before taxes went into a pool, which was divided among the officers based on their salaries. For example, if the return-on-equity for the company reaches 20 percent, then senior officers can wind up with as much as 190 percent of their base salaries and 115 percent on top of that in stock. Half of the bonus was paid in cash and half was deferred. Individual bonuses ranged from zero to several hundred percent, averaging 75 to 150 percent.

However, the opposite was true as well. In 1982 the return was 8 percent and the executives received no bonus. Iverson's pay in 1981 was approximately $300,000 but dropped the next year to $110,000. "I think that ranked by total compensation I was the lowest paid CEO in the *Fortune* 500. I was kind of proud of that, too." In his 1997 book *Plain Talk: Lessons from a Business Maverick*, Iverson said, "Can management expect employees to be loyal if we lay them all off at every dip of the economy, while we go on padding our own pockets?" Even so, by 1986 Iverson's stock was worth over $10 million, and the former Vulcraft manager was a multimillionaire.

In lieu of a retirement plan, the company had a profit-sharing plan with a deferred trust. Each year 10 percent of pretax earnings were put into profit sharing for all employees below officer level. Twenty percent of this was set aside to be paid to employees the following March as a cash bonus, and the remainder was put into trust for each employee on the basis of a percentage of their earnings as a percentage of total wages paid within the corporation. The employee was vested after the first year. Employees received a quarterly statement of their balance in profit sharing.

The company had an Employer Monthly Stock Investment Plan into which Nucor added 10 percent to the amount the employee contributed to the purchase of any Nucor stock and paid the commission. For each five years of service with the company, the employee received a service award consisting of five shares of Nucor stock. Moreover, if profits were good, extraordinary bonus payments would be made to the employees. For example, in December 1998 each employee received an $800 payment.

According to Iverson:

I think the first obligation of the company is to the stockholder and to its employees. I find in this country too many cases where employees are underpaid and corporate management is making huge social donations for self-fulfillment. We regularly give donations, but we have a very interesting corporate policy. First, we give donations where our employees are. Second, we give donations that will benefit our employees, such as to the YMCA. It is a difficult area and it requires a lot of thought. There is certainly a strong social responsibility for a company, but it cannot be at the expense of the employees or the stockholders.

Having welcomed a parade of visitors over the years, Iverson became concerned with the pattern apparent at other companies' steel plants: "They only do one or two of the things we do. It's not just incentives or the scholarship program; it's all those things put together that results in a unified philosophy for the company."

Building on Their Success

Throughout the 1980s and 1990s, Nucor continued to take the initiative and be the prime mover in steel as well as the industries vertically related to steel. For example, in 1984 Nucor broke the industry pattern of basing the price of an order of steel on the quantity ordered. Iverson noted, "Some time ago we began to realize that with computer order entry and billing, the extra charge for smaller orders was not cost justified." In a seemingly risky move, in 1986 Nucor began construction of a $25 million plant in Indiana to manufacture steel fasteners. Imports had grown to 90 percent of this market as U.S. companies failed to compete. Iverson said "We're going to bring that business back; we can make bolts as cheaply as foreign producers." A second plant, which opened in 1995, gave Nucor 20 percent of the U.S. market for steel fasteners. Nucor also acquired a steel bearings manufacturer in 1986, which Iverson called "a good fit with our business, policies, and our people."

In early 1986, Iverson announced plans for a revolutionary plant at Crawfordsville, Indiana, that would be the first mini-mill in the world to manufacture flat-rolled or sheet steel, the last bastion of the integrated manufacturers. This market alone was twice the size of the existing market for mini-mill products. It would be a $250 million gamble on new technology. The plant was expected to halve the integrated manufacturer's labor cost of $3 per ton and save $50 to $75 on a $400-per-ton selling price. If it worked, the profit from this plant alone would come close to the profit of the whole corporation. *Forbes* commented, "If any mini-mill can meet the challenge, it's Nucor. But expect the going to be tougher this time around." If successful, Nucor would have the licensing rights to the next two plants built in the world with this technology. Nucor had spent millions trying to develop the process when it heard of some promising developments at a German company. In the spring of 1986, Aycock flew to Germany to see the pilot machine at SMS Schloemann-Siemag AG. In December the Germans came to Charlotte for the first of what they thought would be many meetings to hammer out a deal with Nucor. Iverson shocked them when he announced Nucor was ready to build the first plant of its kind.

Keith Busse was named general manager and put in charge of building the Crawfordsville steel sheet plant. The process of bringing this plant online was so exciting it became the basis for a best-selling book by Robert Preston, which was serialized in *The New Yorker*. Preston reported on a conversation during construction between Iverson and Busse. Thinking about the future, Busse was worried that Nucor might someday become like Big Steel. He asked, "How do we allow Nucor to grow without expanding the bureaucracy?" He didn't want to see Nucor end up like other companies with overlapping people doing the same job. Iverson agreed. Busse seriously suggested, "Maybe we're going to need group vice-presidents." Iverson's heated response was, "Do you want to ruin the company? That's the old Harvard Business School thinking. They would only get in the way, slow us down." He said the company could at least double in size before it added a new level of management. "I hope that by the time we have group vice-presidents I'll be collecting Social Security," he said.

The gamble on the new plant paid off, and Busse became a key man at Nucor. The new mill began operations in August 1989 and reached 15 percent of capacity by the end of the year. In June 1990 it had its first profitable month and Nucor announced the construction of a second plant in Arkansas.

The supply and cost of scrap steel to feed the mini-mills were an important future concern to Iverson. In 1993 Nucor announced the construction of plant in Trinidad to supply its mills with iron carbide pellets. The innovative plant would cost $60 million and take a year and a half to complete. In 1994 the two existing sheet mills were expanded and a new $500 million, 1.8-million-ton sheet mill in South Carolina was announced, to begin operation in early 1997.

In 1987, in what *The New York Times* called their "most ambitious project yet," Nucor began a joint venture with Yamato Kogyo, Ltd. to make structural steel products in a mill on the Mississippi River in direct challenge to the Big Three integrated steel companies. John Correnti was put in charge of the operation. Correnti built and then became the general manager of Nucor-Yamato when it started up in 1988. In 1991 he surprised many people by deciding to double Nucor-Yamato's capacity by 1994. It became Nucor's largest division and the largest wide-flange producer in the United States. By 1995, Bethlehem Steel was the only other wide-flange producer of structural steel products left and had plans to leave the business.

Nucor started up its first facility to produce metal buildings in 1987. A second metal buildings facility began operations in late 1996 in South Carolina and a new steel deck facility in Alabama was announced for 1997. At the end of 1997, the Arkansas sheet mill underwent a $120 million expansion to include a galvanizing facility.

In 1995, Nucor became involved in its first international venture, an ambitious project with Brazil's Companhia Siderurgica National to build a $700 million steel mill in the state of Ceara. While other mini-mills were cutting deals to buy and sell abroad, Nucor was planning to ship iron from Brazil and process it in Trinidad.

Nucor set records for sales and net earnings in 1997. Although sales for 1998 decreased 1 percent and net earnings were down 10 percent, the management made a number of long-term investments and closed draining investments. Startup began at the new South Carolina steam mill and at the Arkansas sheet mill expansion. The plans for a North Carolina steel plate mill in Hertford were announced. This would bring Nucor's total steel production capacity to 12 million tons per year. Moreover, the plant in Trinidad, which had proven much more expensive than was originally expected, was deemed unsuccessful and closed. Finally, directors approved the repurchase of up to five million shares of Nucor stock.

Still, the downward trends at Nucor continued. Sales and earnings were down 3 percent and 7 percent, respectively, for 1999. However, these trends did not seem to affect the company's investments. Expansion was under way in the steel mills and a third building systems facility was under construction in Texas. Nucor actively searched for a site for a joist plant in the Northeast. A letter of intent was signed with Australian and Japanese companies to form a joint venture to commercialize the strip casting technology. To understand the challenges facing Nucor, industry, technology, and environmental trends in the 1980s and 1990s have to be considered.

Evolution of the U.S. Steel Industry

The early 1980s were the worst years in decades for the steel industry. Data from the American Iron and Steel Institute showed shipments falling from 100 million tons in 1979 to around 85 million tons in 1980 and 1981.

A slackening in the economy, particularly in auto sales, led the decline. In 1986, when industry capacity was at 130 million tons, the outlook was for a continued decline in per-capita consumption and movement towards the 90 to 100 million-ton range. The chairman of Armco saw "millions of tons chasing a market that's not there: excess capacity that must be eliminated."

The large, integrated steel firms, such as U.S. Steel and Armco, which made up the major part of the industry, were the hardest hit. The *Wall Street Journal* stated, "The decline has resulted from such problems as high labor and energy costs in mining and processing iron ore, a lack of profits and capital to modernize plants, and conservative management that has hesitated to take risks." These companies produced a wide range of steels, primarily from ore processed in blast furnaces. They found it difficult to compete with imports, usually from Japan. They sought the protection of import quotas.

Imported steel accounted for 20 percent of the U.S. steel consumption, up from 12 percent in the early 1970s. The U.S. share of world production of raw steel declined from 19 percent to 14 percent during the period. *Iron Age* stated that exports, as a percentage of shipments in 1985, were 34 percent for Nippon, 26 percent for British Steel, 30 percent for Krupp, 49 percent for USINOR of France, and less than 1 percent for every American producer on the list. The consensus of steel experts was that imports would average 23 percent of the market in the last half of the 1980s.

By the mid-1980s, the integrated mills were moving fast to get back into the game: they were restructuring, cutting capacity, dropping unprofitable lines, focusing products, and trying to become responsive to the market. The industry made a pronounced move toward segmentation. Integrated producers focused on mostly flat-rolled and structural grades; reorganized steel companies focused on a limited range of products; mini-mills dominated the bar and light structural product areas; and specialty steel firms sought niches. There was an accelerated shutdown of older plants, elimination of products by some firms, and the installation of new product lines with new technologies by others.

The road for the integrated mills was not easy. As *Purchasing* pointed out, tax laws and accounting rules slowed the closing of inefficient plants. Shutting down a 10,000-person plant could require a firm to hold a cash reserve of $100 million to fund health, pension, and insurance liabilities. The chairman of Armco commented: "Liabilities associated with a planned shutdown are so large that they can quickly devastate a company's balance sheet."

Joint ventures were formed to produce steel for a specific market or region. The chairman of USX called them "an important new wrinkle in steel's fight for survival" and stated, "If there had been more joint ventures like these two decades ago, the U.S. steel industry might have built only half of the dozen or so hot-strip mills it put up in that time and avoided today's over-capacity."

The American Iron and Steel Institute reported steel production in 1988 of 99.3 million tons, up from 89.2 in 1987 and the highest in seven years. As a result of modernization programs, 60.9 percent of production was from continuous casters. Exports for steel increased and imports fell. Some steel experts believed the United States was now cost competitive with Japan. However, 1989 proved to be a year of "waiting for the other shoe to drop," according to *Metal Center News*. U.S. steel production was hampered by a new recession, the expiration of the voluntary import restraints, and labor negotiations in several companies. Declines in car production and consumer goods hit flat-rolled steel hard. AUJ Consultants told MCN, "The U.S. steel market has peaked. Steel consumption is trending down. By 1990, we expect total domestic demand to dip under 90 million tons."

The economic slowdown of the early 1990s did lead to a decline in the demand for steel through early 1993, but by 1995 America was in its best steel market in 20 years and many companies were building new flat-roll mini-mills. A *BusinessWeek* article at the time described it as "the race of the Nucor look-alikes." Six years after Nucor pioneered the low-cost German technology in Crawfordsville, competitors were finally gearing up to compete. Ten new projects were expected to add 20 million tons per year of the flat-rolled steel, raising U.S. capacity by as much as 40 percent by 1998. These mills opened in 1997, just as the industry was expected to move into a cyclical slump. It was no surprise that worldwide competition increased and companies that had previously focused on their home markets began a race to become global powerhouses. The foreign push was new for U.S. firms who had focused on defending their home markets. U.S. mini-mills focused their international expansion primarily in Asia and South America.

Meanwhile, in 1994, U.S. Steel, North America's largest integrated steel producer, began a major business process re-engineering project to improve order fulfillment performance and customer satisfaction on the heels of a decade of restructuring. According to *Steel Times International*, "U.S. Steel had to completely change the way it did business. Cutting labor costs and increasing reliability and productivity took the company a long way towards improving profitability and competitiveness. However, it became clear that this leaner organization still had to implement new technologies and business processes if it was to maintain a competitive advantage." The goals of the business process re-engineering project included a sharp reduction in cycle time, greatly decreased levels of inventory, shorter order lead times, and the ability to offer real-time promise dates to customers. In 1995, they successfully installed integrated planning/production/order fulfillment software, and results were very positive. U.S. Steel believed that the re-engineering project had positioned it for a future of increased competition, tighter markets, and raised customer expectations.

In late 1997 and again in 1998, the decline in demand prompted Nucor and other U.S. companies to slash prices in order to compete with the unprecedented surge of imports. By the last quarter of 1998, these imports had led to the filing of unfair trade complaints with U.S. trade regulators, causing steel prices in the spot market to drop sharply in August and September before they stabilized. A press release from William Daley, the U.S. Secretary of Commerce, stated, "I will not stand by and allow U.S. workers, communities and companies to bear the brunt of other nations' problematic policies and practices. We are the most open economy of the world. But we are not the world's dumpster."

The Commerce Department concluded in March 1999 that six countries had illegally dumped stainless steel in the United States at prices below production costs or home market prices. The Commerce Department found that Canada, South Korea, and Taiwan were guilty only of dumping, while Belgium, Italy, and South Africa also gave producers unfair subsidies that effectively lowered prices. However, on June 23, 1999, the *Wall Street Journal* reported that the Senate decisively shut off an attempt to restrict U.S. imports of steel despite industry complaints that a flood of cheap imports were driving them out of business. Reportedly President Clinton would have vetoed the bill anyway because it would violate international trade law and leave the United States vulnerable to retaliation.

The American Iron and Steel Institute reported that in May 1999, U.S. steel mills shipped 8,330,000 net tons, a decrease of 6.7 percent from the 8,927,000 net tons shipped in May 1998. They also stated that for the first five months of 1999, shipments were 41,205,000 net tons, down 10 percent from the same period in 1998. AISI president and CEO Andrew Sharkey III said, "Once again, the May data show clearly that America's steel trade crisis continues. U.S. steel companies and employees continue to be injured by high levels of dumping and subsidized imports … In addition, steel inventory levels remain excessive, and steel operating rates continue to be very low."

As the 1990s ended, Nucor was the second-largest steel producer in the United States, behind USX. The company's market capitalization was about two times that of the next smaller competitor. Even in a tight industry, someone can win. Nucor was in the best position because

the industry was very fragmented and there were many marginal competitors.

Steel Technology and the Mini-Mill

A new type of mill, the mini-mill, emerged in the United States in the 1970s to compete with the integrated mill. The mini-mill used electric arc furnaces initially to manufacture a narrow product line from scrap steel. The leading U.S. mini-mills in the 1980s were Nucor, Florida Steel, Georgetown Steel, North Star Steel, and Chaparral. Between the late 1970s and 1980s, the integrated mills' market share fell from about 90 percent to about 60 percent, with the integrated steel companies averaging a 7 percent return on equity, the mini-mills averaging 14 percent, and some, such as Nucor, achieving about 25 percent. In the 1990s, the integrated mills' market share fell to around 40 percent while mini-mills' share rose to 23 percent, reconstructed mills increased their share from 11 percent to 28 percent, and specialized mills increased their share from 1 to 6 percent.

Some experts believed that a relatively new technology, the twin shell electric arc furnace, would help mini-mills increase production and lower costs and take market share. According to the *Pittsburgh Business Times*, "With a twin shell furnace, one shell—the chamber holding the scrap to be melted—is filled and heated. During the heating of the first shell, the second shell is filled. When the heating is finished on the first shell, the electrodes move to the second. The first shell is emptied and refilled before the second gets hot." This increased production by 60 percent. Twin shell production had been widely adopted. Nucor Steel began running a twin shell furnace in November 1996 in Berkeley, South Carolina, and installed another in Norfolk, Nebraska, which began operation in 1997. "Everyone accepts twin shells as a good concept because there's a lot of flexibility of operation," said Rodney Mott, vice president and general manager of Nucor-Berkeley. However, this move toward twin shell furnaces was destined to affect scrap availability. According to an October 1997 quote in *Pittsburgh Business Times* by Ralph Smaller, vice president of process technology at Kvaerner, "Innovations that feed the electric furnaces' production of flat-rolled (steel) will increase the demand on high quality scrap and alternatives. The technological changes are just beginning and will accelerate over the next few years."

According to a September 1997 *Industry Week* article, steelmakers around the world were now closely monitoring the development of continuous "strip casting" technology, which many thought would prove to be the next leap forward for the industry. "The objective of strip casting is to produce thin strips of steel (in the 1-mm to 4-mm range) as liquid steel flows from a tundish—the stationary vessel which received molten steel from the ladle. It would eliminate the slab-casting stage and all of the rolling that now takes place in a hot mill." Strip casting was reported to have some difficult technological challenges but companies in Germany, France, Japan, Australia, Italy, and Canada had strip-casting projects under way. In fact, all of the significant development work in strip casting was taking place outside the United States.

Larry Kavanagh, American Iron and Steel Institute vice president for manufacturing and technology, said, "Steel is a very high-tech industry, but nobody knows it." The most-productive steelmaking facilities incorporate advanced metallurgical practices, sophisticated process-control sensors, state-of-the art computer controls, and the latest refinements in continuous casting and rolling mill technology. Michael Shot, vice president of manufacturing at Carpenter Technology Corp., a maker of specialty steels and premium-grade alloys, said, "You don't survive in this industry unless you have the technology to make the best products in the world in the most efficient manner."

Environmental and Political Issues

Not all stakeholders were happy with the way Nucor did business. In June 1998, *Waste News* reported that Nucor's mill in Crawfordsville was cited by the Environmental Protection Agency for alleged violations of federal and state clean-air rules. The Pamlico-Tar River Foundation, the North Carolina Coastal Federation, and the Environmental Defense Fund had concerns about the state's decision to allow the company to start building the plant before the environmental reviews were completed. According to the Charlotte *News & Observer,* "The environmental groups charge that the mill will discharge 6,720 tons of pollutants into the air each year."

Moreover, there were other concerns about the fast-track approval of the facility being built in Hertford County. This plant was to be located on the banks of one of the most important and sensitive stretches of the Chowan, a principal tributary to the Albemarle Sound and the last bastion of the state's once-vibrant river-herring fishery. North Carolina passed a law in 1997 that required the restoration of this fishery through a combination of measures designed to prevent overfishing, restore spawning and nursery habitats, and improve water quality in the Chowan. Another issue regarded the excessive incentives the state of North Carolina gave Nucor to build a $300 million steel mill there. Some questioned whether the promise of 300 well-paying jobs

in Hertford County was worth the $155 million in tax breaks the state was giving Nucor.

Management Evolution

Only five members of the board of directors were in attendance during their meeting in January 1999 due to the death of Jim Cunningham. Near the end of the meeting, Aycock read a motion, drafted by Siegel, that Ken Iverson be removed as chairman. It was seconded by Hlavacek and passed. This came as a surprise to Iverson. Prior to this time, in the spring of 1998, as Iverson approached his seventy-third birthday, he commented, "People ask me when I'm going to retire. I tell them our mandatory retirement age is 95, but I may change that when I get there." Now he was being forced out. It was announced that Iverson would be a chairman emeritus and a director, but after further disagreements, Iverson left the company completely. It was agreed, Iverson would receive $500,000 a year for five years. John Correnti succeeded Iverson in January 1999; but, he was voted out of this position in June 1999. At that time, David Aycock came out of retirement to become chairman, CEO, and president of Nucor.

All of this was a complete surprise to investors and brought the stock price down 10 percent. Siegel commented, "The board felt Correnti was not the right person to lead Nucor into the twenty-first century." Aycock assured everyone he would be happy to move back into retirement as soon as replacements could be found.

Aycock moved to increase the corporate office staff by adding a level of executive vice presidents over four areas of business and adding two specialist jobs in strategic planning and steel technology. When Siegel retired, Aycock promoted Terry Lisenby to CFO and treasurer and hired a director of IT to report to Lisenby (see Exhibit 3 for the organizational chart in 2000).

Jim Coblin, vice president of human resources, believed the additions to management were necessary, "It's not bad to get a little more like other companies." He noted that the various divisions did their business cards and plant signs differently; some did not even want a Nucor sign. Sometimes six different Nucor salesmen would call on the same customer. "There is no manager of human resources in the plants, so at least we needed to give additional training to the person who does most of that work at the plant," he stated. With these new additions there would be a director of information technology and two important committees, one for environmental issues and the second for audit.

Coblin believed the old system might have worked well when there was less competition. Aycock considered it "ridiculous." "It was not possible to properly manage,

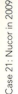

Exhibit 3 Nucor Organization Chart, 2000

to know what was going on. The top managers have totally lost contact with the company." Coblin was optimistic the use of executive vice presidents would improve management. The three meetings of the general managers had slowly increased in length from about a day and a half to two-and-a-half days and became more focused. The new executive vice presidents would bring a perspective above the level of the individual plants. Instead of 15 individual detailed presentations, each general manager would give a short, five-minute briefing and then there would be an in-depth presentation on the group, with team participation. After some training by Lisenby, the divisions became pretty good with SWOT analysis. Coblin thought these changes would make Nucor a stronger global player.

To Jeff Kemp, the new general manager of strategic planning and business development, the big issue was how to sustain earnings growth. In the U.S. steel industry there were too many marginal competitors. The U.S. government had recently added to the problem by giving almost a billion dollars to nine struggling mills, which simply allowed them to limp along and weaken the industry. He was looking for Nucor's opportunities within the steel industry. His experience in the chemical industry suggested a need for Nucor to establish a position of superiority and grow globally, driving industry competition rather than reacting. He argued that a company should protect its overall market position, which could mean sacrifices for individual plants. Aycock liked Kemp's background in law and accounting and had specifically sought someone from outside the steel industry to head up Nucor's strategic planning. By June 2000, Kemp had conducted studies of other industries in the

U.S. market and developed a working document which identified opportunities worthy of further analysis.

"Every company hits a plateau," Aycock observed, "You can't just go out and build plants to grow. How do you step up to the next level? I wouldn't say it's a turning point, but we have to get our strategic vision and strategic plans." Nucor had its first-ever strategic planning sessions. Aycock believed Nucor needed to be quick to recognize developing technology in all production areas. He noted the joint venture to develop a new strip caster. This new product could allow Nucor to build smaller plants closer to markets. This would be particularly helpful on the West Coast. Nucor would own the U.S. and Brazilian rights, their partners the rest. He was also looking forward to the next generation of steel mills and wanted to own the rights to them. He praised Iverson's skill at seeing technology and committing to it.

Aycock was very interested in acquisitions, but felt they must fit the company's strategic plans. A significant opportunity existed in pre-engineered buildings. Aycock intended to concentrate on steel for the next five to six years, achieving an average growth rate of 15 percent per year. In about seven years he wanted Nucor to be ready to move into other areas. He said Nucor had already "picked the low hanging grapes" and must be careful in its next moves.

Daniel DiMicco assumed the role of Nucor's president and chief executive officer in September 2000, when Aycock stepped down as planned. Peter Browning was elected chairman of the board of directors. Aycock retired from the board a year later.

Sales for 2000 increased 14 percent over 1999 to reach a record level. Earnings were also at record levels, up 27 percent over 1999. The year began strongly but business weakened by year's end. The good news was that Nucor had record profits while other steel companies faced bankruptcy. A Vulcraft plant was under construction in New York, their first northeastern operation. They were also attempting a breakthrough technological step in strip casting at Crawfordsville known as the Castrip process. They sold their Grinding Ball process and the Bearing Products operation because they were not a part of their core business.

In the company's annual report, DiMicco laid out their plans for 2000 and beyond: "Our targets are to deliver an average annual earnings growth of 10–15 percent over the next 10 years, to deliver a return well in excess of our cost of capital, to maintain a minimum average return on equity of 14 percent, and to deliver to return on sales of 8–10 percent. Our strategy will focus on Nucor becoming a 'Market Leader' in every product group and business in which we compete. This calls for significant increases in market share for many of our core products and the maintenance of market share where we currently enjoyed a leadership position." While pointing out that it would be impossible to obtain this success through the previous strategy of greenfield construction, he added, "There will now be a heavy focus on growth through acquisitions. We will also continue growing through the commercialization of new disruptive and leapfrog technologies."

Steel and Nucor in the Twenty-First Century

In early 2009, DiMicco reflected back on his nine-year tenure as CEO of Nucor with pride. These had been some of the steel industry's rockiest times, and yet under his leadership, Nucor had almost doubled in size (see Appendices 1, 2, and 3).

By October 2001, more than 20 steel companies in the United States, including Bethlehem Steel Corp. and LTV Corp., the nation's third- and fourth-largest U.S. steel producers, respectively, had filed for bankruptcy protection. Over a dozen producers were operating under Chapter 11 bankruptcy-law protection, which allowed them to maintain market share by selling steel cheaper than non–Chapter 11 steelmakers. On October 20, 2001, *The Economist* noted that of the 14 steel companies followed by Standard & Poor's, only Nucor was indisputably healthy. In the fall of 2001, 25 percent of domestic steel companies were in bankruptcy proceedings, although the United States was the largest importer of steel in the world. Experts believed that close to half of the U.S. steel industry might be forced to close before conditions improved.

In 2001, the world steel industry found itself in the middle of one of its most unprofitable and volatile periods ever, in part due to a glut of steel that had sent prices to 20-year lows. While domestic steel producers were mired in red ink, many foreign steelmakers desperately needed to continue to sell in the relatively open U.S. market to stay profitable. The industry was hovering around 75 percent capacity utilization, a level too low to be profitable for many companies. Three European companies—France's Usinor SA, Luxembourg's Arbed SA and Spain's Aceralia Corp.—merged to form the world's largest steel company. Two Japanese companies—NKK Corp. and Kawasaki Steel Corp.—merged to form the world's second-biggest steelmaker. These new megasteelmakers could outmuscle U.S. competitors, which were less efficient, smaller, and financially weaker than their competitors in Asia and Europe. At this time, the largest U.S. steelmaker, USX-U.S. Steel Group, was only the eleventh-largest producer in the world. Furthermore, while in 1990 mini-mills accounted for 36 percent of the domestic steel market, by 2000 the more efficient minimill had seized 50 percent of the market and the resulting competition had driven prices lower for integrated steel as well as mini-mills.

The year 2001 turned out to be one of the worst ever for steel. There were the September 11th attacks, a recession, and a surge of imports. DiMicco broke with Nucor's traditional opposition to government intervention to make a major push for protective tariffs. He stated, "The need to enforce trade rules is similar to the need to enforce any other law. If two merchants have stores side by side, but one sells stolen merchandise at a vast discount, we know that it's time for the police to step in." In March 2002, President Bush, after an investigation and recommendation by the ITC, imposed anti-dumping tariffs under section 201 of the Trade Act of 1974. This restricted some imports of steel and placed quotas of up to 30 percent on others. The move was opposed by many, including steel users. Some criticized the president for abandoning free trade and pointed out that protection would hamper the necessary actions to restructure the steel industry in America by reducing excess capacity. The European Union immediately threatened reprisals and appealed to the WTO. In December, China imposed its own three-year program of import duties. Steel prices rose 40 percent in 2002 after the tariffs. Within a year, the price of hot-rolled steel increased to $260 per ton over the 20-year low of $210 during 2002. In November 2003, the WTO ruled against the tariffs and, under increasing pressure of retaliation, Bush withdrew them.

While many steel companies floundered, Nucor was able to take advantage of these conditions. In March 2001, Nucor made its first acquisition in 10 years, purchasing a mini-mill in New York from Sumitomo Corp. DiMicco commented, It's taken us three years before our team has felt this is the right thing to do and get started making acquisitions." In this challenged industry, he argued it would be cheaper to buy than build plants. Nucor made more purchases. They purchased the assets of Auburn Steel, which gave them a merchant bar presence in the Northeast and helped the new Vulcraft facility in New York. They acquired ITEC Steel, a leader in the emerging load-bearing light-gauge steel-framing market, and saw an opportunity to aggressively broaden its market. Nucor increased its sheet capacity by roughly one third when it acquired the assets of Trico Steel Co. in Alabama for $120 million. In early 2002, they acquired the assets of Birmingham Steel Corp. This $650 million purchase of four mini-mills was the largest acquisition in Nucor's history. However, 2002 also proved to be a difficult year for Nucor. While they increased their steelmaking capacity by more than 25 percent, revenue increased 11 percent, and earnings improved 43 percent over their weak numbers of 2001, their other financial goals were not met.

This did not stop Nucor from continuing its expansion through acquisitions to increase their market share and capacity in steel and by actively working on new production processes that would provide them with technological advantages. They acquired the U.S. and Brazilian rights to the promising Castrip process for strip casting. After development work on the process in Indiana, they began full-time production in May 2002 and produced 7,000 tons in the last 10 months of 2002. Moreover, in April, Nucor entered into a joint venture with a Brazilian mining company, CVRD, the world's largest producer of iron-ore pellets, to jointly develop low-cost iron-based products. Success with this effort would give them the ability to make steel by combining iron ore and coke rather than using scrap steel, which was becoming less available (as was once feared).

During 2003, prices of steel rose in the United States and Asia as global demand outpaced supply. China, with its booming economy, drove the market. World prices did not soar dangerously because the steel industry continued to be plagued by overcapacity, but steel-hungry China and other fast-growing nations added to their steel capacity to balance supply and demand.

In August 2003, imports of steel commodities into the United States fell 22 percent. A weakened dollar, the growing demand from China, and tariffs imposed in 2002 limited imports. Domestic capacity declined as producers consolidated, idled plants, or went out of business, which increased capacity utilization from 77.2 to 93.4 percent. Prices for iron ore and energy rose, affecting integrated producers. Mini-mills saw

their costs rise as worldwide demand for scrap rose. Thus, U.S. steelmakers boosted their prices. By February 2004, a growing coalition of U.S. steel producers and consumers was considering whether to petition to limit soaring exports of scrap steel from the United States, the world's largest producer of steel scrap. The United States had exported an estimated 12 million metric tons of steel scrap in 2003, a 21 percent increase from 2002. Moreover, the price of scrap steel had risen to $255 a ton. At the same time the price of hot-rolled sheet steel rose to $360 a ton. One result was that the International Steel Group (ISG) replaced Nucor as the most profitable U.S. steel producer. ISG was created when investor Wilbur Ross acquired the failing traditional steel producers in America, including LTV, Bethlehem, and Weirton. These mills used iron ore rather than scrap steel.

When 2003 ended, Nucor struck a positive note by reminding their investors that they had been profitable every single quarter since beginning operations in 1966. But, while Nucor set records for both steel production and steel shipments, net earnings declined 61 percent. While the steel industry struggled, Nucor increased its market share and held on to profitability. They worked on expanding their business with the automotive industry, continued their joint venture in Brazil to produce pig iron, and pursued a joint venture with the Japanese and Chinese to make iron without the usual raw materials. In February 2004, they were still "optimistic about the prospects for obtaining commercialization" of their promising Castrip process for strip casting in the United States and Brazil. The mini-mills could not produce sheet steel, a large share of the market. Moreover, Nucor was optimistic because trade laws were curtailing import dumping and Nucor expected higher margins.

Global competition continued. According to the *Wall Street Journal*, Posco Steelworks in Pohang, South Korea, enjoyed the highest profits in the global steel industry as of 2004. Moreover, *Business Week* reported that the company had developed a new technology called Finex, which turned coal and iron ore into iron without coking and sintering and was expected to cut production costs by nearly a fifth and harmful emissions by 90 percent. They had also expanded their 80 Korean plants by investing in 14 Chinese joint ventures. By December 2004, demand in China had slowed and it had become a net steel exporter, sparking concerns of global oversupply.

Global consolidation also continued. In October 2004, London's Mittal family announced that they would merge their Ispat International NV with LNM Group and ISG, to create the world's largest steelmaker, with estimated annual revenue of $31.5 billion and output of 57 million tons. This would open a new chapter for the industry's consolidation, which had been mostly regional. Although the world's steel industry remained largely fragmented with the world's top 10 steelmakers supplying less than 30 percent of global production, Mittal Steel would have about 40 percent of the U.S. market in flat-rolled steel. Mittal, which had a history of using its scale to buy lower-cost raw materials and importing modern management techniques into previously inefficient state-run mills, was buying ISG, a U.S. company which already owned the lowest-cost, highest profit mills in the United States. In January 2005, Mittal also announced plans to buy 37 percent of China's Hunan Valin Iron & Steel Group Co.

In 2004 and 2005, Nucor continued its aggressive geographic expansion and introduction of new products. For example, Nuconsteel ("Nucon"), a wholly owned subsidiary of Nucor which specialized in load-bearing light-gauge steel-framing systems for commercial and residential construction markets, introduced two new low-cost automated fabrication systems for residential construction. In March 2005, Nucor formed a joint venture with Lennar Corporation, named Nextframe LP to provide comprehensive light-gauge steel framing for residential construction. Nucor's 25 percent joint venture with the Rio Tinto Group, Mitsubishi Corporation, and Chinese steelmaker Shougang Corporation for a HIsmelt commercial plant in Kwinana, Western Australia, started up in 2005. In 2004, Nucor acquired the assets of an idled direct-reduced iron (DRI) plant in Louisiana and moved them to Trinidad. By December 2006, construction was completed, and, in 2008, Nu-Iron Unlimited produced 1,400,000 metric tons of DRI from Brazilian iron ore for the United States.

By 2005, Nucor had 16 steel facilities producing three times as much as in 1999. The number of bar mills had grown to nine with capacity of 6,000,000 tons through the addition of Birmingham's four mills with 2,000,000 tons and Auburn's 400,000 tons. The sheet mills grew to four and increased capacity by one-third with the acquisition of Trico. Nucor–Yamato's structural steel capacity was increased by half a million tons from the South Carolina plant. A new million-ton plate mill, their second, had opened in North Carolina in 2000. Ninety-three percent of production was sold to outside customers.

By 2006, DiMicco had made many acquisitions while still managing to instill Nucor's unique culture in the new facilities. A May 2006 *BusinessWeek* article revealed that Nucor's culture and compensation system had changed very little since the 1990s. Michael Arndt reported that "Nucor gave out more than $220 million in profit sharing and bonuses to the rank and file in 2005. The average Nucor steelworker took home nearly $79,000 last year. Add to that a $2,000 one-time bonus to mark the company's record earnings and almost $18,000, on average, in profit sharing." He also noted that executive pay was still geared toward team building as "The bonus of a plant manager, a department manager's boss, depends on the entire corporation's return on equity. So there's no glory in winning at your plant if the others are failing."

Globally, steel mergers and acquisitions boomed during this time. This merger activity was due to a combination of low borrowing costs, high stock prices, and large amounts of cash. Another factor prompting mergers was a rise in the cost of raw materials. Despite all the transactions in 2006, 2007, and 2008, the industry remained fragmented, both domestically and internationally, and more mergers were expected.

Future merger activity was expected to differ slightly as steel companies attempted to become more vertically integrated. Examples included forward integration, such as combining Esmark's service center with Wheeling-Pittsburgh's steel production; and integration backward into scrap, such as the takeover of OmniSource by Steel Dynamics in 2007 and Nucor's acquisition of David J. Joseph Co. in 2008. These moves represented a trend toward becoming less dependent on outside vendors. This was due to the rising cost of scrap, which jumped from $185/ton in January 2006 to $635/ton in June 2008, and the highly concentrated nature of iron ore sources. BHP Billiton Ltd. based in Australia, Rio Tinto plc, headquartered in London, and Brazil-based Vale accounted for 75 percent of iron ore shipments worldwide.

Nucor was also active in mergers. In March 2007, Nucor acquired Harris Steel Group Inc. of Canada for $1.06 billion in cash, adding 770,000 tons of rebar fabrication capacity and over 350,000 tons of capacity in other downstream steel products. This acquisition showed that Nucor saw growth opportunities in finishing steel products for its customers and in distribution rather than additional steelmaking capacity. While many large steel companies were buying other primary steelmakers around the world, Nucor was focusing its investments largely in North America's manufacturing infrastructure such as reinforced steel bars, platform grating, and wire mesh for construction products ranging from bridges to airports and stadiums. According to Dan DiMicco, these moves "significantly advanced Nucor's downstream growth initiatives." Through the acquisition of Harris, Nucor also acquired a 75 percent interest in Novosteel S.A., a Swiss-based steel trading company that matched buyers and sellers of steel products on a global basis and offered its customers logistics support, material handling, quality certifications, and schedule management.

For the previous three years, Nucor had a joint venture with Harris, and in fact already owned a 50 percent stake in the company. Harris kept its name, as a Nucor subsidiary, and was led by the former chairman and CEO John Harris. However, the Harris board consisted of Harris and three Nucor representatives. This was the first time Nucor had broken from its non-union tradition, as about half of Harris's 3,000 employees were unionized. As steel analyst Timna Tanners said, "It's definitely a stretch for Nucor, culturally, since they have managed to keep its other operations non-union by offering higher salaries and production incentives. But there are not many non-union options left in North America when it comes to acquisitions and expansion."

The Harris team was operating as a growth platform within Nucor and had completed several acquisitions, including rebar fabricator South Pacific Steel Corporation in June 2007; Consolidated Rebar, Inc. in August 2007; a 90 percent equity interest in rebar fabricator Barker Steel Company, Inc. in December 2007; as well as smaller transactions. Nucor made several other acquisitions, which combined with the Laurel Steel, Fisher & Ludlow, and LEC businesses that came with the Harris acquisition and some internal organic growth, increased Nucor's cold finish and drawn products' capacity by more than

75 percent from 490,000 tons in 2006 to 860,000 tons at the end of 2007. In addition, it resulted in 90,000 tons of steel-grating capacity, and steel mesh capacity almost tripled, to 233,000 tons per year.

Nucor continued to invest in other downstream and upstream businesses (see Exhibit 4 for the organization chart in 2009). In the third quarter of 2007, they completed the acquisition of Magnatrax Corporation, a leading provider of custom-engineering metal buildings, for $275.2 million. The Magnatrax acquisition, when combined with their existing Building Systems divisions and a newly constructed Buildings Systems division in Brigham City, Utah, made Nucor the second-largest metal building producer in the United States, more than doubling their annual capacity to 480,000 tons of pre-engineered metal buildings.

In 2007, Nucor's seven Vulcraft facilities supplied more than 40 percent of all domestic buildings built using steel joists and joist girders. In both 2006 and 2007, 99 percent of its steel requirements were obtained from Nucor bar mills. Nucor's nine steel deck plants supplied almost 30 percent of total domestic sales in decking; six of these plants were constructed by Nucor adjacent to Vulcraft joist facilities and three were acquired in November 2006 as a wholly owned subsidiary called Verco Decking. These decking plants obtained 99 percent of their steel requirements from

Exhibit 4 Nucor Organization Chart, 2009

Nucor sheet plants in 2006, but only 76 percent in 2007.

In March 2008, Nucor completed the acquisition of the David J. Joseph Company (DJJ), the largest broker of ferrous and non-ferrous scrap in the United States and one of the nation's largest processors of ferrous scrap, for $1.44 billion. The company had been a supplier of scrap to Nucor since 1969. DJJ operated over 30 scrap-processing facilities. This acquisition expanded Nucor's scrap-processing capabilities from 500,000 to 4,000,000 short tons and provided them additional steelmaking raw materials through their brokerage operations, and rail services and logistics through its private fleet of some 2,000 scrap-related railcars. This allowed them to capture further margins in the steelmaking supply chain and to more closely control their raw-materials inputs. In May, they announced a plan to raise $3 billion for expansions and acquisitions, two-thirds to come from selling 25 million new shares.

U.S. steelmakers saw a major transition in 2008. In the first quarter, the combination of higher volume and increased prices led to a sizable gain in profits. Furthermore, data showed that the four leading domestic steel companies, AK Steel Holding Corp., Nucor Corp., Steel Dynamics Inc., and United States Steel Corp., which Standard & Poor's followed as a proxy for industry performance, collectively accounted for 45.5 percent of industry shipments in 2007. The rise in revenues for this proxy group reflected a 9.3 percent increase in revenue per ton, volume gained at the expense of imports, and the impact of acquisitions. At the end of July, major U.S. steelmakers' results were still supported by months of steel-price increases, which eased the burden of rising raw materials prices, as demand from emerging markets kept global steel supplies tight.

However, in September 2008, steelmakers in the United States experienced a sharp pullback from buyers who were concerned with the credit crisis and a slowdown in automobile and construction markets. This caused inventories to rise and prices on some key products to drop by 10 percent. The *Wall Street Journal* reported on November 17 that "Metals prices fell 35% in just four weeks last month—the steepest decline ever recorded, according to Barclays Capital." They also reported that big steelmakers worldwide were cutting production as much as 35 percent and that U.S. Steel planned to lay off 2 percent of its workforce. Chinese demand also slowed. This was a swift reversal in an industry that saw its profits increase 20-fold in five years. The pricing volatility was intensified by the global financial crisis as many hedge funds, pension funds, and other investors desperate to raise cash rapidly sold their commodities holdings. Still, the article said that ultimately the industry's problems were rooted in weakened demand, particularly in China, rather than the financial crisis.

So as 2009 began, with prices for steel, iron ore, and scrap metal plummeting, competition in the global steel industry was expected to increase. And further consolidation was expected as the major players sought to maintain their dominant positions (see Exhibit 5). In a December 2008 interview on CNBC, Cramer said to DiMicco, "Nucor's great CEO," that it was "amazing you can be profitable" with an overnight 40 percent drop in sales. DiMicco said it showed the success of their business model. He believed Nucor's acquisitions over the past 10 years, with their integration into steel products markets and raw materials, would position them to survive and even prosper—where there were threats there were also opportunities.

Exhibit 5 Top 12 Global Steel Producers, end 2007

2007 Rank	mmt	2006 Rank	mmt	Company Name
1	116.4	1	117.2	ArcelorMittal
2	35.7	2	34.7	Nippon Steel
3	34.0	3	32.0	JFE
4	31.1	4	30.1	POSCO
5	28.6	6	22.5	Baosteel
6	26.5	45	6.4	Tata Steel*
7	23.6	5	22.6	Anshan-Benxi
8	22.9	17	14.6	Jiangsu Shagang
9	22.8	9	19.1	Tangshan
10	21.5	7	21.2	U.S. Steel
11	20.4	16	15.1	Wuhan
12	20.0	8	20.3	Nucor

Note: *2007 figure includes Corus.

mmt = million metric tons.

Source: International Iron and Steel Institute, September 21, 2008.

Appendix 1 Balance Sheet 2000–2008 (in millions of U.S.[$])

As of 12/31	2008	2007	2006	2005	2004	2003	2002	2001	2000
Assets									
Cash	2,355	1,394	786	980	779	350	219	462	491
Receivables	1,229	1,612	1,067	1,001	963	572	484	331	350
Total Inventories	2,408	1,602	1,141	945	1,240	560	589	467	461
Other Current Assets	405	283	270	288	193	137	157	134	80
Total Current Assets	6,397	5,073	4,675	4,072	3,175	1,621	1,449	1,394	1,381
Property, Plant, & Equip.	4,132	3,233	2,856	2,856	2,818	2,817	2,932	2,366	2,329
Deposits & Other Assets	667	202	354	212	140	55	n/a	n/a	n/a
Goodwill, Other Intang.	2,679	1,318	n/a	n/a	n/a	n/a	n/a	n/a	n/a
Total Assets	13,874	9,826	7,885	7,139	6,133	4,492	4,381	3,759	3,711
Liabilities									
Accounts Payable	534	692	517	502	472	330	247	189	203
Curr. Long-Term Debt	180	n/a	n/a	n/a	n/a	n/a	n/a	n/a	n/a
Accrued Expense	352	431	478	384	565	300	319	295	355
Income Taxes	199	n/a	n/a	n/a	29	n/a	9	n/a	n/a
Other Cur. Liab., Salaries	580	436	455	369	n/a	n/a	n/a	n/a	n/a
Total Current Liabilities	1,854	1,582	1,450	1,256	1,066	630	592	484	558
Deferred Charges/Inc.	677	593	448	487	515	440	371	329	260
Long-Term Debt	3,086	2,250	922	922	924	904	879	460	460
Total Liabilities	5,945	4,713	2,820	2,665	2,504	1,973	1,841	1,274	1,279
Shareholder Equity									
Minority Interest	327	287	239	194	173	177	217	284	301
Preferred Stock	n/a	n/a	n/a	n/a	n/a	n/a	n/a	n/a	n/a
Common Stock	150	149	149	74	74	36	36	36	36
Capital Surplus	1,630	256	196	192	147	117	99	81	71
Retained Earnings	7,861	6,622	5,809	5,709	3,689	2,642	2,642	2,539	2,479
Treasury Stock	−1,521	−2,078	−1,332	−739	452	453	454	455	455
Total Shareholder Equity	7,929	5,113	4,826	4,280	3,456	2,342	2,323	2,201	2,131
Total Liability & Shareholder Equity	13,874	9,826	7,885	7,139	6,133	4,492	4,381	3,759	3,711

Source: Nucor annual reports.

Appendix 2 Income Statement 2000–2008

Period Ended	12/31/2008	12/31/2007	12/31/2006	12/31/2005	12/31/2004	12/31/2003	12/31/2002	12/31/2001	12/31/2000
Net Sales	23,663,324	16,592,926	14,751,270	12,700,999	11,376.83	6,265.82	4,801.78	4,333.71	4,756.52
Cost of Goods Sold	19,612,283	13,462,927	11,283,123	10,119,496	9,128.87	5,996.55	4,332.28	3,914.28	3,929.18
Gross Profit	4,051,041	3,130,049	3,468,147	2,581,503	2,247.96	269.28	469.5	419.43	827.34
R & D Expenditure	n/a	n/a	n/a	n/a	n/a	n/a	n/a	n/a	n/a
Selling G & A Exps	750,984	577,764	592,473	459,460	415.03	165.37	175.59	150.67	183.18
Depreciation & Amort.	n/a	n/a	n/a	n/a	n/a	n/a	n/a	n/a	n/a
Non-Operating Inc.	n/a	n/a	n/a	−9,200	−79.3	−12.4	−49.57	−82.87	−150.65
Interest Expense	90,483	5,469	−37,365	4201	22.35	24.63	14.29	6.53	n/a
Income Before Taxes	2,790,470	2,253,315	2,693,818	2,016,368	1,731.28	66.88	230.05	179.37	493.52
Prov. For Inc. Taxes	959,480	781,368	936,137	706,084	609.79	4.1	67.97	66.41	182.61
Minority Interest	313,921	293,501	219,121	110,650	80,840	n/a	n/a	n/a	n/a
Realized Investment	n/a	n/a	n/a	n/a	n/a	n/a	n/a	n/a	n/a
Other Income	n/a	n/a	n/a	n/a	n/a	n/a	n/a	n/a	n/a
Net Income	1,830,990	1,471,947	1,757,681	1,310,284	1,121.49	62.78	162.08	112.96	310.91

In thousands of USD

Source: Nucor annual reports.

312

Case 21: Nucor in 2009

Appendix 3 Nucor Valuation Rations, 2005–2008

	2008	2007	2006	2005
P/E(TTM)	7.38		11.76	7.38
Per Share Rations				
Divdend Per Share	1.31		0.67	0.47
Book Value Per Share	25.18		21.54	21.54
EPS Fully Diluted	5.98	4.94	5.68	7.02
Revenue Per Share	77.31		48.1	71.21
Profit Margins				
Operating Margin	13.95		18.26	16.23
Net Profit Margin	7.74	8.9	11.90	9.86
Gross Profit Margin	17.12		23.51	19.88
Dividends				
Dividend Yield	3.17		0.66	1.13
Dividend Yield -5-Year Avg.	3.21		2.17	1.28
Dividend Per Share (TTM)	1.31		0.6	0.52
Dividend Payout Ratio	35.94		37.32	6.66
Growth (%)				
5-Year Annual Growth	96.32		27.76	35.6
Revenue – 5-Year Growth	30.44		27.8	23.19
Div/Share – 5-Year Growth	45.63		71.5	12.57
EPS – 5-Year Growth	97.3		73.34	32.58
Financial Strength				
Quick Ratio	1.93		2.44	1.63
Current Ratio	3.45	3.2	3.22	2.98
LT Debt to Equity	38.92	44.01	19	26.72
Total Debt to Equity	42.09		19	26.72
Return on Equity (ROT) Per Share	27.91		38.61	38.57
Return on Assets (ROA)	16.19	16.62	23.4	25.4
Return on Invested Capital (ROIC)	19.91		29.58	33.33
Assets				
Assets Turnover	1.71		1.96	1.85
Inventory Turnover	9.51		10.82	9.7

Source: Thomson-Reuters Financial.

Oasis Hong Kong Airlines: The First Long-Haul, Low-Cost Airliner in Asia

Gary Chan, Andrew Lee

The University of Hong Kong, Asia Case Research Centre

It was August 2006, and Stephen Miller, chief executive officer (CEO) of the newly founded Oasis Hong Kong Airlines, was busy rallying his management team for the purpose of launching Asia's first long-haul, low-cost carrier. Oasis intended to pioneer the concept of affordable business class and offer one-way economy-class fares between Hong Kong and London for as little as HK$1,000.[1] Miller was confident that with a unique business model, solid financial backing from a few entrepreneurial investors, and almost 30 years of experience in the aviation industry under his belt, he had what it took to make Oasis a success. Meanwhile, Miller stumbled upon a Singapore Airlines advertisement in the *South China Morning Post* offering a special round-trip fare from Hong Kong to London for HK$2,950 (US$378). As he glanced over the advertisement again, he decided that traditional airlines had thrown down the gauntlet and that the time had come for him to prove that his business model would prosper.

The Airline Industry

The International Airline Industry[2]

The shape of the international airline industry was largely the result of deregulation, privatization, liberal air traffic agreements, and economic downturns. The United States led the world in air traffic deregulation in 1977 when it deregulated its domestic air cargo market, allowing carriers the freedom to choose domestic routes and set fares. This was followed by deregulation in the passenger market, which started in 1978, relaxing restrictions on fares, routes, and mergers. By 1981, all restrictions on routes and services had been eliminated and, by 1983, all rate regulations had ended.

Within approximately 20 years after deregulation, the number of airlines operating in the United States had roughly doubled and passenger traffic had nearly tripled.[3] By one estimate, roughly 85 percent of passengers had a choice of at least two airlines in 2001. Meanwhile, air fares had fallen by 35 percent. Major airlines found themselves settling on a few major hubs as the foundation for connecting passenger and cargo traffic to other destinations. This structure came to be known as the hub-and-spoke.

As deregulation forced U.S. carriers to become more efficient and competitive, the competitive pressure was felt throughout the rest of the world and triggered a series of privatizations of flag carriers in Europe and Japan, many of which had been state-owned. British Airways, for instance, was restructured and floated in 1987. Similarly, in 2000, the Japanese government deregulated its domestic market and privatized Japan Airlines. Nonetheless, many European national carriers that sustained losses were still heavily subsidized by their respective governments, and other carriers outside of Europe and Japan, even if not state-owned, still maintained a very close relationship with their governments. For example, such flag carriers and listed companies as Singapore Airlines, China Airlines, and Air China were all majority-held by entities that could be traced back to their respective national governments.

International air traffic remained regulated by bilateral air services agreements that were negotiated between countries. These agreements were often very elaborate, detailing the granting of different traffic rights and specifying which airlines could fly which routes and at what capacity and frequency. Traffic rights described in these agreements were commonly known as Freedoms of the Air (see Exhibit 1). Since 1992, the United States had

Gary Chan and Andrew Lee prepared this case under the supervision of Dr. Venkat Subramanian for class discussion. This case is not intended to show effective or ineffective handling of decision or business processes.

Exhibit 1 Freedoms of the Air

First Freedom of the Air: The right or privilege, in respect of scheduled international air services, granted by one State to another State or States to fly across its territory without landing. This is also known as a **First Freedom Right.**

Second Freedom of the Air: The right or privilege, in respect of scheduled international air services, granted by one State to another State or States to land in its territory for non-traffic purposes. This is also known as a **Second Freedom Right.**

Third Freedom of the Air: The right or privilege, in respect of scheduled international air services, granted by one State to another State to put down, in the territory of the first State, traffic coming from the home State of the carrier. This is also known as a **Third Freedom Right.**

Fourth Freedom of the Air: The right or privilege, in respect of scheduled international air services, granted by one State to another State to take on, in the territory of the first State, traffic destined for the home State of the carrier. This is also known as a **Fourth Freedom Right.**

Fifth Freedom of the Air: The right or privilege, in respect of scheduled international air services, granted by one State to another State to put down and to take on, in the territory of the first State, traffic coming from or destined for a third State. This is also known as a **Fifth Freedom Right.**

   ICAO characterizes all freedoms beyond the Fifth Freedom as "so-called" because only the first five "freedoms" have been officially recognized as such by international treaty.

Sixth Freedom of the Air: The right or privilege, in respect of scheduled international air services, of transporting, via the home country of the carrier, traffic moving between two other countries. This is also known as a **Sixth Freedom Right.**

Seventh Freedom of the Air: The right or privilege, in respect of scheduled international air services, granted by one State to another State, of transporting traffic between the territory of the granting State and any third State with no requirement to include on such operation any point in the territory of the recipient State (i.e., the service need not connect to or be an extension of any service to or from the home State of the carrier). This is also known as a **Seventh Freedom Right.**

Eighth Freedom of the Air: The right or privilege, in respect of scheduled international air services, of transporting cabotage traffic between two points in the territory of the granting State on a service which originates or terminates in the home country of the foreign carrier or (in connection with the so-called "Seventh Freedom of the Air") outside the territory of the granting State. This is also known as an **Eighth Freedom Right** or **"consecutive cabotage."**

Ninth Freedom of the Air: The right or privilege of transporting cabotage traffic of the granting country on a service performed entirely within the territory of the granting country. This is also known as a **Ninth Freedom Right** or **"stand-alone cabotage."**

Source: ICAO, 2006, Freedoms of the air, http://www.icao.int/icao/en/trivia/freedoms_air.htm (accessed November 19, 2006).

been advocating and signing the so-called Open Skies agreements with foreign governments. These bilateral or multilateral agreements included unrestricted landing rights on each other's soil and unrestricted capacity and frequency; however, these agreements did not allow increased foreign ownership or control of airlines, nor did they grant cabotage freedom in the United States or U.S. domestic traffic rights, to foreign carriers. Meanwhile, the European Union (EU) was increasingly behaving like a single nation. In April 1997, the EU took a major step toward deregulation by allowing an airline from one member state to fly within another member's domestic market.[4] In 2000, the EU established the Common European Aviation Area, comprising all 15 member states and within which airlines of member states would have full traffic rights and ability to set fares.

Types of Carriers

There are three primary types of commercial carriers: scheduled airlines, charter airlines, and feeder airlines.

   Scheduled airlines, the most common type and the one with which most passengers are familiar, operate year-round on established schedules. International carriers of this type operate under the framework of the bilateral air services agreements described earlier. Any international carrier that obtains approval to operate under a bilateral agreement is a "designated carrier." Scheduled airlines sell their capacities directly to the public within specified fare levels, which must be filed with and approved by their respective governments.

   Charter airlines differ from scheduled airlines in that they do not operate on established schedules, but rather as ad hoc services, either to support the operations of scheduled airlines or to meet the demands of specific groups of customers. Charter airlines do not operate under the normal bilateral agreements, and each flight is separately approved by the respective governments. Some airlines that had started off as charter airlines eventually became scheduled airlines. From time to time, scheduled airlines also operate charter services.

   The third type of commercial carrier, feeder airlines, are mostly scheduled airlines operating smaller aircraft for the primary purpose of carrying passengers from smaller cities to larger air traffic hubs for connections with other flights. As the aviation industry evolved, many of these smaller feeder airlines either were bought out by their larger competitors or simply perished under the pressure of fierce competition. Because most feeder airlines operate domestic flights, their operations do not involve any bilateral agreements between nations.

Traditional and Low-Cost Carriers

A commercial scheduled airline could be either a traditional carrier or a low-cost carrier. While most commonly known airlines in 2006 (e.g., United Airlines, British Airways, Cathay Pacific Airways, and Singapore Airlines) were traditional carriers, the late 1990s and early 2000s saw a proliferation of low-cost carriers in almost every part of the world. Inspired by Southwest Airlines' impressive success, as indicated by the fact that Southwest was the only major U.S. airline in 2005 that had remained profitable since the September 11, 2001, terrorist attacks,[5] many attempted to replicate this firm's business model either in the United States or in other parts of the world. By 2006, examples of low-cost carriers could be found in all major regions of the world: Southwest and JetBlue in North America; Ryanair and easyJet in Europe; Kingfisher and Air Deccan in India; Tiger Airways, Jetstar Asia, and Valuair in Singapore; Air Asia in Malaysia; and Jetstar and Virgin Blue in Australia.

Traditional Carriers. Traditional carriers usually provide a full complement of options and services throughout the entire passenger experience, from the point when a booking is made to the end of the return flight. They allow passengers to book tickets through various means, including travel agents (usually via one or more global computer reservation systems) and directly with the airline (which could be by phone, in person, or online), and provide a choice of up to four classes of cabin service. Upon check-in, using the International Air Transport Association (IATA) interline system, a traditional airline can check passengers and their baggage through to connecting flights on other airlines and issue onward boarding passes. For premium-class passengers or members of loyalty clubs, a comfortable waiting lounge is provided with complimentary food and beverages, as well as other services. Once on board, passengers are provided with various in-flight amenities, reading materials, in-flight audio and video programs (on a broadcast or on-demand basis via personal TVs or cabin-based screens), and hot meals and beverages. For some overnight flights, lounges are also available for select passengers to freshen up upon arrival. Service agents are present at arrival gates to assist passengers with connecting flights. Most traditional carriers provide these services at no additional cost to passengers.

Operating on a scheduled basis with a hub-and-spoke model, traditional carriers have multiple origins of sales and multiple destinations. For example, Cathay Pacific Airways, a Hong Kong–based traditional carrier that offered service between Tokyo and Los Angeles via Hong Kong, would sell tickets in Tokyo for both the Tokyo–Hong Kong sector and the Tokyo–Los Angeles sector. At the same time, a portion of seats would be reserved to be sold in Hong Kong for the Hong Kong–Los Angeles sector of the same flight. The proportions of seats assigned to the Tokyo–Los Angeles, Tokyo–Hong Kong, and Hong Kong–Los Angeles sectors would vary from flight to flight, based on the forecasted yield and demand at any particular time of the year, with the overall objective of optimizing profit. There are also many different fare classes within each cabin class that carry different validities and restrictions.

Most traditional carriers serve a variety of long-, medium- and short-haul destinations with a variety of aircraft types. British Airways, for instance, serves destinations from its bases in the United Kingdom, ranging from other points in the United Kingdom that are flights shorter than one hour, to trips to New York, which would take 8 hours, and Hong Kong, which would take 14 hours. To serve such a broad range of destinations, British Airways's fleet at this time consisted of a wide variety of aircraft types: Boeing 737s, 747s, 757s, 767s, and 777s; Airbus A319s, A320s, and A321s; and a few other smaller aircraft types.[6]

Traditional carriers often use expensive primary airports as bases and hubs. The major advantage of this model is that airlines can schedule effectively and capture passengers from more origins to more destinations through the hubs. This additional revenue generation allows carriers to operate flights between cities where point-to-point demand alone does not justify the operation economically. By dominating a hub, airlines may also be able to limit competition on certain routes because the supply of slots at leading airports is limited. Nevertheless, any flight irregularities occurring at the hub can wreak havoc on an airline's entire network.

Traditional carriers usually offer loyalty clubs or frequent-flyer programs, which rewarded frequent travelers with such privileges as lounge access, upgrades, and free tickets. Typically, rewards are based primarily on mileage flown, though mileage could also be earned by purchasing from partnering companies or using airline-branded credit cards. To strengthen and expand their hub-and-spoke networks, traditional airlines have chosen to form alliances. These alliances link the networks of their various member airlines and offer alliance-wide loyalty clubs that provide passengers with privileges throughout an alliance's enlarged network. The world's three largest alliances are Star Alliance, Sky Team, and Oneworld. As of 2005, Star Alliance was the largest, with 18 full members (including Lufthansa Airlines, United Airlines, and Singapore Airlines), and an estimated 23.6 percent share of the international air travel market.[7] Sky Team was the second largest, with 10 full members (including Northwest Airlines, Air France-KLM, and Korean Airlines) and a world market share of 20.7 percent. Oneworld was the smallest among the top three, with eight full members (including American Airlines, British Airways, Cathay Pacific, and Qantas Airways) and a world market share of 13.5 percent.

Low-Cost Carriers.

The term "low-cost carriers" commonly refers to airlines that offer low ticket prices and limited services. However, when this term was first used, it referred specifically to carriers with lower operating-cost structures than traditional carriers. As competition and the overall business environment toughened, most airlines, traditional or otherwise, lowered their operating costs significantly, blurring the definition of the term. It was for this reason that low-cost carriers were later distinguished from traditional carriers by ticket prices and services rather than by cost structures.

Unlike traditional carriers, low-cost carriers tend not to use travel agents or computer reservation systems. Instead, they prefer to sell directly and limit their use of travel agents. Low-cost carriers usually provide a single-class cabin and very basic complimentary services such as soft drinks and peanuts. Southwest Airlines, for example, is well known for offering complimentary peanuts. Some also provide limited in-flight entertainment. One such example is JetBlue, which historically provided an in-flight entertainment system that broadcast satellite TV. Low-cost carriers commonly charge for additional services.

Low-cost carriers typically do not adopt the hub-and-spoke network business model. Instead, their networks consist of city pairs that support direct service, or point-to-point traffic. Many low-cost carriers believe that direct service is cheaper than the hub-and-spoke model. One industry observer even suggested that the cost of handling passengers in a hub-and-spoke system was as much as 45 percent higher than in a point-to-point system. With a simpler network, low-cost carriers also tend to have much simpler pricing systems and fewer fare classes than their traditional counterparts. To keep their costs low, low-cost carriers also fly to secondary airports. One example is easyJet, which, instead of flying in and out of London Heathrow, a major air transport hub in Europe, opted to base its London service out of London Gatwick.

Most low-cost carriers focus on short-haul services, flights of less than five hours. Because the type of operations of all the different flights is similar, low-cost

carriers usually use just one type of aircraft. Since its inception, Southwest Airlines has flown only Boeing 737s. Although there were different versions of the 737 in the fleet, including the new generation 737, the commonality among the aircraft reduces the cost of both the spares inventory and the training of pilots, flight attendants, and maintenance personnel, and also facilitates quick turnarounds. Likewise, JetBlue adopted a similar model and flew only Airbus A320s, all with the same engine type.

Low-cost airlines were unlikely to be members of the IATA and did not value receiving feeder traffic or feeding traffic to other airlines. As a result, low-cost airlines do not complete interline check-ins or baggage transfers, nor are they members of an alliance. Indeed, Ryanair encourages passengers not to have any checked baggage[8] by reducing ticket prices by £2.5 for these passengers. In contrast, those with checked baggage have to pay £2.5 or £5.

Although typical low-cost carriers keep to themselves and do not collaborate with other airlines in the form of alliances, some are beginning to deviate a bit from this model. Southwest Airlines, which had an unprecedented 33 consecutive years of profit, is an example of a low-cost carrier doing so. In 2005, Southwest Airlines announced a code-sharing agreement[9] with ATA Airlines, allowing customers to book flights on ATA to fly to such destinations as Hawaii.[10] Some low-cost carriers also offer a simpler version of frequent-flyer programs. For example, Southwest Airlines operates a simple frequent-flyer program where points are accumulated based on the number of one-way trips, not mileage flown, and a free round-trip is rewarded for every 18 points accumulated. Similar to frequent flyer programs of traditional carriers, Southwest also allows spending on partner companies and through Southwest-branded credit cards to be converted into frequent flyer points.

Airline Economics

Airlines operate much like many other businesses in that the primary aim is to generate maximum revenue and incur minimum cost to maximize return on invested capital. For these firms, seats and cargo space, which travel at a particular time from one location to another, are the products. As products, passengers and cargo both have a very short shelf life (from the time the schedule is published to the time the gate closes for departure) and are perishable by nature (once an aircraft departs, any unsold products "perish").

To benchmark themselves against each other, airlines often examine their capacities in available seat kilometers (ASKs) for passenger service or available tonne kilometers (ATKs) for total capacity, including passenger and freight[11] (see Exhibit 2 for a glossary of airline terms). Two closely related benchmarks are

Exhibit 2 Glossary of Terms

Terms	Description
Available seat kilometer (ASK).	A measurement of an airline's passenger-carrying capacity, calculated by multiplying the number of seats available by the distance flown in kilometers. If miles are used, available seat mile (ASM) is used instead of ASK.
Available tonne kilometer (ATK)	A measurement of an airline's total capacity (including both passengers and cargo), calculated by multiplying the capacity in tonnes by the distance flown in kilometers. If miles are used, available ton mile (ATM) is used instead of ATK.
Block hours	The distance of a flight leg between two points, from the time when the aircraft is pushed back for takeoff to the time when the aircraft arrives at the gate. Compare with "flying hours."
Break-even load factor	The percentage load factor that represents the point at which an airline breaks even.
Cost per ASK	A unit cost measurement of an airline, calculated by dividing the total operating cost by ASK or ASM. This is regarded as an appropriate measurement for airlines with a predominant focus on passenger service.
Cost per ATK	A unit cost measurement of an airline, calculated by dividing the total operating cost by ATK or ATM. This is regarded as an appropriate measurement for airlines that provide only cargo service, or passenger as well as cargo service.
Cycle	A measurement of utilization, where one cycle equals one takeoff and landing.
Flying hours	The distance of a flight leg between two points, from the time when the aircraft lifts off the ground during takeoff to the time when the aircraft touches the ground during landing. Compare with "block hours."
Load factor	A measurement of capacity utilization in percentage, calculated by dividing RPK by ASK, or RTK by ATK.
Narrow-body aircraft or single-aisle aircraft	An aircraft that has a fuselage diameter of about 3 to 4 meters and has only one aisle in its seat arrangement.
Revenue passenger kilometer (RPK)	A measurement of passenger volume carried by an airline, calculated by multiplying the number of revenue-generating passengers by the distance flow in kilometers. If miles are used, revenue passenger mile (RPM) is used instead of RPK.
Revenue tonne kilometer (RTK)	A measurement of total volume carried by an airline, calculated by multiplying the revenue tonnage by the distance flown in kilometers. If ton and mile are used, revenue ton mile (RTM) is used instead of RTK.
Seat pitch	The distance between two rows of seats, typically in inches, measured from the back of one seat to the back of the seat directly behind it.
Sector	A sector is a direct flight between two cities and is usually represented by the city pair names. For example, Hong Kong–London is one sector and London–Hong Kong is another sector.
Sector length or stage length	The distance of a flight leg measured either in physical distance in kilometers (or miles) or time in hours. When it is measured in time, it can be represented in block hours or flying hours, depending on the purpose.
Wide-body aircraft or twin-aisle aircraft	An aircraft that has a fuselage diameter of about 5 to 6 meters and has only two aisles in its seat arrangement.

Sources: Adapted from http://moneyterms.co.uk, http://en.wikipedia.org, and industry sources.

revenue passenger kilometers (RPKs) and revenue tonne kilometers (RTKs); these benchmarks measure the number of seat kilometers or tonne kilometers that an airline sold during a particular period of time. To measure their financial performance, airlines published their unit costs in cost per ASK or ATK. The fraction of RPK over ASK yields the passenger load factor while the fraction of RTK over ATK shows the overall load factor.

For airlines focusing on passenger service, cost per ASK is used as a primary measure of unit cost. For airlines that also have a sizeable cargo service, a combined measurement, including cost per ATK, is used. Airlines also measure their ability to generate revenue with revenue per ASK and revenue per ATK.

Armed with these numbers and various other figures and forecasting tools, airlines employ sophisticated inventory management and pricing techniques to maximize revenue and profitability and to lower their breakeven load factors (see Exhibits 3 and 4 for the ASKs, ATKs, RPKs, RTKs, and related data of selected airlines).

Exhibit 3 Income Statements and Company Information of Two Low-Cost Carriers

	Southwest Airlines Year Ending December 31, 2005 (in US$ millions)	EasyJet Year Ending September 30, 2005 (in UK£ millions)
Total operating revenue		
Passenger	7,279	1,254
Freight	133	
Other	172	87
	7,584	1,341
Total operating expenses		
Salaries, wages & benefits	2,702[a]	267
Fuel & oil	1,342	260
Maintenance & repairs	430	119
Aircraft rentals	163	124
Landing fees & other rentals	454	339
Depreciation & amortization	469	37[d]
Other operating expenses	1,204	148
	6,764	1,293
Total operating income	820	49
Other expenses (income)		
Interest expense	122	8
Interest income	(47)	(27)
Other (gains) losses, net	(129)	0
	(54)	(19)
Profit before tax	874	68
Taxes	326	25
Net income	548	43

Exhibit 3 Income Statements and Company Information of Two Low-Cost Carriers *(Continued)*

	Southwest Airlines Year Ending December 31, 2005 (in US$ millions)	EasyJet Year Ending September 30, 2005 (in UK£ millions)
Other information		
Fleet size (averaged)	431[b]	94
Aircraft types	Boeing 737	Boeing 737, Airbus A319
Total trips flown	1,028,639	229,068
Average trips per aircraft per day	6.5[b]	6.7[b]
Average stage length (block hour)	1.84[b]	1.75
Average hours per aircraft per day	12.02[b]	11.70[b]
RPK (thousand)	96,356,960[c]	27,448,000
ASK (thousand)	136,276,472[c]	32,141,000
Passenger load factor	70.7 percent	85.4 percent
Passenger revenue per ASK	5.57 cents	4.17 pence
Operating cost per ASK	4.96 cents	3.97 pence[e]

Notes: Income statement items have been aligned for comparison purposes; [a] included handling charges; [b] estimated by case writer; [c] converted from ASM/RPM; [d] included goodwill amortization of £17.4 m; [e] before goodwill.

Sources: Southwest Airlines, 2005, Annual Report; easyJet, 2005, Annual Report.

Exhibit 4 Income Statements and Selected Information of Two Traditional Airlines

	British Airways Year Ending March 31, 2006 (in UK£ million)	Cathay Pacific Airways Year Ending December 31, 2005 (in HK$ million)
Total operating revenue		
Passenger	6,820	30,274
Freight	498	12,852
Other	1,197[a]	7,783
	8,515	50,909
Total operating expenses		
Salaries, wages & benefits	2,346	9,025
Fuel & oil	1,632	15,588
Maintenance & repairs	473	4,527
Aircraft rentals	112	4,893[e]
Landing fees & other rentals	559	6,947
Depreciation & amortization	717	790[f]
Other operating expenses	1,971[b]	4,996[g]
	7,810	46,766
Total operating income	705	4,143

(Continued)

Exhibit 4 Income Statements and Selected Information of Two Traditional Airlines *(Continued)*

	British Airways Year Ending March 31, 2006 (in UK£ million)	Cathay Pacific Airways Year Ending December 31, 2005 (in HK$ million)
Other expenses (income)		
Interest expense	221	1,605
Interest income	(93)	(1,161)
Other (gains) losses, net	(43)	(269)
	85	175
Profit before tax	620	3,968
Taxes	153	500
Net income	467	3,468
Other information		
Fleet size (averaged)	281[c]	93
Aircraft types	10 major types	4 major types
Total trips flown	368,000	84,000
Average trips per aircraft per day	3.6[c]	2.5[c]
Average stage length (block hour)	2.83[c]	5.06[c]
Average hours per aircraft per day	10.14	12.60
RPK	111,859,000	65,110,000
ASK	147,934,000	82,766,000
Passenger load factor	75.6 percent	78.7 percent
Passenger revenue per ASK	4.61 pence[d]	HK$0.37
ATK	23,106,000	17,751,000
Total revenue per ATK	31.67 pence	HK$2.87
Operating cost per ATK	28.62 pence	HK$2.19

Notes: Income statement items have been aligned for comparison purposes; [a] included fuel surcharge; [b] included selling cost of £449 m; [c] case writer's estimates; [d] before fuel surcharge; [e] for Cathay Pacific this category should be "aircraft depreciation and leases"; [f] for Cathay Pacific this category should be "non-aircraft depreciation and leases"; [g] included commission of HK$555 million.

Sources: British Airways, 2006, Annual Report; Cathay Pacific Airways, 2005, Annual Report.

Airline Cost Structure. Personnel, fuel, capital cost and maintenance cost of assets, selling expenses, and airport and landing fees are the major costs airlines incur. Personnel-related costs are among the largest of the incurred costs for major airlines. Typically, airlines employ large labor forces including pilots, flight attendants, engineers, mechanics, airport service agents, and support staff. Labor in the airline industry is highly unionized, especially in North America and Europe, though strong pilots' and flight attendants' unions were also found in Asia. In 2005, labor costs for a major airline represented 20 to 40 percent of total costs.

The cost of fuel is a major concern for all airlines due to the huge increase in oil prices in the first decade of the 21st century. In 2005 for example, fuel represented approximately 20 to 30 percent of an airline's operating costs in contrast to around 12 to 15 percent during most of the 1990s. A successful fuel hedge program could save an airline a significant amount of money. Southwest Airlines was renowned for its fuel hedging program. In 2005, fuel cost represented about 20 percent of Southwest's operating cost. In 2006, its fuel expenses were approximately 73 percent hedged at about US$36 per barrel, which translated into savings of hundreds of millions of U.S. dollars.

In addition to the costs of offices, fixtures, office equipment, and ticketing equipment, airlines incur substantial capital costs to purchase aircraft and the flight simulators that are used to train pilots. In 2006, the Boeing 737 and the Boeing 777 were the best selling families of the firm's commercial planes. At this time, the list price of a Boeing 737, a single-aisle, narrow-bodied aircraft, ranged between US$47 million and US$80 million. A Boeing 777, a twin-aisle, wide-bodied aircraft, was priced between US$180 million and US$260 million. Although the actual purchase price was usually at least 15 to 20 percent lower than the list price,[12] aircraft capital costs are substantial. Airlines typically finance their purchase of aircraft through a finance/lease[13] arrangement. An operating lease[14] is a viable alternative, but with a typical monthly lease rate of 1 percent of the purchase price for a long-term lease, the rental cost for a brand-new Boeing 737 was still around US$600,000 a year in 2006 while that of a Boeing 777 was US$2.64 million a year.

The cost of maintaining aircraft and engines is another major expense for an airline, accounting for about 6 to 10 percent of operating costs. Managing maintenance costs is interwoven with asset and fuel cost management. For instance, an airline needs to balance the average age of its aircraft (capital costs of older aircraft tended to be cheaper) with maintenance costs, which tend to be more expensive as aircraft age. Also, as aircraft and engines age and enter their heavy maintenance cycles, ground time of up to 45 days for aircraft and 90 days for engines is required, necessitating additional aircraft or engines to uphold schedule integrity. Fuel cost management also plays a part, as older assets are usually less efficient and consume more fuel.

Selling expenses are another category of operational costs for an airline. Traditionally, air tickets were bought through travel agents, who subscribed to global computer reservation systems where airlines made bookings and reservations available. Airlines incurred costs through paying agency commissions and charges for using global computer reservation systems. In the fiscal year ending March 2006, British Airways's selling cost was £449 million (US$829 million), amounting to 5 percent of its total turnover. However, as online bookings and direct sales increased, the cost of agency commissions also came down, especially for low-cost carriers. In 2001, 25 percent of Southwest Airlines's ticket sales were through travel agents, while 24 percent came from reservation centers (where customers could call to make reservations directly) and 39 percent from the Internet. By 2005, Southwest's reliance on travel agents and reservation centers dropped to 11 percent and 15 percent, respectively, while sales generated through the Internet rose to 65 percent.

Operating aircraft incurs airport charges, landing fees, and route costs. For example, British Airways's landing fees and en-route costs amounted to £559 million (US$1.032 billion), or 6.6 percent of total turnover, in the fiscal year ended in March 2006. In stark contrast, easyJet, British Airways's low-cost counterpart, spent £438 million (US$808 million), or 25.2 percent of turnover, on airport charges and navigation expenses.

Airline Profitability. A report published by IATA in 2006,[15] which studied the fiscal performance of 85 of the world's major carriers who together accounted for 85 percent of worldwide passenger numbers and the vast majority of global freight volumes, found that eight of them made operating profits in excess of US$500 million each, among which three made more than US$1 billion. On the other hand, 20 of the carriers surveyed had incurred operating losses, with nine having lost more than US$100 million each. Asian and European carriers were among the highest profit generators, whereas 9 of the 20 who lost money were U.S. carriers. Only 14 carriers had operating margins of greater than 10 percent, many of which were low-cost carriers (see Exhibit 6).

Experience in the United States further suggested that low-cost carriers operating on a point-to-point model displayed higher aircraft utilization rates, lower unit operating costs, and higher staff productivity. For example, in 2004, JetBlue's A320 fleet had an average utilization rate of 13.6 block hours per day, 46 percent higher than Northwest's A320 fleet, and a unit operating cost of US$0.032 per available seat mile (ASM), compared to Northwest's US$0.051.[16]

In Asia, airlines such as Cathay Pacific Airways, Singapore Airlines, Qantas, and Emirates Airlines were among the most profitable commercial carriers in the world, yet they all operated on the traditional hub-and-spoke model. Collectively, these airlines generated over US$6.4 billion in net profits between 2003 and 2005, even after the severe acute respiratory syndrome (SARS) pandemic nearly caused the Asian air travel market to grind to a complete halt in 2003.

Asia also differed from the United States in that the majority of Asian countries did not have large domestic air travel markets, and there were a limited number of secondary airports, which low-cost carriers could use as operating bases. This meant that low-cost carriers were faced with high airport charges, which was contrary to

Exhibit 5 Operating Profits by Airline, Fiscal Year 2005 (* = fiscal 2004)

By Total Operating Profit			By Operating Profit Margin		
Rank	Airline	US$ (mil)	Rank	Airline	%
1	FedEx*	1.414	1	Gol Airlines	23.3
2	British Airways	1,330	2	Ryanair	21.8
3	Air France-KLM	1.200	3	Air Asia	18.9
4	Lufthansa	377	4	COPA	17.3
5	Southwest	820	5	Kenya Airlines	15.6
6	Emirates	786	6	Philippine Airlines	13.7
7	All Nippon	776	7	DHL International*	12.5
8	Qantas*	775	8	Kalitta Air	12.3
9	Singapore Airlines	590	9	Emirates	11.9
10	Cathay Pacific	533	10	Mesa Airlines	11.7
11	Ryanair	459	11	American Eagle	11.3
12	Air China	458	12	SkyWest	11.2
13	Iberia	457	13	Southwest	10.8
14	Air Canada	388	14	Jet Airways	10.3
15	UPS Airlines	293	15	Air China	9.6
16	Thai Airlines	269	16	Virgin Blue	9.6
17	Gol Airlines	266	17	TAM	9.5
18	TAM	232	18	Singapore Airlines	9.1
19	American Eagle	225	19	Royal Jordanian	9.0
20	SkyWest	220	20	Qantas*	8.9
21	Korean Airlines	207	21	Atlantic Southeast	8.5
22	Virgin Blue	184	22	British Airways	8.3
23	China Eastern*	179	23	Aer Lingus	8.2
24	LAN Airlines	142	24	Cathay Pacific	8.1
25	Asiana*	136	25	FedEx*	7.2

Source: IATA, 2006, IATA economic briefing, June 2006.

their basic operating principles. Recently, however, this situation began to change. In 2006, both Singapore's Changi Airport and Malaysia's new airport in Kuala Lumpur opened separate, no-frills terminals that catered to low-cost carriers' needs. However, the airport authority of Hong Kong showed no interest in following suit.

Front-End (Business- and First-Class) Traffic Revenue Contribution. For a typically configured Boeing 747-400 aircraft flying on a popular transatlantic route between the United States and Europe, the revenue split between first, business, and economy classes would be roughly 20 percent, 60 percent, and 20 percent, respectively. In 2006, typical published fares for such a flight would be around US$14,000, US$7,000, and US$750, with the aircraft equipped with 14, 79, and 265 seats, respectively, for the three classes. Because of the differences between carriers in short-haul and long-haul mixes, primary target markets, load factors, aircraft types, and so on, the resulting revenue mix across the three classes could vary significantly.

In the first half of 2006, front-end traffic accounted for 11 percent of all international traffic and 15 percent of long-haul routes. During this period, the top five route areas accounted for 72 percent of all front-end traffic volume, falling from 82 percent in 2000. Routes within Europe accounted for around one-third of all international front-end traffic, while routes between Europe and East Asia contributed 14 percent (see Exhibit 6). Because of the strong rebounds in trade and investment after the decline triggered by the September 11th terrorist attacks in 2001, front-end traffic between Europe and Asia had grown faster than overall traffic, contributing to strong revenues for airlines in 2005 and 2006.[17]

The International Airline Industry in 2006.

In the five years following the September 11, 2001, terrorist attacks, the average financial performance of commercial airlines around the world improved substantially, except for the second and third quarters of 2003, when carriers operating in Asia were badly hit by the SARS pandemic. Between 2000 and 2006, total revenues increased from US$329 billion to a projected US$450 billion while the number of passengers carried increased from 1.672 billion to a projected 2.154 billion, representing an increase of 36.8 percent and 28.8 percent, respectively. Cargo volume grew from 30.4 million tonnes to 39.8 million tonnes, a 30.9 percent increase. Operating profit fluctuated from a high of US$10.7 billion in 2000 to a

loss of US$11.8 billion in 2001 due to the 9–11 terrorist attacks, but rebounded to a projected US$9.8 billion in 2006. However, as fuel expenses skyrocketed from US$46 billion to a projected US$115 billion (a 150 percent increase), airlines' net profit actually decreased from US$3.7 billion to a projected loss of US$1.7 billion. When broken down geographically, North American carriers incurred a US$4.5 billion loss, followed by African carriers at US$0.8 billion. European and Asian carriers earned net profits of US$1.8 billion and US$1.7 billion, respectively.[18]

The Airline Industry in Hong Kong.

Located in southern China and historically an important trade port between the East and the West, Hong Kong's catchment area (within five hours of flight time) included most of the urban centers in East Asia, whose cumulative population was about 2 billion in the late 1990s.[19] With flights connecting to over 40 cities in the Chinese Mainland, Hong Kong was also the leading gateway to the rapidly growing Chinese market. In 2005, over 78 scheduled airlines served the Hong Kong International Airport, providing about 5,300 scheduled passenger and all-cargo flights each week between Hong Kong and more than 140 destinations worldwide. In the same year, the airport handled some 40.7 million passengers and 3.4 million tonnes of cargo, making Hong Kong the fifth-busiest international passenger airport and the busiest airport for international cargo in the world. In 2005, the airport also saw more than 19.8 million passenger departures.[20] Among them, South-East

Exhibit 6 Distribution of Front-End Traffic Volume by Route, January–May 2006

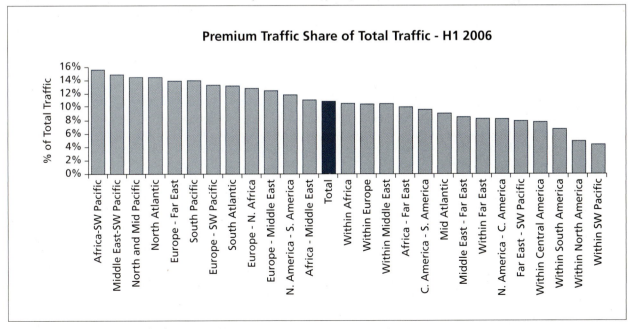

Source: IATA, 2006, IATA economic briefing, August 2006.

Asian destinations contributed 24 percent to the total, followed by mainland China at 21 percent and Taiwan at 19 percent. The remaining traffic was divided among Japan, Europe, North America, Australia, and others.[21]

According to the *Current Market Outlook 2005* published by Boeing,[22] passenger air travel would grow at an annual rate of 4.8 percent from 2005 to 2024, while cargo was forecast to grow at an annual rate of 6.2 percent. In Europe and North America, where the air travel market was mature, a slower growth of 3.4–5.5 percent was expected. The Asia-Pacific region was expected to be a major source of growth. Intra-regional traffic was expected to grow at an annual rate of 5.1 percent, while China was forecast to have an annual growth rate of 8.8 percent in this area. Traffic between Europe and Asia-Pacific was expected to grow 5.4 percent annually, while traffic between North America and Asia-Pacific, 6 percent.

Industry observers believed that Hong Kong, being a major air transport hub between the Far East and the Western world, was uniquely positioned to reap the benefits of this growing trend. However, they cautioned that the growing and rapidly improving mainland Chinese airports might challenge Hong Kong's position as a leading gateway to China. The Guangzhou Baiyun International Airport, Macau International Airport, Shenzhen Baoan International Airport, and Zhuhai Airport are all within 30 minutes by air from Hong Kong and the catchment area of the Pearl River Delta. In addition, direct traffic from Beijing's Capital Airport and Shanghai's Pudong International Airport to Europe and North America was also expected to increase during the 2008 Beijing Olympics and the 2010 Shanghai World Expo.

In response, Hong Kong had been extending its airport's market reach to serve the Pearl River Delta's population of 48 million, as well as the rest of China.[23] Since the early 2000s, Hong Kong International Airport has established multi-modal links that connect Hong Kong with other cities in the Pearl River Delta: the SkyPier provides frequent ferry connections to selected Pearl River Delta cities (including the four airports) and the SkyLimo provides coach services to and from major Pearl River Delta cities. Additionally, there were more than 170 daily coach trips operating between more than 40 Pearl River Delta cities and Hong Kong International Airport. In 2003, the Hong Kong Airport Authority (HKAA) signed a letter of intent with Shanghai Airport Authority to strengthen exchanges and facilitate closer cooperation between the two airports. In 2005, HKAA agreed to buy a major stake in the Hangzhou Xiaoshan International Airport.

Airlines in Hong Kong

In late 2006, seven airlines used Hong Kong as their home base. Among them, six were commercial airlines providing scheduled services to the public: Cathay Pacific Airways, Hong Kong Dragon Airlines, Air Hong Kong, CR Airways, Hong Kong Express Airways, and Oasis Hong Kong Airlines.

Cathay Pacific Airways. Founded in 1946 by American Roy C. Farrell and Australian Sydney H. de Kantzow, Cathay Pacific Airways was Hong Kong's largest airline and de facto flag carrier. The airline started with passenger service to destinations such as Shanghai, Manila, Singapore, Bangkok, and Guangzhou. In 1948, Butterfield & Swire (which later became the Swire Group) bought 45 percent of the airline and subsequently increased its stake to 5.2 percent. Since the 1960s, the airline has undergone significant expansion, both in fleet size and in the number of destinations served. By 2006, Cathay Pacific served 90 passenger and cargo destinations worldwide and had a fleet of 100 aircraft, including the Boeing 747 and 777 series and the Airbus A330 and A340 series. The average age of its fleet was seven years and the longest non-stop flight on its regular schedule was its Hong Kong–New York flight at 12,968 km and roughly 16 hours of flying time. It operated four daily flights to London's Heathrow airport, two using Airbus A340–300s and two using Boeing B747–400s, with all four offering three classes of service.

Cathay Pacific had a reputation as one of the industry's best airlines, with regular and frequent updates of seats, entertainment systems, meal options, and other in-flight amenities. Its latest first-class seats are equipped with 17-inch personal TVs with Audio-Video on Demand ("AVOD"), massage functions, extendable meal tables, and the largest pitch-flat beds available on a scheduled commercial airline, all enclosed within private areas. Meals could be selected and served at any time. Passengers also received preferential check-in service, access to exclusive lounge facilities, priority luggage handling, and other personalized services. Personal TVs with AVOD were also standard for its business-class service. Menus were created in cooperation with leading local fine-dining establishments and a broad wine selection was also available to passengers in both first and business class. Among its numerous industry awards, Cathay Pacific was named "Airline of the Year" by *Skytrax* in 2003 and 2005 and by *Air Transport World* in 2006.[24]

Cathay Pacific was a founding member of Oneworld. The airline had established a large number of code-share agreements with other carriers, including Air China, American Airlines, British Airways, Japan Airlines, Qantas, and Malaysian Airlines. Cathay Pacific had two loyalty programs: the Marco Polo Club, reserved exclusively for Cathay Pacific customers, and Asia Miles, where membership was available to customers of a number of participating airlines and other merchants, such as restaurants, hotels, and entertainment establishments.

Hong Kong Dragon Airlines.[25] In May 1985, Hong Kong Dragon Airlines ("Dragonair") was established as a wholly owned subsidiary of Hong Kong Macau International Investment Co. on the initiative of a local shipping tycoon, K. P. Chao. The airline, however, struggled under the one-airline-one-route policy of the then British colonial government of Hong Kong. In 1990, CITIC Pacific, the Swire Group, and Cathay Pacific acquired an 89 percent stake in Dragonair. As a result, Dragonair transitioned into a regional carrier with a focus on mainland Chinese destinations. In 1996, at the onset of the sovereignty change of Hong Kong from being a British colony to becoming a Special Administration Region of the People's Republic of China, the China National Aviation Corporation ("CNAC") purchased a 35.86 percent interest in Dragonair, becoming the largest shareholder. CITIC Pacific remained the second-largest shareholder, with a 28.5 percent stake, while the Swire Group and Cathay Pacific together held a 25.5 percent stake.

The new shareholding structure allowed Dragonair to develop outside the shadows of Cathay Pacific. The year 2000 marked a watershed for Dragonair, when it introduced its all-cargo service with a Boeing 747-200 special freighter, competing directly with Air Hong Kong, a wholly owned subsidiary of Cathay Pacific. The following five years saw Dragonair's passenger fleet double in size to 30 aircraft and its freighter fleet grow to four. Meanwhile, Dragonair established its own frequent-flyer program; rolled out a new cabin interior with lie-flat seats and personal TVs in the premium classes; competed with Cathay Pacific head-to-head on passenger services to Taipei, Bangkok, and Tokyo; and won numerous accolades for its outstanding service in the mainland Chinese market.

In June 2006, a joint announcement was made by Air China (the parent company of CNAC and China's flag carrier), CNAC, CITIC Pacific, the Swire Group, and Cathay Pacific about a shareholding realignment that resulted in a cross-shareholding between Air China and Cathay Pacific and made Dragonair a wholly owned subsidiary of Cathay Pacific.[26]

Air Hong Kong.[27] Founded in 1986 and initiating charter services in 1988 with a Boeing 707 freighter, Air Hong Kong was Hong Kong's only all-cargo operator. In 1994, Cathay Pacific bought a 75 percent stake in the company, strengthening Air Hong Kong's market and giving it access to Cathay Pacific's distribution system. In February 2002, Cathay Pacific acquired the remaining 25 percent stake in Air Hong Kong, making it a wholly owned subsidiary. In October 2002, Cathay Pacific and DHL Express announced a joint venture in which DHL Express acquired 30 percent of Air Hong Kong. Under the agreement, an initial investment of about US$300 million was to be committed by 2004 and a further US$100 million by 2010 to purchase a fleet of long-range, wide-body freighters to operate DHL Express's network connecting the major cities in the Asia-Pacific region. In March 2003, DHL Express acquired an additional 10 percent stake in Air Hong Kong from Cathay Pacific. By mid-2006, Air Hong Kong's fleet included eight A300-600GFs and one wet lease[28] Airbus A300-600F, and operated a freighter service network between Hong Kong and Tokyo, Osaka, Seoul, Taipei, Bangkok, Penang, Singapore, and Shanghai.

CR Airways and Hong Kong Express Airways. CR Airways was founded in 2001 and began service with Bombardier CRJ200 and CRJ700 regional jets.[29] In December 2005, it was reported that Hainan Airlines, a mainland Chinese carrier based on the island of Hainan, was interested in acquiring a 60 percent stake in CR Airways. In the same month, CR Airways announced the signing of a Memorandum of Understanding with Boeing to acquire thirty 737-800s and ten 787 Dreamliners. Hainan Airlines later revealed that it would reduce its stake in CR Airways to 45 percent to ensure that CR Airways remained a Hong Kong–based airline. In early 2006, the acquisition was given the green light by the government. CR Airways's service network changed rapidly as new routes were tested for viability and as the airline phased in the 737-800s, the first of which was delivered in early 2006 and coincided with the launch of services to Changsha and Tianjin. More destinations were slated to be added to the network in the second half of 2006, including Chengdu, Xian, Nanjing, and Fuzhou in China, as well as Seoul, Taegu, and Pusan in South Korea. CR Airways was also keen to begin long-haul service and was planning to operate Boeing 777s in the interim before the arrival of its Boeing 787s (which were expected to be delivered from 2010 onwards).

Hong Kong Express Airways Limited (formerly Helicopters Hong Kong Limited) was 51 percent owned by Macau casino tycoon Stanley Ho. Hong Kong Express wanted to take advantage of liberalization of air service between Hong Kong and the Chinese mainland. In September 2005, Hong Kong Express launched its first service to Guangzhou. As the fleet expanded, it added such destinations as Hangzhou, Ningbo, Chongqing, and Chengdu in China, as well as Chiang Mai in Thailand. However, six months after starting service to Guangzhou, they cancelled this route because the load factor fell short of the 30 percent target.[30] In May 2006, Hong Kong Express acknowledged that negotiations were under way regarding a possible capital injection from Hainan Airlines and a merger with CR Airways.[31]

Oasis Hong Kong Airlines

Oasis Hong Kong Airlines was founded by ex-Dragonair CEO Stephen Miller, with principal investment from property developer Raymond Lee and his wife Priscilla. Oasis had a definitive positioning as the only long-haul, low-fare airline operating out of Hong Kong. After developing the idea of a long-haul, low-fare carrier, Miller went to Lee with a proposal. Although initially skeptical, Lee eventually agreed to invest in the proposal Miller brought to him. The Lees provided the majority of the seed funding, which was supplemented by additional investments from Allan Wong, chairman and CEO of VTech Holdings (a multinational corporation), and Richard K. Lee, founder of Trinity Textiles.[32]

The Oasis Model

Oasis marketed itself as a long-haul, low-fare carrier that offered exceptional value with customizable options. It offered two classes of service, targeting both economy- and business-class passengers, whereas other low-cost carriers only offered economy-class service and competed primarily on price. While all other low-cost carriers served short-haul routes, Oasis would only serve long-haul routes. The initial network plan of Oasis included Oakland and Chicago in the United States, Berlin and Cologne in Germany, Milan in Italy, and London Gatwick in the United Kingdom, which would be the airline's launch destination.[33]

While Oasis did not position itself to be a low-cost carrier, competitive pricing was nevertheless one of its competitive advantages. Oasis only sold one-way tickets,

which, on the Hong Kong-London route, would sell for as low as HK$1,000 (US$128) for an economy class seat and HK$6,600 (US$846) for a business class seat, excluding taxes and surcharges. In the long run, at least 10 percent of seats would continue to be sold at these fares.[34] In contrast, for a Hong Kong–London round-trip economy-class ticket departing on October 31, 2006, and returning on November 10, 2006, Cathay Pacific's prices varied from HK$5,880 (US$754) to HK$9,550 (US$1,224), depending on the level of travel restrictions, while British Airways's prices ranged from HK$2,250 (US$288) to HK$4,525 (US$580), and Virgin Atlantic's fell between HK$5,532 (US$709) and HK$17,263 (U$4,525). At these prices, Cathay Pacific was 190 to 380 percent more expensive than Oasis, 112.5 to 130 percent more expensive than British Airways, and 180 to 760 percent more expensive than Virgin Atlantic. For business-class tickets, Cathay Pacific charged HK$44,952 (US$5,763), British Airways HK$21,350 (US$2,737), and Virgin Atlantic between HK$44,897 (US$5,756) and HK$46,813 (US$6,002). In addition to attractive prices, Oasis also had a relatively simple, easily understood fare structure, which the firm expected customers would find appealing (see Exhibit 7).

Operating long-haul flights would also allow the airline to have high average aircraft utilization and efficiency. It was expected that Oasis could achieve average aircraft utilization in excess of 15 hours per day. This would give Oasis a low operating unit cost on a per available seat kilometer basis. Furthermore, by spending a large proportion of time in cruise, an aircraft flying long-haul flights would have fewer takeoffs and landings than one flying short-haul, which would translate into

Exhibit 7 Oasis Hong Kong Airlines Fare Types

Fare Type	Description
Flexi Fare	• Available year-round • Reservation held for 72 hours before payment • Unlimited free changes to flight and date • Changes to passenger name allowed on payment of change penalty plus fare difference • Refundable subject to cancellation penalty
Advance Purchase Fare	• Booked 45, 21, or 14 days in advance • Payment must be made at time of flight confirmation • Changes to flight, date, and passenger name allowed with penalty and fare difference • Refundable subject to cancellation penalty
Value Fare	• Semi-flexible fare available year-round • Payment must be made at time of flight confirmation • Changes to flight, date, and passenger name allowed with penalty and fare difference • Refundable subject to cancellation policy
Hot Deal	• Discount value fare • Payment must be made at the time of flight confirmation • Changes to flight, date, and passenger name not permitted • Non-refundable

Source: Oasis Hong Kong Airlines, 2006, Fare types, http://www.oasishongkong.com/hk/en/services/faredetails.aspx (accessed November 19, 2006).

lower maintenance costs for the airframe and engines, as well as lower fuel consumption.

Another area where Oasis would save on costs was airport landing and parking fees because the airline would use secondary airports such as Gatwick instead of Heathrow in London and Oakland instead of San Francisco in California. Other secondary airports under consideration included Milan in Italy, and Berlin and Cologne in Germany. All these secondary airports were also major hubs of leading low-cost carriers: London Gatwick, Milan, and Berlin were hubs for easyJet; Cologne was the main hub for Germanwings; and Oakland was a hub for Southwest Airlines and a busy port for JetBlue. By flying into the hubs of major low-cost carriers, Oasis hoped to receive feeder traffic from them and feed traffic to these carriers. Doing so would require interline ticket sales, check-ins, and baggage transfers, which were not unusual among low-cost carriers.

Oasis's value proposition was to offer products and services that were not significantly inferior to those of the major competitors at a price that would be considered extremely competitive and of solid value. Oasis's two Boeing 747-400s were configured for 81 business-class seats and 278 economy-class seats.[35] All passengers in economy class would be offered standard complimentary hot meals. For business-class passengers, Oasis would offer standard upgraded meals with complimentary drinks. In-flight entertainment, such as video and audio programs with personal TVs and in-flight magazines, was a part of Oasis's standard offerings. Lounge access, if required, would be available at an additional cost.

On the distribution side, Oasis adopted the traditional carriers' model and relied on brick-and-mortar travel agents to sell tickets. Passengers would also be able to buy tickets directly on the company's Web site or through a call center.

The traditional model for low-cost carriers placed little emphasis on cargo revenue. However, because Hong Kong was a major air cargo hub for the Asia-Pacific region, demand for cargo space was consistently high, and hence the corresponding market prices, especially on routes to Europe and North America, were very high. Thus, Oasis was also looking at tapping into this revenue stream by filling the bellies of its aircraft with freight.

The Plan

Oasis planned to launch its inaugural flight to London Gatwick in late October 2006. It had purchased two Boeing 747-400s from Singapore Airlines. The first was to be delivered in September, just in time for the planned inaugural flight, and the second one was to be delivered in November. With just two aircraft, Oasis could only serve one destination, with over 12 hours of idle time at London Gatwick. As Lee admitted, load factors would have to be extremely high to be profitable.[36] With four

aircraft and the added service to Oakland, the break-even load factor would come down to around 85 percent. With six aircraft, the break-even load factor could come under 80 percent.

The airline's five-year plan called for aggressive growth of fleet size, amounting to 25 aircraft. The challenge was finding the right aircraft at the right price.[37] Oasis wanted the Boeing 747-400, but in 2005–2006, this aircraft was in high demand. With high fuel prices and the availability of more efficient aircraft types, many 747-400s were expected to cease being economical as passenger aircraft. However, with a healthy growth forecast for the air cargo market, many of these aircraft were destined to be converted into freighters. Singapore Airlines, for example, not only had sold or pre-sold 11 of its 747-400s to Cathay Pacific and Dragonair for freighter conversions, but also was planning to convert a few of its own into freighters. Meanwhile, some airlines, including Singapore Airlines, had originally planned to replace their 747-400s with Airbus's A380 super jumbos starting in 2006, but were caught off guard by Airbus's 22-month delay in its A380 program, forcing airlines to hold on to their 747-400s longer than they had planned. In 2005, the market value of a 747-400 manufactured in 1991 ranged from US\$33 million to US\$52 million (see Exhibit 8).[38]

Exhibit 8 Market Value of a Boeing 747-400 (in US\$ millions)

| Vintage | Value (market) | Future Value | |
	2005	2009	2012
1989	33.9	19.5	13.7
1991	45.5	26.5	18.9
1993	56.9	33.9	24.5
1995	68.4	41.7	30.5
1997	79.9	50.0	37.1
1999	91.4	59.1	44.6
2001	103.0	68.1	52.5
2003	114.5	76.1	60.2

Source: Aircraft Value News, 2005, Semi-annual jet aircraft value listing, September 5.

Rental Cost per Month (in US\$ thousands)

Vintage	2005
1989–1995	360–490
1996–2002	470–865

Source: Aircraft Value News, 2005, Widebody lease rates (dry) US\$, October 2005.

Other possible aircraft types for Oasis included the Airbus A340-600 and the Boeing 777-300ER. Albeit slightly smaller than the 747-400, the A340-600 could work, but not many were available at this time. Similarly, the 777-300ER, which had been in service for only a few years, was not readily available on the second-hand aircraft market. In 2005, an A340-600 manufactured in 2002 was valued between US$102 million and US$111 million, whereas a 777-300ER manufactured in 2003 was worth between US$117 million and US$132 million. There was always the option of purchasing brand-new aircraft, but because of long production lead times and production slot availability, it would take 36 to 48 months before any new aircraft delivery. Oasis needed to increase capacity and add new services sooner rather than later.

Preparing for Takeoff

Oasis's potential to get off to a successful start depended to a great extent on the global economic situation at the time, as there is a strong positive correlation between gross domestic product growth and the amount of money businesses and individuals are willing to spend on travel and air freight. However, the biggest question was whether Oasis's target customers would readily embrace these services from a newcomer. On its inaugural route from Hong Kong to London, Oasis's service would be judged and compared to such reputable carriers as British Airways, Virgin Atlantic, Cathay Pacific, and Qantas. It was up to Miller and his management team to prove themselves in the marketplace.

NOTES

1. This price excluded surcharges and taxes.
2. This section is adapted from: P. Ferreira, 2001, Systems in transportation: The case of the airline industry, http://web.mit.edu/esd.83/www/notebook/Transportation%20-%20Airline%20Ind.ppt (accessed November 15, 2006); The airline industry and the World Trade Center disaster, Centre for Asian Business Cases, University of Hong Kong.
3. P. Ferreira, 2001, Systems in transportation: The case of the airline industry, http://web.mit.edu/esd.83/www/notebook/Transportation%20-%20Airline%20Ind.ppt (accessed November 15, 2006).
4. The airline industry, http://adg.stanford.edu/aa241/intro/airlineindustry.html (accessed November 15, 2006).
5. M. Schlangenstein, 2005, Southwest Airlines profit jumps: Lower fuel costs let carrier nearly triple its bottom line, Washington Post, April 15.
6. British Airways, 2005–2006 Annual report & accounts.
7. Wikipedia, 2006, Airline alliance, http://en.wikipedia.org/wiki/Airline_alliance (accessed November 20, 2006).
8. 2006, Ryanair turns screw to hold luggage, http://news.cheapflights.co.uk/flights/2006/01/ryanair_turns_s.html (accessed November 21, 2006).
9. A code sharing agreement is a cooperative agreement between two or more airlines whereby a flight operated and marketed by one airline is also marketed by its code share partner(s). In this case, the flight will have more than one flight number—one that is given to it by the operating airline and other one(s) given to it by the code share partner(s)
10. 2005, Southwest Airlines Annual Report.
11. In the parts of the world where the imperial system was prevalent (e.g., the United States), the equivalent terms were Available Seat Mile (ASM) and Available Ton Mile (ATM). Note that "ton" referred to the imperial ton equal to 2,000 pounds, whereas "tonne" in ATK referred to the metric tonne, which was equal to 2,000 kilograms.
12. This was due to the various discounts that aircraft manufacturers would offer to airlines or leasing companies.
13. A finance lease was basically a mortgage arrangement. Typically an airline would set up a special purpose company, which financed the purchase of the aircraft through a syndicate loan and would in turn lease the aircraft back to the airline.
14. As opposed to a finance lease, an operating lease was purely a leasing arrangement between the airline and a leasing company.
15. IATA. 2006, Profitability: Does size matter?, Economics Briefing, June.
16. The airline industry and current challenges, http://web.mit.edu/airlines/www/the-airline-industry/the-airline-industry.htm (accessed November 14, 2006).
17. IATA, 2006, Premium traffic, Economic Briefing, August, 3.
18. IATA Economics, 2006, Industry financial forecast briefing note, September, 4.
19. Trade Development Council, 2006, Air transport, http://logistics.tdctrade.com/ (accessed November 15, 2006).
20. Hong Kong Civil Aviation Department, 2006, Hong Kong International Airport Civil International Air Transport Movements of Aircraft, Passenger and Freight (1998–2006), http://www.cad.gov.hk/english/p-through.html (accessed November 21, 2006).
21. Airport Authority Hong Kong, 2006, Annual report 2006.
22. Boeing Commercial Airplanes, 2005, Current market outlook 2005, 3–5.
23. Airport Authority Hong Kong, 2006, The airport authority, http://www.hongkongairport.com/eng/aboutus/profile.html (accessed October 17, 2006).
24. Cathay Pacific Airways, 2006, Awards and honours, http://www.cathaypacific.com/cpa/en_INTL/aboutus/cxbackground/awardsandhonours (accessed November 29, 2006).
25. This section was adapted from: Hong Kong Dragon Airlines, 2006, History, http://www.dragonair.com/icms/servlet/template?series=98&lang=eng (accessed November 29, 2006).
26. Air China, Cathay Pacific, CNAC, CITIC Pacific, and Swire Pacific 2006, Changes in shareholding structure builds new aviation partnerships in Greater China, Joint Press Release, June 9.
27. This section was adapted from: Air Hong Kong, 2006, History, http://www.airhongkong.com.hk/ahk/en/F300/History/index.jsp (accessed June 21, 2006).
28. A wet lease was an aircraft leasing arrangement between two parties whereby the lessor provided not only the aircraft, but also the crew, maintenance, and insurance to the lessee.
29. Wikipedia, 2006, Hong Kong Airlines, http://en.wikipedia.org/wiki/CR_Airways (accessed November 29, 2006).

30. C. So, 2006, HK Express to drop Guangzhou service, *South China Morning Post*, February 9.

31. R. Barling, 2006, CR Airways and Ho carrier eye merger, *South China Morning Post*, May 9.

32. Asia Travel Tips, 2006, New low cost–long haul Hong Kong-based airline opens for reservations, http://www.asiatraveltips.com/news06/59-OasisHongKongAirlines.shtml (accessed November 23, 2006).

33. Wikipedia, 2006, Oasis Hong Kong Airlines, http://en.wikipedia.org/wiki/Oasis_Hong_Kong_Airlines (accessed November 22, 2006).

34. Wikipedia, 2006, Oasis Hong Kong Airlines, http://en.wikipedia.org/wiki/Oasis_Hong_Kong_Airlines (accessed November 22, 2006).

35. Wikipedia, 2006, Oasis Hong Kong Airlines, http://en.wikipedia.org/wiki/Oasis_Hong_Kong_Airlines (accessed November 22, 2006).

36. R. Barling, 2006, Oasis success still on a wing and a prayer to distant horizon, *South China Morning Post*, October 27.

37. Wikipedia, 2006, Oasis Hong Kong Airlines, http://en.wikipedia.org/wiki/Oasis_Hong_Kong_Airlines (accessed November 22, 2006.

38. Aircraft Value News, 2005, Semi-annual jet aircraft value listing, September 5.

Richard Ivey School of Business
The University of Western Ontario

"I am working harder and longer hours than ever before and making less money," thought Kevin Wilson as he drove his van to work one morning in Knoxville, Tennessee. Wilson was the sole owner and manager of Pro Clean LLC, a carpet cleaning business. He was still the first one to arrive at work and the last one to leave. As a result, he had been neglecting his family lately and the first tensions in his marriage were becoming visible.

The issue was fast becoming not one of working harder and longer and making less money but that of survival. Looking back at his decision to expand his business, he was now close to admitting that he had made a mistake. But was there a chance to rectify his mistake or would his business spiral ever faster to bankruptcy?

Knoxville

Knoxville was the third largest city in Tennessee. It was located in a broad valley between the Cumberland Mountains to the northwest and the Great Smoky Mountains to the southeast.[1]

Knoxville had a population of 183,546 in 2007 and the population had grown by 4.6 per cent since 2000. The estimated median household income in 2005 was $30,473 (it was $27,492 in 2000) and the estimated median house/condo value in 2005 was $100,400 (it was $78,000 in 2000). Knoxville had a land area of 92.7 square miles.[2]

Knoxville had a highly diversified economy with no over-reliance on any industry. The local economy had seen substantial growth in the areas of trade, transportation, utilities and financial activities recently.

The Market

The residential house cleaning market in Knoxville was serviced predominately by independent companies. There were also a few large franchises competing for market share. Residential house cleaning services were divided into different categories: maid or house cleaners, carpet cleaners, window cleaners and a variety of other service providers. The carpet cleaning market consisted of approximately 60 cleaners. The figure was close to 80 if one took into account the cleaners in the distant Knoxville counties. Roughly 90 per cent were owner/operators that had one van. There was one large national franchise, which had seven vans and 18 to 20 employees. The remaining companies operated with two or three vans (see Exhibit 1). The market grew an approximate five per cent per year, which was what Wilson averaged. Pro Clean had built up a respectable five per cent market share in Knoxville.

The commercial cleaning market was serviced by janitorial service providers that offered a one-stop service to commercial businesses and offered diverse services such as general office cleaning, carpet cleaning, window cleaning, etc.

Regardless of the saturated marketplace, a number of national janitorial cleaning and carpet cleaning chains were advertising aggressively to establish new franchises in the city.

Pro Clean

Wilson was an old-timer in the carpet cleaning business. He had run his own carpet cleaning business as an owner/operator in Chicago, Illinois, for seven years and had moved to Knoxville, Tennessee, eight years ago when his wife had gotten an offer to run a medical clinic (the average American family relocated every 12 years). He had worked hard to establish himself in Knoxville and what had worked for him in Chicago had also worked in Knoxville and he was making $75,000 a year as an owner/operator. They had settled in well in Tennessee and had two young children, who were now in elementary school.

Wilson offered both steam cleaning and dry cleaning options to his customers but the method of choice was steam cleaning (see Exhibit 2).

As an owner/operator, Wilson managed the following daily functions:

- Scheduling
- Estimates
- Cleaning
- Inventory management
- Training
- Ordering
- Payroll
- Marketing
- Customer care management
- Van and equipment maintenance
- Accounting

Wilson used QuickBooks software to do his accounting and was not good with numbers. He also was not good at selling and avoided public speaking at all cost. After 15 years of hard work, long hours and incessant back pains he had finally decided that it was time for him to hang up his overalls and leave the cleaning to others.

Business Expansion

He had long envied the high prices that one of his competitors, King Rug, charged and had tried to emulate the business model of that company. Two years ago he had hired three workers to do the cleaning, (see Exhibit 3), moved the business out of his home to a newly rented commercial facility and purchased two new vans on lease. Upon the suggestion of a fellow member of the Knoxville Chamber of commerce who designed web sites, he had also invested in a basic web site.

He had thought "With four employees, three vans and a web site, Pro Clean is now ready to take on even the best in Knoxville." Wilson had targeted to become the new King Rug of Knoxville.

Expansion Pains

The expansion process had been exhilarating at first. A new Pro Clean logo had been designed. He had trained the new employees to clean and had outfitted his employees with Pro Clean-branded overalls. The Pro Clean logo had also been painted on the sides of all the vans to complete the branding effort.

At the onset of the expansion, the business had started to churn cash as a result of the increased payroll expense and the lease payments for the new vans. Cash flow had quickly become a problem, one that Wilson was not used to and he had had to resort to using his business and personal credit cards' overdraft facility to finance his business.

His return on investment, however, was dismal. Increasing capacity threefold had not increased business threefold as originally foreseen and cleaning technicians and their assigned vans were spending at least two thirds of the day idly at the new office.

Looking for answers to get him out of his predicament, he had tried to get help from peers at the Chamber of Commerce, but to no avail. As a last resort, he had sought help online and had found a carpet cleaning guru in Memphis, Tennessee, who went by the title of "King of Klean." The King of Klean had promised guaranteed results and Wilson had enrolled in the program, paying for the $20,000 workshop and tutorials over the duration of a year with his already overextended credit card.

He had tried to the best of his knowledge to enact the standardized marketing templates that had brought fame and glory to the King of Klean. What had worked for the King of Klean and turned him into a millionaire had unfortunately not worked for Wilson, as he was not able to replicate the great man's success.

Restructuring

Accepting that his expansion plans had run into trouble, he had laid off Jeremy Turner, one of his cleaning technicians. Desperately in need of new business and in response to one of the remaining cleaning technicians, who had problems adapting to the rigor of cleaning and the ensuing back pains, he had temporarily transformed the cleaning technician position to that of sales and office administration. The change in position had been made permanent shortly thereafter, along with a pay rise and new title of sales and office manager.

The Restructured Pro Clean Organization

Initially, the new sales/office manager had spent a lot of time stuffing envelopes with direct mail material, answering phones, giving estimates, etc. After six months of spending most of his time in the office and with little additional business to show for, he had started to visit real estate agents and business owners to garner referrals and do in-home estimates for residential prospects that called in. He had also started to visit current business clients to build stronger relationships.

The sales/office manager had now been routinely visiting real estate agents and other referral sources for half of the day and spending the remainder of the day in the office, usually when Wilson was out. He had also seemingly been doing a lot of work from his home, with full online access to the Pro Clean computer network and claimed that he clocked-in at least 60 hours a week. The two men had established a good rapport and Wilson regularly conferred with him before making business decisions.

The other cleaning technician had not been available to clean after hours or on weekends and Wilson himself was back to cleaning on one of the vans for overflow work for after-hours and weekend cleaning jobs. The rest of Wilson's time had been spent trying to develop the business and at the office dealing with administrative and clerical tasks.

Marketing Strategy

Pro Clean's strategy was to target all potential residential customers in Knoxville without bothering to focus on demographics. A paying customer was a paying customer. In the past year, it had done some commercial cleaning and hoped that it could build on that in the present year, targeting small businesses with carpets of not larger than 10,000 square feet/930 square meters. The commercial business was not a cash business and required receivables follow-up and payments were usually late. Pro Clean tried to stay in touch with all its customers by sending out quarterly newsletters.

Pro Clean Customer Profile

- Income greater than $250,000 per year
- Mostly single-income families
- Most homes had pets/young children
- Stay-at-home spouse made the purchasing decision
- Mostly paid in cash
- Want a safe, healthy, quality service
- Want to protect their investments with regular maintenance

Purchasing Patterns

- The average Pro Clean customer had their carpets cleaned every 12 months
- Frequent-use customers had their carpets cleaned every six months
- Frequent-use customers made up approximately 20 per cent of the business
- Most carpet owners cared for their carpets themselves regularly on a weekly or bi-monthly basis using standard household vacuum cleaners

Source of Business

Pro Clean had a loyal and satisfied customer base which provided most of the business. 60 per cent of Pro Clean's business was repeat business, with marketing accounting for 10 per cent, referrals 8.5 per cent, other sources like walk-ups and calls from people that saw the van accounting for 19.5 per cent and internet-based sales for three per cent. The Pro Clean website had not lived up to expectations and Wilson himself had tried to upgrade the website himself with the help of a high school student.

Source of Revenue

Carpet cleaning was the main source of revenue for Pro Clean and accounted for 77 per cent of its revenue. The other service offerings did not bring in that much revenue. Upholstery cleaning accounted for nine per cent, area rug cleaning five per cent, tile and grout cleaning five per cent, carpet and fabric protection three per cent and drapery cleaning a mere one per cent.

Wilson suspected that his competitors generated considerable extra revenue by up-selling customers extra services in addition to carpet cleaning. It was a well-known fact in the carpet cleaning industry of Knoxville that King Rug derived a substantive portion of its revenue from rug cleaning at its place of business and did well with cross selling and up-selling. Pro Clean, however, did not, or as he sometimes admitted to himself, could not, successfully upsell.

Sales Incentives

Pro Clean had a commission system in place for its technicians that paid 10 per cent of each new job. After each job, technicians were encouraged to distribute flyers to the two to three houses across the street and one on each side of the house they were cleaning. The technicians, however, rarely bothered to distribute flyers, as their previous efforts had yielded no results.

Scheduling

Pro Clean had divided Knoxville into zones and tried to schedule cleaning jobs on a one-zone-a-day basis to save fuel. More often than not, trucks would have to service two or more zones a day.

Customers were given time options to accommodate their own schedules. The size of the cleaning job was not prioritized unless it affected Pro Clean's punctuality. Scheduling became even more complicated because the new vans had faster setup and cleaning times versus the older van.

Vans

The new vans gave Pro Clean a better return on investment versus the old van:

- The new vans averaged 40 per cent better fuel efficiency than the old van
- Van setup for each job was faster
- New equipment required less fuel
- New equipment cleaned faster

New Service Offering

Wilson was thinking of offering a new service to his clients. He had carefully studied the competitive landscape and seen that only one company offered hardwood floor cleaning. He planned to introduce the new service as soon as he had been trained for it.

Sales and Cleaning Process

New Customers
See Exhibits 4, 5 and 6.

Potential customers would call to get information and prices as a result of interest sparked by Pro Clean's marketing effort. The sales/office manager would prequalify the sales leads and visit the prospective customer at the agreed day and time and prepare an on-site estimate after measuring the areas to be cleaned. Potential customers would usually take a couple days to come to a decision. Most of them would contact other carpet cleaners and ask for estimates. Once the job was given to Pro Clean, a cleaning technician would be dispatched to clean at the agreed day and time. The technician would also collect the cash payment upon completing the job.

Existing Customers
Existing customers' details were stored on the Pro Clean computer. The price estimate would be given over the phone unless the customer required additional spaces to be cleaned or asked for new services. A technician would then be dispatched at the agreed day and time to clean (see Exhibits 4, 5 and 6).

On-Site Estimates versus Phone Estimates

Only King Rug and Pro Clean made on-site estimate visits. Wilson thought that doing on-site estimate calculations was one way to impress customers and was just one more way to emulate King Rug. At times, he had watched the young, professional King Rug technicians' interactions with customers and admired the way they managed the customer interaction process in a standardized way. The only other cleaner that had a similar level of standardized proficiency was D-Cleaner.

All other cleaners gave approximate estimates over the phone and followed up with a detailed price once they were on-site to clean. This was when the inevitable up-selling began and greatly increased the low estimate given over the phone.

Wilson was not very good at selling and it was Andrew Scott that did most of the visits for Pro Clean. Alexander Martinez preferred just to clean and his closing ratio on the few times that he had made on-site estimate visits was dismal. Scott had a higher closing ratio with elder customers, with whom he claimed he was able to "connect" better. His approach did not work as well with other age groups or with commercial buyers.

The Pro Clean estimate kit consisted of a tape measure, calculator and pre-printed estimate form of which a copy was given to the customer. Wilson had taught Scott and Martinez how to do the calculations and fill out the estimate form in their first week at work after showing them how to clean.

Competitive Field

Pro Clean had more than 80 direct competitors in Knoxville providing carpet cleaning services. The market was very price-competitive and there was a large national chain, D-Cleaner, with high brand recognition that advertised aggressively at the national and local levels. D-Cleaner had successfully acquired a good portion of the market with a standard low price for standard cleaning services. D-Cleaner advertised prices by area rather than by square feet and a favorite ploy was to advertise a $199 all-inclusive price for five areas of a standard home, which was usually upsold by at least 50 per cent by aggressive point of sale bait and switch tactics.

The exception to price-based competition was King Rug, which was able to attract a wealthier clientele. King Rug had 20-plus years of business presence in the Knoxville area, operated four top-of-the-line vans and equipment and worked out of a nice building with a warehouse where oriental rugs were treated. King Rug charged on average 50 to 100 per cent higher for its services than its competitors.

At the bottom of the price spectrum was Kleen Clean, run by Kim Lee, a Korean-American, which offered low-cost dry/chemical cleaning services (see Exhibit 7).

Exhibit 1 Map of Knoxville, Tennessee

Source: Author.

Exhibit 2 Cleaning Methodology

There were two methods of carpet cleaning available in the market:

- Steam cleaning
- Low moisture/chemical cleaning

Steam Cleaning

- 85 per cent of the professional carpet cleaning business in the United States was steam cleaning
- Steam cleaning done with the right equipment and trained technicians dried within three to fours hours of application and dried in full within 12 to 16 hours
- Steam cleaning flushed the carpet with hot water piped in from the van with a long retractable hose at 180 to 220 degrees (steam was the term used to help buyers visualize the service better)
- Carpet manufacturers required steam cleaning every 12 to 16 months to keep maintenance warranties valid

Steam cleaning advantages:

- Preferred by clients as cleaning method of choice
- Required by carpet manufacturers
- Best deep down cleaning (fibers were flushed and extracted to remove all contaminates)
- Better overall results

Steam cleaning disadvantages:

- Average truck-mounted cleaning system started at $17,000 and went up to $40,000 (not including van)
- Longer setup time
- Longer cleaning time
- Longer dry time
- Longer training time for new technicians
- More equipment maintenance and downtime
- More fuel costs to operate equipment

Dry Cleaning/Chemical Cleaning
The cleaning process consisted of using a chemical compound to treat the carpet and then using a cotton bonnet spinning on a rotary machine, with the bonnet absorbing the dirt into the cotton pad.
Low moisture/chemical cleaning advantages:

- Faster dry times — 30 to 60 minutes after initial application
- Faster setup and cleaning time
- Faster learning curve
- No fuel costs to run machines
- Low equipment cost ($700–1000)

Low moisture/chemical cleaning disadvantages:

- Limited to surface cleaning of fibers
- Did not rinse carpet of contaminants
- No extraction
- Most consumers did not prefer it for fear of chemicals

Exhibit 3 Pro Clean HR Data

1. Kevin Wilson – Owner

    - Age: 48
    - Education: Some community college
    - Past Experience: 15 years of experience in the carpet cleaning industry

2. Andrew Scott – Sales/Office Manager

    - Age: 47
    - Education: High school diploma
    - Past Experience: Had owned and operated a limousine rental service for eight years in Kansas before moving to Knoxville (company went out of business); had started work in Knoxville as a call center operator handling customer service complaints for a large national appliance manufacturer
    - Had started out as a cleaning technician before making the switch to sales/office manager
    - Wilson had hired him because of his business experience and his ability to deal with people

(Continued)

Exhibit 3 Pro Clean HR Data (*Continued*)

3. Alexander Martinez – Technician

- Age: 51
- Education: High school diploma
- Past Experience: 20 years' experience in air conditioning installation (company went out of business)
- Had a wife, who had a serious health problem and needed constant care
- Wilson had hired Martinez because he was very eager to work for him (due in part to the good health benefits) and was mechanically inclined

4. Jeremy Turner – Technician

- Age: 27
- Education: High school diploma
- Past Experience: Five years of experience working in different janitorial cleaning service companies in the Knoxville area
- Hired because he had good references, was a hard and reliable worker, and knew the Knoxville area well

Exhibit 4 New Residential Customer Sales, Cleaning, and Collection Process

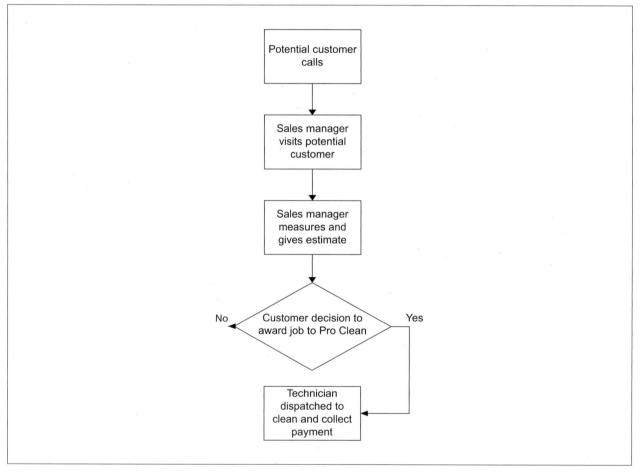

Exhibit 5 Existing Residential Customer Sales, Cleaning, and Collection Process

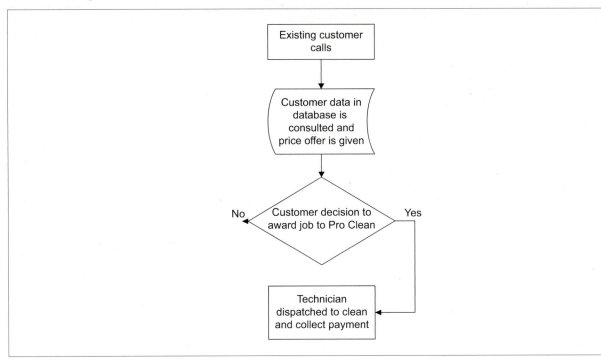

Exhibit 6 New Commercial Customer Sales, Cleaning and Collection Process

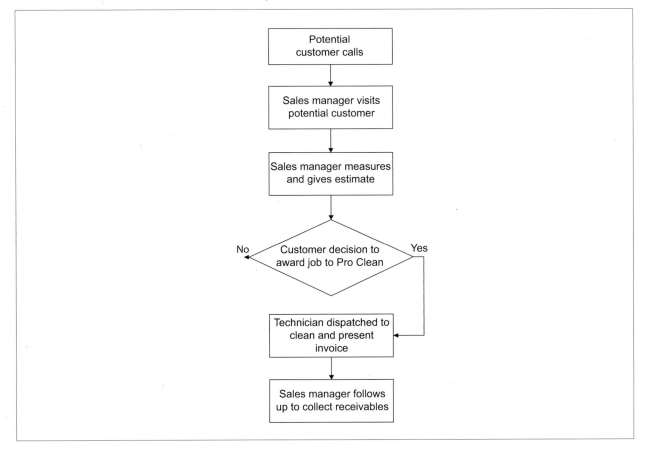

Exhibit 7 Competitive Analysis

Competitive Analysis	Pro Clean	D-Cleaner	King Rug	Green Clean	Right Clean	Kleen Clean
BUSINESS BASICS						
Number of vans	3	7	4	2	2	1
Number of employees	3	18–20	5	3	5	1
Number of years in business	15	50	20	8	18	5
MARKET FOCUS						
Residential	Y	Y	Y	Y	Y	Y
Commercial	N	N	N	N	N	N
CLEANING METHOD						
Steam	Y	Y	Y	Y	Y	N
Chemical	Optional	N	N	N	N	Y
CLEANING SERVICES						
Carpets	Y	Y	Y	Y	Y	Y
Upholstery	Y	Y	Y	Y	Y	Y
Rugs	Y	N	Y	N	N	N
Tiles	Y	Y	Y	Y	Y	N
Drapery	Y	Y	N	Y	Y	N
Air ducts	N	Y	N	Y	Y	N
Odor treatment	Y	Y	Y	Y	Y	Y
Natural stone car	Y	N	Y	N	N	N
House exteriors	N	N	N	N	N	N
RVs, trailers	Y	Y	Y	Y	Y	Y
Hardwood floor restoration	N	Y	N	N	N	N
Hardwood floor cleaning	Y	Y	N	N	N	N
MARKETING						
Carpet cleaning packages	N	Y	N	Y	Y	Y
Referral program	Y	N	Y	N	N	N
Coupons	N	Y	N	Y	Y	Y
Newsletter	Y	N	Y	Y	N	N
Advertising	N	Y	N	Y	Y	N
Loyalty program	N	N	Y	N	N	N
Unconditional guarantee	Y	N	Y	Y	Y	N
Good web page	N	Y	Y	N	N	N

(Continued)

339

Case 23: Pro Clean, Tennessee

Exhibit 7 Competitive Analysis (*Continued*)

Competitive Analysis	Pro Clean	D-Cleaner	King Rug	Green Clean	Right Clean	Kleen Clean
PRODUCT SALES						
Flooring goods	N	Y	N	N	N	N
GEOGRAPHICAL FOCUS						
Focus on metro Knoxville	Y	Y	Y	Y	Y	Y
Focus on other counties	N	N	N	N	N	N
Close to customer base	Y	Y	Y	Y	Y	Y
PRICING						
Carpet	$0.27 per sq. ft.	$36 per room	$0.60 per sq. ft.	$36 per room	$30 per room	$33 per room
Sofa upholstery cleaning (per piece)	$85	$80	N	$75	$60	N
Love seat cleaning (per piece)	$60	$60	N	$55	$50	N
Chair cleaning (per piece)	$55	$50	N	$35	$30	N
Rug cleaning (sq. ft.)	$2.00	$1.50	$3.00	$1.75	$1.50	$1.50
Tile cleaning (sq. ft.)	$0.90	$0.65	$1.25	$0.75	$0.75	N
Drapery cleaning (per pleat)	$1.75	N	N	N	N	N
Upholstery cleaning (by linear foot)	N	N	$15	N	N	N

NOTES

1. http://www.cityofknoxville.org/about/history.asp.
2. http://www.city-data.com/us-cities/The-South/Knoxville-Population-Profile.html.

Edward D. Hess

University of Virginia, Darden School Foundation

Room & Board was a privately owned home-furnishings retailer, offering products that combined classic, simple design with exceptional quality. Approximately $50 million of revenue a year was generated through Room & Board's fully integrated, multichannel sales approach, consisting of its eight national retail stores, an annual catalog, and a Web site. Based in Minneapolis, Minnesota, Room & Board's story is one of contrarian success as a company that had abandoned the standard retail-industry business model, disavowed debt and equity-growth financing, and embraced a unique multiple-stakeholder model that valued quality and relationships ahead of the bottom line while producing stellar financial results. That the company had achieved consistency and harmony between its values and actions also added to its uniqueness. Its culture supported an energized, positive growth environment for its employees that fostered high employee engagement and in turn, high customer engagement.

Room & Board was wholly owned by John Gabbert, who had created it more than 25 years earlier. Having reached the age of 60, Gabbert was now confronting his biggest challenge: how to institutionalize the unusual business model, culture, and employee environment he had built. His primary objective was to preserve and protect his "relationship" business model, which was the heart and soul of Room & Board's success.

History

Gabbert grew up working in a family retail business that sold traditional home furnishings; at the age of 24, he succeeded his father as the CEO. Family dynamics proved challenging, so when he was 33, he left the family furniture business to start his own furniture company initially based on IKEA's business model. He also diversified into other businesses. By the late 1980s however, feeling overextended and unfulfilled, he decided to focus all his energy on building a business with people he liked and on a model that represented quality. All this drew him into the design aspect of the furniture business.

To Gabbert, quality relationships were just as important as quality home furnishings. This belief helped shape Room & Board into a business focused on creating long-lasting relationships with customers, vendors, and employees, who were all fully integrated into the model of selling quality furnishings. At Room & Board, quality was also about providing value. That value was inherent in the firm's products, which lasted and whose style and design were timeless—furniture that customers could count on enjoying for many years. But Room & Board went further by believing that a customer's home should be a place where he or she can create a meaningful environment. This was made possible by offering customers a multitude of special-order products, ranging from fabric choices on throw pillows to customer-designed solid-wood storage pieces.

Supply Chain

The retail-furniture industry was generally controlled by large manufacturers that dictated style, product availability, and price, and that made many products overseas with cheaper labor than could be found in the United States. Room & Board decided early on that it did not want to compete by the traditional rules associated with the retail-furniture industry. In contrast, the firm created its own supply chain of approximately 40 different vendors, nearly all privately owned family businesses, many having grown alongside Room & Board over the years. Soon, more than 85 percent of the

This case was prepared by Edward D. Hess, Professor of Business Administration and Batten Executive-in-Residence. It was written as a basis for class discussion rather than to illustrate effective or ineffective handling of an administrative situation.

company's products were made in the United States—in places like Newton, North Carolina; Martinsville, Virginia; Minneapolis, Minnesota; Grand Forks, North Dakota; Shell Lake, Wisconsin; and Albany, Oregon—by craftsmen and artisans using high-quality hardwoods, granite, and steel. Most of these products were made exclusively for Room & Board, and more than 50 percent of the products were manufactured by 12 key vendors. Room & Board met with its vendors frequently to plan growth, discuss needs, and share financial data and results to ensure that everyone was making a fair living while creating high-quality, well-designed products.

These vendor relationships evolved over the years into true partnerships, which allowed Room & Board to set an annual goal of having 85 percent of its products in stock at all times, contributing to quick deliveries. Special-order products were programmed ahead of normal production with the aim of delivering the product as quickly as possible to the customer.

Under this model, Room & Board was more in control of its destiny; it had control over product quality, inventory availability, and the risk of supply-chain disruptions. This unique model carried its own risks however, as almost all of Room & Board's suppliers were private, family-owned businesses that shared the company's challenge of growing at a rate that sustained their economic health.

Culture

Room & Board had rejected common attributes of private-company culture: hierarchy, command and control from the top, information on a need-to-know basis, and, in the retail industry, high turnover resulting in customer-service challenges. Its culture was based on the principles of trust, respect, relationships, transparency, entrepreneurial ownership of one's job and career, and the importance of a balanced life. Room & Board eschewed rules, lengthy policy manuals, and elitism. Rather, it believed that individuals thrive in an environment where they are empowered to make decisions and everyone's view is heard and respected. These core beliefs were outlined in its *Guiding Principles,* partially based on the following expectation:

At Room & Board we hope you find meaning in your work. There is both tremendous productivity for the company and personal fulfillment for each staff member when someone finds their life's work. It's a wonderful circle of success.

Room & Board tried to achieve this "circle of success" by creating an environment of collaboration and engagement. This engagement was evidenced by deep relationships with customers, fellow employees, and suppliers. Respect for different views, openness to

feedback, and responsibility for one's actions all drove the staff's behavior.

What worked for Room & Board as it tried to achieve balance was defined by Gandhi: Harmony exists when what you feel, what you think, and what you do are consistent. Many businesses talked a good game, but Room & Board actually tried to "walk the talk." In this company environment, there was a heightened sensitivity regarding the impact of actions across functions and an awareness of the real message being communicated.

Room & Board believed that success was rooted in shared accountability; therefore, there were no rules for personal leave or sick pay. All 670 employees were shown the company's annual strategy priorities and a complete detailed financial package every month so that they could understand the goals of the business. All financial and operating numbers were transparent to encourage responsibility for owning and, in turn, affecting Room & Board's success. In discussing the company's normal eight-hour day, Gabbert stated:

I learned a long time ago that most people only have so many productive hours a day—it is the number of productive hours that count, not the number of hours at work. We strive to have an environment which results in energy and productivity. That is why we have a full physical-fitness facility with classes going on during the workday, a masseuse, as well as a great kitchen for employees to prepare healthy lunches.

Room & Board also operated on the principle that people who have a balanced life, with a life outside work, were happier and dealt well with customers and with each other. Gabbert, who recognized that what set his company apart was its engaged employees who tried to make every customer experience special, said, "I never wanted to be the biggest. I never thought about size. I just wanted to be the best and to spend my time at work with good people doing something more meaningful than just making money or keeping score."

Employees

The retail industry is known for high employee turnover, with companies using many part-time employees to keep expenditures on employee benefits low and commission-based compensation to lower fixed costs. But Room & Board was proof that a very profitable, high-quality business could be built by not following any of those common retail practices.

Instead, Room & Board had very low employee turnover, mostly full-time employees, provided full benefits for part-time employees, and pay based on salary rather than on individual sales. The rejection of a commission-based structure, together with its integrated and multichannel purchasing options, allowed Room & Board customers to shop and purchase in the manner that made the most sense to them. "We want customers to rely on us for the best advice and to trust that we have their best interests in mind—sales commissions run against that type of trust," said Gabbert. The breakdown of Room & Board's employees by staff divisions is shown in Exhibit 1.

Room & Board stores more than five years old had average employee tenure of more than five years, which was very high for the retail industry. Delivery and warehouse personnel in delivery centers open for more than four years had an average tenure of five years. Employee tenure was 5.7 years for the central office, and total employee tenure for the company averaged nearly five years.

Room & Board also took a different approach to measuring employee satisfaction: The company tracked how many employees referred family and friends for jobs and how many employees participated in the company's 401(k) program. Room & Board believed that these measures truly contributed to long-term employee engagement. Following the philosophy that employees needed good physical, mental, and financial health, Room & Board offered an extensive physical-fitness facility, a healthy-lunch program, and personal financial-planning services and 401(k) investment advice from an outside financial consulting firm at no cost. In addition, all employees could buy Room & Board products at a substantial discount.

Leadership Team

Room & Board was led by a six-member advisory board made up of John Gabbert and the members (see Exhibit 2). The leadership team received generous bonuses if key company objectives were met.

Key Expectations for Employees and Leaders

Room & Board's *Guiding Principles* was the foundation for the company's expectations and also served as a tool to help employees understand their connection to the business. The document, which spoke primarily to

Exhibit 1 Room & Board Staff Divisions

Type	Number
Store personnel	237
Delivery personnel	220
Store and delivery leadership team	62
Central office staff	100

Exhibit 2 Leadership Team

Member	Title	Tenure
Bruce Champeau	Vice President of Distribution Delivery/Technology	16 years
Kimberly Ruthenbeck	Vice President of Retail Customer Experience & Vendor Managements	15 years
Mark Miller	Chief Financial Officer	11 years
Betsey Kershaw	Director of Brand Experience	5 years
Nancy McGough	Director of Human Resources	16 years

respect individual accountability and engaging the business, included the following statements:

- Respect is foundational to our work environment. Everyone is expected to build relationships based upon mutual respect and collaboration.
- Use good judgment when making decisions and apply principle, not rules, to each situation.
- The more you seek to understand how your role is related to our business objectives and tied to the broader success of the company, the more rewarding, enjoyable, and challenging the effort.

Just as all employees were expected to understand and embrace the core beliefs outlined in *Guiding Principles,* leaders were expected to adhere to their own additional roadmap. Room & Board set forth a number of leadership objectives for its central office, store, and delivery/distribution leadership team, including the following:

- You take ownership for your business—you're independent and therefore do not wait to be told what to do.
- You lead less with rules and rely more on principles.
- You value building relationships; collaboration is much more important to you than competition.
- You appreciate and desire longevity within your role. You do not seek to move from location to location or from department to department to get ahead; your growth occurs from richer experiences within your current role.

Financial Results

The Skokie, Illinois, store opened in 1986; the Edina, Minnesota, store in April 1989; the Denver store in 1991; and the Chicago store in 1993 (see Exhibits 3 and 4).

Exhibit 3 Room & Board Financial Results

Year	Sales (in millions [$])	New-Store Openings
1995	$33	
1996	$45	
1997	$53	Oakbrook, IL
1998	$67	
1999	$82	
2000	$98	
2001	$92	
2002	$95	South Coast, CA
2003	$110	
2004	$132	New York, NY; downtown Chicago store moves to Rush & Ohio location
2005	$173	San Francisco, CA
2006	$208	
2007	$229	

Source: Room & Board.

Exhibit 4 Room & Board Financial Results

Key Metrics	Goals
Sales growth	10% annual
Net profit	8% pretax
Customer satisfaction	>96%
Product in warehouse at time of sale	>85%
Vendor lead time	<7 weeks
Channels of Distribution	**Approximate-Breakdown**
Store sales	70%
Phone sales	2%
Web sales	18%
Markets	**($ in millions)**
Colorado	$18
Minneapolis	$24
Chicago	$44
San Francisco	$33
Southern California	$23
New York City	$46
National sales	$42
Main Product Lines	
Sofas and chairs	36%
Bedroom	17%
Dining room	12%

Source: Room & Board.

Delivery Centers

Another point of differentiation from other retailers was Room & Board's philosophy regarding deliveries. Many furniture chains outsourced their deliveries. Room & Board did not, operating its own delivery centers staffed by full-time Room & Board professionals. These teams delivered all the local products. For national deliveries, Room & Board had an exclusive relationship with a Minneapolis company. To ensure ongoing collaboration, a few employees from the national shipping company's office worked out of Room & Board's central location.

In addition, the company had dedicated delivery teams for just Room & Board products. It was not unusual for customers to assume that these delivery professionals were Room & Board employees, not just because of their Room & Board uniforms, but also because they adhered to the same principles that all Room & Board employees followed: namely, that the customer experience during every step of the process was hassle-free and treated as an opportunity to create long-lasting relationships. The individuals who had the last interaction with customers about purchases were viewed as brand ambassadors and acted as such.

Room & Board's goal of providing a great customer experience at every step of the buying-and-receiving process required delivery personnel to deliver and set up the product and leave the customer happy. Delivery times were scheduled to allow time for customer interaction, discussions, and the proper placement of the new purchases. If there was a problem, delivery personnel were empowered to solve it on the spot because they were trained to "leave the customer in a good place." The focus on interaction with the customer, from the beginning of the experience to the end, drove customer satisfaction, in terms of loyalty and referrals, to a rate of more than 95 percent.

Real Estate

To avoid the high rent typical in retail malls, Room & Board owned most of its locations and searched out freestanding sites with ample parking and easy access for customers. The company often chose to renovate an existing location, blending its store in with a particular environment rather than building a new one. This practice served as inspiration to customers who dealt with similar challenges when designing and furnishing their own spaces. Moreover, it prevented Room & Board from adopting a "cookie cutter" image for its stores and fostered the company's philosophy of unique design. The central-office facility was furnished with Room & Board products, so even employees who were not in customer-facing roles understood what the company sold, its quality, and its lasting design.

Pricing Model

Room & Board's pricing model was simple: no sales, no volume discounts, and no discounts for interior designers. Everyone paid the same price. As John Gabbert put it, "Nothing makes me madder than to buy something and then see it go on sale. I feel taken advantage of. That is why we have no sales, and we guarantee all prices for a year after purchase for each calendar year. If we sell a product within a year of your purchase for less than you paid, we will refund the difference."

Competition

Direct comparison with other retailers was impossible because Room & Board's exclusive designs, corporate structure, and long-lasting heirloom-quality products were not offered by any other company. Ultimately, Room & Board was competing for any of the dollars that customers spent on their homes no matter what the other retailer sold. Design Within Reach and Crate and Barrel were two companies that carried similar modern home furnishings and mid-century products.

Design Within Reach was a public company. In fiscal 2006, it had $110 million in sales through its 63 stores, which ranged in size from 1,100 square feet to 11,000 square feet. Although Room & Board stores were fewer in number, they were much bigger, at 30,000 square feet. Crate and Barrel had grown from a small family business, started in 1962, to a chain of over 160 mall-based stores owned by the private German company Otto, which also owned Spiegel and Eddie Bauer. More than 50 percent of Crate and Barrel products were imported from Europe.

Conclusion

Room & Board achieved the enviable market position of managing its growth and avoiding the capital-market pressures produced by debt financing and equity partners or by being a public company. It built a loyal and highly engaged workforce dedicated to its way of doing things, and managed to be a model of productivity and engagement without sacrificing quality. The company did not strive for the lowest operational costs, but instead embraced a vertically integrated business model and earned good net margins.

The beauty of the Room & Board success story was how it had created a consistent, seamless, self-reinforcing system that cut across culture, structure, execution philosophy, employee hiring, and benefits. The result was a company with a high-performance environment that manufactured 85 percent of its products in the United States, paid its people well, sold high-quality products, and made good profits.

Room & Board adhered to a multiple-stakeholder philosophy of capitalism, much like the European model and less like the sole-stakeholder model more common in the United States. It believed it would do well if its customers, employees, and suppliers did well. To create shareholder value had not been Room & Board's sole purpose. But now the company was looking at expanding—into Los Angeles, Seattle, Atlanta, Miami, and Washington, D.C.—but at its own pace and on its own terms. Room & Board's task was figuring out how to institutionalize its way of doing business beyond the life of its founder and how to strengthen its culture and high employee and customer engagement, while growing at a rate that sustained its economic health.

X. U. Leiping

China Europe International Business School

It was the morning of October 18, 2007. In Beijing, the autumn air was clear and crisp. Zhang Lan, the founder and chair of the board of the South Beauty Group, sat in her office with her management team to discuss the future plans for her seven-year-old company.

As a successful player in China's catering industry, by September 2007 the South Beauty Group had expanded to a total of 20 plush restaurants in the most commercially valuable locations across Beijing, Shanghai, and Chengdu, with three different brands. South Beauty, the Group's flagship brand with 19 restaurants, targeted the upper-middle-class segment of businesspeople; LAN Club, the new luxury brand with two restaurants (one opened), targeted the upper-class dining segment; SUBU, the company's latest brand slated to shortly open its first restaurant in Beijing, would cater to health-conscious youth. All the restaurants were owned and operated by the group. Occupying more than 40,000 square meters in total, employing around 2,600 people, and registering more than 3.5 million footfalls a year, the South Beauty Group was regarded as an innovative and leading player

in the Chinese restaurant market. It won a prestigious contract to become a Food Service Partner of Chinese cuisine for the 2008 Beijing Olympics, which would provide more revenue than the group's estimated revenues in 2007.

However, as Zhang Lan sat with her team that morning, daunting challenges lay ahead for the company as it sought to expand its operations from the existing 20 restaurants in China to a total of 100 worldwide (35 in China and 65 in the international market) over the next three years. To achieve this scale of expansion, the company needed to make critical decisions on a number of issues: the standardization of the process of preparing the dishes to increase efficiency and quality, which was a tough task to achieve with Chinese cuisine; the prioritization of markets to enter (i.e., whether to focus on the local market to realize its full potential before venturing abroad, or to do both at the same time); entry into new businesses, such as airline catering and the supply of semi-processed food to retail outlets such as supermarkets; and the expansion model (i.e., through owned outlets,

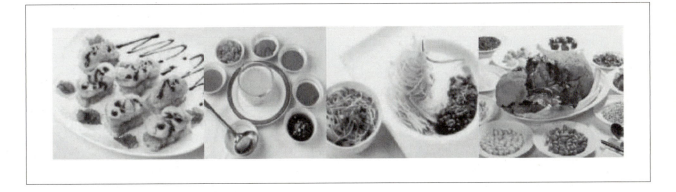

This case was prepared by research fellow X. U. Leiping under the guidance of Prof. S. Ramakrishna Velamuri in collaboration with South Beauty Group for the purpose of class discussion, as opposed to illustrating either effective or ineffective handling of an administrative situation. Certain names and other identifying information may have been changed to maintain confidentiality.

Zhang Lan[1]

as had been the case until now, or through franchising). With so many areas to study, Zhang Lan realized that she and her team had their work cut out for them.

Zhang Lan: The Founder of South Beauty

Zhang Lan was born in Beijing. Her father was a professor of civil engineering at Tsinghua University. However, the Cultural Revolution in China shattered her carefree childhood. Her family was exiled to a farm in an impoverished mountainous area of the Hubei province, which was built to "reform" intellectuals through labor. Although moving to such an environment was devastating for a young girl, she secretly dabbled in drawing and music with her parents. Significantly, at the age of nine, she also learned to prepare simple meals for her parents, who returned exhausted after their daily toil on the farm.

At the age of 17, Zhang Lan and her parents returned to Beijing after the collapse of the Cultural Revolution. At that time, there was no opportunity for young people to study in universities. Her first job was as a worker in a factory. It was much later, in 1985, as a 27-year-old mother of a two-year-old boy, that Zhang Lan decided to study business administration at Beijing Business College[2] through an adult education program. When she graduated in 1987, she joined a civil engineering company as an office worker with a salary much higher than the average level at that time. But she was not content with things as they were, because her life was leisurely and carefree and she wanted something different. In early 1989, she obtained a visa to study in Canada with the help of her uncle, a Canadian resident. Once in Canada,

she worked part time in restaurants, hotels, and hair salons to support herself, working as many as four jobs at a time.

Following the Tiananmen Square protests in the summer of 1989, the Canadian government offered green cards to all Chinese students in the country. Zhang Lan was one of the few who rejected this opportunity. She was faced with the dilemma of staying in a prosperous country for the rest of her life or returning to an impoverished China to stay with her family. She finally decided to return to China as soon as her savings reached USD 20,000 (RMB 108,000 at that time).[3] Just four days before Christmas 1990, Zhang Lan's bank account met the target and she returned to China immediately.

When Zhang Lan reached Beijing with her substantial savings, she was brimming with ideas for possible business ventures—a pizza store, a dumpling-wrapping business, a frozen foods store, and even a paper production plant based on high-quality Canadian paper pulp technology—but soon realized that her savings could only support a business that required limited capital. During windy springtime in Beijing, with a gauze kerchief on her head, she rode a bicycle through the streets in search of business opportunities. She found that consumers' needs for dining out were increasing; however, many old and traditional restaurants could not meet this trend. Opening a small restaurant in Beijing seemed to be a relatively safe venture in that the total investment would be relatively low.

In April 1991, an attractive opportunity presented itself to open a small restaurant of only 96 square meters in Dong Si, Beijing's downtown area. Zhang Lan believed the restaurant business would help her realize her dream of doing something in China while enabling her to benefit from her extensive experience in several Canadian restaurants serving Chinese and Western food. She knew how to operate a Chinese restaurant, from the purchase of raw materials to customer reception. Her friends regarded the restaurant business as unsuitable for Zhang Lan; in spite of this, she remained adamant about pursuing her dream.

In the initial phase, Zhang Lan invested considerable time and effort to formulate her business plan. She selected Sichuan food as the restaurant's main cuisine. She believed that among the eight main Chinese cuisines, Sichuan food best expressed the Chinese culture. Sichuan food is known as "Bai Cai Bai Ge, Bai Cai Bai Wei," literally "a hundred dishes, a hundred flavors," which means that it is liked by people across the world.

Further, Zhang Lan wanted to provide a unique and comfortable ambience in her restaurant. In this pursuit, she traveled to Pi Xian, a county in Sichuan, to transport 13-meter-long bamboo shoots to Beijing by train. Three bamboo weavers designed her restaurant as a bamboo house. Zhang Lan named her restaurant

"A Lan," which sounded like her childhood nickname. "Lan" is the Chinese word for orchid or fragrance. Although bamboo was cheaper than other regular materials, by the time the restaurant was ready to open, Zhang Lan's savings were almost fully depleted.

In the early 1990s, China, especially Beijing, was staid and lacking in diversity because of slow economic and social growth. Zhang Lan's small restaurant was thus able to tap a large customer base as its unique style and offerings contrasted with the environment. Zhang Lan initially managed all operational issues (ordering dishes, purchasing, etc.) pertaining to the restaurant by herself. In a short time, A Lan Restaurant became known as a special small restaurant in Beijing.

In 1997, encouraged by the success of A Lan Restaurant, Zhang Lan opened a larger restaurant, Bai Niao Yuan Seafood and Shark's Fin Restaurant[4] in Beijing, which was quite different from the A Lan Restaurant (Exhibit 1). At that time, expensive shark's fin and abalone were popular in many Chinese cities. This popularity was influenced by Guangdong and Hong Kong cuisines. Zhang Lan capitalized on this business opportunity, seeking to exploit the demand for new tastes and accumulate profits from these relatively expensive dishes. At the same time, she was also occupied with other investments, including real estate, stocks, mobile phone retailing, and even a nightclub. In 1999, Zhang Lan sold all her restaurants and other assets and made a profit of RMB 60 million (USD 7.26 million).[5] She explained this surprising action afterwards: "I thought it was hard to earn high profits through cooking the dishes one by one in a traditional way. After selling out all my assets in 1999, I spent half a year to calm my mind and continuously ask myself … what activity should I pursue in the end?"[6]

After six months of hard and careful reflection, Zhang Lan realized that her heart was still in the restaurant business. Possessing a large cash reserve, she went to France to see her son, who was studying fashion design in Paris. While in Paris, she visited a few well-known restaurants and decided to do something different this time—start a restaurant to carry forward Chinese cuisine to the world, as opposed to the idea of opening an unoriginal restaurant in China. Zhang Lan explained the logic behind her decision:

When I was involved with the restaurant business, I felt that I should take up the responsibility of enhancing Chinese cuisine. Although China has a 5,000-year catering culture, Chinese cuisine is regarded as low-end. French cuisine, on the other hand, is regarded as high-end. I did not agree with this. However, I thought that it would take my whole life to do this job (to prove the detractors wrong). Moreover, it would also require several generations' efforts because the restaurant business is a difficult venture, which needs assiduousness, diligence, thriftiness, zealousness, earnestness, and willingness for undertaking hard work.[7]

The Birth of South Beauty

Zhang Lan took the second step in her journey as an entrepreneur. She discovered that there were only a few restaurants offering Guangdong cuisine in plush office buildings in Beijing. These restaurants were too expensive to attract average businesspeople and their potential buying power. These customers looked for a high-quality, stylish, and comfortable environment as well as hygienic and delicious food presented aesthetically at a reasonable cost. Therefore, she decided to build a top-notch Chinese restaurant brand by targeting these businesspeople:[8] "There is a big misunderstanding of Chinese cuisine in the world. A lot of foreigners regard Chinese cuisine as the Mapo Tofu and Sweet and Sour Pork that you find in Chinatown. In fact, there are deep cultural meanings inside Chinese cuisine. More and

Exhibit 1 Pictures of A Lan Restaurant and Bai Niao Yuan Restaurant

Zhang Lan in A Lan Restaurant, 1991

Mockup Pictures of Bai Niao Yuan Restaurant

Source: South Beauty Group provided the picture of A Lan Restaurant; the mockup pictures were selected from http://food.yoolink.com to simulate the environment of Bai Niao Yuan Restaurant at that time.

more foreigners and businesspeople are in Beijing now. But there are few Chinese restaurants with special and elegant atmosphere. I wanted to build a Chinese restaurant for global business people to understand Chinese catering culture in the shortest time."[9]

Zhang Lan selected a prestigious office building for her first new restaurant, located in the proximity of her target customers—white collar office workers—who were still an untapped niche market in China at that time.

In April 2000, she launched an upper-middle-class restaurant, "South Beauty" (in Chinese: Qiao Jiang Nan[10]), at Guomao (China World Trade Center), a high-end office building in Beijing. In those days, Chinese restaurants were acclaimed for their delicious offerings, while Western restaurants were credited for their ambience. But Zhang Lan had her own intuition: "People prefer visual pleasures to those offered to the taste buds. When customers walk into your restaurant, they first observe the ambience and only then decide what to eat. Therefore, the first glance at the restaurant is critical."[11]

Among 10 designers, Zhang Lan selected Jack Tam, a Chinese-American designer who graduated from Harvard University, to design her new restaurant. It was the first time that a Chinese restaurant in China was designed by a foreign artist. Zhang Lan believed that only Tam could understand both Western restaurant-styling practices and the Chinese catering culture. Once completed, Tam's work did not disappoint Zhang Lan. The targeted customers took to the restaurant almost instantly (see Exhibit 2).

Zhang Lan also decided to provide Sichuan food in her new restaurant, just as she had in her earlier

Exhibit 2 Pictures of the First South Beauty Restaurant at Guomao in Beijing

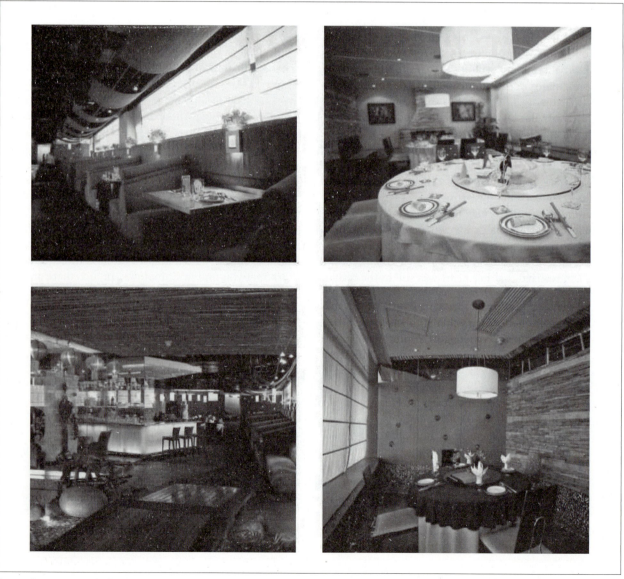

Source: Company internal information.

A Lan Restaurant. Sichuan food was regarded as a kind of low-middle-level cuisine in China due to its popular raw materials. However, South Beauty Restaurant introduced several innovations and improvements with regard to traditional Sichuan food, not only in terms of new raw materials, but also the process of preparing the dishes and the customer experience. For example, South Beauty launched a new Sichuan dish, "Stone-heated Tofu Congee," which was much appreciated by office workers. To prepare this dish, waiters poured cold liquid Tofu into a glass bowl, which contained three Sichuan-origin river stones heated to 200°C, in front of the customers. Then the bowl was covered. After five minutes, the Tofu congee was ready for customers to mix with various flavors. Zhang Lan also devised various creative ways to present Sichuan delicacies. For example, inspired by the countryside experience of washing clothes in the river after work and hanging them up under the setting sun, she created a new way to present a traditional Sichuan dish, "Cold Boiled Pork with Garlic Puree." In a highly innovative and visually impactful way, slices of meat were hung from a bamboo beam. In addition, she renamed this dish as "Hanging Meat." She had utensils of different shapes and colors in her office, allowing her to experiment with food presentation styles (see Exhibit 3).

With its unique positioning as an innovative Sichuan restaurant, providing businesspeople with pleasant ambience and located at prestigious office buildings, South Beauty was a success, although the initial four months were very difficult because of low market awareness. Zhang Lan once explained the difference between A Lan Restaurant and South Beauty Restaurant: "A Lan was just like other normal traditional Chinese restaurants and my purpose with that venture was just to earn money. South Beauty was different. South Beauty is a brand, actually."[12]

Some staff members of the A Lan restaurant moved to South Beauty in the finance and restaurant development divisions. Zhang Lan and her team also surmounted the SARS[13] crisis in 2003. Under a group of experienced managers, the company established a sound reputation and opened more restaurants successfully in other business buildings. Each restaurant was run autonomously and the role of the head office was minimal.

By mid-2007, the South Beauty Group had expanded to 19 restaurants, under the brand name of South Beauty, in three key cities: Beijing, Shanghai, and Chengdu. Zhang Lan also attempted to build new restaurant brands, LAN Club and SUBU. One LAN Club restaurant opened in Beijing in November 2006, a location of more than 5,000 square meters designed by the well-known designer Philip Stark with a total investment of over RMB 100 million. It was profitable from its first month. The Group expected to recover its investment on this first LAN Club in two years. Moreover, one new LAN Club restaurant was to open in Shanghai in April 2008, and one SUBU restaurant was scheduled to open soon in Beijing (see Exhibits 4–7). With estimated revenues of

Exhibit 3 Examples of Innovative Sichuan Dishes from South Beauty

Note: Top row (left to right) Stone-heated tofu congee; hanging meat; shredded chicken with spicy sauce; bottom row (left to right): four seasons; seasonal Williams pear aspic; spare ribs fried deeply with chili and spices; fried mandarin fish with Ziran and spicy sauce.

Source: Company internal information.

Exhibit 4 Coverage of South Beauty in China (2007)

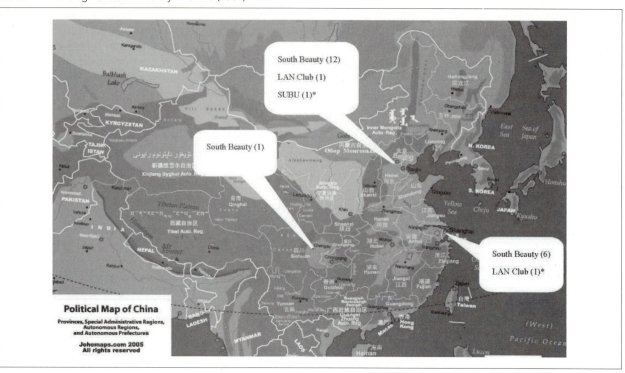

*SUBU and LAN Club's outlets in Beijing and Shanghai, respectively, are currently being furnished and are expected to open shortly.

Source: The map was copied from http://www.xxcha.com/All/449/8224_1.htm and company internal information.

Exhibit 5 Pictures of Various South Beauty Restaurants

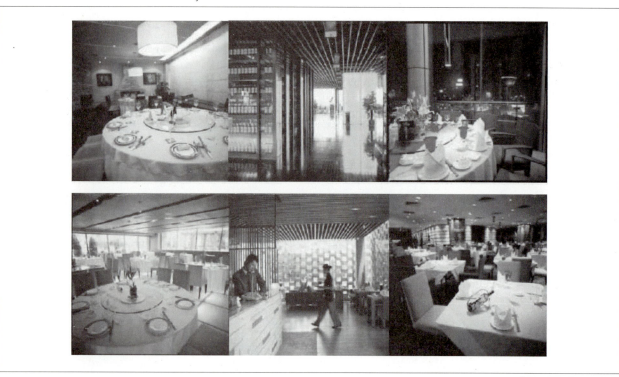

Note: Names of these restaurants (top row, left to right): South Beauty at China World Trade Center in Beijing; South Beauty in Chengdu; South Beauty at Super Brand Mall in Shanghai; (bottom row, left to right) South Beauty at Beijing Yinzuo; South Beauty at Shanghai 881; South Beauty at Beida Resource in Beijing.

Source: Company internal information.

Exhibit 6 Pictures of LAN Club

The internal décor of LAN Club in Beijing

Source: Company internal information.

Exhibit 7 Design Effect of SUBU in Beijing

The design effect of SUBU Restaurant in Beijing, opening soon

Source: Company internal information.

RMB 384 million in 2007,[14] and around 10,000 footfalls every day, the Group became one of the benchmarks of the Chinese restaurant market (see Exhibit 8). Because of the highly fragmented nature of China's catering market, the market share of South Beauty in the total industry was less than 0.1 percent; however its market share in the Chinese dinner category[15] was an estimated two percent in 2006. In terms of the niche market of high-end Chinese dinner, South Beauty's share was more than 7 percent.[16] The company was also regarded as an innovative company, with 55 percent annual growth. The Group had also won the bid for providing food services for the 2008 Beijing Olympics. During the Olympic Games, South Beauty prepared food for around 150,000 people every day. It was the first time for Chinese food to be designated as one of the cuisines for the Olympic Games.

South Beauty's Business Model

From 2005 forward, the South Beauty Group slowed down its speed of expansion and started to develop functional management expertise at its head office with a view to coordinating the management of its restaurants, all of which were directly owned and managed by the Group. Under the recently adjusted structure, the Group had two divisions: one for head office functions and another one for restaurant operations (Exhibit 9).

The head office made decisions regarding the overall development of the Group, such as those pertaining to strategy, financial management, human resources, marketing, market expansion, engineering, R&D, and quality control of the food supply.

The three restaurant brands (South Beauty, LAN Club, and SUBU) had different missions. Within South Beauty, each restaurant handled its own daily business operations. A new department was also set up to manage the franchising business in local and overseas markets, mainly for the South Beauty restaurant brand. Luo Yun, who was personal assistant to the board chairman, commented on the change in the management structure in the following manner:

To select the management direction, we spent two years considering how to conduct our business. Before 2005, we formulated operations for individual restaurants, not considering the overall company strategy. Later, we realized that we were not just a single restaurant business; in fact, we felt that we should use the company's central management to achieve greater synergies. Thus, we decided to move from single-restaurant-based operations to company-based management.

During the last two years, we have also been thinking about ways to differentiate ourselves from our competitors to capture greater market share. In China, we need to distinguish ourselves from numerous restaurants. We also set up the "Restaurant Chain Management Company" to try the franchising model to expand our business size.[17]

The size of a normal South Beauty Restaurant was between 2,000 and 3,000 square meters. In each restaurant, there were 100 to 150 workers, of which 30 to 40 percent worked in the kitchen. Usually, each restaurant offered more than 380 dishes, of which 60 to70 percent belonged to the Sichuan cuisine, while the remaining were Cantonese and other cuisines.

The unique features of South Beauty's business model were related to its brand positioning, menu innovation, location, pricing, interior decoration, IT application, and people management. With these

Exhibit 8 Chronology—South Beauty Group (2000–2007)

Year	Restaurants Number	Employees	Location and Number of Restaurants	Total Revenue (in RMB million)*
2000	2	200	Beijing (2)	10
2001	6	600	Beijing (6)	40
2002	8	800	Beijing (7); Shanghai (1)	60
2003	11	1,300	Beijing (8); Shanghai (3)	110
2004	16	1,900	Beijing (11); Shanghai (4); Chengdu (1)	200
2005	18	2,200	Beijing (12); Shanghai (5); Chengdu (1)	280
2006	20	2,600	Beijing (13); Shanghai (6); Chengdu (1)	350
2007	20	2,600	Beijing (13); Shanghai (6); Chengdu (1)	Est. 384

*Total revenue provided by company.

Source: Company internal information.

Exhibit 9 South Beauty's Organization Structure (2007)

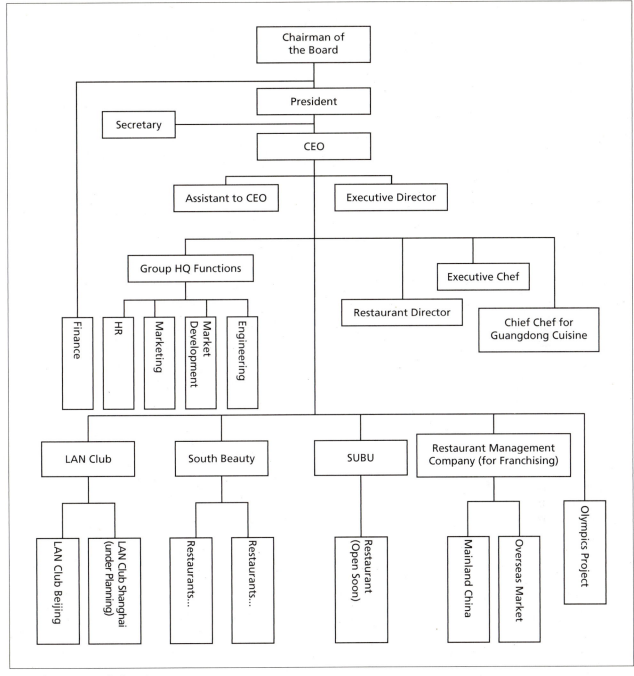

Source: Company internal information.

features, South Beauty could surpass almost all local competitors.

Positioning and Branding

With its positioning as an upmarket restaurant focused on office workers and businesspeople, South Beauty's occupancy rate was quite low during public holidays, such as the Golden Weeks,[18] because its target customers usually went on vacation at this time. In contrast, the business of other popular restaurants or fast food chains, such as McDonald's, fared well during these holidays; this proved the correctness of the brand positioning of South Beauty.

Danny Wang, Zhang Lan's only child and executive director of the Group, was in charge of developing LAN Club and SUBU. He did his high school, university, and MBA education in France and Canada and visited upmarket restaurants all over the world. When he returned to China in 2004, Zhang Lan asked him to consider a multi-brand strategy for the Group. Danny

Wang mentioned the basic consideration of LAN Club brand and SUBU:

At the beginning, the company just wanted to build a flagship restaurant under the South Beauty Brand. But I did not agree with that. As a metropolis, Beijing lacks the attributes of a modern city. I think that Beijing needs a place for leisure with an international standard to provide the 360-degree experience of an exclusive and healthy lifestyle. It is the original positioning of LAN Club. LAN is the name of my mother and also means "orchid," a symbol of Chinese culture.

As the newest brand in the Group, SUBU was to be different from the luxury LAN Club and the business-segment-focused South Beauty. SUBU was to focus on innovative healthy food. Moreover, a special store was to be inside a SUBU restaurant to sell the SUBU-style CDs and tablewares, etc.[19]

In fact, no competitor in the Chinese restaurant market had such brand architecture. Almost all of them just operated their single brands without clear brand positioning, and their brand image was relatively inferior. Luo Yun explained the company's branding strategy thusly: "We focused on brand differentiation to cater to a wide range of customers. Thus, South Beauty targets businesspeople aged 30–45 years. LAN Club targets successful businesspeople aged over 45 years. SUBU targets younger and more fashionable office workers. We hope that our business would be like that of BMW, which rolls out 7-, 5-, and 3-series products at the same time."[20]

In order to promote these three brands systematically, the company built consistent brand identities and launched some outdoor and print advertisement. The company explored cooperation with certain international airlines, including Air France and KLM Royal Dutch Airlines, to provide business travelers flying between China and Europe with South Beauty–branded Chinese dishes (see Exhibit 10). In addition, it wanted to diversify into the business of partially cooked frozen foods—such as dumplings—for retail outlets.

Menu Innovations

The Group developed a range of innovations with regard to Sichuan cuisine. An independent R&D team was placed in charge of creating new dishes, and the executive chef was responsible for food quality. Under a strict assessment system, only 2 percent of all new dishes could be launched. Although many competitors copied the Group's dishes, Zhang Lan reminded her team to focus on continuous innovations to stay ahead of its followers instead of worrying about being copied by them. In addition, to enrich its variety and cater to the tastes of different people, the company also added certain

Cantonese cuisine and other flavors to its menu. As a brochure said:

The South Beauty Group primarily offers Sichuan flavors, but we also offer Cantonese and other dishes. We innovatively combine Chinese and Western cuisine that breaks with tradition and creates original new flavors. It is the first Chinese restaurant to offer Chinese food in a western style, and the first to mix food presentation with artistic elements.... For many years the Group has charged itself with the mission of developing the culture of Chinese cuisine and advocating a stylish and healthy lifestyle. It has always been focused on drawing from China's deep traditional culture while at the same time making bold innovations and improvements.... Some of the factors that make the Group's cuisine different from others are the strict requirements placed on raw ingredients, the innovation on traditional cuisine, the exacting criteria placed on a dish's nutritional value, and the strong emphasis on the visual appeal of each dish.[21]

Location and Pricing

In order to remain close to its targeted customer base, the Group's restaurants were located in top-notch office buildings in key cities. Although the operational costs were higher in comparison with those of other restaurants, meals could be more expensively priced to cover the costs. This combination of high-end location and high pricing was also helpful in developing the upper-middle-class brand image.

Interior Decoration

Each South Beauty restaurant had a different décor, designed by well-known artists in the field. Zhang Lan and her team insisted that people came to the restaurants not only for the food but also for the ambience. South Beauty never hesitated to invest in interior décor, and sought to combine both Chinese and Western designs in the restaurants. On average, the Group invested RMB 8 million (around USD 1 million) on the furniture, interior decoration, and in setting up the kitchen of a new South Beauty restaurant. Moreover, for the luxury LAN Club, the total investment on interior decoration was over RMB 100 million (around USD 13 million), including USD 2 million in design fees. In this way, the Group became unique in the Chinese restaurant market. In contrast, no competitor could invest so heavily in interior decoration.

IT Applications

In the South Beauty Group, advanced IT applications (e.g., portable order placement) were seen as potent tools to enhance the upper-middle-class image of the restaurant and to improve efficiency. Well before other Chinese restaurants constructed CRM systems, the Group built its own CRM system to record customer information

Exhibit 10 Branding Activities of South Beauty

(Left) Restaurant Signage in Shanghai; (Right) Outdoor Advertising in Beijing

Airline Food Cooperation between Air France and South Beauty

The Brand Logos of South Beauty, LAN Club, and SUBU

Source: Company internal information; the pictures of airline food cooperation with Air France were copied from http://www.cnsphoto.com/NewsPhoto/printNews.asp?ID=359106.

and use that information to provide tailor-made services and make promotional communications. An ERP system was established to control the key financial variables and the purchasing process. Meanwhile, the company tested its remote conference system to increase internal communication among various restaurants located at different places. These IT applications were quite innovative for the traditional Chinese catering industry, as most restaurants remain committed to their old ways of operating their businesses.

People Management

Zhang Lan believed that a dedicated workforce could surmount challenges pertaining to financial capital and market potential. In 2003, when the threat of the SARS virus had the population terrified and almost all other restaurants temporarily closed and dismissed their staffs, Zhang Lan resisted this course of action. She paid her more than 1,000 staff members their full salaries and provided them with proper accommodations to limit their risk of catching the disease.

The Group sought to apply performance management techniques with regard to the management team. At the same time, it worked with a consulting firm to design a new people management system to motivate its staff. Danny Wang regarded people management as a key part of the daily operation, stating: "Our industry is a labor-intensive business. Although the top management is critical (for efficient performance), it is the waiters who are the first point of contact with our customers. The process of training and managing these front-line people, who are young and inexperienced, is the most difficult issue. We initiated a large-scale training program for our staff last year."[22]

In 2006, waiters had to undertake a three-month course at a company training center, evaluated on metrics such as setting a table within three minutes. Restaurant managers, meanwhile, had to complete a two-year on-the-job training program. For two weeks each year, they were sent to tour restaurants in Europe, the United States, and Asia in order to compare service levels and bring back ideas. Zhang Lan also recruited Chinese executives who had previously managed the operations of McDonald's and Coca-Cola in China to work for South Beauty.

China's Restaurant Market

The Shandong, Sichuan, Guangdong, Fujian, Jiangsu, Zhejiang, Hunan, and Anhui cuisines, also known as the "Eight Cuisines," are the most popular in China. The essential factors that establish a particular cuisine are complex, and include history, cooking habits, geography, climate, resources, and lifestyles. A typical Chinese restaurant offers one or two cuisines.

Since the 1990s, China's catering industry had been booming with a compound annual growth rate (CAGR) of more than 15 percent. In 2007, the catering market size of RMB 1,200 billion (USD 155 billion) accounted for 4.87 percent of the gross domestic product (GDP) in China. This percentage was only 1.5 percent in 1978. In 2004, Eastern China contributed at least 50 percent of total industry revenue (see Exhibits 11 and 12).

Exhibit 11 Market Development—China's Catering Industry (1995–2007)*

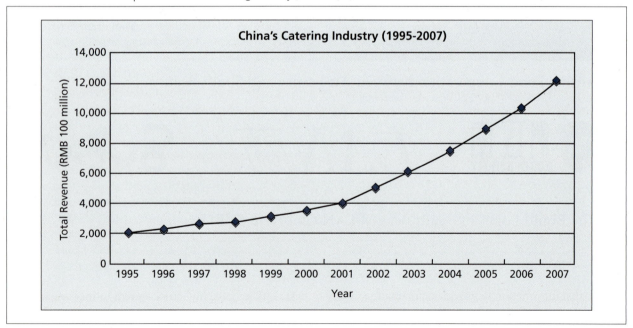

*The data for 2007 were estimated.

Source: Information from industry interviews.

Exhibit 12 Area Difference—China's Catering Industry (2004)

Area	Number of Provinces	Total Revenue of Restaurant Industry (in RMB billion)	% of Total	Annual Growth Rate (in %)
National Total	**31**	**748.6**	**100**	**21.6**
East China	11	418.3	55.7	22.0
Middle China	8	180.0	24.0	20.1
West China	12	152.0	20.3	23.8

Source: 2004, China catering industry analysis, *Economic Daily*, March 16, 2005.

There were three main sections in China's catering industry: breakfast stands, street hawkers, and restaurants. Although there were many breakfast stands and street hawkers, the restaurants section was especially significant (see Exhibit 13). In China, the restaurants section was divided into four subcategories: dinner (mainly Chinese cuisine), hot pot, fast food (Western and Chinese), and teahouses (including coffeehouses). Generally speaking, the growth of the Chinese dinner category was slower than that of the other three categories.

In 2006, the average profitability of the restaurant market was pegged at about 10 percent of total revenues; raw material costs were 43.6 percent of total revenues; labor costs were 11.92 percent; and rental costs were 8.75 percent. The labor costs in China were lower, while the overhead costs were higher, as compared with those in other developed countries.[23]

Beneath the prosperous surface, China's restaurant market faced critical problems. As a result of low entry barriers, thousands upon thousands of new restaurants emerged. However, the service quality, hygiene levels, and managerial capabilities of those in charge were often unsatisfactory.

Growth Dream

China's restaurant market was competitively challenging, not only in terms of the number of players, but also in terms of food varieties. This market was also affected by high rates of turnover (openings and closures) and fragmentation. Since 2001, half of the top 100 restaurant companies in China have been replaced by other emerging companies. In 2006, the sales revenue of the top 50 restaurant companies accounted for just 5 percent of the national restaurant market. In contrast, the sales revenue of the top 50 restaurant companies in the United States represented 20 percent of that market.[24] The global player, Yum! Brands, ranked at the top of China's catering industry, reaching annual revenues of more than RMB 11 billion; however, the revenue of the next biggest player in China was only around five billion, and that of the tenth biggest was less than one billion.[25]

Nevertheless, shocked by the success of Western fast food in China, the leading Chinese players explored how to expand their scale. It was believed that expanding the scale of the leading restaurants in China was critical for the market's healthy development. It was also believed that scaling required standardization. However, for traditional Chinese cuisine, standardization was difficult to implement. As an industry observer commented:

The features of Chinese catering culture are different from those of the Western one. Chinese cuisine has a wider range of raw materials, more varied consumption of dishes per meal, and more flexible ways of preparing dishes. It conflicts with the tenets of standardization, such as few product types, standardized processes and criteria,

Exhibit 13 Structure Difference—China's Catering Industry (2004)

Type	Number (in thousands)	Daily Revenue for Each Outlet (in RMB)	Est. Investment for Each Outlet (in RMB)	Estimated Employee Number
Breakfast Stander	1,900	<100	<500	1
Street Hawkers	1,000	300–400	2,000	2–3
Restaurants (100–400 seats)	600	5,000–10,000	300,000	20–50
Restaurants (400–800 seats)	200	15,000–30,000	2,000,000	150–200
Restaurants (800+ seats)	1	50,000–120,000	5,000,000	300–400

Source: Constraints on Chinese restaurant development: Reason and analysis; *Xinhua Daily*, April 27, 2005, and industry interviews.

etc. Comparatively speaking, it is easier for the sections of hot pot and Chinese fast food to explore standardization and expand scale through chain restaurants. However, for the Chinese dinner section, standardization is not an easy job. That's why the scaling of Chinese dinner restaurants is slower than that of the hot pot and Chinese fast food restaurants.[26]

Expanding Chains

The rapid development of many restaurant chains was notable, both in the hot pot and the Western fast food markets, especially with regard to the trend of franchising (see Exhibits 14 and 15). In 2006, the top 100 restaurants in China had 14,489 outlets, of which about 39 percent were directly owned while 61 percent were franchisees. In addition, the operational indicators of the dinner/hot pot restaurant chains were also distinct from those of fast food chains (see Exhibit 16).

Because expansion required significant investment, in 2006, at least 10 restaurant chains announced their intentions to launch initial public offerings (IPOs). Certain venture capital firms (VCs), which were normally in the business of technology, media, and telecom (TMT) deals, bought stakes in restaurant businesses. They expressed their increasing interest in this evolving traditional industry: "The restaurant business has better

cash flow and lower risk than the TMT businesses. China is at the critical point of the booming consumption economy. There are many opportunities to foster leading companies in a traditional business. The VCs would like to select valuable companies who have the long-term dream to be great players in their industries."[27]

The restaurant chains' expansion was much quicker than the rate of economic growth and raised a great deal of issues. Besides the difficulties inherent in standardizing Chinese cuisine, the lack of human resources and management skills were bottlenecks as well. Although the franchising model became popular for chain expansion, the franchisees sometimes crept out of the control of the principal companies and gradually set up their own similar brands. In addition, a restaurant could quickly and easily copy any new dish created by another restaurant. Because of these issues, few Chinese restaurant chains could build their core competitiveness for the long term.

However, a few far-sighted restaurant chains were planning to avoid the potential risk of unplanned expansion and took actions to improve the quality of their business operations. For example, Little Sheep, which was the biggest hot pot chain and had received USD 25 million from venture capitalists, reduced its outlets from 721 to 326 in the summer of 2007. Even though the

Exhibit 14 Top 100 Restaurants—China's Restaurant Market (2006)

Type	Restaurant Chains	Restaurant Outlets	Total Revenue (in RMB billion)	% of Top 100
Hot Pot	22	6,682	30	36
Fast Food	15	4,375	23	27.8
Chinese Dinner	42	1,690	19.5	23.5
Tea/Coffee House	N/A	N/A	10.6	12.7

Source: The fast development of Chinese key restaurant companies, *China Business Newspaper*, June 15, 2007.

Exhibit 15 Restaurant Chains—China's Restaurant Market (2006)*

Type	Revenue (in RMB billion)			Restaurant Outlets		
	2005	2006	Growth (in %)	2005	2006	Growth (in %)
Western Fast Food	14.7	18.5	25.8	2,330	2,757	18.3
Chinese Fast Food	1.8	2.0	11.6	1,191	1,075	−10.8
Hot Pot	13.1	14.9	14	2,454	2,799	13.6
Chinese Dinner	139.0	151.0	9.5	1,507	1,545	2.25

*Because of various sampling, some data in Exhibit 15 are different from those in Exhibit 14; however, Exhibit 15 reveals the yearly difference between 2005 and 2006.

Source: *China Chain Store Business Year Book* 2007.

Exhibit 16 Dinner/Hot Pot Chains vs. Fast Food Chains in China (2006)

Index	Dinner/Hot Pot Chains		Fast Food Chains	
	2005	2006	2005	2006
Number of Restaurants	4,244	5,066	4,213	4,843
Total Size (10,000 m^2)	338.2	426.6	123.6	140.7
Staff (10,000 people)	27.8	32.9	20.6	20.6
Seats (10,000)	191.6	212.6	49.2	55.7
Total Revenue (in RMB billion)	22.8	27.8	20.4	24.9
Purchased Product (in RMB billion)	9.5	11.24	7.35	8.43
By Central Distribution	3.99	4.74	6.74	7.75
By Owned Distribution Center	2.73	3.54	4.94	5.63
By Third-Party Distribution Center	1.26	1.19	1.79	2.10

Source: Adapted from *China Statistical Year Book 2007.*

majority of the closed restaurants were franchisees, only 30 percent of the remaining restaurants were directly controlled; the rest continued to be franchisees.[28]

Innovative Chinese Restaurants

Certain emerging, innovative Chinese restaurants, including South Beauty, sought to revamp the image of Chinese cuisine. For example, the appearance of the hot pot was considered unappealing and, therefore, it was not treated as refined food. However, the Hot Loft Restaurant in Beijing experimented with certain simple innovations in the dish, thereby elevating the image of the traditional hot pot.

Some of the innovative Chinese dinner restaurants also paid more attention to their brand statement, which dealt with the entire process of daily operations from raw material purchases to service delivery. These restaurants selected their menus carefully and limited customers' choices, although they had the capability to prepare a great variety of dishes in their kitchens. The founders of these restaurants realized the importance of innovative business ideas, a unique menu, and an impressive decoration style. They believed that unless such initiatives were undertaken, Chinese cuisine would not be able to catch up with the changing tastes of consumers. Paul Hsu, owner of Night Shanghai, suggested that "People only want to visit restaurants that have an impressive ambience. The food can be extremely simple, and they order a small number of dishes and enjoy them slowly."[29]

The most important innovation among Chinese dinner restaurants was the attempt to standardize raw material purchases, preparation of semi-cooked dishes, logistics, and customer service. For example, Jade Garden, with 11 top-grade Shanghainese Cuisine chain restaurants in Shanghai and Beijing, set up a central kitchen in 2002. At the beginning, its intention was just to manage various suppliers centrally for the quality control of raw materials. After a few years' operation, the central kitchen evolved into a production center for meals to be heated as well as to prepare dim sums and semi-cooked dishes with packs of well-mixed sauces. The chefs at each restaurant could prepare the food easily according to the required process. Li Jun, one of the founders of Jade Garden, shared her experience:

At the beginning, the Chief Chef was against the central kitchen, because he was worried that he had to make his cooking knowledge public. But I told him, with the central kitchen, he would be a Chief Chef supervising 500 chefs, not just 50 chefs at the current time. Then we separated the food preparing process into many steps, with each chef in the central kitchen just handling part of the entire process.

In this way, except the Chief Chef, nobody can grasp the whole process. But we are able to overcome the bottleneck of production and prepare Chinese dishes in a standardized way. Moreover, we also have unexpected results, such as lower stock of raw materials, and fewer chefs in each chain restaurant.

Operating several restaurants under the same brand does not necessarily constitute a real chain. A real chain requires a consistent business model and operation. With the standardized raw material purchases, food preparation and sauce mix, we believe that we are building a real restaurant chain. However, we would not request standardized interior decoration for each restaurant. We are not McDonald's, which makes simple standardized fast food; we are standardizing complex Chinese dishes to keep steady quality.[30]

Fast Food Players

The growth of international fast food brands such as KFC, McDonald's, and Pizza Hut in China have increased the food options available to consumers. For instance, since November 1987, KFC had launched 2,000 restaurants and covered more than 400 cities. The restaurant chain's next objective in China was to rapidly penetrate into smaller cities, with plans of opening one outlet every day. China had become the second-largest market for KFC, after the United States. Its main competitor, McDonald's, had 820 outlets and intended to reach 1,000 restaurants in 2008.

These Western fast food chains showed what standardization and logistics could achieve in the restaurant business. For example, by 2006, Yum! Brands, the parent company of KFC, Pizza Hut, and Taco Bell, established 16 distribution centers in China. Its newest East China distribution center, which was also the group's largest facility in Asia, was 15,500 square meters in area and nine meters high. It could manage more than 3,500 items to cover more than 300 restaurants and deliver at least five million cartons of food over three million kilometers every year. At the same time, in Shanghai, Yum! was testing its new brand, Dong Fang Ji Bai Chain Restaurant, focusing exclusively on Chinese fast food. This new brand had the same standardized operational system as KFC and showed encouraging results.

Local fast food chains, such as Kungfu, Ajisen Noodle, Malan Noodle, and Da Niang Dumpling, borrowed the best practices of these international brands. For example, Kungfu—a fast-growing local player with 200 restaurants—planned to establish three logistics centers in China to carry out the key functions of raw material procurement, food processing, and delivery. Kungfu also announced plans to open 2,000 restaurants by 2012. Most successful local chains had attracted foreign capital and also planned to offer IPOs to gain greater resources for scaling up their operations. However, they lagged far behind the international brands in some areas, especially food and process standardization and central logistics capability.

South Beauty's Competitors

Being positioned in the high-end Chinese dinner segment, South Beauty would not compete directly with fast food, hot pot, and "ordinary" restaurants. Among the top 100 restaurant companies in China in 2007, 10 were in this segment, including Shanghai Jingjiang (ranked No. 4), Beijing Shunfeng (No. 18), Guangzhou Jiujia (No. 28), Shanghai Xiaonanguo (No. 32), Shanghai Renjia (No. 60), Shanghai Jade Garden (No. 88), Shanghai Shenjia Garden (No. 91), and South Beauty itself (No. 72). These competitors focused on various Chinese cuisines; for example, Beijing Shunfeng and Guangzhou Jiujia mainly served Guangdong cuisine, and Jingjiang, Xioananguo, Renjia, Jade Garden, and Shengjia Garden in Shanghai offered Jiangsu and Zhejiang dishes. Thus, South Beauty, which focused on Sichuan cuisine, did not compete with these restaurants directly in terms of cuisine. Normally, people selected the type of cuisine they were in the mood for first and the restaurant later.

The most crucial issue for South Beauty was that of restaurants claiming to be South Beauty franchises. In 2005, South Beauty found there were at least 16 "fake" restaurants in cities South Beauty had not penetrated, such as Nanjing, Xiamen, Tianjing, Qingdao, and Hong Kong. Generally speaking, the imposters used the same Chinese name as South Beauty (i.e., Qiao Jiang Nan), with one or two additional Chinese characters. The counterfeit logos enlarged the size of the "Qiao Jiang Nan" characters and minimized the other elements. In this way, these counterfeit restaurants attracted innocent customers and provided them with poor service and atmosphere. However, the unhappy customers complained to the "real" South Beauty. South Beauty attempted to use legal means to protect its brand, but because of the local protection the copiers enjoyed in some cities, the process was sometimes quite slow, and the results were not very encouraging.

Consumer Trends and Opinions

In recent years, as Chinese urban consumers' disposable incomes have increased, they have spent more on meals in restaurants. The annual expenditure per capita on restaurant meals increased from RMB 534 (USD 65) in 2004 to an estimated RMB 800 (USD 105) in 2007. However, compared with developed markets, there is still great potential for growth—the corresponding figure in the United States was USD 1,600 per capita, and, in France, USD 1,050.[31] Moreover, in more advanced cities, such as Shanghai, Guangzhou, and Beijing, this number was three to five times higher than the national average. In these cities, consumers had more choices of restaurants and made selections based on word of mouth. According to a Web site survey, 63 percent of consumers obtained restaurant information from word-of-mouth publicity, 15 percent from traditional media (newspaper, TV, radio, etc.), 12 percent from the Internet, and 10 percent from outdoor advertising.[32]

Since the 1990s, consumption in restaurants has evolved into various segments, such as office workers having lunches, family members dining out, friends gathering, lovers dating, and business-related meals. Different segments have different needs. The office workers select fast food (Western 30 percent and Chinese 70 percent) as their lunch for its convenience and quickness. This huge segment constituted one fourth of the total catering industry. The main consideration of families dining out is value for their money. The restaurant selection for a gathering of friends depends on the social status of the people; those with higher status select better restaurants. Lovers prefer a romantic restaurant for their dates.

Because of the booming economy in China, the business meals had more potential than the other segments because they could absorb higher prices. Also, businesspeople were not satisfied with simple eating and drinking—they required more in terms of the restaurant's atmosphere, food taste, location, and so on. These businesspeople were the target consumers of the South Beauty Group.

A popular restaurant review Web site stated:

Promoting "Refined or Improved Sichuan Food," South Beauty has elevated Sichuan food from the level of austerity to one fit for the nobility. The dishes have a unique taste, appearance, and preparation style. The ambience is also excellent—an elegant, grand, Western style—quite different from that offered by ordinary Chinese restaurants. The waiters and waitresses wear well-designed uniforms and are hospitable. It is a good place to entertain guests, although the charges are higher in comparison with normal restaurants.[33]

However, in Chengdu, the birthplace of Sichuan food, customers were of the opinion that the Sichuan food offered by South Beauty was not as spicy as the original cuisine. Others did not view South Beauty as a genuine Sichuan food restaurant. Nonetheless, they were pleased that South Beauty offered a range of innovative dishes that were presented elegantly (see Exhibit 17).

2008 Beijing Olympics Opportunity

The 2008 Olympic Games in Beijing were estimated to generate sales of RMB 18 billion for the catering industry in the city. Thirteen million meals would be provided for athletes, support personnel, media reporters, and other guests for three months. This revenue was divided between Western (estimated at 70 percent of meals) and Chinese cuisine (30 percent).

However, the mainstream international media challenged the food security situation in China. The Chinese government tried to ensure food supply safety for the Olympic Games. Following the completion of the bidding process based on strict food standards, six companies were selected as the food suppliers: South Beauty Group, along with three other local companies and two international ones, McDonald's and ARAMARK. Bian Jiang, the chief secretary of the China Restaurant Association, commented to the press: "The 2008 Beijing Olympic Games will facilitate the internationalization of the Beijing restaurant market. The food suppliers for the Olympic Games will suffer a critical technical transition,

Exhibit 17 Customer Ratings of South Beauty Restaurants (October 2007)

	Beijing (Among 420 customers)	Shanghai (Among 1,153 Customers)	Chengdu (Among 187 customers)
Rating (max. 30)			
Taste	18–21	17–18	17
Environment	24–27	21–26	27
Service	20–22	15–20	22
Consumption (RMB/per person)	**102–141**	**149–180**	**115**
Category Perception (%)			
Business Entertainment	34%	27%	41%
Sichuan Food	23%	18%	10%
Gathering of Friends	13%	8%	0%
Innovative Sichuan Food	0%	0%	33%
Dinner for Dating	16%	8%	16%

Source: Information collected from http://www.dianping.com in October 2007 based on customers' comments on a typical restaurant in each city.

especially in terms of the food and process standardization and logistics capacity, which will also lead to a change in the restaurant market. Restaurants that can upgrade their operations in response to the large-scale requirements of the Olympics are likely to fare well in China's catering industry in the future."[34]

Future Plans

Zhang Lan believed that the Chinese entrepreneurs of her generation should take greater responsibility to rejuvenate Chinese culture because they have access to better opportunities than previous generations:

I am thinking about how to develop Chinese cuisine to enter the mainstream restaurant market in Western countries as opposed to opening the kind of Chinese restaurants you find in Chinatown. The South Beauty Group has catered to more than 100,000 foreign guests from all over the world, and they all enjoyed our food. Thus, now is the time to expand. We have met success in China, and now we wish to build an international brand, which will have a presence in New York, Paris, London, Milan, Geneva, Tokyo, and other important international cities of the world.[35]

Undoubtedly, redefining Chinese cuisine and maintaining quality in the midst of rapid domestic and global expansion will not be an easy job. Luo Yun commented on the difficulties:

Having objectives and ambitions are not enough; we have to act to meet these objectives. Top management is thinking about the big picture. We also need to consider how to execute the tasks and foresee difficulties. For example, we should constantly improve the menu through R&D, improve people management practices, etc.; we also should train people to do things in a standardized way. It is difficult to do so, and until now, no one (in the China's dinner category) has been able to do it very successfully.[36]

The Challenges Ahead

The existing business of the South Beauty Group was flourishing, but the management team did not halt their efforts to improve the Group's operational efficiency through standardization, which was also the foundation for scaling up. To expand, the Group had to consider the prioritization of markets to enter (i.e., whether to focus on the local market to realize its full potential before venturing abroad, or to do both at the same time); entry into new businesses, such as airline catering and the supply of semi-processed food to retail outlets; the expansion model (i.e., through owned outlets as had been the case until now or through franchising); and the way to finance the expansion, which posed many challenges.

Seeking Standardization

It was easier for a fast food chain or a Western restaurant to standardize its food and processes—for example, McDonald's offered only 40 to 50 dishes and T.G.I. Friday's around 100. Each South Beauty restaurant carried 380 items on the main menu, excluding soft drinks and wines. Raw materials depended on local suppliers, and the quality of each dish relied on the experience of the chef. Although there was a team with three main chefs at the head office to develop new dishes and control the quality, the process of standardization was still in its nascent phase.

Jacy Yang, who joined the Group in July 2007 as executive director, had 25 years of experience in Western food companies such as McDonald's, T.G.I. Friday's, and Gino's. He was assigned the task of setting up a system to enhance operational efficiency. He described the challenges and the company's reactions:

In fast-food restaurants, such as KFC and Kungfu, it is easier to handle standardization. However, the same can be quite difficult to manage in high-end Chinese dinner restaurants. Before I came on board, the chefs did not define the inputs because these were regarded as their secrets, and some were even offended when asked to write down the recipes. Subsequently, I looked up the recipes, read the local menu, spoke to professional cooks, and studied the terminology to understand the entire process.

I think it is easy for a restaurant to elaborate on its two success factors. The first is service, which can be stipulated manually and standardized easily through training, rules, inspections, and the right incentive systems. The second is the menu. We are working on an idea for a central kitchen to prepare the main dishes and distribute them to each restaurant to ensure the same taste of key dishes at different times across various restaurants.

At present, in each restaurant, we have a kitchen that is 300–400 square meters in area. The function of a central kitchen that is 2,000 square meters in area is to prepare the main dish packets with uncooked raw materials and send them to the various company restaurants for cooking. The central kitchen will be set up in each city of operation. Currently, we are building two, in Beijing and Shanghai. In this way, we can achieve standardization and control the average cost. Our central kitchen will handle dishes prepared from expensive materials and the ones that can be easily standardized. However, the kitchens in individual restaurants will also prepare some dishes with fresh materials, such as vegetables, and other special requests, so they will still be required to make certain raw material purchases.[37]

Jacy Yang's other role was to standardize the Group's cost management. He explained his ideas this way:

Some people in our company say they have cut 30 percent of the cost, but I am not sure about it. They should provide data. I will set the standard, ask the chef, and nail down the recipe and the input cost, factor in the processing cost, and then arrive at a standard cost for each dish. Meanwhile, we will control the use of raw materials with computer software to calculate the number of dishes sold and the raw materials used, and check the stock situation to evaluate materials usage. In this way, we will be able to control the cost of raw materials, which constitutes the largest part of the cost structure.[38]

Venturing into Newer Markets

The South Beauty Group's domestic business was concentrated in Beijing and Shanghai. The city selection was a critical decision (see Exhibit 18). This same issue was raised with regard to international markets. In 2005, Zhang Lan planned to open two restaurants in Hong Kong, but little progress had been made on this front. Zhang Lan also wanted to test the market in the United Arab Emirates. Recently, the Group had communicated its ongoing projects to open restaurants in well-known international cities such as New York, Paris, and Tokyo, although the details of this plan have not been disclosed.

When Zhang Lan stated her scale expansion objectives, she projected the Group to have 30 restaurants in short term and 100 outlets in the next three years, of which 35 restaurants would be located in China and 65 in the international market in cooperation with strategic partners in Tokyo, New York, and other cities. The Group was also trying to expand its scale through entering into new product areas, such as airline catering in the global market and the supply of semi-processed food to retail outlets in the domestic market.

The scaling up of fast food restaurants has been achieved by several brands, both international and Chinese, but the expansion of upper-middle-class dinner restaurants posed a bigger challenge. Therefore, South Beauty Group's targets looked extremely ambitious and certain observers expressed their worries. According to a well-known international media publication, "There is no other successful national restaurant chain in this market segment, and South Beauty has still not covered all the major Chinese cities. Entering a mature (Western) market will involve working in a radically different operating environment."[39]

Expansion Model

The South Beauty Group was trying to develop a franchising system to expand its restaurant chain in China. There were two new restaurants at the stage of signing franchise contracts. The company also announced its plan to seek franchisees on its Web site and was flooded with questions from interested entrepreneurs. Luo Yun expressed his concerns:

It is a huge and extremely difficult transition for the company, because Chinese cuisine has not been standardized well with regard to operations. We studied the central management style, for example, of the McDonald's chain, which has 16 staff members in its financial division for 800 outlets. However, we recruited

Exhibit 18 Top 10 Cities—China's Catering Industry (2006)

Rank by Size	City	Total Revenue of Catering Industry (in RMB billion)	Rank by Growth	City	Annual Growth (in %)
1	Shanghai	45.2	1	Shanghai	29.0
2	Beijing	36.2	2	Jinan	21.8
3	Guangzhou	35.0	3	Qingdao	21.7
4	Tianjing	21.0	4	Chongqing	20.0
5	Chengdu	20.9	5	Zhengzhou	19.3
6	Chongqing	19.4	6	Hefei	19.1
7	Wuhan	17.7	7	Wuhan	17.9
8	Jinan	14.0	8	Hangzhou	17.9
9	Dalian	13.4	9	Tianjing	17.4
10	Zhengzhou	13.0	10	Changsha	17.2

Source: China's catering industry: Top 10 cities in 2006; *China Chain Store Business Year Book 2007.*

more than 80 people in the same department for only 20 restaurants. That is the big difference.[40]

However, in the international market, both owned and franchised restaurants might be risky models for expansion because of the lack of local market knowledge and the difficulties of managing the franchisees. The Group contacted local partners with complementary resources in target cities to seek cooperation. For example, Royal Company, a potential strategic partner for the group in Japan, controlled over 1,000 restaurants and provided airline food in the Japanese market. In addition, the requirements for the restaurant's size, style, and cuisine in the international market would be different from those in the domestic market. The Group had to adjust its plan accordingly.

Financing by IPO

In China, it was difficult for a private restaurant to apply for a bank loan because banks were hesitant to provide capital to restaurants because of the perceived risks involved in this industry. In addition, the government did not consider this industry as a priority area. The South Beauty Group funded its growth plans by reinvesting its profits. The company's cash flow was sufficient to maintain its current operations and to pursue moderate growth. However, the company needed external funding for its expansion plan and other projects related to standardization, new business development, and the Olympic Games contract.

Several private venture capitalists and investment banks, such as Citigroup and Credit Suisse, had expressed their wishes to cooperate with the South Beauty Group. In 2006, the Group announced the launch of a possible IPO in the international or domestic stock market, although a decision regarding the exact date of the IPO was not made. Zhang Lan discussed her company's IPO:

Our IPO is not just for funding. Our main objective is to build an open company with the supervision of the shareholders. I do not like the family company, because it is difficult to be a giant under family members' management. A long-life company could be built through a well-designed management system and a clear arrangement with the shareholders about their equity and responsibility.[41]

Dream Big but Do Small

At the break of the 2007 meeting with her management team, Zhang Lan looked out of her office window. She saw Beijing National Stadium (the "Bird's Nest") being built for the 2008 Olympics—the stadium's main body had already taken shape.[42] Zhang Lan sat back and pondered:

Should the Group scale up its size at a rapid pace? How can the company improve standardization of Chinese cuisine? Where should the targeted domestic and international markets be located? How can the company achieve the right balance between owned and franchised restaurants? What would be the correct time to invite external capital and launch an IPO?

Zhang Lan realized that she had to dream big for the future, but, at the same time, take small steps to keep everything on track. She knew that the road ahead was just like the Bird's Nest Stadium, which had an exciting outer shape and a complex inner structure as well.

NOTES

1. Picture of Zhang Lan from 2006, Zhang Lan: Planning to open South Beauty in New York and Paris, *China Entrepreneur*, December.
2. This school's name was changed to Beijing Technology and Business University in 1999.
3. Exchange rate in 1991: USD 1=RMB 5.4.
4. "Bai Niao Yuan" means a garden with a lot of birds.
5. Exchange rate in 1999: USD 1=RMB 8.27.
6. 2007, Boss town: Dialogue with Zhang Lan, http://www.sina.com.cn, January 19.
7. Ibid.
8. Businesspeople include entrepreneurs, professional managers, and some middle-level office workers.
9. 2008, LAN Club and its hostess, *Lifeweek*, February 4.
10. Qiao Jiang Nan: "Qiao" means beautiful and "Jiang Nan" stands for the area south of Yangtze.
11. 2006, South Beauty: Chinese food in a Western way, winning with details, *Eastern Entrepreneur*, March 2006.
12. Case writer's interview with Zhang Lan, October 16, 2007.
13. SARS is the acronym for Severe Acute Respiratory Syndrome.
14. This number was provided by the company. As a cautious private company that was contacting venture capitalists, South Beauty was sensitive about providing its financial data. However, some media (such as Zhang Lan: A woman behind South Beauty, *Money Talk*, April 17, 2008) estimated that the annual revenue of the South Beauty Group would be over RMB 1 billion in 2007, with 20,000 to 30,000 footfalls every day. According to another source, the company's actual revenue in 2005 was RMB 460 million, with an average annual growth of 55.6 percent in the past three years (*China Entrepreneur*, May 20, 2006).
15. Dinner is the main meal of the day, whether eaten at midday or in the evening. The Chinese dinner category includes Chinese restaurants that provide the main meals of Chinese cuisine, not fast food or hot pot.
16. The market share of the top player, Yum!, was around 1 percent. The market share of South Beauty was estimated by the case authors and industry observers.
17. Case writer's interview with Luo Yun, October 16, 2007.
18. Golden Week is a twice-yearly week-long Chinese holiday.
19. 2007, South Beauty promotes its multibrand strategy and plans the overseas market expansion, *China New Age*, October; case writer's interview with Danny Wang, October 16, 2007.
20. Case writer's interview with Luo Yun on October 16, 2007.
21. The brochure was printed by the South Beauty Group.

22. Case writer's interview with Danny Wang on October 16, 2007.

23. 2007, The out-of-order competition in China's catering industry," *Economic Policy Information*, January 15.

24. 2008, Who is the biggest in China's catering industry? *Lifeweek*, February 4.

25. 2007, China Catering Industry Report, Hu Nan Science and Technology Publishing Company, October.

26. 2008, Who is the biggest in China's catering industry? *Lifeweek*, February 4.

27. 2007, China's catering industry becomes a hotspot, *China Business News*, January 15.

28. 2007, Little Sheep Restaurant Chain: Plan an IPO in Hong Kong for HK$ 2 billion, *Oriental Morning Post*, August 3.

29. The features of Chinese restaurants, http://brand.hr.com.cn/html/40724.html.

30. 2008, Jade Garden: Dialectic of high end Shanghainese cuisine development, *Lifeweek*, February 4.

31. The data of personal consumption came from "China's catering industry is developing fast," *International Business Newspaper*, October 18, 2006, with adjustment based on *China Statistical Year Book 2004*. Exchange rate in October 2007: USD 1 = RMB 7.5; in 2004: USD 1 = RMB 8.27.

32. 2008, Restaurant consumer survey through Internet, *Pin Week*, March 15.

33. Adapted from the Web site: http://www.dianping.com.

34. 2007, Olympics 2008 will create RMB 18 billion business for China's catering industry, *Consumption Daily*, July 30.

35. Information combined from case interview and the media report, 2006, LV (Zhang Lan's South Beauty wants to be LV brand in the restaurant market, http://www.netease.com, January 26; China's 400 richest, http://www.forbes.com/global/2006/1113/098.html.

36. Case Writers' interview with Luo Yun on October 16, 2007.

37. Case Writers' interview with Jacy Yang on October 16, 2007.

38. Ibid.

39. China's 400 richest, http://www.forbes.com/global/2006/1113/098.html.

40. Case Writers' interview with Luo Yun on October 16, 2007.

41. 2008, LAN Club and its hostess, *Lifeweek*, February 4.

42. Please refer to http://en.wikipedia.org/wiki/Beijing_National_Stadium.

James Francart, Harry Fry, Denis Grigorov,
Leonard Muhammad, Regina Pelkman,
Kyle Schlabach, Robin Chapman

Arizona State University

The worst sort of business is one that grows rapidly, requires significant capital to engender the growth, and then earns little or no money. Think airlines. Here a durable competitive advantage has proven elusive ever since the days of the Wright Brothers. Indeed, if a farsighted capitalist had been present at Kitty Hawk, he would have done his successors a huge favor by shooting Orville down.[1]

—WARREN BUFFETT IN A 2008 LETTER TO BERKSHIRE HATHAWAY SHAREHOLDERS

Some of the best minds in business have entered the commercial airline industry and failed. Included in this group is Warren Buffett, who invested in U.S. Air during the 1990s and was unsuccessful in saving the airline.[2] Since the inception of commercial flight, more than 200 airlines have tried and failed in the commercial airline industry.[3] These companies are a reminder that this business is tumultuous, complex, and in many cases, futile. Herb Kelleher, one of Southwest Airlines's founders, illustrates his awareness of how difficult it is to achieve any modicum of profitability in this industry with his comment, "If the Wright brothers were alive today Wilbur would have to fire Orville to reduce costs."[4]

Financial distress in the airline industry can be tied to the high costs incurred by the airlines to offer their services and low costs demanded by customers to travel. In an already extremely challenging industry, Southwest also faces dilemmas associated with its growth strategy, costs incurred to meet safety regulations on its aircraft, and a dispute with a labor union.[5]

These issues make the current and future decisions of the company more critical than ever. Fortunately for Southwest, the current president and CEO has a vast amount of experience within the company.

Key Leader

Gary C. Kelly replaced Herb Kelleher, one of the founders and chairman of the board, as president when he resigned in May 2008.[6] Kelly began his 22-year career with Southwest in the finance department as controller.[7] In that time, he has risen to the top of Southwest Airlines, holding positions such as vice president of finance, executive vice president, chief financial officer, and vice chairman.[8] Kelly, with such initiatives as fuel hedging, has been instrumental in Southwest's recent success.[9]

History of Southwest

Southwest Airlines, originally known as Air Southwest, was founded by Rollin King and Herb Kelleher. Southwest took its first flight in June 1971, serving three major cities: Dallas, Houston, and San Antonio.[10] Within the first two years Southwest suffered operating losses and was forced to make a difficult decision: lay off employees or sell one of its four aircraft. As an early indication of Southwest's loyalty to its employees, it chose to sell the aircraft.[11] This established the company's "no layoff policy" that is still in force.[12]

Southwest was able to sustain a four-aircraft schedule using only three aircraft by utilizing the "ten-minute turn."[13] Southwest turned its first annual profit in 1973. Southwest's expansion strategy flourished after 1973. By 1977 Southwest operated six airplanes and had transported five million customers.[14] New flight destinations were added such as Rio Grande Valley, Austin, Corpus Christi, El Paso, Lubbock, and Midland/Odessa.[15] Between 1979 and 1980, Southwest established its first interstate service to New Orleans and Albuquerque, followed by Oklahoma City and Tulsa.[16] Southwest expanded west in 1982, when it added service to Phoenix, Las Vegas, and San Diego.[17] In late 1984 the first 737-300 was added to its fleet and was used to service flights to Chicago Midway and St. Louis.[18]

In 1986, Southwest opened a new multi-million dollar training center for flight crews.[19] Since customer satisfaction was Southwest's main focus, it began a frequent flyer program, "The Company Club," in 1987. In 1988,

Southwest won its first monthly Triple Crown award for having the best on-time record, best baggage handling, and fewest customer complaints. All of its achievements allowed it to reach the billion-dollar revenue mark and become a major airline by 1989.[20] In 1990, Southwest created its corporate culture committee to take the lead in preserving the airline's unique culture.[21]

Southwest began to offer service to many new cities such as Nashville, Sacramento, Cleveland, and Columbus, and finally entered the east coast market in 1993 when it offered service to Baltimore/Washington International Airport.[22] With the acquisition and integration of Morris Air in 1994, the company was able to add service to seven new cities, including Seattle, Spokane, Portland, Salt Lake City, and Boise. That same year Southwest became the first airline to introduce Ticketless Travel in four cities, which eventually expanded system-wide in January of 1995.[23] Later in 1995, Southwest became one of the first airlines to have its own Web site, and the following year the Ticketless Travel system debuted online.[24]

After 25 years of service, Southwest owned a fleet of 243 aircraft and it saw an opportunity to introduce a fuel cost management program. The Asian market plummeted in 1998, causing jet fuel costs to drop to 35 cents per gallon. Southwest took advantage of this opportunity and hedged its fuel costs. Within two years fuel costs had increased as crude oil increased from $11 to $34 per barrel.

Further expansion, tangible asset improvements, and technology upgrades continued between 1999 and 2006. Southwest expanded to serve locations such as Long Island and Raleigh-Durham. It teamed up with IBM to introduce approximately 250 self-service check-in kiosks.[25] This project was "part of a nationwide effort to reduce the amount of time Southwest customers spend in line and to improve the airport experience."[26] By 2004, Southwest was offering online boarding passes via its Web site, allowing passengers to go directly to the departure gates without having to stop at the ticket counter.[27] Customer convenience increased even more in 2005, when Southwest "extended online check-in to 24 hours prior to departure."[28] By 2006, Southwest was ranked number one among airlines in customer satisfaction.[29]

Southwest updated its boarding procedure in 2007. Passengers are now assigned a boarding letter and a number that assigns them a specific place in line.[30] Select fare increases aligned with continuous cost-cutting policies resulted in the year-end revenue of $9.8 billion and $645 million in profits.[31]

In November 2008, Southwest purchased one of its main competitors, ATA Airlines, which allowed it to obtain boarding slots at New York's LaGuardia Airport.[32]

Acquiring ATA has the potential to provide Southwest with means to connect to foreign destinations. Southwest also partnered with WestJet Airlines, a low-cost carrier, to synch flights between Canada and the United States.

Southwest followed other carriers in early 2009 by increasing fare prices $10 per leg in the domestic market and up to $40 per leg for international routes.[33]

Southwest's technological innovations, procedure changes, price increases, and recent acquisitions are attempts to overcome the looming challenges in the airline industry.

Industry Challenges

Factors such as increased fuel costs and other high operating expenses, a decrease in business travelers due to budget cuts, and increased regulation have placed strains on airline companies. Many airlines have subsequently been forced out of business or acquired by competitors. This is illustrated by the fact that the large group of airlines that made up the industry 30 years ago has narrowed to six major firms that control a majority of the market (see Exhibit 1). These six carriers constitute five traditional airline companies (American, Continental, Delta, United, and US Airways) and Southwest, the low-cost leader.

Additionally, many airlines have been forced to file for bankruptcy. From 2005 to 2007, US Airways, UAL Corporation (United Airlines), ATA Airlines, Northwest Airlines, and Delta Air Lines all emerged from bankruptcy proceedings.[34] In 2008, Frontier Airlines, Skybus Airlines, Inc., Aloha Airlines, and ATA Airlines (for the second time) filed for bankruptcy.[35] All of these

Exhibit 1 Airline Domestic Market Share (March 2009)

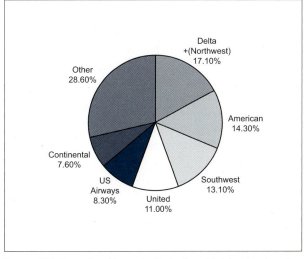

Delta +(Northwest) 17.10%

Other 28.60%

American 14.30%

Continental 7.60%

Southwest 13.10%

US Airways 8.30%

United 11.00%

Source: 2008, Research and Innovative Technology Administration, http://www.transtats.bts.gov.

bankruptcies demonstrate the difficult and competitive nature of the industry.

Competitive Environment

Southwest considers any airline offering a flight on the same route it does a competitor, regardless of the overall size of that competitor's operation. Since Southwest now operates in many geographic markets throughout the United States, essentially every airline that offers service to domestic cities is viewed as a competitor.[36]

New companies still occasionally try to replace Southwest as the low-cost leader. Many of these new airlines have disappeared as fast and unspectacularly as they flashed into existence. For example, Skybus, founded by an ex-Southwest employee, copied Southwest's operating model and began its operations in May 2007. Within one year it discontinued operations, citing the weakened state of the economy and increasing fuel costs as the reasons for its ruin.[37]

Although it was able to sustain operations for a longer period of time, the final days of Frontier were no less tragic. When Frontier filed for bankruptcy in April 2008, six days after Skybus,[38] it was the fourth airline to close its doors that week.[39]

JetBlue, also founded by an ex-Southwest employee, emerged in 1999 and is one of the few new entrants to successfully become a principle competitor to Southwest both in terms of route coverage and low-cost, low-fare strategies.[40] It is currently the seventh-largest airline in the United States and holds 4 percent market share compared to Southwest's 13 percent. It operates mostly with point-to-point routes and reaches 52 destinations in 19 states as well as South and Central America and the Caribbean. It just opened its own terminal at JFK airport in New York and claims it has started a new airline category, the "value airline" based on service, cost, and style.[41]

Traditional carriers have recently also adopted cost-cutting practices to more effectively compete with their low-cost counterparts.[42] More than 200 aircraft were grounded in 2008, Continental cut 3,000 jobs, and airlines offered fewer flights.[43] Although the major carriers are still offering higher fares overall, their business models are beginning to mirror those of low-cost rivals. Thus, Southwest has to increasingly improve its marketing efforts to differentiate itself.

Marketing Strategy

Due to the industry-wide move to promote value, Southwest aims to differentiate itself from its competitors by utilizing quirky, humor-driven advertising.[44] One of its first ads, featuring the slogan, "How do we love you? Let us count the ways" illustrated that by offering many flights throughout the day to its first three destinations, Southwest loved its customers (see Exhibit 2).

Another example relates to the recent checked bags fees charged by most other airlines. In response, Southwest began promoting a "no fees" policy in its advertisements such as with its "The Other Side" ad, illustrating a desk clerk with two faces: one face offering only the competitor's airfare; the other face demanding additional fees.

To further develop its unconventional niche in the airline industry and achieve success as a low-cost provider, Southwest distinguishes itself using both quantitative and qualitative characteristics.

Low Costs

An efficiency technique that has consistently saved Southwest both time and expense is the standardization of its airline fleet. It was the first company to put into practice the "one-model-fleet" tactic,[45] meaning that it has focused on purchasing only one aircraft model. It started in 1971 with a fleet of Boeing 737-200s, and it has used the Boeing 737 model ever since, being one of the launch customers for the Boeing 737-700, 737-500, and 737-300 series.[46] This model has been deemed "the workhorse of the aviation industry" and has gained a reputation of being excellent in the areas of cost, reliability and flexibility.[47] "Having a single airplane model in a fleet also lowers inventory, record keeping and maintenance costs, and it minimizes the number of technical manuals, tools and spare parts. Also, fleet management is greatly simplified [and] maintenance crews do not have to modify their routines to service different models."[48]

Another tactic that Southwest employs to maintain its low costs is fuel hedging. Southwest began this practice in the late 1990s and it has played a major role in its 36 years of profitability.[49] Although Southwest is renowned for using this methodology, the idea of oil futures contracts is nothing new in the airline industry (see Exhibit 3). "All the major airlines have hedged fuel prices since the 1980s, but as the major carriers have run into financial difficulties in recent years, they have no longer had the cash—or the creditworthiness—to play the oil-futures market."[50] Nonetheless, Southwest has successfully hedged "at least 70 percent" of its fuel consumption, saving the company $727 million in 2007.[51] Fuel costs fluctuated significantly during 2008, starting out at $91, hitting $151 during the summer, and closing the year at $51. The significant change in oil prices did not provide Southwest with cost savings like those in 2007, but it

Exhibit 2 Southwest Advertisement

How do we love you?
Let us count the ways.

Dallas/Ft. Worth to Houston		Houston to Dallas/Ft. Worth	
Depart	Arrive	Depart	Arrive
7:30 a*	8:18 a	7:30 a*	8:18 a
8:45 a*	9:33 a	8:45 a	9:33 a
10:00 a	10:48 a	10:00 a*	10:48 a
11:15 a*	12:03 p	11:15 a	12:03 p
12:30 p	1:18 p	12:30 p*	1:18 p
1:45 p**	2:33 p	1:45 p	2:33 p
3:00 p	3:48 p	3:00 p**	3:48 p
4:15 p**	5:03 p	4:15 p	5:03 p
5:30 p	6:18 p	5:30 p**	6:18 p
6:45 p**	7:33 p	6:45 p	7:33 p
8:00 p	8:48 p	8:00 p**	8:48 p
9:15 p**	10:03 p	9:15 p**	10:03 p

Dallas/Ft. Worth to San Antonio		San Antonio to Dallas/Ft. Worth	
Depart	Arrive	Depart	Arrive
7:00 a*	7:50 a	8:15 a*	9:05 a
9:30 a	10:20 a	10:45 a	11:35 a
12:00 n	12:50 p	1:15 p	2:05 p
2:30 p	3:20 p	3:45 p	4:35 p
5:00 p	5:50 p	6:15 p	7:05 p
7:30 p**	8:20 p	8:45 p**	9:35 p

*Except Sunday.
**Except Saturday.

SOUTHWEST AIRLINES
The somebody else up there who loves you.

Source: 2008, Southwest Airlines Historical Advertising Gallery, http://www.southwest.com.

did allow it to secure a good hedging contract through 2013 based on the fourth quarter fuel prices ($51). This is expected to save $600 million in fuel costs annually compared to 2008.[52]

Southwest exercised other cost-saving measures concerning fuel consumption, such as the implementation of blended winglets on all of its 737-700s.[53] These blended winglets would "improve performance by extending the airplane's range, saving fuel, lowering engine maintenance costs and reducing takeoff noise."[54] (See Exhibit 4 for estimates on fuel savings.) Testing on the blended winglets demonstrated "gross fuel mileage improvement … in the range of 4 to 5 percent."[55] In 2003, Southwest announced that performance-enhancing "blended winglets" would be installed on all existing and future aircrafts, though this action was not carried out until 2007.[56]

In 2008, Southwest initiated a contract with Pratt & Whitney to use its EcoPower® engine wash services. EcoPower uses atomized water to wash aircraft engines and prevent potential contaminant runoff. This system is more efficient and effective than traditional engine washing processes and extends on-wing time for Pratt & Whitney, International Aero Engines, General Electric, Rolls-Royce, and CFMI engines. By using this engine wash, Southwest anticipates saving "more than $20 million in fuel costs [at 2008 prices]."[57]

The following measures not only help Southwest save on costs, but also to retain its reputation for being reliable and punctual.

Exhibit 3 Southwest Advertisement

Southwest's Profitable Bet

Percentage of each airline's fuel needs that are hedged against higher fuel prices and have been disclosed, with the price caps of their hedges.

	2007 4th quarter		2008 full years		2009		2010	
	HEDGED	PRICE CAP	HEDGED	PRICE CAP	HEDGED	PRICE CAP	HEDGED	PRICE CAP
Alaska[1]	50%	$62	32%	$64	5%	$68	0	
American[1]	40	69	14	n.d.†	0		0	
Continental[2]	30	93	10*	93	0		0	
Delta[2]	20	99	0		0		0	
JetBlue[2]	47	83	0		0		0	
Northwest[1]	50	73	10*	84	0		0	
Southwest[1]	90	51	70	51	55	51	25%	$63
United[2]	18	93	0		0		0	
US Airways[1]	56	73	15	73	0		0	

[1]Price based on crude oil.
[2]Price based on heating oil, which is more expensive.

*First quarter only. †Price not disclosed.

Source: 2008, Southwest Airlines manages risk through oil price hedges. http://www.artdiamondblog.com/archives/energyenvironment/, March 18.

Exhibit 4 Improvements from Winglets

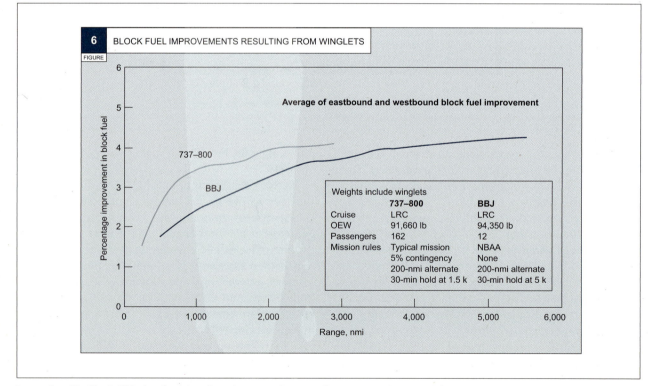

6
FIGURE

BLOCK FUEL IMPROVEMENTS RESULTING FROM WINGLETS

Average of eastbound and westbound block fuel improvement

737–800

BBJ

Percentage improvement in block fuel

Range, nmi

Weights include winglets		
	737–800	**BBJ**
Cruise	LRC	LRC
OEW	91,660 lb	94,350 lb
Passengers	162	12
Mission rules	Typical mission	NBAA
	5% contingency	None
	200-nmi alternate	200-nmi alternate
	30-min hold at 1.5 k	30-min hold at 5 k

Source: Aero 17 – Blended Winglets, fig. 6, http://www.boeing.com/commercial/aeromagazine/aero_17/winglet_story.

Punctuality

Timeliness has been a defining characteristic for Southwest since its beginning. In the 1970s, the company had a 10-minute turnaround time for aircraft while the industry average was four to six times longer.[58] Southwest's "turnarounds now average 23 minutes, but that's still . . . half the time it takes other airlines."[59] It is able to maintain this quick turnaround rate because it uses point-to-point service (curtailing connection times and luggage transfers) and secondary airports for the bulk of its flights (reducing potential congestion).[60] Instead of point-to-point service most legacy carriers use a hub-and-spoke system where small feeder airlines from smaller cities feed into larger international airports such as Delta's hub in Atlanta.

The boarding process with unassigned seating is another of Southwest's differentiating qualities, but one for which it has received mixed reviews from customers.[61] Although this tactic aids in quicker gate turnaround,[62] it is flawed from a customer service standpoint and has a reputation as "cattle call" check-in. It favors customers who are able to arrive at the gate early, no matter when the ticket was purchased (even with an "A" boarding pass—see Exhibit 5). In response to customer complaints Southwest initiated a new check-in process in 2007. Kelleher believes, "Customers are like a force of nature: You can't fool them, and you ignore them at your own peril."[63] The new method gives passengers a group letter (A, B, C) and a number (1 to 60) based on order of check-in, thus it reserves more of a semblance of a place in line than the previous process.[64] Even though this distinction creates perceived value for the customer in terms of time savings, there is still controversy about this method among Southwest customers. Recently, adjustments were made to accommodate families with small children, who did not receive priority seating when the change was first made.[65]

Exceptional Customer Service Begins at Home

A unique aspect of Southwest's customer service perspective is that the end-user is not the primary focus, the employees are; "If [Southwest] can effectively make employees feel good about what they're doing on a daily basis, satisfied employees will deliver [a] . . . sense of friendliness and care to Southwest passengers."[66]

In 2008, Southwest was the highest-rated airline in *Fortune's* list of "America's Most Admired Companies."[67] It ranked first in the categories "people management" and "quality of management." Southwest's reputation for being a great employer is further illustrated by the fact that in 2007, Southwest received 329,200 resumes from job seekers.[68] In 1973, the airline adopted the first profit-sharing plan in the U.S. airline industry, and employees now own at least 8 percent of the company stock.[69] It would be safe to assume that these factors are key contributors to the low employee turnover rate that Southwest enjoys.[70] However, there have been some recent issues related to union activities and contract negotiations that could possibly tarnish Southwest's reputation as an employer (see the Additional Challenges section).

Exhibit 5 Southwest's Boarding Process

How it worked before:

- Each passenger's boarding pass was assigned to Group A, B, or C, based on check-in.
- A and B groups had 45 passengers, with everyone else in Group C.
- Families with young children boarded before the groups were called.
- In the gate area, passengers in each of the groups lined up, often 30 to 45 minutes before boarding, in either the A, B, or C line.
- Passengers boarded by group letter.
- Seats were unassigned.

The new boarding drill:

- Passenger boarding passes will have a group letter (A, B, or C) and a number (1 to 60), based on order of check-in.
- In combination, the letter and number reserves passengers' places in line, leaving them free to relax or get something to eat.
- Groups A and B contain 60 passengers each; those remaining are in Group C.
- Families with young children must now wait until the A group has boarded, unless they hold A passes.
- At the gate, six stainless steel columns divide passengers into groups of five on each side. For example, the first column has passengers holding 1–5 passes on one side and those with 31–35 on the other. The second column has spaces for those holding 6–10 and 36–40.
- Electronic monitors indicate which group is boarding. Those with A passes standing on the first side of the column will board, followed by those on the other side. As the second half boards, Group B will assemble.
- Seats are still unassigned.

Source: S. Marta, 2007, Southwest launches streamlined boarding, *The Dallas Morning News*, http://www.dallasnews.com, October 15.

Reward Programs

Nearly every major airline has attempted to increase customer loyalty through reward programs. These programs offer repeat customers perks such as an accelerated check-in process, upgrades, and even free flights and hotel stays. However, it is debatable how effective these programs are. Leisure travelers may not travel enough to allow these programs to influence their purchasing decisions; and business and other frequent travelers, who are much more concerned about convenience and scheduling, are often members of many, if not all, frequent flyer programs from each airline. The end result is that Rewards programs have not had a major impact on Southwest's bottom line.

Financial Results

Southwest Airlines reported an operating profit of $449 million for the year 2008, despite rising operating expenses marking 71 consecutive quarters of profitability. Total operating expenses for the year increased 16 percent compared to 2007 and were driven primarily by higher fuel costs (44 percent), as well as ongoing maintenance costs (see Exhibit 6). However, Southwest did make 2008 its thirty-sixth consecutive year with annual operating profits.[71]

In 2008, Southwest boasted an operating profit margin (4 percent) much higher than its competitors such as Delta (−36 percent), JetBlue (3.2 percent),

Exhibit 6 Southwest Airlines—Consolidated Statement of Income

	Years Ended December 31		
	2007	**2006**	**2005**
	(In millions, except per share amounts)		
Operating Revenues:			
Passenger	$9,457	$8,750	$7,279
Freight	130	134	133
Other	274	202	172
Total operating revenues	9,861	9,086	7,584
Operating Expenses:			
Salaries, wages, and benefits	3,213	3,052	2,782
Fuel and oil	2,536	2,138	1,341
Maintenance materials and repairs	616	468	446
Aircraft rentals	156	158	163
Landing fees and other rentals	560	495	454
Depreciation and amortization	555	515	469
Other operating expenses	1,434	1,326	1,204
Total operating expenses	9,070	8,152	6,859
Operating Income	791	934	725
Other Expenses (Income):			
Interest expense	119	128	122
Capitalized interest	(50)	(51)	(39)
Interest income	(44)	(84)	(47)

Exhibit 6 Southwest Airlines—Consolidated Statement of Income (*Continued*)

| | Years Ended December 31 | | |
	2007	2006	2005
		(In millions, except per share amounts)	
Other (gains) losses, net	(292)	151	(90)
Total other expenses (income)	(267)	144	(54)
Income before income taxes	1,058	790	779
Provision for income taxes	413	291	295
Net income	$645	$499	$484
Net income per share, basic	$.85	$.63	$.61
Net income per share, diluted	$.84	$.61	$.60

Source: 2008, Southwest Airlines 2007 Annual Report, http://www.southwest.com.

United (−21.9 percent), and American (−7.9 percent).[72] This is an indication of Southwest's ability to control costs in an industry that has historically struggled in this area. Continued emphasis on cost cutting has allowed Southwest to avoid filing for bankruptcy, unlike many of its competitors (see Exhibit 7).

In the airline industry, a high ROA indicates a company's ability to generate high income proportionate to its held assets, which are primarily composed of aircraft and other flight equipment, property (including airport operating slots), and fuel hedge contracts. In 2008, Southwest operated with an ROA of 1.2 percent, double that of the next-closest competitor, JetBlue (−1.3 percent). This demonstrates Southwest's outstanding ability to avoid excess capacity and service outages.

Many airlines rely heavily on debt financing, since many investors avoid sinking cash into this industry. Southwest has been able to maintain low levels of debt and position itself with the lowest D/E ratio (77.6) among major airlines (the industry average D/E is 330). Southwest has been able to generate income, have positive profit margins, and maintain low debt levels because it puts great effort into wisely carrying out its strategies.

Part of Southwest's efforts to maintain positive operating margins and low debt levels is to expand its service to greater destinations.

Expansion Plans
Kelly has expressed a desire to expand Southwest beyond the 64 cities it currently serves, calling the airline "an adolescent" in the airline industry.[73] Although the airline

is cutting certain less profitable routes, the net result of the additional flights will increase the company's overall flights by nine.[74]

In March 2009, flights between Chicago and Minneapolis were added. "The people of Minnesota have been asking for Southwest Airlines' service for many years, and we can't wait to introduce them to our legendary customer service, as well as our low fares, on-time flights, and no hidden fees."[75] Even though its strategy is primarily limited to domestic expansion with a push into Denver, Southwest is exploring ways to launch services to the Caribbean and England.[76] It recently announced the addition of flights to Mexico through code-sharing with Volaris. "Volaris has a stellar reputation for being a highly efficient airline with a dedication to customer service, which makes it a natural fit for Southwest Airlines."[77] Growth initiatives also include possible acquisitions of flights once belonging to now defunct airlines such as Ted (United Airlines attempt at a lower cost approach).[78]

Additional Challenges

Technology
The airline companies' widespread integration of the Internet into the booking process acts as a double-edged sword. Customers value the ease provided by online booking, which in turn draws in customers. Southwest obtained first-mover advantage using this technology when it became the first airline to offer the service. However, now that this has become the industry

Exhibit 7 Financial Analysis of Southwest Airlines and Selected Key Competitors

	Southwest Airlines[1]	JetBlue Airways[2]	American Airlines[3]	Delta Air Lines[4]	United Airlines[5]
Period	*2007*	*2007*	*2007*	*2007*	*2007*
Annual Revenue					
Passenger	9,457	2,636	20,705	11,803	18,317
Freight and other	404	206	2,230	1,555	1,826
Total	*9,861*	*2,842*	*22,935*	*13,358*	*20,143*
Employees (FTE)	34,378	10,219	85,500	55,044	44,861
Operating Profit Margin	8.0%	5.9%	4.2%	6.0%	5.1%
Pre-Tax Profit Margin	10.7%	1.4%	2.2%	3.9%	3.5%
Net Profit Margin	6.5%	0.6%	2.2%	2.4%	2.0%
Return on Equity	9.6%	1.8%	49.1%	−18.0%	17.7%
Return on Assets	4.3%	0.3%	1.7%	1.2%	1.6%
Total Debt/Equity	1.42	4.40	9.75	2.21	9.02
12-month Revenue Growth	8.5%	20.3%	1.6%	nm	nm

[1] 2008, Southwest Airlines 2007 Annual Report, http://www.southwest.com.
[2] 2008, JetBlue Airways Corporation 2007 Annual Report, http://www.jetblue.com.
[3] 2008, AMR Corporation 2007 Annual Report, http://www.aa.com.
[4] 2008, Delta Air Lines, Inc. 2007 Annual Report, http://www.delta.com.
[5] 2008, UAL Corporation 2007 Annual Report, http://www.united.com.

standard, it has significantly increased consumer ability to apply some pressure on ticket prices. Travel search engine sites such as Expedia.com, Travelocity .com, Orbitz.com, Kayak.com, and others have further exasperated this issue for the airlines. Southwest has long refused to submit pricing information or allow the purchase of its tickets from these sites. Since there are many airlines and negligible switching costs, this is truly an industry that has long lacked customer loyalty.

Violations of Safety Requirements. Early in 2008, it was revealed that Southwest had flown at least 117 aircraft that were in violation of mandatory safety checks.[79] As a result, the airline had to temporarily ground 47 of its aircrafts for re-inspection, and the Federal Aviation Administration charged the airline with $10.2 million in fines.[80] Southwest claims, "[it] discovered the missed inspection area, disclosed it to the FAA, and promptly

reinspected all potentially affected aircraft in March 2007. The FAA approved our actions and considered the matter closed as of April 2007." FAA inspectors contest that Southwest continued to use the planes in question before inspections were complete, thus the airline did not take immediate corrective action.[81] Gary Kelly states, "Our interpretation of the guidance that we got from the FAA at the time was that we were in compliance with all laws and regulations … the important point is that at no time were we operating in an unsafe manner, and I think our history proves it."[82]

Union Walkout
The company that once enjoyed superior employee relations compared to its competitors ran into problems in 2008. Complaints of unequal pay for members of ground crew and no raises since 2005 prompted a walkout by the labor union on November 20, 2008.[83] In March

2009 an agreement was reached. The union president admitted that the negotiations were conducted with a spirit of cooperation that is part of Southwest's culture: "Southwest Airlines flight attendants have always been an integral part of the airline's success and it is great news that together they have negotiated a contract that recognizes their contribution."[84] Flight attendants will gain wage increases and a boost in 401k contributions, but only to the degree that such increases will allow Southwest to keep its low-cost advantage.

Questions to Address

As the airline industry as a whole suffers, due to threats from fuel price increases, ever-escalating operational costs, potential security threats, and the current global economic crisis, can Southwest maintain its 36-year streak of profitability? With fluctuating oil prices, can Southwest continue to depend on fuel hedging as an important source of cost control? As it expands its domestic flight operations, will "point-to-point" methodology still prove to be useful? As the major traditional airlines become more like their low-cost counterparts, will they ultimately become more of a competitive threat to Southwest? Using its current strategy, will Southwest be able to expand internationally? Can it maintain its positive relations with employees and avoid future union walkouts and negotiations? If the current economic crisis persists, how will the present expansion plans by Southwest fare? As environmental uncertainties mount, what overall strategies and as well as competitive tactics should Southwest consider to maintain it low cost position and perception of customer loyalty?

NOTES

1. Sykes, 2008, Buffett letter offers great lessons for investors, http://www.bloggingstocks.com, March 3.
2. 2008, Warren Buffett, airlines hasn't always been a successful marriage, Local Tech Wire, http://localtechwire.com, January.
3. 2008, Defunct airlines of the United States, http://en.wikipedia.org.
4. H. Kelleher, 1994, USA Today, June 8.
5. M. McSherry & M. Lewis, 2008, Southwest Airlines union pickets over wages, Reuters, http://www.reuters.com, November.
6. T. Maxon, 2008, Kelleher to preside over his last Southwest meeting Wednesday, The Dallas Morning News, http://www.dallasnews.com, May 20; 2008, Southwest officer biographies, http://www.southwest.com.
7. G. C. Kelly, 2008, Forbes, http://people.forbes.com/profile/gary-c-kelly/73447.
8. 2008, Southwest officer biographies, http://www.southwest.com.
9. S. Taylor, 2005, To provide the best customer service, put customers second, says Southwest President Colleen Barrett, McCombs School of Business, http://www.mccombs.utexas.edu, April 18.
10. 2008, Southwest Airlines, Wikipedia, http://en.wikipedia.org.
11. D. Koenig, 2008, Southwest leader Kelleher steps down, USA Today, http://www.usatoday.com, May 21.
12. 2003, What makes Southwest Airlines fly, Knowledge@Wharton, http://knowledge.wharton.upenn.edu, April 23.
13. 2008, About Southwest Airlines, http://www.southwest.com.
14. Ibid.
15. Ibid.
16. Ibid.
17. Ibid.
18. Ibid.
19. Ibid.
20. Ibid.
21. Ibid.
22. Ibid.
23. Ibid.
24. Ibid.
25. Ibid.
26. Ibid.
27. Ibid.
28. Ibid.
29. Ibid.
30. Southwest Airlines, Wikipedia.
31. About Southwest Airlines.
32. Ibid.
33. M. Schlangenstein, 2009, Delta, Southwest airlines raise most U.S. tickets $20, http://www.Bloomberg.com, June 17.
34. 2008, Southwest Airlines 2007 Annual Report, http://www.southwest.com..
35. J. Bunch & K. Yamanouchi, 2008, Frontier Airlines files Chapter 11, The Denver Post, http://www.denverpost.com, April 11; 2008, Southwest Airlines bids on 14 LaGuardia slots, Queens Chronicle, http://www.zwire.com, November; 2008, Skybus becomes third airline to close this week, CNN, http://www.cnn.com, April 4.
36. 2008, Southwest Airlines 2007 Annual Report.
37. Ibid.
38. J. Bunch & K. Yamanouchi, Frontier Airlines files Chapter 11.
39. Skybus becomes third airline to close this week.
40. 2008, America's most admired companies, Fortune, http://money.cnn.com, March 17.
41. 2009, JetBlue 2008 Annual Report, http://www.jetblue.com, June 17.
42. M. Maynard, 2008, As costs rise, airlines cut services and raise fares, The New York Times, http://www.nytimes.com, June 6.
43. Ibid.
44. 2008, Southwest Airlines historical advertising gallery, http://www.southwest.com.
45. 2002, The secret behind high profits at low-fare airlines, Boeing News Release, http://www.boeing.com, June 14.
46. 2008, Southwest Airlines Fact Sheet, http://www.southwest.com.
47. The secret behind high profits at low-fare airlines.
48. Ibid.
49. D. Reed, 2008, Can fuel hedges keep Southwest in the money? USA Today, http://www.usatoday.com, July 23.
50. E. Roston, 2005, Hedging their costs, Time, June 20.
51. Southwest Airlines 2007 Annual Report.
52. 2009, Southwest Airlines 2008 Annual Report, http://www.southwest.com, June 11, 9.
53. 2003, Southwest Airlines Boeing 737-700 fleet takes wing with sleek new look, Boeing News Release, http://www.boeing.com, June 17.
54. Ibid.
55. Ibid.

56. Ibid.

57. G. Brostowicz & J. Whitlow, 2008, Southwest Airlines to save millions in fuel costs and significantly reduce carbon dioxide emissions with Pratt & Whitney EcoPower® Engine wash services, *Pratt & Whitney*, http://www.pw.utc.com, June 11.

58. 2007, Something special about Southwest Airlines, CBS News, http://www.cbsnews.com,_September 2.

59. Ibid.

60. 2008, Southwest Airlines Company (LUV), Wikinvest, http://www.wikinvest.com.

61. D. Grossman, 2007, New Southwest boarding policy pits business travelers against families, *USA Today*, http://www.usatoday.com, October 28.

62. W. Haas, 2007, How Southwest Airlines plans for success, *Associated Content*, http://www.associatedcontent.com, February 2.

63. B. McConnell & J. Huba, 2001, The wild turkey, *Creative Customer Evangelists*, http://www.creatingcustomerevangelists.com, September 1.

64. S. Marta, 2007, Southwest launches streamlined boarding, *The Dallas Morning News*, http://www.dallasnews.com, October 15.

65. Ibid.

66. To provide the best customer service, put customers second.

67. America's most admired companies, *Fortune*.

68. Southwest Airlines Fact Sheet.

69. Ibid.

70. T. Tripp, Best practices case study: Best perks, Southwest Airlines, *Vault*, http://www.vault.com/nr/newsmain.jsp?nr_page=3&ch_id=402&article_id=19258&cat_id=1123.

71. Southwest 2008 Annual Report; 2008, Southwest Airlines reports third quarter financial results, http://www.southwest.com, October 16; 2008, Southwest Airlines reports fourth quarter earnings and 35th consecutive year of profitability, http://www.southwest.com, January 23.

72. 2009, Delta, Southwest, AMR, UAL, and JetBlue, *Reuters*, http://www.reuters.com, June 11.

73. J. Bottiglieri, 2008, Gary C. Kelly: Aspire to something greater; Southwest Airlines' CEO talks about sustaining profitability and mitigating risk, *Bnet Business Network*, March; R. Velotta, 2008, Southwest Airlines announces code share with Mexican airline, *Las Vegas Sun* http://www.lasvegassun.com, November 10.

74. 2008, Southwest Airlines cuts 31 flights, adds 40 flights, *DWS Aviation*, http://www.dancewithshadows.com, June.

75. 2008, Southwest Airlines announces schedule, fares for its new Minneapolis-Chicago service, *DWS Aviation*, http://www.dancewithshadows.com/aviation, November.

76. Ibid.

77. 2008, Southwest to partner with Volaris on international flights, *Austin Business Journal*, http://www.bizjournals.com, November.

78. 2008, Southwest Airlines bids on 14 LaGuardia slots, *Queens Chronicle*, http://www.zwire.com, November.

79. D. Griffin & S. Bronstein, 2008, Records: Southwest Airlines flew "unsafe" planes, *CNN*, http://www.cnn.com, March 6.

80. Ibid.

81. Ibid.

82. D. Griffin & S. Bronstein, 2008, Southwest Airlines CEO calls FAA's threats of fine "unfair", *CNN*, http://www.cnn.com, March 7.

83. Southwest Airlines union pickets over wages.

84. J. Horwitz, 2009, Arriving today, a tentative agreement for Southwest flight attendants that protects employees and the LUV airline's future, TWU News Room, http://www.twu.org, March 26.

Tesco versus Sainsbury's: Growth Strategies and Corporate Competitiveness

Markus Kreutzer, Christoph Lechner

University of St. Gallen

Introduction

In 2008, the UK-based international food and general merchandising retailer Tesco reached a market share of about 30 percent in the United Kingdom, roughly the same as its rivals Sainsbury's and ASDA combined. In recent years, Tesco has greatly diversified, extending its business lines from food into non-food, clothing, financial services, and telecommunications. It ranks sixth in the international retail market behind Wal-Mart (United States), Carrefour (France), Home Depot (United States), Metro (Germany), and Royal Ahold (Netherlands).[1]

Tesco was not always the dominant player it is today. In 1990, it was a mid-sized food chain far behind its rival, Sainsbury's. Starting in the 1990s, it pursued a broad set of growth initiatives, steadily increasing its market share and gaining importance. In 1995, Tesco surpassed Sainsbury's to become the U.K. market leader. Today, Tesco is the clear market leader. How did that happen? Why was Tesco so successful in growing sales and profits, while Sainsbury's could not keep pace? Where did the competitive actions of these firms differ? Let us start with a close look at their origins.

Sainsbury's, Tesco, and the U.K. Retail Market in 1990

Sainsbury's was established in 1869 by John James and Mary Ann Sainsbury, making it the oldest food retailing chain in Britain. In 1922, J Sainsbury became a private company, with J Sainsbury plc acting as parent company of Sainsbury's Supermarkets Ltd, commonly known as Sainsbury's, a chain of supermarkets in the United Kingdom. In 1973, the company was floated as J Sainsbury plc in what was at the time the largest flotation on the London Stock Exchange. The family currently retains about 14 percent of its shares. The group is also engaged in property and banking, owning real estate worth about £8.6 billion. For much of the twentieth century, Sainsbury's was the market leader in the U.K. supermarket sector, but in 1995 it lost its place to Tesco; in 2003, it was pushed to third place by ASDA.

Tesco was founded by Jack Cohen in London's East End. From a modest background, Cohen began selling groceries in Well Street market, Hackney, in 1919. In the aftermath of World War I, food supplies were low, so he bought damaged goods from other stores and re-sold them at reasonable prices. The Tesco brand first appeared in 1924. The name originated after Cohen bought a shipment of tea from TE Stockwell. He made new labels using the first three letters of the supplier's name and the first two letters of his surname. The first Tesco store opened in 1929 in Burnt Oak, Edgware, Middlesex. Tesco was floated on the London Stock Exchange in 1947 as Tesco Stores (Holdings) Ltd. During the 1950s and 1960s, Tesco grew slowly, until it owned more than 800 stores. The company purchased 70 Williamsons stores (1957), 200 Harrow Stores outlets (1959), 212 Irwins stores (1960), 97 Charles Phillips stores (1964), and the Victor Value chain (1968) (sold to Bejam in 1986). In 1973, Jack Cohen resigned and was replaced as chairman by his son-in-law, Leslie Porter. Porter and managing director Ian MacLaurin abandoned the "pile it high and sell it cheap" philosophy of Cohen, which had left the company stagnating with a bad image. In 1977, Tesco launched "Operation Checkout," which included price reductions and centralized purchasing for all its stores. As a result, its market share rose by 4 percent within two months.

At the beginning of the 1990s, the U.K. retail market slowly became more competitive. Three players dominated the food market: ASDA[2] (which became Wal-Mart's largest overseas subsidiary in 1999), Sainsbury's, and Tesco. ASDA positioned itself as the price leader and held this position for some time, closely followed by Tesco. Sainsbury's targeted the upper price segment, positioning itself between mass market and high end.

In the mid-1990s, competition intensified as a price war among these players emerged, resulting in squeezed margins and cost cutting. It is not surprising that this also had an adverse impact on the service level these corporations provided.

In general, prices of standard brands and private labels at both Sainsbury's and Tesco came closer, while the two firms differed slightly in their discounting policies. Tesco emphasized its low-price private label ("Value") and continued to cut prices, while Sainsbury's emphasized price reductions on the standard private labels. The price cuts were prompted by the increased price pressure from the market entry of discounters. For example, Aldi entered the market in 1990, followed by Lidl in 1994. In 2005, these two hard discounters had acquired a market share of 2.2 percent and 1.9 percent, respectively.

Store Formats

In 1975, Sainsbury's launched the "Sainsbury's SavaCentre" hypermarket format as a joint venture with British Home Stores. This was the first attempt in the United Kingdom to launch supermarkets with a large non-food range. SavaCentre became a wholly owned Sainsbury's subsidiary in 1989. As the hypermarket format became mainstream, with rivals such as ASDA and Tesco launching ever-larger stores, Sainsbury's decided that a separate brand was no longer needed. Over the following years, these stores were converted to the regular Sainsbury's superstore format and, subsequently, Sainsbury's retreated from hypermarkets and changed its store formats. Now, Sainsbury's operates three formats: regular Sainsbury's stores, Sainsbury's local stores (convenience stores), and Sainsbury's central stores (smaller supermarkets in urban locations). For an overview of Sainsbury's U.K. store portfolio at the end of fiscal year 2005–06, see Exhibit 1.

While Sainsbury's retreated from hypermarkets, Tesco expanded Tesco Extra and strengthened its hypermarket formats.[3] Its overarching store strategy is reflected in its core marketing slogan adopted when Terry Leahy became CEO in 1997. "The Tesco Way" implies a shift from a focus on the corporation to a focus on people, both employees and customers. Tesco stores are divided into five formats, differentiated by size and range of products, and are customized to specific segments: Tesco Extra, Tesco Superstores, Tesco Metro, Tesco Express, and One Stop (see Exhibit 2). The approximately 500 One Stop stores are the smallest units. They stay open in the late evening and feature a differentiated pricing and offer system. Tesco Extra, launched in 1997, is the largest format, consisting mainly of out-of-town hypermarkets that stock Tesco's entire product range and offer free parking. Their number has increased about 20 percent annually, mainly by conversions of other formats. Tesco Superstores are the standard large grocery supermarkets, with a much smaller range of non-food goods than Extra. They are referred to as "superstores" for convenience, but not as part of the name. It is the standard Tesco format. Most are located in suburbs of cities or on the edges of large- and medium-sized towns. Tesco Metro stores are sized between normal Tesco stores and Tesco Express stores. They are mostly located in city centers and on the high streets of small towns. The first Tesco Metro was opened in Covent Garden, London, in 1992. Tesco Express stores are neighborhood convenience stores, stocking mainly food, with an emphasis on high-margin products alongside everyday essentials. They are found in busy city center districts, in small shopping precincts in residential areas, and in petrol station forecourts. As CEO Terry Leahy remarked in the company's 2000 annual report:

This obsession with our customers, their needs, and how these must be changing, means that you should not expect us to go on opening large edge-of-town superstores long after the need for new ones has passed. Expect . . . continual evolution: expect us to provide a mix of formats in different locations . . . to meet special needs of customers in each location.

Exhibit 1 Sainsbury's Store Portfolio in the United Kingdom (at the end of 2006)

Format	Number	Area (ft²)	Area (m²)	Percentage of Space
Supermarkets	455	15,916,000	1,467,000	95.1%
Convenience stores	297	821,000	76,000	4.9%
Total	752	16,737,000	1,543,000	100%

Exhibit 2 Tesco's Store Portfolio in the United Kingdom (at the end of 2007)

Format	Number	Total Area (m²)	Total Area (sq ft)	Mean Area (m²)	Mean Area (sq ft)	Percentage of Space
Tesco Extra	147	952,441	10,252,000	6,479	69,741	36.89%
Tesco	433	1,227,434	13,212,000	2,834	30,512	47.55%
Tesco Metro	162	177,073	1,906,000	1,093	11,765	6.85%
Tesco Express	735	145,114	1,562,000	197	2,125	5.62%
One Stop	506	62,988	678,000	124	1,339	2.44%
Tesco Homeplus	5	16,258	175,000	3,251	35,000	0.62%
Total	1,988	2,581,310	27,785,000	1,298	13,976	100%

Much of Tesco's sales increases occurred through increases in total square footage with the opening of new stores, including new formats such as Metro and Express. From 1994 to 1996, selling areas increased by 22 percent for Tesco and 10 percent for Sainsbury's. At the same time, Tesco managed to increase sales per square foot by 14 percent, while Sainsbury's gained only 3 percent. In addition, acquisitions and alliances complemented the organic growth strategy. Tesco, for example, purchased Adminstore in 2004, owner of 45 Cullens, Europa, and Harts convenience stores in and around London. In late 2005, it purchased the 21 remaining Safeway/BP stores after Morrison's dissolved the Safeway/BP partnership. In 1997, Tesco formed an alliance with Esso Petroleum Company Ltd (now part of ExxonMobil Corp.). The agreement included several petrol filling stations on lease from Esso, where Tesco would operate the store under the Express format. In turn, Esso would operate the forecourts and sell their fuel via the Tesco store. Ten years later, over 600 Tesco/Esso stores can be found across the United Kingdom.

Sainsbury's also expanded by acquisition. As part of the acquisition of Safeway Group by Morrison's, Morrison's was to dispose of 53 of the combined group's stores. In May 2004, Sainsbury's announced that it would acquire 14 of these stores, 13 Safeway stores, and one Morrison's outlet, all located primarily in the Midlands and the north of England. The first of these new stores opened in August 2004. In 2004, Sainsbury's also expanded its share of the convenience store market through other acquisitions. Bell's Stores, a 54-store chain based in northeast England, was acquired in February 2004. Jackson's Stores, a chain of 114 stores based in Yorkshire and the North Midlands, was purchased in August 2004. JB Beaumont, a chain of six stores in the East Midlands, was acquired in November

2004. SL Shaw Ltd, which owned six stores, was acquired in April 2005 for £6 million. On September 29, 2004, Sainsbury's established Sainsbury's Convenience Stores Ltd to manage its Sainsbury's local stores and the Bell's and Jackson's chains. The latter two are to be rebranded as Sainsbury's local stores by 2009.

Service Offerings and Distribution Systems

"An inclusive offer" is how Tesco describes its aspiration to appeal to upper-, medium-, and low-income customers in the same stores. According to Citigroup retail analyst David McCarthy, "They've pulled off a trick that I'm not aware of any other retailer achieving. That is, to appeal to all segments of the market." One plank of this program has been Tesco's use of its private label products, including the upmarket "Finest" and low price "Value." Other examples include organic, kids, British specialty food, and "free from" brands. As Edward Garner, the communications director of the TNS Superpanel, remarks: "Tesco's winning formula is largely due to its ability to be all things to all people. According to TNS, over 60 percent of British households shop in Tesco every four weeks. That's 20 percent more than its nearest rival. The store appeals to wide-reaching demographics across the country and has built up a heritage of reliability and trustworthiness, which keeps shoppers returning to its stores. These factors have enabled Tesco to gain close to a third of the British grocery market."

Sainsbury's has also invested in private labels. A large Sainsbury's store typically stocks around 50,000 lines, of which about half are private labels. These lines include, for example, "Basics" (an economy range similar to

Tesco's "Values"), "Taste the Difference" (a premium range similar to Tesco's "Finest"), "Different by Design" (a smaller range of premium non-food lines), "Kids," "Be Good to Yourself" (products with reduced calorific and/or fat content), "Free from," "Sainsbury Organic," "Fair Trade," and "Super Naturals™" (a range of ready-made meals with healthy ingredients).

While service offerings today are quite similar, the rivals' distribution strategies differ significantly. In common with most other large retailers, Tesco decided to draw goods from suppliers into regional distribution centers for preparation and delivery to stores. Tesco is extending this logistic practice to cover collection from suppliers (factory gate pricing) and input to suppliers in a drive to reduce costs and improve reliability.

In contrast, Sainsbury's has heavily invested in fully automated depots. On January 14, 2000, Sir Peter Davis was appointed Sainsbury's CEO. This decision was well received by investors and analysts, as in his first two years he raised profits above targets. By 2004, however, the group had suffered a decline in performance relative to its competitors and fell to third in the U.K. food market. Davis oversaw an almost £3 billion upgrade of stores, distribution, and IT equipment. Part of this investment included the construction of four fully automated depots, which, at £100 million each, cost four times more than standard depots.

Loyalty Programs

Retailers try to gain the loyalty of their customers in various ways. Tesco was the first to launch a Clubcard system. It was introduced in 1995 and has become the most popular card in the United Kingdom, with around 13 million active Clubcard holders. Customers collect one Clubcard point for every £1 (€1 in Ireland) they spend in a Tesco store, Tesco Petrol, or at Tesco.com. Customers also collect points by paying with a Tesco credit card or by using Tesco Mobile, Tesco Homephone, Tesco Broadband, selected Tesco Personal Finance products, or by using its Clubcard partners, Powergen or Avis. Each point is worth 1p in-store when redeemed or 4p when used with Clubcard deals (offers for holidays, day trips, etc.). Every three months, holders receive a Clubcard statement offering discount coupons that can be spent in-store, online (if opted into eVouchers), or on various Clubcard deals. The program has numerous partners (e.g., hundreds of British pubs), but the Clubcard belongs to Tesco alone. Tesco implemented the Clubcard rewards program to gather customer information, which is then used to cater to specific potential customer needs and wants. When shoppers sign up for the card, they automatically submit their ages, genders, and incomes.

Tesco segments their shoppers on the basis of these factors. As soon as the shopper uses the card online or in-store, product information is automatically uploaded into the Tesco database. Product information is used to cross-sell additional products and services, such as food delivery.

Tesco is the most customer-focused business that I have ever worked for. They are absolutely obsessed with the customer.
—**John Hoerner, Non-Food Director, Tesco**

Sainsbury's was "wrong-footed" in its original reaction to the Tesco Clubcard, showing "no immediate response apart from disdain."[4] It lost market share in subsequent years. In 2004, the *London Times* quoted a former executive and others who viewed this event as the start of the company's downturn due to management failures by David Sainsbury and his successors, Dino Adriano and Peter Davis. David Sainsbury, who in 1992 replaced his cousin, the long-time CEO John Sainsbury, first dismissed Tesco's Clubcard. After long internal debates, Sainsbury introduced the Sainsbury's reward card in 1996. A multiparty card program, "Nectar," was launched in the autumn of 2002. Nectar gives the customer a versatile and powerful point-gathering system to be used and redeemed at a variety of stores. In Nectar, Sainsbury's has strong partners such as Barclaycard, British Petroleum, and the department store chain Debenhams. The Nectar card was re-launched in summer 2007 to celebrate its fifth anniversary. The scheme was changed from a reward- to a treats-based program. In its early days, the Nectar scheme was criticized as being among the worst card schemes offered. At the time, it was said that some consumers who spent £5,000 on Barclaycard received as little as £12.50 in points to redeem, while Sainsbury's customers had to spend as much as £1,000 just to get two tickets to the cinema. Today, points on spending in-store are earned at a rate of two points per £1 spent (except 1 point per liter of fuel); 500 points can subsequently be exchanged for a voucher worth £2.50 to spend in Sainsbury's. The card scheme is run by a third-party company, Loyalty Management UK (LMUK), which collects information on behalf of the partner sponsors.

Online Sales Channels

Toward the end of the 1990s, both firms targeted online distribution channels that promised large growth potential. Non-store retailing growth rates were expected to be higher than store-based rates, as online usage gained popularity among British consumers (see Exhibit 3). Following these predictions, the United

Exhibit 3 Retailing: Growth in Value Sales by Broad Sector/Sector 2001–2006 (percentage of current value growth)

	2005–2006	2001–2006 CAGR	2001–2006 Total
Non-store retailing	13.3	13.8	91.2
Internet retailing	24.8	32.9	313.9
Vending	2.5	5.0	27.7
Home shopping	2.8	3.8	20.6
Direct selling	−1.0	−1.5	−7.4
Store-based retailing	2.4	3.7	19.8
Food retailers	3.0	4.0	21.7
Non-food retailers	1.9	3.4	18.3
Retailing	3.1	4.2	23.1

Source: 2007, Official statistics, trade associations, trade press, company research, trade interviews, Euromonitor International estimates; Euromonitor, U.K. Retail Market: Market overview.

Kingdom has evolved into a leader of Internet retailing in Europe, and growth is continuing.

Tesco[5] has operated on the Internet since 1994 and was the first retailer in the world to offer a robust home-shopping service in 1996. Tesco.com was formally launched in 2000. It also has online operations in the Republic of Ireland and in South Korea. Food sales are available within delivery range of selected stores, goods being hand-picked within each store, in contrast to the warehouse model followed by most competitors (e.g., Ocado[6]), which allows rapid expansion with limited investment. In 2003, Tesco.com's then-CEO, John Browett, received the Wharton Infosys Business Transformation Award for the innovative processes he used to support this online food service. Today, Tesco operates the world's largest food home-shopping service, as well as provides consumer goods, telecommunications, and financial services online. As of November 2006, Tesco was the only food retailer to make online shopping profitable.

Sainsbury's has been involved in e-business and home-shopping development since 2000, when it launched Sainsbury's to You in April of that year. Although some employees transferred from the traditional side of the business, Sainsbury's also hired new staff with Web and marketing skills. Specific training was provided on e-business, as well as cross-functional training. Sainsbury's to You did not completely spin off

but occupied a separate building, thereby combining entrepreneurial flexibility with the strength and security of a strong brand. Sainsbury's Online currently operates from 144 stores and uses two dedicated picking centers that are not open to the public. In addition to food, also available are flowers, wine, gifts, and electronics. In October 2007, Sainsbury's was receiving around 80,000 online orders per week. This represents quite strong growth, but is far less than Tesco, which processes weekly orders of 250,000. Sainsbury's did not release any e-commerce sales figures, but said it was still on track to expand its Web service to 200 stores by March 2010. Tesco.com captured two-thirds of all online food orders in the first seven months of 2007, generating sales of approximately £2.5 million per day. Sainsburystoyou.com took third place with 14 percent, behind ASDA with 16 percent. Customers of Sainsbury's, however, spent the most per order, averaging almost £90, compared to £80 for both Tesco and ASDA. ASDA and Sainsbury's online shoppers also bought more items per order, with both averaging 69 units per order compared to 58 for Tesco. Sainsbury's online customers incurred the lowest average delivery charge during the period, at just over £3. Tesco online customers paid over £4 per delivery, and ASDA online customers paid nearly £5.50.

Diversification into Non-Food

A number of retailers have created such sense of nearness with customers in terms of perception, safety and security that you can refer to them as brands.
— **KAREL VUURSTEEN, CHAIRMAN & CEO, HEINEKEN**

Originally specializing in food, Tesco began to diversify into areas such as discount clothes, consumer electronics, consumer financial services, DVD sales and rentals, compact discs and music downloads, Internet service, consumer telecoms, consumer health insurance, consumer dental plans, and budget software. In these new product segments, Tesco heavily built on its skills in private labels. For example, it introduced brands such as "Cherokee" and "F+F" in clothing, "Technika" and "Digilogic" in consumer electronics, and other labels ranging from DVD players to televisions and computers. Tesco used its food brands "Finest" and "Value" to expand into non-food items. In its Extra stores, Finest health and beauty, home, and clothing lines resulted.

In 1997, Tesco Personal Finance was launched as a fifty-fifty banking joint venture with the Royal Bank of Scotland. Products offered included credit cards, loans, mortgages, savings accounts, and several types of insurance, including car, home, life, pet, and travel. They are promoted by leaflets in Tesco stores and through its

Web site. All of its offers are simple, providing customers few but clear options and choices. Profits were £130 million for the 52 weeks prior to February 24, 2007, of which Tesco's share was £66 million. This move toward the financial sector has diversified the Tesco brand and provides opportunities for growth outside the retailing sector. For example, Tesco offers Clubcard points or free petrol when consumers purchase Tesco car insurance. The company is currently conducting trials at a finance center in the Glasgow Silverburn Extra store, providing free financial advice and quotes for insurance and loans; this service is staffed by trained Royal Bank of Scotland employees. The center also has a Euro cash machine providing commission-free Euros and a Bureau de Change run by Travelex. If successful, this service will be rolled out to more key and flagship stores.

Tesco also entered the telecommunications sector. Though it launched its Internet service provider in 1998, the company was not seriously active in telecommunications until 2003. Rather than purchasing or building its own telecom network, Tesco paired its marketing strength with the expertise of existing telecom operators. In autumn 2003, Tesco Mobile was launched as a joint venture with O2, and Tesco Home Phone was created in partnership with Cable & Wireless. In August 2004, Tesco Broadband, an ADSL-based service delivered via BT phone lines, was launched in partnership with NTL. In January 2006, Tesco Internet Phone, a Voice over Internet Protocol service, was launched in conjunction with Freshtel of Australia. Simple and clear offering logic is also evident in the strategic move into telecommunications. Tesco Mobile offers only four different pay-as-you-go tariffs: Value, Standard, Extra, and Staff (for employees). Tesco announced in December 2004 that it had signed up 500,000 customers to its mobile service in the 12 months since launch. By December 2005, one million customers were using its mobile service, and by April 2006, Tesco claimed over one and, one-half million telecom accounts in total, including mobile, fixed line, and broadband. On December 19, 2006, Tesco Ireland announced that it would enter into a joint venture with O2 Ireland to offer mobile telecommunications services, also under the Tesco Mobile brand.

Recently, Tesco entered the housing market with a self-advertising Web site, Tesco Property Market. Other strategic initiatives into non-food items include, for example, following a successful trial in 2006, "Apple" zones in 12 outlets, where the iPod range is sold alongside Mac computers and other Apple products.

Sainsbury's was much more reluctant to move into non-food retailing. Inspired by the success of its main rivals (ASDA had also moved strongly into the non-food area) and the sheer size of the U.K. non-food retail market (in 2003, it was estimated at over £100 million), it launched 2,500 home and cookware products in September 2003. Copying Tesco, Sainsbury's also used its own food brands and transferred them to non-food items. For example, it extended its clothing range with an organic line. In addition to food and non-food items, Sainsbury's expanded into retail banking and property development. In 1997, Sainsbury's bank was established as a joint venture between J Sainsbury plc and the Bank of Scotland (now HBOS). Sainsbury's bank offers services similar to Tesco's, including travel (insurance and money), savings, and lending; it also offers a Sainsbury's credit card. By 2010, Sainsbury's expects to achieve sales of £3.5 billion, with 33 percent of its total sales coming from non-food businesses.

International Diversification

These results show that our new growth businesses—in international, in non-food and in services—have contributed as much profit as the entire business was making in 1997.

—CEO TERRY LEAHY, 2005

Tesco's international expansion[7] began in the late 1970s with the purchase of a small company in the Republic of Ireland. The small-scale nature of this first foray was seen as a weakness, and the company was eventually sold in the mid-1980s. In 1994, Tesco acquired the Scottish supermarket chain William Low. Tesco successfully fought off Sainsbury's for control of the Dundee-based firm, which then operated 57 stores. This paved the way for Tesco to expand its presence in Scotland, where it was weaker than in England. Inverness was recently branded "Tescotown" because well over 50p in every £1 spent on food is believed to be spent in its three Tesco stores. In March 1997, Tesco announced the purchase of the retail arm of Associated British Foods, which consisted of the Quinnsworth, Stewarts, and Crazy Prices chains in the Republic of Ireland and Northern Ireland, as well as associated businesses, for £640 million. This acquisition gave Tesco both a major presence in the Republic of Ireland and a larger presence in Northern Ireland than Sainsbury's, which had begun its move into the province in 1995.

In the 1990s, Tesco strongly expanded overseas by increasing investments in emerging markets such as Hungary, the Czech Republic, Thailand, and South Korea. Tesco was buying into successful companies, a strategy that resulted in strong positions in these markets. In 1997, the new CEO, Terry Leahy, enforced Tesco's international growth strategies beyond Great Britain. However, outside the United Kingdom the supermarket firm's position was far from dominant and remained in the shadow of larger, more high-profile international operators such as Wal-Mart and Carrefour. Tesco then analyzed countries for expansion, putting high emphasis on two dimensions: the market potential for growth and the competitive situation in the market. Only if a market was characterized by relatively high growth potential and relatively low rivalry was it considered a real target market and approached in an orderly fashion.

In 2002, Tesco purchased 13 HIT hypermarkets in Poland. In June 2003, Tesco purchased the C Two-Network in Japan. It also acquired a majority stake in the Turkish supermarket chain Kipa. Another acquisition was the Lotus chain in Thailand. In mid-2006, Tesco purchased an 80 percent stake in Casino's Leader Price supermarkets in Poland, which were subsequently reconfigured as small Tesco stores.

Many British retailers attempting to build international businesses have failed. Tesco has responded to the need to be sensitive to local expectations in foreign countries by entering into joint ventures with local partners, such as Samsung Group in South Korea (Samsung-Tesco Homeplus), and Charoen Pokphand in Thailand (Tesco Lotus), and by appointing a high proportion of local personnel to management positions.

In late 2004, the amount of floor space Tesco operated outside the United Kingdom surpassed its home market space for the first time, although the United Kingdom still accounted for more than 75 percent of group revenue due to lower sales per unit area outside the territory (for an overview of Tesco's international store portfolio, see Exhibit 4). Tesco regularly continues to make small acquisitions to expand its international businesses. For example, in the 2005–06 fiscal year, acquisitions were made in South Korea, Poland, and Japan.

In September 2005, Tesco announced that it was selling its operations in Taiwan to Carrefour and purchasing Carrefour stores in the Czech Republic and Slovakia. Both companies stated that they were concentrating their efforts in countries where they had strong market positions. Tesco entered China by acquiring a 50 percent stake in the Hymall chain from Ting Hsin of

Exhibit 4 Tesco's Store Portfolio "International"

Country	Entered	Stores	Area (m²)	Area (sq ft)	Turnover (£ million)
China	2004	47	392,422	4,224,000	552
Czech Republic	1996	84	381,459	4,106,000	807
France	1992	1	1,400	16,000	Note 3
Hungary	1994	101	448,164	4,824,000	1,180
Republic of Ireland	1997	95	205,780	2,215,000	1,683
Japan	2003	109	29,078	313,000	287
Malaysia	2002	19	174,750	1,881,000	247
Poland	1995	280	606,935	6,533,000	1,135
Slovakia	1996	48	225,475	2,427,000	498
South Korea	1999	81	473,340	5,095,000	2,557
Thailand	1998	370	698,166	7,515,000	1,326
Turkey	2003	30	102,936	1,108,000	256
United States of America	2007	6	Unknown	60,000 (est.)	Unknown

Note 1: The store numbers and floor area figures are as of February 24, 2007, but the turnover figures are for the year 2005, except for the Republic of Ireland data, which are for the year ending February 24, 2007, like the U.K. figures. This information is taken from the 2007 final broker pack.

Note 2: China: Joint venture in February 2006; now a 90 percent–owned subsidiary.

Note 3: France: Tesco owned a French chain called Catteau between 1992 and 1997. Its existing single store in France is a wine warehouse in Calais (opened in 1995 and targeted at British day trippers).

Note 4: Malaysia: Tesco Stores (Malaysia) Sdn Bhd was incepted on November 29, 2001, as a strategic alliance with local conglomerate, Sime Darby Bhd of which the latter holds 30 percent of total shares.

Taiwan in September 2004. In December 2006, it raised its stake to 90 percent in a £180 million deal, which was just after Tesco lost out to Wal-Mart to partner with the Indian group, Bharti, to develop a national retail chain in India.

In February 2006, Tesco announced its intention to move into the United States, opening a chain of convenience stores on the West Coast (Arizona and California), Fresh & Easy Neighborhood Market. The first store was opened in November 2007, with 100 more openings scheduled in the first year. By planning to open a new store in the United States every two-and-one-half days, Tesco intends to mimic the successful expansion of U.S. pharmacy chains such as Walgreens. Tesco's strategy and unorthodox tactics have not been without controversy. In 2005 and 2006, the company covertly sent an advance team consisting of executives in disguise to conduct intelligence on potential competitors. Like a James Bond movie, the company's agents sought to keep their plans secret by posing as Hollywood film producers making a movie about supermarkets, according to *BusinessWeek*. The bold operation collected intelligence on the U.S. market and on competitors such as Wal-Mart, Kroger, Safeway, Albertson's, Whole Foods, and Trader Joe's. The covert operation was so unusual and unsettling that some potential rivals hired security teams to infiltrate Tesco and obtain information about executives involved in the operation. In the end, Tesco did obtain the necessary information to proceed with its store openings. A Tesco senior manager said, "For me, it is remarkable that in five years Tesco has moved from being a U.K.-based supermarket chain to become an international mixed retail and services business. This rapid transformation is based on clarity at the top and a tremendous creativity and energy in making it happen quickly." Sainsbury's international strategy can be described as that of a fast follower, albeit with varying results and to a lesser extent. It expanded its operations into Scotland, opening a store in Darnley in January 1992. In June 1995, Sainsbury's announced its intention to move into the Northern Ireland market, which had until that point been dominated by local companies. Between December 1996 and December 1998, the company opened seven stores. Two others at Sprucefield, Lisburn, and Holywood Exchange, Belfast, would not open until 2003 due to protracted legal challenges. Sainsbury's move into Northern Ireland was undertaken in a very different way than that of Tesco. While Sainsbury's outlets were all new developments, Tesco (apart from one Tesco Metro) instead purchased existing chains from Associated British Foods (see Tesco Ireland). In 1999, Sainsbury's acquired an 80.1 percent share of the Egyptian Distribution Group SAE, a retailer in Egypt with 100 stores and 2,000 employees. However, poor profitability led to the sale of this share in 2001.

Management Teams

At the end of March 2004, Davis was promoted to chairman and was replaced as CEO of Sainsbury's by Justin King. Justin King joined Sainsbury's from Marks and Spencer plc, where he was a director with responsibility for its food division and Kings Super Markets, Inc, a subsidiary in the United States. King was also previously a managing director at ASDA, with responsibility for hypermarkets. In June 2004, Davis was forced to resign as chairman in the face of an impending shareholder revolt over his salary and bonuses. Investors were angered by a bonus share award of over £2 million, despite poor company performance. In July 2004, Philip Hampton was appointed chairman. Hampton had previously worked for British Steel, British Gas, BT, and Lloyds TSB.

King perceived Sainsbury's to be not sufficiently focused on its customers or its main competitors. King ordered a direct mail campaign to one million Sainsbury's customers, asking what they wanted from the company and where the company could improve. Results re-affirmed the commentary of retail analysts; that is, the group was not ensuring that shelves were fully stocked, partly due to the failure of the IT systems introduced by Peter Davis. In October 2004, King unveiled the results of the business review and his plans to revive the company's fortunes. This was generally well received by both the stock market and the media. Immediate plans included terminating 750 headquarters staff and recruiting around 3,000 shop floor staff to improve the quality of service and the firm's problem of stock availability. Another significant announcement was the decision to halve the dividend in order to increase funds available to offer price cuts and to improve quality. The company's fortunes have improved since the launch of this recovery program.

In 2004, King hired Lawrence Christensen, previously an expert in logistics at Safeway, as supply chain director. Immediate supply chain improvements included the reactivation of two distribution centers. In 2006, Christensen commented on the four automated depots introduced by Davis, saying, "[N]ot a single day went by without one, if not all of them, breaking down ... the systems were flawed. They have to stop for four hours every day for maintenance. But because they were constantly breaking down you would be playing catch up. It was a vicious circle." Christensen felt that a fundamental mistake was to build four such depots at once, rather than building one and testing it thoroughly before building the others. In 2007, Sainsbury's announced an additional £12 million investment in its depots to keep pace with sales growth and to remove the failed automated systems from its depots.

The Competitive Landscape Today

The situation today is clear. Tesco has outpaced its closest rival in its local and international markets. Edward Garner, communications director of the TNS Superpanel, said, "TNS supermarket share information shows that the retailer's market share has grown consistently and strongly over the last decade and shows no sign of abating."

These events led to shifts in the competitive landscape. The U.K. retail industry has become highly concentrated. The top four store-based retailers—Tesco, Sainsbury's ASDA, and Morrison's Supermarkets—dominate the market; all are original food retailers. This illustrates the status of food retailers in the market (see Exhibit 5). All are British, except ASDA, which was acquired in 1999 by the U.S. retail giant Wal-Mart.

Discounters adapted to this less-favorable environment by slightly improving their meager U.K. presence by expanding their number of outlets and moving upscale. This was helped by the trend of consumers to increasingly combine bargain shopping with purchases of luxury products or services. This "schizophrenic" shopping behavior blurs previously separate boundaries. The traditional structure of upper, middle, and mass market has been more or less abolished.

Since the launch of King's recovery program, Sainsbury's has reported nine consecutive quarters of sales growth, most recently in March 2007, even outpacing Tesco, making the company's performance the best since its glory days of the 1980s and early 1990s. Sales increases were credited to solving problems with the company's distribution system. More recent sales improvements have been attributed to significant price cuts and the company's focus on fresh and healthy food. On October 4, 2007, Sainsbury's announced plans to relocate their Store Support Centre from Holborn to Kings Cross in 2011. This office, part of a new building complex, will allow both cost savings and energy efficiency.

Despite this positive news, according to the latest Taylor Nelson Sofres rankings published in March 2007, Sainsbury's market share in food retailing remains third in the United Kingdom at 16.37 percent compared to Tesco's 31.35 percent, ASDA's 16.83 percent, and Morrison's 11.08 percent (see Exhibit 6). Tesco remains the clear market leader. In the past, Tesco showed itself

Exhibit 5 Retailing: Company Shares by Value 2004–2006 (in percentage of retail value)

	2004	2005	2006
Tesco plc	10.2	11.0	11.4
J Sainsbury plc	5.4	5.8	5.9
Asda Stores Ltd	4.7	4.9	5.1
Wm Morrison Supermarkets plc	3.7	3.7	3.5
Marks and Spencer plc	2.7	2.7	2.7
Alliance Boots plc	—	—	2.1
Dixons Group plc	1.3	1.4	1.4
Argos plc	1.3	1.4	1.4
B&Q plc	1.5	1.5	1.4
Somerfield Ltd	1.7	1.7	1.3
Waitrose Ltd	1.0	1.0	1.2
Co-operative Group (CWS) Ltd	1.3	1.3	1.2
Next plc	1.0	1.0	1.1
Spar Ltd (UK)	0.8	0.9	0.9
Debenhams Retail plc	0.7	0.8	0.8

Source: 2007, Official statistics, trade associations, trade press, company research, trade interviews, Euromonitor International estimates; Euromonitor, U.K. Retail Market: Market overview.

to be the quickest at seizing expansion opportunities. Furthermore, it has succeeded in building an image of providing good value at low prices.

The recovery in the Sainsbury market share builds on the positive picture already established. This strong performance has been achieved in the face of relentless pressure from Tesco, which continues its recent run of double-digit turnover growth. . . .

Whilst Tesco remains dominant, there are signs that it is experiencing increased competition. It is still growing, but the year-on-year share increase is below the average we were seeing last year. Looking towards the future, Tesco will continue to face challenging competition from its nearest competitor Asda as well as the likes of Sainsbury's, which is showing positive growth trends and Morrisons once the Safeway store conversions are complete. Tesco will need to prove its ability to meet increasingly challenging consumer demands and stay a step ahead of the competition. . . .

Exhibit 6 Food Retailing: Company Shares by Sales 1990–2007 (in percentage of retail value)

	1990	...	1994	1995	...	2002	...	2004	2005	2006	2007
Tesco plc	9.7		11.4	13.4		16.7		27.5	29.8	31.1	31.35
J Sainsbury plc	11.0		12.3	12.2		11.7		15.5	15.9	16.0	16.37
Asda Stores Ltd	6.8		6.7	7.2		10.6		16.6	16.5	16.4	16.83
Wm Morrison Supermarkets plc (Safeway included)						7.5 (only Safeway)		14.4	12.2	11.3	11.08

Source: TNS (Taylor Nelson Sofres) World Panel market-share data released June 2007.

Future Internationalization: It has a long way to go before it overhauls Wal-Mart as the world's biggest grocer—but analysts said the same about overhauling Sainsbury's in the U.K. market 15 years ago and now Tesco is almost double its size.

—EDWARD GARNER, COMMUNICATIONS DIRECTOR OF TNS SUPERPANEL, 2007

New Challenges Ahead

After a relatively long period of economic growth during the review period, conditions may well stagnate in the coming years, thus dampening the forecast performance of store-based retailing. Consumer debt levels have reached record highs and, with the United Kingdom's negative saving rate, there is less room for continued growth in consumption. As a result, discounters (both food and non-food) are well placed to gain importance. Euromonitor predicts food retailers to outperform non-food retailers with a value compound annual growth rate of 1 percent. Recent trends, such as health and wellness and ethical concerns, have opened opportunities, even in the saturated food category; however, most food retailers' growth is expected to stem from non-food items.

Consolidation is expected to continue (see the Safeway takeover), with independent shops closing, being taken over, or joining larger chains. This is evident in the decline of the number of total outlets, particularly independent ones.

Sainsbury's might be the target of additional takeover bids, since family investment in the company is only 18 percent. A first private equity bid was considered by CVC Capital Partners, Kohlberg Kravis Roberts (which later left the consortium in order to focus on its bid for Alliance Boots), and Blackstone Group; in February 2007, this also included Goldman Sachs and Texas Pacific Group. The initial offer submitted in April 2007 of 562p a share was rejected after discussions between Sainsbury's top management and the two largest family shareholders. A subsequent offer of 582p a share was also rejected. As a consequence, the CVC-led consortium abandoned its quest, stating "[I]t became clear the consortium would be unable to make a proposal that would result in a successful offer." In April 2007, Delta Two, a Qatari investment company, bought a 14 percent stake in Sainsbury's (causing its share price to rise 7.17 percent); this stake was increased to 25 percent in June 2007. On July 18, 2007, BBC News reported that Delta Two had tabled a conditional bid proposal. On November 5, 2007, it was announced that Delta Two had abandoned its takeover bid due to the "deterioration of credit markets" and concerns about funding the company's pension scheme. Following the withdrawal of the interest of Qatari investment, shares in Sainsbury's dropped about 20 percent (115p) to 440p on the day of this announcement.

Appendix 1 Retail: Number of Employees: 2001–2006 (in thousands)

	2001	2002	2003	2004	2005	2006
Retail employees	3,048	3,077	3,136	3,308	3,329	3,316
% growth	—	1.0	1.9	5.5	0.6	−0.4

Source: 2007, Official statistics, trade associations, trade press, company research, trade interviews, Euromonitor International estimates; Euromonitor, U.K. Retail Market: Market overview.

Appendix 2 Number of Employees of Food Retailers (full-time equivalents)

Employees	2006	2007
Tesco	380,000	318,283
Asda	150,000 90,000 part-time 60,000 full-time	143,125
Sainsbury's	96,200 104,100 part-time 49,200 full-time	95,500 98,100 part-time 48,800 full-time

Appendix 3 Tesco's Financial Figures

52 weeks ended	Turnover (£m)	Profit before Tax (£m)	Profit for Year (£m)	Basic Earnings per Share (p)
2007	46,600	2,653	1,899	22.36
2006	38,300	2,210	1,576	19.70
2005	33,974	1,962	1,366	17.44
2004	30,814	1,600	1,100	15.05
2003	26,337	1,361	946	13.54
2002	23,653	1,201	830	12.05
2001	20,988	1,054	767	11.29
2000	18,796	933	674	10.07
1999	17,158	842	606	9.14
1998	16,452	760	532	8.12

Note: The numbers include non-UK and Ireland results.

Appendix 4 Growth Rates (Tesco vs. Sainsbury) 1990–2007

Growth Rates (%)	Sales	Operating Income	Net Income	Div. Per Share	Equity	Total Assets
Sainsbury's Y2007				21.88		
Tesco Y2007	8.08	5.88	20.51	11.70	12.00	9.86
Sainsbury's Y2006	5.65	7.55	−64.67	2.56	−0.21	9.24
Tesco Y2006	16.50	13.40	16.82	14.15	9.03	11.97
Sainsbury's Y2005	−10.10	−53.04	−84.60	−56.50	−15.48	−7.11
Tesco Y2005	10.26	12.47	24.18	10.53	13.76	10.12
Sainsbury's Y2004	−1.66	−2.03	−12.78	0.70	2.05	4.70
Tesco Y2004	17.00	19.78	16.28	10.32	22.50	12.68

(Continued)

Appendix 4 Growth Rates (Tesco vs. Sainsbury) 1990–2007 (*Continued*)

Growth Rates (%)	Sales	Operating Income	Net Income	Div. Per Share	Equity	Total Assets
Sainsbury's Y2003	1.56	11.46	24.73	4.99	3.30	8.76
Tesco Y2003	11.35	12.49	13.98	10.71	18.24	21.91
Sainsbury's Y2002	7.57	9.95	38.93	3.63	−1.31	6.85
Tesco Y2002	12.70	13.29	8.21	12.45	4.02	16.00
Sainsbury's Y2001	−1.95	−5.78	−24.93	—	3.23	−1.94
Tesco Y2001	11.66	12.55	13.80	11.16	12.05	18.80
Sainsbury's Y2000	−0.99	−25.32	−41.64	—	0.65	4.32
Tesco Y2000	9.55	7.92	11.22	8.74	9.58	13.88
Sainsbury's Y1999	13.33	8.48	22.79	3.02	12.89	10.13
Tesco Y1999	7.81	5.03	20.00	6.54	10.42	15.58
Sainsbury's Y1998	8.25	11.58	20.84	13.01	12.01	25.23
Tesco Y1998	14.60	18.09	−2.88	12.09	−0.36	12.32
Sainsbury's Y1997	6.08	−11.94	−17.42	1.65	3.88	7.88
Tesco Y1997	14.83	6.91	11.59	7.81	8.78	6.74
Sainsbury's Y1996	11.18	−4.09	−8.87	3.43	7.45	15.81
Tesco Y1996	19.73	17.34	22.63	11.61	15.21	5.01
Sainsbury's Y1995	7.31	13.36	278.18	10.38	8.21	6.22
Tesco Y1995	17.45	18.38	27.43	10.99	12.92	18.84
Sainsbury's Y1994	9.27	1.80	−71.84	5.99	0.36	3.95
Tesco Y1994	13.43	−5.53	−28.59	9.13	−0.15	9.82
Sainsbury's Y1993	11.39	17.48	14.74	14.29	14.68	12.26
Tesco Y1993	6.82	15.06	5.56	12.71	12.50	9.03
Sainsbury's Y1992	11.29	14.29	23.37	20.41	57.92	22.22
Tesco Y1992	11.84	20.48	30.69	20.00	13.29	13.01
Sainsbury's Y1991	12.74	23.83	13.23	20.50	18.98	14.75
Tesco Y1991	17.48	25.63	19.27	25.72	72.23	50.90
Sainsbury's Y1990	22.47	17.16	24.88	20.79	20.38	16.97
Tesco Y1990	14.50	20.50	36.23	22.86	21.60	19.75

Source: Thompson Database 2007.

Appendix 5 Financial Leverage and Return on Equity/Assets 1990–2007

Profitability (%)	Financial Leverage Tesco	Financial Leverage Sainsbury's	Return on Equity Tesco	Return on Equity Sainsbury's	Return on Assets Tesco	Return on Assets Sainsbury's
Y2007	42.41	45.42	18.81		8.62	
Y2006	41.59	30.62	17.50	1.67	8.11	1.02
Y2005	44.13	36.50	16.20	−1.10	7.86	1.56
Y2004	42.72	40.12	15.65	8.09	7.31	3.70
Y2003	39.29	41.16	16.17	9.49	7.37	4.59
Y2002	40.51	43.34	15.65	7.71	7.72	4.21
Y2001	45.18	46.92	15.62	5.60	8.30	3.34
Y2000	47.91	44.57	15.26	7.55	8.54	4.12
Y1999	49.78	46.20	14.99	13.71	8.56	6.94
Y1998	52.11	45.07	13.01	12.56	8.08	6.79
Y1997	58.74	50.38	13.98	11.21	8.74	6.63
Y1996	57.64	52.32	14.02	14.29	8.90	8.48
Y1995	52.54	56.39	13.00	16.88	8.08	10.04
Y1994	55.29	55.36	10.84	4.70	6.96	2.77
Y1993	60.81	57.34	16.07	17.74	10.58	10.39
Y1992	58.93	56.13	17.17	19.88	11.18	11.96
Y1991	58.79	43.44	19.36	23.11	11.12	12.05
Y1990	51.51	41.90	21.05	24.40	12.82	12.20

Source: Thompson Database 2007.

Appendix 6 Margins 1990–2007

Profitability (%)	Gross Margin Tesco	Gross Margin Sainsbury's	Op Profit Margin Tesco	Op Profit Margin Sainsbury's	Pretax Prof Margin Tesco	Pretax Prof Margin Sainsbury's
Y2007	7.60	6.83	5.02	3.00	5.91	2.78
Y2006	7.67	6.95	5.13	2.22	5.46	0.65
Y2005	7.77	7.20	5.89	2.21	5.49	0.10
Y2004	7.65	8.89	5.78	4.22	4.92	3.56
Y2003	7.50	8.20	5.64	4.24	4.96	3.83
Y2002	7.51	7.41	5.58	3.86	4.97	3.33

(Continued)

Appendix 6 Margins 1990–2007 (*Continued*)

Profitability (%)	Gross Margin Tesco	Gross Margin Sainsbury's	Op Profit Margin Tesco	Op Profit Margin Sainsbury's	Pretax Prof Margin Tesco	Pretax Prof Margin Sainsbury's
Y2001	7.53	6.69	5.56	3.78	5.01	2.72
Y2000	7.39	6.96	5.51	3.93	4.91	3.12
Y1999	7.77	7.87	5.60	5.22	4.87	5.33
Y1998	7.68	8.05	5.74	5.45	4.67	4.85
Y1997	7.27	7.43	5.57	5.29	5.40	4.40
Y1996	7.65	8.36	5.99	6.37	5.58	5.49
Y1995	7.70	9.29	6.11	7.38	5.45	7.07
Y1994	8.13	9.00	6.06	6.99	5.06	3.48
Y1993	9.33	9.68	7.28	7.50	7.66	7.57
Y1992	8.98	9.44	6.76	7.11	7.69	7.21
Y1991	8.46	9.21	6.27	6.92	6.87	6.63
Y1990	8.39	9.06	5.86	6.30	6.69	6.49

Source: Thompson Database 2007.

Appendix 7 Sales per Share, EPS, and Dividends 1990–2007

Profitability (%)	Sales per Share Data Tesco	Sales per Share Data Sainsbury's	EPS Tesco	EPS Sainsbury's	Dividend Tesco	Dividend Sainsbury's
Y2007	5.37	10.14	0.24	0.19	0.10	0.10
Y2006	5.04	9.57	0.20	0.04	0.09	0.08
Y2005	4.41	8.81	0.18	−0.03	0.08	0.08
Y2004	4.22	10.24	0.15	0.24	0.07	0.18
Y2003	3.77	10.42	0.14	0.27	0.06	0.18
Y2002	3.43	10.28	0.12	0.22	0.06	0.17
Y2001	3.09	9.59	0.11	0.16	0.05	0.16
Y2000	2.81	9.72	0.10	0.21	0.04	0.16
Y1999	2.59	9.84	0.09	0.36	0.04	0.16
Y1998	2.43	8.87	0.08	0.30	0.04	0.16
Y1997	2.14	8.34	0.08	0.25	0.03	0.14
Y1996	1.92	7.94	0.07	0.31	0.03	0.14
Y1995	1.68	7.22	0.06	0.34	0.03	0.13
Y1994	1.46	6.79	0.05	0.09	0.03	0.12
Y1993	1.30	6.27	0.07	0.33	0.02	0.11

Appendix 7 Sales per Share, EPSs and Dividends 1990–2007 (*Continued*)

Profitability (%)	Sales per Share Data Tesco	Sales per Share Data Sainsbury's	EPS Tesco	EPS Sainsbury's	Dividend Tesco	Dividend Sainsbury's
Y1992	1.22	5.83	0.07	0.29	0.02	0.10
Y1991	1.28	5.81	0.06	0.26	0.02	0.08
Y1990	1.13	5.19	0.05	0.24	0.01	0.07

Source: Thompson Database 2007.

Appendix 8 Retailing: Company Shares by Value 2004–2006 (in percentage of retail value)

Company	2004	2005	2006
Tesco plc	10.2	11.0	11.4
J Sainsbury plc	5.4	5.8	5.9
Asda Stores Ltd	4.7	4.9	5.1
Wm Morrison Supermarkets plc	3.7	3.7	3.5
Marks and Spencer plc	2.7	2.7	2.7
Alliance Boots plc	—	—	2.1
Dixons Group plc	1.3	1.4	1.4
Argos plc	1.3	1.4	1.4
B&Q plc	1.5	1.5	1.4
Somerfield Ltd	1.7	1.7	1.3
Waitrose Ltd	1.0	1.0	1.2
Co-operative Group (CWS) Ltd	1.3	1.3	1.2
Next plc	1.0	1.0	1.1
Spar Ltd (UK)	0.8	0.9	0.9
Debenhams Retail plc	0.7	0.8	0.8

Source: 2007, Official statistics, trade associations, trade press, company research, trade interviews, Euromonitor International estimates; Euromonitor, U.K. Retail Market: Market overview.

Appendix 9 Food Retailing: Company Shares by Value 2004–2006 (in percentage of retail value)

Company	2004	2005	2006
Tesco plc	23.0	24.4	25.2
J Sainsbury plc	12.5	13.1	13.3
Asda Stores Ltd	10.9	11.0	11.2
Wm Morrison Supermarkets plc	8.7	8.5	8.1
Somerfield Ltd	4.0	3.8	3.1
Waitrose Ltd	2.3	2.3	2.8

(*Continued*)

Appendix 9 Food Retailing: Company Shares by Value 2004–2006 (in percentage of retail value) (*Continued*)

Company	2004	2005	2006
Co-operative Group (CWS) Ltd	2.7	2.6	2.5
Spar Ltd (UK)	2.0	2.0	2.0
Musgrave Group plc	1.6	1.8	1.8
Lidl Ltd	1.0	1.1	1.1
Aldi Stores Ltd	0.9	1.0	1.1
Iceland Frozen Foods Ltd.	1.2	1.1	1.0
Others	26.6	24.8	23.6

Source: 2007, Official statistics, trade associations, trade press, company research, trade interviews, Euromonitor International estimates; Euromonitor, U.K. Retail Market: Market overview.

Appendix 10 Food Retailers: Value Sales by Sector 2001–2006 (in millions of pounds, current rsp)

Retailer Type	2001	2002	2003	2004	2005	2006
Supermarkets	40,502.8	42,591.0	43,106.1	44,356.0	45,198.8	46,284.0
Hypermarkets	22,766.5	24,677.2	27,569.9	31,698.9	35,521.1	38,175.9
Convenience stores	10,514.3	11,895.7	13,729.7	14,306.0	14,577.8	14,875.2
Food/drink/tobacco specialists	12,074.0	11,460.6	11,100.0	10,700.0	10,144.0	9,667.0
Independent grocers	8,563.0	8,135.0	7,647.0	7,119.4	6,592.5	6,203.6
Discounters	2,395.0	2,582.6	2,672.2	2,725.4	2,980.2	3,375.5
Other food retailers	2,365.7	2,395.0	2,218.9	2,159.0	2,129.0	2,088.0
Food retailers	99,181.2	102,737.0	108,043.9	113,064.6	117,143.4	120,669.1

Source: 2007, Official statistics, trade associations, trade press, company research, trade interviews, Euromonitor International estimates; Euromonitor, U.K. Retail Market: Market overview.

Appendix 11 Food Retailers: Growth in Value Sales by Sector 2001–2006 (percentage of current value growth)

Retailer Type	2005/2006	2001–2006 CAGR	2001/2006 TOTAL
Hypermarkets	7.5	10.9	67.7
Convenience stores	2.0	7.2	41.5
Discounters	13.3	7.1	40.9
Supermarkets	2.4	2.7	14.3
Other food retailers	−1.9	−2.5	−11.7
Food/drink/tobacco specialists	−4.7	−4.3	−19.9
Independent grocers	−5.9	−6.2	−27.6
Food retailers	3.0	4.0	21.7

Source: 2007, Official statistics, trade associations, trade press, company research, trade interviews, Euromonitor International estimates; Euromonitor, U.K. Retail Market: Market overview.

Appendix 12 Share Price Tesco vs. Sainsbury (1990–2007)

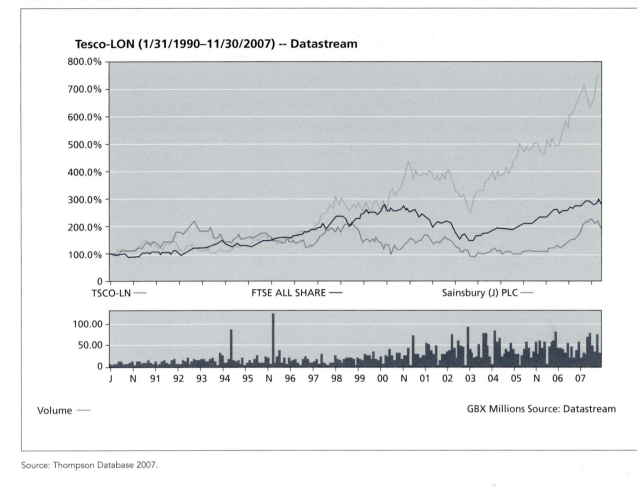

Source: Thompson Database 2007.

NOTES

1. The largest retailers in the world ranked by sales in 2005, http://www.chainstoreage.com.
2. For more information on ASDA and how the purchase of Asda by Wal-Mart in 1999 changed the competitive scenario of the U.K. retail industry, see, for example, Dhar & Sushma, 2005,: Tesco vs. Asda: UK's retailing battle, ECCH Case: 305-623-1.
3. For more detailed information on Tesco's store formats in 2003, see, for example, Padmini & Himansu, 2003, Tesco in 2003, ECCH Case: 304-173-1.
4. The article "Surpassing Sainsbury" describes Tesco's market-share dominance since the introduction of the Clubcard.

5. For Tesco's online sales strategy, see also Pole, 2007, Tesco's online sales strategy, ECCH Case: 507-024-1; Mukund, 2003, http://www.tesco.com: A rare profitable dotcom, ECCH Case: 903-034-1.
6. Ocado was launched in January 2002, in partnership with Waitrose and is today available to over 13.5 million households in the United Kingdom.
7. For Tesco's global expansion strategies, see also Bhavika & Phani Madhav, 2005, Tesco: The British supermarket chain's global expansion strategies and challenges, ECCH Case: 305-350-1.

Andrew Inkpen, Michael Moffett

Thunderbird School of Global Management

In July 2008, BP was embroiled in a dispute with the Russian shareholders of its TNK-BP joint venture. The Russian shareholders, a group led by billionaires Mikhail Fridman, Viktor Vekselberg, and Len Blavatnik, were demanding the removal of TNK-BP Chief Executive Robert Dudley. The Russian shareholders maintained that BP was not adequately controlling costs and was blocking efforts to expand TNK-BP outside of Russia because that would compete with BP's own operations. They also claimed that BP was employing too many highly paid expatriates in Russia. BP's response was that the venture's main area of operation was always meant to be Russia and Ukraine. According to Dudley: "The company's corporate governance is being tested and the fate of the company is a bellwether for Russia's progress in improving the way its companies are run ... For five years, one of my roles has been trying to balance all the issues of shareholders. And I think the ability to keep this balance is important, and I will try to keep that balance."[1]

In comments made to the French newspaper, *Le Monde*, Russian Prime Minister Vladimir Putin said that he had warned both sides that the 50-50 structure would be problematic: "You shouldn't do this ... Work it out between yourselves so someone has a controlling stake...There needs to be a boss ... You see the result: There's always friction over who's in charge."[2]

With events escalating, Robert Dudley and BP senior management were faced with a challenging situation. Losing its stake in TNK-BP would have serious financial implications for BP. TNK-BP accounted for nearly one-quarter of BP's oil production, and close to one-fifth of its reserves. How the situation was resolved would have a lasting impact on BP and its presence in Russia. The resolution would also impact Russia's overall reputation for attracting and supporting foreign investment.

BP

BP, formerly British Petroleum, was the world's third-largest oil and gas supermajor. Originally founded as the Anglo-Persian Oil Company, BP went from a public company to a British state-owned entity, and then back to being publicly traded during the Thatcher years. BP made many acquisitions over the past century, including Standard Oil of Ohio, Amoco, Castrol, Aral, and Arco. BP's upstream business operated in various countries, including the United States, the United Kingdom, Australia, Angola, Azerbaijan, Canada, Egypt, Russia, Trinidad, Tobago, and Indonesia. The company also operated a diverse range of pipeline, refining, chemical, and retail assets around the world. In recent years, the company had adopted the tagline "Beyond Petroleum" as a way to distinguish itself from its hydrocarbon-based competitors.

Like its supermajor competitors, BP's biggest challenges were increasing oil and gas production and replacing reserves. Most host governments in oil-producing nations were looking for better contractual terms, and the so-called easy oil and gas discoveries were already made. Reserve replacement and equity ownership of new discoveries was becoming difficult. In 2003, then-CEO John Browne told analysts that BP's daily oil production would rise 1.0 million barrels to 4.5 million barrels per day by the end of 2007. The result was less than half the projection, and targets were scaled back to 4.3 million barrels per day by 2012. In 2008, the company planned to invest $15 billion in its upstream business. Relative to its competitors, BP's production growth was constrained by its mature oil fields. Thus, BP was aggressively looking for new reserves, and the stake in TNK-BP was a major part of expected production growth.

BP's financial performance in many areas lagged behind that of ExxonMobil and Shell, especially in the refining sector, which was planning 2,000 job cuts in 2008. The company was also planning about 2,500 head-office job cuts to eliminate bureaucracy and restructure the organization around global businesses rather than geographic sectors. In addition, BP's safety record was under close scrutiny after a recent series of incidents, the most serious being the 2005 explosion in Texas City (southeast of Houston, Texas) which killed 15 people.

The Oil and Gas Industry in Russia

Russia was the world's largest natural gas producer and second-largest crude oil producer. The share of oil and gas in Russia's GDP was believed by many analysts to have more than doubled since 1999 (although some reports, such as a 2007 report from Alfa Bank, said the oil and gas GDP share was declining). Oil and gas revenues made up about 50 percent of Russian budget revenues, 65 percent of exports, and 30 percent of foreign direct investment. According to *The Economist*, "The flow of petrodollars has created a sense of stability, masked economic woes, and given Russia more clout on the world stage."[3] Russia's proven reserves ranked number seven in the world, and there were huge opportunities for further exploration. To manage the windfall from high energy prices, the Russian government created a sovereign wealth fund that held almost $160 billion at the end of 2007.

The Russian oil and gas industry was dominated by six large firms: TNK-BP, Lukoil, Gazprom, Rosneft, Surgutneftegaz, and Tatneft (for comparable financial information see Appendix 4). The latter four were government controlled. Gazprom, with 436,000 employees, was Russia's largest company, the world's largest gas producer with about 93 percent of Russian gas production, and the dominant exporter of gas to Europe (Gazprom supplied about 25 percent of the European Union's gas). In recent years, Russia had been accused of using gas exports as a means of achieving foreign policy objectives. Gazprom had made many acquisitions of small Russian companies that had been privatized in the rigged auctions of the 1990s. Gazprom's oil subsidiary, Gazprom Neft, formerly the independent company Sibneft, was Russia's fifth-largest oil-producing company. Two oligarchs and former partners, Roman Abramovich and Boris Berezovsky, acquired Sibneft for US$100 million; in 2005, Gazprom paid $13 billion for majority control (an "oligarch" is a term for a small group of businessmen who acquired significant wealth and political influence in post-Soviet Russia). Gazprom announced that it planned to make major oil and gas investments outside Russia. Before becoming Russia's president, Dmitry Medvedev was chairman of Gazprom.

Rosneft, the largest oil producer, was a remnant of the Soviet Union's Ministry of Oil and Gas. Rosneft was broken up in the early 1990s and was left with few assets. After 2004, with the acquisition of assets from the now-defunct Yukos, Rosneft became a major firm. In 2006, Rosneft sold 15 percent of its shares in one of the world's largest IPOs. Surgutneftegaz was believed to be closely tied to the Kremlin. The controlling share-holder of Tatneft was the Russian Republic of Tatarstan. Ownership of Lukoil, the largest nongovernment-controlled oil company, included two oligarch share-holders with a 25 percent stake, and Conoco-Philips with 20 percent.

Despite the size and importance of the oil industry in Russia, all was not well. Production in 2008 was declining because of a combination of factors: (1) aging oil fields and poor maintenance; (2) a tax and regulatory regime that was increasingly viewed as confiscatory by oil companies; and (3) a dearth of Russian and foreign investment in exploration and development. The future of foreign investment was unclear. In May 2008, Russia's legislature approved a bill under which Gazprom and Rosneft would have exclusive rights to develop the country's offshore reserves in the Arctic and Far East (not the Caspian). This included the Sakhalin area, where Shell was forced in 2006 to transfer majority control of the Sakhalin II project to Gazprom. In May 2008, Russian President (and soon to be Prime Minister) Putin signed into law a bill limiting foreign investment in strategic industries, including major oil and gas fields. The law prohibited companies with less than 50 percent Russian ownership from bidding for strategic fields, allowing them to participate only as minority partners. The government retained the right to make a decision to issue a license to a foreign-controlled company in special cases.

BP's First Foray in Russia

In November 1997, BP paid $571 million to Uneximbank, one of Russia's most powerful financial and industrial groups, for a 10 percent ownership stake in Sidanco, Russia's fourth-biggest vertically integrated oil company. Sidanco owned three refineries and six production facilities. The deal gave BP 20 percent of the voting rights, a seat on the board, and the right to nominate chief operating and financial officers in the company. The intent was that BP and Sidanco would set up a joint venture to develop and operate Russian oil discoveries. The two companies would have an equal vote in how the venture was run. John Browne, CEO of BP, described the deal as a "major opportunity for BP in one of the great oil and gas provinces of the world … We believe the time is now right and, more importantly, that we have found in Sidanco a partner with a strong, established position at the heart of Russia's oil industry." Uneximbank said, "The agreement signed today is of great importance, both for Sidanco and the Unexim Group, which is the controlling shareholder of Sidanco. For successful development, Sidanco needs a strategic partner with considerable experience and a leading position in the international oil business. BP is this kind of partner."

In 1998, problems began to emerge with Sidanco's oil-producing subsidiary, Chernogorneft, in which Sidanco held 73 percent control. Although BP thought Chernogorneft was financially stable, oil sold to Sidanco had not been paid for, and large tax arrears had accumulated. This helped turn Chernogorneft's management against its parent, Sidanco. Also, the Russian financial crisis of 1998 undermined Uneximbank and sharply reduced oligarch Vladimir Potanin's political influence. Alfa, a rival conglomerate, became interested in Sidanco. As BP was drawn into daily management of Sidanco, Chernogorneft's debts continued to rise.

Alfa Access/Renova. In December 1998, Chernogorneft was driven into bankruptcy by Tyumen Oil Company (TNK), a company held 50–50 by a group known as Alfa Access/Renova, or AAR. TNK was created in 1997 from a cluster of 600 upstream and downstream companies in Russia and Ukraine acquired through various privatization auctions.

AAR was a complex alliance involving three private investment companies: Russia-based Alfa Group and Renova Group, and New York–based Access Industries. Each of the investment companies was headed by an oligarch:

- **Mikhail Maratovich Fridman**, president of Alfa Group Consortium, was born in 1964 in Lvov, on the western border of Ukraine. Fridman attended Moscow Institute of Steel and Alloys, where he had his first business ventures, including window washing, running a discotheque, and scalping Moscow theater tickets—all illegal under Soviet rule. In 1988, Fridman set up a photo cooperative, Alfa Foto, and subsequently ALFA/EKO, a commodities trading firm, which gave him the capital to establish Alfa Bank in 1991, which became one of Russia's largest banks. He hired a Russian foreign trade minister to head up the bank. As his wealth grew, Fridman was able to acquire significant oil interests in Russia. He was a member of a group that funded President Boris Yeltsin's 1996 re-election campaign. Alfa Group, one of Russia's largest privately owned financial-industrial groups, controlled Alfa Bank, Alfa Capital, several construction material firms (cement, timber,

glass), food processing businesses, and a supermarket chain. In 2008, *Forbes* listed Fridman's wealth as $20.8 billion, making him the twentieth richest person in the world.

- **Viktor Vekselberg** was born in 1957 in the Ukraine. He graduated from the Moscow Institute of Transportation Engineering and later went on to complete his master's degree and Ph.D. in mathematics. Vekselberg worked at the special design office of state-owned Rodless Pumps (OKB BN). He started as a technician and eventually became research manager. Vekselberg joined the world of business in 1990. In 1993, he became chairman of the board of directors of Renova Group, which became one of Russia's largest investment and business development companies. Through Renova, Vekselberg orchestrated Russia's first successful hostile takeover, acquiring the Vladimir Tractor Factory in 1994. He rose to prominence after Boris Yeltsin's re-election in 1996, when he started to purchase shares of oil companies, including Tyumen Oil (TNK). In 1997, he became a member of the board of directors of TNK. Vekselberg was ranked the sixty-seventh richest person in the world by *Forbes*, with a net worth of $11.2 billion.

- **Len Blavatnik** was born in Russia in 1958. After attending Moscow Institute of Transportation Engineering, he emigrated with his family to the United States in 1978. He received a master's degree in computer science from Columbia University and an MBA degree from Harvard Business School in 1989. In 1986, Blavatnik founded Access Industries, a privately held U.S.-based industrial group. After the fall of the Soviet Union, Access began making investments in Russia in industries such as oil, coal, aluminum, petrochemicals and plastics, telecommunications, media, and real estate. With his friend from university, Viktor Vekselberg, Access and Renova collaborated in various investments. Blavatnik was ranked the 113th richest person in the world by *Forbes* magazine with a net worth of $8.0 billion.

BP Writes off $200 Million. In February 1999, BP wrote off $200 million of its investment in Sidanco. In November 1999, Chernogorneft was sold out of bankruptcy for $176 million dollars to TNK. BP's director for external affairs in Russia commented: "The entire bankruptcy has been subject to major manipulations. We do not consider it to be valid. In many ways, this decision has damaging implications for foreign investors. BP Amoco will be very carefully reviewing its business position in Russia in the light of these events."[4]

Simon Kukes, chairman of TNK, said that his company had upheld "international standards of corporate governance and ethical behaviour," and stressed that "the purchase had been made in a competitive auction."[5] He offered BP the chance to enter a strategic alliance with him. Although TNK denied doing anything illegal, it appeared to most outside observers that the company used its political influence and the weaknesses of Russia's laws and judicial system to ensure that a succession of court cases went its way.

BP and TNK

In December 1999, TNK and BP announced an agreement under which Sidanco would regain Chernogorneft in return for TNK receiving a 25 percent stake in Sidanco. AAR, TNK's principal shareholder, would receive 25 percent plus one share in Sidanco. In exchange, TNK's shareholders would return Chernogorneft debt-free. The deal would cost TNK about $200 million, compared with $484 million paid by BP for its 10 percent stake. In 2000, after lengthy negotiations, AAR's controlling shareholders replaced Unexim Group as the dominant shareholders of Sidanco.

In February 2003, BP announced a major strategic alliance with the same companies with which it had battled for control of Sidanco. Under the terms of the alliance, BP and AAR would combine their interests in Russia to create the country's third-largest oil and gas business, in which both parties would have a 50 percent stake. The new company, TNK-BP, would be made up of various assets: TNK, Sidanco, and most of BP's Russian assets. BP's Russian assets included a retail network in the Moscow region, minority stakes in Sidanco Rusia Petroleum, and several other equity investments.

For its 50 percent stake, BP would pay AAR $3 billion in cash and three subsequent annual payments of $1.25 billion in BP shares. In describing the deal, BP CEO John Browne said that BP had instituted new governance mechanisms to protect the interests of all parties. He also said that changes in Russia's legal system and an increasing commitment to international rules of trade convinced BP that it was time to deepen its partnership with AAR. Browne called the experience with Chernogorneft and Sidanco a key learning experience in Russia. A BP executive said, "Of course, we had qualms, given the history. But sometimes you don't get the chance to choose your partners. It was the only deal available."[6]

When the JV was announced (see Exhibit 1), there was speculation that the Russian government had reservations about the desirability of foreign investment in energy reserves. There was also speculation that the speed with which the deal was done caught the government off guard.

Joint Venture Structure

The joint venture was legally created in August 2003. In 2004, a major restructuring simplified the complex TNK-BP holdings (a dozen subsidiaries and hundreds of legal entities). In 2005, further restructuring occurred. Three holding companies (TNK, Sidanco, and ONAKO) were merged into TNK-BP Holding. Approximately 70 percent (by value) of minority shareholders in 14 key TNK-BP subsidiaries exchanged their shares for shares in TNK-BP Holding through the voluntary share

Exhibit 1 Agreement on Structure of TNK-BP Holding Signed in London

TASS, Thursday, June 26, 2003

British Petroleum and the Russian Alfa Group (Access-Renova) signed an agreement in London on Thursday, determining the structure of a deal on establishing a TNK-BP joint venture. Under the agreement, all commercial and financial obligations of the sides are formalised, which opens a way for the final creation of a holding.

"The history of the TNK-BP Company starts from this moment," said chairman of the board of directors of the Alfa Group Mikhail Fridman. "I'm sure that this new unique entity will play a leading role in the Russian and, later, in the world oil industry." "We hope that merging trends in the Russian and world fuel and energy complex will not be limited to this deal," said, in turn, TNK board chairman Viktor Vekselberg. "This deal is an international recognition of rising political stability in Russia and its progress in the economic development," he noted.

Holding President Robert Dudley admitted in an interview with Tass that "it was not an easy thing" to take a decision on expanding BP business in Russia. The company carried out a painstaking assessment of assets over the past nine months, and spent enough time on making feasibility estimates. BP participated in a number of major deals over the past five years, and not a single one was concluded with greater carefulness than the present one: "this is true both of assets and obligations as well as legal formalities," the president said.

TNK-BP will have substantial assets in the most important oil-bearing areas of Russia: production will total 800,000 barrels a day in Western Siberia, and 370,000 barrels a day in the Volga-Ural area. Besides, Dudley continued, the company will continue the development of deposits, which was already conducted. There are now 8,000 mothballed wells, he went on to say, and the company mulls over a possibility of resuming their operation gradually. It will be necessary to restart several thousands of wells annually, the president stated. British Petroleum intends to use skilled Russian personnel and to bring machinery and methods from other areas of the world to organize production so as to optimize deposits, wells, and land infrastructure to boost efficiency of recovery, Dudley emphasized.

exchange program. Upon completion of the voluntary share exchange program, minority shareholders owned approximately 5 percent of publicly held TNK-BP Holding. An independent valuation by Deloitte & Touche put a value of $18.5 billion on TNK-BP Holding. See Exhibit 2 for the ownership structure in 2008.

Key elements of the joint venture agreement were as follows:

- Ten-member board with equal representation from BP and AAR.
- AAR nominates the chairman of the board and the chairman of the remuneration committee.
- BP nominates the vice chairman of the board and chairman of the audience committee.
- BP appoints the CEO and holds half the top management positions.
- The Russian shareholders have management control over government relations, legal affairs, and security.
- Dividends will be a minimum of 40 percent of TNK-BP's U.S. GAAP net income.
- The debt ratio must be kept at 25 to 35 percent.
- The business scope of TNK-BP is limited to oil and gas in Russia and Ukraine.
- Management is particularly focused on certain actions: to improve safety, focusing on reducing high-risk practices; to improve planning and forecasting, so that delivery can be assured and there are no surprises; to improve internal control systems and ethical conducts; to curb the chances of fraud,

illegal payments, and misjudgments; to improve the reporting of results, continuously diligent and appropriate disclosure; and, finally, to increase export and production, and reduce cost through the use of better technology.

- TNK-BP holds a 49.8 percent interest in Slavneft through TNK-BP International Ltd. Slavneft operates as a separate entity. TNK-BP and Gazprom Neft have equal representation on the Slavneft Board of Directors.
- The partners are not allowed to sell their interests in the venture until after December 31, 2007 (termed the "lock-in period").

BP appointed Robert Dudley as CEO. Dudley, an American and graduate of Thunderbird School of Global Management, was a veteran Amoco and BP executive. In the mid-1990s, Dudley worked for Amoco in Russia, and saw Amoco outmaneuvered on a deal by the Russian company Yukos.

Shareholder Comments about the JV Formation

At an analyst meeting in New York on October 17, 2003, BP Chairman John Browne made the following comments:

We regard this group of shareholders as one of the best in Russia, with a strong track record. We've built a strong relationship, tested by past difficulties, notably over Sidanco. We continued to build trust, and less and less viewed each other's motives with suspicion. AAR is a vital

Exhibit 2 TNK-BP Ownership Structure, 2008

part of the future success of TNK-BP. It brings not only assets and people, but also experience and judgment on the right things to do in the Russian context. They've made it clear that they're committed to making TNK-BP not only a successful operation, but a company which can compare favorably with BP in terms of the quality of governance, transparency, safety, and ethics. In these matters, I know they are reinforcing President Putin's agenda for modernization. BP, as a powerful, globally connected company, brings not only technology to improve the business, but also credibility and experience in modern management. It is a partnership of mutual advantage. Finally, it's about people. And we've selected some of the very best people. Whether they've come from outside, or from TNK, or from Sidanco, or from BP.

At the same meeting, Mikhail Fridman (the lead oligarch shareholder) said:

Of course, we made quite significant profits from the deal but, frankly speaking, we've done this deal not because we just want to realize the profits, but because we do believe that the most important way for us as investors to increase our benefits and potential growth, we do believe that to create a joint venture with a company like BP at the end of the day, we'll benefit after all.

It is obvious to everybody here that the biggest challenge we have is probably the cultural gap between the Russian style of doing business and Western style of doing business. And it is not so easy to overcome that. And from this point of view, we are quite happy that we have a long story of relationship between us and BP. And this not very smooth story—not just, you know, [a] story of friendship and partnership that started from quite tough, you know, competition … We do believe that there are only two things we need as a shareholder. I think it's trust and, second, probably patience.

And it seems to me that both sides have enough of that. So, that's why I'm quite optimistic about the future of our company.

TNK-BP Assets

In 2008, TNK-BP was Russia's third-largest oil and gas company in terms of liquids production, and accounted for almost 20 percent of Russia's total oil production. TNK-BP employed about 65,000 people, including 85 foreign managers, many of whom had formerly worked for BP. The main oil production assets of TNK-BP were located in West Siberia and the Volga-Urals region (Exhibit 3), with new provinces being opened in East Siberia via the planned development of the Verkhnechonskoye oil field (concurrently with the construction of the Transneft-operated East Siberia Oil Pipeline) and in the south of the Tyumen region. The main gas business assets included the Rospan project in Novy Urengoi, which is 100 percent owned by TNK-BP, and the Yugragazpererabotka gas processing joint venture with SIBUR Holding in Nizhnevartovsk. TNK-BP owned 49 percent of Yugragazpererabotka. Some specific data on TNK-BP assets are as follows:

Exhibit 3 TNK-BP's Asset Map, 2008

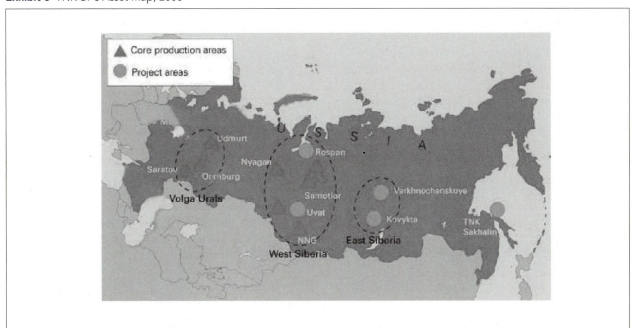

Source: BP.

- TNK-BP held approximately 200 exploration and production licenses.
- Twenty-seven new licenses were acquired in 2007.
- TNK-BP's top 10 fields delivered two-thirds of its production.
- Top 20 fields held 80 percent of proved reserves.
- Average well productivity was 15 tons per day.
- Approximately 25,000 km of infield gathering pipelines (following divestment of assets).
- TNK-BP had four refineries located in Russia (Ryazan Refinery, Saratov Refinery, Nizhnevartovsk Oil Refining Enterprize, and Krasnoleninsk Refinery) and one refinery in Ukraine (Lisichansknefteorgsintez), all close to production areas and export routes.
- The company operated approximately 1,600 retail outlets branded either as BP or TNK in Russia and Ukraine.

JV Financial Results

TNK-BP's revenues, profitability, assets, and cash flow grew substantially over its brief life span (see Exhibit 4; also see the various appendices). However, the revenue structure was heavily constrained by export duties (the Russian government captured about 90 percent of crude prices), and the domestic market prices earned were complex combinations of contracts and regulated rates.

TNK-BP Strategic and Financial Objectives

TNK-BP's strategic objective was to "become a world-class oil and gas group that is an industry leader in Russia, with a clear focus on the sustainability and renewal of its resources and the efficiency of its operations." The company was committed to being an integrated oil and gas company, but the partners were not in agreement as to the level of non-Russian growth. The company was also committed to growing its gas business and was involved in various different discussions with Gazprom.

The joint venture's financial objectives were as follows:

- To maintain a strong balance sheet providing flexibility, liquidity, and cost-effective borrowing.
- To target a gearing range of 25 to 35 percent (net debt/net debt + equity, U.S. GAAP basis).
- To maintain a conservative debt structure with a significant percentage of long-term debt.
- To maintain a dividend policy of at least 40 percent of net income.
- To attain an investment grade credit rating over time.
- To improve the timeliness and quality of financial reporting based on centralized financial management.

In 2008, TNK-BP accounted for about one-quarter of BP's total production, one-fifth of its reserves, and about one-tenth of net income.

Key Joint Venture Events 2003–2007

June 2003—Uncertainty

According to Robert Dudley, TNK-BP CEO: "With all due respect for BP, it had a fairly vague idea about what was going on in Russia. It knew about Russian risks, but it had never had to deal directly with tax authorities, customs officers, monopolies, and relationships with regions …This is more than just an oil deal. And if we fail, it will be more than just a setback for one foreign investor. It will be a setback for the whole country—and the Russian government understands that very well … We will insist on the same level of transparency and governance as in BP."[7]

June 2003—Russians Say the Expatriate Costs Are Too High

Victor Vekselberg commented on expatriate costs: "Bonuses and entitlement for expatriates has been one of the most hotly debated issues. Foreigners who come to Russia want to bring a piece of their own life here."[8]

May 2004—The Russian Partners Want the Deal Changed

The Russian partners informed BP that they wanted the payments for their share of the JV to be made earlier. BP made the following statement:

We have an excellent set of agreements. We expect all partners to stick to those agreements. As we announced in February last year, BP, under the terms of the agreement, will pay three annual tranches on the anniversary of completion of dollars 1.25bn in BP shares valued at market prices prior to each annual payment. What our partners do with those agreements is a matter for them. The agreements provide for AAR to be 50 percent owners of TNK-BP through 2007.[9]

August 2004—Yukos Is Dismantled

The Russian government began the process that would see the bankruptcy and dismantling of oil company Yukos, and the jailing of its prominent and outspoken CEO, Mikhail Khodorkovsky. Yukos was charged with tax bills and other claims of about $28 billion.

April 2005—TNK-BP Faces a Huge Tax Bill

Russian tax authorities announced a $1 billion tax claim relating to 2001 earnings. Viktor Vekselberg said, "We cannot possibly have such liabilities, and will therefore dispute them … There can be no risks, no parallels with Yukos."[10] A few months later, the tax liability was reduced.

Robert Dudley made the following comments:

The significance of this (tax claim) goes far beyond our company. Everyone will watch this as a test of whether

Exhibit 4 TNK-BP's Financial Results, 2002–2007

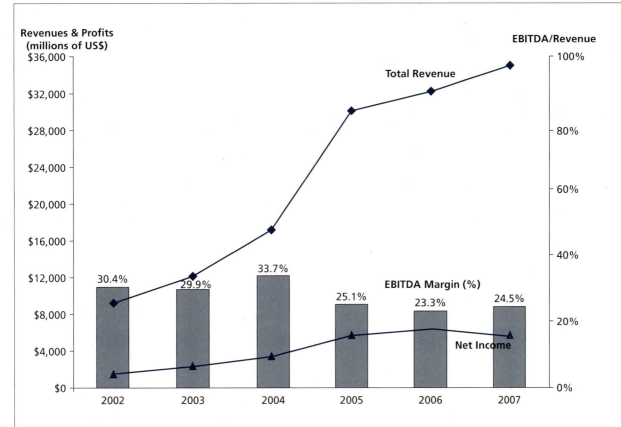

- Revenues grew from $9.2 billion in 2002 to $35 billion in 2007. Net income rose from $1.5 billion in 2002 (16.8 percent) to $5.7 billion in 2007 (16.1 percent).
- Total assets doubled between 2002 and 2007, from $12.6 billion in 2002 to $25.3 billion. The net debt/equity ratio (debt – cash/equity) decreased from 30.2 percent to almost zero in 2007 (0.1 percent). As a result, TNK-BP earned more in interest income than it paid in interest expenses in 2007.
- Operating cash flow grew from $1.385 billion in 2002 to $5.053 billion in 2007.
- The growth in cash flow was deployed between both the owners and the business. Capital expenditures (capex) rose from $595 million in 2002 to $2.23 billion in 2006, with another major jump to $3.285 billion in 2007.
- Dividends paid grew from $139 million in 2002 to $6.664 billion in 2006 and then down to $4.379 billion in 2007.
- Cash and liquid assets were $2.587 billion at end-of-year 2007.
- The share price for TNK-BP Holding fell from a high of $3.40/share in early 2006 to $2.00/share in mid-2008.

Russia can integrate with the world economy. I don't think it is in the interest of the Russian government to destroy TNK-BP. Russia is inadvertently becoming increasingly difficult to navigate for well-intentioned investors— Russian and foreign alike. The state has progressively asserted its influence over the commanding heights of the economy, and state-owned companies have begun to play an increasingly prominent role. At the time when Russia's economy is in need of knowledge and management skills, *it is becoming increasingly difficult to bring in managers and executives.*[11]

April 2005—TNK-BP May Not Be Allowed to Bid for New Oil Fields

A senior official in the Natural Resources Ministry said that that an auction for three major fields was canceled in March in order to exclude TNK-BP. Later in the month, Vladimir Putin told John Browne, BP CEO, "We were not mistaken when we supported your decision two years ago. The profits of the joint company have increased 20 times over. This is proof of the quality of management."[12]

October 2005—Foreign Oil Companies Cannot Participate in Auctions

Russia's natural resources minister announced that companies more than 50 percent foreign-owned will not be allowed to take part in 2006 auctions for new oil fields.

March 2006—TNK-BP in Major Dispute Over Gas Field

One of TNK-BP's most valuable assets was the Kovykta gas field in eastern Siberia. The license to develop Kovykta was held by Rusia Petroleum, 62.89 percent owned by TNK-BP and previously controlled by Sidanco. TNK-BP wanted to develop the gas for Asian markets, and Gazprom (the Russian government-owned natural gas company) said the gas should be developed for Russia. There was speculation that Rusia Petroleum's license for the field would be revoked. The Natural Resources Ministry accused TNK-BP of producing too little gas at the field. TNK-BP argued it could not produce the 9 billion cubic meters per year stipulated in the license since Gazprom had blocked construction of a pipeline to China, and local demand was insufficient. TNK-BP had been lobbying for years for the license to be amended.

October 2006—Robert Dudley Says TNK-BP Will Survive

Dudley stated, "We are confident there is a solid future for TNK-BP. Much has been written about the consolidation of the state … But I believe having companies like this is a good thing for the industry … As long as we continue to get good results, I think the company will more than survive, I think it will thrive. I have seen no evidence that they [the Russian partners] are working to sell their interest."[13]

An oil industry analyst had the following observation: "BP has found it is not only dancing with the wrong partner, but that the dance tune has changed, too. They got in at a good price, and they got in at a good time. It's better for the company to adjust rather than try to go against the tide."[14]

October 2006—TNK-BP Engineer Killed

The chief engineer for Rusia Petroleum, which held the license to develop the Kovykta gas field, was shot dead in Siberia. Rumors about a contract killing immediately began circulating.

June 2007—Putin Angry about the Kovykta Gas Field Dispute

In Germany for a G8 meeting, Putin said to reporters: "How long should we tolerate it if participants of that consortium do nothing to implement the license? This is not about BP, not about the foreign partner, but about all the shareholders that took the obligations to develop this field and, unfortunately, didn't meet the license terms … I won't even talk now about how the license was purchased. Let's leave this up to the conscience of those who did it a while ago, also in the early 1990s."[15]

Late June 2007—TNK-BP Sells Its Stake in the Kovykta Gas Field

TNK-BP sold its 62.89 percent stake in Rusia Petroleum to Gazprom for about $800 million, less than a third of its real value, according to some analysts. TNK-BP had invested about $450 million in developing the field. TNK-BP had the option to buy back 25 percent of the field at market price.

Gazprom Approaches BP about a Deal in 2007

In mid-2007, Gazprom initiated discussions with BP about a possible alliance. Gazprom's goal of becoming a global oil and gas company was being stymied by opposition from Western governments. Gazprom was interested in stakes in BP assets outside Russia. In return, Gazprom would contribute large stakes in its Russian oil business. A key element of the alliance would involve Gazprom buying AAR's TNK-BP stake, which would then allow BP and Gazprom to combine their various Russian oil assets and create the largest Russian oil producer.[16] Gazprom officials told BP privately that they believed AAR would sell. AAR said publicly that they had no intention of selling.

BP's country manager for Russia, James Dupree, handled most of the discussions with Gazprom. BP CEO Tony Hayward made several trips to Russia to meet with Gazprom CEO Alexei Miller. Based on the many meetings that were held, BP was confident that a deal would happen, and that the TNK-BP partner issues would be resolved.

2008: Can the JV Survive?

On March 19, 2008, Russian security services raided TNK-BP offices and detained an employee, Ilya Zaslavsky, on charges of espionage. On March 21, Russia's environmental agency announced an investigation of TNK-BP's largest oilfield. The investigation was to be led by the same official that investigated the Sakhalin II project operated by Shell. Shell was later forced to sell a stake in the project to Gazprom. On March 25, the Interior

Ministry said it was investigating a $40 million tax evasion case against Sidanco, a former TNK-BP subsidiary.

Expatriate Visa Problems for BP.

President Putin had complained about the dearth of Russians in top management positions in natural resource companies. In early 2008, BP had problems renewing visas for expatriate employees, allegedly because of a "lack of clarity." In May, a Siberian court refused to allow visas for 148 technology specialists seconded from BP. The court order was initiated by a Moscow brokerage, ZAO Tetlis, that owned a small stake in a publicly traded unit of TNK-BP, and alleged that the fees TNK-BP paid for the BP specialists amounted to an illegal dividend for BP. BP maintained that without the specialists, TNK-BP's production could be reduced. When the expatriates, already in the country, showed up for work, TNK-BP security refused to let them enter the office. Robert Dudley blamed a TNK-BP executive, German Khan (a billionaire investor and colleague of Mikhail Fridman), for orchestrating the visa issue, and sought his and two other executives' ouster from the venture for gross insubordination. BP said that Khan ignored instructions and applied for fewer than half the required visas. The Russian shareholders responded with a statement saying that TNK-BP should be allowed to expand outside Russia even if it would compete with BP's own operations, and called for reducing the venture's reliance on foreign specialists. The statement also called Dudley's recent comments about the visa issue deeply inappropriate.[17]

In July, immigration authorities approved only 71 visas, far fewer than the 150 BP requested. BP reassigned the 148 seconded employees to other BP units.

The Gazprom Deal Collapses.

Despite the various problems, BP remained hopeful that a deal with Gazprom would be worked out. In April 2008, BP CEO Tony Hayward visited Igor Sechin, a powerful Putin confidant and chairman of Rosneft (the following month, Sechin was promoted to deputy prime minister in charge of the energy industry). At the meeting, Hayward discussed BP's efforts to reach a deal with Gazprom. Sechin explained that Gazprom was not always able to deliver on its ambitions for making major international deals. In May, Hayward met with a former Kremlin official who informed him that his talks with Gazprom were "indecent" and that BP should be less confrontational with AAR. Hayward was also told that the Kremlin would not force AAR to sell. On May 14, 2008, Hayward met Gazprom officials in Manchester, England, at a football match. At this meeting, Gazprom was noncommittal and, in a surprise to BP, suggested holding off on any decisions for a month or so.

Partner Disagreements over JV Strategy.

In late May, the stakes escalated when the three Russian oligarchs met with Tony Hayward and demanded that Robert Dudley be removed as TNK-BP CEO. According to a statement released by the Russian shareholders, Dudley was favoring BP over the Russian shareholders. A spokesperson for the Russians said, "He [Dudley] is acting in the interests of only 50 percent of the shareholders. We want someone who will pursue the interests of all shareholders, not just run TNK-BP like a BP subsidiary."[18] The Russian shareholders were particularly upset with Dudley's five-year strategic plan forecasting lower shareholder returns in the coming years because of high taxes, increasing costs, and stagnant production. The Russian shareholders refused to approve the plan. They argued that Dudley was too focused on increasing reserves, and should be increasing the production of existing oil fields. They wanted the 2008 investment plan of $4.4 billion cut by $900 million and the money paid as dividends. BP argued that TNK-BP was the best-performing oil company in Russia. According to Mikhail Fridman: "There's a strategic conflict of interests between TNK-BP and BP itself. We had a company that was strong, energetic, and aggressive in the good sense of the word. BP turned it into a typical bureaucracy … We don't plan to leave, and I don't think that they plan to leave. So, ultimately, we're destined to come to some agreement.[19] The attempt to portray this conflict as a dispute between a respectable Western company and some Russian oligarchs who are trying to take control using dirty methods is completely cynical. It is our partners who are using methods from the 1990s. There is a good English word: arrogance … We sensed this condescending attitude towards what we were saying [for months] … This is about the type of foreign investors Russia needs. We don't need foreign investors who limit the development of the company."[20]

Hayward refused to remove Dudley. The Russian shareholders threatened legal action to strip BP-appointed directors of their powers. BP was contemplating its own lawsuit against the partners to recover a recently paid portion of back taxes. BP maintained that the taxes paid for the period prior to the formation of the JV should be borne entirely by the previous owners of TNK (which would include Fridman, Vekselberg, and Blavatnik) and its subsidiaries, and not BP.

BP Chairman Peter Sutherland expressed his frustration: "This is just a return to the corporate raiding activities that were prevalent in Russia in the 1990s. Prime minister has referred to these tactics as relics of the 1990s but, unfortunately, our partners continue to use them, and the leaders of the country seem unwilling or unable to step in and stop them. This is bad for us, bad for the company and, of course, very bad for Russia."[21]

"The Alfa Playbook." BP took several steps to deal with its partners. In early June, Tony Hayward met with Igor Sechin to discuss AAR's pressure tactics. BP moved Lamar McCay, an executive with Russia experience, from the United States to Russia to be executive vice president of TNK-BP. BP hired a consulting firm to study other foreign joint ventures involving AAR companies. The outcome of the study became known in BP as the "Alfa Playbook."[22] BP learned, for example, that other Alfa joint ventures had run into various difficulties. For example, Altimo, an Alfa subsidiary, had a joint venture with Norway's Telenor A/S. In 2007, Telenor accused Altimo of dirty tricks in the midst of a business dispute over a Ukrainian mobile phone company. Telenor accused Alfa of paying journalists in Ukraine to publish negative articles about Telenor. Altimo filed a lawsuit in Ukraine and received a favorable ruling. Telenor was never informed that the lawsuit was under way. The result of the lawsuit was sent to a Telenor address that was unoccupied, and by the time Telenor learned of the ruling, the Ukrainian judge on the case had disappeared (the day after giving the decision), and it was too late to appeal. According to BP officials, the Alfa Playbook was "playing out to the letter" in the TNK-BP dispute.

BP's Options

In late July 2008, it was looking increasingly likely that Robert Dudley would not be granted a visa and would have to leave Russia. There was also concern that Russia's Federal Labor and Employment Service would try to prosecute a group of TNK-BP managers for violating labor law. Because of the uncertainty, Dudley had not left Russia since March. The Russian partners maintained that his contract expired at the end of 2007, while BP said his contract was automatically renewed. In an interview, Dudley said: "Running the company now is like driving a car, and sometimes the brakes work and sometimes they don't. I spend a lot of time holding meetings out on the balcony of my office …. It's not me personally, it can't be performance; it's the role, the check and balance between the interests of the shareholders. I've got an obligation to hold the line for both sets of shareholders."[23]

Without a Gazprom deal to buy out AAR, Robert Dudley and his BP colleagues considered other options. One option was to take the dispute to the highest levels in the Russian government, perhaps even to Putin himself. The results of earlier meetings with Igor Sechin, deputy prime minister, suggested that this option would have limited value. A second option was to seek British government help, which had been offered. Prime Minister Gordon Brown was going to be in Russia in July for meetings with President Medvedev. A third option was legal action against AAR for violating the shareholder agreement. Finally, BP could sit tight, continue to run the business, and resist the Russian shareholders. Meanwhile, the Russian shareholders continued to push for Dudley's dismissal, with Victor Vekselberg calling for a July board meeting to discuss Dudley's infringement of Russian employment, immigration, and tax laws. Although BP said Dudley would keep his job, it was hard too see how he could remain CEO if he was outside Russia.

Appendix 1 TNK-BP Holding, Consolidated Statements of Income (millions of U.S. dollars)

	2002	2003	2004	2005	2006	2007
Sales revenue	$9,172	$12,114	$17,169	$30,106	$32,114	$34,995
Operating expenses	(6,381)	(8,497)	(11,390)	(22,536)	(24,684)	(26,399)
EBITDA	2,791	3,617	5,779	7,570	7,430	8,596
EBITDA margin	*30.4%*	*29.9%*	*33.7%*	*25.1%*	*23.1%*	*24.5%*
Depreciation & amortization	(580)	(814)	(1,039)	(1,206)	(1,250)	(1,341)
EBIT	2,211	2,803	4,740	6,364	6,180	7,255
Equity income					71	4
Net interest income					79	182
Interest expense	(273)	(177)	(29)	(111)	(210)	(167)

(Continued)

Appendix 1 TNK-BP Holding, Consolidated Statements of Income (millions of U.S. dollars) (*Continued*)

	2002	2003	2004	2005	2006	2007
Exchange gain (loss)					(104)	8
Gains on disposal of subsidiaries	133	189	—	766	2,677	105
Profit before tax	2,071	2,815	4,674	6,975	8,693	7,387
Income tax expense	(190)	(227)	(1,221)	(1,220)	(2,115)	(1,453)
Minority interest	(337)	(214)	(37)	(70)	(169)	(202)
Net profit	$1,544	$2,374	$3,416	$5,685	$6,409	$5,732
Return on sales	16.8%	19.6%	19.9%	18.9%	19.9%	16.4%
Weighted average shares (m)	15,448	15,448	15,448	15,448	15,448	15,448
EPS	$0.10	$0.15	$0.22	$0.37	$0.41	$0.37
DPS	$0.01	$0.04	$0.25	$0.25	$0.43	$0.16
Payout ratio	9.0%	25.0%	112.8%	68.6%	105.7%	42.2%
Export duties (part of operating expenses)					9,327	9,256

Source: TNK-BP Holding, TNK-BP, and author calculations.

Appendix 2 TNK-BP Holding, Consolidated Balance Sheet (millions of U.S. dollars)

	2002	2003	2004	2005	2006	2007
Cash and other liquid assets	1,083	869	477	485	827	635
Fixed assets	7,751	10,121	11,050	11,704	11,259	13,901
Long term investments	823	1,679	81	90	94	20
Other assets	2,948	3,445	4,826	6,609	9,530	13,348
Total Assets	12,605	16,114	16,434	18,888	21,710	27,904
Interest-bearing debt	3,167	2,755	1,669	1,811	1,515	1,859
Other liabilities	2,533	4,101	5,291	7,844	8,103	9,752
Total Liabilities	5,700	6,856	6,960	9,655	9,618	11,611
Shareholders' equity	5,099	8,530	8,958	8,606	11,488	15,585
Minority interest	1,806	728	755	866	604	708
Total Liabilities & Shareholders' Equity	12,605	16,114	16,434	18,888	21,710	27,904
Net debt	2,084	1,886	1,192	1,326	688	1,224
Net debt/equity	30.2%	20.4%	12.3%	14.0%	5.6%	7.8%
Change in working capital	(327)	661	(499)	(214)	2,453	3,369

Source: TNK-BP Holding and author calculations.

(*Continued*)

Appendix 3 TNK-BP Holding, Cash Flow (millions of U.S. dollars)

	2002	2003	2004	2005	2006	2007
Cash flow from operations	1,980	4,082	4,687	5,042	7,877	5,485
Net capital expenditures (capex)	(595)	(849)	(1,293)	(1,764)	(2,234)	(3,266)
Free cash flow	1,385	3,233	3,394	3,278	5,643	2,219
Dividends paid	(139)	(594)	(3,854)	(3,901)	(6,594)	(2,420)
Discretionary cash flow	1,246	2,639	(460)	(623)	(951)	(201)
Net change in borrowings	(472)	(807)	580	264	(2,026)	305
Equity capital raised, net	—	—	—	—	—	—
Other investing/financing activities	(72)	(2,111)	(338)	1,203	3,319	(296)
Net cash flow	702	(279)	(218)	844	342	(192)

Source: TNK-BP Holding.

Appendix 4 Public Comparables

Company	Country	Capitalization Million USD	Market Multipliers				Financial Multipliers				
			P/S	P/E	EV/ EBITDA	P/BV	ROE	ROA	ROIC	WACC	ROIC/ WACC
Gazprom	Russia	305,152	3.23	12.06	9.13	1.99	21.28%	12.70%	16.51%	8.89%	1.86
LUKOIL	Russia	64,090	1.06	8.50	5.62	1.69	25.07%	16.90%	21.97%	9.50%	2.31
Gazprom Neft	Russia	27,794	1.45	7.50	5.24	2.71	41.63%	29.59%	36.09%	10.15%	3.56
Surgut- neftegas	Russia	38,076	1.55	10.20	0.00	0.97	9.83%	9.15%	9.71%	10.84%	0.90
Tatneft	Russia	13,537	0.94	10.49	5.66	1.26	13.84%	9.90%	13.59%	11.30%	1.20
TNK-BP	Russia	29,634	1.27	4.38	0.00	2.44	73.96%	31.86%	60.87%	10.50%	5.80
Transneft	Russia	9,186	0.79	3.15	3.06	0.41	15.09%	10.38%	13.94%	9.86%	1.41
Rosneft	Russia	86,799	2.04	7.66	11.64	3.31	24.11%	9.20%	14.82%	9.86%	1.50
NOVATEK	Russia	23,531	9.91	34.44	21.34	7.20	22.42%	17.27%	20.78%	9.86%	2.11
Russia's Average			**2.47**	**10.93**	**6.85**	**2.44**	**27.47%**	**16.33%**	**23.14%**	**10.08%**	**2.29**
Petro- China	China	538,994	2.61	13.77	15.07	3.08	25.81%	17.24%	23.21%	17.20%	1.35
Petroleo Brasileiro SA	Brazil	253,141	2.29	17.58	9.83	3.39	29.39%	13.15%	19.85%	13.66%	1.45
Sasol	RSA	33,667	2.54	15.77		4.07	29.82%	15.33%	23.82%	14.09%	1.69
Sinopec	China	9,752	0.47	28.43	16.94	1.20	4.47%	3.11%	4.86%	17.49%	0.28

(Continued)

Appendix 4 Public Comparables (*Continued*)

Company	Country	Capitalization Million USD	Market Multipliers				Financial Multipliers				
			P/S	P/E	EV/ EBITDA	P/BV	ROE	ROA	ROIC	WACC	ROIC/ WACC
Emerging Markets Average			**1.98**	**18.89**	**13.95**	**2.94**	**22.37%**	**12.21%**	**17.94%**	**15.61%**	**1.19**
Murphy Oil	USA	15,409	0.83	18.85	11.15	3.16	16.99%	9.24%	14.32%	9.00%	1.59
Norsk Hydro	Norway	18,363	0.58	5.30		1.72	24.17%	11.16%	21.05%	13.13%	1.60
Occidental Petroleum	USA	64,736	3.48	14.91	6.29	2.85	25.67%	15.66%	24.14%	10.67%	2.26
Petro-Canada	Canada	24,295	1.11	9.96	3.66	2.00	24.50%	11.76%	19.69%	12.41%	1.59
Repsol YPF	Spain	42,498	0.54	8.73	4.37	1.51	18.54%	6.87%	12.30%	10.36%	1.19
Developed Markets Average			**1.31**	**11.55**	**6.37**	**2.25**	**21.97%**	**10.94%**	**18.30%**	**11.11%**	**1.65**
BP	Great Britain	205,892	0.73	10.03	5.94	2.20	23.38%	9.19%	18.64%	9.41%	1.98
Chevron Texaco	USA	186,271	0.92	10.25	5.68	2.49	26.04%	13.26%	22.56%	10.09%	2.24
Conoco-Phillips	USA	131,370	0.80	8.66	4.98	1.58	13.86%	6.94%	11.33%	10.09%	1.12
Exxon-Mobil	USA	488,394	1.36	12.28	6.91	4.12	35.11%	18.49%	33.43%	10.03%	3.33
Royal-Dutch	Holland	227,019	0.64	7.22	4.33	1.81	27.28%	12.41%	23.34%	9.18%	2.54
Total SA	France	182,004	0.83	8.61	4.33	2.52	30.95%	12.05%	22.81%	10.12%	2.25
Global Average			**0.88**	**9.51**	**5.36**	**2.45**	**26.10%**	**12.06%**	**22.02%**	**9.82%**	**2.24**

Source: Veles Capital, 2008, June 16, 17. Original data drawn from Bloomberg, Estimation, and Veles Capital.

NOTES

1. G. White, 2008, BP in Russia—plagued from start? Putin says venture structured poorly, clear boss is needed, *Wall Street Journal*, June 2, B2.
2. Ibid.
3. 2008, Trouble in the pipeline: Russia's oil industry, *The Economist*, May 10.
4. A. Jack, 1999, BP Amoco to review its Russian interests, *Financial Times*, November 27, 15.
5. Ibid.
6. G. White & G. Chazan, 2008, Boardroom brawl roils BP's Russia venture, talks break down; Kremlin's role murky, *Wall Street Journal*, June 12, A1.
7. C. Hoyas & A. Ostrovsky, 2003, Aiming to clean up in Russia with record deal: The success of BP's huge project will not only be judged in oil and money, *Financial Times*, June 26, 26.
8. Ibid.

9.   C. Hoyas, A. Jack, & A. Ostrovsky, 2004, Russian partners seek to change BP deal, *Financial Times*, May 4, 1.

10. I. Gorst & A. Ostrovsky, 2005, TNK-BP hit by a dollars lbn tax bill, *Financial Times*, April 12, 21.

11. I. Gorst & A. Ostrovsky, 2005, TNK-BP chief attacks Russia's uncertain investment climate, *Financial Times*, April 13, 8.

12. C. Belton, 2005, Putin allays TNK-BP worries, *Moscow Times*, April 25.

13. C. Belton, 2006, Dudley dismisses talk of sale, *Moscow Times*, October 4.

14. Ibid.

15. A. Medetsky, 2007, An irritated president steps into Kovykta fray, *Moscow Times*, June 5.

16. G. White & G. Chazin, 2008, Misreading the Kremlin costs BP control in Russia venture, *Wall Street Journal*, December 16, A1, A6.

17. G. White & G. Chazan, 2008, BP venture is threatened as criticisms spill into the open, *Wall Street Journal*, May 28.

18. G. White & G. Chazan, 2008, Intrigue in Russia ensnares BP venture, *Wall Street Journal*, May 30, A1.

19. White & Chazan, Boardroom brawl roils BP's Russia venture.

20. C. Belton & E. Crooks, 2008, Fridman accuses BP of arrogance, *Financial Times*, June 17, 18.

21. R. Anderson, C. Belton, & E. Crooks, 2008, BP accuses Russians of corporate raiding, *Financial Times*, June 13, 1.

22. G. White & G. Chazan, 2008, BP is in the dark in struggle to save its Russian venture, *Wall Street Journal*, June 30, B4.

23. G. White, 2008, The bitter battle to lead TNK-BP: Dudley pushes back as Russian group seeks his ouster, *Wall Street Journal*, July 23, B1.

Mark Brewer, Brandi Chauvin, Eric Mitchell,
Eric Partington, Mark Rade, Don Riddle,
Yinghong (Sara) Song, Robin Chapman

Arizona State University

Millions of people each year try to come up with a "million dollar" idea. Many believe that it requires an "unfathomable" idea, but sometimes going back to the basics is the key. That's what allowed Kevin Plank, the founder of Under Armour performance apparel, to find success. The task at hand was to simply make a superior T-shirt and nothing more. It all began in 1996 when the former University of Maryland football player wanted to create a shirt that would help control the temperature of an athlete's body, not just soak up the sweat during intense activities. He wanted a shirt that enhanced performance rather than detracted from it. As a result, Plank created a synthetic shirt made of high-tech material that had a snug fit designed to feel like a second skin.

The technology behind Under Armour's diverse product lines for men, women, and youth is complex, but the message is simple: wear HeatGear when it's hot, ColdGear when it's cold, and AllSeasonGear between the extremes. Under Armour's mission is to enhance the experience for all athletes by applying passion, science, and the relentless pursuit of innovation to create clothing with temperature control, comfort, and flexibility.[1]

Under Armour's stated goal is to be "a leading developer, marketer, and distributor of branded performance products." It has been able to successfully penetrate the sports apparel market by using the image and influence of: domestic and international professional teams, collegiate teams, Olympians, and individuals.

Utilizing broad-based, frequently free endorsements and well-received publicity, Under Armour has also reached regular athletes, active outdoor enthusiasts, elite tactical professionals, and active lifestyle consumers.

Under Armour is quickly becoming a leader in the sports apparel industry, and it could be argued that it is an opposing force to Nike in sports apparel, with its widespread popularity amongst top-name athletes and sports programs and teams. This is further evidenced by a 133 percent compound annual growth rate and an equally enormous increase in operating income from $5.7 million to $52.5 million between the years 2003 and 2007. As of 2007, Under Armour had $606 million in sales revenue, far surpassing its first year's revenue in 1996 of $17 thousand (see Exhibits 1 and 2).

Under Armour's products are sold worldwide, with the company's headquarters located in the United States and support offices in Hong Kong and Guangzhou, China. Primary sales are achieved through wholesale distribution and licensing to distributors. Products are offered through the company website and retailers, and company stores in the United States, Europe, Japan, Canada, South Africa, Australia, and New Zealand (see Exhibit 3). Under Armour operates in a highly competitive industry where the dominant competitors have significant breadth of market coverage that it is difficult to find an entry point. The main competitors have been advertising and establishing distribution channels, marketing agreements,

Exhibit 1 Under Armour Net Revenue: 2003–2007

	Year Ended December 31				
(In thousands, except per share amounts)	2007	2006	2005	2004	2003
Statements of Income data:					
Net revenues	$606,561	$430,689	$281,053	$205,181	$115,419

Source: 2008, Under Armour, Inc., Form 10-K 2007 Annual Report, December 31, 26.

Exhibit 2 Under Armour Income Growth from 2005 to 2007

Under Armour, Inc. and Subsidiaries Consolidated Statements of Income (In thousands, except per share amounts)			
	Year Ended December 31		
	2007	**2006**	**2005**
Net revenues	$606,561	$430,689	$281,053
Cost of goods sold	301,517	215,089	145,203
Gross profit	305,044	215,600	135,850
Operating expenses			
Selling, general and administrative expenses	218,779	158,682	100,040
Income from operations	86,265	56,918	35,810
Other income (expense), net	2,778	2,169	(2,836)
Income before income taxes	89,043	59,087	32,974
Provision for income taxes	36,485	20,108	13,255
Net income	52,558	38,979	19,719
Accretion of and cumulative preferred dividends on Series A Preferred Stock	—	—	5,307
Net income available to common stockholders	$52,558	$38,979	$14,412

Source: 2008, Under Armour, Inc., Form 10-K 2007 Annual Report, December 31, 46.

and recognition for many years. Thus the battle for Under Armour was much more uphill than most other new entrants to an established market. However, Under Armour has succeeded in breaking into a mature market and is no longer simply an amateur player in the sports apparel arena. The question is: "How does the company stay on top of its game?"

History of Under Armour

As previously mentioned, when Plank was a football player he grew tired of having to change his damp, heavy t-shirt under his jersey, so he set out to create a unique product that would meet the needs of all athletes. His laboratory was his grandmother's basement in Maryland. After many prototypes, Plank created his first shirt; it was a shiny tight shirt made of high-tech fibers that wicked away moisture, keeping athletes cool, dry, and feeling "light."[2] Plank's shirts truly did regulate athletes' body temperatures, lending to improved performance.[3]

Starting Small
Plank believed that he could make a profitable apparel business with his advanced feature shirts, so he used

Exhibit 3 Net Revenue by Geographic Region

(In thousands)	Year Ended December 31		
	2007	**2006**	**2005**
United States	$562,439	$403,725	$266,048
Canada	23,360	16,485	9,502
Subtotal	585,799	420,210	275,550
Other foreign countries	20,762	10,479	5,503
Total net revenues	$606,561	$430,689	$281,053

Source: 2008, Under Armour, Inc., Form 10-K 2007 Annual Report, December 31, 68.

$20,000 of his savings and ran up $40,000 in credit card debt to launch Under Armour.[4] Success was initially slow in coming, but once Plank made his first big sale to Georgia Tech University,[5] Under Armour grew rapidly. Plank marketed his product by focusing on the value-added concept, and now many high school, college, and professional teams use Under Armour athletic gear.

At the end of its first year of operations, Under Armour had five lines of clothing made for every climate, and the company's operations were moved out of Plank's grandmother's basement into a manufacturing warehouse in Maryland.

Growing into a Recognized Brand

In the late 1990s, Under Armour achieved national recognition. By 1998, it was the official supplier of performance apparel to NFL Europe. In 1999, it signed a contract to feature Under Armour in Warner Brothers' movies. By 2000, Under Armour had become a globally recognized brand and was supplying performance apparel to the National Football League, National Hockey League, and Major League Baseball, USA Baseball, and the U.S. ski team as well as other professional leagues abroad.[6] Currently players from 30 of 32 NFL teams wear Under Armour products.

As of 2005, Under Armour was supplying over 100 NCAA Division 1A football programs and thirty NFL teams, but it was still looking for other areas to branch into within the performance apparel industry.[7] Consequently, Under Armour introduced a loose-fit clothing line and added women's clothing to its product line.[8] Also in 2005, the company went public, seeking to sell as much as $100 million in shares of common stock. Ben Sturner, president of Leverage Sports Agency, a New York–based sports marketing firm, said, "Under Armour is no longer an up-and-coming brand. [It] [has] positioned [itself] as a real player in the industry and in the eyes of consumers in only a few years' time."[9]

During 2007, Under Armour increased its marketing initiatives by opening self-owned retail and outlet stores. Plank recognized that "You can't be a world-class athletic brand without the ability to outfit the athlete head to toe,"[10] so Under Armour developed athletic footwear. As of the first quarter of 2008, Under Armour had 43 percent of the total U.S. performance apparel business sold through sporting goods stores, versus 32 percent for Nike and 5.1 percent for Adidas.[11] A marketing consultant has said, "Under Armour is identified with performance the way Starbucks is identified with better coffee, and that is a huge advantage in entering new categories."[12] Plank attributes the company's success to the fact that "[it] ha[s] grown and reinforced [its] brand name and image through sales to athletes and teams at all levels, from youth to professional, as well as through sales to consumers with active lifestyles around the globe."[13]

Current Product and Sales Profile

Geographic Distribution

Approximately 93 percent of sales in 2007 were in the United States. with the remaining 7 percent split between Canada [4 percent] and all other international markets [3 percent] (see Exhibit 3). Under Armour sells products in 13 countries, including in-house distribution in the United Kingdom, Germany, and France. Sales in other Western European and Asian countries are done through partnerships and third-party distributors. The limited sales outside of the North American market were primarily the result of an emerging international penetration plan that received new emphasis in 2006 with the opening of a European headquarters. In an effort to increase the geographic diversity of sales, these headquarters were opened to manage sales and distribution channels, and additional experienced industry talent was brought on board in 2007 (Exhibit 4 shows where offices and stores are located).

Exhibit 4 Geographic Diversity

Location	Use
Baltimore, MD	Corporate headquarters
Amsterdam, The Netherlands	European headquarters
Glen Bumie, MD	Distribution facilities, 17,000 square foot quick-turn, Special Make-Up Shop manufacturing facility, and 4,500 square foot retail outlet store
Denver, CO	Sales office
Ontario, Canada	Sales office
Guangzhou, China	Quality assurance & sourcing for footwear
Hong Kong	Quality assurance & sourcing for apparel
Various	Retail store space

Source: 2008, Under Armour, Inc., Form 10-K 2007 Annual Report, December 31, 20.

Product Segment Distribution

Under Armour's sales results are broken into apparel, footwear, accessories, and licensed products (see Exhibits 5 and 6). Apparel dominated in 2007 with 84 percent of total sales. Men's apparel made up the "lion's share" of Under Armour's business, representing 68 percent of apparel sales and 57 percent of total sales. The second largest apparel segment was women's with 23 percent of apparel sales and 19 percent of total sales, representing a significant growth and diversification opportunity. Youth products made up the balance of apparel sales.

Under Armour's non-apparel product segments made up the remaining 16 percent of sales: footwear (7 percent), accessories (5 percent), and licensed products (4 percent). Footwear is a new product line that was launched in fourth quarter of 2006. Initially this line only offered baseball, softball, and lacrosse cleats designed for high performance through a highly breathable and lightweight design. The footwear line now includes shoes for golf, football, running, and cross-training. In the near future it will likely introduce basketball shoes and soccer cleats. It captured 20 percent of the U.S. football

Exhibit 5 Net Revenue by Product Category

(In thousands)	Year Ended December 31		
	2007	2006	2005
Men's	$348,150	$255,681	$189,596
Women's	115,867	85,695	53,500
Youth	48,596	31,845	18,784
Apparel	512,613	373,221	261,880
Footwear	40,878	26,874	—
Accessories	29,054	14,897	9,409
Total net sales	582,545	414,992	271,289
License revenues	24,016	15,697	9,764
Total net revenues	$606,561	$430,689	$281,053

Source: 2008, Under Armour, Inc., Form 10-K 2007 Annual Report, December 31, 68.

Exhibit 6 Net Revenue by Product in 2007

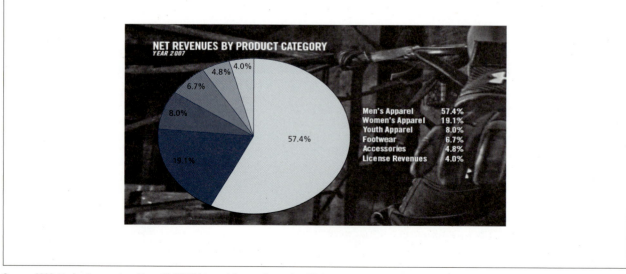

Source: 2008, Under Armour, Inc., Form 10-K 2007 Annual Report, December 31, Intro.

shoe market in the first year.[14] The company's 2009 first quarter earnings beat analysts' expectations, which the company attributes largely to the new running shoe.[15]

Under Armour's accessories category is developed and managed directly by Under Armour. The primary accessories products are performance gloves for football, baseball, running, and golf aligned to the Heatgear and Coldgear product lines with unique performance features.

Under Armour also licenses its brand name to independent manufacturers for other miscellaneous products such as bags, socks, headwear, eyewear, and watches. The company works with multiple licensees directly throughout the product development process to ensure that the products are aligned with its brand and quality expectations.

Seasonality

There appears to be a trend that sales are higher in the third and fourth quarters of each year, aligning with the football and basketball seasons and the traditional holiday gift-giving season in the United States. Under Armour has contemplated putting more emphasis on its baseball product line to improve the sales balance and reduce the seasonal variability in sales, inventory efforts, and distribution.

Operations and Distributions/ Distributors

Under Armour possesses an efficient operations and distribution network. As with any corporation, this requires a blend of physical-location metrics and strategic qualities.

By leveraging its licensing partners (JR286, Inc. and USG), Under Armour can provide a wider range of branded products to its customers. This broader range of products adds value by reinforcing the brand and generating revenue without having to organically develop capabilities in these adjacent product categories. Through keen selection and effective partner relationships, Under Armour has developed unique products that consumers value.

For the first ten years of its existence, the company was able to sustain operations by using "off the shelf" software programs, but after it went public in 2006, Under Armour invested in a new SAP system. This system is key to the company's ability to add products to its list of offerings, as it allows Under Armour to manage a more diverse inventory and to ship directly to distributors.[16]

Under Armour does not have a patent on any of the materials[17] used in its products. Therefore, it needs to be cautious in its licensing agreements so companies do not steal its know-how and introduce their own versions. Though the materials and technology used to create its products are not exclusive, by implementing an effective corporate strategy Under Armour has been able to fashion itself as a profitable business and remain a key player among competitors.

Major Competitors

There is stiff competition in the athletic apparel industry with companies of various sizes employing different strategies in order to attract consumers to their product and brand. The athletic apparel industry is so diverse that some smaller companies may choose to target a specific area such as yoga; whereas the larger companies try to capture the whole market. The larger companies continuously increase the competition by spending large amounts of money on product innovation, advertising, and sponsorships. Under Armour's three largest competitors in the industry are Nike, Adidas/Reebok, and Columbia Sportswear.[18] There are also smaller competitors such as SportHill that could possibly break through to become larger threats.

Nike[19]

Nike was founded in 1964 by a University of Oregon track star, Phil Knight. Knight saw a need for better running shoes and began selling shoes imported from Asia out of the trunk of his car. By 1972 he severed his relationships with suppliers abroad because they had become strained and developed his first shoe branded as Nike. Nike over time became known as a high-quality, innovative product that consumers and athletes wanted to wear and were willing to pay a premium price to own.

By 1980, Nike had captured 50 percent of the athletic shoe market and in the 1980s began expanding into other areas of the market through acquisitions and product innovation. It produces its three main product segments (footwear, apparel, and equipment) mostly through contract manufacturers rather than operating its own plants. Nike has relationships with some 700 factories in 52 countries, with most in China, Vietnam, and India.[20] Nike is the leader in athletic shoes, apparel, and equipment and grossed $18.6 billion in fiscal year 2007. It sells products for every sport and climate and strives to be the best in every segment. Nike advertises its brand through high-priced endorsement deals, media advertising, event sponsorships, and partnerships and alliances. Nike currently has 30,000 employees spread across six continents and operates in 160 countries. Nike is an industry leader that is continually striving to stay ahead of the competition.

Adidas[21]

Adidas, combined with Reebok (through an acquisition), is the second largest athletic apparel manufacturer in the world. Adidas was founded in 1924 in Germany by Adolf Dassler. Dassler created the first running shoe made by hand without electricity in his mother's kitchen. Dassler's big break came in 1954 when the German soccer team beat Hungary in the World Cup wearing Adidas cleats. From that point forward, Adidas was the industry leader in soccer shoes and apparel.

Changes in leadership during the late 1980s led Adidas to branch out into other markets, but it struggled to find its niche. Through acquisitions and better management it was back on track by the mid-1990s. Adidas acquired three smaller companies: TaylorMade, Salomon Group, and Maxfli. These acquisitions gave it access to the golf and winter sports market segments. In 2006, it merged with athletic apparel and equipment giant Reebok making it the second largest athletic apparel manufacturer in the world. Today the Adidas product line includes shoes and athletic apparel for basketball, soccer, fitness, golf, and outdoor adventure. Adidas operates globally and has 25,000 employees worldwide with 80 subsidiaries and reported $15.6 billion in profits in 2007.

Columbia Sportswear[22]

Columbia Sportswear Company started in the 1930s as a family-owned and operated hat company in Portland, Oregon. Founder Paul Lamfrom grew tired of working with inadequate suppliers and decided to manufacturer his own products. Columbia quickly gained a reputation for its innovative, high-quality products.

Columbia's introduction of waterproof, breathable fabrics triggered the growth it has experienced since the 1980s from a small family-owned business to a billion dollar publicly traded company. Columbia continues to grow thanks to its innovative product development and the acquisitions of Sorel, Mountain Hardware, Pacific Trail, and Montrail. These acquisitions enabled the company to branch out into other market segments.

Columbia Sportswear is now one of the largest manufacturers and sellers of outdoor apparel specializing in skiwear, snowboard gear, and hunting, fishing, hiking, camping, and casual wear. Columbia currently operates in North America, Europe, and Asia, and its products are available in 90 countries. Columbia has 3,000 employees worldwide. In 2007, Columbia posted record net sales of $1.36 billion.

SportHill[23]

SportHill was founded in 1985 by a University of Oregon track runner who saw the need for cold weather track gear. His athletic apparel design concept merged the best American fabrics with European style to make unique athletic apparel. SportHill clothing is designed for use in any climate and for any sport. SportHill utilizes the expertise of elite athletes to perfect its design and innovate new products. It is well known for quality, comfort, and reliability. SportHill's clothing can be found globally in most major retailer stores and can be purchased online. The success of SportHill is apparent in the number of sponsorships it has, including many Olympic athletes and collegiate running teams; however, it is a privately held company so financial information is not available.

Under Armour has been able to remain successful among its competitors in large part due to the strength of character of its founder and other leaders.

Under Armour's Leaders

Under Armour's success may seem unbelievable at first, but it's no accident. Plank's drive to keep trying even during difficult times when it seemed the company might never flourish is what made it possible. In the beginning, when customers would request products that Plank had not created, he would respond, "Of course we make that!" and then immediately go to work with suppliers and contractors to deliver on his promise. Two such examples were when the equipment manager for the Atlanta Falcons wanted long-sleeve Under Armour shirts, and when the equipment manager for Arizona State wanted clothing for cold weather.[24]

"He's one of the hardest workers I've known in my life," says Plank's mother.[25] Plank's humble beginnings give him valuable insight into his business. He knows every aspect of it because at one time he actually did the work himself. Many of his first employees were his college classmates and teammates. Most of them are still with Under Armour and play important roles in management.

He spent five months driving round-trip from Baltimore to Moundsville at least twice a week to help Ella Mae Holmes produce and ship Under Armour products. He left Baltimore at 4 AM, arrived in Moundsville about 8 AM, and worked with Holmes and her boyfriend throughout the day. At 8 PM, Plank would take his shipment to the local FedEx office and drive back to Baltimore.[26]

Plank effectively uses his athletic experience and connections to help Under Armour's marketing and sales teams earn new business. In the athletic world, he is considered by his customers to be "one of them" rather than a CEO of a very profitable business. It frequently takes competitors years to develop a loyal customer, but Under Armour has been able to quickly earn loyalty after a customer has had one or two good experiences with their purchase. Most of the sports teams feel that Plank is truly helping them by providing a better product and not simply trying to sell his brand. Plank embraces and nurtures this connection respectfully and gracefully. He regularly seeks feedback regarding existing products and the need for new products.

Management Style

Having been part of a sports team, Plank manages his company with a unique team-driven style. "Under Armour is one team and my job is to help ensure we operate and execute as one team. Because there's a lot of noise and clutter surrounding our brand, I try to simplify our story and objectives for the team to help keep everyone running on the same wavelength and working towards the same goal: to become the world's number one performance athletic brand."[27]

To remind him of his critical role every day, Plank has written on a whiteboard in his office four things that define his job: (1) make a great product, (2) tell a great story about the product, (3) service the business, and (4) build a great team. Every morning when he arrives at the office and every evening before he leaves, he looks at the board. Plank said, "If I don't work toward those things, I'm not doing my job …. You can overcomplicate your job … It's important that you don't allow the clutter to grow too loud […] and distract you from your mission."[28]

International Leadership

In order to facilitate its international expansion, Under Armour hired several new executives with experience in international business, most notably Peter Mahrer. Mahrer was appointed as president and managing director for Under Armour Europe, B.V. Mahrer, a seasoned industry executive, will oversee Under Armour's European operations headquartered in Amsterdam. Mahrer previously served as head of international sales and general manager for Puma AG.[29]

Under Armour's Business Strategies

Ever since its inception in 1996, Under Armour's leaders have strived to achieve the company's vision of becoming the world's leading performance athletic apparel brand by employing a differentiation strategy through innovation. Under Armour attains physical differentiation through the value chain activities of technological development and procurement. As CEO Kevin Plank puts it, "The key driver is to offer products that are better than what is currently in the market, best in class."[30] Additionally, Under Armour is able to exploit psychological differentiation through its marketing campaign, which has hundreds of professional athletes that not only volunteer to wear Under Armour gear, but actually want to wear it. Most budding stars or wannabe weekend recreational athletes want to wear the gear the pros wear. Plank is fixated on maintaining differentiation from Nike, and uses "authenticity" as his guiding principal to grow or advertise the brand. Under Armour, for example, identifies

itself with team sports, rather than individual sports and fashion. "Everything we do is centered on performance … we aren't ever going to develop products to fill up a sales table," says Plank. Specifically, Under Armour will never use cotton to produce its clothing.[31]

Under Armour's corporate level strategy consists of a low level of diversification. While it does offer more than one product, 84 percent of its revenue comes from athletic apparel and gear. Incorporating a shoe line is helping the company with its diversification efforts, but it is still highly dependent upon premium priced products that are closely related. There is obviously a degree of economic risk associated with the premium pricing and Under Armour is feeling the effects of the current declining retail consumer market that is affecting the broader economy. Additionally, Under Armour is exposed to a degree of risk by offering closely related, nonessential products that are, to a degree, subject to the fashion whims of its customers. Plank said Under Armour is "cautiously optimistic about 2009" and is looking at the year with the "appropriate degree of conservatism."[32]

Under Armour added new domestic sales channels by introducing its first independent retail sales outlet in 2007 in Annapolis, Maryland. However, due to the conservative approach to growth in 2009, no new retail stores will be opened during the year.

Under Armour has placed major emphasis on international expansion. In addition to creating a broader consumer base, "Researchers have found that international diversification can lead to greater operational efficiency, which ultimately leads to higher financial performance."[33] Because its product transcends cultural differences and is appealing to many athletes, regardless of nationality, Under Armour is pursuing a worldwide scope via regionalization. Over the past three years, revenues from foreign sales other than Canada have increased at a rate of 100 percent per year and are expected to increase even more quickly with the international growth emphasis (Exhibit 3). Under Armour is fortunate because performance sports apparel appears to transcend any jingoistic trends and exporting does not require an in-depth knowledge of local customer service. Additionally, Under Armour's products are already manufactured overseas in China; therefore, the new offices in Europe are primarily geared toward marketing and distribution and do not have to contend with the challenges associated with establishing manufacturing plants in foreign countries.

Marketing

Under Armour's marketing strength is twofold. First, its products have proven to be so effective that professional athletes want to use them. Second, Under Armour has become a master of product placement in movies, TV shows, and video games.

Plank believes that word-of-mouth advertising is the most effective method. Plank has said, "We always build a product for the athlete's needs." The customer is willing to pay the price because the Under Armour product has value in it. "Without value, our product is just an expensive t-shirt. But we have the technology in the fabric [and] the design and the features satisfy what the athlete needs."[34] "Our model is getting to the athletes—supplying them with great product that helps them perform better."[35]

Athletes are a valuable marketing resource and the mouthpiece for Under Armour. The company signed a five-year partnership agreement in April 2009 with Cal Ripken, Jr., a retired professional baseball player, to be their official uniform representative. Under Armour feels this is a great opportunity because Ripken previously was partnered with Nike.[36] The company has reached out to capture much of the youth sports industry by sponsoring recreational teams and major youth tournaments, including the Under Armour All-America high school football and lacrosse games (see Exhibit 7).[37]

Under Armour has initiated other sponsorships that help get its name out in public, such as the Baltimore Marathon, which is now named the Under Armour Marathon. In an effort to boost the women's clothing line, Under Armour sponsored the women's U.S. field hockey team and some of the U.S. women's softball and volleyball athletes during the 2008 Olympic Games.[38]

During the first three months of 2008, Under Armour apparel appeared in cable shows nearly 3,000 times, more than any other company, according to Nielsen Media.[39] Ironically, movie studios are asking to use Under Armour's products as opposed to Under Armour having to purchase product placement time. The desire of athletes and movie studios to use Under Armour's products leads to a lower-cost, more effective, grass roots ad campaign. While Under Armour did sponsor its first Super Bowl commercial in 2008, the company will continue to use more guerrilla tactics than traditional expensive ad campaigns.

Strategic Challenges

Like most up-and-coming companies, Under Armour faces several issues and challenges. These challenges include the current economic downturn, competing against major rivals such as Nike and Adidas/Reebok, and maintaining a positive brand image despite setbacks, such as the recent recall of its men's protective athletic gear.[40] In addition, some of the most critical issues involve protection of the differentiation strategy, improvement of production and procurement capabilities, and continued implementation of a sound international expansion strategy.

Under Armour's differentiation strategy has been successful to date; however, the lack of proprietary product rights, intellectual property rights in foreign countries, and a heavy reliance on relatively few third-party suppliers and manufacturers could adversely affect the long-term sustainability of the firm. "The intellectual property rights in the technology, fabrics, and processes used to manufacture our products are generally owned by our suppliers and generally not unique to us."[41] The company's ability to obtain patent protection for its products is limited, and as previously mentioned it does not currently own any fabric or process patents.[42]

Intangible assets such as trademarks are very important to the Under Armour brand, as are licensing arrangements and other legal agreements. The intellectual property rights laws and regulations of countries in the global market vary dramatically. Under Armour relies heavily on suppliers and manufacturers outside of

Exhibit 7 Sponsorship and Other Marketing Commitments

(In thousands)	December 31
	2007
2008	$14,684
2009	14,660
2010	13,110
2011	10,125
2012 and thereafter	1,005
Total future minimum sponsorship and other marketing payments	$53,584

Source: 2008, Under Armour, Inc., Form 10-K 2007 Annual Report, December 31, 60.

the United States. Seventy to 75 percent of the fabric used in its products come from only six suppliers,[43] lending to Under Armour's weak position relative to its suppliers. Additionally, some of its supplies are commodities and thus are subject to price fluctuations; for example, petroleum-based materials are used in Under Armour's products and the petroleum industry has experienced significant swings in price and relative availability in recent months and years.[44]

Under Armour has achieved a level of success in the U.S. domestic market and limited foreign markets, but is relatively small in size and financial strength compared to its major competitors (Nike and Adidas) with similar or competing product offerings. Does Under Armour run the risk of diluting the brand relative to its competitors? Is an acquisition strategy feasible due to the company's current debt situation? Although a cooperative strategy may be beneficial to bridge barriers to entry into desirable markets such as China, how likely is it that Under Armour would pursue this option due to its emphasis on innovation and premium branding? Overall, has Under Armour done a good job in finding key strategic leaders with the experience necessary and does it have the right organization in place to help execute its international growth strategy? Going forward, how can it maintain the product quality that it has nurtured thus far?

Additional questions that Plank and other managers are pondering are: Can Under Armour maintain strong relationships with its suppliers so that it becomes the customer of choice? Should Under Armour pursue patents or strike agreements to limit the chance of competitors offering identical products? If so, will this effort actually be a defense or will counterfeit merchandise undermine such an investment? Does Under Armour possess appropriate supplier relationships and have an understanding of the inherent economic impacts on raw materials? If not, how will Under Armour acquire or develop these capabilities? What capabilities should Under Armour develop to ensure international success? What barriers to entry exist in additional markets, and is licensing or some other method the best approach based on its current cash position? Will the international strategy be different from Under Armour's overall differentiation and growth strategy? As its founder and CEO has stated, "Under Armour's success in 2010 and beyond will be significantly impacted by the decisions we make in 2009."[45]

NOTES

1. 2008, Investors Relations—About Under Armour, Inc., http://www.underarmour.com.
2. 2008, Five questions with Under Armour CEO, Kevin Plank, *Sports Business Journal*, http://www.sportsbusinessconferences.com/sss-pov/entries/2008/five-questions-with-kevin-plank, August 15.
3. Ibid.
4. Ibid.
5. S. Lyster, 2008, The history of Under Armour—A mastermind for performance apparel, http://www.ezinearticles.com, December 4.
6. 2008, Under Armour performance apparel, *Funding Universe*, http://www.fundinguniverse.com, December 4.
7. Ibid.
8. Ibid.
9. D. Rovell, 2005, Under Armour could offer up to $100 million in stock, http://sports.espn.go.com, August 26.
10. S. N. Mehta, 2009, Under Armour reboots: The sports apparel maker is sprinting into footwear—and trying to take on Nike—with the help of software and science, *Fortune*, http://www.money.cnn.com, March 5.
11. D. Kiley, 2008, Under Armour steps into footwear field: Sports apparel maker set to do battle with Nike and Adidas, *BusinessWeek*, http://www.businessweek.com, January 31.
12. Ibid.
13. 2008, Under Armour 10-K 2007 Annual Report, http://www.underarmour.com/annuals.cfm, February.
14. D. Kiley, 2008, Under Armour steps into footwear field.
15. A. K. Walker, 2009, New shoe helps Under Armour beat expectations, *Baltimore Sun*, http://www.baltimoresun.com, April 29.
16. S. N. Mehta, 2009, Under Armour reboots.
17. D. Kiley, Under Armour steps into footwear field.
18. 2008, Under Armour, *Hoovers*, http://premium.hoovers.com.ezproxy1.lib.asu.edu/subscribe/co/competitors.xhtml?ID=fffrfjjfkrrrhkxsxh.
19. 2008, Nike history, http://www.nikebiz.com/company_overview/history, December 4.
20. 2009, Nike company overview fact sheet, http://www.nikebiz.com; 2009, Nike pulling production from four Asian factories, *Reuters*, http://www.reuters.com, March 24.
21. 2008, Adidas group history, Adidas Group, http://www.adidas-group.com/en/overview/history/default.asp. December 4.
22. 2008, Columbia Sportswear, *Funding Universe*, http://www.fundinguniverse.com/company-histories/Columbia-Sportswear-Company-Company-History1.html, December 4.
23. 2008, http://www.sporthill.com, December 4.
24. M. Hyman, 2003, How I did it: Kevin Plank: For the founder of apparel-maker Under Armour, entrepreneurship is 99% perspiration and 1% polyester, *Inc.*, http://www.inc.com, December.
25. S. Graham, 2004, Kevin Plank's drive makes Under Armour an industry overachiever, *Sports Business Journal*, http://www.sportsbusinessjournal.com/article/36213, January 19.
26. Ibid.
27. 2008, Five questions with Under Armour CEO, Kevin Plank.
28. 2008, How do you define your job? *Business Management Daily*, http://www.businessmanagementdaily.com, November 8.
29. 2007, Under Armour appoints Peter Mahrer as president & managing director, Europe; Experienced sporting goods industry executive to lead sport performance brand's European growth strategy, Baltimore, MD, Under Armour press release, http://www.underarmour.com, July 9.
30. T. Heath, 2008, In pursuit of innovation at Under Armour: Founder Kevin Plank says Super Bowl commercial has generated "buzz," *Washington Post*, February 25, D03.

31. D. Kiley, 2009, Under Armour steps into footwear field.

32. R. Sharrow, 2009, Plank: Under Armour eyeing '09 "with appropriate degree of conservatism," *Baltimore Business Journal*, http://www.baltimore.bizjournals.com, January 29.

33. R. E. Hoskisson, M. Hitt, R. Ireland, & J. Harrison, 2008, *Competing for Advantage*, Thomson Southwestern, 286.

34. 2007, I am, Video interview with Kevin Plank, *CNBC*, http://www.cnbc.com/id/25191722, September 11.

35. M. Hyman, 2003, How I did it: Kevin Plank.

36. R. Sharrow, 2009, Under Armour, Ripken Baseball swing for fences with sportswear pact, *Baltimore Business Journal*, http://www.baltimore.bizjournals.com, April 22.

37. R. Sharrow, 2009, Cal Ripken Jr. nears deal to promote Under Armour, *Baltimore Business Journal*, http://www.baltimore.bizjournals.com, March 20.

38. R. Sharrow, 2008, Under Armour entering an Olympic contest of its own, *Baltimore Business Journal*, http://www.baltimore.bizjournals.com, August 1.

39. A. K. Walker, 2008, Under Armour in public eye, *The Baltimore Sun*, July 24.

40. J. Alper, 2009, Under Armour recalls 200,000 cups: Injuries involve cutting and bruising, *NBC New York Sports*, http://www.nbcnewyork.com/sports, April.

41. 2007, Under Armour, Inc., Form 10-K Annual Report, http://investor.underarmour.com, December 31, 18.

42. Ibid.

43. 2008, Under Armour, Inc., Form 8-K, http://investor.underarmour.com, 6.

44. Ibid.

45. R. Sharrow, 2009, Plank: Under Armour eyeing '09 with appropriate degree of conservatism.

*Analia Anderson, Jake Johnson, Pauline Pham,
Adam Schwartz, Richard Till, Craig Vom Lehn,
Elena Wilkening*

Arizona State University

*Air transportation powers the U.S. economy—this is an
industry that drives economic and social development.
Air transportation is a critical part of our nation's infrastructure and should play a vital role in our country's
economic recovery … enabling our cities and smaller
communities to connect and compete domestically and
globally. It is, therefore, hugely ironic that we enable
such economic and business development in the United
States—to the tune of more than $1 trillion a year and
contribut[ing] some 5 percent of GDP—but have historically and systemically been incapable of earning our cost
of capital.*

—GLEN TILTON, CHAIRMAN, PRESIDENT, AND
CEO OF UNITED AIRLINES[1]

In early 2009, the U.S. economy was mired in its worst
recession since the Great Depression. With airline
industry business cycles closely mirroring larger economic trends, United Airlines felt the effects of the
downturn. United, the fourth-largest U.S. passenger
airline, lost more than $5 billion in 2008 and reported
further declines in both revenue and traffic in the first
quarter of 2009.[2] Even before the economy soured,
United managed only minimal profits in 2006 and 2007,
which were considered great years for the U.S. airline
industry. Prior to that, the company spent three years
in Chapter 11 bankruptcy protection as a result of losses
early in the decade. In addition, United encountered
challenges related to expanding service internationally,
introducing subsidiaries in an effort to compete with
low-cost carriers (LCCs), and maintaining positive relations with its employees and the unions that represent
its employees. Thus, more than just waiting for economic recovery, United is exploring tactics to become
profitable again and reclaim the image and success it
once experienced.

Early History

United Air Lines, Inc. came into existence in 1931 to
provide mail service and passenger transport.[3] United
was born uniquely national, with Eastern and Western
subsidiaries, and diversified by virtue of its ownership of
Boeing Air Transport, an aircraft manufacturer.[4] Early
growth in the fledgling industry was funded largely
by U.S. government payments for mail service. When
accusations of collusion arose from the allocation of
routes by the postal service, the government stepped in to
regulate both the process and the industry.[5] The resulting
Civil Aeronautics Act of 1938 transferred power over
route allocation to the newly created Civil Aeronautics
Authority,[6] which required United to divest Boeing and
several airports it owned, but awarded the company
"grandfather certificates on U.S. transcontinental and
West Coast routes it was operating when the law took
effect."[7]

Like most airlines, United prospered and grew
under government regulation. Pricing was regulated,
and approval from government regulators was required
for an airline to enter or exit a particular route.[8] While
the market for passenger travel grew significantly after
World War II, artificially high prices limited air travel
to wealthier travelers and businessmen. Under regulatory protection, carriers developed hub-and-spoke
networks that allowed them to centralize operations
and provide convenient connections to passengers. The
beginnings of United's network can be seen in Exhibit 1,
which shows the airline's route map in 1940. Hubs in
Chicago, San Francisco, and Los Angeles were beginning to take shape. Eventually they would be joined by
hubs in Denver and Washington D.C.[9] Larger airports
often were dominated by one or two carriers, such as
United in Denver and Chicago.[10] As a result of regulation

Exhibit 1 United Air Lines Route Map, 1940

and network distribution, competition was restrained, with carriers making small but reliable profits based on the uniqueness of their networks and the convenience of schedules and connections, but deregulation changed all of this.

Deregulation

In 1978, the passage of the Airline Deregulation Act eliminated government oversight of routes and fees, allowing carriers to compete along a much broader range of parameters.[11] Deregulation brought about a glut of new airlines "causing airfares to plummet 40 percent in real terms between 1978 and 1997."[12] For United and its competitors, business cycles have been much more dramatic under deregulation, with profits in years when the economy is strong and heavy losses when it is weak.[13] Along with the challenges came opportunities for expansion. United secured its first Trans-Pacific route in 1983 and subsequently purchased 13 additional Asian routes from the ailing Pan American Airways.[14] In 1990, the company launched service to Europe, and in 1992 it operated flights to South America.[15] By 1995, with the introduction of service to Mumbai, India, United could advertise that it offered "Round the World" service.[16]

Although United was taking advantage of the opportunities that deregulation made possible, the company was struggling with the higher oil prices that resulted from the Persian Gulf War and the emergence of successful low-cost carriers such as Southwest Airlines. By the early 1990s, United was losing money. In 1993, the company attempted to remedy its financial problems by exchanging $5.15 billion of salaries and benefits with its employees for a 53 percent stake in the company.[17] As a result, in 1994, United became the "largest majority employee-owned corporation in the world."[18] Also in 1994, United launched "Shuttle by United" to compete against the low-cost carriers in the western United States; however, in 2001 when air travel diminished and cost savings had not materialized, the Shuttle was assimilated back into the main business.[19] Business took a sharp turn for the worse at the beginning of the new millennium when United declared bankruptcy and confronted other challenges.

Bankruptcy and Beyond

At the end of 2001, United recorded a $2.1 billion loss, the largest in airline history. With losses continuing to mount, United, under newly appointed CEO Glenn Tilton, filed for Chapter 11 bankruptcy protection in December 2002.[20]

Under bankruptcy protection, the company restructured its labor contracts and defaulted on its employee pension plan. United took out a $3 billion loan from investment banks in order to gain approval to exit bankruptcy, which it did on[21] February 1, 2006.[22] The timing was auspicious for the company as the U.S. economy was once again on the rise and airlines, including United, earned profits in 2006 and 2007.[23] The good times came to an end in 2008, however, as the U.S. economy slipped into recession, and United posted its largest-ever loss of $5.2 billion.[24]

In an unusual move for a bankrupt company, United also formed a new business line called Ted, which was a second attempt at creating a low-cost subsidiary.[25] Ted failed to meet expectations and the company announced its closure in 2008.[26]

Company executives have tried to reposition the company since 2006. United bid to merge with Delta in 2007[27] and with both Continental[28] and US Airways in 2008, but none of these negotiations were successful.[29] United was forced to make significant cuts once again, and by June 2008 the company had announced plans to ground 70 planes, eliminate 950 pilot positions, and cut up to 1,600 salaried positions.

While United has suffered many trials since deregulation, it has managed to survive. Many airlines have not been so fortunate, as competition in the airline industry is intense.

Competition

Within the last 30 years the airline industry has undergone significant contraction, as healthier carriers acquired failing competitors or their assets. Exhibit 2 shows the 51 mergers and acquisitions that brought the airline industry to its current state.[30] Six airlines now control 71.4 percent of the U.S. market (see Exhibit 3). The top six carriers consist of five traditional carriers—American, Continental, Delta, United, and US Airways—along with Southwest, the most successful of the LCCs (Exhibit 4 shows relevant financial data).

Competition is becoming more intense among the traditional carriers because the amount of business travel is decreasing.[31] Among the factors contributing to the decline in business travel are the use of video-conferencing, e-mail, and other Internet-based interactive technologies that make it easy to convey information without a face-to-face meeting.[32] Even more significant, perhaps, are cuts in corporate expenditures and increased governance, which lead to fewer approved trips and more price sensitivity among business travelers. The end result of this shift is that "the leisure segment of demand now constitutes the dominant one in air transport today."[33]

The similarities between United and its major competitors (excluding Southwest Airlines) are far greater

Exhibit 2 The Evolution of the U.S. Airline Industry

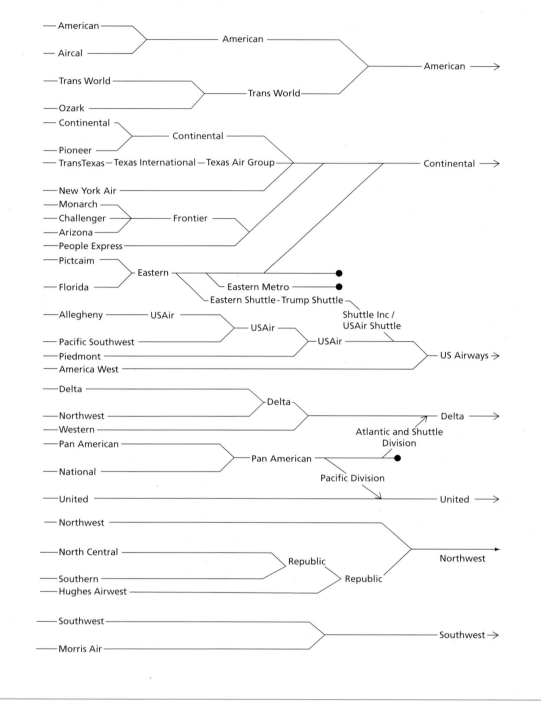

Source: B. Vasigh, K. Fleming, & T. Tacker, 2008, *Introduction to Air Transport Economics*, Ashgate Publishing, 16.

than their differences. All operate a hub-and-spoke route network, seeking to efficiently transfer passengers across the country. They all run a mainline service with large jets and extend their reach through networks of regional affiliates and global alliances. They all focus on the business traveler, offering service upgrades and frequent flyer loyalty programs to appeal to the business segment

of the market. These companies differ, however, in their history, size, and hub locations.

American Airlines

Founded in 1934 as the Robertson Aircraft Corporation, American Airlines has grown from a small airmail service to one of the largest passenger airlines with 84,000

Exhibit 3 Airline Domestic Market Share, March 2009

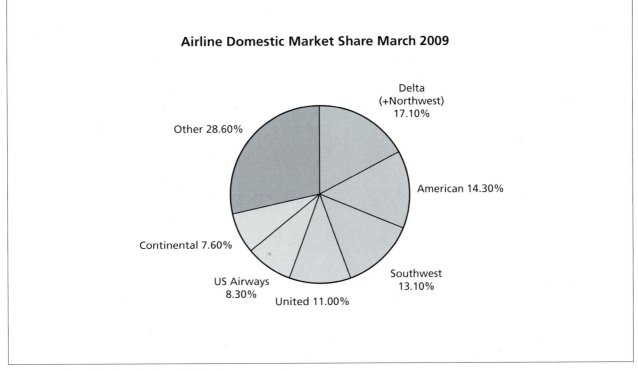

Source: 2009, Chart by authors, data from RITA, http://www.transtats.bts.gov.

Exhibit 4 Comparison of Net Profits between United and Top Competitors

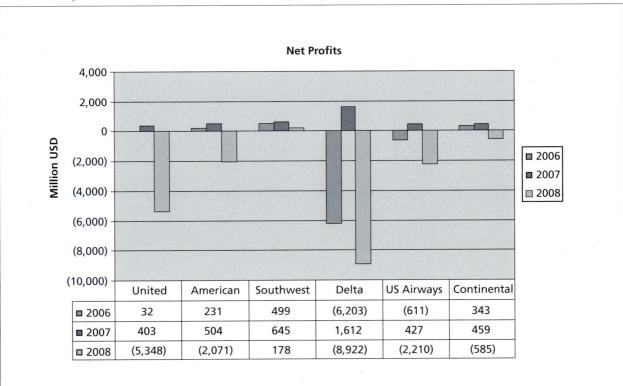

	United	American	Southwest	Delta	US Airways	Continental
2006	32	231	499	(6,203)	(611)	343
2007	403	504	645	1,612	427	459
2008	(5,348)	(2,071)	178	(8,922)	(2,210)	(585)

Source: 2009, Chart by authors using data from the 2008 10-K reports of each company.

employees and a fleet of 900 aircraft.[34] From its corporate headquarters in Dallas and additional major hubs in Chicago, St. Louis, and Miami the company transports 270,000 passengers on 3,300 flights to 250 domestic and international destinations every day.[35] Like most traditional carriers, American operates a mainline business serving larger cities and a regional affiliate network (American Eagle) serving smaller airports. American Eagle accounts for 300 of American's planes, flying 1,800 daily flights to 150 destinations in the United States and the Carribean.[36] American's network is further extended by its participation in the Oneworld global airline alliance.

American is the only large traditional domestic carrier that has not filed for bankruptcy, narrowly avoiding this fate in 2003.[37] In 2008, the company posted the fourth-largest loss among domestic carriers, just under $2.1 billion.[38]

Continental Airlines. Unlike American, Continental Airlines has filed for bankruptcy protection twice—once in 1983 and again in 1990.[39] Since the second bankruptcy, the company's fortunes have improved significantly, leading *Fortune* to name Continental, "The World's Most Admired Airline" for five years running.[40] While several competitors posted multi-billion dollar losses in 2008, Continental's loss was modest by comparison, $585 million.[41]

Continental and its regional affiliates, Continental Express, Continental Micronesia, and Continental Connection, fly more than 2,600 flights per day to 265 domestic and international destinations using a network based on hubs located in Newark, Houston, Cleveland, and Guam.[42] Continental has more than 42,000 employees, 44 percent of whom are covered by collective bargaining agreements.[43]

In 2007, Continental entered into merger talks with United Airlines. The talks subsequently failed to produce a merger, but did result in an alliance that involved Continental terminating its membership in the SkyTeam global alliance (anchored by Delta and Air France KLM) and becoming part of the Star Alliance dominated by United, Lufthansa, and US Airways.[44]

Delta Airlines. Founded in Georgia in 1924 by a cropduster named Huff Daland, Delta's first decades of operation were dominated by agricultural and public service flights, with the majority of its domestic flights dedicated to mail handling, and then for military purposes during World War II.[45]

From the 1940s through the late twentieth century, Delta aggressively pursued a differentiation strategy, known for its innovation and contribution to the art and science of aviation. There were many "firsts" for Delta, such as being the first airline to offer night service, the first to employ interchange service among flight attendants, the first airline to transport living vegetables and plants, the first airline to use the Douglass DC-8 and DC-9 (which would become standard in the industry for decades), and the first to offer passengers an in-flight telephone system (Airfone). In 1962, Delta had the quickest flight time from coast to coast (Atlanta to Los Angeles); its record time of just less than three hours remains the fastest cross-country passenger flight to date. The hub-and-spoke system was Delta's innovation that improved passenger plane transfers with coordinated flight arrival and departure times.[46]

However, this airline giant has experienced financial trouble in recent years. In September 2005, Delta Airlines filed for Chapter 11 bankruptcy.[47] Goodwill and deferred tax asset write-offs, significant declines in passenger miles, and high fuel costs led management to conclude that "… these results underscore the urgent need to make fundamental changes in the way we do business."[48] A more fundamental shift in industry strategy, however, seemed to underlie the firm's demise. The continued growth of low-cost carriers, intense competitive rivalry within the industry (most notably increased price sensitivity), and increased customer use of the Internet for travel information challenged Delta's differentiation strategy that was framed around exceptional customer service and innovative aviation.

To counter the increasing threats to its firm, Delta finalized its merger with Northwest Airlines in October 2008. Although the combined organization lost $8.9 billion in 2008,[49] Delta hopes to obtain three major benefits from the merger: (1) larger market share by including Northwest's mid- and northwest U.S. routes, along with its Asia routes; (2) improved financial capacity to sustain cyclical downturns in the economy and associated volatility in fuel costs; and (3) synergy of resources created by the combination of the Delta SkyMiles and Northwest WorldPerks frequent flyer programs, facilitated by both airlines membership in the SkyTeam alliance (including over 20 other commercial carriers).[50] As a result of the merger, Delta offers the largest variety of domestic and international commercial routes (378 destinations in 66 countries) and is the largest commercial airline in the world.[51]

US Airways. Headquartered in Tempe, AZ, US Airways is the nation's fifth-largest airline. It employs over 33,000 people and has more than 3,000 departures a day using a fleet of 351 mainline and 299 express aircraft serving 155 domestic and 46 international destinations in 27 different countries from its major hubs in Phoenix, Charlotte, and Philadelphia.[52]

As a result of its acquisition by America West Airlines in September 2005, US Airways avoided filing a second bankruptcy in three years and inevitable liquidation.[53] The new US Airways (under the America West leadership team and CEO Doug Parker) was able to offer "more non-stop flights and better connecting service than either the West-Coast-oriented America West or the old, East-Coast-centric US Airways had before," and even "branded [itself] as 'America's largest low cost carrier.'"[54] The post-merger airline earned $427 million in profit on reported $11.7 billion in revenue in 2007 and $304 million on $11.6 billion in revenue in 2006. The firm reported a net loss of $2.2 billion on increased revenue of $12.1 billion in 2008.[55]

As with many of its competitors, US Airways relies on its regional affiliate, US Airways Express, to provide jet service to passengers traveling in and out of the smaller airports across the country, as well as flying during off-peak hours when it becomes inefficient to operate a larger jet.[56] In addition, US Airways is a member of the Star Alliance, which provides customers with even more access to various destinations across the globe without additional costs for the airline.[57]

US Airways competes on price, flight availability, and level of service provided with both low-cost carriers such as Southwest and AirTran, and full service traditional airlines such as American, Delta, and United.[58] The weakened state of the U.S. economy, a higher operating cost structure than that of true low-cost carriers, and fluctuations in fuel prices make it extremely difficult for the airline to earn profits on an annual basis. In fact, according to the airline officials, "one cent per gallon change in fuel prices will result in a $14 million increase/decrease in annual fuel expense."[59] However, US Airways is determined to be successful by providing the best customer service. But according to the 2008 American Customer Satisfaction survey conducted by the University of Michigan, the airline only scored 59 out 100 and thus has significant room for improvement in this regard.[60]

Southwest Airlines. Founded in 1971, Southwest Airlines introduced a new business model in the U.S. airline industry. It originally flew only intra-state routes in Texas, allowing it to operate outside the price and route regulations inter-state carriers faced.[61] Thus it was able to focus on providing low-cost no-frills travel to price-conscious consumers. When the industry was deregulated in 1978, Southwest began to expand beyond the borders of Texas. By 2007, Southwest had carried nearly 102 million passengers, more than any other airline in the world.[62] At the end of 2008, the company had a fleet of 500 Boeing 737 aircraft that flew 3,300 flights to 65 U.S. cities daily.[63]

Unlike its traditional competitors, Southwest does not rely on a hub-and-spoke network, using instead a point-to-point service between medium and large metropolitan areas.[64] Southwest minimizes costs by standardizing its fleet to reduce training and maintenance expenses, by using secondary airports that charge lower access fees, and by minimizing downtime for both aircraft and employees.[65] While traditional hub-and-spoke networks attempt to coordinate hub arrivals to facilitate shorter layovers for passengers, Southwest makes regular, frequent flights throughout the day. The result is a flatter demand for labor (less peaks and valleys) and higher aircraft utilization because of turnarounds that take half as long as the industry average.[66]

The customer experience on Southwest is described as "no-frills" because the company uses first-come, first-served seating and does not provide complimentary meal service. Southwest was also a pioneer in online bookings, e-ticketing, and self-check kiosks, reducing the cost of the ticketing and check-in process.[67]

Although "no-frills" might indicate a lack of commitment to service, industry statistics and surveys confirm that passengers feel otherwise. In fact, "Southwest Airlines has consistently received the lowest ratio of complaints per passengers boarded of all major U.S. carriers that have been reporting statistics to the Department of Transportation (DOT) since September 1987."[68]

The company earned profits during every year from 1975 to 2008, including recessionary periods in the early 1990s and 2000s when traditional carriers suffered losses.[69] In 2008, while every major traditional U.S. carrier posted a loss, Southwest turned a profit of $178 million.[70] The extent of the threat posed by Southwest and its model is evident in the number of low-cost carriers that have been launched around the world and the extent to which traditional carriers have tried to change their business models in direct response to the growth of low-cost airlines. Primarily, traditional carriers have tried combating low-cost carriers by creating "low-cost" subsidiaries of their own. American Airlines is the only major competitor to avoid this temptation.

Southwest has not posed a threat in regard to international travel because its operations do not yet extend beyond the borders of the United States.

International Transport

Generally speaking, an airline is permitted to carry passengers from a domestic airport to a foreign destination, drop them off, pick up passengers at that airport, and return to its country of origin.[71] Airlines are usually not permitted to carry passengers to other airports in other countries or within any country other than their home nation. Obviously, this situation presents problems for a traveler who wishes to go for example from a small airport in the United States to a small airport in Russia. This traveler would need to purchase separate tickets on a U.S. and a Russian carrier, transfer his or her own baggage, and assume the risks of missed connections between the carriers.

One obvious way around this dilemma is a merger of carriers with domestic rights in both countries. Unfortunately, "U.S. law limits the amount of foreign ownership in its domestic airlines to a maximum of 49 percent, with a maximum of 25 percent control."[72] Because other nations have similar restrictions, international airline mergers are essentially impossible at this time.

To circumvent the limitations related to international routes and restrictions on ownership, airlines have formed global strategic alliances.

Global Alliances

Alliances allow passengers to book end-to-end itineraries to a much larger pool of international destinations through airlines code-sharing on their joint networks.[73] In addition to extending a carrier's network, alliances also allow airlines to expand the value of their Frequent Flyer Programs (FFP) by providing passengers the opportunity to accumulate and redeem awards for other member airlines.[74] These alliances have extended beyond code-sharing and agreements on FFP programs to include food service agreements and maintenance contracts for each other's aircraft. There are three main airline alliances that compete against one another: Oneworld, SkyTeam, and Star. Exhibit 5 shows the airlines participating in each alliance as of June 2009, along with key statistics from 2008 for each alliance.

Star Alliance. The Star Alliance is the largest and the oldest formed by an agreement between United Airlines, Lufthansa, Air Canada, Thai Airways, and SAS (Scandinavian Airlines) in 1997.[75] In its 12-year existence, Star Alliance has grown to 21 member airlines and 3 regional members. The extent to which the alliance has been successful in covering the globe is evident in the combined route map shown in Exhibit 6.

Exhibit 5 Global Alliances

Global Alliances			
Alliance	**Oneworld**	**SkyTeam**	**Star**
Year formed	1999	2000	1997
Countries served	134	169	159
Unique airports	673	905	912
Daily departures	8,419	16,787	16,500
Passengers (thousands)	328,626	462,000	499,900
Lounges	550	447	805
Fleet (operated)	2,226	2,496	3,325
Employees	302,753	356,998	393,559
Full members	American Airlines	Aeroflot	Air Canada
	British Airways	Aeromexico	Air China
	Cathay Pacific Airways	Air France	Air New Zealand
	FinnAir	Alitalia	ANA
	Iberia	China Southern Airlines	Asiana Airlines
	Japan Airlines (JAL)	Continental Airlines*	Austrian
	LAN Airlines	CSA Czech Airlines	bmi
	Malev Hungarian Airlines	Delta Air Lines	EGYPTAIR
	Mexicana	KLM Royal Dutch Airlines	LOT Polish Airlines

Exhibit 5 Global Alliances (*Continued*)

Global Alliances			
Alliance	**Oneworld**	**SkyTeam**	**Star**
	Qantas	Korean Air	Lufthansa
	Royal Jordanian	Northwest Airlines	Scandinavian Airlines
			Shanghai Airlines
			Singapore Airlines
			South African Airways
			Spanair
			SWISS
			TAP Portugal
			THAI
			Turkish Airlines
			United Airlines
			US Airways
Associate/regional members	Air Nostrum	Air Europa	Adria Airways
	American Connection	Copa Airlines	Blue1
	American Eagle	Kenya Airways	Croatia Airlines
	BA Citiflyer		
	Click Mexicana		
	Comair		
	Dragonair		
	J-Air		
	JAL Express		
	JALways		
	Japan Transocean Air		
	Jetconnect		
	LAN Argentina		
	LAN Ecuador		
	LAN Express		
	LAN Peru		
	QantasLink		
	Sun-Air of Scandinavia		

* Continental is transitioning from SkyTeam to Star in 2009.

Source: 2009, Table compiled by authors using data from http://www.oneworld.com, http://www.skyteam.com, and http://www.staralliance.com.

Exhibit 6 Star Alliance Route Network

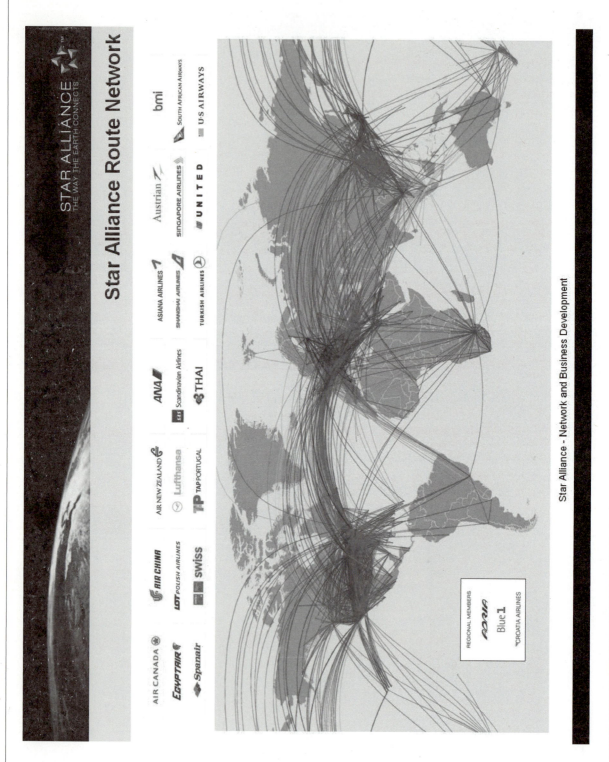

Star Alliance - Network and Business Development

Source: 2008, Network facts & figures, Star Alliance, http://www.staralliance.com, July.

Star Alliance exemplifies both the advantages and disadvantages of global airline alliances. Member airlines have been able to reduce costs and increase convenience for passengers through initiatives such as Star's dedicated terminals in Tokyo, Bangkok, Miami, and elsewhere.[76] Placing Star Alliance member airlines in a single terminal allows passengers to connect faster with shorter walks between gates. It also allows airlines to share lounges as well as personnel and resources used in check-in and ground handling activities.[77]

However, critics of alliances claim that code-sharing arrangements can lead to a reduction in competition, as "all the flights on a route carry the codes of [all] the 'competitors' and are jointly marketed by [all] the airlines."[78] Too many alliance members flying the same routes can also adversely affect the airlines involved, "as new airlines are added to the alliance, the importance of an existing airline may be reduced."[79]

Additionally, airlines face expenses when they join an alliance. Service levels must be standardized, information technology systems must be integrated, and costs are incurred for running the alliance itself.[80] Still, on the whole, there is general agreement that the benefits of alliances outweigh their drawbacks.

Oneworld.   Oneworld is the smallest of the three major alliances. Offering the same basic benefits as Star, Oneworld also consolidated operations in dedicated terminals in Madrid, London Heathrow, Tokyo Narita, and elsewhere.[81] Oneworld seeks to distinguish itself from the Star and SkyTeam alliances by offering innovative fare structures that are designed to appeal to adventurous pleasure travelers as well as frequent business travelers.[82] In the United States, American is the primary Oneworld carrier.

SkyTeam.   Formed in 2000, SkyTeam is the youngest of the major alliances. Like its competitors, SkyTeam is working to reduce member costs and "has opened more than 40 co-locations."[83] Member airlines are currently in the process of repainting some aircraft to emphasize the SkyTeam brand and de-emphasize the individual carrier brands.[84] Exhibit 7 shows a standard Delta branded plane and a new SkyTeam-Delta co-branded model. In 2007, the U.S. market was served by SkyTeam carriers Delta, Northwest, and Continental. Delta acquired Northwest in 2008 and Continental is scheduled to switch to the Star Alliance in 2009, leaving Delta as the sole U.S. airline in SkyTeam. Continental's defection is not surprising given Delta's acquisition of Northwest coupled with "Delta's and Continental's battle on transatlantic routes."[85]

Of the six largest U.S. airlines, Southwest is the only one that is not a member of a global alliance. In fact, no LCC is currently a member of any alliance. LCCs have traditionally avoided global alliances because of the service level requirements that membership places on them, although they do have some domestic code sharing agreements (Southwest had a code sharing agreement with ATA Airlines, for example, until ATA ceased service in 2008). A particularly enlightening case is Aer Lingus, which was in Oneworld, but quit the alliance as part of its attempt to restructure itself as an LCC.[86]

In addition to extending its network globally through the Star Alliance, United extends its network to smaller domestic airports through its regional affiliate, United Express.

United Express.   The goal of this air carrier service is to transport passengers from smaller airports to United hubs for convenient connections to other United and Star Alliance flights.[87] United maintains agreements with regional carriers such as Chautauqua Airlines, Colgan Airlines, Go Jet Airlines, Mesa Airlines, Shuttle America, SkyWest Airlines, and Trans States Airlines, all of which fly planes bearing the United Express insignia; as such, passengers are generally unaware of the relationship and consider these flights to be United Airlines flights.[88] United Express conducts more than 2,000 flights daily and all of the same elements apply, such as acquiring points for the United frequent flier program.

Not only are alliances and networks important considerations for airline companies, but factors of production may be even more crucial.

Factors of Production

Aircraft Manufacturers.   The most visible tangible asset of any airline is its fleet of aircraft. For large jet aircraft (more than 100 seats), Boeing and Airbus are currently the only two suppliers in the world.[89] The two companies are relatively evenly matched in terms of capabilities, and "since both manufacturers price their aircraft almost identically, competition occurs in the area of additional services, such as financing agreements or agreed buy-back of older aircraft."[90] Most airlines, including United, tend to maintain a relationship with both manufacturers to avoid becoming overly dependent on either supplier.

Fuel.   With recent increases in the cost of oil, fuel has become the largest and most volatile expense for airlines.[91] In 2008 oil prices escalated to a high of $145 per barrel in July, then dropped to $70 a barrel in October, making it difficult for airlines to forecast expenses.[92] To smooth the variance, airlines routinely participate in fuel hedging, but this is not a foolproof practice. United lost $519 million in just the third quarter of 2008 when price decreases lowered the

Exhibit 7 Delta Planes with Traditional Delta Branding and New SkyTeam Branding

Source: 2009, Delta Air Lines N702DN and N844MH, http://www.flickr.com, March 30.

value of its hedges.[93] American, Delta, Continental, and even Southwest also posted losses due to fuel hedges.[94]

Airport Slots. The relationships between airlines and airports are quite complex. While airports generally have significant latitude with regards to the fees they charge airlines to use their facilities, the resulting agreements give airlines significant power over gates, terminals, ticket counters, and slots for takeoffs and landings.[95]

Of particular interest is something called an "airport slot." Essentially, airport slots grant the holder "the right to land or take off from an airport at a given time."[96] Once these slots are granted, they exist in perpetuity as long as the owner uses the slot at least

80 percent of the time.[97] This provides a significant incentive to slot owners to continue flying in every slot they own to keep those slots from becoming available to other carriers.[98]

Labor. Labor relations can be challenging for any company, but for the airline industry, where a large percentage of airline workers are represented by labor unions, it is a very critical component of the business. Unfortunately for United, the firm's history of problems with the labor unions representing its workers continues to plague the company today.

After years of strikes and bitter negotiations, 1994 was something of a watershed moment for United's labor relations. As part of contract negotiations, it became the largest company in the world to be majority owned by its employees. Pilots bought 25 percent of the company, machinists, 20 percent and salaried and management workers, about 10 percent, and several seats on the board of directors were granted to union representatives.[99] It seemed that United and its unions were finally working together; however, that perception ended quickly. While the company's Employee Stock Ownership Plan (ESOP) provided job security for the so-called new "owners," there was little change in employee relations, airline efficiency, or customer satisfaction as workers still had little control over the critical decisions the company made. In retrospect, it seems that there was no intention to create an "ownership culture" by either side. Instead, union leaders "wanted to use ownership to prevent United from breaking up into regional carriers ... and outsourcing work performed by union members," while the company's management saw ESOP "primarily as a way to get wage concessions."[100]

Results of a 2008 employee survey showed that a staggering 70 percent of United's employees remain dissatisfied working for the airline, and only 38 percent were proud of the company, "compared with the average *Fortune* 500 Company, where 84 percent of employees express pride in their employer."[101]

United's pilots, along with the Air Line Pilots Association (ALPA), criticized CEO Glenn Tilton based on the fact that his compensation package remains the highest in the industry by a considerable margin, even while his airline was reporting negative earnings, its employees are being laid off, and customers are being charged extra service fees.[102] Further, United's decision in June 2008 to eliminate 950 pilot jobs, lay off 1,600 salaried positions, and ground 70 aircraft was not received well by the ALPA community.[103] In fact, the union's pilots went on strike; in response, United sued the ALPA claiming it organized an illegal and disruptive "sickout" that caused hundreds of flight cancellations costing the airline millions of dollars in potential revenue and "damaging its reputation with the flying public and disrupting travel plans of about 36,000 passengers."[104] In November 2008, the federal court ruled against United's pilots, stating that their actions were illegal.[105]

Financial Results

During fiscal year 2008, five out of six major domestic carriers sustained losses on their income statements (see Exhibit 8a). Low-cost carrier Southwest Airlines was the only exception to this outcome. Most of these firms, because of liabilities that exceed their total assets, maintain a negative equity position (see Exhibits 8a, 8b, 8c). The extraordinarily high ROE shown simply demonstrates the significant amount of

Exhibit 8a Industry Financial Statistics 2008 (in millions except ratios and per-share figures)

Year Ending 2008	United	American	Southwest	Delta	US Airways	Continental
Income Statement						
Sales	20,194	23,766	11,023	22,697	12,118	15,241
Average daily sales	55	65	30	62	33	42
EBIT	(4,856)	1,348	383	(8,336)	(1,957)	(352)
Total interest	523	723	105	705	253	332
Lease obligations (capital leases)	1	1	25	473	752	195
Net income	(5,348)	(2,071)	178	(8,922)	(2,210)	(585)
Balance Sheet						
Current assets	4,861	5,935	2,893	8,904	2,418	4,347
Accounts receivable	977	811	574	1,844	293	669

(Continued)

Exhibit 8a Industry Financial Statistics 2008 (in millions except ratios and per-share figures) (*Continued*)

Year Ending 2008	United	American	Southwest	Delta	US Airways	Continental
Inventory	237	525	203	388	201	235
Finished goods	NA	NA	NA	NA	NA	NA
Fixed assets	10,312	15,735	11,040	20,627	3,286	7,327
Total assets	19,461	25,175	14,308	45,014	7,214	12,686
Current liabilities	7,281	9,374	2,806	11,022	3,044	4,474
Long-term debt	8,286	9,001	3,498	15,411	3,634	5,371
Total debt	21,926	28,110	9,355	44,140	7,719	12,581
Annual dividend per share	0	0	0	0	0	0
Current market price per share	12	10	9	12	9	19
After-tax earnings per share	(42)	(8)	0	(19)	(22)	(6)
Common shares outstanding	140	285	741	772	114	124
Owner's equity	(2,465)	(2,935)	4,953	874	(505)	(105)
Statement of Cash Flows						
Net change in cash	780	43	(845)	1,607	(914)	37
Profitability						
Profit margin	−26.48%	−8.71%	1.61%	−39.31%	−18.24%	−3.84%
Asset turnover	103.77%	94.40%	77.04%	50.42%	167.98%	120.14%
Return on assets	−27.48%	−8.23%	1.24%	−19.82%	−30.63%	−4.61%
Financial leverage	789.49%	857.75%	288.88%	5,150.34%	1,428.51%	12,081.90%
Return on equity	216.96%	70.56%	3.59%	−1,020.82%	437.62%	557.14%
Liquidity						
Current ratio	0.67	0.63	1.03	0.81	0.79	0.97
Quick ratio	0.64	0.58	0.96	0.77	0.73	0.92
Inventory to net working capital	−0.10	−0.15	2.33	−0.18	−0.32	−1.85
Leverage						
Debt to assets	1.13	1.12	0.65	0.98	1.07	0.99
Debt to equity	−8.89	−9.58	1.89	50.50	−15.29	−119.82
Long-term debt to equity	−3.36	−3.07	0.71	17.63	−7.20	−51.15
Times interest earned	−9.28	1.86	3.65	−11.82	−7.74	−1.06
Fixed-charge coverage	−9.26	1.86	3.14	−6.67	−1.20	−0.30
Activity						
Inventory turnover	NA	NA	NA	NA	NA	NA
Fixed assets turnover	1.96	1.51	1.00	1.10	3.69	2.08

Exhibit 8a Industry Financial Statistics 2008 (in millions except ratios and per-share figures) (*Continued*)

Year Ending 2008	United	American	Southwest	Delta	US Airways	Continental
Total assets turnover	1.04	0.94	0.77	0.50	1.68	1.20
Accounts receivable turnover	20.67	29.30	19.20	12.31	41.36	22.78
Average collecting period	17.66	12.46	19.01	29.65	8.83	16.02
Shareholder's Return						
Dividend yield on common stock	0.00	0.00	0.00	0.00	0.00	0.00
Price-earnings ratio	−0.28	−1.25	37.50	−0.63	−0.41	−3.43
Dividend-payout ratio	0.00	0.00	0.08	0.00	0.00	0.00
Cash flow per share	5.57	0.15	−1.14	2.08	−8.00	0.30

Source: 2009, Table compiled by authors using data from the 2008 10-K reports of each company.

Exhibit 8b Industry Financial Statistics 2007 (in millions except ratios and per-share figures)

Year Ending 2007	United	American	Southwest	Delta	US Airways	Continental
Income Statement						
Sales	20,143	22,935	9,861	19,154	11,700	14,232
Average daily sales	55	63	27	52	32	39
EBIT	1,337	1,398	1,127	2,471	707	922
Total interest	642	894	69	652	273	356
Lease obligations (capital leases)	1,106	846	39	526	765	183
Net income	403	504	645	1,612	427	459
Balance Sheet						
Current assets	6,095	7,229	4,443	5,240	3,347	4,561
Accounts receivable	966	1,027	279	1,208	374	865
Inventory	242	601	259	262	249	271
Finished goods	NA	NA	NA	NA	NA	NA
Fixed assets	11,359	17,153	10,874	11,701	2,488	6,558
Total assets	24,220	28,571	16,772	32,423	8,040	12,105
Current liabilities	7,979	8,483	4,838	6,605	2,434	4,449
Long-term debt	7,521	10,093	2,050	7,986	3,031	4,366
Total debt	21,431	25,914	9,831	22,310	6,601	10,555
Annual dividend per share	0	0	0	0	0	0
Current market price per share	32	13	12	13	13	20
After–tax earnings per share	3	2	1	5	5	4

(*Continued*)

Exhibit 8b Industry Financial Statistics 2007 (in millions except ratios and per-share figures) (*Continued*)

Year Ending 2007	United	American	Southwest	Delta	US Airways	Continental
Common shares outstanding	117	255	808	772	114	124
Owner's equity	2,418	2,657	6,941	10,113	1,439	1,550
Statement of Cash Flows						
Net change in cash	2,573	26	823	614	832	5
Profitability						
Profit margin	2.00%	2.20%	6.54%	8.42%	3.65%	3.23%
Asset turnover	83.17%	80.27%	58.79%	59.08%	145.52%	117.57%
Return on assets	1.66%	1.76%	3.85%	4.97%	5.31%	3.79%
Financial leverage	1,001.65%	1,075.31%	241.64%	320.61%	558.72%	780.97%
Return on equity	16.67%	18.97%	9.29%	15.94%	29.67%	29.61%
Liquidity						
Current ratio	0.76	0.85	0.92	0.79	1.38	1.03
Quick ratio	0.73	0.78	0.86	0.75	1.27	0.96
Inventory to net working capital	–0.13	–0.48	–0.66	–0.19	0.27	2.42
Leverage						
Debt to assets	0.88	0.91	0.59	0.69	0.82	0.87
Debt to equity	8.86	9.75	1.42	2.21	4.59	6.81
Long-term debt to equity	3.11	3.80	0.30	0.79	2.11	2.82
Times interest earned	2.08	1.56	16.33	3.79	2.59	2.59
Fixed-charge coverage	1.40	1.29	10.80	2.54	1.42	2.05
Activity						
Inventory turnover	NA	NA	NA	NA	NA	NA
Fixed-assets turnover	1.77	1.34	0.91	1.64	4.70	2.17
Total-assets turnover	0.83	0.80	0.59	0.59	1.46	1.18
Accounts-receivable turnover	20.85	22.33	35.34	15.86	31.28	16.45
Average collecting period	17.50	16.34	10.33	23.02	11.67	22.18
Shareholder's Return						
Dividend yield on common stock	0.00	0.00	0.00	0.00	0.00	0.00
Price–earnings ratio	9.58	7.30	14.29	2.49	2.79	4.94
Dividend-payout ratio	0.00	0.00	0.02	0.00	0.00	0.00
Cash flow per share	22.01	0.10	1.02	0.80	7.28	0.04

Source: 2009, Table compiled by authors using data from the 2008 10-K reports of each company.

Exhibit 8c Industry Financial Statistics 2006 (in millions except ratios and per-share figures)

Year Ending 2006	United	American	Southwest	Delta	US Airways	Continental
Income Statement						
Sales (millions USD)	17,880	22,563	9,086	17,171	7,117	13,128
Average daily sales	49	62	25	47	19	36
EBIT	511	1,232	867	(6,098)	(379)	752
Total interest	729	1,001	77	870	242	383
Lease obligations (capital leases)	1,350	927	51	387	956	200
Net income	32	231	499	(6,203)	(611)	343
Balance Sheet						
Current assets	6,273	6,902	2,601	5,385	1,413	4,129
Accounts receivable	942	988	241	1,317	252	747
Inventory	218	506	181	181	177	217
Finished goods	NA	NA	NA	NA	NA	NA
Fixed assets	11,463	17,763	10,094	12,973	3,370	6,263
Total assets	25,369	29,145	13,460	19,622	8,422	11,308
Current liabilities	7,945	8,505	2,887	5,769	2,383	3,955
Long-term debt	8,803	12,041	1,567	6,509	2,637	4,859
Total debt	22,860	29,751	7,011	33,215	8,856	10,961
Annual dividend per share	0	0	0	0	0	0
Current market price per share	46	32	15	20	54	45
After-tax earnings per share	197	1	1	(32)	4	3
Common shares outstanding	140	285	808	772	114	124
Owner's equity	2,148	(606)	6,449	(13,593)	(434)	347
Statement of Cash Flows						
Net change in cash	2,183	(17)	(890)	26	(191)	400
Profitability						
Profit margin	0.18%	1.02%	5.49%	−36.12%	−8.59%	2.61%
Asset turnover	70.48%	77.42%	67.50%	87.51%	84.50%	116.09%
Return on assets	0.13%	0.79%	3.71%	−31.61%	−7.25%	3.03%
Financial leverage	1,181.05%	4,809.41%	208.71%	144.35%	1,940.55%	3,258.79%
Return on equity	1.49%	−38.12%	7.74%	45.63%	140.78%	98.85%
Liquidity						
Current ratio	0.79	0.81	0.90	0.93	0.59	1.04

(Continued)

Exhibit 8c Industry Financial Statistics 2006 (in millions except ratios and per-share figures) (*Continued*)

Year Ending 2006	United	American	Southwest	Delta	US Airways	Continental
Quick ratio	0.76	0.75	0.84	0.90	0.52	0.99
Inventory to net working capital	–0.13	–0.32	–0.63	–0.47	–0.18	1.25
Leverage						
Debt to assets	0.90	1.02	0.52	1.69	1.05	0.97
Debt to equity	10.64	–49.09	1.09	–2.44	–20.41	31.59
Long-term debt to equity	4.10	–19.87	0.24	–0.48	–6.08	14.00
Times interest earned	0.70	1.23	11.26	–7.01	–1.57	1.96
Fixed-charge coverage	0.90	1.12	7.17	–4.54	0.48	1.63
Activity						
Inventory turnover	NA	NA	NA	NA	NA	NA
Fixed-assets turnover	1.56	1.27	0.90	1.32	2.11	2.10
Total-assets turnover	0.70	0.77	0.68	0.88	0.85	1.16
Accounts-receivable turnover	18.98	22.84	37.70	13.04	28.24	17.57
Average collecting period	19.23	15.98	9.68	28.00	12.92	20.77
Shareholder's Return						
Dividend yield on common stock	0.00	0.00	0.00	0.00	0.00	0.00
Price–earnings ratio	0.23	32.65	24.59	–0.63	15.38	13.72
Dividend-payout ratio	0.00	0.00	0.03	0.00	0.00	0.00
Cash flow per share	15.59	–0.06	–1.10	0.03	–1.67	3.23

Source: 2009, Table compiled by authors using data from the 2008 10-K reports of each company.

financial leverage that is commonplace in the airline industry.

Competition from low-cost carriers, recent emergence from bankruptcy, and intense competitive rivalry (because of high fixed costs and the need for high turnover) among carriers has forced United to contract its operations. With negative cash flows from operating and financing activities, United was forced to finance its activities by forgoing future investment and liquidating its assets (see Exhibit 9). In 2008, the firm permanently removed 100 aircraft from its fleet, reduced capital spending by $200 million, and cut 6,000 employees from its workforce.[106] In addition, in 2009 the company plans to eliminate 1,400 more workers, limit capital expenditures to $450 million, and reduce premium seats on domestic flights by 20 percent. Net sales of short-term investments accounted for the majority of United's liquidity in 2008 ($2.2 million of $2.7 million on the Statement of Cash Flows).[107]

Volatile fuel costs remain the most significant threat to financial stability for the airline industry as whole, but for United in particular. For the airline industry as a whole, fuel accounts for approximately 30 percent of total operating expenses. In 2008, United witnessed a 59 percent increase in the cost of fuel, leading to a $3.1 billion increase in overall costs related to hedging or direct fuel costs.[108]

United, along with competitors American, Continental, Delta, and Northwest, have implemented fees and reduced service in order to cope with rising fuel costs and decreased traffic. While charging fees for checked baggage seems intuitively counterproductive to increasing passenger traffic for United Airlines, according to CFO Kathryn Mikells, "a la carte pricing is proving to be a very large opportunity," and is expected to provide $700 million in additional income for 2009.[109] However, in many instances, such fees have caused an increase in public ire toward the airline industry. Thus, in an attempt to win back passengers and generate

Exhibit 9 UAL Statement of Cash Flows, 2006 to 2008

Period Ending	12/31/08	12/31/07	12/31/06
Net income	−5,348,000	403,000	22,876,000
Operating Activities, Cash Flows Provided by or Used in			
Depreciation	981,000	925,000	882,000
Adjustments to net income	3,374,000	496,000	636,000
Changes in accounts receivables	195,000	−59,000	43,000
Changes in liabilities	−591,000	638,000	1,447,000
Changes in inventories	—	—	—
Changes in other operating activities	150,000	−269,000	−1,411,000
Total Cash Flows from Operating Activities	−1,239,000	2,134,000	1,539,000
Investing Activities, Cash Flows Provided by or Used in			
Capital expenditures	−415,000	−658,000	−362,000
Investments	2,295,000	−1,951,000	−235,000
Other cash flows from investing activities	841,000	49,000	347,000
Total Cash Flows from Investing Activities	2,721,000	−2,560,000	−250,000
Financing Activities, Cash Flows Provided by or Used in			
Dividends paid	−253,000	—	—
Sale purchase of stock	96,000	24,000	10,000
Net borrowings	−702,000	−2,253,000	770,000
Other cash flows from financing activities	157,000	82,000	2,000
Total Cash Flows from Financing Activities	−702,000	−2,147,000	782,000
Effect of Exchange Rate Changes	—	—	—
Change in Cash and Cash Equivalents	$780,000	−$2,573,000	$2,071,000

Source: 2009, UAL Corporation cash flow, *Yahoo! Finance*, http://finance.yahoo.com.

brand loyalty, United has embraced several marketing strategies.

Marketing Initiatives

In 2008, United began its "Travel Options by United" program in an effort to provide passengers with greater choice and flexibility.[110] The program is comprised of six services that passengers can elect to add to their ticket price: economy plus, Premier Line, door-to-door baggage, travel insurance, award accelerator, and Red Carpet Club.[111] Through the Travel Options program, United is attempting to offer travelers services they will value—even if the service must be purchased by the passenger. The Premier Line, for example, was the result of market research aimed at uncovering customer needs and desires. Dennis Cary, senior vice president and chief marketing and customer officer, described the process as follows: "when we asked our customers what travel services were most important to them they told us the access to priority lines was something they value highly."[112] The Premier Line provides priority access at check-in, security, and boarding for a starting fee of $25.[113]

Another marketing strategy that United is using is its Premium Service, or p.s., flights. According to the company Web site, "in its essence, p.s. is about doing a few things extraordinarily well." The p.s. flights offer the only domestic lie-flat bed in first class, more leg room, laptop power, and a premium menu.[114] Currently, p.s. flights only service three cities: Los Angeles, New York, and San Francisco, providing special accommodations for a select few.[115] For United, p.s. flights are a confirmation of the belief that "to get business travelers to pay more and not simply shift to discount airlines, big airlines may have to find ways to offer premium service travelers will value."[116]

In addition to its marketing efforts to increase passenger transport, United Airlines maintains cargo service to supplement its revenues. United Cargo is the seventh-largest domestic freight company.[117]

Additional Revenue Streams

In 2008, cargo accounted for approximately 4 percent of the United's operating revenue, generating $854 million in freight and mail revenue.[118] While United and most of its competitors derive some revenue from the freight market, "competition in the freight market has grown steadily, and it is becoming less and less likely that airlines treating freight purely as a by-product will be successful."[119] The bulk of the market (which is expected to grow more rapidly than passenger service) is expected to fall to dedicated air freight companies.[120]

Despite all of United's attempts to improve its financial situation and future viability, it faces multiple challenges.

Strategic Challenges

Just three years removed from bankruptcy, United Airlines is suffering financially once again. The company's losses in 2008–2009 combined with its high levels of debt and low liquidity placed the company on shaky ground. The growth of LCCs, especially Southwest, and United's failed attempts at countering their influence are also troubling trends for the firm.

The company must decide how best to face the changing landscape of the passenger airline industry. Can United find a viable merger opportunity? If so, does a merger only postpone resolution of United's problems? Most importantly, can United neutralize the market erosion caused by low-cost carriers, or must it find a way to compete with them directly by lowering its own cost structure? Glenn Tilton and his executive team must find the most viable answers as the pathway for United Airlines to operate in ways that will satisfy all stakeholders, certainly including shareholders.

NOTES

1. 2009, Glenn Tilton remarks to the Phoenix Aviation Symposium, http://www.united.com, March 27.
2. 2009, UAL Corporation reports first quarter 2009 results, United Press Release, http://www.united.com, April 21; 2009, UAL Corporation 2008 Annual Report, http://www.united.com.
3. 2009, Era 2: 1926–1933 Timeline, http://www.united.com.
4. 2009, Era 3: 1934–1940, http://www.united.com.
5. R. Freeman, Walter Folger Brown: The postmaster general who built the U.S. Airline industry, U.S. Centennial of Flight Commission, http://www.centennialofflight.gov/essay/Commercial_Aviation/Brown/Tran3.htm.
6. E. Preston, The Federal Aviation Administration and its predecessor agencies, U.S. Centennial of Flight Commission, http://www.centennialofflight.gov/essay/Government_Role/FAA_History/POL8.htm.
7. Era 3: 1934–1940 Timeline.
8. S. Shaw, 2007, Airline Marketing and Management, 6th ed., Ashgate Publishing, 52.
9. 2008, Star Alliance Facts & Figures, Star Alliance, http://www.staralliance.com, December 11.
10. B. Vasigh, K. Fleming, & T. Tacker, 2008, Introduction to Air Transport Economics: From Theory to Applications, Ashgate Publishing, 227.
11. S. Shaw, Airline Marketing and Management.
12. B. Vasigh, K. Fleming, & T. Tacker, Introduction to Air Transport Economics, 308.
13. Ibid., 2.
14. 2009, Era 7: 1970–1989 Timeline, http://www.united.com.
15. 2009, Era 8: 1990–1993 Timeline, http://www.united.com.
16. 2009, Era 9: 1994–1999 Timeline, http://www.united.com.
17. 2002, United, CBS News, http://www.cbsnews.com, December 9.
18. Era 9: 1994–1999 Timeline.
19. 2009, Era 10: 2000–... Timeline, http://www.united.com.
20. United, CBS News.

21. Ibid.
22. Ibid.
23. 2009, UAL Corporation 2008 Annual Report, http://www.united.com.
24. Ibid.
25. Ibid.
26. M. Maynard, 2008, More cuts as United grounds its low-cost carrier, The New York Times, http://www.nytimes.com, June 5.
27. 2007, Delta, United deny being in merger discussions, MSNBC, http://www.msnbc.msn.com, November 14.
28. M. Maynard, 2008, United and Continental form alliance, The New York Times, http://www.nytimes.com, June 20.
29. United, CBS News; M. Maynard, United and Continental form alliance.
30. B. Vasigh, K. Fleming, & T. Tacker, Introduction to Air Transport Economics: From Theory to Applications, 51.
31. S. Shaw, Airline Marketing and Management, 37.
32. Ibid., 70.
33. Ibid., 37–39.
34. 2009, American Airlines History, http://www.aa.com, March; 2009, AMR Corporation 2008 Annual Report, http://www.aa.com, June.
35. 2008, AMR Corporation – American's Parent Company, http://www.aa.com, August.
36. 2009, American Eagle Airlines: At a glance, http://www.aa.com, May.
37. 2003, American Airlines avoids bankruptcy, BBC News, http://news.bbc.co.uk, April 1.
38. 2009, AMR Corporation 2008 Annual Report, http://www.aa.com.
39. A. Salpukas, 1990, Continental files for bankruptcy, The New York Times, http://www.nytimes.com, December 4.
40. 2008, Continental Airlines ranked No. 1 world's most admired airline by Fortune magazine, Reuters, http://www.reuters.com, March 11.
41. 2009, Continental Airlines 2008 8-K, http://www.continental.com, April, 24.

42. 2009, Continental Airlines facts second quarter 2009, http://www .continental.com; 2009, Continental Airlines 2008 Annual Report, http://www.continental.com, February.

43. Ibid.

44. 2009, Continental to join Star Alliance, Continental Airlines News Release, http://www.continental.com, April 16.

45. 2009, Delta through the decades, http://www.delta.com, April.

46. Ibid.

47. Ibid.

48. 2009, Delta Air Lines 2005 Annual Report, http://www.delta.com, April.

49. 2009, Delta Air Lines 2008 Annual Report, http://www.delta.com, April.

50. Ibid.

51. Ibid.

52. 2009, US Airways fact sheet, http://www.usairways.com, April; 2009, US Airways 2008 Annual Report, http://www.usairways.com, April.

53. 2009, US Airways chronology, http://www.usairways.com, April.

54. D. Reed, 2008, US Airways highlights drawbacks of consolidation, USA Today, http://www.usatoday.com, May 3; 2009, US Airways & America West Airlines combined route network map, http://www .airlineroutemaps.com, April; 2008, Is US Airways a low-cost carrier?, http://www.associatedcontent.com, February 14.

55. 2009, US Airways 2008 Annual Report, http://www.usairways.com, April.

56. Ibid.

57. Ibid.

58. Ibid.

59. Ibid.

60. S. McCartney, 2009, For the first time in awhile, airline customer satisfaction is up, Wall Street Journal, http://online.wsj.com, May 20.

61. We weren't just airborne yesterday, http://www.southwest.com.

62. 2008, Scheduled passengers carried, World Air Transport Statistics, http://www.iata.org.

63. 2009, Southwest Airlines Fact Sheet, http://www.southwest.com, April 27; 2009, Southwest Airlines Investor Relations, http://www .southwest.com.

64. Ibid.

65. B. Vasigh, K. Fleming, & T. Tacker, Introduction to Air Transport Economics, 309–318.

66. S. Shaw, Airline Marketing and Management, 96.

67. We weren't just airborne yesterday.

68. 2009, Southwest Airlines 2008 Annual Report, http://www .southwest.com, April.

69. S. Shaw, 2007, Airline Marketing and Management, 90.

70. Southwest Airlines 2008 Annual Report.

71. B. Vasigh, K. Fleming, & T. Tacker, Introduction to Air Transport Economics.

72. Ibid., 138.

73. S. Shaw, Airline Marketing and Management, 112.

74. Ibid., 255.

75. 2007, Backgrounder: 10 years Star Alliance from "The airline network for Earth" to "The way the Earth connects"—A chronological history, Star Alliance Press Office, May 14, 2.

76. Ibid., 3.

77. 2009, SkyTeam airline member benefits, http://www.skyteam.com, April.

78. S. Shaw, Airline Marketing and Management, 112.

79. B. Vasigh, K. Fleming, & T. Tacker, Introduction to Air Transport Economics, 173.

80. Ibid.

81. 2007, An introduction to Oneworld: The alliance that revolves around you, http://www.oneworld.com, July 11.

82. Ibid.

83. SkyTeam airline member benefits.

84. 2009, SkyTeam names managing director, introduces aircraft livery, http://www.skyteam.com, April 1.

85. B. Vasigh, K. Fleming, & T. Tacker, Introduction to Air Transport Economics, 173.

86. Ibid.

87. 2009, United Express, http://www.united.com, April.

88. 2009, United Airlines 2008 Annual Report, http://www.united.com, April.

89. B. Vasigh, K. Fleming, & T. Tacker, Introduction to Air Transport Economics, 212.

90. Ibid.

91. J. Lowy, 2008, Pilots: To cut costs, airlines forcing us to fly low on fuel, The Huffington Post, http://www.huffingtonpost.com, August 8.

92. M. Maynard, 2008, United, citing fuel hedging, loses $779 million in quarter, The New York Times http://www.nytimes.com, October, 21.

93. Ibid.

94. Ibid.

95. B. Vasigh, K. Fleming, & T. Tacker, Introduction to Air Transport Economics, 190.

96. Ibid., 191.

97. Ibid.

98. Ibid.

99. Era 9: 1994–1999 Timeline; 2003, United Airlines likely to lose employee ownership, USA Today, http://www.usatoday.com, January 16.

100. C. Rosen, 2002. United Airlines, ESOPs, and employee ownership, The National Center for Employee Ownership, http://www.nceo .org, November.

101. 2008, United Pilots: Leadership void costly for UAL in 2008, UPI, http://www.upi.com, December 29.

102. Ibid.

103. 2008, United Airlines to lay off 950 pilots—cuts in addition to those announced earlier, domain-b.com, http://www.domain-b.com/ aero/unitedairlines/20080624_united_airlines.html, June 24.

104. 2008, United Airlines sues pilots' union, says it caused hundreds of flight cancellations, domain-b.com, http://www.domain-b.com/ aero/unitedairlines/20080731_united_airlines.html, July 31.

105. 2008, Injunction halts United Airline's pilot strike, RoutesOnline, http://www.routesonline.com, November 19.

106. United Airlines 2008 Annual Report.

107. D. Koenig, 2008, Major airlines ready to cut more flights in 2009, Associated Press, http://www.news.yahoo.com, December 2; 2009, United Airways 2008 Annual Report, http://www.united .com; L. Stark, M. Hosford, & K. Barrett, 2008, Layoffs continue for airlines in crisis, ABC News, http://www.abcnews.go.com, June 5.

108. United Airlines 2008 Annual Report.

109. A. Karp, 2008, Downsizing United, Air Transport World, http:// www.atwonline.com, November.

110. 2009, United Airlines, Wikitravel, http://wikitravel.org/en/United_ Airlines, April.

111. 2009, Travel Options by United, https://www.united.com, April.

112. Ibid.

113. 2009, Travel Options by United—Premier Line, https://store.united .com; 2008, Take the fast track through the airport with United's new Premier Line service, http://www.united.com, December 8.

114. S. McCartney, 2008, A posher domestic first class; United sells space and comfy beds on "p.s." flights, Wall Street Journal, http:// online.wsj.com, July 29.

115. 2009, p.s. Experience the comfort of our exclusive coast-to-coast service, http://www.unitedps.com, April.

116. S. McCartney, A posher domestic first class; United sells space and comfy beds on "p.s." flights.

117. Scheduled Freight Tonne—Kilometres, IATA Web site, http://www .iata.org/ps/publications/wats-freight-km.htm.

118. United Airlines 2008 Annual Report.

119. S. Shaw, Airline Marketing and Management, 40.

120. Ibid.

Case Title	Manu-facturing	Service	Consumer Goods	Food/Retail	High Tech-nology	Internet	Transportation/Communication	International Perspective	Social/Ethical Issues	Industry Perspective
Alibaba		●				●		●		
Baidu		●				●		●		
Barclays		●						●		
Biovail			●		●			●	●	
Blockbuster			●	●		●				●
CEMEX	●						●	●		
Citibank		●			●	●		●		
Computime	●		●			●		●		●
Dell	●		●		●	●				●
eBay, Inc.		●			●	●		●		●
Great Lakes	●								●	
Henkel	●		●					●		
Kroger, Safeway, Costco, and Whole Foods			●	●					●	●
Apple Computer, Inc.	●	●			●	●	●	●		●
Three Generations of Family-Entrepreneurship	●		●						●	
Cinemaplex		●		●						●
Motorola, Inc.	●		●					●		●
The New York Times Company		●				●	●			●
Nike	●			●				●	●	
Nintendo			●		●	●		●		●
Nucor	●						●	●		●
Oasis Hong Kong Airlines		●					●	●		
Pro Clean		●		●						
Room and Board				●					●	
South Beauty Group		●		●				●		
Southwest Airlines		●					●			●
Tesco versus Sainsbury's			●	●				●		
TNK-BP	●							●		
Under Armour		●						●		●
United Airlines		●					●	●		●

Case Title	Chapter												
	1	2	3	4	5	6	7	8	9	10	11	12	13
Alibaba				●		●		●			●		
Baidu			●		●			●					
Barclays	●	●	●			●						●	
Biovail								●		●	●	●	
Blockbuster			●			●	●						
CEMEX		●	●				●	●			●		
Citibank		●	●	●				●	●		●		
Computime	●	●		●							●		●
Dell		●		●	●						●	●	
eBay, Inc.	●				●	●			●				●
Great Lakes	●	●		●								●	
Henkel			●	●			●	●			●		
Kroger, Safeway, Costco, and Whole Foods	●	●								●		●	
Apple Computer, Inc.			●	●	●				●				●
Three Generations of Family-Entrepreneurship	●		●									●	●
Cinemaplex		●	●	●	●				●				
Motorola, Inc.		●		●		●	●					●	●
The New York Times Company	●	●		●					●			●	
Nike		●		●				●	●		●	●	
Nintendo		●	●	●				●			●		
Nucor		●	●	●	●						●	●	
Oasis Hong Kong Airlines		●	●	●				●					
Pro Clean		●	●	●								●	●
Room and Board			●	●					●			●	●
South Beauty Group	●	●		●								●	●
Southwest Airlines		●	●	●	●							●	●
Tesco versus Sainsbury,					●	●	●						
TNK-BP		●				●	●			●			
Under Armour	●		●	●				●				●	●
United Airlines		●		●				●	●				